CLUES
I CLU ES 0631091 E

P9-APW-490

# THE DESTRUCTION OF THE DUTCH JEWS

# The Destruction of the Dutch Jews

*by* Dr. J. Presser

*Translated by*

Arnold Pomerans

E. P. Dutton & Co., Inc.   New York   1969

First published in the U.S.A. 1969
by E. P. Dutton & Co., Inc.



First published in Holland by Staatsuitgeverij,
's-Gravenhage under the title of *Ondergang*.
English translation first published in Great Britain
under the title *Ashes in the Wind*.



Library of Congress Catalog Card Number: 68-12445

A07725

Yet there comes a time for forgetting,
for who could live and not forget?
Now and then, however, there must also
be one who remembers.

ALBRECHT GOES
*Das Brandopfer*

# CONTENTS

# ILLUSTRATIONS

# TO THE READER

THIS book was commissioned by the *Rijksinstituut voor Oorlogsdocumentatie* (Netherlands State Institute for War Documentation) on January 13, 1950, after a number of long discussions with its Governors and the Director, Dr. L. De Jong. In these discussions it was anticipated that the work would run to 500 pages and would be completed in 1952 at the latest. Now, so many years later, I can only marvel at our optimism.

What I was not deceived in during all these years was the support vouchsafed me by the Institute. This it has given unstintingly and in a manner that deserves my heartfelt gratitude. In the course of labours extending over fifteen years I have come to know what privilege it is to be encouraged by an Institute unsurpassed anywhere in the world. Three names in particular must stand here for all, those of B. A. Sijes (whose critical acumen and painstaking examination of the entire text was invaluable), C. J. F. Stuldreher (my irreplaceable and indefatigable famulus) and above all Dr. L. De Jong, who by omitting much of purely local interest, prepared the Dutch text for the present English edition. Needless to say, any shortcomings remain my sole responsibility.

I have spoken of fifteen years, but the reader will understand that, as a university teacher, I had to undertake this work as an addition to my professional duties. Now that the task is done I must confess that more than once I despaired of its completion, and not only because of the labours involved.

Yet complete it I did. What sustained me in my efforts was not only the support and devotion of all those I have mentioned but also a growing awareness of what, in all humility, I felt to be my duty: to speak up for all those thousands now doomed to eternal silence, whose last cries of despair went unheard, and whose ashes no one was allowed to gather up. And while on the subject of my personal feelings, I should like to say something to those of my readers, Jews among them, who simply do not want to be reminded of what happened during those terrible years. I have met many of them in the course of my work, and I fully sympathize with their attitude. Others may react differently, but one thing has become clear to me while writing this work: no single Jew who has lived through that period can think dispassionately about the events here recorded. At best, the terrible experiences have been repressed, but never completely forgotten; the wound in the psyche has not had time enough to heal. Perhaps it never will, while this generation is still alive. Nor can the writer, who is himself one of them, pretend to have achieved an Olympian objectivity. His choice was only to write or to remain silent. He chose to write, his heart demanded it. For the rest, the reader must be his judge.

As to the facts, the choice was between crowding every page with source references or omitting them altogether. I have tried to steer a middle course, but would like to add that the original MS. deposited with the *Rijksinstituut voor Oorlogsdocumentatie* is fully documented and that anyone is free to consult it. For the rest, the reader may content himself with my solemn assurance that I have reported the facts as conscientiously as lay within my power.

Finally, it must be said that a labour stretching over fifteen years would have been impossible without the sympathetic understanding and loving atmosphere of my own home and family. It would be idle to try to put into words what I owe to them.

J. PRESSER

# INTRODUCTION

THIS book tells the story of murder—of murder on a scale never known before, with malice aforethought and in cold blood. The murderers were Germans, their victims Jews—in the Netherlands they mounted up to a hundred thousand, less than 2 per cent of the total of those killed by the Nazis in the course of their final solution of the Jewish problem. In this process, Dutch Jewry was put outside the law, isolated, robbed of all its possessions, deported and cut down with near-scientific precision—town-dwellers and country-folk, believers and free-thinkers, the whole and the sick, old and young, Dutchman and foreigners, men, women and children. All this was done without great haste, with typical German thoroughness, and with due regard for the proper formalities. Many of the murderers were mere thugs and illiterates, but others were educated men with an undeniable love of literature, art and music; many were good family men, not without sensibility; most of them celebrated Christmas, taking time off from the massacre of their fellow-creatures.

Since their campaign, in the Netherlands and elsewhere, was mainly directed from Germany, we must briefly recapitulate what every reader knows about Hitler's rise to power in 1933. Neither the structure nor the fate of the Third Reich can be understood without constant awareness that Hitler's demoniacal hatred of the Jews formed the very core of his policy and that he was still mouthing anti-Semitic obscenities on his death-bed. Not a few people in Germany and elsewhere had imagined that, once the Nazis had come to power and were allowed to let off some steam, they would not put their propagandistic threats into action—after all, *un jacobin ministre n'est pas un ministre jacobin.* But if this historical principle did not apply to Robespierre, it certainly was not true of Hitler. Even before 1939, and assuredly afterwards, he left the outside world few illusions about his real intentions—except for a brief interlude during the Olympic Games in 1936 when he put on a show of amiability for the benefit of foreign visitors at whose credulity we today can only blush. It was not long afterwards that the persecution of the Jews in Germany was stepped up to an unprecedented pitch—we have only to remind the reader of the so-called *Reichskristallnacht,* the pogrom of November 9, 1938, during which German Jews were ill-treated and seized in their hundreds, synagogues were burnt, and robbery and theft were the order of the day.

It is worth stressing this escalation of violence, not only because it ought to have shown Dutch Jews what was happening to their brethren in Germany, but also because they, too, were soon afterwards to become its victims. It may be said that in persecuting the Jews in Germany the Nazis mainly used two methods: a campaign of incitement and mob violence followed by more systematic oppression. The latter, which at first seemed the less fearsome of the two, did in fact help to develop the bureaucratic machine that was to carry the Nazi policy to its bitter end.

We have mentioned the attitude of foreigners at the time of the Olympic Games. It seems beyond doubt that, from it, the Nazis concluded that they had a free hand; that, at worst, the outside world would issue protests on paper. We have also mentioned the pogrom of 1938, an action in which the mob and the police clearly acted in concert. But to the outside world the whole affair had to be presented as a spontaneous outburst, and this part of the business was entrusted to Goebbels, who had no equal in that sort of stage-management. As a result, the hand of the Goebbels faction, which was in favour of mob action and of frightening the Jews out of Germany, was greatly strengthened. Soon afterwards, however, Goering, Himmler, Heydrich and those other Nazi leaders who preferred a more bureaucratic solution, put pressure on Hitler to come down in favour of the "orderly" mass extermination of the Jews.

All this is a highly simplified account of what was, in effect, a most complicated process, though we might add that what differences there were between the rival Nazi factions generally resolved themselves in sharper measures against the Jews. That was the only constant, the only ever-present element in a development that was, in reality, more planless and improvised than its horrifying results would lead one to suppose.

This process was given a new impetus by the outbreak of the Second World War and certainly by the German attack on the Soviet Union, that home of "Jewish Bolshevism", where Hitler's initial victories earned him hundreds of thousands of Jews—in addition to the 2,000,000 that had already fallen to him in the autumn of 1939, with the fixing of the Polish demarcation line. We cannot tell when precisely Hitler determined to get rid of them all; what we do know is that he was still wavering in 1940, for it was in that year that the Germans put forward their so-called Madagascar plan, by which 4,000,000 Jews were to be herded as slaves into an African island under German supervision—it is an open question whether this "solution" would have given them any better chances of survival. Soon after the beginning of the Russian campaign, however, the Germans dropped this plan in favour of their so-called "final territorial solution". The real meaning of this term was never in doubt to those who coined it, but the use of the euphemism was an essential part of their campaign to mislead public opinion and lull the Jews themselves into a sense of false security. Thus on July 31, 1941, when Goering conferred powers on Heydrich, Head of the *Reichszentrale für jüdische Auswanderung* (State Centre for Jewish Emigration), to deal with the Jewish problem, he spoke of "evacuation" but not of "extermination". But as we know from Eichmann's testimony in Jerusalem, the two had become synonymous by then.

However, before the "final solution" could be fully implemented, the Germans had first to set up an elaborate organization. This they did at the notorious *Wannsee Konferenz*, which was convened on January 20, 1942, by Heydrich, and attended by a large number of high officials, representing all the departments concerned with, or involved in, the destruction of the Jews. When this conference was over, Heydrich, Eichmann and Müller (his immediate chief) remained behind for a "fireside chat" and, over a bottle, worked out the details of mass-murder. The report of the conference was still couched in the usual euphemistic terms, but after that there was no going back. The *Wannsee Konferenz* may be called a turning-point in the history of Western civilization, for it ushered in an era of human sacrifice such as not even the barbarians could have imagined. Eichmann spoke on one occasion of 6,000,000 victims; another time he put it at 5,000,000. In essence the "final solution" was the same in all countries where the Germans could carry it out; what differences of policy there were (for instance, in Holland and Belgium) were entirely due to local circumstances.

As we know now, the whole operation was directed from Berlin, or more precisely from Section B 4 of Bureau IV of the *Reichssicherheitshauptamt* (State Security Headquarters). This does not, of course, mean that IV B 4 was the only agency involved; far from it. One small department could not possibly have carried out the whole extermination programme by itself, nor was it asked by Hitler to do so. For this work the *Führer* could also call on the Ministry of the Interior, the Ministry of Justice, the Ministry of Foreign Affairs, the Ministry of Finance, the German Bank, the Chancellery, the High Command of the *Wehrmacht*, and on "all the departments of the German Government and the National Socialist Party, whose work impinged in any way upon the Jewish question, and who vied with one another in working for the common aim; the eradication of the Jews, as enemies of the *Reich*, by every conceivable means and as thoroughly and as quickly as possible". So spoke Eichmann's judges, who might also have mentioned the noble few in these departments, who tried to stem the tide with what pitifully small means they had at their disposal.

We think it best to refrain from extended treatment of the origins of the *Reichssicherheitshauptamt* under Heydrich and, after the latter's death, under Kaltenbrunner; all that concerns us here is that in March 1941 Eichmann was appointed head of IV B 4, and that it was this section which, *inter alia*, directed the persecution of the Jews in the Netherlands; more than once, Eichmann appeared in our country for consultations with the local machine.

Before proceeding to the main narrative, we should like to give the non-Dutch reader a few details about the administrative organization set up by the Germans in the Netherlands and about the structure of its hierarchy. This will help him to identify some of the leading figures he will meet in the following pages.

On May 13, 1940 Queen Wilhelmina and the Dutch Government arrived in England. One day later the Dutch Army was forced to capitulate and the Netherlands fell into the hands of the Germans or, as they preferred to put it, under their administrative control (*Aufsichtsverwaltung*). This meant that, to begin with, the pre-war Dutch Civil Service continued to discharge all its duties though, in the course of time, an increasing number of important posts was entrusted to Dutch National Socialists. In the absence of the Ministers themselves, the day-to-day direction of the various administrative departments in The Hague became the responsibility of the Secretaries-General, whose role was roughly comparable to that of British Permanent Secretaries. However, the Dutch Secretaries-General were working in an occupied country and it is worth remarking that at his first meeting with them, the highest German official in the Netherlands, *Reichskommissar* Dr. Seyss-Inquart, declared that if any one of them disliked a particular German order he was always free to resign. And this is precisely what some of them did.

Seyss-Inquart was represented by special Delegates in Amsterdam, Rotterdam and the eleven Provincial capitals of the Netherlands; the Delegates had "administrative charge" of the provincial and through them of the municipal authorities. On the national level, Seyss-Inquart was aided by four *Generalkommissare*: Dr. F. Wimmer (Administration and Justice), Dr. H. Fischböck (Economy and Finance), H. Rauter (Security and Police) and F. Schmidt (Political Affairs and Propaganda). Schmidt was also the representative at The Hague of the Chancellery of the German Nazi Party, and (after 1941) of Martin Bormann, its influential chief. As for Rauter, he regarded himself as the spokesman of the SS, and he was utterly devoted to Heinrich Himmler, the *SS Reichsführer*. Representing as they did various conflicting tendencies within the Reich itself, these men were often at loggerheads, but there was one thing on which they all saw eye to eye: the treatment of the Jews.

As a rule, Seyss-Inquart would bring his four *Generalkommissare* together once a week. It was at these so-called *Chefsitzungen* (top-level discussions) that all the most important decisions were taken; for these Seyss-Inquart was directly responsible to Hitler. Others present usually included Otto Bene, the representative at The Hague of the German Foreign Office, and Dr. W. Harster, the Commander of the Security Police and the German Intelligence Service in the Netherlands. Just as Rauter was answerable to Himmler, so Harster was responsible to the *Reichssicherheitshauptamt* (German State Security Centre) in Berlin and its chief, first Heydrich and then Kaltenbrunner.

Many of the decisions taken at the *Chefsitzungen* were communicated to the Head of the German Armed Forces in the Netherlands: General of the Air Force Friedrich Christiansen, who might be described as a garrison commander.

We have mentioned Eichmann. His own Section IV B 4 was, as we said, part of the *Reichssicherheitshauptamt*, and so was its offshoot in The Hague, which began operations in 1941 under the overall direction of Harster, though its immediate chief was Willi Zöpf. Zöpf took his orders direct from Eichmann, but had to adapt them to the general policy laid down by Seyss-Inquart and his coterie. The Jews he had to deal with were chiefly concentrated in Amsterdam, where they were represented, from 1941 onwards, by a Jewish

Council that the Germans had foisted upon them. Zöpf himself had no direct contact with the Jewish Council, but dealt with it through the *Zentralstelle für jüdische Auswanderung* (Central Bureau for Jewish Emigration), an organization formally responsible to W. P. F. Lages, Harster's deputy security chief in Amsterdam. However, Lages generally had his hands full with the Resistance, and so left the Jewish Council to the tender mercies of F. H. Aus der Fünten, another official of the Security Police.

Since the German machine was ostensibly no more than a controlling body, what measures were taken against the Jews invariably involved the participation of Dutch officials—from the Secretaries-General in The Hague down to the lowliest village policeman. The evil policy was, of course, that of the Germans themselves, but while bearing this in mind throughout the book, the writer has also thought it necessary to look at the actions of their—willing and unwilling—accomplices among Gentile and Jewish officials in the Netherlands.

The writer fully realizes the story he has to tell is utterly appalling, and often involved to the point of confusion. He hopes that the foregoing outline will help the reader to find his way through the labyrinthine paths pursued by the German persecutors.

CHAPTER ONE

# TOWARDS ISOLATION

*May 1940–September 1941*

## THE FIRST FEW MONTHS

WHEN the Germans marched into Holland in the early morning of May 10, 1940, they ushered in a new phase in Dutch history in general and in the life of Dutch Jewry in particular.

Few Jews were in any doubt, even in those early days of May, that a train of disastrous events had begun; but even the most pessimistic among them could hardly have guessed the full horror that lay in store for them. There was widespread fear and dejection, not only among Jews but also among other Dutchmen, and many tried to escape along one of two routes: into freedom abroad or death at home. Most of those who fled across the Southern border were forced to return within a few days; others—among them a number of Dutch Jews domiciled in Belgium—managed to escape to America and other parts of the world through France, Spain and Portugal. Their subsequent fate does not concern us here.

Others again made for Ijmuiden and nearby coastal towns, in the hope of getting away by boat. In his story *De Adem van Mars* ("The Breath of Mars"), Leo Vroman has given us a vivid account of the scramble at Scheveningen as people packed into boats for England. Such scenes must have been common: Jews who were turned away from Ijmuiden tried their luck elsewhere, though generally without success. They returned home, tired and dispirited, to watch the trap close round them.

There has been much talk of the "drama" of Ijmuiden, but the word does not do justice to the tragedy of errors, confusion and self-sacrifice that was played out there. Thousands of Jews flocked into this harbour, though not nearly as many as remained home in Amsterdam—some by choice, others because they had no means of getting away. A journalist[1] later described the situation as "a combination

[1] Report by S. Davids, July 1957, p. 1.

of passivity, stubbornness, misplaced trust in the law and exaggerated ideas of the risks involved". Another journalist[1] has admitted that while "patriotism and a love of adventure drove me to escape, patriotism and love of adventure also urged me to stay". He, at least, had the choice; the vast majority—those lacking motor-cars—did not, though quite a few are said to have taken to their bicycles (there are conflicting reports as to the possible use of taxis).

Of the many rumours that were rife at the time, the best known was probably the one that the Dutch Government had provided a special ship to carry Jews from Ijmuiden to England. This report was passed on—inasmuch as anything could be passed on in a city without a telephone service and with regular air-raid alerts—by the Special Committee for Jewish Affairs, founded in Amsterdam in 1933. Rather than speculate about what else the Committee might have done, we shall merely mention one of the few courageous people who actually did something. Somehow, Mrs. G. Wijsmuller-Meijer managed to procure five large cars in which she drove a number of Jewish children, originally from Germany and Austria and now in the Amsterdam Municipal Orphanage, to Ijmuiden. There she put them on board the *Bodegraven* just before that ship sailed out at 7.50 p.m. "If only I could have laid my hands on more cars," she told me,[2] "I could have saved a good many more people."

Yes, more cars were needed, but more permits as well, for without permits the refugees were in danger of being sent back by the Dutch patrols. Why, one may ask, were so many stringent controls applied at that late hour—was it fear of the fifth column? Perhaps the most charitable explanation is that, in the confusion, various departments issued contradictory orders. In any case, though the Dutch Government was supposed to have provided a special boat, the potential passengers were not allowed to get to it.

Quite understandably, many writers have expressed pain and resentment at this state of affairs, assuming hostility, obstruction and even worse on the part of Dutch officials. I, for one, could find no positive evidence to support such allegations.

It is claimed that of the many hundreds of Jews who did manage to embark, most, though not all, reached England safely. One who

[1] H. Wielek: *De oorlog die Hitler won* (The War that Hitler Won, Amsterdam, 1947), pp. 11–12.

[2] Conversation with the author, January 13, 1951.

did not was the famous Amsterdam art dealer, J. Goudstikker, who had done so much for German-Jewish refugees in Holland. In the dark, he tripped and fell into the ship's hold, where his body was discovered hours later. A few months after his death, on a very hot day in July, a corpulent figure wearing a white uniform and clutching a baton appeared at his gallery in the Herengracht. *Reichsmarschall* Goering was paying a visit. An eye-witness has described what happened a few days later: "Huge lorries and barges drew up outside, and were soon filled to overflowing with valuable paintings and antiques. Goudstikker's was left empty. Everything went to Germany." This is perhaps the place to mention that Goering's "court jeweller", Dr. Kurt Hermann, purchased diamonds to the value of 368,000 gulden from the firm of Asscher, the first of a series of profitable purchases, as early as June 7, 1940.

One Jewish family drifted about in a small boat for a week. Luckily the weather was good and they eventually reached England, unlike the many thousands who were turned back to blazing Amsterdam, a city which, on the darkest night in its history was more brightly lit up than on many a more glorious occasion. Here, they sheepishly rejoined their old neighbours, who helped them to burn piles of anti-Nazi newspapers and other incriminating literature, including English dictionaries.

We need not enter into further details; suffice it to say that panic was rife everywhere. Typical of this attitude was the rumour that a pogrom was about to start. One witness, who heard the story from a relative of a police officer, barricaded his house, and lay awake throughout the night listening to every footstep. Others preferred death to waiting, and not a few behaved with great serenity. Let the psychologist pronounce on the differences—if he can.

Though it is impossible to tell how many Jews attempted suicide, since the available statistics can, at best, only give us some idea of how many succeeded, De Monchy,[1] the burgomaster of The Hague, speaks of just under thirty suicides in The Hague alone. Herzberg[2] has drawn attention to the existence of many Jewish family graves bearing the dates May 15 and 16. Undoubtedly family suicides did

[1] S. J. R. de Monchy: *Twee ambtsketens* (Two chains of office) (Arnhem, 1946), p. 251.

[2] A. J. Herzberg: "*Kroniek der Jodenvervolging*" (Chronicle of the Persecution of the Jews), in *Onderdrukking en Verzet*, part 3 (Amsterdam, 1949–54), pp. 11–12.

occur, and according to Meyers, there were also death pacts between people living in the same house and not necessarily related.[1] Meyers, who has analysed the various methods of suicide (or, in the case of young children, of murder) most commonly employed, concluded that "most of these Jews took an overdose of veronal, though gassing, hanging, shooting, wrist-slashing and injections of morphine were also used". Many reports speak of an "epidemic of suicides", a term that may be justified if the many unsuccessful attempts are also taken into account. When, a few days after the Dutch capitulation, the rumour went round that Jews could still leave the Netherlands, many who applied for exit permits appeared at the relevant offices with bandaged wrists and throats. Similar epidemics occurred wherever the Germans attacked or gained control. Drees[2] mentions the suicides of J. Limburg, a much-respected member of the Liberal-Democratic Party, and of Joels, a Liberal and a well-known city-councillor, who considered himself a Dutchman first, and only then a Jew, and who could not bear the idea of being hounded and driven into exile. People everywhere were particularly struck by the sudden disappearance from public life of Jews who had previously played a very active part, including Alderman Boekman (Amsterdam) and Professors Van Gelderen and Polak Daniëls; some schools lost a noticeable number of children, and quite a few families were reduced to only one member—saved by chance, ineptitude or other causes. Our knowledge of this period would be greater if more of the survivors of May 1940 had also survived until May 1945.

Meanwhile, the remaining Jews tried to resume their old lives in a new situation, one that made great demands on the Dutch people as a whole and on Jews in particular. At first nothing at all happened: there were no pogroms; there was no persecution; the dead were buried. Life went on. There was an unusually large number of widows, widowers, orphans and abandoned husbands, wives and children, but people made the best of it. Back to work they went, in towns and villages where German uniforms had become a common sight. People got used to them now that the threatened pogrom had not materialized; non-Jews brought soothing reports. Thus when

[1] Dr. F. S. Meyers: "Social-Psychiatric Reports on the Amsterdam Jewish Community during the years 1940–1943," *Proceedings of the Studieclub voor Sociale Psychiatrie* (1946), p. 188.

[2] W. Drees: *Van mei tot mei* (From May to May, Assen, 1958), p. 14.

De Monchy[1] asked "the first German officer I met", what the German attitude towards Dutch Jews really was, he was told that, as far as the Germans were concerned, there was no Jewish problem in Holland. Dutch Jews would be treated as ordinary Dutchmen. Nor was De Monchy asked to keep this conversation to himself, but "despite my many requests, my report was never published". Similarly, the Burgomaster of Amsterdam, Dr. W. de Vlugt, summoned a number of Jewish dignitaries to the Town Hall, to tell them of the assurance by the German military commander that Dutch Jews would not be molested. Can we blame them for accepting this assurance with great alacrity when the Secretary-General for Justice repeated it in a telephone call to Professor Cohen? And as if that were not enough, Cohen was expressly told by a German officer that "we have no plans against the Dutch Synagogue".

By then, military control had been joined by political control—Seyss-Inquart was establishing himself in the saddle. We shall be discussing his character and precise function in a later chapter; here we need merely mention that his inaugural address, given in The Hague on May 29, 1940, already contained sinister allusions to "blood and honour". Jews found some solace in the fact that they had not been referred to by name. Moreover, a proclamation issued on the same day assured the people that Dutch law would remain in force (though the proclamation also contained an inconspicuous clause that rendered it worthless). Such assurances, coupled to threats and escape clauses, were typical of most of the proclamations issued by the Germans at the beginning of the Occupation. Seyss-Inquart made a fateful remark when, during an official conference, he told (*Generalkommissar*) Schmidt, his chief political adviser, that he would prefer people not to analyse his speeches too carefully. And no doubt, only a very few did. The first time Seyss-Inquart referred to Jews in a speech was on March 12, 1941, and we may take it that the February strike was one of the causes. Moreover, his general report on conditions in Holland during the period May 29, to July 19, 1940, once again made no mention of Jews, although the first stringent measures against them had already been taken. In the light of later events, we may conclude that the Germans were soft-pedalling the whole question as a sop to the West, where anti-Semitism was not nearly as popular as it was in the East. Thus our records include the photostat of a document dated July 19, 1940,

[1] *Op. cit.*, p. 253.

and signed by one Bohl, of the German *Volkstum und Archiv* (Ethnology and Records) organization in Holland. In it we can read: "The Jewish question must be treated with great care . . . The main task remains . . . Am expecting orders soon . . . Then we shall pounce on them." The "pouncing" probably referred to Jewish archives and libraries, but from there it was but a short step to the Jews themselves.

The first act of public discrimination against Jews was their expulsion from the ARP service, but we must first mention another anti-Jewish measure of about the same time, whose effects were hardly noticed in the beginning. On July 2, 1940, R. A. Verwey, Head of the National Insurance and Labour Service, issued a circular defining what sort of people were unsuitable for work in Germany by virtue of "physical or psychological defects". They were expressly stated to include "anti-social elements, e.g. people who have served long prison sentences, those with a clear communist history, and Jews".

As for the expulsion of Jews from the Dutch ARP Service, the matter was dealt with in a circular dated July 1, 1940, and signed by *Generalmajor der Ordnungspolizei* (Police Major General) Schumann. It contained orders to clear the ARP Service of:

(*a*) all Jews;
(*b*) all subjects of countries at war with Germany;
(*c*) all Dutchmen with known anti-German sentiments.

On July 5, 1940, the Dutch Secretary-General for Internal Affairs, *mr.* K. J. Frederiks,[1] sent a copy of this circular to Dr. F. Wimmer, the German *Generalkommissar für Verwaltung und Justiz* (Commissar-General for Administration and Law) and asked him to explain whether the instructions could be reconciled with "your assurance to me that as far as the Germans are concerned there is no Jewish problem in Holland". Had Frederiks asked *how* rather than *whether* the instructions could be reconciled with the German assurance, his question would have been more pertinent: the answer, of course, would have had to be "not at all". We have a copy of Wimmer's note to H. A. Rauter, *Generalkommissar für das Sicherheitswesen und Höhere SS und Polizeiführer* (Commissar-General for Security and Higher SS and Police Commander), stating in the

[1] The Dutch legal title of *mr.* (*meester*) is roughly equivalent to the French *Maître*.

Gothic script so popular under Hitler: "I have spoken personally to Frederiks on this subject. Matter closed. File. W." Unfortunately, we have no further information about this conversation, although from the subsequent course of events it appears that Frederiks fought one, perhaps the first, of a series of "unsuccessful rearguard actions". In his post-war apologia,[1] he tells us that Wimmer was really quite "unreliable and weak, where Rauter was concerned". All he apparently said on the subject of the ARP expulsions (p. 72) was that "circumstances have changed".

It goes without saying that the Dutch authorities did not feel obliged to do more than simply pass the German orders on. Little is known of their reaction outside Amsterdam and Eindhoven, where the German orders were "dressed up" by the head of the local ARP organization. He had marked them "Very Urgent" on top, adding the words "Re: Expulsion of undesirable elements from the ARP."

From Amsterdam we have a special form of declaration, and five circulars signed by the head of the local ARP. In the form, dated July 10, 1940, all members of the organization had to confirm that they did not belong to any of the three groups specified by General Schumann. The original German text referred to "all Jews", and was correctly translated in Eindhoven; in Amsterdam, a strange mis-translation turned it into "all members of the Jewish race". The word "race" reappeared, this time underlined, in a circular dated July 18. Seeing that "members of the Jewish race" had felt free to sign the declaration, the Head of the Amsterdam ARP added the following rejoinder:[2] "Anyone with one or more Jewish parents must put himself down as a Jew irrespective of his religion."

Wielek[3] tells us that, in many parts of Amsterdam, the ARP became completely disorganized, not only as a result of the expulsions but also because many non-Jews resigned in protest. Thus the director of the Amsterdam YMCA, Dr. Eykman, refused to sign.[4] "He simply tore up the paper and refused to go along with them. He realized better than most that resistance had to start there and then, and he was one of the first to act accordingly." At the special

[1] K. J. Frederiks, *Op de bres* (In the breach) (The Hague, 1945), p. 16.

[2] Amsterdam Air-Raid Service Circular No. 666, July 9, 1940 and July 18, 1940.

[3] Wielek: *op. cit.*, p. 13.

[4] N. G. J. van Schouwenburg: *Dwing hen binnen te komen; Dr. J. Eykman* (Amsterdam, 1946), p. 20.

request of the Burgomaster, Jews were allowed to stay on in some predominantly Jewish districts; later the employment of professional air-raid personnel made this type of "evasion" unnecessary.

What of the Jews themselves? Their reactions were confused, a mixture of despondency, annoyance, hatred, resignation, indifference and shame. "For the first time," wrote Herzberg,[1] "we have become officially and publicly disqualified."

At a Staff Conference attended by *Generalkommissar* Schmidt on July 16, came the first official reference to another measure which must have been under consideration for some time. In the minutes (Section 10) we read: "Ritual slaughter must be prohibited. Propaganda is being directed to this end."

Now this measure did not take anyone by surprise, the more so as anti-ritual slaughter legislation had been among the first passed by the Nazis in Germany itself—in Blau's chronological list of anti-Jewish laws[2] it accounted for numbers 4 and 5 out of 400 measures (April 21–22, 1933). Why ritual slaughter should worry anti-Semites as much as it apparently does is a problem for the psychologists. References to the proposed law can be found in the minutes of the Secretaries-General. The first is dated July 22, when it was decided that ritual slaughter fell in the province of the Department of Economic and Social Affairs and that "Mr. Scholtens must try to get the matter settled". The Minutes conclude with a sentence worth special mention in the light of subsequent events: "It would be desirable to avoid the impression that the Jewish question is being brought into the open in this way." On July 25, Scholtens reported that, after consultation with "the Dutch Rabbis" agreement had been reached on the question of ritual slaughter. The minutes of July 31 reveal that a German order was about to be issued: "Although it is highly desirable to keep the matter under Dutch control, the Germans are unlikely to change their minds."

It is reasonable to conclude that the Dutch authorities had pleaded with the Germans in vain. In any case, the Germans passed their law and, in the circumstances, neither the College of Secretaries-General nor the Jews themselves were too downcast. If nothing worse lay in store for them . . .

Moreover, was the measure, in fact, *really* directed against the

[1] Herzberg, p. 44.

[2] B. Blau, *Das Ausnahmerecht für die Juden in Deutschland 1933–1945* (Düsseldorf, 1945), p. 19.

Jews? The law was entitled "Avoidance of Cruel Practices in Slaughter" and its four clauses contained no references to Jews as such. Nor was it a "special" measure, for as No. 80 it was part of an apparently innocuous series: No. 81 dealt with the prevention of bestiality and No. 82 with anti-typhus vaccination. The new regulation simply called for the stunning of warm-blooded animals before slaughter, stipulated fines, and stated that the measure would become law on August 5. Nothing sinister in that, one might say, and many, at the time, said just that.

Thus on July 31, 1940, a small stone was thrown into the water, its ripples spread out, and then the surface became calm again. Or at least relatively so. For on July 20, 1940, Simon de la Bella, Vice-President of the Dutch Federation of Trade Unions, was arrested. He had managed to transfer 5 million guilders from union funds to England just in time, and when the Germans struck against the Socialist leaders, he was their first victim. The Secretary-General of the Department of Social Affairs lodged a vain protest (the Germans found that *Herr* Scholtens "does not grasp the situation, and that his attitude leaves much to be desired"; a few weeks later he was removed from office for this and other reasons).[1] De la Bella died in Dachau concentration camp on July 11, 1942. His arrest must have alarmed many Jews; others must have taken comfort in the thought that he had been carried off in his capacity of trade union leader rather than as a Jew. But why pick on a Jew when there were so many other union leaders? Was it because of the money? You could believe that, if you wanted to. And most Jews wanted to, desperately. No, nothing at all had happened, they told themselves, the whole business was highly embarrassing but no more.

August and the first weeks of September passed without further trouble; there seemed little need to worry about the law of August 20 (Vo. 108/1940) by which the *Reichskommissar* was authorized to dismiss civil servants at will. Did this refer to Jews? There was no reference to them by name. True, German Jews were ordered to leave The Hague and the coastal area, and all Jewish refugees from Germany were asked to report to the Aliens Department. But that was all; no other harm befell them, and then, they were not even Dutch.

[1] *Onderdrukking en Verzet*, III (Oppression and Revolt), 371–2.

## THE ARYAN ATTESTATION

Alas, the Germans were merely biding their time before presenting an even more stringent measure: the suspension and ultimate dismissal of all Jewish civil servants. Did the civil servants themselves know what to expect? The author agrees with his former Jewish colleagues at the Vossius Gymnasium in Amsterdam that only after the summer holidays of 1940 did people begin to get an inkling of the Germans' intention. Still, nothing definite was known; there were rumours, of course, but everyone was disinclined to give credence to them, to play the pessimist to himself or to his fellows. Indeed, it was the Germans' chief trump card that no one ever knew where and when they would strike next. People still believed in their good faith, that things were bound to get better. Danger signals appeared in the minutes of the College of Secretaries-General; for instance, on August 12, when there was a discussion of the German refusal to employ a harbour official on the grounds that his wife was apparently "non-Aryan". Professor de Quay, who was responsible for labour relations, considered this an ominous step but felt that "little could be done about it". Not everyone present agreed with this conclusion, and some members proposed "that the College take a firm stand". However, the President, Jhr. A. M. Snouck Hurgronje did not "deem it expedient to make an official protest". All they could do at this stage was to insist that the German authorities "take full responsibility for this measure".

But did the College do even that? On August 28, Dr. Wimmer, the German Commissar-General for Administration and Justice, wrote a letter to the College instructing them to ensure that in future no one of Jewish blood was appointed, elected or promoted to public office; the order was to apply to anyone having a Jewish grandfather. The reaction of the Secretaries-General is found in the minutes of a meeting of August 30: "This instruction will cause friction in a number of respects." The President was asked to inform Dr. Wimmer that "we are forced to comply, but after having been told repeatedly that there is no Jewish problem in the Netherlands, we do so most reluctantly". Wimmer's attention was also drawn to the fact that "although the new order will not be published in accordance with German wishes, its implementation will affect so many people that the truth must needs become known, and this is bound to irritate the nation".

Now Wimmer was an "easy-going Austrian who would listen to what you have to say"[1] but even he "failed to understand why anyone should wish to treat the Jews as ordinary people". And if an easy-going Austrian could make remarks like that, what could be expected of such compulsive people as Rauter, Seyss-Inquart and . . . Hitler? The College must have known that none of these gentlemen was open to reason, and that Wimmer could have done nothing in the matter, even if he had wanted to. All the same, as the minutes of September 2 show, the President did protest to Dr. Wimmer. Then, on September 4, the College discovered that the German order, in fact, violated Article 5 of the Constitution stating that "every Dutch citizen is eligible for public service". The College went on to discuss the meaning of "public service" and concluded that it was to be taken in its widest sense. Hence it would be impossible for the College to implement the German order "in this form". A further search revealed that, by Article 176 of the Constitution, "members of different religions shall enjoy full civic and civil rights and . . . have equal titles to holding all public positions and honours". Surely this clause must protect the Jews? Alas, it had been forgotten that the Germans used race and not religion as their chief criterion. In any case, the meeting decided to contact the "easy-going" Austrian once again in order to explain their discovery. No record of the resulting conversation exists, but we do have a copy of a letter bearing the imprint of the Dutch Ministry of the Interior and sent on September 10 to Dr. Carl Stüler, a high German official. It states:

"In connection with the drafting of the law governing the appointment of Jews, I have thought it desirable to consult and follow the so-called Neuremberg (*sic!*) laws. In this connection, I wondered whether it would not be best to use a definition of Jews and people of mixed blood, based as closely as possible on the tekst (*sic!*) of the Neuremberg law."

The author cannot help recalling that these and similar letters were being written by Dutch officials at the very time when, to the mounting air attacks on England, the British people, under the inspired leadership of Winston Churchill, made it clear that they preferred death to slavery and honour to humiliation. The Nuremberg laws seemed to have held a strange fascination for the Dutch

[1] States-General: *Commission of Enquiry into Government Policy in 1940–1945*, part VIIc (The Hague 1955), p. 589.

Ministry of the Interior, as we can also judge from a document written eight days later, on September 18. In it, Frederiks informed Wimmer that all the ministries were badly in need of a yardstick for judging who precisely was of Jewish blood, and that he had accordingly sent a set of directives to the other Secretaries-General. And where, precisely, had Frederiks himself obtained these directives? From a memorandum issued by the German delegate to the Ministry of . . . Public Works.

Meanwhile, another apparently innocuous decree (137/1940) had appeared, again without mentioning Jews by name. Its first clause was the most important: "The legal and financial status of public servants, and especially the conditions of their employment and dismissal may, if necessary, be amended in disregard of the existing laws." As the reader will realize, this decree was merely an amplification of the one promulgated on August 20, 1940 (Vo. 108), it would, however, have needed a jurist to explain why the *Reichskommissar* should have considered that there was need for amplification. The layman might consider this further proof that the Germans were always sticklers for detail and correct form. Perhaps Article 2 is even more revealing: "Orders for the implementation of Article 1 will be issued in due course. They may be published in the Government Gazette."

The publication of the new decree must have caused great uneasiness to even the most defiantly optimistic Jews. And, indeed, the next blow fell even before the month was out.

Circular No. 47176 (Personnel Dept.) of September 30 addressed to all Provincial Authorities dealt once again with the appointment and promotion of persons of Jewish or of partly Jewish blood, including those holding honorary positions. Jews were defined to be all those with one grandparent known to have been a member or temporary member of the "Jewish community". Anyone unfortunate enough to be married to such a person was also to be included in this category. On October 3, another circular, No. 47177, followed in which all government, provincial and municipal authorities were asked to send the relevant returns to the Commissar-General for Administration and Justice by November 1 at the latest.

One day later, on October 4, came a German newspaper report[1] which expressly mentioned the disqualification of "Jews". It was

[1] *Deutsche Zeitung in den Niederlanden.*

a short article of only eight lines, headed: "Public Service to dispense with Jews and people of mixed blood." The sub-heading read: "No new posts or promotion."

No new posts or promotion—but at least the Jews could console themselves that there was no question of dismissal. Wielek[1] remembers that in Amsterdam and The Hague many were reassured because the instructions were sent out over the signatures of S. J. van Lier and J. J. Boasson, the Jewish town clerks of Amsterdam and The Hague.

This brings us to the so-called Aryan attestation. The reader will remember that Jews had previously been excluded from the ARP service, but at that time the Germans were newcomers and no one suspected what further evils that small injustice foreshadowed. Since then the meaning had become far more obvious. On October 18, the Amsterdam City Council sent a copy of Circular No. 47176 to the heads of all education departments. Attached were two forms of attestation: A for Aryans and B for non-Aryans, the latter to be completed in duplicate. All forms had to be returned by October 26 at the latest. This, as we have said, was to be the acid test for all Dutch civil servants, from the top of the hierarchy to the lowliest volunteer. Jew or non-Jew, each of them received one Form A and two Forms B. All alike found themselves on the horns of a grave dilemma. Many wavered, angry and disconsolate, but signed all the same, only to reproach themselves when it was too late. As Herzberg[2] put it: "We recalled our grandparents, we signed, but none of us really knew what we were doing." He continues: "Each signed his own death warrant, though few appreciated this at the time." Nevertheless, one senior official in the Finance Department did remark in a letter to the Paymaster-General that "the time will surely come when all of us will feel deeply ashamed of our behaviour and of our attitude". Another wrote that, as Dutch authorities, they ought to have realized what would happen, since, after all, they had been able to observe the rise of Hitlerism in Germany. He added: "I am sorry that I signed the Aryan declaration; only the confused circumstances of the time could have allowed me to do such a thing."

The author must share these regrets, while making allowances for the pressure of circumstances. In fact, there was no one who called

[1] Wielek: *op. cit.*, p. 15.
[2] Herzberg: *op. cit.*, p. 46.

for a general boycott of the forms, and it was only when all the declarations had been collected that the majority began to realize what they had done. Knowing what we do today, we can only agree with Professor Cleveringa of Leyden University,[1] that it would have been a great blessing indeed had the High Court listened to the urgent appeal of Professor Telders (of Leyden University) not to be blinded by expediency or convention in dealing with this vital question of principle. "Naturally," the Professor went on to say, "it is far easier to let events run their course but can we really reconcile such passivity with our duty as Dutchmen?" He urged the High Court to "return these despicable forms uncompleted, with the remark that neither the Court as such nor its members were willing to sign a document that was nothing but an instrument of injustice".

His advice was neither heard nor heeded. Most non-Jews signed Form A without really knowing what they were doing, while Jews signed Form B in much the same spirit. In his account of resistance in the Dutch Reformed Church, Touw remarks ironically that one Christian educational organization advised its members to sign the attestation since "after all, we have no objection to declaring our religion on the decennial census forms". The staff of The Hague Christian High School after long reflection, signed "with misgivings" though "many regretted their action later".[2] Luckily many Christian teachers decided not to take the path of least resistance. Thus Ad Goede tells us that at another Christian school in The Hague, teachers refused to sign the declaration *en bloc*, and so did the staff of the Amsterdam Lyceum.

This brings us to the reactions of the universities during these weeks. Here students and staff alike realized full well that this was the time to make a public stand.

The first blow against the German measure was struck in late September 1940 at Amsterdam, where the famous jurist, Professor Paul Scholten, who died shortly after the Liberation, hearing of the impending anti-Jewish measure, drafted a petition to Seyss-Inquart. We know the text of this petition, and also the contents of the covering letter, with which it was sent to university teachers throughout

[1] R. P. Cleveringa: *Telders' geschriften over volkenrecht* (Telders on international law) in *De Gids* (1949), pp. 12–14.

[2] Dr. J. C. H. de Pater: *Gedenboek van het 's-Gravenhaags Christelijk Gymnasium, 1908–1958* (Memorial Volume of the Christian High School in The Hague) (The Hague, 1958), pp. 63–4.

the Netherlands. In it, Scholten pointed out that most of his Amsterdam colleagues had expressed their full agreement with the contents of the petition and that the majority of Dutch teachers elsewhere would no doubt also wish to give their assent to its presentation. He assured them of its legality and moderate tone. The petition was, in fact, a well-prepared and noble document; it emphasized above all else "the simple fact that there is no Jewish question in the Netherlands", and that as far as university teachers are concerned "it is a matter of indifference whether a scholar is Jewish or not". "In the Dutch view, all learning is service to a single, universal truth, involving all mankind, and it is from this service that education derives its moral value and social importance". The use of social discrimination "far from solving a problem would merely create one and, moreover, be an infringement of the traditions and freedom approved and vouchsafed us by Your Excellency". The petition and another covering letter, signed, *inter alia*, by Professor Telders, were sent to Seyss-Inquart on October 13, though "with little hope" of success. Some claim the petition was signed by one Dutch professor in two; others mention a smaller figure. The *Meldungen aus den Niederlanden* of October 22, 1940, reported an attempt by the students of Leyden to collect at least 2,000 signatures for a separate petition to Seyss-Inquart. We are told by another source that, though only 1,700 signatures were obtained, the petition was presented all the same. The *Meldungen* also gave a vague account of petitions, prepared or actually presented, by other universities.

As we see, Dutch resistance hardened as soon as the Germans passed their second anti-Jewish measure, and called for the submission of "Aryan" attestations. This time no one could pretend that the whole thing had nothing to do with him, for everyone was expected to sign the form in person. Professor Cleveringa[1] blames the equivocating attitude of the High Court for the fact that the academic staff at Leyden acted with such lack of decision. The opposition of Telders, professor in international law, at first strengthened their resolve to ignore the German demand, but eventually the majority decided to sign under protest (among them, Cleveringa writes, some who later distinguished themselves in the Resistance). Telders and the others who had refused to sign altogether, decided to hold out if they could muster at least twenty-five supporters; failing this, they would follow the example of the "protesters"—"on the

[1] Cleveringa: *op. cit.*, pp. 14–15.

grounds that a united front would be more effective than individual refusals". Cleveringa recognized not only the artlessness but also the wrongness of this decision. In fact, only eighteen refused to sign the attestation in the end, but sixty agreed to put their names to a protest prepared by Telders. Little is known of what happened at other universities, but Professor Van Meurs of Groningen is said to have been the last Dutch professor to sign the Aryan declaration and, a biographer wrote,[1] "I know at what cost to himself."

On October 4, 1940, the Drion brothers published the first edition of an illegal student paper, *De Geus onder Studenten*. In the second issue they told their readers that the Germans had started "a cold pogrom" in the Netherlands despite assurances to the contrary, and added: "the only surprise is that they have kept their promises so long". The article concluded with the following forceful pronouncement: "The Jewish problem does not exist . . . but what does exist is an anti-Semitic problem." In this connection we must mention that Councillor J. H. Scheps[2] of Zeist (Utrecht) asked his colleagues throughout the Netherlands to resist the mass dismissal which, he anticipated, would follow the Aryan attestation.

What, the reader may ask, did the Churches say to all this, the Churches to whom so many Dutch people looked for help and guidance in those troubled days? In fact, they did raise their voices, but those voices were by no means unanimous. They proceeded, as Herzberg[3] noted, "in a typically ponderous but precise Dutch manner", and it was only after the Germans intensified their anti-Jewish campaign, that Church leaders became far more outspoken. The Roman Catholic Archbishop, Mgr. Dr. Johannes de Jong, an avowed opponent of the Nazis, wanted to lodge a strong protest with Seyss-Inquart as soon as he heard about the attestation; he even intended to make the matter a subject of a pastoral letter. Aukes, his biographer, speaks of "strong pressures" and uncertainty as to the most opportune moment for presenting a protest which, in the event, was not made. As for the Protestant Churches, it was thanks to Professor Slotemaker de Bruïne that mutual consultations on the German measures were initiated in June. At the beginning of October, the Rev. J. J. Buskes raised the question of anti-Jewish

[1] *Groningen University Yearbook* (1945), p. 50.

[2] J. H. Scheps: *Een ernstig woord aan de leden van de Gemeenteraden in Nederland* (A warning to the members of the town councils in the Netherlands) (Den Dolder, 1940).

[3] Herzberg: *op. cit.*, p. 45.

discrimination and suggested that "these measures are bound to have important spiritual repercussions and, moreover, are in direct conflict with the concept of Christian charity". He also mentioned the promise made by Seyss-Inquart on May 29 in the Ridderzaal not to "force an alien ideology on our country". This and very much more was proclaimed on Sunday, October 27, to many thousands of worshippers in churches all over the country. However, not all Protestant Churches joined in, as Delleman[1] has observed, the Church as a whole, like the Dutch people themselves, was not yet completely aware of the insidious nature of the German demands. Thus the two Lutheran communities failed to sign the first protest, chiefly for legalistic reasons.

The newspapers were not allowed to publish news of the proclamation from the pulpit, but this prohibition was disregarded by the anti-Semitic *De Misthoorn*, which printed it in full under the heading *One in Judah*. Seyss-Inquart himself ignored the protest, but many throughout the nation welcomed its message as a deliverance from uncertainty; one preacher later reported that he felt he had been handed his battle orders; "even irregular churchgoers came again that afternoon to hear it read once more".[2]

These collective petitions are the only protests recorded during that time. In retrospect, we know that their effect was not very great, but in the light of the times we must commend the fact that any initiative was taken at all. Much greater respect still is due to those who did not wait for a lead, but followed the voices of their own consciences. How many there were we shall never know for much of the evidence has disappeared.

We must be content to mention only a few of these brave individuals. Lt.-Colonel Pierre Versteegh, who was later shot as one of the leaders of the Resistance, resigned his commission in the Dutch Army rather than sign the required form; N. H. de Graaf, an official in the Department of Social Affairs, and leader of the Youth Service, resigned as early as September 12, the day an investigation into the racial origins of all new officials was decreed. Four days later he sent his former staff a short mimeographed letter of explanation which undoubtedly made a deep impression on them. An even greater impact was made by a pamphlet distributed by the

[1] T. Delleman: *Opdat wij niet vergeten* (Lest we forget) (Kampen, 1950), p. 79.

[2] L. de Jong: *De Bezetting* (The Occupation) (Amsterdam, 1961), p. 137.

ten thousand: Dr. J. Koopmans' *Bijna to Laat* (Almost too late). His story has been told by H. C. Touw,[1] who praised this young theologian for his unflinching and self-sacrificing labours on behalf of persecuted Jews, and reserved for him a place of high honour in his book. Koopmans, too, expressed his dismay that the Churches should have remained so "correct" in their protests, and above all that Dutch Christians should not have been instructed from the pulpit to withhold their signatures from the Aryan attestation. "Now it is too late," he added. "Though most of those who filled in the forms did so without thinking, they must nevertheless bear some measure of responsibility for what was done to the Jews."

In the second part of his pamphlet, Koopmans made a passionate appeal to all Secretaries-General, Burgomasters, public servants and governors of Christian schools who "had adopted the safe policy of not employing anybody of Jewish blood", to the managers of the Christian broadcasting companies who, anticipating censorship by the enemy, were trying to give as little offence as possible, on the assumption that "preaching half a gospel is better than preaching no gospel at all", and finally to the Bishops, urging them to denounce the "godlessness of our enemy, the horrors which plague our country, and the consequent confusion".

These angry words sprang from the realization that the country was already in the throes of a terrible catastrophe. Dr. Koopmans seems to have caught a fleeting glimpse of the *via dolorosa* that would eventually lead to the crematorium, an apocalyptical vision of despair, destruction and death. "They have been put out—soon they will be put down." Dr. Koopmans spoke up because he could do no other. But to the Dutch Nazis he was neither a prophet nor a Cassandra—a leading article in the *Storm* of November 14, 1941, pilloried him as a "dangerous saboteur" and "a jumped-up paper tiger", who championed the cause of the "Jewish rabble", that "cancer to our German blood". Together with his publishers, the Uitgeversmaatschappij Holland, he would surely receive his just deserts. "What we want to know," the article concluded, "is how long such filth will be allowed to continue pouring forth its poisonous drivel?"

We know today that the Aryan attestation was merely a stepping-stone to the next measure: only when the Jews had been separated

[1] H. C. Touw: *Het verzet der Hervormde Kerk* (Resistance by the Reformed Church), Part 1 (The Hague, 1946), pp. 606–8.

from their non-Jewish colleagues could they be dismissed as such. Quoting Article 2 of Decree No. 137 (September 13, 1940), Wimmer instructed the Secretaries-General on November 4, 1940, to see to the immediate dismissal of Jewish officials and to the withholding of their salaries pending a further decision. The Secretaries-General did not treat the matter lightly. After much conferring, they decided on November 15 to agree to the temporary *suspension* (rather than dismissal) of Jewish officials, at the same time making it clear that they were acting on the express orders of the *Reichskommissar*. This was the second item in the minutes of the meeting held on November 15; the first item on November 18 was the dropping of the word "temporary".

But this concession did not satisfy the Germans, as can be seen from a letter they sent to Frederiks which, *inter alia*, complained of the Dutch failure to realize that the chief concern was not with religion but only with blood and race.

The Secretaries-General remained unmoved and replied that the instructions of November 4 were causing them a grave crisis of conscience. It was only after "prolonged discussion" that they had agreed to implement the order in the first place and then only on the understanding that it would be a temporary measure for the preservation of public order and safety. Once more they insisted that they were having qualms of conscience, adding that the measure was bound to arouse the hostility of the Dutch people.

Was the *Reichskommissar* impressed? Not if we are to judge from the short letter of acknowledgment he sent on December 2. Nor could the Secretaries-General have expected anything else, ignorant though they were of the full implications of the new measure.

In any case, the dismissal or rather "suspension" was now unopposed and took place during the second half of November. The whole game was nearly given away by the *Deutsche Zeitung in den Niederlanden* which, on November 28, 1940, proclaimed the *dismissal* of Jews in banner headlines. ANP, the Dutch Press Agency, also used the word "dismissal" but quickly amended it to "suspension". Apparently the Germans found it necessary to hold a special press conference in order, as they said, to clear up this "horrible misunderstanding". There was no question, they insisted, of their taking any permanent steps, but all manner of evil rumours were now circulating, and unfortunately found credence in the prevailing atmosphere. Few documents from the time of the Occupation equal this one in cynicism and hypocrisy, the more so as the Germans did not take very long to drop their mask. No doubt, their chief purpose was to lull the College of Secretaries-General into a sense of false security. For by demanding the permanent dismissal of Jews, the Germans would undoubtedly have exceeded the rights bestowed upon them by the Occupation Statutes. Yet they did succeed in ousting Jewish officials and, *mirabile dictu*, even found a Dutch apologist for this step in the highly respected Dutch jurist, Professor J. P. A. François, the legal adviser to the College of Secretaries-General who, after the War, wrote in his *Handboek van het Volkenrecht* (Handbook of International Law) that the German measure was justified by the "pathological aversion of National Socialists towards Jews".

And so the Jews were "put out" before they were "put down". But not all at once. In the meantime, the vital question of who was a Jew had been solved by the all-important Decree No. 189/1940 of October 22 to which we shall be returning. All those who qualified were "suspended", not only from the Civil Service but also from municipal councils, and other public positions—paid or honorary. Once only did Frederiks try to throw a spanner in the German works. When the special German representative in Amsterdam, Dr. Böhmcker, ordered the Burgomaster to implement the German dismissal orders in full, adding the words "irrespective of whether you have received instructions from the Secretary-General in the Ministry of the Interior or not", Frederiks protested in a long letter dated December 3, stating that in his interpretation, members of town councils did not fall under the German instructions of November 4. On the following day he received a reply which contained the telling argument that, since many burgomasters had already interpreted the order of November 4 in the "widest possible" terms, *mr.* Frederiks had nothing to worry about.

And so, as we said, the Jews were dismissed. One morning the bell rang, and on the steps stood an unknown but expected messenger, bearing a notice addressed to a Dutchman of Group B by a Dutchman of Group A. On the Amsterdam telephone exchange, Jews were not even allowed to enter the hall to say goodbye to their non-Jewish colleagues—as if they were so many lepers. Even the highly respected *mr.* L. E. Visser, President of the High Court, was treated as if he were unclean. This is not the place, nor does the writer have the ability, to do more than state the fact that the High Court "permitted" its Jewish President to be thrust aside by the Occupying Power as an inferior Dutchman, without making a public protest against this breach of one of the most fundamental principles of Dutch law, and without appreciating the consequences to themselves.[1]

Fortunately we have evidence that a great many people behaved far more honourably and nobly at that time. Thus quite a few universities and schools once again took a positive stand against the Germans. Here we must confine ourselves to citing only a few instances. To begin with there was a spontaneous student demonstration and strike at Delft, following the dismissal of Professors Van Dantzig, Waterman and Jitta. Special mention must be made of the outstandingly courageous bearing of Frans Van Hasselt, President of one of the Student Councils. His fellow-students will always remember his fiery address to them upon finding Professor Jitta's room closed. "Another professor turned up and told them to disperse. No one listened to him. But when Frans Van Hasselt began to speak from the top of the staircase, you could have heard a pin drop."[2] This brave young man was arrested in the summer of 1941, and died in Buchenwald in 1942.

We know more about the resistance at Leyden where Professors Meijers and David, and another member of the staff, Gans by name, had to leave the university. In Leyden, unlike Delft, it was the professors themselves who took the lead. Special mention must be made of a speech which Professor Cleveringa, the Dean of the Legal Faculty, delivered on November 26, in honour of his Jewish colleague, the famous jurist Professor E. M. Meijers: "Their actions are beneath contempt. All I ask is that we may dismiss them from our sight and gaze instead on the heights, up to that radiant figure in whose honour we are assembled here." Professor Cleveringa went on to contrast "power based on nothing but force" with "this noble son of our people, this man, this father to his students, this scholar, whom foreign usurpers have suspended from his duties . . . a man

[1] N. C. M. A. van den Dries: *De Hoge Raad der Nederlanden tijdens de bezetting* (The Dutch High Court during the Occupation) (Leyden, 1945), p. 4; *De Hooge Raad; antwoord aan Mr. N. C. M. A. Dries* (Amsterdam, 1945), p. 28.

[2] *Gedenkboek van het verzet der Delftsche studenten en docenten gedurende de jaren 1940–1945* (Resistance by students and lecturers at Delft during the years 1940–1945) (Delft, 1947), pp. 9–12; L. de Jong, *De Bezetting* (The Occupation), I, 146–8.

who, as all of us know, belongs here and God willing, shall return to us". The address was duplicated the same night[1] and the first forty-eight copies were distributed by post and subsequently re-duplicated, so that thousands of Dutchmen were able to read the full text within a few days. Professor Cleveringa was arrested the next day and kept in prison for eight months.

The universities of Delft and Leyden were closed by the Germans. Of the other universities, little remains to be told. The Rector of Amsterdam University, Professor Dr. B. Brouwer, declared an early vacation in an attempt to prevent student demonstrations against the dismissal of Professors Palache, Van den Bergh, Bregstein, Laqueur, Van Creveld, Cohen, Frijda and Kohnstamm, and their junior colleagues Leefmans, Van Zanten and Van Praag. In a leading article, the students' weekly, *Propria Cures*, took its farewell of these men with bold words: "We are proud to have been your students and colleagues, and pray that you may return to us before long." On November 26, Professor Donkersloot, speaking *ex cathedra*, expressed his profound respect for "those whom I deem my peers as colleagues and my betters in experience, learning and wisdom", and whom aliens were now keeping from their students. He spoke of his sadness and dismay at the violation of national and spiritual rights, and looked forward to the time when "this crying injustice to all Dutchmen would be ended".

In Utrecht, where Professors Ornstein, Wolff and Roos were dismissed, the students considered calling a strike, but eventually decided against the idea. It is said that what weighed most with the students was a proclamation by the Rector-Magnificus, Professor Dr. H. R. Kruyt, that a strike, far from achieving its ends, would merely be suicidal. The students agreed to wait and trust in Professor Kruyt's assurance that he and his fellows would determine the right moment for action. But that moment never came. It was also in Utrecht that Professor Koningsberger told an enthusiastic and excited audience of his great sadness and revulsion at the German decree. When he had finished his address he left a typewritten copy on the desk with the words: "Anyone wishing to report me to the Germans or to the NSB (the Dutch Nazi Party) will find the full text here." As the audience was streaming out at the end of the lecture, one of the students went up to the desk and tore up the paper.[2]

[1] *Gedenkboek*, p. 108.

[2] Letter, May 6, 1963, from Mr. A. J. Andrée Wiltens.

At Wageningen, some of the students went on a protest strike against the dismissal of Messrs. Polak, Schweizer and Berger; at Groningen, the axe fell on Professor Polak, and his colleagues Kahn, Van Praag and Lifschitz; Nijmegen lost Vidos, and Rotterdam lost Blazer, Polak and Stibbe (the latter after February 20, 1941).

When dealing with the reactions at some high schools to the dismissal of their Jewish teachers, the author must be excused if he makes particular mention of the strike which broke out spontaneously among the pupils of his own school, the Vossius Gymnasium in Amsterdam. The initiative came from two fifth-form pupils—Lucas van der Land and Bartjoost Romein; the former stayed away from the school altogether and took private lessons from his former Jewish teachers, and so successful was this arrangement that he passed the final state examination a year earlier than his less rebellious classmates. We also have some evidence that a strike was called at Doetinchem Lyceum and that, at the Government High School in Tiel, an attempt was made to draw up a petition in support of two dismissed teachers. The *Meldungen aus den Niederlanden* mentioned a school in Friesland where, after the dismissal of a Jewish woman teacher, eight of her "Aryan colleagues", all members of the *Nederlandse Unie*, signed and published an advertisement that the dismissed teacher would give private sewing lessons. The German paper was particularly incensed that the minister had seen fit to endorse this "kind of propaganda" in church.

We leave it to the reader's imagination what nationwide upheaval the dismissals must have caused, particularly in their effect on young children, who lost their trusted teachers overnight and must have realized that this was no ordinary parting.

And so the first phase in the destruction of Dutch Jewry was completed. So many are now dead that even conversations with survivors and the examination of letters leave an obscure picture of what actually happened. In the autumn of 1940 few could have predicted what was to follow and many still hoped that the Germans had done their worst. In this hope they were strengthened by the attitude of their non-Jewish neighbours, many of whom felt a bit envious that the Jews could "strut about idly like princes" while still drawing their salaries. Jewish officials were replaced, but many honorary posts (for instance, in the States Provincial and the Town Councils) remained unfilled. Often the newcomers would openly declare that their tenure of office would be short. Many Jews, above all the intellectuals among them, made the most of their unexpected Sabbatical year; some found a new occupation, some utilized their scientific training, others could at last write that long-postponed book or begin new studies. Five days after my own dismissal, the director of the Elsevier Publishing Company called on me with a commission to write a history of the Eighty Years War; this offer was immediately and eagerly accepted and the work tackled with quite unusual speed. Others were less fortunate, among them many who had given years of loyal service and now found themselves in the street without a future or even recognition of their past achievements. "Never did I think such heartlessness was possible," one of them wrote, "when before the war we all got on so well together. At night, I could not fall asleep, but lay wondering why it had to happen. A school which meant everything to me, to which I had given my all . . ." But many more must have consoled themselves with the fact that, after all, they had only been relieved of their responsibilities and not dismissed—had not the ANP stated this fact quite unequivocally? Relatives and friends were constantly reassured on this point, as the weeks passed, the New Year came in, and still nothing happened.

But even while the Germans were reassuring the Dutch Press, they were already making ready to break their word. Within a month of the "suspension", they began to reopen the question of dismissal with the Secretaries-General.

The first mention of the new line appears in the minutes of the Secretaries-General on December 23, 1940. Frederiks was told by the Germans that the order regarding the Jews had been misunderstood—they should have been dismissed, not merely suspended. Frederiks replied with four points:

(*a*) Dismissal was incompatible with the wording of the decree.
(*b*) The Jews were being paid an agreed annuity.
(*c*) The Germans themselves had expressly stated, even in print, that the dismissal of Jews was not intended.
(*d*) Dismissal would be in conflict with the intention of the decree whereby only "anti-German elements" were to be removed.

The minutes end with this sentence: "Several Secretaries-General stated bluntly that the sending out of further letters of dismissal would be quite intolerable."

From the minutes of January 20, 1941, it appears that Frederiks, in a further conversation with Wimmer "told him that it was an inopportune time to take new measures". But the Germans were merely playing a cat and mouse game with the College. At one moment it was: no dismissal, well and good, but then also no financial restitution; at the next moment it was dismissal with less than the agreed restitution. And all the Secretaries-General, despite their "bluntness" and alleged intransigence could do was to inform Seyss-Inquart that they themselves could take no further measures against the Jews; the more so as to do so would "in any case be impossible at such short notice". Would the *Reichskommissar* therefore deal with the matter himself. For the rest, the question of restitution would have to be the subject of further discussions with Wimmer.

Wimmer, however, seemed to be beyond reach and so the College was forced to deal with Althaus, one of his chief assistants, who, on February 21, 1941, sent them a letter from the *Reichskommissariat* dealing with the dismissal and the financial arrangements. All the Secretaries-General would have to do was to send this letter to the Jews in question.

In a circular, also dated February 21, 1941, Frederiks told his colleagues that as far as finance was concerned he had succeeded in getting better terms. Once again, the Dutch administrators had been fooled into believing that they had achieved something. The German policy was simply to make exceptionally harsh proposals and then "allow themselves" to be talked into something less stringent, only to repeat their original demands at a later date. In any case, in his circular (No. 678) Frederiks advised his colleagues to comply with the German request. This they did, but at the same time they resolved to write a letter to Seyss-Inquart pointing out once again that the new steps were in total conflict with their own views, and that they were transmitting the German notification under protest. The compensation was to be as follows:

| | *Breadwinners* | *Others* |
|---|---|---|
| First three months | 85% of last salary | 75% of last salary |
| First five years thereafter | 70% ,, ,, | 60% ,, ,, |
| Second five years | 60% ,, ,, | 50% ,, ,, |
| Thereafter | 50% ,, ,, | 40% ,, ,, |

Luckily both the letter of the Secretaries-General to Seyss-Inquart (dated February 24), Seyss-Inquart's own annotations of the letter, and the final reply have been preserved.

In its letter, the College reported that it had, in fact, passed on the German order for the dismissal of Jews but refused to accept responsibility for its contents. The College went on to complain that the Dutch people would nevertheless conclude that the College, simply by transmitting the German orders, was partly responsible for them. The Secretaries-General once again stressed the "disappointment" that the dismissal would cause after the assurance that it was only suspension that was intended and not dismissal. Such changes were bound to cause misunderstanding between the German authorities and the Dutch people.

At the bottom of this letter, Seyss-Inquart added a brief note to Dr. Wimmer, asking him to inform the College of his views. The word Jew was not mentioned; the *Reichskommissar* merely stated that as far as he was concerned, the College of Secretaries-General simply did not exist. He finished by saying: "If individual secretaries should feel that they cannot take responsibility for an order, even after discussion, they are always at liberty to resign."

It is highly interesting to see what Wimmer made out of all this. We have his drafts reply of March 12, with annotations in Seyss-Inquart's own hand and a copy of the final document sent out the same day. Seyss-Inquart had obviously decided to soft-pedal the whole issue. Thus Wimmer's "The Secretaries-General must realize" was amended to "You, Gentlemen, will understand", and in many other places, too, the *Reichskommissar* toned down the brusqueness of his Austrian colleague. What is most striking, however, is that the gratuitous advice mentioned at the end of the last paragraph is missing, the letter ending instead with the request in future to refrain from collective petitions to the *Reichskommissar*. Were the Germans afraid that the "gentlemen" would down tools? A certain answer to this question is impossible, though we have another document which might throw some light on the subject and which we shall discuss later. Here we must merely mention that the College became so immersed in long discussions with the Germans about its own existence, that little time was left for the Jews. And so the Jews were forced out, and the College could console itself with the fact that the actual number of those involved was small—hardly one per cent of a total of 200,000 officials.[1]

We end this section with yet another telling document. On September 15, 1942, Althaus sent a letter to the German representa-

[1] Herzberg: *op. cit.*, p. 47.

tive in Amsterdam on the subject of the agreed compensation which the Germans were apparently trying to cut down. Althaus thought this rather precipitate and wrote: "May I draw your attention to the fact that, when instructions of November 4, 1940, were issued, the Secretaries-General made great difficulties and seriously considered resigning their offices. It was only after much trouble that I succeeded in keeping them on the rails (*sic!*)."

Here the winning chess player affords us a glimpse of the rules by which he proposed to conduct the game. His opponent—the College of Secretaries-General—had made a forcing move. It had been difficult to find the right reply, but in the end the advantage had been regained. The Jews were wiped off the board.

## THE REGISTRATION OF BUSINESSES AND INDIVIDUALS

The next German measure was the now notorious decree of October 22, 1940. We quote the most significant provisions, since they also served in part to pave the way for many subsequent steps. The new decree required the registration of a wide range of enterprises, thus defined in Article 1:

"1. Businesses required to submit accounts in terms of the Trade Registration Act of 1918;

"2. Businesses controlled by companies, including institutions, foundations and all similar organizations engaged in economic activities;

"3. Businesses connected with agriculture and forestry (including horticulture and fishery) if conducted for profit;

"4. Businesses, other than those covered by (1), owned by artisans or street-vendors."

Even a reader unfamiliar with legal jargon may conclude that these categories were fairly comprehensive. If by no means all Dutch enterprises were scheduled, that was because the decree was specifically aimed at the Jews and, in Article 2, the Jews were openly named for the first time in any measure taken by the Occupying Power.

All businesses owned by Jews or having even one Jewish partner or director were obliged to register as at May 9, 1940. This proviso extended to a great many undertakings, including the Netherlands Bank, which had one Jewish director. But the meshes of the net were made yet finer: all enterprises with predominantly Jewish capital or Jewish shareholders must register. And "predominantly" did not merely signify the greater part. If as little as a quarter of the capital belonged to Jews, or if Jewish shareholders between them could muster so much as half the total votes—they were, in this singular definition, "predominant". Moreover, lest some suspect enterprises should nevertheless escape the new regulations, there was yet another clause: registration was also compulsory for enterprises that were under predominantly Jewish "influence". Just how this Svengalian "influence" was to be understood was not defined.

Now once they had mentioned Jews by name, the Germans also had to give their own precise answer to the question "What is a Jew?" They did so in what was probably one of the most far-reaching measures they took against Dutch Jewry:

*Article 4*
*Definition of Jews*

1. Jews are all persons whose grandparents included three or more full Jews by race. (And see 3 below.)
2. Persons with only two fully Jewish grandparents are deemed to be Jews if they either
   (*a*) belonged to the Jewish religious community on 9 May 1940 (or subsequently joined it);
   (*b*) or were married to a Jew on 9 May 1940 or after that date.
3. A grandparent is deemed a full Jew if he was at any time a member of the Jewish religious congregation.

We shall frequently advert to Article 4, since it was to rear its ugly head in all the principal instruments of Nazi oppression. The reader will recall the definition of Jew used by the Germans during the expulsion of Jewish personnel from the ARP service; the new definition was, of course, far more extensive, but it, too, was still far from watertight. That was not yet the main point, however; what most exercised German officialdom was whether their new measures were practicable. No doubt they did not deliberately leave loopholes, but it is characteristic of their whole administrative strategy in the Netherlands, that they were always able to pursue their policies by enforcing their decrees or by ignoring them, whichever best suited them at any given moment. To this, too, we shall return all too often.

The second part of the Decree (Articles 5–8) prescribed the method of registration. The first mention of the notorious *Wirtschaftsprüfstelle* (Bureau of Economic Investigation) of which, too, much more will be heard in these pages, occurs in § 3 of Article 6. The third part stipulated the heavy fines that could be imposed in case of non-compliance. In view of what followed, special mention must also be made of Article 10, which threatened to punish misrepresentation by confiscation of the whole property involved. The fourth part carried this ominous sentence: "The *Reichskommissar* for the Occupied Netherlands is taking the necessary steps to implement this decree and is issuing the requisite instructions."

When the Jews learned what was demanded of them, they complied in every respect. They applied for the appropriate forms, and completed them in accordance with the "hints" thoughtfully issued by the *Wirtschaftsprüfstelle* (forms, enclosures and envelope—50 cents). These forms were in quintuplicate and in five colours: white, blue, violet, dark and light green with carbon papers interleaved—value for money, if you look at it that way.

Before the year was out, there appeared the decree of December 19, 1940, prohibiting the employment by Jewish householders of "persons of German nationality, or of German and related blood". This was followed, early in 1941, by the sweeping Decree No 6 of January 10, ordering the registration of *all* Jewish persons: full Jews, half-Jews, quarter-Jews, orthodox or not. Later, on October 2, 1941, Böhmcker, the German delegate in Amsterdam, was able to write to Seyss-Inquart: "Thanks to Decree 6/41, all Dutch Jews are now in the bag (*erfasst*)."

Article 2 of that decree (6/41) is a masterpiece of conversion by definition. It was no longer necessary to have had *three* Jewish grandparents. *One* would do just as well. And this single grandparent need not have had a Jewish ancestor at all. It was quite enough that he should at any time have been "a member of the Jewish religious congregation". But this might sometimes be a little difficult to prove, and indeed the Germans afterwards discovered that it was far easier merely to declare Jews inferior than actually to ferret them out. Article 3 tried to take care of that. In case of doubt, the *Reichskommissar* himself would adjudicate. If this resulted in many judgments of Solomon, the compliment is one that Seyss-Inquart himself would not greatly have appreciated. Against his decision there could be no appeal.

All Jews, thus defined, had to register with the burgomaster or the Census Office (Articles 5 and 6) within four (ten in Amsterdam) weeks. This had to be done in writing (Article 7) and nothing could be left out. Registration had come to mean compulsory submission of a complete personal history. In return the person received a yellow card. (The colour, as Herzberg has pointed out, was hardly accidental.) The *Joodse Weekblad* (Jewish Weekly) of June 13, 1941, announced the dates on which these cards would be available. The price ("fee") was one guilder, payable in advance: the fee of the impecunious must be paid by the "local Israelitic congregation", if the person belonged to one—otherwise he could get his card free. The Census Office received half the guilder, when there was one. Failure to register was punishable with five years' imprisonment and/or confiscation of property.

The Decree itself took effect from January 24, and on February 3 the *Government Gazette* published the regulations of January 27 (January 25–26 was a weekend) on the procedure for implementing it. This distinguished Jews = J from "Bastard Jews" = B. Frederiks defined the former in terms of Article 4 of Decree No. 189 of 1940; but the "bastards" were now subdivided into B I (two Jewish grandparents and B II (one Jewish grandparent). Burgomasters receiving registrations were instructed to check the information supplied against identity cards or police registers, and to endorse the respective index card J, BI or BII in white or black by means of a special tab approved by the Head of the Government Inspectorate.

The completed forms had to reach the Head of the Inspectorate "before the sixteenth day of each month" and the Inspectorate itself was charged with the full implementation of the new measures.

This, by and large, was the genesis of a piece of legislation that was to have particularly profound effects on the life of Dutch Jewry. If it was to succeed, it was vital that both Jews and Dutch officials should co-operate. Here, if anywhere, the choice they made can be appraised only in the context of the time. How could anyone have anticipated the horrifying outcome? It is for the reader to decide whether or not ignorance was sufficient extenuation.

What, first of all, did the Jews themselves do? Those who have written on the subject or whom the author has consulted are agreed: with few, indeed with very few, exceptions, they all registered. There have been various explanations, many of them coloured by wisdom after the event. Certainly there was a general lack of appreciation of the full extent of the threat. Was there an element of pride and defiance as well? Herzberg's assertion[1] that many who had never

[1] Herzberg: *op. cit.*, p. 50.

been members of the Jewish congregation now joined it for reasons of principle is strong evidence that these factors did, indeed, play a part. Fear? No doubt that, too, was a powerful agent. Moreover, Dutch Jews had always lived in a well-regulated society, in which one's name stood on all sorts of index cards and registers. These records still existed and might be used to trace and punish anyone who attempted evasion or resistance. Immediately after the capitulation, Professor N. W. Posthumus offered to hide (not destroy) the records of the Amsterdam Jewish Community—who refused without hesitation. It did not seem that the time had yet come for throwing files into the canals. In any case, the German orders were obeyed and, what is more, obeyed promptly.

Nor did Dutch non-Jews behave with less circumspection. As early as November 12, 1940, the Head of the Dutch Census Office passed on the German demand for the establishment of Jewish registration offices, which had to be kept open day and night, in the centre of every town with Jewish inhabitants. In a document dated January 15, 1941, the Census Office expressed its satisfaction that, thanks to the German measure, here had been "an untold administrative simplification and a saving of tens of thousands [of guilders] for the country".

Among the surviving German records are several surveys of the number of people who had registered by a certain date. One might think they dealt with a famous victory. Few fail to sing the praises of the Census Office. As early as March 24, 1941, when the grim business had barely started, they spoke of the Dutch organization as being "exemplary". But two things seemed to bother them: there were delays and the number registered did not come up to the estimated figure. On April 9, J. L. Lentz, the Head of the Census Office, gave them a number of excuses for the delay; one was that not all Dutch burgomasters read the *Government Gazette*. Still, a report of April 30, 1941, tells that of the 1,050 municipalities, 1,019 had discharged their duty. One of the others was Amsterdam. Another was Apeldoorn—where delay was due to the "difficulty of registering the inmates of the local Jewish Insane Asylum"; there was "no reason to think that the Dutch were in any way sabotaging the measure". A week later, on May 5, Apeldoorn had done its duty; only twelve burgomasters now lagged behind. 555 had sent in returns. Another 483 had no Jews to register.

On September 5, 1941, Wimmer took stock: from the statistics submitted by the Census Office on August 27, it appeared that there had been a total of 160,820 registrations: 140,552 Jews, 14,549 half-Jews (B I) and 5,719 quarter-Jews (B II). He expressed great surprise at the relatively small number of "half-breeds"—clearly there was far less intermarriage in Holland than there had been in Germany. He went on to say, with some satisfaction (p. 3): "With the establishment of a Central Register of Jews and Jewish half-breeds by the Census Office in The Hague there has been created an instrument and a central information bureau for all branches of government, police and law officers, whose use I recommend and request in all cases of doubt. Close links between the Central Register and the Municipal Census Offices in the Netherlands ensure the speedy detection of all changes (of residence, for instance) and thus guarantee that the register at all times reflects the actual state of affairs in individual cases and for statistical purposes."

Had all Jews at last been caught in the net? The Germans thought so, but Lentz was not so sure. At the beginning of 1942 he warned that there were "reasonable grounds" for supposing that some Jews had not done their duty; quite a few Kohns and Levys whose names appeared on the old rolls had not put down their names on the new. Clearly Lentz went to some trouble in the matter. Thanks to his vigilance, the Germans considered asking the bearers of such compromising names to produce proof of their origins; the available records do not tell us whether they ever implemented this decision.

Here we may mention a letter addressed by Lentz to the relevant German authorities on October 7, 1942. He expressed his joy that the Germans thought so favourably of his (and his associates') work. "This," he said, "encourages us to strive with utter devotion to do justice to our slogan 'To record is to serve'. For my part, I would like to express appreciation of the confidence you repose in myself and my staff. Thanks to this and to your co-operation, the Census Office was able to contrive ways and means of carrying out its often difficult task. May I express the hope that we shall continue to enjoy your confidence." This was written when the deportation of Jews to unknown destinations had been proceeding for three months, when Jews were being dragged out of their houses at night, thanks not least to the "utter devotion" with which the Census Office was discharging its "often difficult" task! As an epilogue to all this, we quote from the answer by Seyss-Inquart's deputy in Amsterdam to Wimmer's question of who had to bear the cost of this "sorting" of the Jews. The answer was "the Dutch state". For "our action is helping to remove Jews from the Netherlands and thus ensure that the Dutch state will have less expenditure in the future". So much for our brief digression; we can now return to the beginning of 1941 and earlier.

The issue of identity cards to Jews was closely connected with the registration. On the antecedents of these cards we can be brief. Their legal basis was Ordinance No. 197 signed by Frederiks on October 17, 1940. This is not the place to discuss the general merits of identity cards; we freely grant that the measure was useful in itself. In the event, however, it strengthened the grip of the invader on all Dutchmen, and hence on the most vulnerable among them, the Jews. This grip became a stranglehold, thanks to the precautions taken at The Hague against possible forgeries. The identification card was extremely detailed: it must include two photographs, two sets of fingerprints, a stamp, two signatures of the bearer, one signature and the initials of the official. To keep these souvenirs in pristine conditions, they had to be preserved in a special container. Finally, the date of registration and the bearer's serial number were recorded in the card index. And was that all? Not if you were a Jew. The general issue of identity cards began in Amsterdam in April 1941—first to non-Jews. Not a priority to be envied, perhaps. However, when Jews were eventually issued with their cards in a special department, these bore the letter J in ominous and large black type.

We know part of the early history of this fatal letter. In the Netherlands it was first mentioned in a memorandum sent by Lentz to the German authorities on January 8, 1941. From a letter by Rauter (June 12) it would appear further that, on May 5, Lentz had submitted the design of an identity card for Jews, though the records do not tell us on whose initiative. In his reply, Rauter suggested that a black J on a red background should appear twice on every Jewish identity card. Even before that date, on June 3, Frederiks had sent a circular to all burgomasters (No. 23953) in which he informed them that Rauter had ordered the letter J (= Jew) to be stamped in black ink on the identity cards of all those who, according to Decree No. 189/1940, qualified for it: twice on the identity card itself, once on the notice to report and once on the receipt. The circular also specified the form and size of the J, a letter which "in many cases, was the bearer's death warrant . . . Jews are often blamed for not having sabotaged this measure more effectively. Much more blameworthy, however, were those officials who went out of their way to implement every detail of the measure."[1]

Not all officials did so, of course. There was the case of a sixty-two-year-old ship's carpenter with four Jewish grandparents, but baptized, with a Christian wife and seven children, all married to Christians. This man wrote desperate letters to the German authorities: (". . . Your Excellency may imagine my dismay, I who have grown up in Christian society . . . who have absolutely nothing in common with anything Jewish . . .") An Amsterdam official broke a lance for him since, after all, "a ship's carpenter holds a highly responsible position . . .". Moreover, "his looks completely belie his Jewish origins. On the contrary, his appearance—round face, honest grey eyes—is that of the Dutch seaman . . . He had gone through a lot—he was torpedoed in the last war, braved fire on board ship and a host of other dangers, but as he himself puts it: Being forced, in my old age, to bear a J on my identity card is the worst thing that ever happened to me." And the Dutch official "knew just how he must feel." No comment is needed.

There were some Jews who went to even greater lengths. A fifty-year-old man declared in a petition to the *Reichskommissar* that he had had no dealing with Jews or Jewish matters (except for four Jewish grandparents, J.P.), that he had always been proud of his non-Jewish appearance, that he was married to an Aryan ("the thought of marrying a Jewish woman has always filled me with abhorrence"); his twelve-year-old daughter had no idea that her father was a Jew. Another petitioner, a fanatical member of the Dutch Nazi Party, wrote four long pages to Seyss-Inquart. She was in utter despair, ever since she had found out that she was of Jewish blood, although "my blood speaks 100 per cent German". Her husband knew nothing of all this, she felt utterly wretched . . .

Among the records is the story of a Jew who had the impertinence to obtain identity cards without a J for himself and his family ("in an underhand way"). From the tone in which this matter was discussed by Dutch officials and from the way the Dutch police apprehended the culprit, we might suppose that they considered him a dangerous criminal. Indeed, the annual report of the Amsterdam Criminal Investigation Bureau mentions three Jewish failures

[1] *Het grote gebod* (The great commandment), Part I (Kampen, 1951), p. 615.

to register in the same breath as theft, embezzlement and fraud. This, too, needs no comment.

To discuss other important developments we must go farther back in time. One of the earliest was the "Aryanization" of the Dutch Press Agency, the ANP, at the outset of the Occupation. On the day after the capitulation, the Press attaché to the German legation in The Hague, H. Hushahn, Jr., had the Jewish staff of the Press Agency put into the street without paying them a single cent. The director of the ANP eventually succeeded in getting them one and a half months' salary. In The Hague, the Bureau fell into the hands of Dr. H. W. van der Vaart Smit, a member of the Dutch Nazi Party (NSB). As late as May 19, 1943, when the deportation of Jews was at its height, the *Deutsche Zeitung in den Niederlanden* still saw fit to devote an entire page to Jewish "control" of the Dutch Press, and made the (by then) somewhat musty revelation: "Jews and their stooges used to control the Dutch press, and exploited it to proclaim their own excellence." What is remarkable about this denunciation is that it came so late in the day. After a brief struggle, in which the chief protagonists were Dutchmen and Dutch organizations, with the Germans in the background, the Press had been among the first Dutch professions to allow itself to be forced to toe the Nazi line. This process began even before the capitulation, but only got into its stride afterwards, due not least to defeatism within the Dutch ranks. Thus *De Telegraaf* dismissed three journalists as early as August 1, 1940, because, as contributors to the foreign section, they had carried on too virulent a "Jewish-Bolshevik" smear campaign against the Germans. Many other "Jewish Bolsheviks" were to follow, though the Germans believed, or gave out they believed, that others still lurked about the Presses. On November 23, 1940, when the *Nederlandse Journalistenkring* (Dutch Journalists' Circle) was turned into the *Nederlandse Journalisten Verbond* (Dutch Journalists' Union) to which no Jew could belong, it appeared that of a total of 700 journalists only 37 were Jews, and that of the 400 editors in the Association of Dutch Newspapers (*De Nederlandse Dagbladpers*) only a single one was Jewish. This last organization introduced the leadership principle by regulation and also agreed to comply with the German "wish" that no more Jews should be admitted. On the credit side, however, more than one Dutch witness praised the speech of Gerard Hoek (NCRV) who, at a meeting of the Utrecht branch, made a strong protest against all discrimination.

Some Dutch journalists were rather less heroic. With the coming of the Germans, Jew-baiting by the section of the Press subservient to the invader was freed from all restraint. Their choicest gems will presently be noticed. Here we need only say that some Dutch Nazi papers tried to out-Stürmer *Der Stürmer* itself; *De Misthoorn*, for instance, a paper founded before the war, proved too virulent for even the NSB, who had it closed down.

Then there was the Nazi campaign against Jewish authors, which would also be very funny if it were not so tragic. German interference in the book trade made itself felt as early as May 1940, although not yet directed at Jewish authors as such: Heine was proscribed, but so was Niemöller. Soon afterwards there were signs of "grave confusion and irregularity" due to the fact that in Holland, unlike Belgium and France, no lists of prohibited books had been published. Wielek reports that, as early as the summer of 1940, two Jewish publishers were forced to resign from the publishers' association.

The records contain a letter by Wimmer to the Secretaries-General, dated August 22, 1940, ordering them to remove from Dutch libraries all writings hostile to the German people, the *Führer*, the Nazi Party, the German State, the German Government and the German Army, and to submit a full list of all the offending volumes within a few weeks, giving titles in alphabetical order, author's names, place and year of publication.

In 1940 all textbooks, and particularly school textbooks, were already heavily doctored. In a school history in which the present writer had some part, space could no longer be given to the portrait of Karl Marx. So Marx, as well as my name on the title page, disappeared. When my *History of the Eighty Years War*, commissioned by Elseviers in 1940, appeared in May 1941, it did so under the name of a friend (Dr. B. W. Schaper) who lent it at no small personal risk. Many other Jewish writers received similar assistance, particularly when things got even worse in the years that followed.

Another anti-Jewish measure was the exclusion of Jews from cinemas. As early as May 1940, the *Nederlandse Bioscoopbond* (Dutch Cinema Union) forced its Jewish members to resign.[1] The *Meldungen aus den Niederlanden* complained of anti-German demonstrations and of frequent catcalls, which could be made with individual impunity in the darkness of the cinema. What is less plausible is their claim

[1] Wielek: *De oorlog die Hitler Won* (The war that Hitler won) (Amsterdam, 1947), p. 22.

that all these demonstrations in the dark were, in fact, the work of Jews. In any case, that was the pretext for barring Jews from all but two cinemas as from January 5, 1941. Nor did the *Nederlandse Bioscoopbond* do things by halves. On January 8 it published a report in which it "regretfully" declared that "despite repeated warnings" the disturbances had recurred; the Union was therefore obliged to expel the intractable Jews from the remaining two theatres as well. Members of the Union were also doubtful whether it was fitting to retain Jewish employees; one cinema sacked them all while the discussions were still proceeding. Particularly embarrassing must have been the position of Jewish cinema owners forced to put up posters with the words *Für Juden verboten*—it is said that quite a few displayed these notices in the required format but with small letters. Non-Jewish members of the *Nederlandse Bioscoopbond*, whose co-operation seemed less than wholehearted, were forced to conform on pain of getting no films, and by still less reputable measures. Soon afterwards, twenty-five Jewish-owned cinemas were placed under the "management" of the German *Filmreferent*, Dr. Zimmer. On January 17, 1941, the *Liberale Weekblad* published an attack on the *Nederlandse Bioscoopbond* by *mr.* J. Rutgers, who called its attitude "un-Dutch in the highest degree". The paper was promptly shut down. At first there was a clear boycott of cinemas by non-Jews, but soon afterwards many took a "soft attitude", particularly towards German comedies.[1] The Jews could console themselves with the fact that they were not missing very much, certainly not the repulsive newsreels that were everywhere being shown. Moreover, they were spared the indignity of having to watch such scurrilous films as "The Eternal Jew"—which all Dutch cinemas had to put on, on the orders of the Secretary-General for Propaganda and Arts. When the Burgomaster of Utrecht, G. A. W. ter Pelkwijk, asked, for purposes of entertainment tax assessment, into what category this film fell, he was told on behalf of the German Delegate that it was cultural. "I informed him that, in view of its content, this could not possibly be the case."[2]

Another matter, too, takes us back to 1940. As early as May 31 of that year, Frederiks informed the College of Secretaries-General that the Burgomaster of Zandvoort had telephoned him for a ruling

[1] *Onderdrukking en Verzet*, II, 173.

[2] G. A. W. ter Pelkwijk: *Utrecht in de eerste jaren van de bezetting* (Utrecht during the early years of the Occupation) (Utrecht, 1950), p. 34.

on the German request that signs bearing the words "Jewish business" must be affixed outside the relevant shops and offices. The College was unanimous in its advice to the Burgomaster to refuse all co-operation. The same thing happened again at a meeting on August 12, which received similar enquiries from councils all over the south of the country; the College again vetoed the German demand. Precisely one month later, Wimmer informed Frederiks and Tenkink, Secretary-General for Justice, that he would like to see all Jewish businesses clearly marked as such; both men refused, but the "measure was nevertheless implemented by the Germans themselves". In early June 1940 the College had to instruct the Burgomaster of The Hague to order the removal of anti-Jewish posters in a local café. The Hague was also the first town to mark a park-bench "Not for Jews". This campaign got into its stride soon after the New Year, particularly in Amsterdam. On January 4, 1941, the Nazi *Het Nationale Dagblad* treated its readers to the good news that Leyden Square was full of notices proclaiming "Jews not wanted here", and added: "It is almost too good to be true."

The records include a lengthy account by Volmer, the manager of the American Hotel in Amsterdam, which provides us with a clear picture of how the Germans and the NSB played their game, and of the general reaction to it. Thus on December 30, 1940, a German Army spokesman alleged that there had been "repeated complaints by German officers against being treated by the public, and by Jews in particular, in an insulting manner"; similar complaints had been lodged by lower ranks. The *Kommandant* further alleged that he had "positive reports" of "rowdy scenes" in various businesses, adding that "if one of his men were injured in any way, for instance by the throwing of beer glasses and the like, the proprietor or owner of the business would be held responsible".

How these "rowdy scenes" came about was no secret to anyone. In Amsterdam and elsewhere, NSB-men, Dutch storm-troopers (WA-men) and similar elements banded together for deliberate provocation, often causing grave damage. Bystanders often witnessed scenes that made a much deeper impression on them than many a more far-reaching measure. Here they could see with their own eyes what was happening around them, witness humiliation and violence —no one who watched the Nazi gangs at work could fail to realize what was going on. They were behaving like licensed thugs—for the moment directing their venom against the Jews, but in future perhaps against everyone else as well. Meanwhile, these thugs succeeded in sticking up their anti-Jewish signs everywhere, down to the smallest snack bar.

At the same time, non-Jews were being urged by duplicated letters to boycott all discriminatory establishments and to oppose the German measures as contrary to elementary justice and human decency. Without success, rejoiced Böhmcker, the German Delegate in Amsterdam, adding that the staff of these establishments was happy to be rid of their "miserly and arrogant Jewish employers". Everywhere the symptoms of anti-Semitism were increasing, although Böhmcker felt impelled to complain of the attitude of orthodox Calvinist circles who for "so-called" reasons of conscience thought fit to side with the Jews. Nevertheless there was good reason to think that "the anti-Semitic movement in Amsterdam could be strengthened even further". This was written on February 4, 1941.

Before the month was out Böhmcker had reason to reconsider his prediction.

## THE FOUNDING OF THE JEWISH COUNCIL AND THE FEBRUARY STRIKE

In the stream of events that was to carry the Jews to their final destruction, there were violent eddies against the even flow. One of these occurred in February 1941, when it must have become crystal clear to all Jews—and to many non-Jews as well—that the pogrom had begun in earnest. For the first time Jews were being robbed, beaten up and carried off on a large scale.

The reason for this sudden intensification of the anti-Semitic campaign was probably the German feeling that it could do no harm to try the effect of giving the Dutch Nazis free rein for a short time; the more so since by bringing them under control again they might hope to impress the Dutch with their own discipline and propriety. What they did not reckon on was the reaction of the Dutch people, whose February strike took them completely by surprise.

Violence was largely organized by the WA, the storm-troopers of the NSB and, here and there, by active members of other Nazi groups. B. A. Sijes[1] has given us a lengthy—but presumably incomplete—summary of the outrages committed by these men,

[1] *De Februaristaking, 25–26 February 1941* (The February Strike) (The Hague, 1954).

particularly in Amsterdam (where the Jews were chiefly concentrated) but also elsewhere. Most of the thugs came away disappointed. The vast bloodbath for which they had hoped eluded them; far from taking control of the streets, they were beaten back, time and again, albeit after first hurting a host of innocent people.

What strikes us most in the excesses of the WA is not the undisciplined behaviour of people who prided themselves on their sense of discipline, nor the craven manner in which they retreated at the first sign of opposition (unless they could rely upon the support of German soldiers), nor yet their thieving, but that they stole chiefly from the poorest of the poor, whose meagre possessions they carried off, while leaving many richer Jews completely unmolested. Perhaps the simplest answer to this puzzle is that they concentrated their attack on the most densely populated Jewish quarters, and had no time to get round to the rest. The whole thing makes a sad story of human wretchedness, or rather depravity. It is scant consolation that this pales into insignificance in the perspective of the coolly calculated mass murder, systematically organized by the Germans themselves.

However, in the story of those days there were two encouraging elements. The first was that the Jews refused to knuckle under. They did not seek out their enemies but neither did they allow themselves to be led like sheep to the slaughter. Determined to defend their hearths and homes—however poor—they formed the first resistance groups in the country. The second positive element was the support they were given by their non-Jewish neighbours. The feeling that they were not alone undoubtedly encouraged the Jews; those who came to provoke them in their own districts did so at grave risk. WA-man Hendrik Koot, who was wounded in one of the many fights that occurred in those days, died soon afterwards. The Dutch Nazi Weekly, *Volk en Vaderland*,[1] took the occasion of his funeral to proclaim in large print: "Judah has dropped its mask at last. Murdered? No, cut down with sadistic lust. Crushed under the heel by a nomadic race of alien blood."

It is not surprising that both NSB-men and Germans should have painted the victim's death and the circumstances surrounding it in the most lurid colours, though what they did, in fact, was to betray their own bestiality rather than describe the actual facts. According to Rauter, for instance, a Jew had ripped open the victim's artery

[1] February 21, 1941.

with his teeth and then sucked the blood; another "authority" had the Jews throw vitriol out of the windows; Böhmcker claimed that a Jew had fastened his teeth into Koot's face, and so on. This was his pretext for sealing off the Jewish quarter of Amsterdam on February 12, 1941, at 6 a.m.—not even doctors were allowed to leave—but nor was the WA allowed to enter.

And so the Jews found themselves in a sort of ghetto, a prison they knew neither from experience nor from memory. Böhmcker legalized the whole thing with a series of proclamations. There is no point in listing them all, since the Germans failed to implement them. Much more important was another of his measures: the very day he sealed off the Jewish quarter, he also sent for the President of the Council of the Great Dutch Synagogue, A. Asscher (the merchant Asscher as Böhmcker chose to call him), L. H. Sarlouis, Chief Rabbi of the German-Jewish (Ashkenazi) Congregation, and D. Francès, the Rabbi of the Portuguese-Jewish (Sephardic) Congregation. Others present at the conference were the acting town clerk, Franken, and *Kriminalkommissar SS-Hauptsturmführer* Ditges. Böhmcker began with a brief account of the events of the past few days, as he saw them, made it clear that uniformed party members would not enter the Jewish quarter in future and demanded the immediate formation of a Jewish Council as responsible representatives of Amsterdam Jewry. The three Jewish leaders were then "requested" to form such a body. After consulting with the two rabbis, Asscher told the Germans that Professor Cohen and he would act as joint presidents and that he would co-opt the rest in consultation with the two rabbis. Böhmcker thereupon informed "the merchant Asscher", that the Jewish Council, and its joint presidents in particular, would have to preserve order in the Jewish quarter, and start by calling upon all Jews to surrender their weapons. This, he claimed, was a great concession, for the only alternative was a police raid on the Jewish quarter and the arrest of all those in illegal possession of arms. Whether Asscher was pleasantly surprised at the German's generosity, or whether he saw through him, we cannot tell; but we do know that he later described Böhmcker as a very polite person.

And so Dutch Jewry was suddenly saddled with a German-sponsored Council. Asscher's co-president, Professor D. Cohen, had previously been President of the Committee for Jewish Refugees, set up in 1933. The two rabbis stepped down, but Asscher and Cohen agreed without hesitation to serve, as did many—though not all—the members they invited to join them. The only one to refuse on principle was Professor Frijda, who declared that the Council could never be anything but a tool of the Germans; A. van Dam declined on medical grounds; *mr.* Kisch agreed, after consultation with *mr.* Visser, ex-President of the High Court, and then only as observer on behalf of the Jewish Co-ordination Committee, of which more anon. Some of those asked to join did so only after a great deal of discussion. All the members were prominent Jews, but since Asscher felt that the ordinary Jewish workers, too, should be represented, he telephoned I. Voet, the President of the Dutch Diamond Workers' Union, who agreed to serve after some hesitation; on April 17, 1941, the *Jewish Weekly* reported that he had resigned for reasons of health, so that the working-class element soon disappeared from this "representative" council of Dutch Jewry. A local representative from the (poorer) Jewish quarter also resigned very quickly; his function was taken over by a small residential sub-committee.

The list of council members submitted to Böhmcker (with one subsequent addition) included the two Presidents together with Dr. J. Arons; *mr.* N. de Beneditty; A. van den Bergh; *mr.* A. B. Gomperts; I. de Haan; A. de Hoop; *mr.* M. L. Kan; *mr.* I. Kisch; A. Krouwer; *mr.* S. J. van Lier; A. J. Mendes da Costa; Professor Dr. J. L. Palache; Dr. M. I. Prins; Rabbi L. H. Sarlouis; Dr. D. M. Sluys; A. Soep; I. Voet; Dr. I. H. J. Vos.

We have the minutes of a meeting held by the Council at Asscher's factory on February 13, 1941, at 11 a.m., and a reference to a meeting of the previous evening of which no details are known. From the brief minutes, it would appear that neither the name nor the character of the organization had been settled; one suggested title was "Representative Committee of Amsterdam Jewry", and all agreed that the Council would have a "predominantly executive and mediatory task, but could bear no responsibility for the orders it had to transmit, nor could it accept orders that were dishonourable to the Jews".

On the same day, some 5,000 inhabitants of the Jewish quarter met in the Diamond Exchange in two separate sessions, to hear what Asscher had to tell them. Among those present were most members of the newly-formed Council, a few uniformed German policemen, and a number of detectives. "There were no incidents," Böhmcker wrote in his report, which also included a German translation of Asscher's address. The gist of it was the order to hand over to the police "all fire-arms, clubs, knives and other weapons", and to do so without delay. The ultimatum expired at noon the next day.

It will probably never be possible to reconstruct the reaction of the audience to the demand that they hand in their "fire-arms, clubs, knives and other weapons" as if they were a private army![1] Asscher[2] later declared that he himself was convinced that whatever weapons the Jews may or may not have had, fire-arms were not among them. Cohen told the author that he himself never discovered whether there were any effective weapons at all, though many inhabitants of the Jewish district assured him that there were. Asscher, in any case, urged the Jews to hand their arms in although he—unlike Cohen—was at first in favour of the Jews being armed, and only gave in when Böhmcker threatened to shoot 500 Jews as an act of reprisal.

May we take it that, since hardly any weapons were handed in, none, in fact, existed? It certainly points in that direction. True, many Jews were afraid to put in an appearance at the police station—an unnecessary risk when all they would have had to hand in was a piece of wood or iron. Sijes[3] tells us that many people have reproached Asscher because "his call for the handing in of weapons broke the Jewish will to resist and their active solidarity with non-Jews". Even so, Böhmcker was dissatisfied with the poor response to his express orders, and told Asscher on February 17: "The number of arms handed in so far does not correspond with the actual state of affairs"; as a result, he would be forced to take official steps. Asscher replied on February 19 that the Jewish Council had once again made the German instructions known in the Jewish quarter; the ultimatum was extended until February 21 at 4 p.m. The result was no better.

Meanwhile the closure of the Jewish district had been partially lifted, but so many other vexatious restrictions continued that the people of Amsterdam were not appeased. In particular, they resented the fact that the remaining barriers still cut off an important part of their city; they were appalled at the sanctimonious way in which the Germans explained their behaviour in the Press; and

[1] Wielek: *op. cit.*, p. 39.
[2] Examination, November 3, 1947, p. 5.
[3] *De Februaristaking* (The February Strike), p. 93.

many felt repugnance at the film of the funeral of WA-man Koot. The tension was increased further by a fresh incident—this time not in the Jewish quarter but in South Amsterdam, where about one quarter of the city's Jews lived—mostly the more prosperous. This was the so-called Koco affair.

"Koco" was the name of two ice-cream parlours run by Messrs. Cahn and Kohn, two refugees from Germany, and both extremely popular with Jews and non-Jews alike, and hence an obvious target for the Nazis. A number of regular clients accordingly decided to offer them protection. They bought pocket torches and improvised weapons (covered gas pipes with straps), and helped one of the owners to fix a special 20-inch ammonia flask to the wall of his parlour. Everything went well—in fact, too well. A few minor successes with Dutch Nazis so increased the defenders' self-confidence that they abandoned all pretence to secrecy; for many of the younger participants, the whole thing was as thrilling as a good Western.

On February 19 when a German police patrol, in the area more or less by chance, wanted to enter one of the parlours, the flask was set off and they were suddenly sprayed with the irritant fluid; they emptied their guns and then arrested Cahn, Kohn and some other Jews involved in the affair. Ernst Cahn was shot by a firing squad on March 3, 1941, after he had refused, even under torture, to tell which "conspirator" had fixed the bottle in his shop. Thus the first man in our country to die at the hands of a German firing squad was a Jewish refugee from Germany.

The Koco affair, which we have reported very briefly, made a great impression on the Germans. "I did not like that Koco business at all," the German police-chief in Amsterdam, W. P. F. Lages, told the author after the war.[1] He thought everything had been handled far too sensationally; if the man had to be put out of the way, it would have been far better to do it quietly. In any case, in his report to Himmler on February 20, Rauter felt obliged to describe the event in a manner most unfavourable to the Jews, adding an exaggerated account of the general disorderliness of the Jewish quarter. Something would have to be done, he suggested. Needless to say, his appeal did not fall on deaf ears: a Jew "gnawing through an Aryan's artery and then sucking out his blood", another "squirting poisonous fluids at policemen pursuing their duty"—such Jewish treachery

[1] Conversation of July 15, 1952.

clearly called for retribution. The Germans had only been waiting for a pretext and now they had it. On February 22 and 23 they descended on the Jewish quarter *en masse.*

Only those who—like the author—have been present at German raids can have any idea of the feelings of those unsuspecting and innocent young men who, on Saturday, February 22, and again on the following morning, were snatched off the streets and, after much humiliation and ill-treatment, thrown into a camp which proved to be—although they did not then realize it—the beginning of their end. We shall have further occasion to discuss the German terror raids; here we shall merely mention that the present one had the object of arresting some 400 Jewish "hostages" between the ages of twenty and thirty-five years. This objective was achieved with German thoroughness, including beatings, kicks, insults and screams. The man in command, *SS Oversturmbannführer* Knolle, then acting Chief of the Security Police, saw fit to take his dog to the raid, and set an example for the future—no hunt without hounds. The police officers in Jonas Daniel Meyer Square station, long familiar with the inhabitants of the district, were completely taken aback; some managed to save a few Jews. The whole raid was recorded on film—another token of German "thoroughness". The repeat performance on Sunday morning was watched by a far larger number of non-Jews, who came to visit the picturesque area over the weekend. What they saw and heard was brutality on the one hand; despair and complete helplessness on the other. One survivor reports[1] that he saw the German police form a ring into which they threw the first victim they found, and then tossed him about like a ball. The "hostages" were all carried off first to Schoorl in North Holland, then to Buchenwald and finally to Mauthausen.

The first phase, at Schoorl, was very short; on February 27 the young captives were packed off to Germany—a journey without food but with plenty of viciousness ("they seemed to have a special predilection for people with glasses, whom they would hit straight in the face"). From Weimar they were herded, or rather kicked, up the Ettersberg to Buchenwald, some five miles away—389 Jews "of Asiatic type", as Rauter later described them. He, too, insisted that they were not prisoners but hostages. In Buchenwald, mark you! But such was his self-deception that he may even have believed it. When the College of Secretaries-General heard where the men

[1] M. Nebig: Evidence given on April 5, 1948.

had ended up, it consoled itself with the fact that the story had not been confirmed or denied officially.

Now Buchenwald did, in fact, contain a number of non-Jewish hostages and short-term prisoners. It is to some of these that we owe what knowledge we have of this phase of the operation. Dr. Van der Wey[1] witnessed the arrival of the young Jews: "They were very cheerful and even cracked jokes about their new-fashioned attire and large clogs." Indeed, they pitied the prisoners they met there; "these young men had not the least idea of what lay in store for them". One of them looked completely disconcerted when an old camp-inmate tried to console him with the story that he would be back home in three months. Three months struck the young man as far too long.

If the "hostages" did not at once realize what was happening to them, the Germans did not defer their rude awakening—certainly not of those forty whom they put to work in the so-called "quarry". But the others, too, were soon given a better glimpse into their true situation, as sheer chicanery, bad food and ill-treatment were increasingly used to break their spirits. One of our sources denies that they were ill-treated, but adds that "they died all the same, or rather as the saying had it, they were encouraged to do so". Those who tried to escape were shot. This went on until May, when 340 had to leave these relatively congenial surroundings for Mauthausen. Of three survivors, one remained in Buchenwald because he had the incredible fortune to fall into the hands of SS-surgeon Dr. Hans Eisele as a "guinea pig". According to Kogon,[2] Eisele's "actions between 1940 and 1943 exceeded in foulness anything done by any other SS doctor". This healer of the sick, who after the Liberation was first sentenced to death and then to eight years' imprisonment, was reprieved after serving only five and, thanks to a government grant of 10,000 Marks to all "homecomers", was able to resume his practice in Munich. Accusations by former prisoners were disregarded until June 28, 1958, when the Public Prosecutor finally ordered his arrest. Eisele fled one day earlier, but his subsequent fate does not concern us nearly so much as that of M. Nebig, the young Jew on whom he practised vivisection, incidentally subjecting him to a completely unnecessary stomach operation ("I still have an

[1] A. van der Wey: *In het voorgeborchte der hel* (In the antechamber of hell) (Heemstede, 1946), p. 48.

[2] E. Kogon: *Der SS Staat* (Frankfort, 1961), p. 146.

8-inch scar"). Later, when Nebig was about to be given a fatal injection, he was saved by German prisoners at the risk of their own lives, and kept hidden in Buchenwald until 1945. Lest the reader should suppose that out of sight was out of mind, he will be reassured to hear that Mauthausen enquired after Nebig's whereabouts on fourteen successive occasions.

Why were these young men transferred to Mauthausen? According to the Germans themselves, as a punishment for the tone used by the Jewish Council when writing on the subject of the hostages. It need hardly be said that the offending letters were to the point but far from discourteous. And the punishment for a crime that had never been committed, and in any case, not by the victims? A death sentence comparable to that meted out to the Athenians in the fourth century B.C. when they were packed off to the Sicilian quarries.[1]

The environs were glorious: "These green hills, with their pink and white cottages set among pine trees—and in the distance the white Alpine crests and glaciers . . . was the backcloth they chose for their drama of blood and mire, sadism and hatred."[2]

And here the first batch of young Dutch Jews was soon afterwards joined by several hundred victims of the second raid (June 1941) to which we shall return. Not one of them lived to tell the tale, but that was not, of course, the object of the exercise.

Mauthausen, "those three evil syllables which will forever haunt the conscience of mankind", is today once again a favourite tourist resort. Here, the visitors can inspect the 148 steps where so many Jews were maimed. "They were not allowed to come down by the steps themselves, but had to slide down in the loose pebbles at the side, in which process many were killed or seriously injured."[3] On the third day the guards started machine-gunning the climbers; on the fourth, some ten young Jews linked hands and jumped to voluntary death. What particularly annoyed the Nazis was that the spattered brains and flesh of the suicides (the Germans referred to them humorously as "parachutists") spoiled the beauty of the famous steps. In order to spare German feelings and to prevent a recurrence, a hundred or so of the prisoners were placed under the

[1] B. Bettelheim: *The informed heart* (London, 1960), p. 243.

[2] Michel Riquet: "L'Europe à Mauthausen," *Tragédie de la Déportation 1940–1945* (Paris 1945), p. 75.

[3] E. Kogon: *op. cit.*, pp. 197–8.

charge of two bully-boys, one known as "the blonde fräulein", the other as "Hans the killer".[1] We shall not mention what happened next, except to add that by the autumn there were no survivors.

But our silence on the subject should not be misunderstood. Paul Tillard and other eye-witnesses have described a wide-ranging list of foul horrors. And what could you expect in a place whose *Kommandant* "gave his son fifty Jews for target practice as a birthday present",[2] a place that had been specially set up as a horror and murder camp, and that today, like so many of its kind, has become a museum of death?

When Dr. J. J. C. van Dijk, a leading figure in the Church resistance movement, complained to *Generalkommissar* Schmidt that most of the 700 Jews from Amsterdam had died in Mauthausen, the Commissar asked him: "Is it our fault that they choose to jump off mountains?" Still, he must have known that the causes of death listed by the German authorities—sunstroke, dysentery, heart-failure, nephritis—were a tissue of lies. Did others believe them? For instance, the victims' families and friends, the Jewish Council or the Dutch authorities? The Jewish Council informed the afflicted families just as soon as it received the notifications of death, but reluctance to face the plain truth was strong. Was it not obvious that the Germans were merely trying to intimidate the Jews with false reports? The Chief Rabbi of The Hague made it known that no one need go into mourning; he had "good" reason to believe that the notifications need not be taken seriously.[3] People went on seeking reassurance, clinging to any straw; for instance, to fortune-tellers who "saw" that the victims were still alive, that they had merely been reported dead because the Germans would not publicly admit that the boys had made a successful escape. Some were said to have sent secret messages. Lawyers were engaged at staff fees payable in advance to help get the boys back; many poorer Jews borrowed the necessary amount from their richer co-religionists. Swiss contacts of a thirty-two-year-old Jew deposited 20,000 francs with the *Schweizerische Bankgesellschaft*, to be transmitted to the *Dresdner Bank* in Germany as soon as their man presented himself in person at the

[1] P. Tillard, *Mauthausen* (Paris, 1945), p. 20–1.

[2] Grete Salus: *Eine Frau erzählt* (A woman recounts) in Supplement to the weekly *Das Parlament*, October 30, 1957.

[3] F. Weinreb: *War Reminiscences* (unpublished), p. 43.

Swiss Consulate in Amsterdam. He never did so, nor was any other of the Dutch Jews sent to Mauthausen ever seen again.

Some parents published obituary notices in the newspapers, so many, in fact, that in July 1941, the Jewish Council was given orders to prevent such publications. The Council complied, and it did more. When it had heard that the Jewish boys had been sent to Mauthausen it wrote to the Dutch Red Cross asking for the precise location and address of Mauthausen, and whether the deportees were allowed to receive money and food-parcels, and to send and receive letters. The Red Cross was "reluctantly forced to advise you to take the matter up elsewhere". In September 1941 the Jewish Council considered asking permission to send winter clothes to the camps, and also decided to enquire whether the urns with the ashes of the deceased could be sent to Amsterdam, and what amounts of money could be sent to the prisoners. They also wanted to know the precise format of the letters they were permitted to send. The Emigration Section of the *Reichsvereinigung der Juden in Deutschland* (Association of Jews in Germany) had already replied in May that the prisoners were not allowed to receive parcels, adding that "everything can be bought in the camp". But as Asscher[1] stated after the war, he for one was certain that the boys had been murdered (and in what ways) because he was told the whole story by an anonymous German soldier as early as 1941. He claims that he passed this information on to "all Jews", with the advice that they went into hiding. The writer could, however, find no evidence in support of this claim; rather the opposite.

Far more forceful was another action, albeit unsuccessful in the end. From a "Note on my efforts on behalf of the Jewish hostages" dated December 11, 1941, and written by the former President of the High Court, *mr.* L. E. Visser, we gather that he prevailed upon the College of Secretaries-General to intercede with the Germans on the hostages' behalf, after he himself had addressed a moving plea to Rauter and had received no reply. The College thereupon asked Frederiks to see what he could do. He called on Rauter, who received him most ungraciously, but nevertheless admitted that it was "a bit thick" to send the Jews to the hardest of all camps, into the quarries; he and Wimmer promised to send someone to Berlin "with the message that the German authorities in the Netherlands could not accept responsibility for such treatment of the Jews". The

[1] Examination on November 7, 1947.

discussion, which must have taken place about November 1, 1941, is remarkable for yet another reason. Rauter asked Frederiks what he would do were he (Rauter) to deport Dutch Jews to Poland. Frederiks told him that he would protest most strongly, that "he and his colleagues would not continue in office for another minute, and that most Dutch civil servants would follow their example. The Germans would have to clear up their own mess."

But we are running ahead of our story. It is known that the capture and deportation of the young Jews was very largely responsible for one of the most heroic episodes in recent Dutch history, the famous strike of February 25 and 26. Although the author is filled with great admiration and respect for those involved in it, he mentions the strike in passing only—the full story can be found in B. A. Sijes' *De Februaristaking*. Moreover, the Jews as a group, though the cause of the strike and to some extent involved in its conclusion, did not as such participate in the demonstration itself—the strike was not a Jewish but a Dutch, and quite particularly a local Amsterdam, affair, with a few repercussions in other parts of the country.

Nevertheless we must not omit to say that the February strike was for many Jews the greatest experience of the whole war. The reason for this was simple: for once, albeit for but a little while, they did not feel that their Dutch compatriots were leaving them in the lurch. Behind them there now stood openly a group of their fellow-citizens, men with whom they had lived at peace for centuries. This group dared to brave a ruthless enemy, and was ready to sacrifice life and property—for them. Rightly the statue of the Docker now looks down from his pedestal in the Jewish quarter as an unforgettable witness to human solidarity.

So far as the Germans were concerned, the strike was entirely the work of the Jews. Whether they really believed that story or merely concocted it makes little difference now. Those "underhand", "hole-and-corner" Jews had incited the Dutch to strike and they must put an end to it. That is the simplest and perhaps the fairest explanation of why Rauter and Böhmcker delivered an ultimatum to the leaders of the Jewish Council on the very first day of the strike—according to Sijes, they threatened to arrest another 300 Jews unless the strike was ended the very next day. Further "Jewish contingents" would follow; according to Herzberg 500 Jewish leaders were threatened with the concentration camp. Asscher[1]

[1] Examination on November 7, 1947.

claimed in 1947 that when he was called to appear alone before the German Security Police at noon on February 25, four Germans told him of their "irrevocable" decision to shoot 500 Jews on the next day. Professor Cohen, who was also summoned to Böhmcker's office, claims that he was met by a man of "savage appearance" who yelled at him that the Jews had unleashed the strike—had not a Jewish woman said so? It was at this point that they were joined by Asscher. In any case, whatever the truth of the matter, Asscher got in touch with some forty industrial leaders that very day and implored them to end the strike; after all, the whole affair had started because of the deportation of a few hundred Jews and it was best to prevent the deportation of hundreds more.

It has been alleged, particularly by Jews, that the February strike must be called a fiasco, since far from forcing the Germans to stop the persecution of Dutch Jewry, it convinced them that machine-guns and threats sufficed to overcome any resistance to anti-Semitic excesses. The writer feels that to pursue this point would mean venturing too far into the realms of speculation. The fact is that though the strike may have been a spoke in the invader's wheel, it did not remain there long; in the end it merely gave him yet another pretext for persecution.

## NEW MEASURES

To keep as far as possible to the chronological order of events we must, by way of introduction to the next German measure, mention the sad fate that befell one of the most prominent and respected Jews in our country: Leo Polak, Professor of Philosophy at Groningen University. Thanks to the Secretary of the Dutch section of the Kant Society, Dr. H. W. van der Vaart Smit, Polak had for long been known in Berlin as a "wily Jew". From the very start he had staunchly defended the Dutch point of view, refusing to truckle to the invaders—whom, in a letter written after his suspension, he described openly as "the enemy". The Germans apparently found this letter so important that they printed it in full in their weekly *Meldungen aus den Niederlanden*, not excluding the following reproach to his colleagues: "The faculty seems to think fit to treat me as if I were no longer a Professor at Groningen, no longer a member of the Senate or the Faculty!" Clearly Professor Polak was a man who refused to surrender any of his Dutch rights. The *Meldungen* reported further that this suspended Jewish professor simply continued to deliver lectures at the University and that his students attended them as if nothing had happened. The article concluded with the ominous sentence: "Steps are being taken by the Security Police."

Polak was arrested on February 15, 1941. "You are the most dangerous man in Groningen," he was told by the man who heard his case. This meant the concentration camp, in the event Sachsenhausen, and death that very year (December 9, 1941)—a demise which "robbed our country of a noble and brilliant man, one of its most enlightened sons".[1] The Vice-Chancellor of Groningen, Professor J. M. N. Kapteyn, from whom the Germans obtained Polak's "impertinent" letter, cannot be said to have played a particularly glorious role in this matter.

On January 6, 1941, the Secretary-General of the Department of Education, Science and Culture, Professor Van Dam, informed his colleagues that Seyss-Inquart had promised to consider the possibility of allowing a limited number of Jewish students to attend university classes. The word "promised" clearly implied a concession—and so it must have looked in view of the fact that the *Reichskommissar* was considering—or alleged to be considering—the total expulsion of Jewish students from all universities. Van Dam was asked to collect material "so as to be able to decide what recommendations should be submitted to the *Reichskommissar* in this matter". The tone of the article of the *Deutsche Zeitung in den Niederlanden* reporting these deliberations on February 16 suggests strongly that Seyss-Inquart was once again playing his well-tried game of threatening worse measures than he had in mind for the moment, then modifying his demands so as to gain Dutch support for his actual plans, and leaving the College with the illusion that they had wrested major concessions from him. In the case of Van Dam, it would seem that the German was able to play this game with particular ease.

Two decrees settled the matter of the students. In the first, issued on February 11, 1941, Seyss-Inquart made it known that the enrolment of Jewish students in Dutch universities and colleges would be governed by rules to be issued by the Department of Education, Science and Culture. Any Jew who was not officially enrolled already, would only be allowed to sit his preliminary or final examinations by special permission of the Secretary-General. In his own decree issued on the same day, Van Dam made it known that

[1] H. J. Pos: *Dr. Leonard Polak—6 January 1880—9 December 1941* in *De Nieuwe Stem* (1946), pp. 180–4.

Jewish students wishing to enrol for the academic year 1941–2 might do so only with his express approval; applications would have to be handed in not later than March 31, 1941. Those who had not enrolled by that time, would not be admitted "pending a further decision"—this last point was no doubt a further "concession" obtained by Van Dam.

"Jewish predominance in university life broken," the *Deutsche Zeitung* blazoned forth in large letters. The restrictions, it added, were no more than just retribution for the "incitement by Jewish elements" in Leyden and Delft. The public was also told by the paper that, far from being a discriminatory bill, the decree was precisely the contrary: it merely put an end to the preferential treatment of Jews. Nevertheless the two decrees produced a strong reaction, so much so that a proposed strike at Amsterdam University was only called off after a "report" that the Queen considered such action inopportune—a "report" that, after the war, was found to have been completely false. The *Meldungen aus den Niederlanden* gives us some idea of the other reactions, particularly at Groningen, where all the protests apparently came from the students' side, none from the professors, many of whom even obstructed the protest movement. A later issue of the paper claimed that things had again settled down. Characteristic was its opinion of a proclamation issued by the University authorities at Leyden. In it the students were told that, though the authorities had hoped that no anti-Jewish measures would be taken, now that this hope had proved vain there was nothing for it but to submit and in "no way whatsoever to resist the new measures". Far from being satisfied with this declaration, the German paper complained of its "negative" tone!

Before February was out, the Germans took two further steps that were not particularly hurtful at the time. On February 18, the *Deutsche Zeitung in den Niederlanden* reported that Wimmer had charged the Secretary-General for Social Affairs with removing all Jews from the list of blood donors before March 1. The *Government Gazette* of February 28 shows that Secretary Verwey had not tarried in communicating this decision to all doctors and hospitals. A small problem arose when the Red Cross informed the Secretary-General that many "acceptable" donors had refused to continue giving their blood in these circumstance; would he please discuss the matter with *Herr* Wimmer. We do not know whether he did so; in any case, the Germans did not change their minds.

Towards the end of February came news that the German *Kommandant* in The Hague had confiscated the houses and apartments of members of the B'nai-Brith Organization, described as a Jewish Freemasons' Lodge, and that he had put them at the disposal of the *Reichskommissar*. An article in the *Deutsche Zeitung in den Niederlanden* of March 14 lists some of the "unspeakable" horrors that came to light during the dissolution of this and other lodges. And speaking of horrors, we might mention that it was in the self-same month that Dutch cinemas showed that "outstanding production of the German film industry", the tendentious *Jew Süss*, of which the *Meldungen* could proclaim triumphantly that "all its performances had an extraordinarily good propaganda effect". We know, however, that Böhmcker was forced to fill the seats with WA-men; Dutch public interest in the film was not very dependable.

March 1941 was a quiet month compared with its predecessor; what little happened in it was generally dismissed by the Jews with the now familiar "if only nothing worse befall us".

Decree No. 48 of March 12, 1941, could have come as no surprise to anyone—it was merely an extension of the old decree No. 189/1940 governing the registration of businesses. At the same time, the Jews were, however, faced with another measure that was subsequently to affect them most profoundly. Our information on this subject is largely based on Berkley; his report has been fully corroborated and amplified by subsequent investigations.

Berkley tells us that, in a letter dated March 18, 1941, Böhmcker placed the Jewish Council in charge of all Jewish organizations, except religious associations; to that end he requested a list of all such organizations with headquarters in Amsterdam. On March 20, a number of German police raided the Refugee Committee and declared the Committee for Special Jewish Affairs and all its subcommittees dissolved; the same fate befell the so-called Emigrants' Associations. On the evening of March 20, the Germans confirmed the new measures in a discussion with the Presidents of the Jewish Council; they gave out that financial support to needy Jews was in no way impeded, that the blocked funds would be released whenever necessary and that all they were interested in was efficiency; once the Jewish Council assumed responsibility for all Jewish organizations in accordance with Böhmcker's well-intentioned suggestion, there would be no further need for police surveillance. So much for Berkley's report.

On April 2, many newspapers published an ANP report (the *Deutsche Zeitung in den Niederlanden* gave it the banner headlines—"Haarlem cleans up") dealing with the action of "Comrade S. L. A. Plekker", the burgomaster of Haarlem and a member of the Dutch Nazi Party. By a proclamation aiming at the "preservation of order", Jews were prohibited from entering hotels, restaurants, cafés, cinemas, theatres, public libraries, public meeting halls, public baths and washhouses within the municipality, and all these institutions would henceforth display "No Jews" signs in prominent places. Moreover, Jews were forbidden to take up residence in Haarlem; those who had moved there after February 25 would have to apply at once for a special permit. Nor could Jews henceforth move house within Haarlem itself. It would not be worth paying so much attention to "Comrade Plekker's" proclamation, were it not that this was merely the beginning of what was to become a far vaster scheme. Nor was this the last time that the Jews of Haarlem would make the headlines.

This brings us to the end of April 1941, another relatively quiet month with a host of petty annoyances and only one fact of great importance: the creation of the *Jewish Weekly* (*Joodse Weekblad*) which deserves further treatment, not only for its own sake but also because of the people involved in its publication. For that purpose, we shall once again have to depart from the strictly chronological treatment of events.

## THE JEWISH WEEKLY

The Germans in The Hague must have had a list of all Jewish newspapers and journals as early as July 1940; on September 13 *Generalkommissar* Schmidt requested the Head of the German Security Police and Intelligence Service, Dr. Harster, to proscribe three Jewish papers, namely the *Nieuw Israëlitisch Weekblad*, the *Joodse Wachter* and *Achawa*, because "I intend to allow only one Jewish paper—the *Joodse Weekblad*". The same request was repeated in a special telex message. In April 1941, another paper, *Haïsha*, the organ of the Jewish Women's Council in the Netherlands was added to the prohibited list, but by then the first issue of the paper which Böhmcker had approved in a letter of March 22 had come out: on April 11, 1941, the *Joodse Weekblad* (*Jewish Weekly*) appeared for the first time, under the editorship of J. de Leon—the German nominee.

It is difficult to arrive at a balanced judgment as to the character of this man, for whom few people have anything but scorn; when the Court of Honour apportioned blame after the war, they were almost as critical of him as they were of Messrs. Asscher and Cohen. A German source described him as "an object of hatred to the Jews, who called him a nebulous dreamer and even a Fascist". For many, he was quite simply a traitor, if not of the Jewish cause at least of that of the Netherlands and her allies. Others thought him neither wicked nor avaricious but simply mad, and . . . exceedingly dangerous.

Jacques de Leon had previously held all sorts of jobs. He had been to Palestine a few times, and was an ardent exponent of Revisionism, a militant Zionist faction demanding a Jewish state on both sides of the Jordan and opposing the acceptance of Balfour's much smaller "national home". According to Herzberg,[1] De Leon first approached the Germans with a plan to use unemployed Jews for the reclamation of heathland, in preparation for a massive post-war emigration to Palestine; the fact that his plan incidentally helped the German war effort was allegedly just so much bait. In any case, the Germans asked De Leon to form a publication committee, for which purpose he called on Herzberg, our chief witness in this matter. In his book, Herzberg devotes a great deal of space to the question of whether or not the Germans intended to use De Leon as a kind of "rat-catcher". What happened next is not quite clear; Cohen alleges that, together with *mr.* M. L. Kan, the then President of the Dutch Zionist Federation, he took the wind out of De Leon's sails by suggesting to Böhmcker that the Jewish Council proposed publishing its own paper; Böhmcker (or some other German official) agreed but insisted that De Leon would, in any event, have to be its editor. We might add that De Leon's activities have been used as a justification for the existence of the Jewish Council, though it is impossible to tell today whether the Jews would have fared better or worse under De Leon than they did under Asscher and Cohen—the records show that De Leon remonstrated with Asscher in Spring 1942, asking him to change his tactics and quoting examples of Asscher's false optimism. We shall return to this question in another chapter.

As we have said, the first issue of the *Joodse Weekblad*, a paper that was to remain the official organ of Dutch Jewry until the autumn of 1943, appeared on April 11, 1941.

[1] Herzberg: *op. cit.*, p. 176.

Herzberg[1] challenges the general view that the Germans foisted the paper on the Jews so as to have a means of publishing their anti-Semitic measures without the knowledge of the non-Jewish public. He emphasizes that the Jews themselves felt the strong need for an official organ, not only as a means of holding their sorely-stricken community together but also for the publication of pastoral messages. Moreover, the Germans published many of their measures in the daily Press all the same, and some prohibitions were not even published in the *Joodse Weekblad* but simply passed on by word of mouth. Even so, the author cannot help feeling that the Germans benefited greatly from not having to bombard the non-Jewish section of the population with their threats against the Jews, as they appeared week after week in the *Joodse Weekblad.* Moreover, Böhmcker is on record as having stated that it was "quite undesirable" for the "Aryan" Press to discuss the Jewish question and that the Jews must be "educated" to read only their own paper. As early as 1940—on October 11 and again on December 18—the Dutch Press was ordered not to write "commentaries or articles on matters affecting the Jews"; the order itself was "not for publication".

While there is no doubt that the *Jewish Weekly* (as we shall from now on call that paper) helped to bind the Jewish community together, the question is whether it did not, perhaps, bind them too tightly, tending to drive them along what the Jewish Council deemed the only possible road. Moreover, it must have made a great deal of difference to the average Jewish reader whether he read a decree without comment in any paper or with admonition by his "own" Council. In any case, the newspaper helped to isolate him even further from his non-Jewish compatriots. This applied to all but the few Jews who refused to read the *Jewish Weekly* on principle.

We have a record of an editorial meeting on April 6, 1941, attended by the Presidents of the Jewish Council and the entire editorial board: Rabbi I. Vredenburg (Religious matters), *mr.* A. J. Herzberg (Jewish culture), S. Pinkhof (Home Affairs), H. Heymans (Home Affairs), J. de Leon (City News).

The whole paper was to be vetted every Wednesday night by Asscher and Cohen, who were directly responsible to the Germans. This amounted to a kind of censorship by these two gentlemen; later the Germans added their own censorship, or rather they replaced

[1] Herzberg: *op. cit.*, pp. 181–2.

that of the two Jewish leaders with that of the *Zentralstelle*. It is said that the paper had also to be approved by the *Expositur*, one of the most important sub-committees of the Jewish Council, and one to which we shall be returning. Very peculiar was the position of J. S. Joachimsthal, who was a member of the secretariat and technical branch of the paper on the one hand, and a director of the best-known firm of Jewish printers.

The editorial board did not remain unchanged. Differences of opinion occurred almost daily as to the presentation of the German information; Herzberg was one of those who eventually resigned. By February 1942 the board included Dr. W. Diamand; according to Herzberg, De Leon had by then ceased to attend editorial meetings. He never forced his view on, nor wrote anything for, the paper although, again according to Herzberg, he was the only one to be paid a salary—at German insistence.

There would be little point in saying any more about this man, all of whose plans came to naught and who ended up in the gas chambers, were it not that the records show that Asscher had insisted on De Leon's deportation, and later proclaimed his great satisfaction that De Leon was forced to share the fate of other Jews.[1] According to Asscher, De Leon was an out-and-out scoundrel and, knowing him for a German spy, he had only done his "bounden duty" in denouncing him. Cohen,[2] on the other hand, declared that no one in the Jewish Council pressed the Germans to deport De Leon; on the contrary, he, Cohen, had even interceded on De Leon's behalf with Aus der Fünten, at the request of Joachimsthal. Nor had Cohen ever heard of Asscher's alleged part in the matter—if he did denounce De Leon, "he did so entirely without my knowledge". The reader will have to form his own opinion both of Cohen's evidence and also of Asscher, who apparently saw fit to denounce a fellow-Jew to the common enemy.

Whatever its faults, the *Jewish Weekly* provides the historian with an incomparable source of information. Increasingly, this paper became the funnel through which German repressive measures were poured upon the heads of the Jewish population—often with the apparent sanction, indeed support, of the Jewish Council. The

[1] Examination of November 7, 1947.

[2] Examination of December 17, 1947; Professor Dr. D. Cohen *et al.*: *History of the Jews in the Netherlands during the Occupation* (unpublished report), p. 13.

Council's excuse was that they had been able to "persuade" the Germans to withdraw many of their measures after "stormy scenes"; had the Council refused to co-operate altogether its mediating influence would have stopped there and then.

## SPRING AND SUMMER OF 1941

At 4.45 p.m., on April 10, 1941, the Presidents of the Jewish Council were summoned to German police headquarters, where *Hauptscharführer* Blohm informed them that no Jews would henceforth be allowed to move from Amsterdam to other parts of the country. In retrospect, we can see how advantageous to the Germans it was to round up their victims into a single pen; at the time their purpose seemed more obscure, and everyone was waiting for the "further regulations connected with this measure", which the *Jewish Weekly* promised would be published "in the near future". When they eventually were, the Jewish Council kept sending this kind of petition to the German police: "Mrs. (name) resident in (street), Amsterdam, aged seventy-nine years. Moved to Amsterdam to recuperate after her husband's death. Has fully recovered now, and would like to return to her original home in Dordrecht, where she spent seventy-seven years of her life. She accordingly requests permission to leave." Needless to say, permission was refused.

Not to be outdone by Blohm, *SS*-Chief Rauter ordered Jews to surrender their radio sets before the month was out.

The minutes of a conference held at German police headquarters on January 11, 1941, had previously mentioned the drafting of a "law to prevent Jews from listening to wireless reports"; to facilitate this measure, all wireless sets—owned by Jews and non-Jews alike—had to be registered at the Post Office. We cannot help gaining the impression that two sets of German officials were in keen competition, for on April 15, Rauter, not waiting for the promulgation of the special law by the German police chief, took matters into his own hands and declared all Jewish wireless sets forfeit; they would have to be surrendered within fourteen days and in working order—any repairs would have to be paid for by the former owners.

But Rauter was not yet satisfied, as we can see from a circular sent by the Acting Secretary-General for Justice to public prosecutors throughout the country: a large number of Jews, this circular stated, were trying to "misappropriate" radio sets, and handing in inferior ones instead. Henceforth all Jews handing in their sets would also have to sign a declaration to the effect that no such substitution had taken place. Those who had already handed in their sets would have to return specially to make that declaration.

In the same months came a decree affecting the employment of Jews in the Amsterdam city abattoirs, where several clashes had occurred between Jews and Nazi provocateurs. On March 24, 1941, the subject had already been discussed at some length during a meeting of the Secretaries-General; from their discussion it appears that Böhmcker had promised them to revoke a number of anti-Jewish measures "pending clarification of the Jewish problem". According to a report in the *Nationale Dagblad*, Böhmcker nevertheless decided to order the segregation of Jews and "Aryans" in the abattoirs. A small matter, you may say, and many Jews at the time even considered it a blessing in disguise.

But elsewhere, too, the Germans went out of their way to force the separation of Jews and non-Jews. On the stock-exchange, for instance, Jews were debarred by order of the German Commissioner-General for Finance and Economics, on May 1, 1941. According to the *Deutsche Zeitung* of the same date, this measure would "close up a source of unnecessary speculation and anti-social activity" in an institution that was in any case "enslaved to America" and a "den of speculation". The *Meldungen* of May 13, however, reported that Jews, anticipating the measure, had made "illegal" arrangements with non-Jewish firms; moreover, the Amsterdam produce-exchange, from which Jews had not yet been barred, shared a passage with the stock-exchange, so that pro-German stock-brokers had to sit by watching the Jews sabotaging the German measure.

In the musical field, too, German sensitivity had long been outraged by the continued presence of Jews. Thus the minutes of a meeting of the Secretaries-General held on July 19, 1940, contain a report by Professor Van Poelje to the effect that the famous conductor Willem Mengelberg was about to be asked by the Germans to take charge of the "Aryanization" of the Concertgebouw Orchestra; Van Poelje advised dismissing Mengelberg if he complied. Similarly, Scheveningen Corporation was asked by the Germans to replace Sam Swaap, the leader of the Residentie Orchestra. At a meeting on July 22, these questions were raised again by the Secretaries-General, who thought it best to arrive at a compromise rather than "bringing these problems to a head". Now, a compromise might still have seemed feasible in 1940. The Germans heard with "great satisfaction" that Sam Swaap was "not putting in too many appearances", and that his "chair had been moved towards the back". The programme of the Concertgebouw Orchestra, on the other hand, continued to displease *Reichskommissar* Seyss-Inquart, for Mahler, Mendelssohn and Hindemith had not yet been removed; after many threats, it was decided to give in to him, though the management thought fit to point out that Hindemith was no Jew and was, moreover, still being played in Germany. At the same time, the management agreed not to engage any new Jewish players, and to change the existing composition of the orchestra. Meanwhile the Wagner Society, which was associated with the Concertgebouw Orchestra, dismissed all its Jewish members. At the time, twenty-one Jews were still playing in the Concertgebouw Orchestra and eight Jews in the Residentie Orchestra; all of them were allowed to stay on for the time being although not in their former positions. But in April 1941 the Germans decreed that, as from May 15, all Jews who "ought to have been dismissed months earlier" had to disappear from government-subsidized orchestras. "To prevent technical difficulties", however, they could continue longer, "if the winter season of a particular orchestra should end after that date". And this brings us to May 1941.

On the very first day of that month came a regulation by which Jewish professional men were segregated from the rest. After the dismissal of civil servants in the autumn of 1940, the new measures came as no surprise; indeed, most people were astonished that the Germans had seen fit to wait for so long. The earliest report on the subject is dated December 9, 1940, and refers to a circular the Germans had sent to the Secretaries-General on November 4 on the "employment of persons sworn into office". The report, signed by a keen German official, Dr. Kurt O. Rabl, deplores the absence of a complete list of the professions concerned, though advocates, attorneys, doctors, dentists, chemists and midwives must, of course, be included. Apparently the Secretaries-General refused their co-operation in this matter for a long time, but in the end Frederiks drafted the necessary forms. These were sent out by the Departments of Justice and Social Affairs on February 5, with covering letters signed by the Secretaries-General J. C. Tenkink and R. A. Verwey. Jewish recipients were expected to complete the form in duplicate and to return it to the department within eight days; they must cease doing professional work for anyone but Jews as from May 1.

In addition to the professions we have mentioned, sworn interpreters and translators were also to be included.

This was a far-reaching measure indeed. When *mr.* Tenkink, the then Secretary-General for Justice, was questioned by the Enquiry Commission of the Second Chamber on March 18, 1952, *mr.* B. J. Stokvis, who had himself been a victim of the German measures, put it to him that "this circular caused a great stir at the bar, particularly in Amsterdam" not least because "by issuing it, the highest Dutch authority was helping the Germans to implement a measure that ran completely counter to Dutch law".

The *Jewish Weekly* of May 9, 1941, published numerous advertisements by Jewish doctors and dentists who, henceforth, could treat none but Jewish patients. One of them, a retired physician from Leyden, sent all his ex-patients and former colleagues a black-bordered notice, with the heading "Israel mourns in the Netherlands" in which he alluded to the rebellion of 1574. It is gratifying to note that many non-Jewish doctors went out of their way to alleviate the worst consequences of a measure that they themselves were unable to avert.

Towards the end of the month, came a further set of repressive measures, this time from quite a different quarter. The first of these was unlikely to cause the Jews any kind of a headache—Article 6 of Decree 97 of May 23, 1941, barred them from participation in the Dutch Labour Service. Four days and five regulations later, the Germans published the far more serious Decree No. 102 on the registration and usage of agricultural land owned by Jews.

In view of the Nazis' avowed mystical ties to the land and peasantry, this measure took no one by surprise. The decree itself was drafted by no less a personage than *Graf* Friedrich Grote, the Germans' Agricultural *Führer* for the Netherlands. It was he who enriched the German language with so magnificent a noun as *Landwirtschaftsentjudungsvordnung* (Agricultural Dejudification Decree). This ingenious word tells a whole story: the registration of Jewish farms; their sale by September 1, 1941, and transfer to the new owner by January 1, 1942. No exceptions whatsoever were allowed.

In the event, this measure affected but a small number of Jews. But no one was to escape another regulation passed at about the same time (May 31). The full text was published in the *Jewish Weekly* of June 27. The new regulation was an extension of Decree No. 20 of February 7, 1941, and barred Jews from

(*a*) bathing in public baths or swimming pools;
(*b*) entering public parks and other amenities in spas, or renting public rooms (hotels, boarding-houses, hostels) in them or any tourist centres;
(*c*) attending race meetings.

"The North Sea will no longer be used for the ablution of Jewish flesh," the *National Dagblad* proclaimed triumphantly, adding that the "glory of Dutch horsemanship will be resurrected in the absence of Jewish profiteers and gamblers, who are more fitted to Oriental camels than to German horses."

This particular measure gave rise to an inordinate number of enquiries and directives. Thus the Secretary-General for Education, Science and Culture felt impelled to send out a special circular (June 17, 1941) barring Jewish apprentices from participating in mixed swimming galas anywhere. Another difficulty was the precise interpretation of the German word "*Kurort*" (spa)—for though Jews had been ordered to keep away from such places, it was an open question which precisely they were. A list of doubtful cases was specially compiled by the Department of the Interior. A ticklish problem was also raised by the Haitian Consul-General in Rotterdam, who asked whether Haitian Jews were exempt from the new regulations. Luckily, they were, provided only that they carried their passports on their persons at all times.

This brings us to the anti-Jewish raid of June 11, 1941, which affords us a good idea not only of the methods used by, but also of the morality of, those responsible for it. Our main source is a report in the *Deutsche Zeitung in den Niederlanden* on June 14, of a "criminal bomb plot" against the headquarters of the *Wehrmacht* in Amsterdam South. There was no doubt, the paper added, that the plotters had intimate knowledge of local conditions, that the responsibility must therefore rest with Amsterdam Jewry (even the *Nationale Dagblad* omitted this causal "nexus"), and especially with German-Jewish refugees, who had been trying to incite anti-German feelings for months. The *Generalkommissar* for Public Security, Rauter, had accordingly ordered the confiscation of the property of "several" Jews. Moreover, a number of Jews, chiefly refugees, would be arrested and sent to work camps. So much for the report.

No one has denied that an attack on the *Wehrmacht* was, in fact, made at the time. Herzberg speaks of a "bomb-explosion in a club for German naval officers"; Ypma[1] credits the attack to the Dutch resistance; as far as we can gather from the names (Theo Dobbe and friends), the explosives were not, in any case, handled by Jews. Whether the Germans knew this or not, the way they played their game on June 11 was more revolting even than their customary behaviour.

After the February raids they had promised to make further mass arrests only after a previous warning. At the beginning of June a German policeman by the name of Barbey appeared at the offices of the Jewish Council, shook hands with Professor Cohen, and after this unaccustomed greeting asked for the latter's help in compiling a list of the names and addresses of all the Jewish apprentices who had recently been transferred from the training camp at Wieringermeer to Amsterdam. The Germans were anxious to have them resume their training, and wished to notify them beforehand, so that "they would not panic on being fetched". Cohen immediately contacted the Wieringermeer management, who told him that the Jewish apprentices would be more than welcome there. On hearing that, he gave Barbey the required list. In the afternoon of June 11 Asscher and Cohen were called to German Police Headquarters, where they were cut off from contact with the outside world until the evening, when Lages informed them he had arrested 300 young Jews as a reprisal for the bomb attack. Cohen and Asscher did not at first connect the arrests with the boys from Wieringermeer; when they saw them lined up they could do no more than whisper a few words of encouragement. None of their protests were of any avail, no more than those of the Secretaries-General. Not all the boys were from Wieringermeer; the Germans carried off anyone in the same age group who happened to live in the houses they called on—the author lost two of his favourite and most promising pupils in this way. Berkley tells us that Dutch as well as German policemen took part in these raids. The boys, who were once again described as "hostages", followed their unfortunate predecessors to Mauthausen; soon afterwards death notices started pouring into Amsterdam.

Cohen has repeatedly expressed his surprise that he did not resign from the Jewish Council there and then. On July 18, 1941, the illegal *Het Parool* had this to say on the subject: "While German sadists are torturing, persecuting, flogging and slaying their innocent victims, they yet have the temerity to call on us to save European civiliza-

[1] Y. N. Ypma: *Friesland annis Domini 1940–1945* (Dokkum 1953), p. 68.

Anlage-

Ubcrsicht

über die z.Zt. einsitzenden Häftlinge.

(Stichtag : 28.12.1941 )

| | | |
|---|---|---|
| 1.) | Geiseln im Internierungslager Haaren ...... (einschliesslich " Antirevolutionäre") | 238 |
| 2.) | Juden im KL. Mauthausen.................... | 8 |
| 3.) | Im KL. einsitzende Schutzhäftlinge ........ | 1354 |
| 4.) | Häftlinge z.Vorbereitung eines Strafverfahrens .................................. | 1433 |
| | Gesamtzahl der Häftlinge ... | 3033 |

Hiervon befinden sich im Lager Amersfoort .. 540 (ohne Russen)

| | | |
|---|---|---|
| 5.) | An die Gerichte abgegeben .................. | 43 |

German tally of number of Dutch prisoners and "hostages" in various camps on 28th December 1941. There were only 8 survivors at Mauthausen.

tion. Their insolence is if anything worse than their lust for blood." The saving of Western civilization was, of course, a reference to the "explanation" for Germany's attack of the Soviet Union on June 22, 1941.

When we look at July 1941 it appears that the German coercive machinery came to a temporary standstill. Not completely, of course, but still most Jews could shrug off the new measures and carry on. One of the new regulations was Decree No. 121 by which a German was put in charge of Unilever—few Jews if any realized what tremendous repercussions this measure was to have. Even less did they worry about the instructions by the Secretary-General for Education and Culture ordering Dutch cinemas to show *Der Ewige Jude*, that scurrilous bit of anti-Semitic propaganda to which we have referred earlier. Jews were, in any case, spared this spectacle, since all cinemas had been closed to them long before. And then there was Decree No. 140 of July 25, 1941, governing the keeping of pigeons. By Article 6, this activity could henceforth no longer be carried on: (1) on ships; (2) by Jews; (3) by aliens and stateless subjects.

Whatever other faults the invaders may have had, no one can deny that they showed inordinate zeal and devotion in a sphere where at best they ran into opponents but never into serious resistance or dangerous risks—Jew-baiting was their least dangerous and most rewarding field of "war operation". Here there were no reverses; here the struggle went on without interruption. The Germans were particularly busy in the holiday months. Thus August of 1941 and 1942 saw the coming of a spate of portentous regulations to which we shall be devoting the next chapter. Before we deal with these measures, however, we must mention two further regulations with fateful consequences for Dutch Jewry.

The first, Decree No. 148/1941, covered the "management of Jewish monetary effects". The word "management" was, of course, a misnomer, for what was intended was expropriation, not at first absolute, mind you, for this was a pleasure the Germans reserved for the future. A number of immobile effects had previously been reserved for people of German blood by Decrees No. 189/1940 and 48/1941. Now it was the turn of cash, cheques, bank deposits, etc., all of which had to be transferred to Messrs. Lippmann, Rosenthal & Co., an organization used by the Germans for the express purpose of milking the Jews. The German order mentioned all sorts of exemptions and exceptions which we need not discuss here because all of them were revoked with inordinate speed. What matters is that of the eleven articles of this Decree, five dealt with penalties: Article 9 stated quite bluntly that the *Reichskommissar* was free to declare forfeit whatever he chose by "departmental decision", and Article 10 that he was taking the necessary steps to implement the new measure. By August 15 the Jewish Council and the Jewish Co-ordination Committee, after discussion with Lippmann, Rosenthal and Co., published a memorandum on the subject, in which they tried to guide the victims through this new tangle of petty-fogging restrictions, but "with the clear understanding that the authorities might take quite a different view of specific cases". Hence readers were advised to contact their "normal consultants" (bankers, lawyers, accountants, etc.) and . . . "in conclusion it cannot be emphasized too strongly that it is in the interest of all concerned to observe the regulations in every least detail".

Three days later came Decree No. 154, a worthy successor to *Graf* Grote's earlier Decree (No. 102) governing the disposal of Jewish estates. By Article 7 of this new regulation, the *Niederländische Grundstücksverwaltung* (Dutch Estate Management Organization), a German body established at The Hague, was authorized to take over all Jewish properties, or else authorize non-Jewish persons to do so. Once again the penalties were stipulated at length. On August 29 the Jewish Council issued a very long circular, on much the same lines as that published in connection with the earlier Decree (No. 148). But here, too, many questions were left unanswered, so much so that *mr.* M. M. G. T. de Kort saw fit to write a special *Treatise on the Decree affecting Jewish property* (*No. 154/41*) and to publish it under the imprint of Holdert & Co., Amsterdam. We cannot tell whether or not its readers found it more helpful than they did the circular.

Before we come to the next major event, the author would like to refer briefly to an affair that cannot be dated precisely, but that became increasingly important in the course of 1941, and thus makes a fitting ending to this chapter. This was the affair of the *Nederlandse Unie* (Netherlands Union) or rather the relationship between that organization, established at the beginning of the Occupation, and Dutch Jewry. The earliest records show what happened as the new political movement, which quickly gained a vast following, gradually came face to face with German anti-Semitism—the only consistent German policy in the Netherlands. In essence, the three leaders of the Union had to face much the same problems as the College of Secretaries-General or the Jewish Council; the basic question exercising them all was whether, and when, it was best to accept the lesser of two evils.

The *Nederlandse Unie* counted a number of Jews among its members —it is no longer possible to establish just how many. After the war, the Commission of Enquiry was told by L. Einthoven, one of the Union's three leaders, that at a time when the (legal) Dutch Press generally kept silent, their weekly *De Unie*, was the only paper to criticize the invader's actions. (In point of fact, the *Liberale Weekblad* kept protesting as well.) Einthoven was referring to an article which *De Unie* published on October 12, 1940, under the heading: "A frank opinion on the fate of Dutch Jewry." This article argued that when it came to employment and promotion of Jewish civil servants, a distinction must be made between Jewish refugees from other countries and Jews who had "lived and worked in the Netherlands for generations". Regarding the former, some regulations were "necessary", but when it came to the latter, changes were both unnecessary and undesirable. "Unnecessary because, in the Netherlands, Jews do not hold the positions nor adopt the attitudes that have made the Jewish question so acute in other countries . . . Undesirable because Christian tolerance and a Christian sense of justice demand that no group living amongst us be ostracized merely because of its origins."

Forced as they were to choose between the devil of complete silence and the deep blue sea of an out-and-out attack of the Germans, the three leaders of the Union chose a middle course—which was still offensive to the Germans but struck many Dutch people as being far too weak. The men who were calling for the political support of the Dutch nation had clearly learned mighty little from the course of events since 1933. Like so many others, they would find that once on the slippery slope of compromise, their further descent was inevitable. A commission set up by the Dutch Premier, Professor W. Schermerhorn, on January 29, 1946, has thrown some fresh light on this unfortunate business; *inter alia* the commission found that "there was much criticism of the Union's decision to bar Jews from membership of the so-called group of active members, founded in the spring of 1941". Since that group meant to play a prominent part in political life, the commission felt, however, that the exclusion of Jews may have been decided upon in the interest of the Jews themselves. The report added that many Jews disagreed with this view. Herzberg mentions two meetings in 1941 between the leaders of the Union and *mr.* Visser, President of the Jewish Co-ordination Committee,[1] in which the latter took very strong exception to the suggestion that Jews might be asked to leave the Union. We quote his letter of April 6, 1941, to Messrs. Linthorst Homan and De Quay, two of the Union's three leaders:

"You have asked our Committee to advise Dutch Jews to withdraw from the Union in the interest of our Fatherland, since their continued presence is likely to weaken the Union's effectiveness. Your request is tantamount to calling for our co-operation in the segregation of Jews from the body politic—in other words in the setting up of a moral ghetto that is quickly bound to turn into a material one. All I can say in reply is, that the Dutch nation has shown quite unmistakably that it does not hold with such a separation and that, were we to agree to your request, we should be acting against what all Dutchmen consider a basic principle of justice."

This brings us to the end of this interlude and to the measure we have alluded to. It was passed in the summer of 1941, and took the separation of Dutch Jews from the rest of the Dutch public one vast step forward. The invader was becoming more and more blatant in the implementation of his plan, and now felt free to usher in what we may call the second phase in his campaign to eradicate Dutch Jewry.

That phase began with an attack on the Jewish child.

[1] Herzberg: *op. cit.*, pp. 152–3.

CHAPTER TWO

# FROM ISOLATION TO DEPORTATION

*September 1941–July 1942*

## EDUCATIONAL SEGREGATION

WHILE most Jews had felt the German lash in public and in private life, Jewish children had so far been left alone. Naturally the children, too, were affected by repressive measures, but never directly. All that was now to change: Jewish children were to be educated separately, and to be fenced in special enclosures for easier control and eventual capture.

The *Meldungen aus den Niederlanden* paved the way for the new measures with reports on a growing stream of complaints about "untenable conditions arising out of the continued association of Jewish and non-Jewish children at school". The paper quoted a great many instances in support of this view; in particular, it alleged that many Dutch teachers gave preferential treatment to Jewish children and rewarded them with unearned high marks simply as a token of their anti-Nazi attitude. Schools known to be "pro-Jewish" were said to have an incredible number of new enrolments—thus the Amsterdam Lyceum, run by Dr. C. P. Gunning, which broke up before the summer holidays with only two or three first grades, resumed with five first grades in the autumn.

Clearly something drastic had to be done to repair this unsatisfactory state of affairs.

The minutes of the Jewish Council show that the members had been looking into the matter as early as July 17, 1941, when reports were first received of attempts to register Jewish children as such in Amsterdam and in various other towns. The supporting documents included a circular by the headmaster of a secondary school informing parents that the Germans had called for the registration of Jewish pupils; the circular is dated July 10 and states that the necessary returns must be made that very day. On the same day, another headmaster sent out similar instructions to parents, the information to be given *by return of post* (twice underlined in the original). Even the "pro-Jewish" Dr. Gunning was apparently forced to follow suit on August 30. The registration was originally restricted to government schools. The minutes of the Jewish Council also mention that a number of headmasters and teachers had begun to dismiss Jewish children. What was to be done, the Council wondered?

In fact, something had already been done. The Jewish Coordination Committee had established an "Advisory Committee for Education", which had held its first meeting on December 10, 1940, under the chairmanship of Rabbi J. H. Dünner of Amsterdam, and which, in January 1941, published a series of recommendations for action that proved extremely useful when the time for action came. In due course the Jewish Council formed its own sub-committee, the Central Committee for Jewish Education, which met for the first time on August 14, 1941, under the chairmanship of Professor Cohen. This sub-committee had its work cut out, for on August 16 the Secretary for Education, Science and Culture, Professor Van Dam, a man who, through weakness rather than malice made concession after concession to the Germans, sent out a document marked "not for publication in whatever form", and stating that the *Reichskommissar* was about to promulgate measures for the establishment of separate Jewish schools. To that purpose, he had asked Van Dam to supply him with the number of Jewish schoolchildren with the utmost speed. The problem was discussed by the Jewish Council on August 19; the members wondered how special Jewish schools could possibly be opened in the smaller towns and villages.

The whole thing came into the open on August 29 when the daily papers published Van Dam's edict that Jewish children would henceforth have to attend separate schools, euphemistically described as "unsubsidized institutes of special education". The papers added that, since local councils would "temporarily" continue to run and pay for the upkeep of these institutions, they would continue to be "public". In the *Misthoorn* of February 21, 1942, Keuchenius, a Dutch Nazi "expert" in matters of race and genealogy, explained that the children affected by the new measure were of "Near Eastern–Oriental–E. Baltic–Alpine–Mongolian–Norse–Hamitic–Negro mixed stock". Half-Jewish children were exempt; the author remembers with what unseemly haste those found to be half Jewish after a long "racial investigation", rushed from Jewish to non-Jewish schools, as if the former had been visited by the plague.

The Jewish Council saw itself forced to build up a whole educational apparatus—under the nominal leadership of Professor Cohen, but under the actual direction of Dutch educationalists—we shall return to the whole subject below. The first step was a national investigation, for which purpose eight experts were engaged. They assembled a host of data, noted the number of pupils and teachers and the qualifications of the latter, dealt with special requests, answered questions, and formulated procedures (especially on dealings with the authorities).

This brief account of a very lengthy operation illustrates how the Jewish Council was quickly changing from bad to worse, as it increasingly began to play its new role of state within a state, or rather of nation within a nation—a role to which the Germans were determined to relegate the Jews. In this process its activities and organs began to proliferate on a vast scale—an early case of Parkinson's law, perhaps.

But let us not digress too far and return to the autumn of 1941. The acute shortage of Jewish teachers which then made itself felt had to be remedied by the recruiting of Jews who held diplomas in primary education but had chosen a different career, and even of unqualified people—a school in Gouda was run by a young advocate and two educated ladies. Primary schools (attended by 1,550 Jewish pupils) were largely run by students. Special Boys' and Girls' High Schools were set up in Amsterdam and The Hague; the Council also considered setting up a boarding-school for pupils living outside the capital.

More difficult still was the problem of technical education: in the provinces alone, Jewish children were expelled from more than 110 technical colleges. Lacking materials, lecture halls and teachers, hundreds of pupils were thus kept idle, a problem that was eventually solved by "labour service" in Germany.

And then there were the schools for the blind, the deaf and dumb and other handicapped pupils. In the three leading cities, these children were sent to special schools or classes; elsewhere they were "temporarily" reinstated in their former schools. In Amsterdam, special teachers' and nursery school teachers' training courses were quickly instituted, and attracted a fairly large number of pupils.

Groups of no more than three Jewish pupils could receive instruction from non-Jewish teachers or lecturers. In September, 399 senior Jewish students were given permission to finish their university studies at Amsterdam. Then there were all sorts of other courses and classes that Jewish students could attend. A number of Jewish teachers founded the Athenaeum Club which prepared students for various external examinations; others helped in whatever ways they could.

In short, in the autumn of 1941, things were still being managed somehow. True, the Germans were sweeping victoriously through Russia, but Jewish children could still be taught by Jewish teachers in Jewish schools. There were some difficulties, of course, not least because some examinations were held in halls barred to Jews. Special rooms were accordingly made available, but this caused so many administrative complications that the German authorities declared the examination halls exempt from the regulations governing the admission to "public buildings" while examinations were in progress. This did not, however, apply to oral examinations, during which the danger of contamination by Jews must have been particularly great.

Not everyone took the new regulations lying down. Thus the Jewish Co-ordination Committee protested to Van Dam on September 12, 1941, that the new measures violated both the letter and the spirit of the Constitution. Moreover, they ran counter to "an age-old tradition deeply rooted in the spirit of the Dutch nation". Among those who made personal protests, two teachers in Haarlem threatened to resign if their Jewish pupils were forced to leave; the author has since ascertained that one of them left her post there and then; the other at the end of her service contract. J. C. Haspels, Mayor of Enkhuizen, informed Van Dam that the new measures were illegal and that he accordingly refused to implement them. Van Dam replied that he fully agreed, and that he had said just that to the German authorities—who had ordered him to implement them all the same.

According to the *Meldungen aus den Niederlanden*, a weekly which gave a confidential survey of the situation in the Netherlands as seen by the German security service, Catholic and Protestant school authorities alike challenged and even sabotaged the new measures. To prove its point, the survey printed a letter by the Archbishop of Utrecht and another by the Management of the Union for Christian Trade Education. The Archbishop's letter is also quoted in

Stokman's book; the prelate ordered Catholic schools neither "to expel nor refuse admission to children baptized into the Catholic faith because of their Jewish origins", and to continue teaching such children as heretofore. Touw called the attitude of all Christian schools to Van Dam's circular "unequivocal, forceful and persistent"; there was a complete refusal to comply. But Van Dam thought of a way out: he simply threatened the parents or guardians of Jewish children with dire punishment if they continued to send their children to non-segregated schools. "What cowardice!" Touw remarks, adding that there followed "an exhaustive and time-consuming enquiry" into the number of Jewish children of the Christian faith. The number was incredibly low—in all Amsterdam there were only twenty of them, including six foreigners. Little could be done for them, the more so as fresh anti-Semitic measures soon occupied the full attention of all those who were opposed to the invader's policies..

### RAIDS IN EASTERN HOLLAND

In September the Germans started a fresh round of activities, possibly galvanized by the fact that this was the month of the Jewish High Festivals, or else because many of them had just returned from their annual holidays full of fresh ideas and new vigour. Or again, it may have been pure chance—the historian's way of dismissing unknown causes—which was responsible for the German raids in Arnhem and Enschede in the middle of that month.

The February raids had ostensibly been a reprisal against the rebelliousness of the Jewish quarter in Amsterdam; the June raids a reprisal for an alleged bomb or dynamite attack; the new ones were ostensibly a retribution for sabotage, particularly near Enschede where a number of cables had been cut. The Germans "accordingly" arrested over 100 (mostly young) Jews in the night of September 13, 1941, and sent them as "hostages" to a "concentration camp" (read Mauthausen). One of these deportees, unable to find a place in the train at Enschede, asked the conductor for one. "Get the hell out of here," he was told, with the result that his life was spared—only his suitcase reached Mauthausen. The Jewish Council cannot be said to have ignored the new "reprisals" entirely. Thus on October 11, Asscher and Cohen sent a letter to Seyss-Inquart pleading for the return of Messrs. Palache and Krukziener, whom they described as indispensable to Jewish education. In retrospect, it seems quite laughable to think they really believed this last point would have made the slightest impression on the *Reichskommissar*. They also had an interview with Böhmcker and Lages on October 27, when they referred to the "extraordinarily large number of Dutch Jews who had died in Mauthausen". They were pleased to hear that "*Herr* Lages was looking into the matter". Then they mentioned that a number of Jews had fled from the provinces since the raids, and were again reassured to hear that "*Herr* Lages agreed to look into this matter as well".

At a meeting of the Secretaries-General held on November 4, 1941, it transpired that Rauter, too, had been "astonished" to learn that of the 105 Jews from Enschede and environs, most of them youngsters, sixty-five had died within a few weeks of their departure; Rauter had promised to send someone to Germany with special orders to "draw attention to this state of affairs". In a letter, Schrieke, the Secretary-General of Justice and a member of the Dutch Nazi Party, told H. W. B. Croiset van Uchelen, the acting Inspector-General of Police, who had protested vigorously against the Arnhem raid, that it was only with the "utmost reluctance" and as a "last resort" that Rauter and the German authorities had been forced to take these "reprisals". At about the same time, the burgomaster of Enschede, speaking for all his colleagues in Twente, called on the President of the College of Secretaries-General to tell him of the grave qualms of conscience the German measures were causing them all. Luckily, Rauter proved most "sympathetic", and promised that future "diversions" of Jews would be delegated to the German police and that in any case, there would be no more such diversions "in the foreseeable future"—unless there were further acts of sabotage. Many Dutch officials and especially members of the Constabulary, had previously put on record their refusal to be in any way connected with the arrest of people who had neither committed a crime nor caused a public disturbance, and were thus fully protected by Dutch law.

When the Rev. Nanne Zwiep, representing all churches in Enschede, carried a round robin to General Christiansen, a man who was reputed to be "extremely kind-hearted", he was welcomed with cigars and coffee, but failed to obtain the release of even a single Jew (not even when the real saboteur was apprehended); six months later, the Rev. Zwiep himself was carried off to Dachau where he perished before the end of 1942.

## THE ATTACK ON JEWISH CULTURE

It was also in September 1941 that the Germans began their raids on Jewish libraries. It is a well-known fact that they joined hatred of Jews to an intense love of Jewish possessions, a love shared by Nazis great and small, believers and free-thinkers, illiterates and intellectuals alike. As for the latter, who prided themselves quite particularly on their interest in German culture and learning, they now concentrated their attention on Jewish libraries. So keen was the competition, that it required a great deal of skill and cunning to be the first in a long queue.

A document produced during the Nuremberg trial mentions the incorporation of the Rosenthal Library (20,000 volumes) and the library of the Sephardic Community in Amsterdam (25,000 volumes; chiefly Hebraica) into the German *Bibliothek zur Erforschung der Judenfrage* (Library for Investigating the Jewish Question), part of an institute by the same name founded by Alfred Rosenberg, the Nazi ideologist and as such the leader of a gang of licensed robbers. A document produced at the Nuremberg Trial (176–PS) tells us further that the Germans carried away the books of the Societas Spinozana in The Hague and of the Spinoza House in Rijnsburg in eighteen large cases marked "extremely valuable". "Not without reason," one of the German experts explained, "did the former director of the Societas Spinozana try to swindle us out of this library; luckily we discovered his ruse in time." Whenever the German Army "confiscated" the possessions of a Jewish emigrant, the Commander of the *Wehrmacht* in The Netherlands (the "kind-hearted" Christiansen) himself, would make the books available to Rosenberg's Institute. The Germans had great hopes of making stupendous discoveries in these books; *inter alia* they were confident they would discover more about Cromwell's attitude to the Jews and the part Jews were playing in the British Secret Service. A German report concludes with the statement that the group charged with this special study worked overtime for weeks on end, and "being as soldiers on active service, they laboured even on Sundays".

The reader will by now be familiar with a host of German regulations, all aimed at segregating Dutch Jews from their fellow-countrymen. Each one struck the Jews as onerous, harsh and insulting. However, in the middle of September, the Germans passed a new decree that made all the old ones look mild by comparison.

Dr. J. Koopmans

Professor R. P. Cleveringa

Frans van Hasselt

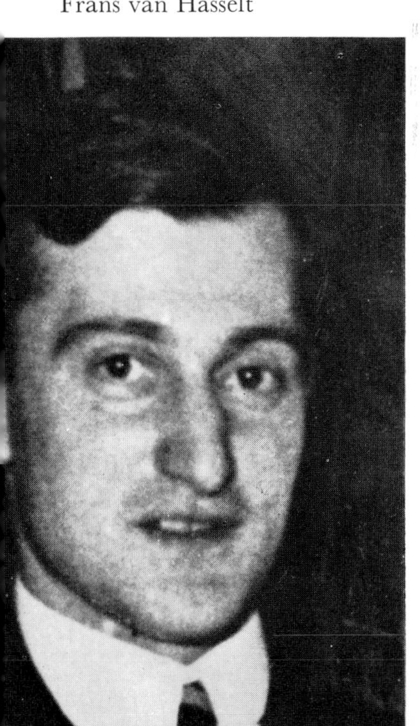

Page from the author's identity card

On February 9, 1941, Dutch Nazis assisted by German soldiers raided the Alcazar café in Amsterdam, where Jewish artistes were still appearing, and smashed all the fittings. Twenty-three policemen were wounded during the affray.

On February 11, nineteen Jewish boys were arrested in the Jewish quarter of Amsterdam. Three of them were forced to pose with their "weapons". Rauter forwarded the photograph to Seyss-Inquart, "just to show what types we have to deal with".

The raid on Jonas Daniel Meijer Square

The raid on Jonas Daniel Meijer Square

Article 45 of Decree No. 138 passed on July 25, 1941, empowered the *Generalkommissar* for Public Security (Rauter) to take whatever measures he thought necessary in the interests of public safety and to promulgate appropriate bye-laws. This was Rauter's chance to use his weight.

Article 1 of his "Proclamation on the Movement of Jews" prohibited them from:

Participation in public meetings and recreational facilities.

In particular, Jews were debarred from:

(*a*) public parks and zoological gardens;
(*b*) cafes, restaurants (including station buffets), hotels and boarding-houses;
(*c*) wagon-lits and buffet-cars;
(*d*) theatres, cabarets and cinemas;
(*e*) sports-grounds, bathing beaches, indoor and outdoor swimming pools;
(*f*) art exhibitions and concerts;
(*g*) public libraries, reading-rooms and museums.

By Article 2 Jews were further barred from "direct or indirect participation in public markets, public auctions and abattoirs".

Article 3 was less prohibitive for it merely required Jews "to obtain permits for making temporary or permanent changes of residence".

Article 4 dealt with possible exemptions under Articles 1 and 2 "with liability to pay costs". According to Article 5, meetings and public institutions open to Jews and hence exempt from the provisions of Articles 1 and 2 must display notices and issue tickets with the words "Jewish hall (or meeting), open to Jews only".

For safety's sake, Article 5 added to this the obvious rider that non-Jews "must not go to such places or attend such meetings".

In the section dealing with penalties for possible transgressions, we find the inevitable proviso that "these regulations do not in any way limit the powers of the Security Police".

All these Articles came into effect on September 15, 1941, the day on which they were promulgated, with the exception of the second which was to come into force fourteen days later.

The attentive reader will have noticed two things. First, the new decree merely reiterated a number of established facts. As Berkley has remarked, the provisions concerning cafés, etc., were, in fact, an improvement, for Jewish enterprises were at last placed on a legal basis, thus saving the proprietors and customers a great many headaches. On the other hand, the decree gave the German authorities many fresh opportunities of persecuting their victims by chicanery, withholding of permits, unexpected prohibitions, new penalties and what have you. The rather hopeless task of "interpreting" the new measures was tackled by the Co-ordination Committee, soon to be dissolved, and by the Jewish Council. A few examples will show how they set about that task.

Jews were no longer admitted to public parks. But what about public gardens, and particularly those in the Jewish quarter? This problem was studied by a special legal committee of the Jewish Council. And their decision was a weighty one indeed, for the lives of many people depended on it. Luckily for the lawyers, the decisions had all to be submitted to the Germans, who generally vetoed favourable interpretations.

And what of boarding-houses? Here, too, there was a "good side", for many new Jewish boarding-houses sprang up, including a number of old-age homes—all under the supervision of the Jewish Council. Yet it was precisely these separate establishments which served the Germans as ready-sprung traps when the time of the deportations came. Meanwhile, the Jewish Council issued a special circular (No. 29 of September 19, 1941), giving a precise definition of "boarding-house", and stating what was allowed to happen in them and for how long. The circular also told all those unable to find accommodation in boarding-houses what to do: to apply without delay (*sic!*) for an extension to the chief of the Security Police, Dept. J., at The Hague. The application, which had to be in German, had to include a declaration—also in German—by the owner of the old boarding-house that he was prepared to continue harbouring his Jewish lodger. While waiting for a reply Jewish applicants were allowed to use a copy of the application as proof that they had not committed a crime. So far so good, but on September 21—only two days later—the Co-ordination Committee saw fit to replace Circular No. 29 with Circular No. 30, which stated that its predecessor was not entirely correct and promised further information "probably within a few days". Circular No. 35 (October 2, 1941) gave Jews another two months at vegetable sales and one month at fruit sales; No. 37 which followed precisely a week later, gave them two months for both fruit and vegetables, but only one month for flowers.

As regards market trading and street selling, the Jewish Council published a report,[1] from which we shall merely quote the conclusion: "Market trading in the Netherlands, both retail and wholesale, is of extremely great economic importance to the country. The expulsion of Jewish traders from markets and streets will have catastrophic repercussions on Dutch economic life as a whole, will seriously dislocate the distributive process, and will cause the non-Jewish population financial damage to the tune of several million guilders per year." It is no longer possible to tell whether the Council was able to bring this conclusion to the notice of the Germans who, in any case, would have paid it no heed. They had taken the first step in reducing the Jewish poor and working class to conditions of abject misery.

The measure also brought immense social handicaps in its wake: no more Jewish bridge clubs, no Jewish dance halls, no visits to museums or zoological gardens, no more attendance of football matches—as referees, linesmen, players, or even as mere spectators.

Of course, some Jews ignored the new regulations. Thus on September 29, 1941, a Nazi journalist from North Holland saw fit to send a lengthy letter to the *Generalkommissar* for Administration and Justice in The Hague complaining, *inter alia*, of the continued appearance of two Jewish footballers, and the attendance by several Jews (mentioned by name) of football matches. As a result of these and similar complaints and the dire consequences that followed, it is reasonable to assume that even the most recalcitrant were gradually brought to heel. Still, it is gratifying to record that in this, as in other fields, many Jews continued to offer resistance and to keep up their morale.

In this connection we should like to dwell briefly on the Foundation inaugurated in Amsterdam on August 26, 1941, by the well-known industrialist B. van Leer and his son, who made available the sum of 150,000 guilders for the "advancement of art and science among Dutch Jews" (according to Berkley, a further 600,000 guilders were added after the enforced liquidation of the van Leer concern). The Foundation, which was originally directed by *mr.* L. E. Visser, was taken over by Albert Spanjaard after the former's

[1] "The economic consequences of the decree issued on September 15, 1941 . . ." (Amsterdam, Autumn 1941).

death; Dr. Paul Cronheim acted as secretary and artistic adviser, and Professor D. Cohen as delegate from the Jewish Council.

We know a great deal about the artistic activities of the Foundation, thanks largely to the *Jewish Weekly*, which not only published reviews of concerts, exhibitions, etc., but also advertised a host of cultural events, the high quality of which is not astonishing when we consider the prominent role Jews had previously played in the artistic life of the Netherlands. The works allowed to be performed at "Jewish" concerts were often the subject of controversy; thus the Germans could not quite make up their minds as to the racial purity of various composers. All programmes had to be submitted to the Germans well in advance by Professor Cohen who, no great connoisseur of music himself, was easily misled into mistaking for Jewish the works of various non-Jewish composers. Thus it came about that, on one and the same night, the Concertgebouw Orchestra and the Jewish Symphony Orchestra both performed the same work of Saint-Saëns. Soon afterwards, Saint-Saëns graduated as a Full Jew, so that this particular problem no longer arose.

From an article which the *Jewish Weekly* (October 17, 1941) published on the Jewish Symphony Orchestra under the leadership of Albert van Raalte, we know that the players were recruited from the Concertgebouw Orchestra, the Utrecht City Orchestra, the Arnhem Orchestral Society, the Groningen Orchestral Society, the Radio-Philharmonic Orchestra and many other Dutch orchestras of high repute; some difficulty was experienced in filling the horn parts: four wind instrumentalists accordingly took special instruction in the spring of 1941. The orchestra contained some of the best Dutch musicians of the time; there was even a choice of guest-conductors. At the time the *Jewish Weekly* published this article, the critics were still under the illusion that the orchestra would be able to play what it liked, "including" the work of Jewish composers—a German decree soon afterwards changed the "including" into "only". And so it came about that after rehearsing Bach, Mozart and Wagner, the orchestra was reduced to playing nothing but Mendelssohn at the opening concert of November 16, 1941. The names of the players appeared on the back of the original programme; most of them were subsequently murdered by the Germans. From a survey published by the *Jewish Weekly* of July 3, 1942, we know that only twenty-five of the fifty odd concerts planned had been performed by that date, mostly Mendelssohn and Mahler, but also Dukas, Goldmark,

Saint-Saëns, Wieniawski, Moszkowsky, Sinigaglia, Milhaud and Rubinstein. On July 9 the Orchestra gave its twenty-fifth concert—a kind of jubilee—and the programme fittingly included Saint-Saëns' *Danse Macabre*. The deportation began less than a week later . . .

The *Jewish Weekly* is also our chief source of information about what was happening on the Jewish stage. A play entitled *Cape of Good Hope* saw the light of day on April 17; its cast included a number of well-known names. It would take us too far afield to list them all or indeed all the plays performed by them; however, two plays advertised on October 17, 1941, deserve special mention, namely Rudolf Nelson's *Travel-book*, a musical which appeared at a time when free travel had just been suspended, and Willy Rosen's extremely witty *Tempo! Tempo!* It is interesting to note that many quite well-to-do people were applying for the job of stage assistant in the various Jewish theatres—at the time it seemed safer to be employed in whatever humble capacity.

We now jump forward in time to the issue of the *Jewish Weekly* dated April 1, 1942, from which we gather (on p. 5) that the Van Leer Foundation made a point of purchasing the work of Jewish artists. Twenty-six established painters and sculptors had been asked to submit three works each, and the Foundation selected one work from every one. The same issue of the *Jewish Weekly* also contains a number of interesting announcements. The New Jewish Chamber Orchestra advertised two concerts and published glowing "press reviews" of its work (the only paper reviewing Jewish performances was, in fact, the *Jewish Weekly*); the Jewish Theatre announced a virtuoso performance by the Great Jewish Entertainment Orchestra under Bernard Drukker. *Cape of Good Hope* was still being shown at the same theatre, and Kalman's *Bayadère* at the Jewish Comedy Theatre. The Jewish Theatre also advertised a new Nelson musical entitled *Fortissimo*, and the Comedy Theatre, Willy Rosen's *Bashful Susanna*. Finally the Jewish Orchestra was playing the ubiquitous Mendelssohn and Mahler, together with Playel and Dukas. In the issue of April 17 there is no mention of the New Jewish Chamber Orchestra, of the Great Jewish Entertainment Orchestra or of the Nelson musical; but on July 3, 1942, there appeared advertisements by Rudolf Nelson who had apparently turned to teaching light music, by the New Jewish Chamber Orchestra (Saint-Saëns, Offenbach, *et al.*), the Jewish Light Ensemble, the Willy Rosen Revue and the Jewish Symphony Orchestra.

We know little about attendance at these performances; many must have found them a great relief from the increasing pressures of daily life, though a large number of non-Jews, who had decided to boycott all segregated performances, objected to them on principle. Similarly many Jews refused to go to theatres exclusively reserved for Jews.

Much more can be said on the consequences of Rauter's proclamation of September 15, 1941, and we shall deal with these in due course. Here we shall conclude with a report of a service conference convened by *Generalkommissar* Schmidt on the same day. It was there that Schmidt revealed his plan to "rid the provinces of Jews" after first forcing them to wear yellow stars. Once that was done, it would be "a simple matter to apply the same measures against Jews resident in the city".

### THE END OF 1941

In September the Germans also passed a number of minor anti-Jewish measures to which we shall be referring elsewhere. All of them filled the Jewish population with forebodings, for instance the order prohibiting the removal of household goods and effects without prior permission. Still, all these measures paled into insignificance when compared with the three decrees of October 22, 1941.

The first, Decree No. 198, covered the employment of Jews. By Article 1, the Germans reserved the right to make the employment of Jews subject to special permits, or to prohibit it altogether; by Article 6, labour contracts subject to three months' notice could be terminated on the first day of every calendar month; those subject to longer notice terminated automatically on January 31, 1942. On that date, as Herzberg has pointed out,[1] every Jew could legally be thrown into the street.

Nor was that all. If an employer made use of this new opportunity he was further granted the right to pay a single sum (if necessary by instalments) in lieu of compensation, pension claims, etc. Jews were granted a maximum of one month's salary after five years' service, and six months's salary after twenty-five years' service.

This decree, too, brought a host of problems in its wake, the solution of which kept many a German and Jewish official busy for a long time. Still, the Germans must have set to with great glee, for not only were they enjoying the misery of the Jews at close hand but

[1] Herzberg: *op. cit.*, p. 74.

they also had the satisfaction of serving their *Führer* far from the battle front.

And in case the Jews were not sufficiently discomfited, the Germans added Decree No. 199, by which Jews were debarred from participation in non-profit making associations and companies other than those run by Jews and for Jews.

It is no longer possible to assess just how hard this measure hit the Jewish community; all we do know is that in the twentieth century more than at any other time, Jews were playing their part in a very great number of Dutch institutions and public associations. Fortunately, many Dutch officials took enforced leave of their Jewish associates in the kindest manner possible, thus coating the bitter pill the unfortunate victims had to swallow. The new repressive measure aroused a great deal of hostility at the universities, where Jewish students were suddenly forced to leave the various fraternities of which they had been welcome members. It seems likely, moreover, that the five resignations from the Royal Dutch Academy of Science were largely in protest against Decree No. 199, although the official reason was "disquiet at restrictions of scientific freedom and of the Academy's right to choose its members irrespective of political conviction or race". The signatories were Professors L. G. M. Baas Becking, N. W. Posthumus, W. J. de Haas, H. A. Kramers and J. H. Oort; Professor J. C. Naber had already resigned on August 10, 1940, when the Germans ordered the removal of the word "Royal" from the title of the Academy.[1]

Nor were Jews allowed to gather freely even in purely Jewish associations; thus the *Jewish Weekly* of October 31, 1941, reminded its readers that Rauter's proclamation of September 15, 1941, debarred Jews from all bridge clubs, dance halls, tennis clubs, etc.—many a Jew was still to lose his life for taking an over-lax view of the "etc." in this reminder.

As for the third decree of the same date (No. 200), it debarred non-Jews from doing work in Jewish households or in households where Jews were continuously resident for periods exceeding four weeks. Article 4 stipulated possible exemptions from this decree, which was said to supersede No. 231/1940.

Once again the Jewish Council had a great deal of work to do if it was to remain faithful to its chosen task of interpreting and miti-

[1] Letter from the Royal Dutch Academy of Science dated September 11, 1959.

gating the effects of the invader's repressive measures. To begin with, it tried to get as many exemptions as possible in terms of Article 4. It soon appeared that households with a Jewish head could not be excepted under any circumstances; nor could mixed households with a male Jewish member below the age of sixty-five hire non-Jewish female employees below the age of forty-five. The age limit of such females was soon afterwards raised to fifty. In addition, the Jewish Council had to register the non-Jewish staff of all Jewish institutions. To deal with the many problems involved—and particularly to answer the many questions that kept pouring in—the Council had to open yet another special office. All in all it dealt with 2,300 applications for exemption; the *Reichskommissariat* dealt with a further 1,000. The Council had no means of assessing the German reaction —the German decisions were communicated directly to the applicants. Today we can tell from the official figures for the first six months of 1942, that the Germans were relatively "lenient"; no doubt they were guided by the realization that the employment of unqualified staff in Jewish hospitals and similar institutions would have had dire repercussions on the health not only of the Jews themselves but also of the entire population.

One of the reasons the Germans gave for the new measure was the prevention of sexual contact between members of the Aryan and Jewish races. However, even where non-Jewish staff was discovered in Jewish households made up exclusively of women, the consequences often proved fatal to the employers.[1]

In any case, the Germans felt that their new measures did not go nearly far enough, for they had to be passed at a time when marriages between "Aryans" and Jews had not yet been proscribed in Holland. "It is still possible . . . to sleep with and even marry Jews in the Netherlands," remarked Calmeyer, a German official, who nevertheless refused a petition by a Jew from Naarden, supported by his burgomaster, to retain a half-day help for his twenty-seven-year-old daughter, who was in poor mental health. The help had accompanied the patient on walks for many years, and the girl was very much attached to her . . .

The Jewish Council also devoted much energy to its new task of organizing domestic service. In the *Jewish Weekly* of November 14 the Council called upon women, girls, men and boys to undertake the work in Amsterdam and The Hague. Since the response was

[1] Herzberg: *op. cit.*, p. 56.

exceedingly poor, the Council considered a publicity campaign and the possibility of exerting pressure in recruiting people; what precisely that pressure was to consist of does not appear from the report. Instead, we find the portentous remark that "circumstances would probably ease the situation". Meanwhile the demand for domestic staff greatly exceeded the supply, with the result that there was keen competition, and less well-to-do families had very little chance of obtaining help; the Presidents of the Jewish Council once again urged all members "to do what they could to improve the situation". It looks as if few heeded the new appeal. No more was achieved by other methods; during their first discussion of the matter with the German Delegate in Amsterdam the two presidents of the Council made a point of emphasizing "the misery caused by the departure of domestic help in families of old, frail and sickly people". It is difficult once again not to feel cynical at the Council's belief that their representation would have had a sympathetic hearing from a German official who himself did so much to implement and adapt these repressive measures.

In the same month—October 1941—there appeared two new German measures which "clarified" existing legislation on the movement of Jews.

The reader will remember that Article 3 of the proclamation of September 15, 1941, required Jews to obtain a permit before changing their addresses temporarily or permanently. This matter, too, was dealt with by a special department of the Jewish Council called "Travel and Removals", and by the German *Zentralstelle für jüdische Auswanderung* (Central Office for Jewish Migration), which, as we shall see, became increasingly important as the war continued. From the very beginning, a distinction was made between temporary travel permits and those valid for more than four days. The former could, at first, be granted verbally by the Jewish Council in cases of "urgent business or family needs". The drawback of this arrangement was that the traveller had no document to produce, but this was overcome by means of a slip proving that the so-called administrative costs had been paid. In order to restrict the Jewish passion for travel even further the German Delegate decreed on February 13, 1942, that the verbal permits could not extend to periods longer than two days. However, even this restriction must have proved ineffective, since Berkley reports that the Jewish Council granted 340,000 permits up to May 1942. On May 29, 1942,

*SS-Hauptsturmführer* Aus der Fünten of the *Zentralstelle* ordered the Jewish Council not to issue any more travel permits until further notice. This task was henceforth reserved for the *Zentralstelle.*

At this stage of our story we can only refer briefly to the problem of changes of address—we shall have occasion to deal with this more fully when we come to the German attempts to establish a ghetto. It is only against the background of the latter that some of the new measures can be understood. The reader will remember the decree of April 1941 prohibiting Jews from leaving Amsterdam. Now Rauter's proclamation of September 15 made it possible to fence them in even further.

On December 9 the Jewish Council reported that removals to Groningen and Overijsel would no longer be permitted. We cannot tell why these provinces should have been selected for such a signal honour. A document of January 2, 1942, lists all the names of the streets in Amsterdam to which Jews could still move—if they had a permit; the removal figures quoted in the same document and in another dated January 1, 1942, show the capricious nature of the German administration—one week a deluge of permits, another a deluge of refusals. The strain on the officials of the Jewish Council can be imagined.

A memorandum of January 1942 indicates that in the provinces of North Holland, South Holland and Zeeland (with the exception of Amsterdam and Haarlem) changes of residence within or between localities were forbidden on principle; where a removal was unavoidable, the people concerned were obliged to go to Amsterdam. There was the remote chance that "indispensable" Jews (for instance, teachers in Jewish schools) might obtain exemptions; however, no Jew whatsoever was allowed into Haarlem because of a local bye-law. On February 25, 1942, came the report that this bye-law no longer applied—but it was still not clear whether Jews could or could not enter Haarlem. This brings us to 1942, and a period in which Jews were to suffer far greater hardships still.

On October 31, 1941, the *Jewish Weekly* headlined the following report:

"On the orders of the German authorities, the competence of the Jewish Council has been extended from Amsterdam to the whole of the Netherlands. Representatives and deputies of the Jews will be appointed for every province and for the city of Rotterdam, and will be responsible to the Jewish Council in Amsterdam. All requests, petitions and other submissions by Jews to official sources must be submitted through the Jewish Council of Amsterdam, if necessary via the provincial or local representatives."

It appeared after the war that this measure was first mentioned to Asscher and Cohen by Böhmcker and Lages on October 27, 1941, on which occasion it was also made known that no statutes for the Jewish Council would be published, and that the Jewish Co-ordination Committee would have to suspend its activities. On November 3 that Committee sent out its fortieth circular, in which *mr.* L. E. Visser, as president, and *mr.* Henri Edersheim, as secretary, took leave of all those with whom they had been in any way connected.

On November 25 all German Jews living abroad—including the Netherlands—were deprived of their German nationality. All their possessions were declared forfeited to the German State which would use them to further the solution of the Jewish problem. This was the notorious Eleventh Decree,[1] and as Dutch Jews were to say later, it was one of the many writings on the wall. And those who still failed to see, should have had their eyes opened by the decree of December 5, 1941, ordering all non-Dutch Jews to report for "voluntary emigration" to the *Zentralstelle*. Herzberg[2] who mentions the "almost endless stream of forms" these unfortunates had to fill in, also reports that this new measure caused a new wave of suicides and increasing unrest among Jews in general, on the principle of *hodie tibi, cras mihi*. No doubt, there were many German and stateless Jews who welcomed this measure, since after all they were allowed to emigrate, whereas Dutch Jews were forced to stay at home to be looked up in ghettos; some even regretted the fact that they had become naturalized before 1940 and were thus prevented from leaving.

On New Year's Eve, 1941, no Dutch Jew could disguise from himself the fact that, unbeknown to his non-Jewish neighbours, things had got infinitely worse in the course of the year. The Germans had caused severe economic hardship, freedom of movement had been drastically restricted, and a series of repressive measures had begun to dog his every step. Yet even so, the historian finds it difficult to evoke the mood of the Jewish people as a whole. Many pinned their hopes on the likelihood of Germany eventually losing the war, and consoled themselves with the knowledge that

[1] Blau: *Das Ausnahmerecht für die Juden in Deutschland 1933–1945*, p. 99 c.v.
[2] Herzberg: *op. cit.*, p. 60.

however bad the position, it could have been much worse. Moreover, few Jews believed that the Germans would carry their policy to the limit. True, there had been raids and hundreds had died, but, thank God, most Dutch Jews had been allowed to remain in their old homes. True also, the Germans had sounded the ugly word of "emigration", but had they not prefixed the comforting adjective of "voluntary" and was not the measure directed at foreign rather than Dutch Jews?

Few suspected the next measure that lay in store for them, a measure that, seen in historical perspective, was a fatal step of the path towards the final catastrophe. This measure was the deportation of Jews to Dutch work-camps, beginning in January 1942 and continuing through most of that year. Seeing that, after only six months, it was aggravated by the large-scale deportation of Jews from the Netherlands, we must once again interrupt the chronological order of events if we are to see the whole episode in proper perspective.

## THE JEWISH WORK-CAMPS

The first Jews to be sent to work-camps were the unemployed, or rather those whom the Germans had rendered so. Being completely unorganized, they had to rely upon the Jewish Council, which offered them only the one slogan: "Go!" Those who felt reservations or the will to resistance were given no support anywhere. In the records we nevertheless have sporadic accounts of such resistance; Berkley[1] speaks of "violent scenes" when these poor men noticed how the promises made to them had been broken; few were, in any case, prepared to take as rosy a view of the camps as the Jewish Council did at the beginning. The author remembers that when he himself reported for medical examination for one of these camps, another victim, a Jewish workman, summed up the whole thing in the words: "We're all going to cop it, every one of us!"

This was not, of course, the way the Jewish Council looked at it. Here more clearly than anywhere else, the ambiguous character of that body reveals itself. While there is no reason to doubt that its members tried to oppose the Germans, all they could do in practice was to try delaying tactics while hoping for the speedy ending of the war. This might be called an attempt at sabotage, though just how successful we cannot say, since we have no means of assessing the

[1] Berkley: *op. cit.*, p. 51.

ratio of the number of Jews intended for the camps by the Germans to those actually working there in the autumn of 1942. In view of the German threats, the estimated number of 5,000 inmates seems very low indeed, the more so as non-Jewish unemployed were also eligible for "relief work" and the measure could not, therefore, be opposed on principle. (Needless to say, most of the Jewish unemployed had been rendered so as a result of German legislation.)

Of course, the Jewish Council was not the only authority dealing with the employment of Dutch Jews; there were also the Dutch Labour Office in The Hague, the Amsterdam Labour Office and the Amsterdam Communal Bureau for Social Affairs. The records contain as many critiques as they do praises for the officials in these organizations. Many were members of the Dutch Nazi Party and as such displayed a characteristic attitude. Luckily not all these collaborators were very bright—but there were enough of them to make things unpleasant for the Jews. Thus the Amsterdam Labour Office alone employed 123 Nazis among a total of 600 officials. The position of the "good" Dutchmen could in many respects be compared with that of the Jewish Council. We shall be discussing the whole question in a wider context; suffice it to say here that a number of Dutch officials went out of their way to be helpful to Jews, often at considerable personal risk to their own lives.

In Amsterdam many of them would wait for closing time; as soon as the Nazis had left they would start destroying cards, forging permits and fabricating fictitious doctor's certificates, etc. Some succeeded in sending Jewish unemployed to Germany as "Aryans" with false passports. Sabotage attempts were reported from many offices; Hilversum is probably the most striking example, for it was here that the forgers had the support of the German technical adviser. Arnhem was so successful in delaying the round-up of Jews that an exasperated Nazi sympathizer was heard to exclaim that it was high time all these yellow stars disappeared from the streets; there were enough of them in the sky as it was. In Gouda 120 Jews were called up by the Dutch authorities, but only one was "approved" for labour service by the Dutch officials.

And then, of course, there was the invader himself with his *Geschäftsgruppe Soziale Verwaltung* (Executive for Social Administration) under the control of the *Generalkommissar* for Finance and an Economics at The Hague; with his *Zentralstelle für jüdische Auswanderung* (Central Office for Jewish Emigration) in Amsterdam, and above all, with the *Referent für Soziale Fragen* (Commissioner for Social Questions), the fanatical H. Rodegro, who instructed the Jewish Council in all these matters, and who taxed to the limit the self-control of all who were forced to appear before him. According to Professor Cohen[1] he was a stupid man, but being one of the oldest Nazis in the office of the German Delegate in Amsterdam, he was very influential. "Rodegro was of the opinion that we (working hand in glove with the Labour Exchange) were sparing the more prosperous Jews and conscripting only the lower classes. This was true, but we could not convince him that it was not policy, but merely reflected the (social) composition of Amsterdam Jewry."

It was in 1941 that the idea of special work-camps for Jews was first hatched, in line with the general German tactic of isolating and seizing all Jews. Wielek[2] reports the arrival at The Hague of a high-ranking official from Berlin with a plan to conscript 3,000 Jewish unemployed. From the minutes of the Jewish Council we know that this matter was discussed at length in the summer of 1941; a meeting on July 29, 1941, specially convened for this purpose, dealt with the correspondence on this subject between Böhmcker and the two Presidents. On July 16 the German Delegate had informed the Council of a plan to provide work for Jews in Germany but close to the Dutch border, on the grounds that they would there be taught proper camp discipline and then be rehabilitated. Before going to Germany itself, the conscripts would be sent to a "training camp". Böhmcker suggested a pioneer corps of sixty (including a doctor, office staff, artisans, etc.) and also stipulated their precise equipment. The training camp was never set up; it is said that the Germans themselves disliked the idea. Professor Cohen has stated that a non-Jewish investigator who went to spy out the land discovered that the camp was to be run by Dutch Nazis; aware that Böhmcker held these men in utter contempt, Cohen[3] told him what he had heard. "You know more than I do," Böhmcker snorted. "Please investigate for yourself," came the reply. We do not know if that investigation was ever held, but in any case no training camp was set up. Incidentally, the Jewish Council did, in fact, call up a number of individuals, on the grounds that a refusal might have endangered hundreds, including the physically unfit. The enthusiasm for the whole plan among the Jews was predictably small.

[1] Cohen, *Herinneringen* (Memoirs), p. 55.
[2] Wielek: *op. cit.*, p. 81. [3] Cohen: *op. cit.*, p. 54.

Most of them thought at once of Mauthausen; on August 18 the Presidents of the Jewish Council pointed this out to Böhmcker and asked "for his help in this matter". Böhmcker thereupon gave the two Presidents "powers to put forward a scheme for relief work inside the Netherlands"; we probably do no injustice to the Jewish leaders when we suggest that they did not tackle this task with over-great haste—Cohen asserted after the War that the failure of this plan had, in any case, gained the Council a year's time. The facts do not, however, seem to bear out this high estimate.

Needless to say, the Germans became more pressing as their plans for the complete destruction of Jewry took shape under direct orders from Berlin. In this connection, the remark by *Generalkommissar* Schmidt (August 20, 1941) that the *Führer* no longer desired the rehabilitation of *Jews* but their exclusion, was a bad omen.

The records contain a report of a conversation on November 27, 1941 between Böhmcker (and his staff), Aus der Fünten, and some, other officials. The meeting agreed that Aryans were to be given better work centres than Jews; and to leave the recruiting of the Jewish contingent to the Dutch Labour Office, the Moorland Reclamation Society, and various local labour offices. The report continues that "the responsibility for supplying the necessary number of workers rests with the Jewish Council. That body will have to decide whether a medical examination of candidates is necessary or whether the choice could be made without this. In any case, the Council will have to inform the Labour Office in good time of the names of Jewish workers, and will be responsible for their suitability. The meeting further agrees that tests of suitability will have to be scaled down so as to obtain the necessary number of workers . . . The crucial consideration is not the restoration of normal labour conditions but the employment of Jews, who must disappear from the streets."

The Germans also devoted a great deal of time to a discussion of the labour conditions and decided that Jews must be paid 20 per cent less than Aryans; "out of this they would have to pay the full cost of their keep to the Land Reclamation Society". The Germans were aggrieved to find that children's allowances could not be stopped, because these were laid down by law. Luckily, however, maternity, wedding and burial benefits could be suspended. While working in the vicinity of Amsterdam, Jews must travel on foot; when distances of more than 10 kilometres were involved, train fares would be refunded "in certain circumstances". Unemployment benefit would be maintained at the same rate "for the time being".

This is an important report, both on account of its programme and also because of the light it throws on the ideas and aims of the Occupying Power. In particular, it foresaw a division of labour between a number of Dutch authorities, mentioned by name, and the Jewish Council—an arrangement that left some scope and, under favourable conditions, a fairly wide one, for delaying tactics and flight. The fact that "the Jews" disappeared from Dutch streets was certainly not the result of Dutch and Jewish co-operation in this field, for though thousands were sent to the camps, they got there *despite* concerted efforts to sabotage the whole plan.

On December 20, 1941, the *Generalkommissar* for Economy and Finance informed Secretary-General Verwey that all the details concerning the Labour Service had at last been worked out. Jews would have to report for work as speedily as they could, and in the largest possible numbers. The German Delegate for Housing and Settlement would initiate work projects, and the Amsterdam Labour Exchange would then be asked to conscript the necessary number of men for work in specific places, through the Jewish Council. The conditions of labour were stipulated and an adjustment in the law concerning children's benefits was promised.

On January 7, 1942, the Jewish Council convened an emergency meeting to discuss the new situation. Two days earlier the two Presidents had been summoned by telephone to the office of the Delegate, where Rodegro informed them that the Jewish Council was expected to supply 1,402 Jewish unemployed for transport to labour camps in Drente from Amsterdam Central Station on Saturday, January 10 at 10 a.m. No further delay could or would be tolerated. The Presidents replied that they were unable to accept responsibility for this measure. They agreed that unemployed Jews ought to be put to work, but could not agree to the transportation of these people on the Sabbath. Rodegro had threatened at first, but had then asked the Presidents to a meeting on the morning of January 6 at 10 a.m., together with officials of the Amsterdam Labour Office and the Department of Labour in The Hague. At this meeting he repeated his demand, the Presidents persisted in their objections, whereupon Rodegro departed, leaving the others to continue the discussion. The Presidents then argued that the raising of this labour force was the job of the Dutch authorities, which latter set to work that self-same day and called up all 2,600 Amsterdam Jews on public assistance. Of these, 1,400 were to be selected by Jewish doctors at the Diamond Exchange. All requests to postpone the transport until after Saturday were rejected.

When they returned from their meeting with Rodegro, the two Presidents issued a circular urging all those called up by their local labour bureaus to report immediately and without fail "since otherwise very much stricter measures may be expected". Thus while refusing to recruit the labour force, the Jewish Council nevertheless gave support to the German measure. The circular ended with the assurance that labour conditions would be the same as prevailed in all Dutch relief camps—only the wages would be somewhat lower.

There were other clouds in the sky, as well. Urban Jews from Amsterdam were being moved to the country in the middle of January. What that meant is perhaps best illustrated by a quotation:[1]

"The camps were quite unfit for winter habitation . . . Each day the cold increased, or else snow fell and remained thick on the ground. It was like a Russian winter. The snow lay yards deep on the roads and froze . . . Imagine yourself at such a time on a lonely moor . . . The Germans had seen fit to close these camps to ordinary workers on 8 January, but they were satanic enough to reopen them for the Jews on 12th . . . What unspeakable cruelty, to condemn people to such an existence . . ."

The age limit in these camps was sixty-five years. Still, the Jewish Council could take comfort from the fact that no one in work was being sent there. Moreover, camps in the vicinity of Amsterdam were still thought to be ordinary centres of training and rehabilitation. When it was made known that camps would also be opened near Groningen, the Council merely expressed its agreement with the views of its adviser, Meijer de Vries, who had stated that the required number would probably not be reached "because of the very large number of unavoidable medical exemptions". Nevertheless, the Dutch authorities, with the co-operation of the Jewish Council, succeeded in obtaining the full quota of conscripts and informed Rodegro accordingly.

On January 7 the Director of the Central Labour Office had sent a circular to the managers of local labour offices; in it he told them

[1] D. C. A. Bout: *In de strijd om ons volksbestaan* (The Struggle for National Survival) (The Hague, 1947), pp. 14 and 17.

of the German directive to send 1,400 Amsterdam Jews to labour camps. Since a second levy on January 20 had to include Jews from outside Amsterdam, the managers were requested to send urgent returns of the number of Jews registered at their offices and eligible for labour service. A subsequent telex message even called for a summary list of those eligible for heavy, medium or light work respectively. How did the managers react? We have the answer of one of them, the manager of the Labour Office in Hengelo, who stated on January 12 that he knew of no regulations by which unemployed Jews should not be sent to labour camps in the ordinary way. "Hence I can see no reason why Jews resident in my area should be considered for service in special camps. They are being placed in the normal relief projects."

By a lucky chance we know the reaction in The Hague to this resolute stand. On January 21 the National Labour Office simply replied that at the "urgent request of the German authorities" a number of Jews would be placed into special relief projects "against a fixed wage and with local increments where applicable". The letter also contains a remonstrance worthy of record: "I should like to remind you that you were sent an order by me and that it is not up to you to decide whether or not the order shall be followed. All you are required to do is to carry it out. It should not have been necessary for me to point this out, but since you obviously fail to grasp your responsibilities, I must tell you so with all emphasis."

The Jewish Council, too, did its best to admonish all those called up—quite a few have survived—to obey the German orders. On January 8 it added a special warning which the victims received via the Labour Office, and in which they were told "emphatically" that "serious measures against you will be taken in the event of non-compliance". The Council gave the "urgent advice" not to "shirk your unavoidable duty" and "to forestall worse measures". The admonition ended with the sentence: "We strongly advise you to co-operate in your own interests."

It would be difficult to cram together into so short a space a greater collection of warnings and admonitions. Even so, the Jewish Council felt impelled to send a further two exhortations on the next day. The first appeared in large type at the head of the *Jewish Weekly*. It contained the urgent (and italic) advice to go to Drente "in your own interests". The other told holders of pedlars' licences that they would have to hand in their permits that very day and that they, too, were eligible for labour service in one of the camps in Drente. Added to this information was a "final warning". It contained the usual peroration and the instruction: "Do not fail to catch the train on Saturday night", followed by a repeated appeal "in your own interest" to obey the order. The article ended with the following memorable sentence: "We repeat, what you are asked to do is ordinary relief work in ordinary Dutch camps under ordinary Dutch instructors."

The result was that on Saturday, January 10, 1942, 905 Jews departed for Drente, while 170 of those selected stayed away.

At the meeting of the Jewish Council on Monday, January 12, the Presidents reported that the Germans had called for another thousand Jews. The meeting expressed its confidence that the Presidents would do everything in their power to protect the interests of those concerned.

There are few records about further progress in this matter during January; all we know is that, at a meeting of the Jewish Council on Thursday, January 29, Meijer de Vries reported that weather conditions made the transport of people to one of the camps in Drente impossible, but that "those drafted would eventually be sent". The question of leisure activities was given "a great deal of attention"; though the rabbis deserved praise for their tireless activities, it seemed desirable to employ "lay preachers" as well. Asscher paid homage to De Vries for his great work in this field and this was unanimously endorsed.

Not everyone was equally appreciative of the "great work". In a manifesto published towards the end of January 1942 as a supplement to the illegal *De Vonk*, of which 100,000 copies were distributed (more were later run off), it was stated that the so-called unemployed had been sent to what amounted to concentration camps, that the Germans intended deporting these and all other Dutch Jews to Poland for extermination, that "relief work" was merely a pretext, and that no one ought to be left in ignorance of these facts.

As early as February 4 the Presidents of the Jewish Council felt impelled to complain to the German Delegate that the promised leave had not been granted to the relief workers, and added that this omission would undermine Jewish faith in the Council. Other complaints were added soon afterwards: the sick were kept in the camps, the wages were less than "just a little" lower; men in work were being sent on "relief", and so on. All this was said to cause a great deal of unrest; Rodegro promised that, as soon as "the consequences of this unrest had been removed" he would grant leave to 100 Jews; if all of them returned to camp, he would "consider" restoring leave to the rest. Meijer de Vries[1] declared after the Liberation that the camp inmates were at first given too much food "which led to their selling and bartering some of it and even sending food home, on which subject articles appeared in the National Socialist Press". He had warned against this, particularly against the trading. He need not have worried, for this state of affairs was quickly ended, so much so that the camp inmates began to suffer from starvation, and their rations had to be supplemented by food parcels from home. De Vries moreover, derived some satisfaction from the fact "that it was not exclusively the poorer Jews who were being called up for the camps"; as he declared "emphatically" he knew "not a single case of social discrimination". When asked whether the transportation of Jews to work-camps did not amount to denial of their liberty, he replied that "as he then saw it, this was not entirely true in the beginning".

At the emergency meeting of the Jewish Council on Thursday, March 5, it appeared that Rodegro had asked for another 3,000 Amsterdam Jews, and when this was refused by the Presidents, he had referred them to the District Labour Office. This consultation took place the same evening. The new age limit was to be from eighteen to fifty-five years, and the draft would have to consist of 600 unemployed, and 2,400 others. The Director of the Labour Office declared that he would not supply the latter without direct orders from the Germans; once these were received, he would, in any case, have to ask the Presidents of the Jewish Council for a list of suitable candidates, since he himself lacked any means of choosing these. The Presidents then told the Council that they were in two minds as to whether or not they should supply the names, "bearing in mind the grave consequences of a refusal to Amsterdam Jewry".

The reader will notice two things. First, by accepting the new conditions the Jewish Council was tacitly abandoning its former view that the camps were ordinary centres for the training and rehabilitation of unemployed workers, and second, that by granting the request of the Director of the Labour Office (and this was done) the Jewish Council took upon itself the even graver responsibility of deciding who had to go to the camps and who could stay at home.

[1] Meeting of the Jewish Court of Honour held on December 15, 1946.

As we have said, the Council accepted this responsibility, but in order to cause as little dislocation as possible it resolved to give only the names of unmarried men aged from eighteen to about forty years and to exempt clergymen, teachers, doctors and technicians.

In this way 1,702 Jews were designated, and of these 863 were selected. However, Rodegro demanded a further "500 or 1,000" Jews on March 23; when asked to defer this matter until after the Passover, he refused. He subsequently insisted that well-to-do Jews should also be included, threatening that "if we send him too many people from the poorer classes, he would order us to replace them with more prosperous ones." The Presidents replied that their list was made up alphabetically "without distinction between rich and poor", and that Rodegro could not really expect them to participate in the "pauperization of the Jewish community". The Council also succeeded in obtaining the release of sick-camp inmates, on the understanding that they would be replaced; Rodegro took the view that all camps had to pay collective fines if one of their members failed to return. After a complaint about the black market carried on from some of the camps, Rodegro enquired into this and also into "the cause of the great number of marriages contracted by Jews during the past two weeks". (This was, in fact, a consequence of the exemption of married men.) Finally, Rodegro drew the attention of the Presidents to the "large number of mixed marriages in the recent past"; the Presidents replied that they knew nothing about this. They were to discover the deeper meaning of this rider a few days later.

During the second quarter of 1942 things went very much from bad to worse. From the few surviving documents we can see clearly how the German pressure grew and how the Jewish Council, supported by various Dutch officials, sank more and more into conformity with the German demands; the reading of the relevant minutes, circulars and reports conjures up the image of a child building sandcastles against a rising tide.

From April, too, we have an admonition by the Council to those called up. "*If you refuse, we shall no longer be able to do anything for you, and you yourself must bear full responsibility for the consequences.*" The Director of the District Labour Office added his little bit with a circular telling all those concerned that "a refusal of an order from the higher authorities" was an offence, and that it was "in your own interest" to obey "without delay".

On April 7 the Presidents of the Jewish Council informed their colleagues that they had asked for an interview with Böhmcker, during which they "would use all their powers to urge the Germans to temper or abandon their present line"; failing which they would have to ask the Council for authority to "carry on as heretofore". They received this authorization, albeit after "some discussion"; the records still contain traces of complaints by various Jewish circles, some of which expressed the view that protests no longer sufficed, "not even violent protests"—it would be far better for the Jewish Council to refuse responsibility for Jewish matters.[1] But the reason given for this suggestion merely emphasized how little the real dangers were appreciated at the time; the writer was merely protesting at the fact that the new labour conditions were creating inhuman conditions for the families of the camp inmates. Just as surprising in retrospect is the reaction of Messrs. Asscher and Meijer de Vries who boasted at the meeting of the Jewish Council on April 16 of a number of minor successes; *inter alia*, they had "with great difficulty" been able to obtain a deferment in the transportation of a thousand Jews from April 20 to April 25.

An undated report (probably from April 25 or 26) suggests that, by April 1, only 756 of a draft of 850 had, in fact, left for the camps; "extra workers supplied by the district labour office", subsequently helped to make up the full contingent. But what of the "thousand" whose departure had been deferred until April 25? Let us look briefly at the figures.

At first, 350 persons were called up every day and this was soon afterwards increased to 600. Altogether, 4,500 people were involved. Of these, 1,300 had to be rejected. (Duplication of names, non-Jews, deceased, non-appearance, objections, etc.) of the remainder, 1,488 were permanently rejected, 808 were temporarily rejected and 145 approved for work in the vicinity of Amsterdam only. Thus of the 4,500 designated, only 759 remained available for transport to the camps (including 87 available for light work only). Luckily, there was a reserve of 250 from an earlier list whose previous objections were now overruled. Did this make a thousand? Alas, only 626 appeared at the Relief Centre to ask for their travel vouchers and of these only 486 reported at the station.

[1] Letter by E. Spier to the Presidents of the Jewish Council for Amsterdam, April 14, 1942.

From the minutes of the meeting of the Jewish Council held on May 7, 1942, it appears that a large number of those who had failed to report were summoned to the German Delegate's office in Museum Square; the Presidents begged Rodegro "not to punish these men but, inasmuch as there were valid reasons for their non-compliance, to take these into consideration, and to give the rest an opportunity to obey the order now". From a report by Meijer de Vries, we may take it that at the time there were some 3,200 Jews in camps already, that 1,500 more had been called up, of which a contingent of 300 was being made ready; clearly there was very little enthusiasm for these resorts, even though the Presidents were doing their best to restore leave and adequate provisions.

That was on May 7. Four days later the Presidents were summoned very early in the morning to Rodegro, who was asking for another 3,000 men and who, as a result of thirty-one escapes, announced more vigilant surveillance. He added that for this reason and also because the required thousand had not yet been sent, he would stop all leave. As to his promise that Jews would enjoy the same conditions as non-Jews, they were no longer being sent to ordinary relief work-camps and so the question of equality of treatment no longer arose. In future the Dutch Labour Relief Service would be in charge of material welfare, the Moorland Reclamation Society for organizing the work, while he himself, Rodegro, would take over the general direction of the camps. He added that if the draft did not yield the desired results he would have to entrust the selection to non-Jewish doctors and also seize any Jews who looked fit for work. If all his demands were met he would restore leave—"probably in four or five months' time". A new situation had arisen to which "precedent no longer applied". "We were told to reckon with great severity and with the fact that no Jews fit for work and below sixty or sixty-five years would be allowed to remain in Amsterdam." Shortages from Amsterdam would, moreover, have to be made good from the provinces. The Presidents discussed the whole matter with the Director of the Amsterdam Labour Exchange and on May 18 sent a circular to the representatives of the Jewish Council in the provinces with the notification that people between eighteen and fifty-five years of age were liable to conscription, and giving a number of conditions of exemption, fifteen in all. Non-Jewish officials also took action; a circular from the Department of Labour mentioned the following three categories as exempt:

(*a*) Those legally married to a non-Jewish woman.
(*b*) Skilled workers employed in the metal, textile and fur trades working under the orders of the *Wehrmacht*.
(*c*) Ragpickers with a permit issued prior to April 1, 1942.

Other exemptions could also be applied for. This circular included a list of the names and addresses of Jews not on the normal lists of unemployed; the thirty-six Area Labour Officers were asked to consider these names in conjunction with local representatives of the Jewish Council. Circular No. 11,132 was amplified a number of times and was discussed by the Jewish Council on several occasions. Thus on May 28 they suggested that "wherever possible", the new conscripts be given a few weeks leave soon after arrival in camp "with the known strict provisos about their return". On June 25 it was reported that this had been refused, because some defaulters had allegedly failed to return to camp. The same meeting also discussed the great hardship suffered by the dependants of the detainees and the "extremely serious fact" that in the provinces of Groningen, Friesland and Drente all male Jews aged eighteen to fifty-five had come before a Selection Board made up of members of the National Socialist Medical Association. That same day, the Amsterdam Labour Exchange sent out Circular No. 11,225, stating that henceforth only Aryan doctors, delegated by the provincial German representatives, would decide the suitability of Jewish conscripts; moreover, 6,000 Jews would have to be in the camps by July 31. In other words, the whole matter had been taken out of the hands of the Jewish Council, whose Presidents now protested that the consequences were bound to be chaotic. The only exemptions the Council could henceforth obtain were for Rabbis, a few doctors and some nurses. They discussed the matter once again with Rodegro, who merely told them that De Leon had guaranteed the supply of the requisite number of Jews; in a letter written by Rodegro on June 18, 1942,[1] the number required by July 15 was given as 4,500. In this letter Rodegro also wrote tellingly of De Leon: "I am convinced that the assistance of this gentleman will go a long way to help the Department of Mr. De Vries in supplying the requisite quota."

This brings us to June 30, the date with which we wish to conclude this chapter. Before we do so, however, we must first mention

[1] Wielek: *op. cit.*, p. 58.

a few incidental matters. For instance, we are in possession of a "highly confidential" note sent on June 10, 1942 by Meijer de Vries to fourteen Jews including the two Presidents and also to the Information Bureau of the Jewish Council; this note contains a report of a conversation between him and a number of Dutch officials on the subject of Rodegro's threat to employ foreign guards for the camps as a reprisal against "the massive defection of Jewish workers". That threat, De Vries now contended, could be averted by the opening of a Dutch punitive camp in Friesland, one and a half miles from the nearest village. It would be under the command of an ex-sergeant-major in the Marines; there would be censorship, smoking would be prohibited, there would be fatigue duties in special cases, the camp would accommodate a hundred people. "We for our part must . . . make it perfectly clear to all those concerned that these arrangements have been made to spare them a worse fate." The fact that the opening of a punitive camp was now regarded as a palliative measure by both the Jewish and the Dutch authorities shows just how far the situation had deteriorated in the early part of 1942.

We have spoken of Selection Boards to which the Jews had to present themselves. Their reactions are variously reported. In The Hague, it is said, the selections were made light of, with the remark that "the whole thing is silly, but after all the Germans must show that they are doing something". "Smart" Jews reported with a bottle of urine collected from a diabetic, and the more prosperous felt they could escape the measure anyway. In Amsterdam the Selection Board met in the Diamond Exchange, and of its first meeting Professor Cohen wrote later that he would not easily forget the despair of many who reported or the ruses used to obtain exemption. Shortly afterwards the Board was transferred to another building, but not until the manager had been given proof that the Germans would allow him to have Jews in it.

For a long time the selection was left in the hands of Jewish doctors. Conflict of conscience, so common at the time, is best illustrated here by a concrete case. A young Jewish doctor appointed by the Jewish Council agreed to serve; he was to receive 15 guilders *per diem*. After having worked for a day he realized that the men he was examining were not genuinely unemployed but people who had been deliberately put out of work by the Germans. He accordingly resigned in the face of strong pressure by the Jewish Council. Other

Jewish doctors also withdrew and at the end only one remained. We know the arguments used by the Jewish Council: it was only with the help of Jewish doctors that they could use their much vaunted delaying tactics. If Nazi doctors got the job, "every examinee would be given a one-way ticket to Mauthausen".

And Berkley tells us that, when Nazi doctors were, in fact, employed, they passed everyone, including "acute asthmatics, serious heart cases and the like". In Groningen, half a dozen Jewish physicians were forced to work with a Nazi heart specialist and a Nazi "doctor" who had failed to qualify. An expert medical witness has explained what happened there: "In six to seven hours on June 24, 1942, they passed some 1,400 men, including those with artificial limbs, heart conditions, etc." No one was weighed or had his urine examined. Only ten were rejected. Many Jews came with medical certificates but no notice was taken of these.[1]

Another witness, also a doctor, reported that of 800 examinees, only three were rejected. "Invalids, diabetics, heart and hernia cases, imbeciles and asthmatics were all selected. Their medical certificates were simply thrown away."[2]

As long as Jewish doctors were in charge something could still be done. "If the whole thing had not been so serious, the selections would have been a rich source of humour," wrote one of the witnesses. The best thing, naturally, was to have a "useful" complaint, of which stomach disorders, rheumatism of the joints and high blood pressure were the most popular. There is the apocryphal story of the doctor who asked, "Do you have headaches?"—"No." "Then perhaps you can't walk very well?"—"On the contrary." "Then it must be your heart?"—"Not at all." "In that case I will have to reject you, you must be crazy."

Far less amusing was the fact—which at the time attracted a great deal of notoriety—that rich Jews called up for selection found it so much easier to obtain exemption than did the poor, and that, even without obvious corruption, they obtained their "specialists' certificates" much more readily.

And so the Jews went to the camps. This brings us to the question of their life there, if life it could be called, and that of their dependants at home. It is a pity, but understandable, that we have so little information about this matter—very few of them lived to tell

[1] Statement by E. A. Cohen.

[2] Letter by Dr. I. Van der Hal, September 28, 1946.

the tale. Some, who were needed for special duties, have survived; there are also a few documents, but this is not enough to paint the full picture in all its horror. We catch occasional glimpses of an ever-changing reality, transformed from month to month and from camp to camp. We cannot really know what bad weather meant to men in these conditions, how they depended on the character of individual guards, or the particular mixture of men in the camp, or form a clear picture of the work they had to do. In a report on April 8, the *Generalkommissar* for Finance and Economics was told by one of his officials that the 2,000 or so Jews in the camps had "such good quarters and food that these conditions must not be allowed to continue". From about the same time we have the text of a telex message to Rauter. It states that each of the inmates of the eleven camps was given a daily ration of 38 oz. of potatoes, 18 oz. of bread, 3 oz. of fat, 2½ oz. of meat, 1½ oz. of milk powder, 12½ oz. of greens, ½ oz. of sugar, 0·6 oz. of marmalade, 0·3 oz. of flour, ½ oz. "*Nährmittel*" and 0·3 oz. of groats—this was the ration for heavy labour decreed for Jews by the Food Office.

What is interesting is that the Jewish authorities—in this particular case Meijer De Vries himself—at about the same time, told the so-called Central Committee that "all in all, the workers are very satisfied with the conditions and treatment they receive in the camps". A letter written by one of the camp inmates states that, from January 10 to March 28, he had been exempted from work on account of the extremely low temperature, and that the food had been "fairly good under these circumstances";[1] however, at the beginning of April the rations had been drastically reduced to 2·8 oz. of butter per week, approximately 7 oz. of bread and one ladle of warm food per day, "which latter looks more like a mass of liquid than a solid meal". The writer added that "for a working day of 9½ hours of heavy labour, this was less than inadequate". "Moreover the treatment is extremely harsh and the restrictions placed upon us most severe . . . The wages are quite hopeless, amounting on average to 10–11 guilders a week. Hygienic conditions, too, leave much to be desired." Another "grumbler"[2] had not seen his family in fifteen weeks and was nearly demented with hunger.

We also have some knowledge of the activities of the so-called cultural workers in the camps. The earliest report goes back to

[1] Letter by S. Wurms to Dr. F. Grewel, June 1, 1942.
[2] Undated letter by S. de Jong to Dr. F. Grewel.

June 15, 1942, and speaks of "excellent libraries", "courses of instruction" and "lectures". It adds that it is "a great pity that those chosen get so little home leave". "A camp with so many idlers, hoping to get home at any moment, is not conducive to cultural activity." Moreover, this particular place was a punitive camp, "knowledge of which has spread like wildfire. This is bound to have a salutary effect. Inmates of normal camps who have hitherto lived in fear and trembling of what would happen to them if one of their comrades escaped, need fear no longer. As regards leave, people in general have become fatalists, but few are reconciled to the prohibition of smoking."[1]

Another reporter had this to say: "Unable to use my bicycle even for cultural purposes, I put on stout shoes and walked most of the way to the camp. The journey took me four hours . . . in broiling sun on an unshaded road. I wonder if there is any chance of getting my good old bike back?" When he arrived he found everyone in a good mood. A very fine sports field was close to the camp but "because of the hostility of the local peasantry" Jews were "naturally" debarred from it. Though the mood was good, the clothes and footwear of the inmates "left much to be desired".[2] A visitor to yet another camp also reported that the mood was good, even though four inmates had escaped that very week. They knew that if caught they would be sent to a punitive camp. "But that did not seem to bother them overmuch." The visitor observed further to his horror—that a number of Jewish women had visited their husbands—by rail and what is worse without wearing a star.

This brings us to the question of Jewish women, children and other dependents. We can do no better than reproduce a letter sent to the Superintendant of one of the camps. It reads as follows:

> Dear Sir,
>
> I, the undersigned, address you with deep respect in the hope of receiving your sympathetic understanding.
>
> My husband has been in your camp for four weeks, having spent the preceding five months in Diever A. Since then I have not seen my husband. Your Excellency will understand how we long for each other, and how our two-year-old child is pining to see her father, and I would therefore beg you to grant my husband two

[1] Letter by S. Cohen to Meijer de Vries, June 15, 1942.

[2] Undated letter to the Jewish Council by A. Levy.

days leave during which I may feel that I have a family once again. You would make me unspeakably happy, for my husband is a good family man who has a good military service record and I am convinced that, should you grant this request, my husband will be in the seventh heaven. In the hope that Your Excellency will treat this request with favour, I remain, Yours, etc.

—and beneath it a Jewish name.

There are many other documents among the records to throw some light on the condition of the women and children left behind, all hoping against hope to see their loved ones again. The historian poring over these letters with their awkward spelling, their faltering language, reads them in the knowledge that, in this very summer of 1942, within a short hundred days, all these families would suddenly be reunited—in the horrible death of the gas chambers in far-distant Poland.

### THE BEGINNING OF THE EVACUATION TO AMSTERDAM

In the light of the approaching catastrophe, all the other German measures during the first half of 1942, however unpleasant, can only be regarded as so many pin-pricks. Even so, life had become one long series of persecutions, chicanery and oppression, to which every Dutch Jew might fall victim at any given moment—yesterday it was the turn of a neighbour, when was it to be one's own? Everyone tried to keep his head, at the very time that Berlin was putting the finishing touches to its plans for the "final solution". They would have to die, all of them, some almost at once, but none before they had been driven to extremity, humiliated and robbed of their last belongings. As we look back on that half year, we ask ourselves whether the German machine, had it consisted exclusively of sadists (which, of course, it did not) could have contrived with more infernal ingenuity the details of its plan to destroy a people. Whether or not so intended, every measure that the Germans took did, in fact, tend remorselessly towards the fatal end.

A good example of this is the herding into Amsterdam of provincial Jews in the first half of 1942, which paved the way for their later deportation. It all began in Zaandam, where Jews were informed on the evening of January 14, 1942, that they had to be ready on January 17 for removal to Amsterdam. That day, too, was a Jewish Sabbath, and this, too, could not have been a coincidence.

Perhaps "removal" is a euphemism, for these unfortunate people were allowed to take with them only what they could carry; their homes were sealed up. On the appointed day, 270 Jews actually left for Amsterdam; a further ninety-eight—all stateless people—were deported to Westerbork in Drente. This was not the only distinction; those married to non-Jews also had to go, but were given a further fourteen day's grace and could take their furniture with them. The Jewish Council again did its bit, this time by helping to find cccommodation for the newcomers (in one of the Jewish quarters of Amsterdam); and, as the process of evacuation accelerated, this was to become a major activity.

Hilversum followed suit soon afterwards; here some fifty stateless families (137 persons) were selected, probably at random, from a much larger number. They were ordered to leave on January 29, again only with what they could carry on their persons, but including pillows and blankets. They, too, were sent to Westerbork. Before leaving, the evacuees were required to hand to the police a list of the articles they were taking with them and the keys to their homes. Gas, water and electricity had to be cut off. Those who failed to comply would have their names and addresses published in the *Police Gazette*. At this very time a further list was already in preparation; 240 persons were soon afterwards evacuated, not to Westerbork but to Asterdorp, an area of Amsterdam set aside for "asocial elements". So much for the stateless Jews of Hilversum. Dutch Jews in that city received orders on June 2 to remove to Amsterdam—between June 15 and 19. But before pursuing this matter we must briefly refer to earlier events.

On February 9, 1942, 150 stateless Jews were ordered out of Utrecht into Westerbork; their number included thirty German-Jewish children in the local Jewish orphanage. People over sixty-five were permitted to remain "until further notice". In Arnhem thirteen named families were ordered to Amsterdam on January 27. Stateless Jews in the province of Zeeland were ordered out by March 24; those in a large number of places in the province of North Holland had to leave in March and April.

At the beginning of March the Jewish Council discussed the whole question with Lages, the head of the German Security Police in Amsterdam, who appreciated that the evacuation and particularly the rehousing of the new arrivals "caused great difficulties", but insisted that the process must go on. When the Council lodged a "strong protest" against the confiscation of money and valuables, it was told that the matter would be investigated. The Council was also told that Jews would have to register all their household goods at a special centre. And Lages had more to say. He declared "emphatically" that the Jewish Council and its representatives would have to refrain from "spreading alarm" about the evacuation. Someone had already been arrested in this connection, but would be released in a few days time. "We pointed out that what alarm may have been spread did not originate from that man but from the measures themselves."

The Jewish Council continued to do what it could, but little trace remains of this activity. A memorandum of June 29 contains a number of practical complaints by the two Presidents, *inter alia*, that because of the "quick influx of evacuees" the Jewish authorities were unable to solve the housing problem. In reply, the Germans simply pleaded "military necessity", and that was that. The best the Council could do now was to gain a few minor concessions. Thus they persuaded *SS-Hauptsturmführer* Wörlein, on May 13, 1942, to concede that non-Dutch Jews bearing the Iron Cross First Class or German decorations for those wounded in action could come to Amsterdam instead of having to go to Westerbork. Those working for the Jewish Council would have to be evacuated as well, but were allowed to take their furniture with them.

The Jewish Council was also quite powerless to prevent the intervention of that German creation, the Commissariat for Non-Commercial Associations and Foundations, a body that gorged itself on Jewish loot. Nor could the Council do anything to solve the problem of deserted synagogues and cemeteries, the payment of their officials, or a host of other problems, unimportant in historical perspective but a grievous hardship to those concerned.

Thus Professor Cohen tried vainly on March 19, 1942, to get permission for those who had paid for graves in their own towns to be buried there. Permission was also refused for the return of a number of confiscated Scrolls of the Law—the reason being that these articles were considered to be "of special importance" to Rosenberg's organization. And when Asscher wrote a long letter complaining that for "completely inexplicable reasons" an entire Amsterdam storehouse containing all sorts of materials for the housing of evacuees and including a quantity of cardboard for erecting partitions had been seized, adding that this "confiscation greatly hampers the work of the Jewish Council which is certainly contrary to your wishes", the reply of *Herr* Lages is not hard to guess. The Jewish Council had all sorts of other concerns as well, but all of these were swamped by the events of the second half of 1942.

The story of the rehousing requires a few words more. Since the newcomers had to be lodged in Jewish quarters and with Jewish families, the inevitable result was the establishment of a virtual ghetto. As long as they could, the Jewish Council called for voluntary hospitality, often appealing to Jewish ethical tradition and principles, but making it clear that if the carrot did not work the stick would be used. At the time the Council had no compulsory powers, an obstacle that the Germans soon helped to remove. Cohen[1] later agreed that it was quite possible that he and Asscher asked for these powers, simply because as leaders of the Jewish community they could not leave people in the streets. However, they did not take the powers into their own hands but delegated them to the "Municipal Bureau for Jewish Accommodation" (a public body staffed mainly by Jews and supported entirely by the Jewish Council). To the outside world it thus looked as if Jewish accommodation was being handled by the Amsterdam municipality.

As the number and tempo of the forced removals increased, so the need for using pressure mounted as well; in May the Jewish Council sent out a circular, a summary of which was also published in the *Jewish Weekly*. In it the Council spoke quite plainly of "everyone's bounden duty", which if necessary would be imposed with a "strong hand". These threats continued for many months—until the very time, in fact, when the whole problem was solved by the disappearance of hosts and guests alike.

### MARCH AND APRIL 1942

Labour camps and evacuation caused very great hardship in the first half of 1942, but not, of course, enough to satisfy the Germans. Possibly February 1942 may be called a lull in this storm—no doubt because the Germans were taking time off to prepare new measures. Even so, they ordered Jewish owners of libraries throughout the country to register their names by the 13th and also placed further restrictions on travel. Then, in March, the German machine went into full action again.

[1] Examination of December 17, 1947.

ᴠᴇ: Mauthausen extermination camp

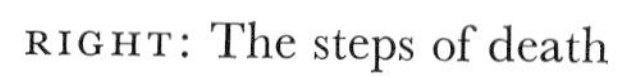

RIGHT: The steps of death

Rembrandt House, Amsterdam. The sign reads "Jewish Quarter".

Dutch storm-troopers posing beside "No Jews" sign

Jewish market in Amsterdam. "Jews only"

Workers in Jewish Labour Camp

Courtyard in the *Hollandse Schouwburg*

The coveted "exemption stamp"

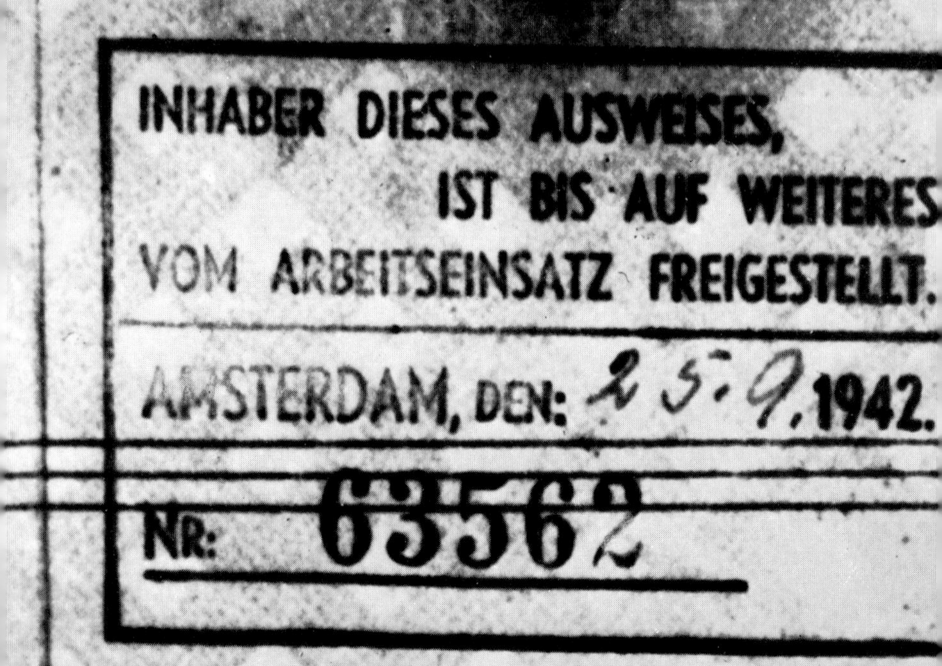

INHABER DIESES AUSWEISES,
IST BIS AUF WEITERES
VOM ARBEITSEINSATZ FREIGESTELLT.

AMSTERDAM, DEN: 25.9.1942.

NR: 63562

On the first page of the *Jewish Weekly* of March 20, 1942, the Jewish Council made it known that Jews would no longer be allowed to travel in motor-cars. From a letter by Böhmcker it appears that this matter was communicated telephonically to Professor Cohen on March 7 by *Herr* Rombach of his department, who also dictated the full list of exceptions "which must not, however, be divulged". These were: (*a*) ambulance services; (*b*) business connected with the German war effort; (*c*) hearses.

The reader will understand that exemptions under headings (*a*) and (*b*) would not be granted without the necessary certificates. Nor will he see anything astonishing in the fact that Jews went scot-free for riding in motor-cars between March 7 (the day on which Rombach communicated the measure) and March 20 (the day it came into force). However, the Germans soon afterwards ceased to be so tolerant: subsequently they punished everyone who disobeyed an order even when it had not yet been promulgated, with death if necessary.

As we said earlier, the Germans were dismayed to find that in The Hague—and no doubt in Amsterdam as well—there had been "a marked increase" in the number of mixed marriages between Jews and non-Jews; in the third week of March 1942 alone, the number was said to be double that recorded in the previous week, or so Wimmer wrote on March 31 to Schrieke, Secretary-General of the Department of Justice, whom he also told to instruct registrars throughout the country to inform the Commander of the German Security Police of the publication of banns for any such marriage.

A marriage was at that time said to be mixed when either partner bore a "J" on his identity card. The order was passed by Schrieke on April 8, 1942; it was modified in a number of respects on May 5, 1942, and again on January 8, 1943.

Meanwhile something else happened. In Amsterdam the Germans, in their understandable dismay at the increase in mixed marriages, had simply arrested some thirty Jewish people who had published their intention of marrying non-Jews. It goes without saying that these unfortunates were not aware of having committed any crime or that the protests lodged by the Jewish Council with the Germans in this matter were quite useless; when the two Presidents remonstrated with Rombach and Lages at noon on 25 March, they were simply ordered to place the following proclamation in the *Jewish Weekly*: "We are informed by the competent German authorities that Jews are prohibited from contracting marriages or having sexual relations with non-Jews." This announcement had to be signed by the two Presidents who protested that:

1. This decision was not based on any existing law. (Reply: it had the force of law.)
2. They could not accept responsibility for such a measure; nor did they have—or desire to have—the means of applying sanctions. (Reply: the Presidents do not have this responsibility—they are merely passing on an order.)
3. No penalty for transgression had been stipulated. (Reply: the Germans themselves would determine penalties in individual cases.)

And so this sad proclamation appeared in the *Jewish Weekly* on March 27, just before the Passover. The Jewish Council now tried the proven tactic of gaining small privileges, ameliorations, etc. In short, they continued to harass the German authorities, if harass is the right word in this context. At first, on April 7, they received "highly reassuring promises"; there was great hope that those arrested would "quickly be released again". On April 10, however, the reports were "no longer quite so encouraging"; on April 16 came the news that only two of the thirty prisoners had been released; on April 21 the Germans in Amsterdam promised to "discuss" the matter; on May 7 the Council was told that the unfortunates had been transferred to Amersfoort concentration camp.

On June 1, 1942, Asscher approached Lages, with whom he had obviously discussed the whole matter. He had this to say about the death of one of the thirty at Amersfoort: "You will understand what panic this news has caused among the dependants of the other prisoners. I must repeat to you, that all these people have already withdrawn their banns and broken off relationships. Could you not use your great influence and your active benevolence to free those who are still alive now? May I thank you in anticipation for your help."

We know little about *Herr* Lages' "benevolent" reaction, other than that, on June 23, he promised to arrive at a "speedy decision" We do know, however, what was in the reports that the Jewish Council had so euphemistically described as "not quite so encouraging". Bearing a large "R" (Race Defiler) sewn on to their clothes, the poor men arrived in Amersfoort,[1] where they were given "special treatment". Those who have any idea of the "normal" treatment of Jews in that camp can imagine what this meant. One man, on whose behalf Asscher intervened with Lages, was "so consistently hounded and ill-treated that he died after three days" (report by a non-Jewish eye-witness).

Seen against this background, the next measure the Germans passed in this ugly month seems to be rather minor; here we shall merely quote the text as it was featured on the front page of the *Jewish Weekly* on March 20.

"Every Jew occupying his own or rented accommodation must under paragraph 3 of the Decree of September 15, 1941, obtain permission in writing from the Central Office for Jewish Migration (*Zentralstelle*), through the agency of the Jewish Council of Amsterdam, before removing furniture, fittings, household equipment and other possessions. Breaches of this order will be severely punished . . ."

Before we come to April 1942, we must mention a few more minor details. There was, to begin with, a report by an *SS-Oberführer* to Security Police Headquarters in Berlin of the following "crass" incident: "At the works of Ringers Ltd., the chocolate manufacturers, in Alkmaar, 5,000 kg. of confectionery has been prepared under rabbinical supervision for use during the Passover. The costs of the supervision were paid by the firm, and the products sold through the Central Sugar Company. The sugar, too, has been refined according to the Jewish ritual." Another German official complained that Jews were being issued with *kosher* candles by the Dutch National Bureau for Chemical Products. No wonder Berlin pressed for stronger Dutch action in these matters.

And so the first quarter of 1942 passed. The second was notable for the appearance of Article 5 (subsection 1) of Decree No. 47/1942, dated April 30:

"Eligible for full membership in the Dutch Labour Front, are all those Dutchmen who earn their livelihood wholly or partly by their own work, and who are not, by Article 4 of Decree No. 189/1940 governing the registration of Jewish businesses, scheduled as Jews."

Soon afterwards came the announcement of the order prohibiting Jews from contracting civil marriages in Town Halls.

[1] J. Overduin: *Hel and hemel van Dachau* (Heaven and Hell of Dachau) (Kampen, 1945), pp. 108–9.

But these were mere pinpricks, for at the end of that very month, the Germans took a far more serious step, perhaps the most serious prior to the final act—they introduced the Yellow Star.

### THE YELLOW STAR

The Yellow Star had been rightly considered a relic of medieval barbarity. The Nazis with their weakness for history rescued it from oblivion and thus became the first to use it after the Lateran Council of 1215. With it, they branded Jews as farmers commonly brand cattle for the market. Perhaps the unenviable distinction of having resuscitated this badge of shame belongs to Reinhard Heydrich, though as P. Friedman[1] has pointed out, demands for such a badge of shame were raised by all sorts of Nazi leaders. In any case, the Nazis, when they overran Poland, immediately introduced special signs for the Jews—two years before such signs came into use in Germany itself.[2] In Germany the police decree governing the wearing of Jewish badges of September 1, 1941, required Jews over the age of six to wear "saucer-sized" yellow stars with a black inscription over their left breast whenever they appeared in public. The *Reichsgesetzblatt* (Government Gazette) published this decree on September 5. The order came into effect on September 19. A number of later regulations dealt with exceptions and refinements; Article 2 of the order of February 10, 1942, stipulated that the badges had to be treated "with great care", and Article 4 defined as "public", "every place in which a Jew obliged to wear such a badge might meet any person not belonging to his household".

On March 26, 1942, German Jews were ordered, as from April 15, to affix a star in black print on white paper to their house doors; on June 12 followed the warning that the star must also be affixed to working clothes (jacket, smocks, shirts). Probably there were other regulations of which we have no knowledge.

The star was also introduced into Czechoslovakia, whence it travelled to Western Europe. Here the Germans were compelled to take far more account of local opposition than they did in the East. They nevertheless decided to introduce this system simultaneously into France, Belgium and the Netherlands. On March 4, 1942, this matter was discussed at a special conference of "experts" on the

[1] P. Friedman: The Jewish Badge and the Yellow Star in the Nazi Era, in *Historia Judaica*, Vol. XVII, No. 1 (1955).

[2] Blau: *Die Judengesetzgebung* (The Anti-Jewish Laws), pp. 86–7, 99–103.

A Jewish star

Jewish question in Berlin; Eichmann was probably the evil genius of this gathering. There was talk of a further conference on March 14 in Paris; the records include an invitation to Lages from Knochen, the head of the Paris department, and also Lages' reply, to the effect that, since his deputy was absent from Amsterdam, he would not himself be able to attend and would therefore welcome a postponement. However, so keen was Paris that the conference was held all the same. But then something very odd happened: the French Commissar for Jewish Affairs, Xavier Vallat, refused to entrust the treatment of French Jews to the Germans and, during a quarrel, told a high German official: "*Je suis un antisémite bien plus ancien que vous! J'aurais pu être votre père!*"[1] In fact, Vallat insisted on his own anti-Semitic prerogatives to such an extent that he had to disappear from the Vichy régime, which naturally caused further delays.

Perhaps it is as well to compare conditions in Holland. Here Rauter was told by A. A. Mussert, the Dutch Nazi leader, that the yellow star "would be badly received in the Netherlands". But having already decided upon the deportation of the Jews, the Germans felt that the star would have to come all the same.

The relevant decision was communicated to the two Presidents of the Jewish Council by *SS-Hauptsturmführer* Aus der Fünten on April 29, 1942; the official text was published on May 9, 1942, by the *Generalkommissar* for Public Security and also as Decree No. 13, dated April 27 and published over Rauter's signature on April 29. The most important provisions were the following:

Art. 1 (1) All Jews appearing in public must wear a Jewish star.

Art. 1 (3) The Jewish star shall be a black, six-pointed star on yellow material, the size of a palm, and bearing the black inscription *Jood*. The star shall be clearly visible and affixed to the outer clothing over the left breast.

Art. 1 (4) Jews are debarred from wearing orders, decorations and other insignia.

Article 2 threatened transgressors with the usual penalties, a maximum sentence of six months' imprisonment and a fine of 1,000 guilders, "provided no more severe penalty is stipulated by other regulations".

As for the consultation on this subject between Aus der Fünten and the two Jewish Presidents, we have two reports, one from the

[1] L. Poliakov: *L'étoile jaune*, Paris, 1949, p. 26.

Jewish side and one from the Germans, the latter probably written by *SS-Hauptsturmführer* Wörlein, who was present at the meeting, and of whom Professor Cohen had this to say later: "I considered him the most unintelligent member of the *Zentralstelle* but one who could write excellent reports." In any case, he seems to have done so on this occasion.

The substance of the Jewish report is simply that Asscher and Cohen protested officially against the new measure. The German report describes the events as follows: "Asscher and Cohen were completely dumbfounded by this news. Clearly they had not expected anything like it. They said that, though it was unpleasant news for Jewry, they personally would be proud to wear the star as a sign of honour among Dutch citizens. Cohen went on to ask why the colour of the star had to be yellow, which was obviously intended to be a humiliation. *Hauptsturmführer* Aus der Fünten replied that the colour had merely been chosen as readily distinguishable and that in Germany, too, the stars were of that colour. The stars (569,355 of them) were then issued for distribution to the Jewish Council, who objected that this could not be done within three days. They were told that no postponement could be permitted (in Cohen's report we read that the three days in question included the Sabbath). The Council then asked whether they could publish the news in the daily press. This was refused. After Cohen had repeated the view that this was a dreadful measure, Asscher said blithely: 'It won't be long now, one or two months at most, before the War is over and we are free.' Altogether, the Jewish Council tried to protest against the introduction of the stars as strongly as possible. As Cohen said: 'You will understand our feelings *Herr Hauptsturmführer*. This is a terrible day in the history of Dutch Jewry.'"

In Cohen's own report we can also read about a telephone conversation between him and Aus der Fünten, who agreed on two days' grace for all those Jews who had found it absolutely impossible to obtain a star. To this we shall return later.

On April 30 the Jewish Council held an emergency meeting, at which the two Presidents explained the latest developments and added that they had reluctantly agreed to distribute the stars: "Quite apart from other motives, this could not be refused since otherwise many Jews would have been unable to obtain their stars and would have been thrown into gaol."

The office staff of the Council worked throughout the night.

Gertrud van Tijn-Cohn[1] tells us that there was keen opposition to the new measure among those present. A well-known Zionist protested that the Jewish Council should never have agreed to distribute the stars since, had the Germans been forced to do it themselves, they would have taken weeks and weeks over it.

A circular dated April 29, 1942, informed the Jewish population of the new measure. It stated that every Jew was entitled to a maximum of four stars against one clothing coupon; the price was 4 cents per star. The circular went on to give a number of addresses in Central, South and East Amsterdam where the stars could be purchased. The new regulations were also the subject of Police Telegram No. 38 sent at 6.35 p.m. on April 30, which added that children under six years would be exempt for the time being. The telegram gave the precise addresses and hours of distribution, called for police surveillance of the operation, and added that Jews disregarding the new measure must be apprehended and turned over to the German Security Service. By Telegram No. 36 of May 1 (5.10 p.m.) the Germans were also to be informed of all non-Jews who wore the star as a protest. Telegram No. 30 of May 3 (8.40 p.m.) instructed all police officers on street patrol to investigate "complaints" by non-Jews about the failure of "presumably Jewish passers-by" to wear the badge, and to hand possible culprits over to the Germans. Two minutes later—at 8.42 p.m.—came Telegram No. 40 ordering the release of anyone with written proof from the Jewish Council that their failure to wear a star was due to a temporary shortage of supplies. This idyllic state of affairs came to an end with Telegram No. 31 of May 4 (5.10 p.m.); at this stage there were apparently enough stars to obviate any exemptions. The police were also ordered to see to it that the stars were so affixed as to "make it difficult to conceal them". Thus the star "must not be affixed to the lapel or to a stole, but must be sewn on the jacket or coat itself at breast height". At 11.50 p.m. there followed Telegram No. 43, adding that all certificates of exemption by the Jewish Council countersigned by *Hauptsturmführer* Aus der Fünten of the *Zentralstelle* continued to have legal force.

Something had clearly gone wrong; precisely what it was became clear on May 5, during a conversation between Aus der Fünten and

[1] Gertrud van Tijn-Cohn: *Bidrage tot de Geschiedenis der Joden in Nederland van 10 May 1940 tot June 1944* (Contribution to the History of Dutch Jewry from 10 May 1940 to June 1944) (unpublished), p. 17.

Blumenthal on the one hand, and Cohen and Sluzker on the other.[1] On that occasion Aus der Fünten was so highly incensed that, contrary to his normal custom, he kept Cohen standing throughout their discussion. Had he not assured Cohen that no innocent people would be arrested? And yet Cohen had apparently seen fit to issue certificates without the agreement of the *Zentralstelle*! Cohen's argument that he had simply done it to obviate false arrests was unacceptable. So was his contention that he had wished to prevent unauthorized persons from claiming that they had been unable to obtain a badge. The examination continued throughout the day and Cohen fully expected that he would be arrested. Late in the afternoon he was informed by Blumenthal that the authorities had decided to close their eyes because they were convinced of the President's good intentions; they would not, however, be as lenient another time. Cohen for his part admitted his mistake which, he pointed out, resulted merely from the zeal of the Council to do its job. Everything ended on an amicable note, and Cohen left with a warning that starless Jews must no longer venture into passages, Jewish cafés, Jewish offices and schools; the question of Jewish actors on the stage was left open.

On May 7, at 9 a.m., Aus der Fünten gave Cohen and Mrs. van Tijn-Cohn a number of supplementary instructions. It appeared that the Germans had sent stars even to the prison authorities; oddly enough, Jews in one Dutch prison had been forced to wear white armbands with a Star of David even earlier.

At 11 a.m. on the same morning Cohen told a meeting of the Jewish Council that, in cases of doubt, it was best to wear the star. In the *Jewish Weekly* of those days we find many references to the whole matter, for instance the excellent advice in the issue of May 8 that the stars could be made colour-fast by washing in alum or vinegar solution. On May 15 we read that stars must also be worn in courtyards, gardens, parks and at open doors. On May 21 came the instruction that stars must be sewn on firmly—fastening them with pins was declared a punishable offence. The paper added that, in view of the new penalties, it had to be emphasized once again that any infringement of the new regulations could have "very serious consequences".

Today we know what these very serious consequences were—the death sentence. But few at the time could have had the least inkling

[1] Cohen: *Herinneringen*, p. 60.

of that. The same issue of the *Jewish Weekly* contained fifteen announcements of engagements, seven of weddings, four of births and seven of barmitzvahs.

But let us return to the star, and particularly to the reaction of both Jews and non-Jews. It is not unfitting to compare the attitude of Dutchmen with those of other West Europeans, particularly with Germans and Frenchmen about which we have some information. Thus we find that even in Germany there was no lack of public sympathy for the Jews. Countless men and women showed great kindness to the new pariahs and many touching stories were told, so much so that, according to Goebbels' diary, he felt impelled to speed up the deportation of the Jews from Berlin. Even Ernst Jünger[1] wrote that, seeing three young girls walking about with yellow stars in Paris, he felt ashamed of his German uniform.

In France, yellow apparently became the fashionable colour; all sorts of people came out with yellow handkerchiefs, yellow handbags, yellow feathers and yellow stars with derisive mottoes. Students were said to be wearing stars with the inscription "*Bon à rien*"—a pun on "*bon Aryen*".

Now for the Netherlands. Our records include a large and diverse number of data on the attitude of the man in the street. Thus we know that, though a Hague daily[2] wrote: "Truly, stars in the streets are as numerous as buttercups in May," its obvious pleasure was not shared by everyone. Herzberg[3] has called the reaction of the Dutch public to the yellow star extremely fierce and profound, the result of a strong sense of solidarity, "indeed, of identification with the oppressed minority". In his diary the writer Sam Goudsmit spoke of "unmistakable and strong" Dutch sympathy; the journalist Sem Davids[4] tells of an "old lady who came up to me to say that it was an honour, and another who congratulated me on 'having to wear the orange'". When he went to the Post Office and said good morning, he was greeted by an embarrassed silence that "I shall not forget". The clerks did not know how to avoid looking at the offensive badge.

A Jewish lady wrote that while she was waiting for a bus, "a nice young lad of about fourteen standing next to me entered into conversation about the weather. When we boarded the bus, he sat right

[1] Ernst Jünger: *Strahlungen* (Tübingen, 1947), p. 125.
[2] *De Residentiebode*, May 15, 1942.
[3] Herzberg: *op. cit.*, pp. 66–7. [4] Report, 1957, p. 5.

next to me and kept the conversation going. He told me about his school, teachers and homework and suddenly said: 'I am glad to be able to sit next to you for, do you know, I'm at the Lyceum, and my class has decided that whenever any of us meet anyone with a star we are going to keep them company, so that they won't feel so lonely.'"

Abraham Asscher, too, was congratulated on the wearing of the orange emblem by a leading Dutchman, who said he felt envious of this honour. We could quote many other examples, for instance, of people lifting their hats to Jews and paying them little attentions. As early as May 1, 1942, the editors of the illegal *De Vonk* printed 300,000 paper stars with the inscription "Jews and non-Jews are one". The hostile *Storm*, the weekly organ of the Dutch SS, indignantly reported the "Orange Bolshevik" activities of some printing works near Arnhem, where the employees all put on stars on the day the Jews were ordered to do so. In Deventer a number of schoolchildren decorated themselves with yellow stars bearing the words "Protestant" or "Roman Catholic"; twenty-three students at the Colonial School of Agriculture were sent to Amersfoort Concentration Camp for two weeks.

Thus in Holland as in France, many "Aryans" wore their yellow stars as fanatically as many Jews refused to do so. And in both countries the Germans took counter-measures. In his commentary on Herzberg's account,[1] Lages claims that all these measures were passed on the personal orders of Himmler. He added: "Undoubtedly the wearing of the star was meant to degrade the Jews. But was that reaction achieved in the Netherlands? Among Dutchmen only to a very small extent, and even among Germans in Holland, not very much."

The records contain an interesting German report. When the German Security Police in Paris wanted to follow the Dutch example they wrote to The Hague for advice, which was given by Zöpf on June 8. He told them that all pro-German circles in the Netherlands were elated about the star, but that—"as is only to be expected"—the enemies, including the Churches, showed antipathy to the measure and great sympathy with the Jews. "Even in N.S.B. circles this order was partly misunderstood at the beginning." Zöpf went on to report various manifestations of solidarity with the Jews, but

[1] W. Lages: *Gedanken und Aufmerkungen zur "Kroniek der Jodenvervolging"* (Ms., 1952).

added: "The members of the Jewish race who at first wore the star with pride, have since climbed down, afraid as they are of further legislation by the Occupying Power." With some justification, we may add, for in his very report Zöpf mentioned three new measures that were to come into force during the next week.

As Zöpf said, the Jews at first wore their stars with pride; this brings us to the very difficult question of the Jewish reaction in various parts of Europe. About this matter we simply do not know enough. Enquiries among the few survivors would probably yield much the same result as Poliakov obtained in France: at first many Jews felt that their self-esteem was not infringed since, after all, the compulsory wearing of a yellow star was neither an attack on their persons nor on their possessions. Yet it was, in fact, more than that—here, after many centuries, a section of the population was being pilloried and held up to public ridicule. No doubt the reaction varied from country to country; thus, the introduction of the star was followed by a peak in the number of suicides among Berlin Jewry; in Poland, particularly at the beginning, there were reports of a general feeling of humiliation and dejection; "on reflection" this feeling gave way to one of pride and to other more positive attitudes, culminating in sabotage and demonstrations. In France demonstrations occurred right from the beginning; about Holland we have the following report:

"The reaction of Dutch Jews to the star was often strange. The children thought it great fun. They revelled in the lovely yellow badge and were extremely proud of it. Five-year-old boys, who were not obliged to wear it, pestered their parents for one. Older people had mixed feelings about it. Many of them simply did not care. Others, and those of whom one would least have expected it, were ashamed and tried to conceal the stars. Some were too embarrassed even to visit their non-Jewish friends. One person is said to have gone further still, and never to have ventured forth, rather than be seen abroad wearing the badge."

The same writer tells us that the Jewish quarter, with its many stars, became known as Hollywood (a joke that also flourished in Warsaw); Waterloo Square became known as the Place de l'Étoile; the Jodenbreestraat was called the Milky Way; the yellow star itself was referred to as the *Ordre pour le Sémite*; P. Mechanicus reported seeing a man in Westerbork who had fastened the star to his naked chest with elastic tape, and so on.

A teacher at the Jewish Lyceum,[1] who at first refused to wear the star, reports that he was asked by his fifth-form pupils why he did not do so. "Because I do not recognize their authority, because I will not let them humiliate me, because I will not be led as a lamb to the slaughter." "But we have been told that the star is a badge of honour, something to be proud of." "Let those who think so wear it, I will not." After long and rather sad discussions with all sorts of people, well-disposed towards the Jews, he gave way, "and in the end my wife, with tears in her eyes, sewed the star to my jacket. In the morning she cycled with me to Alkmaar station. I sat in the train with my star and was ashamed despite myself." A week later, he took it off again, ready to brave the enemy.

We cannot tell just how many Jews lost their lives as a result of this act of defiance. One of these was a son of L. E. Visser, the President of the Supreme Court. The Jewish Council later explained that this was precisely why they had constantly urged all Jews to wear the star.

We conclude with a brief reference to something deserving much more extended treatment: the practical consequences of the yellow star. There is little doubt that it helped to seal the fate of Dutch Jewry, that it marked them out for slaughter. Every informer and extortionist could now recognize his defenceless victims on sight; the Germans could apply their measures with greater precision and even introduce a number of new ones. Herzberg[2] claims that, during raids and round-ups for deportation, the star acted as a target. But while it is possible to miss a target, the German rarely missed the Jews.

## TOWARDS THE DEPORTATIONS

Although only one German Decree (No. 58/1942 of May 21) was passed during the following month of May, we know now that the Germans were far from idle.

A draft for a plan of robbery and murder on an unprecedented scale had been considered by them as early as January 30, 1942, and this was probably not the first such draft. A document of February 5, 1942, revealed the object of this plan: the seizure or "Aryanization" of the remaining Jewish property (claims, precious metal objects,

[1] J. Hemelrijk, Sr.: *Zeven maanden concentratiekamp* (Seven months in a concentration camp), part I (Alkmaar, 1952), pp. 3–4.

[2] Herzberg: *op. cit.*, p. 68.

jewels, household goods, etc.). When the new Decree finally appeared, it was in seven parts, of which Sections IV, VI and VII dealt with the usual penalties. Section I (Articles 1 to 7) was merely a tightening of Decree 148/1941 and others, and required the registration of all outstanding claims, however small. Section II stipulated the permitted cash limit, including money owing (Articles 8 and 9); the monthly maximum drawings were now reduced from 1,000 to 250 guilders, no longer per person but per family. Section III (Articles 10 to 16) dealt with "collections, *objets d'art*, precious metal objects and jewels" in which field the Germans showed the sort of collectors' enthusiasm with which they so bitterly reproached the Jews; all such objects (Article 13) had to be handed in, even if they were merely on loan or held in trust for others. Article 12 stipulated what the Jews could keep:

"1. their own wedding rings including those of their deceased marital partners;
"2. silver wrist and pocket watches in personal use;
"3. table silver, not exceeding four pieces per person;
"4. gold and platinum teeth."

Section V (Article 18) called for the registration of horses and vehicles.

Even the reader unversed in law will understand what suffering, difficulties, anxieties, obstacles and dangers lay hidden in this new measure. Many of the enquiries sent to the Jewish Council at the time (for instance, what about engagement rings?) would make us laugh, were it not for our knowledge that the wrong answer to them often led to Mauthausen and Auschwitz. So the Jews filled in their forms, listing the number, race, age and breed of their horses, the horse-power, registration number, year, kilometer reading, and description of their cars, stating whether their carriages were equipages, sulkies, landaus, enclosed coaches, gigs; whether their boats had motor or sail or were hand-propelled, etc., etc. As to the few personal possessions they were allowed to retain, cutlery and jewellery were seized when they were sent to the gas-chambers, and wedding-rings and teeth were collected in due course—together with their hair.

But we must not anticipate too much. On June 12, 1942, the *Jewish Weekly* wrote in answer to "many enquiries" that "every form of outdoor sport, including rowing, canoeing, swimming, tennis, football, fishing, etc., must be deemed prohibited to Jews". On May 29, the paper had already reported that the Amsterdam municipal authorities had been instructed not to issue fishing permits to Jews.

The same issue contained another unpleasant surprise: henceforth Jews would be forced to buy their vegetables exclusively in Jewish shops and at Jewish markets. This at first applied to Amsterdam alone. The only extant document relating to the matter is a signed denunciation of a Jewish greengrocer who bought his goods at the public market. The informer added the remark: "I think a work-camp will do him no harm."

By Decree No. 58/1942 of May 21 Jews had previously been ordered to register their bicycles. The *Jewish Weekly* of June 12 informed its readers that the necessary forms were now available, how much one had to pay for the privilege of getting them, and that the completed forms had to be submitted before June 30. This was on the orders of the *Reichskommissar* himself (who promised that the bicycles would not be confiscated). But meanwhile Rauter had concocted a regulation of his own, No. 14 of June 22, ordering Jews to hand in their bicycles not later than 1 p.m. on June 24, that is within forty-eight hours, in good working condition and "not forgetting spare tyres and tubes". To make quite sure, Article 2 added: "It is prohibited to sell, hire or lend bicycles to Jews." However, Article 3 conceded that this provision was not applicable to:

1. bicycles belonging to Jews resident in Amsterdam;
2. bicycles stocked by dealers.

Not that Jewish dealers were allowed to keep these bicycles for long. As for Jewish bicycles in Amsterdam, they were seized under another decree, No. 16 of July 20, 1942.

The Jewish Council was not idle, and as early as June 23 sent out a letter describing the insurmountable difficulties this measure would entail and asking exemption for six categories, including cripples and those living more than 4 km. from their work. A reply dated June 25 told them to refer the matter to The Hague, which they did. This measure also gave rise to a number of questions, for instance which outlying districts could be considered as part of Amsterdam, and if the regulations applied to children's and other tricycles.

Berkley[1] reports that a number of temporary exemptions were, in

[1] Berkley: *op. cit.*, pp. 58–9.

fact, granted to certain employees of the Jewish Council and associated organizations; moreover, hospitals and other institutions for the old and sick were allowed to issue exemptions at their own discretion, provided they sent a full list of them to the *Zentralstelle*.

In short, whatever differences the *Reichskommissar* and Rauter may have had on the bicycle question at the beginning, they were happily reconciled again. This brings us to the end of June, a fitting climax to the first half of the year.

At about this time the *Reichskommissar*'s office also issued an "instruction" signed by the *Generalkommissar* for Finance and Economics, Dr. Hans Fischböck, and based on Decree No. 198/1941 governing Jewish professional activities. The reader will not be surprised to find that it limited such activities even further: no more auctioneers, pawnbrokers, employment agents, vocational, economic, financial and tax consultants, no more pharmacists, marriage-brokers or tourist guides. So much for Article 1. Article 2 excluded Jewish accountants, specialist teachers, gymnastic instructors, naturopaths, oculists, chiropodists, manicurists, pedicurists, masseurs, beauty specialists, hairdressers, etc. Article 3 restricted the sale of old metal, rags and offal. The rest of the instructions dealt with possible exemptions (against payment) and the penalties. While many Jews were hit by these new measures, a great many more were unaffected. What comfort they may have derived from this fact was quickly damped by Rauter's order of the same day, published in the Dutch Press. It was his "Second Order governing the appearance of Jews in public".

Article 1 was short and to the point: "Jews must remain in their own homes from 8 p.m. to 6 a.m.". Article 2 debarred Jews from entering rooms, gardens and other private accommodation belonging to non-Jews and used for purposes of recuperation and relaxation, unless by official invitation or under an existing rent or labour agreement. As a result, Jews could no longer visit their non-Jewish friends or rent accommodation from them. According to Berkley,[1] the interpretation of this last proviso was left to the arbitrary discretion of the pro-Nazi Amsterdam police authorities, a fact against which the Jewish Council "protested without success".

Article 3 was mainly directed against the Jewish housewife: she was henceforth allowed to shop in non-Jewish businesses (other than greengrocers, butchers and fishmongers, from which she was com-

[1] Berkley: *op. cit.*, p. 60.

pletely debarred by Böhmcker's earlier order) between the hours of 3 and 5 p.m. only. Home deliveries to Jews were proscribed. Berkley has suggested that the purpose of this new prohibition was to force the Jews to do their shopping after non-Jews had had the pick; he also reports that "most" shopkeepers kept aside a proportion of their best goods for their Jewish customers. Other reports say that the prohibition of deliveries was often ignored: one Jewish woman[1] tells us that she continued to receive flowers from the florist's shop she had patronized for years, and from other florists as well.

The writer can only say that this lady had unusually sympathetic neighbours: in Vught concentration camp she could have found a great many non-Jewish shopkeepers who disregarded this measure and their customers fared even worse.

Article 4 debarred Jews from non-Jewish hairdressers, pedicurists, masseurs, etc. On June 9 the Presidents of the Jewish Council had already been asked by two officials from Böhmcker's department to prepare a list of Jewish hairdressers. One of the Germans had told them that there was no intention of taking any action against these people, "on the contrary, their businesses would be left untouched". It was only when the Presidents, somewhat suspicious of this unexpected show of paternal interest, asked for the purpose of the list, that they were given the real reason. In any case, the list was published in a number of issues of the *Jewish Weekly* (July 10, 17 and 31); the continued existence of these establishments was, however, by no means as assured as the Germans had so emphatically promised. Jews outside Amsterdam were at a particular disadvantage; here and there they were allowed to visit non-Jewish hairdressers at fixed hours. Elsewhere they ignored the order at considerable risk to themselves.

Article 5 debarred Jews from "railway yards and any kind of public or private transport". Naturally there were exceptions. Thus, Jews could still use ferry-boats, bicycles (only in Amsterdam, and, as the reader knows, Rauter stopped even this after only three weeks); carrier bicycles for legitimate business purposes; ambulances for the seriously ill, and special conveyances for invalids. With special permits, Jews could also board trains, provided they used smoking compartments of the lowest class not occupied by non-Jews. The number of such special permits was strictly limited; Jews

[1] G. van Tijn-Cohn: *op. cit.*, p. 21.

working for the German war effort found it easier to get them than did members of the Jewish Council. Moreover, their issue (like that of so many other permits) was, according to Wielek[1] in the hands of "a sadistic lout . . . one of the most feared Dutchmen in the German police headquarters".

Article 6 denied Jews the use of public telephone installations. Soon afterwards, private Jewish subscribers also had their telephones disconnected; in the provinces they were sent notices of termination of service on July 15; in Amsterdam all subscribers were required to declare their race. Once again many non-Jews experienced a crisis of conscience; thus the Synod of the Reformed Church judged that by refusing to fill in the new forms they would lose their telephones and thus a valuable means of helping some Jews. One cannot help smiling at the plaint of the Dutch Nazi paper, *Volk en Vaderland*, that even the editors of this pure-blooded periodical had to certify their racial integrity before they could get a new telephone line. Those who did admit to being Jewish received a letter from the Chief of the Telephone Service terminating their contract. Even doctors were not exempt, except for a happy few who had to be available throughout the night.

The rest of the decree contained the usual stipulations, except for Article 8 which announced that further administrative details would be published in the *Jewish Weekly*. By 5 p.m. on the day this fatal decree appeared, the Presidents of the Jewish Council, together with Dr. E. Sluzker called on Aus der Fünten who greeted them with the remark that they must have seen the latest regulations in the paper and that he could tell them something more about them. In particular, he would like the Jewish Council to designate five doctors and five midwives for night service in Amsterdam, two of each in The Hague, Rotterdam, Utrecht; and one of each in Arnhem, Eindhoven, Enschede, Nijmegen, Groningen and a number of other towns.

What followed is much more interesting. After the Presidents had pressed for several exemptions they asked earnestly that in future they might be informed before new regulations were issued "so that we can make our wishes known before it is too late". They were promised that their request would be given "serious consideration".

Thus the mouse was asking the cat to warn it before pouncing, and the cat agreed to give this request "serious consideration".

[1] Wielek: *op. cit.*, p. 136.

"We protested officially and with emphasis against the fact that the new measures bound Jewry throughout the Netherlands hand and foot. We were told that this also would be considered.

"To our question why exemptions granted to Jews in Germany were not also granted to Dutch Jews, we were told that German Jews were German citizens while Jews here were in Occupied territory."

The issues of the *Jewish Weekly* published immediately after June 30, 1942, give a few more details. Thus laundries could still use the tram service and make home deliveries; Jews (with permits) could only use the front platform of a tram; a list of the five doctors doing night service four times a week appeared (but no midwives were mentioned); in connection with Article 1 (curfew from 8 p.m. to 6 a.m.) it was forbidden to lean out of windows or to use balconies and gardens open to the street. Back gardens were all right. And finally, stars must be worn when standing at open windows.

Looking through the advertisement pages which fill more than half the paper and which give us a glimpse of Jewish life at the time, we find that in addition to the usual engagement, wedding, birth and death announcements, all sorts of new businesses had sprung up—there was, for instance, an inordinate number of pedicurists. There was also a great demand for housemaids and male house-help, and one request for a "sociable and tactful nursemaid for a little boy". Quite a number of people were advertising for work, accommodation was offered and sought, some dutifully adding "in the permitted quarters". Of the seven advertisements for marital partners, three contained the words "home-owners". Many lessons were advertised, including two offers of tuition in French conversation. In The Hague there was a school of window-dressing; in Amsterdam a school for cantors. A teacher from Hilversum was giving lessons at an Amsterdam address. A gymnasium was offering training, not in sport, of course, but in massage. "Not travelling?" another advertisement read. "Let us help you keep in touch with your clients by means of good business letters." The last page advertised a course in ventriloquism; everyone could apparently learn this great art at home. Wedding photographs, flowers, corsets to measure, piano tuning were advertised as well. There were two advertisements for rucksacks, straps and similar goods. The rest of the paper consisted of editorial matter, with the exception of one advertisement by a firm of funeral directors.

As we contemplate all these people with their own little concerns, activities and worries, we cannot help being filled with compassion, pity and grief. For we know what they did not know and could never even have suspected: grim death was even then knocking at the door of most of them.

CHAPTER THREE

# THE DEPORTATIONS

*July 1942–September 1943*

## THE BEGINNING

WE now come to the period beginning in July 1942 and ending in September 1943—fifteen months that saw the wholesale deportation of Dutch Jewry. Some Jews had been deported even before July 1942—the reader will remember the raids of February, June and September 1941—others survived in Holland even after September 1943, but one can say that, in the period under review, the Germans greatly accelerated the tempo of their attacks, and successfully blocked most of the remaining loopholes.

The writer will not presume to decide whether or not Dutch Jews had anticipated their wholesale deportation. Even before 1940, many of them had begun to feel unsafe in their homeland—constant reassurances from the more optimistic notwithstanding. Needless to say, this fear must have increased greatly after the invasion, and particularly when the common enemy began to reveal himself in his true colours. Still, only a very few could have anticipated that what lay in store for them was so infinitely worse than persecution, dire poverty and want.

Then, in 1942, rumours began to circulate, and these rumours gave way to near-panic when Quaker sources let it be known that the Germans intended to deport all alien Jews first, and all Dutch Jews after that. Even then some of the more obdurate victims continued to persist in their blind optimism. Thus A. de Hoop, one of the most powerful and trusted Jewish officials at Westerbork, informed Professor Cohen that the deportations would be discontinued after December 15, 1942;[1] even in March 1943, the leaders of the Jewish Council still called it an "irrefutable fact" that as far as the inmates of Westerbork and Vught were concerned, the

[1] Letter dated November 23, 1942.

Jewish Council would have to continue running, and indeed expanding, the special department dealing with their affairs.

In a later chapter we shall look more closely at the Germans' "final solution of the Jewish problem"; here we need merely point out that on June 22, 1942, Eichmann confirmed a telephone conversation he had had two days earlier with Councillor Rademacher of the Foreign Office in Berlin to the effect that, starting in mid-July or early August, thousands of Jews would be taken in special trains for "labour service" in Auschwitz, among them 40,000 French, 40,000 Dutch and 10,000 Belgian Jews. The Foreign Office had raised no objections in principle but deemed it wise to consider the possible "psychological repercussions" and to begin the good work with the deportation of stateless Jews, of whom there were some 25,000 in Holland alone. Now, this group included refugees from Hungary and Rumania, and Eichmann was given express instructions to account separately for their property, no doubt out of respect for the Germans' allies.

When did the representatives of the Jewish Council know that a mass deportation was being planned? It is said that Aus der Fünten gave them several indications; in any event he summoned the Council at 10 p.m. on Friday, June 26 (once again on the Sabbath!). At first the members believed that it was a routine meeting; in fact Asscher, who never concerned himself with these, went to Noordwijk for a rest. Thus Cohen, Sluzker and De Hoop alone represented the Council; Cohen says he remembers feeling that something ghastly was in the air.

They were received by both Aus der Fünten and Wörlein with the "important news" that "police-controlled labour contingents" of men and women from sixteen to forty years old would be sent to Germany. Dutch as well as German Jews would have to be registered on simple forms of which the Council members were shown a prototype. The Council would have a day in which to tell the Germans how many people per day they could "handle".

"We were completely stunned by this unexpected news," Cohen has since explained. "'You know, of course,' I told the two SS leaders, 'that this type of labour service runs directly counter to all the tenets of international law?' To which Aus der Fünten replied without hesitation: 'It is we who decide what is international law.' I picked up pen and paper and told him that I would like to record that remark, but he interrupted me by saying: 'What I meant is that we decide who has to go on labour service.' Later he added: 'After all, we are the victors.' I pointed out that that was immaterial and put down my pen."

According to another account of this meeting, Cohen argued that, in the First World War, the Germans themselves had contended that the conscription of civilians from occupied territories was contrary to international law. Their answer to this was, that this time Germany thought otherwise. In any case, many Jews would remain in Holland, so there was nothing to complain about.

And what did Cohen do? In his memoirs, dictated many years later, he wrote: "At this point I picked up my briefcase to show that I considered the interview closed and that we were not prepared to implement these orders. But then I noticed a look of triumph in the eyes of Aus der Fünten and Wörlein, and I sat down again. Wörlein then told me that my attitude suggested we were not prepared to co-operate. This merely increased my suspicions and I said that as it was a matter of such high importance, I had decided to resist my first impulse."

De Hoop, too, claims that he noticed a "malicious gleam" in the eyes of the two Germans; according to him "they would have found it easier to carry out the deportations by using physical force rather than through the persuasion of the Jewish Council". Cohen, though in full agreement with this view, has added: "I must admit that Aus der Fünten, when in charge of the first raid, seemed to dislike it a great deal."

There are no minutes of the meeting held by the Jewish Council on the following afternoon; Berkley's version of the proceedings[1] has, however, been endorsed by Cohen. Berkley reports great resentment on the part of "some members" who rejected all thought of co-operation and derided the idea of requesting a reprieve of leading Jews—such a request would clearly have suggested that the Jewish Council, instead of doing its duty and protecting all Jews, was now merely looking after its own. Other members, however, believed that

1. by continuing its work, the Jewish Council might be able to delay the implementation of the new measures;
2. obtaining exemption for leadings Jews would mean the retention of a strong core, on which the rebuilding of Jewish society in Holland so largely depended;

[1] Berkley: *op. cit.*, pp. 68–9.

3. the winding up of the Jewish Council would play right into the hands of the "rougher elements", who would give the Germans a pretext to intensify rather than temper their repressive measures (this remark was probably aimed at De Leon).

The pros and cons of all these arguments will be analysed later. In any case, as Berkley correctly points out, even those members who opposed co-operation with the Germans did not resign from the Jewish Council. No doubt Cohen could console himself with the fact that the "look of triumph" he had seen in Aus der Fünten's eyes was wiped out by that great decision. In fact, during a further meeting with Asscher and Cohen, on June 30, Aus der Fünten stressed that the whole affair was really no more than simple labour service.

It is almost incredible that the leaders of the Jewish Council should have swallowed this tale after all that had happened in the Dutch work-camps. They did ask, however, why it was thought necessary to place the new contingent under "police" control. To which Aus der Fünten replied that the police were best fitted to look after the safety of the Jews in the work-camps. The age limit would "probably" be forty years. The report of the interview ends with the words: "It was expressly stipulated that the camps had to be in Germany, and it was also explicitly defined how the transportations were to be organized . . ." It seems that all this emphasis must have been used by the two Presidents to convince the Jewish Council—or was it perhaps themselves?—that all the evidence to the contrary, everything was, in fact, being done for the best. Indeed, "when we asked that the deportees be allowed religious guidance, we were told that the Germans never interfered with the work of any church". Then came the notorious haggling and bidding for higher stakes. The Presidents offered 350 to 375 persons per day; Aus der Fünten called for 600.

The two Presidents: "Our technical advisers consider this impossible."

Aus der Fünten: "We shall make the forms even simpler than they are already."

The two Presidents: "Let us start with 350 per day."

Aus der Fünten: "All right, but for eight days at the most."

As a further "concession" he exempted all members of the Jewish Council, "seeing that they were already doing labour service in Holland". "Finally the Council was told on behalf of *SS-Gruppen-*

*führer* Rauter that there was a rumour to the effect that the two Presidents had called for a strike against the deportations to Germany. If that rumour should prove true, very strong measures indeed would be taken."

What was the reaction of the Jewish Council to this terrible allegation? "We protested strongly against the very idea that the Presidents of the Jewish Council, set up by the German authorities, should take their responsibilities so lightly as to even contemplate such action."

From the minutes of the meeting of the Jewish Council held on Sunday, July 5, 1942, at eleven o'clock, it appears that the deportations were the subject of a host of further arguments. The Council took note that the Germans had called for 1,200 registrations per day, but were prepared, at first, to "make do" with only 800. But whatever the rate, they insisted that a total of 4,000 Jews be sent to "Germany" during July 14–17. Fortunately the Germans were willing to consider exempting anyone whose name was submitted by the Jewish Council. "Such lists of people essential to the life of the Jewish community in the Netherlands are being compiled at this very moment." The minutes of the meeting held at 11.30 a.m. on July 9 state regretfully that some of the proposed exemptions had not been accepted by the Germans, who also threatened to carry off to concentration camp the parents of all those who had refused to come forward.

Needless to say, agitation among ordinary Jews increased as the transportations began to look more and more unavoidable, and this despite the fact that the "indispensable" few made light of the consequences. So great was the agitation, that the Police authorities felt impelled to send a telegram to all stations on July 13 ordering the "immediate dispersal of any Jews congregating on the public highway, if necessary by force". In case these instructions were not explicit enough, the telegram added: "German police patrols will be specially sent out to supervise the activities of the Dutch police."

In short, the Germans anticipated a good deal of resistance on the part of Jews and other Dutchmen.

Were their fears justified?

What few records we have do not really help us to answer this question. It appears that, at most, individual Jews would refuse to answer their call-up papers, and in view of the attitude of their leaders, very little more could, in fact, be expected of them. One eye-witness wrote bitterly: "I often asked myself what I could do about it all. Since I had no wish to be sent to Poland myself, I had to advise others against it as well. But what was the good of such advice when I could not offer them the alternative of a hide-out or escape to Switzerland? Try and change the policies of the Jewish Council? That was a waste of time. Most members believed that they were doing their duty and working in the best interests of the Jews. Set up a rival organization challenging their leadership? I had often discussed that possibility with my friends. But time and again we reluctantly concluded that this was not a practical alternative—now less so than ever before. Far too many people had placed their trust in the Jewish Council as their last hope. There was nothing at all we could do except work in small groups, get false papers for our families and friends, find safe addresses here and there. And that was all."

Meanwhile the first call-up notices were sent out by special delivery on Sunday, July 5, 1942. Herzberg[1] has given a full description of the forms used on that occasion. Herzberg rightly draws attention to the clever way the document was phrased; it suggested that the conscripts would be put to work, and gave no hint of what the Germans really had in store for them. And the poor victims were, of course, only too willing to swallow the yarn. "The Germans need labour, that was clear, they told each other. That is precisely why they want so many Jews, and why it is in their own interest to treat us well." False optimism was also fed from other sources. There were, for instance, those young Zionist pioneers, who "as patriotic and religious Jews felt it their duty to serve wherever the Jewish community stood in greatest need of their material and moral support". And who was more fitted to give material support in the camps than they, who had enjoyed so much hard training in hard manual labour? A group of these young people entered the transit camp cheerfully singing Hebrew songs; they, too, ended up in the gas-chambers.

Still, pessimism and uncertainty must have been the far more prevalent feelings. Thus Sam Goudsmit tells us that when he took leave of some friends on July 17, he had the clear premonition that they would perish and that he would never see them again. "For our enemies blatantly threaten every least one of us with death and extinction."

[1] Herzberg: *op. cit.*, pp. 105–6.

In these circumstances it is no wonder that so many Jews clutched at whatever straws offered themselves and joined wholeheartedly in the rat race to safety. Safety meant a job with the Jewish Council, or a job in a "protected occupation" such as the scrap metal and diamond trade, or in Jewish shops.

The Jewish community would have had to consist of saints, if corruption, nepotism and all that went with them had not proliferated—we use the term advisedly. People chased after papers, after exemptions, begged for a week's delay, produced doctor's certificates to the effect that they were dope addicts, mutilated or invalids. All hell broke loose at the headquarters of the Jewish Council where the door-keepers had their hands full, endeavouring to keep out a jostling mass of people all of whom were trying to get in by hook or by crook. "Once inside, they pleaded, cajoled and implored. Others shouted and gesticulated." They stood in queues for hours, hating themselves for doing it, but doing it none the less. They lined up for specialists' certificates, legal advice, testimonials from their religious leaders or from the "friend" of an important German, who might use his influence. If only one could achieve recognition as an "indispensable" Jew! Or find some sort of refuge from the Germans, an imaginary oasis! We have a letter sent months later, but that does not matter, from the director of one such "oasis", who stated that "to his great consternation" he had just learned of the call-up of one of his colleagues with his wife and child. "I must stress that the work of this man is of such great importance [twice underlined] that we cannot spare him under any circumstances [underlined]."

There were other petitions as well. On July 16 Professor Cohen was sent one with an impressive letterhead but of tenuous reality, asking help for a "young friend". This friend had originally been told by the Germans that if he reported for work in Germany his children aged four and eight would be allowed to stay in Holland. One hour after he had left, a letter was received cancelling this concession. "By then my young friend had left; he is probably in Germany by now. The two children will now have to go to Germany by themselves and may never be reunited with their parents. Is there nothing you can do?"

Knowing that the Germans were no barbarians, and that they liked to keep families together, the Jewish Council petitioned Böhmcker, asking that young men in the Dutch work-camps be allowed to marry so that "in the event of their being sent to Germany" their wives could go with them. A Jew from Utrecht, wrote to the Commander of the *Wehrmacht*, General Christiansen, pleading for exemption and including documentary proof that he had been wounded in action in May 1940; as a result, his right leg had been amputated, his left leg was badly damaged, and his left foot was crushed; he was confined to an invalid chair. This letter has been preserved with an annotation in red which has since been identified as Christiansen's. It was brief and to the point and simply read: "A Jew is a Jew, legs or no legs." A similar comment also appeared on a petition from a man of seventy-eight who had twenty-seven years military service behind him and who enclosed certificates to show that he was partially paralysed. He, too, was deemed fit for "labour service" in "Germany".

Dr. J. Hemelrijk, a teacher at the Jewish Lyceum, had this to say: "The shadow of death hung heavily over the first graduation ceremony (it was also the last) at my school. Girls over the age of fifteen had all received orders to report for transportation to Central Station at 1 a.m. Destination unknown. All the parents knew was that they had to send their daughters out into the night, defenceless prey, never to be seen again. No one was allowed to accompany these children. The girls went, often after heart-rending domestic scenes, in the hope that by doing so they were sparing their parents. Not that they did.

"I witnessed some of these domestic scenes myself, and had to go away helpless because I did not know what to say. 'Don't go,' I urged some of them. 'And what then?' the desperate parents demanded. Thus most of the girls left—only a very few had the sense to go into hiding. At the graduation ceremony, the threat hanging over us all made the atmosphere unbearably stifling. There were many dignified and serious speeches. Some of the pupils played music, beautifully and expressively. A mixed choir sang Hebrew songs, old, poignant melodies of suffering. Meanwhile the claws of the German police were already stretching towards these children."

The writer himself, who was present at the ceremony, still vividly recalls that after the speech from the headmaster and the presentation of the certificates, a girl from the top form stood up and asked what she and her sister, who had both been called up, were to do. There she stood, erect, a girl of seventeen, with her diploma in her hand, quite alone and unprotected, asking her elders for advice. One of us involuntarily exclaimed, "Don't go!" and several murmured approval. Others sat silent, with their heads bowed. The writer also remembers that when the headmaster had just given a diploma to a boy, a non-Jewish woman suddenly dashed forward, snatched the diploma from his hand and hurried out. She was hiding the boy, who has survived the war and is now a doctor in Amsterdam.

On July 14, one day before the victims were due to report for deportation, the Germans carried out a raid on the Jewish quarters. Perhaps they just wanted to scare, perhaps they wanted to make sure of the full numbers, perhaps they had wanted for a long time to make a raid, perhaps it was for all these reasons together, perhaps for none of them. But then the reasons made little difference to the victims.

## THE RAIDS OF JULY AND AUGUST

The most coherent accounts of the raid of July 14 are found in the minutes of a meeting of the Jewish Council held at 6 p.m. on the same day. Some 700 Jews were seized in the street in all parts of the city and "brought in procession to German Security Police headquarters in Euterpe Street". At noon the two Presidents were summoned there as well, and given no less than four reasons for the arrests by Blumenthal:

1. Jews had been inciting workers to strike.
2. Jews had refused to go to German labour camps.
3. Many Jews were not wearing their stars.
4. Many Jews had gone into hiding.

The Jews seized in the streets would be held as hostages until the 4,000 designated for Germany had presented themselves, failing which the hostages would be sent to a concentration camp. Thus the responsibility for rounding up the intended deportees was thrust upon the Jews themselves. Meanwhile the Jewish Council had succeeded in obtaining the release of its own employees among the arrested 700. We have a letter signed by thirty-one of them in which they express to Professor Cohen their "heartfelt thanks for your brave intervention by which you have succeeded in freeing us so speedily". It remains an open question, however, whether this concession was not bought too dearly, whether the contrast between privileged and unprivileged Jews was not thereby accentuated. Moreover, we must remember that, by this "speedy" release the

Germans were merely showing their appreciation of the work they were expecting the Jewish Council to do for them.

But let us return to the latter. On the one hand, they were faced with 700 hostages possibly, indeed probably, intended for Mauthausen; on the other, there were the 4,000 conscripts who probably faced a life of great hardship as well. A dilemma of the kind that the Jewish Council had been forced to face since the outset had now grown to terrible dimensions; the Council must either resign or else choose between 700, who would probably never return and 4,000 who might do so. The members opted for the 700 and addressed two grave warnings to the 4,000. The first, of which we reproduce a facsimile on p. 145, reads as follows:

"The Security Police informs us:

"Some 700 Jews have been arrested in Amsterdam today. If the 4,000 called up for work-camps in Germany do not leave this week, the 700 now detained will be sent to a concentration-camp in Germany."

In addition, those called up were sent a circular with the same text and the added warning: "We feel obliged to impress on you the gravity of the situation. Think carefully. The fate of 700 fellow-Jews is at stake."

If this did not amount to moral pressure on the 4,000, what would?

Meanwhile, the 700 men and women were being detained in the courtyard of Security Police Headquarters; Blumenthal placed the women in the centre and made the men march round them. German female employees hung out of the windows taking snaps for their albums and, judging by their screams of laughter, were having a highly enjoyable time; several German police officers joined in the merriment, which increased to hilarity when a young Jewish woman, suddenly wrenched away from her pram and child, had a fit of hysteria. Not that the Germans were sadists or vicious, it was just that the incident appealed to their particular sense of humour. Asscher and Cohen came and looked in several times; Asscher protested so vehemently against this degrading march round that Blumenthal ordered him to keep his voice down—nothing at all would happen to these Jews.[1] But many of the detainees heard Asscher's protest and were greatly cheered. They needed to be, for most of them were forced to spend two nights on stone floors, in a state of terrible anxiety. Then, on the morning of July 16, the German

[1] Examination on November 13, 1947.

NIEUWE EDITIE: 2e JAARGANG No. 14a
10 JULI 1942 (25 TAMOEZ 5702)

Het Joodsche Weekblad

Uitgave van den Joodschen Raad voor Amsterdam
Onder verantwoordelijkheid van
A. Asscher en Prof. Dr. D. Cohen

# EXTRA EDITIE

Amsterdam, 14 Juli 1942

De Sicherheitspolizei deelt ons het volgende mede:

Ongeveer 700 Joden zijn heden te Amsterdam gearresteerd. Als deze week niet de 4000 daartoe aangewezen Joden naar de werkkampen in Duitschland vertrekken, zullen de 700 arrestanten naar een concentratiekamp in Duitschland worden overgebracht.

De voorzitters van den
Joodschen Raad voor Amsterdam,

A. ASSCHER
Prof. Dr. D. COHEN

Special edition of *Jewish Weekly*. Unless 4,000 Jews report for "labour service in Germany", 700 hostages will be sent to a German concentration camp.

cat released its mice, but of course not all of them; characteristically, thirty or forty of them were kept behind. Lages simply explained that there were "various reasons" for this; however he "promised" to look into the matter, adding that most of the detainees would be transferred to an Amsterdam Prison. Among them was a pupil of the Jewish Lyceum, and the first thing the writer did after being released himself was to call on the boy's parents in a vain effort to console them. The boy was sent to the gas chambers, the parents followed soon after.

The time had now come for the first contingent of the 4,000 to leave for Germany. Rumour had it that the British would smash Central Station to smithereens. They did not come. There would be a strike of railway workers. It did not materialize. The invasion would begin just in time. It did not. The Communists would spirit away all those who went to the station. They failed to do so. "Think of the 700", was all the solace the Jewish Council had offered these poor men. Had they been completely abandoned to their fate, was there no one to help them?

This is perhaps the place to remind the reader that all these events did not take place in a vacuum. There were the Dutch non-Jews. There were Dutch authorities in The Hague and in London. There was the rest of the world.

What of the Dutch police? Later, in a different context, we shall be discussing their dealings with the Jews at greater length, here we should merely like to mention one detail of their behaviour.

We have already mentioned that they were ordered to keep the Jews in their mouse-holes. From Police telegrams Nos. 4 and 6 of July 12 we may take it that the Dutch were undoubtedly giving the German police some help in rounding up the Jews; Telegram No. 4 of July 25 warned them to take special note of Jews carrying bags. Telegram No. 2 of August 5, 1942, called for the affixing of a list of Jewish suicides in Room 128 of Police Headquarters every morning at 8.45 a.m.; Telegram No. 5 of August 28 returned to this question and stipulated that the homes of suicides had to be guarded until an official of the Bureau of Jewish Affairs appeared; nothing whatsoever was to be removed from these homes. We can only hope that, as well as heeding all these telegrams, many Dutch policemen took note of an impassioned appeal published in the illegal *De Waarheid* (August 3) ". . . think of your human and professional duty—arrest no Jews and only make a show of carrying out orders directed against them. Let them escape and go into hiding. Remember that every man, every woman and every child you arrest will be killed and that you are their murderer."

The paper added a call to railwaymen: "Drivers! Remember that every slave train you drive is taking its cargo straight to the shambles."

But as we shall see, no train, no single train, failed to run on schedule. And Radio Orange, the voice of the Dutch Government in exile, had to tell the world from London, on July 25, that "tens of thousands of Dutchmen have been dragged from the land of their fathers and forefathers, from the midst of the people among whom they had grown up, and to whom they belong. Not content with fleecing and plundering their victims, the Germans have condemned them to an infinitely worse fate."

And on July 29 Radio Orange asked: "Just how does it help the German war effort to herd together thousands of defenceless Jewish Poles and do away with them in gas-chambers? How does it help the war effort when thousands of Jewish Dutchmen are dragged out of their country?"

Luckily, illegal protests were joined by legal as well as illegal deeds; luckily, not everyone was indifferent or merely ashamed. We shall be returning to this subject; here we shall merely give a few examples of the action of the Churches, a subject on which many books have been written.

On July 11 ten Christian Churches sent a joint telegram to the German authorities, in which they expressed their profound disquiet at the earlier anti-Jewish measures and their "sense of outrage" at the latest developments—"the deportation of Jews into the German *Reich* and its dependencies". According to the Churches, these measures went against "the deepest moral feelings of the Dutch people", and ran counter to "the divine commandments of justice and charity". The Churches accordingly addressed "the urgent request" to the Occupying Power not to proceed with the intended measures and concluded: "As for the Christians among these Jews, our appeal is given added force by the fact that your measures will cut them off from participation in Church life."

In the event, the Germans seized upon the final paragraph, on the proven principle that minor concessions merely furthered the major end. So long as tens of thousands of Jews could be dragged away, it served the Nazi purpose to make a show of magnanimity (albeit temporarily) towards the small number of baptized Jews; but even here they made sure of sowing discord by differentiating between Roman Catholics and other denominations. As early as July 14 the Acting Secretary of the Synod of the Dutch Reformed Church (the Permanent Secretary, the militant K. H. E. Gravemeijer, was in prison) received assurances from the *Reichskommissar* that Jews baptized before 1941 would be exempt from deportation. This was something the Churches had not asked for but of which Touw has rightly asked: "Were the Churches really justified in accepting favours for a small number of Jews, thus singling them out for preferential treatment? This was to become a most agonizing question, as time went by."

We know that the Churches also considered sending a formal letter of protest and having their telegram read out from the pulpits. Before they could do so, however, it became clear that, despite the German promises, baptized Jews were among the deported. The Synod accordingly made urgent representation to the Germans by telephone and telegram on July 17, and did in fact succeed in preventing the further deportation of such Jews. "In view of this result, the Synod thought it best not to send a further protest."

Nor was that all. Shortly before July 26, the day on which the telegram of July 11 was to be read out in the churches, the Germans asked the Synod not to do so. They added that this was "an urgent request and not an order". The Synod agreed for a number of reasons, one of which was "the fear that what little we have achieved for Jewish Christians might be lost again". The Germans had scored another success, at least with the Reformed Church, though not with the Roman Catholics and other denominations, who replied very quickly that, not having instructed their ministers to read out the telegram in the first place, they could not now prevent it. The Germans thereupon seized a number of Catholic Jews and sent them first to Westerbork and later to the gas-chambers. The Archbishop of Utrecht, Mgr. Johannes de Jong, pleaded twice on their behalf with Seyss-Inquart but in vain. Perhaps the best-known victim among this group was Edith Stein, a German Jewess who had studied philosophy under Husserl, and lived as a Catholic nun in Holland. During the few days she spent in Westerbork, she was an example to all, helping and consoling wherever she could.

According to Touw, some 400 baptized Jews survived the war with the help of the Dutch Churches. We for our part feel that it is extremely difficult to determine to what extent Church intervention was in fact the main reason for their survival. Even Touw is not sure whether, in keeping quiet, the Synod had not perhaps succumbed to "the promptings of the devil . . . betraying her Master to save the lives of her own flock". But then, when all is said and done, the Jewish Council itself did not do so very much better.

A Police Telegram sent "to all stations" early on July 15, read as follows: "Between midnight and 2 a.m. on July 15, 16 and 19, three tramcars from line number 8, one from line number 9, two from line number 16 and two from line number 24 will be diverted to Central Station for the transport of Jews. The crew of these trams is, on the above-mentioned dates, excused from observing the curfew." The rest of the telegram dealt with police supervision of the operation. A further telegram of July 18 made similar arrangements for the nights of July 21, 24 and 27, this time between midnight and 3 a.m.

The reader would be wrong to assume that all Jews were allowed to go to the station in trams. Boys and girls of sixteen had to go on foot from whatever distance. "There was no moon, the darkened city was black. The children's parents were not allowed to wave them goodbye, not even from the doorway. Once the door had shut behind these children, they had seen them for the last time."

On July 15, 16 and 17, 1942, Dutch Railways put on two separate trains, each holding some 700 people; the first left at 2.16 a.m., and arrived at Hooghalen at 5.48 a.m. (after stopping in Amersfoort and Zwolle). From Hooghalen, this train, followed twenty minutes later by another, continued to Assen; the carriages of both trains were brought back to Amsterdam at 7.15 a.m. Altogether, 962 victims had travelled in them. The Germans had previously submitted a list of deportees to the Jewish Council, from which the latter had deleted the names of indispensable persons; of the rest, quite a few had failed to report, so that the total was considerably less than the Germans had anticipated. The difference was made up from Westerbork; henceforth the inmates in that camp went in fear and trembling lest Amsterdam "failed them" again in this matter. Otto Bene, the Delegate of the German Foreign Office, reported on July 17 that the first trains "went off quite smoothly" and Rauter drew the conclusion that in future, it would be possible to dispatch 4,000 Jews a week. On July 31 he could report again that everything was going smoothly and "that there was no reason to anticipate any difficulties or obstacles to the smooth operation of next week's transport". And there were not—all the Jews left "smoothly" on a long journey; according to Otto Bene, their ultimate destination was Rauschitz in Upper Silesia.

A soothing note for the Jews was sounded at the Jewish Council on July 29. Here Lages was reported as having said that "all Jews taken to Germany are undoubtedly doing ordinary work". Unfortunately there was as yet no "reliable" report of the precise nature of that work. The transports from Westerbork had, moreover, been greatly improved since the Presidents' intervention; the men were now being conveyed in passenger carriages. Admittedly, the Germans made up shortages with people from the work-camps, but they made absolutely certain of keeping families together (*sic*). Most of this news was given to the meeting by A. de Hoop, "who was in charge of this aspect of the Council's work and received the warm thanks of the Presidents and the meeting for his efforts".

In pursuance of "this aspect of its work", the Jewish Council also organized all sorts of emergency services, both for the deportees and also for their dependants. To that end, a number of Council employees had to be transferred to Westerbork where they were said to be "enjoying full freedom of movement, etc.". (It is a pity that the report does not tell us what exactly the "etc." meant.) A special committee held daily meetings to discuss the merits of exemption requests "as objectively as possible". The Council also regretted that the age limit had been increased from forty to fifty, but added that "negotiations were taking place to reduce it to forty-five years". In short, they were trying to split the difference. All this, as we said, was happening in July 1942. In August the Council had to revise all its opinions once again, for by then many Jews had begun to wonder whether work in "Germany" was indeed the lesser of two evils, and came forward in ever-decreasing numbers. This is clearly expressed in a message by Bene on August 13; "Since my earlier report (of July 31) the position has changed considerably. The Jews seem to have become wise to the true meaning of labour conscription for the East, and have ceased to report for weekly transport."

We cannot fully endorse Bene's report, since "the true meaning of labour conscription" was far from clear to the victims—at best they had a slight inkling of what was going on. Their suspicions had, however, been increased by the general absence of letters from the "German" camps, and also by the increasingly threatening language of German officials in Holland, and quite especially of *Generalkommissar* Schmidt, who had said as early as June[1] that the Nazis were aiming at the total destruction of the Jews. We find it difficult to comprehend today how such prominent Dutchmen as Secretary-General Frederiks and Hirschfeld, who must have read it all in the newspapers, failed to draw the necessary conclusions.

On August 2 Schmidt addressed the oldest local group of German Nazis in the Netherlands, at Waubach in Limburg, on the occasion of the group's tenth anniversary. Much of the speech was devoted to a discussion of the Jewish problem, and "the applause proved that the words of the *Generalkommissar* had struck home". It is almost impossible to follow this orator on to the lonely heights of his thinking. Since the Jew was Germany's worst enemy, he would have to be expelled "from the West". In the East, he would have to "work and make good what damage he had caused in this war through his incitement". However, "we are not Barbarians and shall allow the Jew to take his family along, but insist that over there, in the desolated East, he will busy himself with clearing up the rubble. His lot will be a hard one but we must not forget that, after all, the Jew came to our lands poor and lice-ridden."

According to a Jewish official, it was only after this speech that many Jews began to realize what was going on. Quite suddenly, they saw that all that talk about relief programmes, labour camps, and "the whole thing is in your own interest" was so much wishful thinking on the part of the Jewish Council. Their lot would be hard—that was the only true and terrible reality. The obvious consequence was that fewer and fewer of them came forward voluntarily. They had no desire to grub among the rubble in desolate cities. They did not even appreciate the fact that their families could go with them. The extra trams went back to the depots and the trains for Westerbork remained in Amsterdam. Oddly enough, this news reached Westerbork at the same time as British aeroplanes flew over the camp, so that the inmates became convinced that the invasion had begun.

In the week of August 3 to 10 there were eleven conferences between different German officials (including Lages, Aus der Fünten and Wörlein) and the Presidents of the Jewish Council, most of them on the subject of filling the trains for "Germany". On August 5, the Presidents pleaded in vain for permission to send the following

[1] *De Telegraaf*, June 15, 1942.

notice to all concerned: "The labour for which you are being called up is in special work-camps in Germany, where your family will also be accommodated. The Germans have no intention of sending anyone to remote parts of the East. The main purpose of the work is to provide materials for the reconstruction of destroyed areas. As far as possible, everyone will be given work in his own trade. Postal connections with Holland will be re-established as soon as possible."

As we have said, the Germans refused to let this notice go out, and we are left to wonder why. We know that they never scrupled about what promises they made, and we also know that they were most anxious to help the Presidents paint as glowing a picture of life in the camps abroad as they could. Thus even the rather unpleasant Rodegro showed unexpected kind-heartedness when he promised to grant leave to 1,000 men in Dutch work-camps provided only that the Jewish Council would return the seventy-three who had run away—and this at a time when the Germans had already decided on the Amsterdam raid of August 6, Black Thursday, otherwise known as the Raid of the Two Thousand.

This raid lasted throughout most of the day and part of the evening; the Germans picked up Jews in the street or dragged them out of their houses, often with a great deal of brutality; there were quite a few suicides. The writer and his wife were visiting friends on that day. They watched the German squad approach the house and climb up the steps. Then we heard the people downstairs tell them: "There are no Jews here—but there are some upstairs." Outside was waiting a large car surrounded by a dozen boys and girls from the neighbourhood, all wearing N.S.B. badges and making appropriate comments. The writer still remembers that the driver, obviously a stranger to Amsterdam, did not know the way to the *Zentralstelle* and had to be told by one of the Jews inside. He also remembers how some Jews with "too much" money on them pushed a considerable amount into the author's pockets.

Dr. Hemelrijk who, that day, was walking up Schelde Street in Amsterdam, not wearing his star, had this to say: "What I saw there was so shocking and humiliating that you needed all your self-control to remain a passive bystander."

Professor Cohen[1] has given us a report of his visit to Aus der Fünten on the morning of August 6: "I found him in his room, in a state of great, and as it struck me and still strikes me, genuine agita-

[1] *Herinneringen*, p. 73.

tion. He explained that the raid had been ordered simply because too few Jews were reporting for transportation and the trains simply had to be filled. But looking at me, he added: 'Believe me, *Herr* Cohen, it is the last thing I wanted.' I then took both his hands and said: 'But, *Herr Haupsturmführer*, then please don't do it.' He turned to the window, as he always did when trying to hide his tears, and then turned back again to tell me: '*Herr* Cohen, I have no alternative!' I pleaded with him again, but he simply repeated his words."

It so happens that the author is able to fill in the picture: Leo de Wolff, a former pupil who held an important office in the notorious *Expositur*, told him a few days after the raid how bitterly Aus der Fünten had complained about the distasteful job he had to do: "Why don't those who want it done, do it themselves?"

Because there is little reason to doubt Aus der Fünten's sincerity, it seems doubly strange to see how he set to work on the next day. Here the writer can rely almost completely on his own memory, for as we saw, he was one of the 2,000 picked up on August 6 and who had spent the night with them in the open yard of the *Zentralstelle*. Throughout the next day, they had ample opportunity to watch Aus der Fünten at work—had he been a sadist he could have done no worse. He acted precisely like the German SS officer whom John Hersey has described in his novel *The Wall*, dividing the victims to left and right, to death and respite. Yes, on that August 7, 1942, the writer was able to watch him from early morning until five that evening, with long intervals during which the prisoners were consumed with unbearable anxiety. When Aus der Fünten first appeared on the steps, he was smoking one cigarette after another, and leant nonchalantly against the wall. He was accompanied by a number of officials of the Jewish Council including Leo de Wolff. Speaking very softly, he said as he looked across the courtyard: "There's too much noise here," and you could have heard a pin drop. Then he set to work.He had people placed in rows, usually no more than fifteen to twenty at a time, had them file before him, looked at them, inspected their papers, asked a few questions of De Wolff and then decided, without a single word, simply by waving his hand to the right or to the left. The writer was able to follow the whole spectacle from a corner near the steps. He saw and heard a conversation between Aus der Fünten and two old people, a man and a woman of about seventy, whose answers he could not quite make out, because they had their backs to him. But judging from Aus der Fünten's reactions, it must have gone something like this:

Aus der Fünten: "Papers?"

The old man handed him some documents which Aus der Fünten read while lighting a fresh cigarette. De Wolff glanced at the papers.

Aus der Fünten: "I see you run a home. Well, well, a home! Just fancy that. For old people? Since when?"

The old man mumbled something and pointed to the paper.

Aus der Fünten: "Since August 1? That's not very long is it? Not quite a week, what?"

The old man mumbled something else.

Aus der Fünten: "Well, well! Very good!"—waving the old man to the left and his wife to the right.

The old man: "My wife . . ."

Aus der Fünten: "Your wife? What's the matter with your wife?"

The old man: "She's old."

Aus der Fünten: "Old? You tell me she's old? Well, if she can work here she can certainly work for us as well."

The old man mumbled again, probably to the effect that he couldn't let her go by herself. So Aus der Fünten waved him to the right as well—two for Poland instead of only one.

As we have already said, the pauses were the worst part. Aus der Fünten would stop from time to time, while a whole row of quivering people was left standing, wondering when he would resume the inquisition. Rumour had it that he would stop at 5 p.m. and that all those left over would be sent to Westerbork and from there on to Poland. The tension became unbearable in the afternoon. The writer will never forget his last glimpses of some of those he knew personally. There was a young girl from his school, a Rose of Sharon, whose turn never came and who was never seen again; a friendly old bookseller who, as he knew, would long since have gone into hiding with his wife, had she not insisted on looking after her ailing mother, stood there ashen-faced; a woman teacher all alone; a boy who had escaped during the raid on July 14, but had since been recaptured. There we were, hundreds of us, anxiously watching the clock. At ten to five, at what turned out to be the last muster, the writer and his wife came face to face with Aus der Fünten who looked at their papers, waved him to the left and then, turning to De Wolff, said: "She's still very young."

What De Wolff replied, I cannot say, but my wife was waved to the left as well. A moment later we were in the street with ordinary people and children playing. The solitary woman teacher came out soon afterwards, and then the ring closed inexorably on the rest—some 600 were sent off to Westerbork and on . . .

That evening, the *Jewish Weekly* published an Extra Edition with the following proclamation:

"1. All Jews who have been called up but have not reported for labour service in Germany will be arrested and sent to Mauthausen concentration camp. This provision does not apply to Jews reporting before 5 p.m. on Saturday, August 9, 1942, or undertaking to go.

"2. All Jews not wearing the yellow star will be sent to Mauthausen concentration camp.

"3. All Jews changing their addresses without express permission by the authorities—for however short a period of time—will be sent to Mauthausen concentration camp."

The last two provisions had obviously become necessary since Jews had begun to go into hiding in ever-increasing numbers. Otto Bene, for instance, reported on August 13: "Escape into Belgium is in full swing. Jews are being helped across for money and glib words. They are said to be crossing at the rate of a thousand a day, which strikes me as being somewhat exaggerated . . . In any case, we shall have to take much stricter measures in organizing the transports."

But even the thrice-repeated threat of Mauthausen did not produce any more enthusiasm for "German labour camps". Thus even the extra edition of the *Jewish Weekly* produced a crop of only twenty-eight people, and the Presidents of the Jewish Council offered to "send out a team of 200 or 300 of our own people to persuade the men that it was in their interests to go"; Cohen later declared that they merely made this promise so as to prevent a further raid by the Germans.

As it turned out, the Council might have saved its breath, since two days later, on August 9, the Germans had hundreds of Jews dragged from their houses in some parts of Amsterdam South. The story went round that by raiding these more prosperous areas, the invader was trying to make a show of his "socialism". Now it was

K 247 NIEUWE EDITIE: 2e JAARGANG No. 17a · 7 AUGUSTUS 1942 (24 MENACHEM 5702)

# Het Joodsche Weekblad

UITGAVE VAN DEN JOODSCHEN RAAD VOOR AMSTERDAM

ONDER VERANTWOORDELYKHEID VAN A. ASSCHER EN PROF. DR. D. COHEN

SECRETARIAAT DER REDACTIE:
JODEN BREESTRAAT 93 · AMSTERDAM · TELEF. 31736 41830
ADMINISTRATIE EN EXPLOITATIE:
JOACHIMSTHAL'S BOEKHANDEL
UITG.- EN DRUKKERIJBEDRIJF N.V.
JODEN BREESTRAAT 63 · AMSTERDAM · TELEF. 04340 · 04700

# EXTRA EDITIE

## De Duitsche autoriteiten maken bekend:

1. Alle Joden, die niet onverwijld gevolg geven aan een tot hen gerichten oproep voor de arbeidsverruiming in Duitschland, worden gevangen genomen en naar het concentratiekamp Mauthausen gebracht.

   Deze of andere straf wordt niet toegepast op die Joden, die zich nog achteraf voor uiterlijk Zondag 9 Augustus 1942, te 5 ure aanmelden, of verklaren, dat zij bereid zijn, aan de werkverruiming deel te nemen.

2. Alle Joden, die geen jodenster dragen, zullen naar het concentratiekamp Mauthausen gebracht worden.

3. Alle Joden, die zonder toestemming der autoriteiten van woonplaats of woning veranderen - ook indien zij dit slechts tijdelijk doen - worden naar het concentratiekamp Mauthausen gebracht.

Special edition of *Jewish Weekly* after the raid of 6 August 1942. "All Jews refusing to report for labour service in Germany, will be sent to Mauthausen. All Jews found without a Jewish Star will be sent to Mauthausen. All Jews changing address without official permission will be sent to Mauthausen."

the turn of the well-connected, some of them members of the Jewish Council.

There was an envoy to this event, which better than anything else illustrates the impasse the Council had reached. This is how Professor Cohen himself put it:[1] "I told Aus der Fünten that if he deported these people before we had time to check up on them, he would be disrupting the Jewish Council and Jewish life in Amsterdam. He then placed several slips in front of Asscher and myself and told us to pick out twenty people whom we considered indispensable. Asscher could not bear this and went out. I stayed beside Aus der Fünten who was half drunk. The arrested men then filed past us and I had to make the choice. Since the Jewish Council had always been able to obtain exemptions for those doing important communal work, and since I knew most of these men, my task was fairly simple in practice. But later I kept thinking much more of those I had turned away than those I had helped to free.

"There came a moment when I thought I simply could not go on.

"This was when it was the turn of one Calff, a valued member of our Financial Committee. I exempted him. With him were his three children, wonderful children, two sons and a daughter, as nice as you could wish to meet. But Aus der Fünten refused to exempt them as well. I said that this was against our agreement, but he remained adamant. When the father insisted, in that case, on going along with the children, they begged him to stay with the mother instead. He finally gave in.

"I would have told Aus der Fünten there and then that, as he had broken his word, I could not go on with the ghastly business, had I not spotted so many other men with young children, men who had worked hard for the Jewish community and whom I simply could not leave in the lurch, now that it was in my power to free them. And I was, in fact, able to save many of these, including a recent widow who, I felt, had suffered enough already and must not now be parted from her children. Professor Sinzheimer and his wife were also among those apprehended; I told Aus der Fünten who he was and asked him to exempt these two in addition to the other twenty. He agreed and both survived the war.

"When all was over, I reproached Dr. Sluzker with having left me alone. He told me: 'I waited for you to finish and then set to work myself, succeeding in freeing another eighteen of our people.' "

[1] Cohen: *Herinneringen*, p. 74.

So much for Professor Cohen's reminiscences. The writer knows from a reliable source that Asscher, too, made a choice between two people—one of whom was closer to him than the other.

Those rounded up on August 9, followed the victims of August 7 to Westerbork. Many arrived there without even the barest necessities and the Jewish Council had to provide them with these. At the meeting of August 12, Dr. Arons expressed "the general appreciation of what the Council was doing for these poor people". Clearly the Council would have been unable to do so had it not inaugurated a number of special bureaus, including a mending department. In this way it was able to create a whole number of "essential posts"—in fact, the number of such posts went up in proportion as the number of those whose interests they were meant to serve declined.

### FURTHER RAIDS

In the later summer of 1942 the Germans struck harder still. In particular they decided that, as the Jews were not reporting for "labour service" of their own free will, some more of them would have to be dragged out of their houses. This measure was facilitated by the curfew; anyone found at home could be carried off, and those away were in any case criminals to be apprehended by the police.

The report of the meeting of the Jewish Council of September 3 gives us some idea of the effect of the new measures on the members assembled there: because of these "extremely serious problems" and "disastrous events" the Council saw fit . . . to inform "Jews throughout the Netherlands by word of mouth that at the moment call-ups and deportations were taking place at such short notice that there was often no possibility of making ready for the journey. Hence it was best to keep one's bags packed at all times."

From these minutes, we may also conclude that, during two successive nights, 400 to 500 people were seized in their homes; of these some 10 per cent were released, another 10 per cent detained in Amsterdam and the rest sent to Westerbork. At a meeting on Tuesday, September 8 at 4.30 p.m., Aus der Fünten was informed by the two Presidents of the Jewish Council, who were later joined by Dr. Sluzker of the *Expositur*, of the "disquiet" that had been caused by the "new method" of seizing people, including men of ninety, at such short notice that there was far too little time to investigate each case individually or to apply for exemptions. The German answer was that "the main job was to complete the transports".

The leaders of the Jewish Council then made the following recommendations:

1. The Germans should give the call-up method another chance, which was bound to work now that people knew the alternative. (This requires no commentary from us.)
2. The Dutch labour bureaus should be asked to help the Council in making selections. (The Germans agreed, provided only the Presidents would supply a thousand young Jews. In that case, they would also spare all older people. Appreciating as we do now, that the Germans intended to deport all Dutch Jews, we know just how much this promise was worth.)
3. That people be given more time to answer the call-up. (That, too, had to be refused because many conscripts would simply disappear, and no arrangements could be made to accommodate those who did turn up and had to wait for the rest.)
4. That exemption be granted to the parents of officials of the Jewish Council. (While the Germans understood this request "from the purely human point of view" they could not grant the many exemptions involved.)
5. That no transports be sent during the approaching high festivals. (The Germans replied that this was precisely why they were trying to expedite the call-up.)
6. That special consideration should be given to invalids; the last transport had included one man with a twisted spine and another who was blind. (The German reply: "The system simply cannot be changed.")

The only concession the Council succeeded in obtaining was the promise that the identity cards and the records of all those working for the Jewish Council, the Jewish community, Jewish institutions, Jewish schools, Jews married to non-Jews and having children, baptized Jews and those working for the German war effort would be marked with a special stamp. This was the beginning of the stamp drama with which we shall be dealing at greater length. But to convey the full flavour of these negotiations we must add one thing more: "Our request that clergymen be given a night pass to visit dying people was refused on the grounds that no such provisions existed even at the front."

Meanwhile the "new method" continued, though not as smoothly as it might have done. Thus, a special meeting of the Jewish Council had to be convened on September 18 "at the request of a number of leading Jews (only one of whom is mentioned by name) to consider if the arrest of some members of the Council (they were later released) did not call for extra measures concerning the safety of these members". After much discussion, the meeting decided not to take any further steps, "since such steps might prove prejudicial to other sections of the community". Whereupon, some members of the Council thanked Sluzker, Bolle and other officials of the *Expositur* "most cordially" for their efforts in freeing the arrested men as speedily as possible. (Applause.)

The meeting also dealt with leading Jews who were not members of the Council. Some of these, the Council succeeded in saving; the others included Rabbi Dünner, a young man of exceptional integrity. In his reminiscences, Professor Cohen had this to say:[1] "I begged and implored Aus der Fünten but he was immovable. Rabbi Dünner accepted his fate with the calm of the truly pious man. At this point his two children and their grandfather appeared at the door. The children, who had been dragged from their beds, were wearing only coats over their nightdresses. Then Rabbi Dünner could no longer contain himself and cried out: "Professor, save my children!" I pleaded even more fervently with Aus der Fünten, but he remained adamant, although the heartbreaking appearance of the small children, frightened out of their sleep, defies description."

Two other points in the minutes of the meeting of September 18 are also worth mentioning. Firstly, the Council believed that the arrests might continue for another few weeks, but that there would then be a pause during which the new stamps would be introduced, and that those without stamps would probably be sent to Dutch camps. The reasons for this assumption were not stated. There followed one paragraph which we quote in full and without comment: "Most regrettably a report has reached us of the death in Auschwitz, Silesia, of one (*sic!*) Jewish inmate born in 1905."

Let us now turn to those Jews—old, young, sick—sitting day in and day out in their houses, just waiting. Their mood is perhaps best sensed from the entries in the diary of Sam Goudsmit:

"*Thursday, September 10, 1942*. 9.30 p.m. We have been sitting here for nights waiting for the bell. It is generally believed that exemptions will not save anyone from being dragged away to the assembly point. Will they come for us tonight? 10.30 p.m. Can we relax now?

[1] Cohen: *Herinneringen*, pp. 85–6.

No, for last night they were still dragging Jews away at midnight. Who can tell if we shall not be among tonight's crop? How many others must now be sitting like us, with sunken eyes and ashen faces, wondering if they will sleep in their own beds tonight . . .?

"*Continuation, same night, 2 a.m. Relief.*

"They did not come—I am still awake and writing. At five past twelve, J. gave me a kiss, saying 'They won't be coming tonight after all . . .' At last we could breathe again. I went upstairs and even took a cup of coffee to bed with me, because the tension had been so great. Coffee and a cigar, because we are still free and will probably remain so until 8 p.m. tomorrow—a full twenty hours. Then the game will start all over again for the hundreds of thousands of Jews remaining in Amsterdam and for the four of us among them.

"Except that we shall be wincing with pain tomorrow morning at hearing of tonight's harvest."

A Jewish woman described a visit to her parents as follows: "Shaking with fright, Mother told me how she had been sitting at the dark window every evening while all round her people were being dragged away like beasts. She was rigid with fear, thinking it would be her turn and Father's next, while the large squad cars stood outside, crammed with people terrified and screaming . . . Father sat all the time tensely listening. At the least noise he pricked up his ears, only to fall back exhausted into his chair again, reassured for a brief moment."

One Jew who was lucky enough to escape to Palestine with his family had this to say:

"(In the evening the door-bell rang . . .) I asked who it was. It was a woman and a child. What was she to do? I quickly shut the door behind us, so that the light would not be seen from the street and led them upstairs. The woman had jumped off a squad car with her child and rucksack, just outside the *Hollandse Schouwburg*, and had crept along past the houses while seeking for a Jewish name and a *mezuza* fixed to the doorpost . . . I asked her if she had any papers. Yes, and a call-up notice, which she had snatched up before leaving. Without even looking at them, I burnt the whole lot. I let her sleep in peace until five o'clock next morning when I sent her away. I later had her things fetched by the Jewish Council. I have no idea what happened to her."

And what of the old people? On August 30, 1942, just before the beginning of the round-up, Amsterdam counted some 150 Jewish rest homes, and the provinces another thirty or so (shortly before that, the Jewish Council had closed down another 150 as being "below standard"). Now such "rest" homes were particularly easy prey for the Germans—what could be simpler than dragging off completely defenceless old people, many of them very sick besides?

This is how the illegal *Vrij Nederland* described it all on October 10, 1942: "At the stroke of eight, as darkness falls, the dread ordeal of waiting begins once again for our Jewish fellow-citizens. Each footstep is a threat, each car an approaching doom, each bell a sentence. The squad cars are out, the boys in green and the Dutch Jew-baiters ready for their deadly night's work. Every evening the doors are flung open, and women, children, old people, the sickly and the rest are dragged out like so many fish from a pond, defenceless, without appeal, hope or help. Night after night. By the hundred, dragged away, always to one and the same destination: death. When the morning comes, those left behind do the rounds of their friends and relations to see who is left. Next come the removal vans, taking away what furniture is left, and in the evening it all starts over again . . ."

For many, the moment when the squad cars stood outside the door was the breaking of an unbearable tension, a kind of relief. Of this fact, too, we have many records: "Day-time was still just about bearable, but as night approached the pressure became intolerable. Food stuck in our throats. Friends who came to visit us with the very best of intentions were a burden—one could hardly wait for them to leave . . . But just as we thought we had reached breaking point, we were overcome by a strange kind of self-possession and feeling of peace. I cannot tell whether this was a conscious acceptance of unavoidable fate, or merely the peace of exhaustion." But self-control remained, anyway, "bestowing dignity on every single one, down to the very least of us".

We must say a few words, no more, on the new technique employed to round up Jews. While the Germans added a few refinements here and there and adapted their policy to local conditions, what it all usually amounted to was that, every evening, Jews would wait in dread for the ring at the bell—the signal for deportation. Every car that passed down the street might be *the* car; every night one must settle one's small affairs all over again and have one's rucksack packed—according to minute instructions given by the Jewish Council. The blacked-out street windows only added to the oppressive threat which might come any night and, indeed, was bound to come sooner or later. Many Jews faced up to it all with dignity and self-control, but still the stark fact remains that, in September 1942, death stalked the streets of Amsterdam.

### THE HOLLANDSE SCHOUWBURG

The arrested Jews were forced to make their way, on foot or by car, at first to the *Zentralstelle* on Adama van Scheltema Square. Soon afterwards, some of them were also sent to the Hollandse Schouwburg, the "Dutch Theatre" which, in the autumn of 1941, had been renamed the Jewish Theatre. (The candle-lit Portuguese Synagogue was at first considered an alternative to the Theatre but was rejected as being difficult to black out.) After October 14 the *Zentralstelle* was no longer used, and all Jewish captives were herded into the Theatre and kept there until their transfer to Westerbork, hours, days or even weeks later.

"During the day, the chairs were arranged in rows facing each other, with a central aisle between them leading to the stage. In the evenings, the chairs were stacked at the side, straw mattresses were brought out from behind the scenery, thrown into the auditorium and fitted together like a jig-saw puzzle. Everything was rather primitive . . ."

Still, people managed somehow to live there.

"We decided to marry before they sent us away. A lawyer came to make all the necessary arrangements. The happy event took place on . . . (date), in the presence of a registrar. Just as I was signing his book, a rose-petal settled on my pen, something I had always considered a very good omen. The Jewish Council and I made the day as happy an occasion as we could. There was lemonade and little cakes. Various prisoners sang for us. That night we were given a little room behind the stage. We could easily have run away, but we did not do so because the other boys were standing surety for us, and also because I did not want to leave my parents in the lurch."

Yes, people "lived" there—but only just. One day a distress signal went out for another 800 portions of salad—there were 1,400 Jews in the Theatre that day. Sometimes the crowd was even larger. People found it hard to sleep and conditions were far from hygienic. Some had great difficulty in coming to terms with their new environment; a well-known judge asked for a clean collar after only two days. Quite a few committed suicide. At night it could be terrible, particularly when there were screaming children everywhere—in the corridors, foyers, balconies, the pit, the staircases, the stalls. Then there were those who could not lie still and kept walking about all over the building. On top of it all there was the gnawing anxiety of uncertainty.

"One evening, the SS officer in charge turned up; he spoke to no one but kept drinking steadily. After a while, clearly drunk, he began to inspect the building. Because it was late at night, most people were asleep. He ordered the lights to be put on, everyone had to get up and take off their shoes and stockings. He then began to inspect their feet and came to the conclusion that only ten people had clean ones. These were allowed to go home. To the rest he said: 'Your feet are filthy. You obviously can't leave like that.' "[1]

"Some people stayed for several weeks, sleeping on chairs meant for spectators, tortured by constant thirst caused by the stuffy atmosphere, living day and night by artificial light, never getting a breath of fresh air."[2]

We shall be returning to this squat building that was swallowing up so many victims. There was apparently something very odd about it, so much so that many Jews simply could not keep away; they had to walk past it and look up. The *Jewish Weekly* warned them of the "serious consequences", and still they came. Many of them were in fact dragged inside. Like the rest, they would eventually be escorted to Central Station by a police detachment of fifteen to twenty men—in the dead of night. According to one well-informed source, all the Germans had to do was to pick up a telephone and Burgomaster Voûte's underlings would let them have as many tramcars as they needed. It was all reminiscent of the days of the Terror in France, when great numbers of people were carted off to the guillotines in tumbrils—but these went in broad daylight and, moreover, carried no children. The Germans, with greater consideration, kept families together all the way.

## THE STAMPS

We now come to a subject that is among the most delicate and difficult in this whole story: the matter of the official German exemptions. This was a question of life and death for the Jews, though in the end even the exemptions proved worthless. But in

[1] H. Umrath: *Verslag* (Report), p. 15.

[2] Cf. Wielek: *op. cit.*, pp. 262–85.

1942 few could have known that; all people did know was that it was best to hang on in the Netherlands as long as possible.

This story is yet another example of the way in which the Germans played their cat-and-mouse game with the Jews. Their main object was to get rid of the Jews smoothly and by stages, so as to cause the minimum disruption in Dutch public life. To do that, they needed the co-operation of the victims themselves—by granting temporary privileges to a minority, they succeeded in liquidating the rest without too much fuss or bother. As for the Jewish community, their leaders, too, were interested in averting chaos;[1] moreover, they were trying to preserve a nucleus from the shipwreck, a nucleus that, incidentally, was identical with the leadership. This turned out to be a miscalculation, for as the mass of the Jewish people disappeared from the Netherlands, so the need for preserving the nucleus disappeared as well. Hence the Jewish Council became inextricably involved in a *danse macabre* with Satan calling the tune.

It is difficult to say when it all started. The whole thing was probably implicit in the establishment of the Council, by which a small but growing group of privileged men emerged above the mass of ordinary Jews. Their role became a particularly invidious one after the spring of 1942, when the Council agreed to apply for exemptions on behalf of some and, in that way, appointed itself an arbiter between life and death.

In the summer of 1942 the "Bolle stamp" came into use; it was so called after the General Secretary of the Jewish Council, and served as a safe conduct for important people, though in the event it did not serve to save even the Secretary himself. In a circular of July 30, 1942, Bolle called upon all local representatives of the Jewish Council to submit "a very careful and final list" of indispensable Jews "in order of their indispensability"; if too many names were submitted those at the bottom would be deleted—clearly, a case of devil take the hindmost. The families of those remaining on the list were to be exempted as well, provided only that the total exemptions did not amount to more than 20 per cent of the Jewish population in a particular district. There were five categories of exemptions, the first of which comprised members of the Jewish Council, the second leaders of the Jewish community, etc. Clearly, this opened wide the door to favouritism and caused moral disruption on a vast scale.

[1] See Berkley: *op. cit.*, pp. 75 ff.

In a letter of August 3, 1942, Professor Cohen protested to Böhmcker against the round-up of Jewish Council staff; the Council was being hampered in "carrying out the duties delegated to it by the German authorities". Professor Cohen accordingly requested that all his staff be temporarily exempted from labour service, and that those already detained be released and allowed to return to their former occupations. Lists of all such indispensable people had been prepared.

We have an unsigned instruction dated September 7 calling for the submission "within eight to ten days" of lists (ten copies) of all those connected with the Council, or doing essential work for the Jewish community, Jewish institutions, Jewish schools, etc. "These lists (which had to include the names of wives and children under sixteen) will constitute the basis of all exemptions."

On September 16 and 18 Bolle called for the submission of new lists, completing and correcting those called for in his circular of July 30; we may take it that these lists defined the categories of people whose identification cards would be stamped with the inscription "*bis auf weiteres freigestellt vom Arbeitseinsatz*"—exempted from labour service until further notice. The new stamps were issued from September 28, at the rate of about 800 a day.

The total number of exemptions was a subject of animated discussion, the Jewish Council submitting some 35,000 names and Aus der Fünten refusing to accept more than 17,500. Thus, 8,000 provincial candidates were rejected out of hand because the provinces in question were about to be cleared of Jews. "We took note of this with deep regret," Asscher told a meeting of the Jewish Council. As for the 17,500, "the Presidents felt they had to accept this figure for the sake of preserving a core which, in the conditions of the time, was quite understandable". The reader will have noticed that the "core" had already shrunk considerably, and will rightly anticipate that it was fated to shrink considerably further.

It was like a sinking ship that had suddenly lost all the life-boats on one side. The survivors were divided into the following categories by the Germans:

Nos. 10–20,000: foreign Jews, including Portuguese (Sephardic) Jews. We shall be dealing with them in due course; the number of "true" foreign Jews was given as seventy-five; these would be among the first to receive the "Bolle" stamps on September 14.

Nos. 20–30,000: Jews baptized in the Protestant faith; of these the Council had a list of 1,500 people, all of whom were to receive their stamps on September 16.

Nos. 30–40,000: Those whose Jewish descent was still being investigated by the German official, Dr. H. G. Calmeyer; this list consisted of 1,800 people. Stamps to be issued on September 17 and 18.

Nos. 40–50,000: 800 Jews enjoying various forms of German protection. Stamps to be issued on September 19.

Nos. 60–80,000: Jews working in military industries (uniforms, furs, raincoats, diamonds, old metal, rags). Some 3,800 people were involved and would receive their stamps on September 21. Berkley also mentions the group number 70,000 exempted "for special reasons".

Nos. 80–100,000: people connected with the Jewish Council.

Nos. 100–110,000: Jews of mixed marriages—stamps from October 1; later the Jewish partner of childless mixed marriages was placed in the special category 108,000.

Sick people and mental patients needed no stamps of any kind. This did not make very much difference for, with a few exceptions, all the stamps lost their value within the year, anyway.

When the ship sinks people will clutch at straws, and it is often every man for himself. Bolle's stamps may have delayed the collapse of organized Jewish life, but they certainly hastened its demoralization. Let the witnesses speak for themselves:

"When the first stamps were issued, the scenes at the Jewish Council were quite indescribable. Doors were broken, the staff of the Council was attacked, and the police had often to be called in . . . The stamps quickly became an obsession with every Jew . . ."[1]

The writer can still remember how one of his pupils, a young girl of barely sixteen, suddenly got married to a boy of much the same age, simply because he had a stamp. In this way her parents believed she would be saved. Alas, both were seized soon afterwards. The Germans, moreover, gave out that they were wise to this kind of trick, that they considered all such unions fraudulent, and threatened to withdraw exemptions from anyone behaving in this way. So yet another escape route was closed. The only thing to do

[1] G. van Tijn-Cohn: *op. cit.*, p. 48.

now was to nag and threaten the Jewish Council and, if that did not help, to smash doors and attack the officials . . .

Of all the threats, the most common—and at the same time the most ludicrous—was that unless Bolle's stamps were granted to them, various individuals would be prevented from doing valuable work for the Jewish community. Thus, when the Germans carried off the parents of various officials working in the same department in the Jewish Council, one of these officials wrote an appeal to the Presidents: " . . . You will understand that such happenings are bound to damp our enthusiasm for the work . . . It strikes me that the resulting uncertainty so paralyses the work of the Jewish Council that a very strong stand must be taken. I therefore humbly beg you to approach the German authorities as soon as possible, with the request that, in future, they respect the persons of all those whose identity cards bear the proper stamp."

Did the Germans in fact take any notice of this appeal? Did they respect any Jew at all? Barely three months later the man who signed this letter, a very high official in the Jewish Council, and as such protected by a super-stamp, was himself on the way to the gas-chambers.

The reader can have no conception of the intensity of the various pressures exerted on the Council leaders. Herzberg[1] observes that the main opponents of this whole "stampede" and of the activities of the Jewish Council in general, capitulated as soon as their own dependants were threatened. Thus, an incredibly heavy responsibility rested on the shoulders of those who were ultimately responsible for the issue of the stamps. Professor Cohen[2] mentions a special committee consisting of himself and two other leaders of the Jewish community. The surviving letters show clearly under what strain this committee must have worked; it is an extremely embarrassing and sad experience to discover that one of its members, a man of unshakeable rectitude, who had done outstanding work for the Jewish community and who refused on principle to listen to any special pleading, fell down when it came to his own family—whom he "judged objectively" to merit exemption. And when there was talk of further restrictions, he asked Professor Cohen to include him in the selection board. He ended his letter with the following sentence: "I would even make so bold as to suggest that, when the time

[1] Herzberg: *op. cit.*, pp. 157–60.
[2] Cohen: *Herinneringen*, p. 87.

comes, the final decision about exemptions be left in your and my hands." In view of Professor Cohen's other responsibilities, this was tantamount to a request to leave it all to him. And this from a man whom Professor Cohen has described to the present writer as "my conscience". Yet was it really surprising that corruption had begun to stalk the corridors of the Jewish Council?

It would have been a wonder had the issue of stamps not evoked furious resentment as well, "particularly on the part of those Jewish circles that did not succeed in obtaining exemptions".[1] The writer clearly remembers how much people round him commented on the fact that one woman teacher had "received her stamp" weeks before the rest—not because she was particularly good at her work but because her brother was closely associated with one of the Presidents of the Jewish Council. Professor Cohen later admitted that few so-called proletarians got stamps; he called this unavoidable discrimination—unavoidable because "the work called for training in administrative duties". But if these "proletarians" were not so trained, neither were so many sons of brothers of more influential Jews. In any case, the poor were the first to go.

Only the first, mark you, since as Herzberg[2] has pointed out so correctly, "the stamps were mere scraps of paper that saved no one in the long run . . . At best, they gave the odd fugitive time to go underground, and at worst they lulled many people into a false sense of security and prevented them from deserting their posts."

## THE END OF THE WORK-CAMPS

"Deported." This word was to dominate German policy during the coming few months, so much so that the Jews ceased to heed all appeals and threats to come forward for "labour service"—what threats could avail against those who knew they were sentenced to death anyway? Throughout the period September 1942 to September 1943, deportations of Jews occurred on several, often most, evenings of each week, and sometimes also during the day. Day-time, as we saw, was best for getting hold of the most defenceless—sick people, invalids and children, and quite particularly children in orphanages. Old men and old women would henceforth be seen roaming the streets, afraid to stay at home. They strayed about, sitting on steps (park-benches were forbidden to them), trying to find out what was going on, and asking odd passers-by if everything

[1] Berkley: *op. cit.*, p. 78. [2] Herzberg: *op. cit.*, p. 160.

was quiet their way. Then they would shuffle on, sooner or later to fall into the hands of their persecutors.

But when all was said and done, these people were only small fry for the Germans. A man like Rauter, faithful servant of Hitler and Himmler that he was, could not be content with just these. His plan was to round up a record number of Jews at one fell swoop early in October 1942. Other German officials, too, seem to have worked on this principle.

Before dealing with this matter we must, however, revert to the German work-camps in Holland. The reader will remember that in the early part of 1942, many Dutch Jews were "put to work" there with the help of the Jewish Council, which considered this part of their delaying tactics. These tactics sprang from the conviction that work-camps were the worst that could befall the unhappy victims. But what had happened in the latter half of 1942? Deportations to Germany and house-to-house raids had by then created such terrible conditions that the Dutch camps came to look like so many havens of refuge for the Jews.

On August 29, 1942, J. A. Knetsch, the acting Director-General of the National Labour Office, sent a telex message to the managers of all local labour offices instructing them on Böhmcker's orders, to speed up the "recruitment" of Jews for service in the "labour camps"—the present rate must be doubled. On that self-same day, the provincial representatives of the Jewish Council were informed from Amsterdam that deportations to Germany would be suspended for the time being. Wielek[1] has given an evocative account of the general relief that this announcement produced, of how delighted people were that they could once again "stop trembling and spend the evening at home peacefully. It no longer seemed necessary to put old and sick people to bed before eight o'clock, with doctor's certificates and the largest possible number of bottles and powders beside them . . ." On Friday night, even the Jewish Council could take a well-deserved rest, for Seyss-Inquart himself was going to the Amsterdam *Stadsschouwburg* to attend a performance by the *Deutsche Theater*, and his presence there required the full attention of the Security Police. That night, pious Jews enjoyed their Sabbath—by courtesy of the invader.

We need not linger over the play that Seyss-Inquart saw, because we are more concerned with another programme, sent out at about

[1] Wielek: *op. cit.*, pp. 162 ff.

that time by the Chief of the German Security Police and Intelligence Service at Amsterdam. It concerned the "total evacuation" of all Jews in Dutch labour camps, "including their families": 5,242 male Jews in 42 camps, drawn from 85 towns, villages and parishes, with 8,877 dependants in 3,911 households. In addition, the order affected 900 Jews doing "relief work" in Westerbork and in the SS-School at Avegoor.

Nor was that all. The German "programme" also called for the deportation of 5,066 Jews and dependants (2,411 households) in Amsterdam. This called for the combined efforts of all available German and Dutch police in the city: some 120 regular German policemen, 400 Dutch policemen, 50 officials of the *Zentralstelle* and associated bodies; some 200 German Nazi Party officials, 50 Dutch SS men.

The whole operation was directed by *SS-Sturmbannführer* Lages and *SS-Hauptsturmführer* Aus der Fünten who gave orders to seize all the "wanted" Jews at 6 p.m. on Friday night and to take them to an assembly point in Ter Gouw Street. In addition, the men were to bring in all Jews from camps in the neighbourhood of Amsterdam. A "special notice" contained a number of further hints to be communicated by word of mouth to everyone engaged in the operation. Thus, they were to seize the Jewish partners of childless marriages or of mixed marriages with children over sixteen, but had to pass over Jews baptized into the Protestant faith and Jews having the requisite exemption documents. There was to be no age-limit whatsoever; everyone "transportable" must be brought in, with the exception of those suffering from scarlet fever, typhoid and diphtheria. Foreign Jews without the necessary documents had to come along unless they were of Argentinian, Danish, Estonian, Swedish, Swiss, Spanish or Turkish nationality. All Jews had to bring their keys and documents to Westerbork; the windows of their houses were to be shut, the doors sealed, the taps turned off, lights put out. Jewish sub-tenants were to be brought along as well, and so on.

We have the texts of a number of police telegrams from that day, showing that the whole operation had been prepared in great detail. It appears further that the good work was continued on Saturday, October 3; Telegram No. 47 calling the hunt off was not sent until 10 p.m. We also have a number of German accounts of the events. In one dated October 6, we read that the Dutch were not nearly as efficient as the Germans, who had consequently been forced to do most of the work—although the Dutch police accounted for more than half the total force, they only brought in the trifling number of 700 Jews. The reason was that they "failed to carry out their orders with real conviction and hence lacked the necessary energy and severity". As a result, many Jews were allowed to take with them more luggage than they were entitled to, so much so that quite a few came away with four or five large suitcases. But all in all, as a telex report by Dr. Schroeder, Böhmcker's successor, to Seyss-Inquart put it, the operation went off "quite according to plan", while "the Dutch population stood by and watched the round-up with curiosity. There were no demonstrations anywhere." True, the results would have been "better still" had the Dutch police not tipped off so many Jews. Moreover, the raiders came across a large number of bed-ridden people, so that only a total of some 14,000 Jews had been apprehended—Schroeder could not give a precise figure because "the rush was continuing into the night". In his letter to Himmler of October 7 Rauter reported that he had caught 13,000 Jews, 3,000 of whom had had to sleep on the ground in Westerbork. A German official who had "protested on humane grounds" had been "removed", and "the whole liquidation business was now in the hands of the [German] police . . . As you can see, *Herr Reichsführer*, I am fairly well satisfied with the course of events."

Others were far less satisfied, among them the Presidents of the Jewish Council who, at 10 p.m. on October 2, had an interview with Lages and Blumenthal. Both Germans were profuse with reassurances that the operation would cease that very evening, that the arrest of sub-tenants had been a mistake, that all sorts of omissions would be made good in Westerbork, that the Germans themselves would send clothes and blankets to the camps (they did so, but not for the Jews), that old people would not be arrested in future, and so on.

On the following morning, the two Presidents protested that the Germans had arrested a number of leading provincial Jews and urged that these "indispensable" people be released forthwith. Their long letter ended with the phrase: "We thank you in anticipation for your favourable attitude to this important request."

Let us now turn from these two supplicants to the victims themselves. There can be only very few surviving Jews who do not remember that black Friday of October 2, 1942. Something had leaked out early in the morning, and as the day went on rumour mushroomed until, by evening, there was panic in many Jewish circles. Why so many police, people kept asking themselves? Why so many extra trains at Central Station? The writer recalls very vividly how the headmaster of his school assembled the pupils at lunchtime and then ordered them to go home and to pack their rucksacks, how these children scattered in all directions as if a bomb had exploded, how frightened passers-by stopped to ask them what was happening, and how another long, long vigil began. Wielek[1] has told us in nerve-racking detail, how husbands were dragged away from their wives, women from their children, children from their parents, in a process of organized chaos. The writer remembers one of his pupils being snatched up, while the boy's mother, who was a neighbour, screamed into the night from her balcony. On Monday morning, when lessons at the school were resumed, there were many more empty benches than usual.

We also have a report of what happened outside Amsterdam. At Groningen, the local police chief, a Dutch Nazi by the name of P. Blank, told his men that he had a most enjoyable job for them: to reunite the many separated Jewish families. The reporter wondered whether the local police appreciated the irony of this remark, but added that "though most local policemen were sympathetic to the victims, they thought it better to do the unpleasant work themselves rather than leave the Jews to the mercy of the SS or WA". In fact, many Dutch policemen helped the Jews to pack their suitcases and even carried those of older folk. Still, this was little compared with the attitude of the Burgomaster of Beilen, Dr. H. J. Wytema, who was arrested on October 2, 1942, for his categorical refusal to co-operate with the Germans—the only known case of such a refusal—and who, after eight weeks in prison, was banished from Drente and Groningen.

All the Jews rounded up in this latest drive were first sent to Westerbork; their ordeal there will be the subject of a separate chapter.

## THE WINTER OF 1942

Very little if anything, happened for weeks, even for months, after October 2. There were, of course, such minor pin-pricks as the order barring Jews from public benches in The Hague, or the news (on November 17) that 800 Jews from Overijssel and Gelderland had been sent to Germany via Westerbork, but these events passed almost

[1] Wielek: *op. cit.*, pp. 162–8.

unnoticed. Similarly, in the Terror of 1793—4, it was the first tumbril to the guillotine that attracted attention, and perhaps the second as well, but after that people took the whole ghastly business as a matter of course.

We can reconstruct the sort of life people must have been living at that time from the *Internal Information Bulletin* (*I.I.*), a daily news-sheet compiled by one Dr. G. Fränkel and sent to all leading members of the Jewish Council from August 14, 1942, onwards.

We shall begin with the *I.I.* of October 1, not only because it was the beginning of a new quarter but also because that day's issue brought a most soothing report: that the deportation of Jews from Holland would cease forthwith. It also gave news of the issue of a new set of stamps, which, it seemed, would solve everybody's problems. We know what happened on the very next day. After the big raid no Amsterdam Jews were arrested for a short while, but thirty were caught at Rotterdam on October 6, and this figure grew to seventy-five on October 9; Rotterdam was said to have supplied altogether 1,500 conscripts of whom 1,000, "including many old people", were still awaiting transfer. On October 14 came news that twenty-seven men from Gouda and fifteen from Schiedam were taken to the *Zentralstelle*. That day's issue of the *I.I.* also contained a cheerful report about the ghetto in Warsaw ("great attention is being paid to hygienic conditions"). The issue of October 16 carried a gay letter from Theresienstadt by an eighty-year-old man who promised that in case he changed his address he would "if possible" give his new one. On October 18 the bulletin included two letters from the hospital in Sosnowitz, adding that "the spirit of these letters gives us cause for satisfaction". On October 20 came the news that no further reports would be published on labour camps in the Netherlands since all of them had been evacuated. The *I.I.* of October 21 published an enthusiastic and detailed report about "social services" in Poland, and of the wonderful care that was being bestowed on Jewish children there. The work of the Jewish Councils in that country was called difficult but "extremely important", particularly when it came to the prevention of infectious diseases.

From the issue of November 1 we gather that the *Hollandse Schouwburg* was practically empty, though a few new arrivals from Gouda and other provincial places were brought in on that day. On November 3 there was another report from Poland, this time on schooling in that country. It "appeared" that the Warsaw Jewish

Council was having much success with the laying out of playing fields in squares in the middle of the city. On November 5 came a detailed report about 170 "approved" Jewish rest-homes with 2,125 beds. It appeared that these houses were under very strict rabbinical supervision. By November 7 many of these excellent homes had been closed down, and most of the inmates transferred to Westerbork. Among the 450 people taken into custody that day there were many who had the exemption stamp. On November 9 the *Schouwburg* was once again empty, except for four people. But on that day 1,010 Jews were sent or about to be sent from Westerbork to Germany. Six hundred followed for certain on November 10.

On November 11 the Germans raided the Hollandia works in Amsterdam which employed 367 Jews. All of them thought that they were safer than anyone else: their factory had been declared vital to the war effort and hence enjoyed the special protection of the German inspectorate. During previous arrests, the non-Jewish staff manager had always managed to get them back—often by putting in a good deal of overtime, as one of the surviving witnesses has testified. Eight of the Jewish staff even had special permission by General Christiansen to walk in the streets without their star and, what is more, after the curfew. But the allegation that one Jewish worker in this factory was involved in underground communist activity now gave the Germans a pretext to carry off all the others in a raid led by Lages himself. Both during this raid and also during the subsequent investigations in Amsterdam and Scheveningen, the Germans and some of their Dutch henchmen are said to have acted in a most abhorrent manner—the details of their brutalities have been described by a number of independent witnesses. On November 26 the Scheveningen branch of the Hollandia works was raided as well, and the victims plus their families, 121 people in all, sent to Westerbork, whence all Hollandia workers with their families (825 people) were deported on November 30. Eight of them survived the war, all of them men.

But let us go back to the *Schouwburg*. It was empty on November 12; the next night, the Germans brought in the families of the Hollandia workers; the *I.I.* of November 30 also reported the "evacuation" of a number of Jews from Limburg and Groningen and even gave an account of the activities of the "Socio-pedagogical Bureau", which was apparently suffering from the fact that some of its clients had "departed for Germany". On the sunny side was the bureau's attempt "through constant contacts, gradually to improve the attitude of both children and parents". There seemed to be an excellent understanding between this bureau and the Jewish Medical Education Bureau, the Psychiatric Consultation Bureau, the Association of Jewish Family Counsellors, the Housing Bureau, the Pastoral Committee and the Relief Committee for non-Dutch Jews; and "a great deal of attention was being paid to contact with Jewish schools".

The *I.I.* of November 17 contains an important account of the work of the Displaced Persons' Aid Bureau, which during October 1942 supplied Westerbork and other provincial centres with (in round figures): 2,100 rucksacks, 2,000 kitbags, 700 sets of men's underwear, 70 suits, 400 overalls, 350 pairs of shoes, 200 night-shirts, 300 aprons, 50 coats, 125 blouses, 100 pairs of children's shoes, 2,000 mugs, 2,000 spoons, 2,500 pairs of socks, 150 jackets, 800 items of women's underclothing, 500 dresses, 500 pullovers, 900 packets of sanitary towels, 60 articles of girl's underclothing, 100 girl's pullovers, 1,000 caps, 4,000 plates, 2,000 tubes of toothpaste, 600 pairs of boots, 700 shirts, 700 pairs of stockings, 350 overcoats and ladies' two-piece suits, 350 skirts, 100 brassières and corsets, 100 girls' dresses, 80 girls' skirts, 70 pairs of boys' socks, 250 boys' trousers, 500 diapers, 400 lumber jackets, 900 towels, 300 boys' shirts, 125 baby jackets, 725 mittens, 500 ear-muffs, 500 sets of babies' underclothing, 1,000 blankets, 3,000 handkerchiefs, 500 scarves, in addition to provisions, first-aid kits, medicines, etc. The reader may take it that most of these comforts brought some cheer into the lives of the German guards at Auschwitz—the children's supplies almost immediately.

We shall now pass to the issue of December 15, from which we gather that eighty-three letters and eighteen postcards had been received from Birkenau and another thirty-seven letters from Theresienstadt and Monowitz; in Birkenau, work was said to be rather hard but supplies and living conditions not unsatisfactory; in Monowitz, things were positively idyllic: "The food is good, with hot lunches, cheese and jam sandwiches in the evenings . . . We have central heating and sleep under two blankets. There are magnificent shower arrangements with hot and cold water." In the issue of December 16 it "transpired" that the letters from Theresienstadt amounted to no more than two postcards. But on that day a further twenty-nine letters and twenty-four postcards arrived from the same place: "a friendly town with broad streets and lovely gardens, and single-storey houses. The women and children seem to be very well looked after." The letters also suggested that it was possible to get help with rough work, that those who wished could take a nap in the afternoon, that there were small but comfortable single rooms—so glowing were the descriptions that one is surprised the paper did not add an invitation to readers to go and see for themselves.

A great deal of space was devoted to Professor Cohen's sixtieth birthday celebrations. On December 30 Professor M. Brahn, the President of the *Beirat* (to which we shall revert), handed Dr. Cohen an "artistically bound first edition of the *Handbook of the Jewish Council*, prepared by the Internal Information Bureau and "testifying to the creative genius and great organizational talent of the man whose birthday we celebrate". On the same day there was a "solemn gathering" at which the first speaker, Meijer De Vries, said that those assembled represented "the best part of the Jewish Council and of Jewish communal life". In more than one address the hope was expressed that the absence of the deportees would be only temporary; Professor Cohen was repeatedly compared to Moses—the climax came with Chief Rabbi Dasberg, who concluded his speech with a prayer that Cohen, like Moses, "would lead us past Sinai into the Promised Land". Professor Cohen was presented with an armchair and an album of photographs of the work of the Jewish Council. It must be admitted that the whole thing was done extremely well and the photographs were most becoming. One photograph, No. 28, bore the legend "Departure of one Contingent". It shows a motor-car packed with rucksacks and other luggage and one can still read the labels "To Westerbork". It was probably this photograph that gave rise to the rumour that the whole album was full of Jews being shunted off. In any event, album and speeches alike provide us with matchless historical material, for if we had no other documents at all, they would throw a searchlight into the attitudes prevailing among "the best part of the Jewish Council and of Jewish communal life". Less exalted Jewish circles may have had other feelings; the writer still remembers a young Jewish official, then lodging with him, who expressed his utter disgust at the fact that the Council should have seen fit to hold this kind of celebration under the prevailing conditions, even closing its offices for the occasion. He, for one, failed to appreciate that this sort of thing helped to "increase the unity of and hence co-operation in our organization" (Professor Cohen's apologia).

On January 15, 1943, the *Jewish Weekly* carried a new German proclamation, the first for some time: "Because so many children have recently been abandoned by their parents, the German authorities have decided in future to treat all foundlings as Jewish children and to send them to the appropriate institutions." Quite a few families who had taken in such children were now forced to surrender them again. There is no doubt that many Jews did, in fact, adopt this desperate remedy. The *Police Gazette* had for long been full of reports such as this: "On July 22, 1942, at approximately 11.15 p.m. a male child was abandoned in the corridor of the Overtoom police-station in Amsterdam. Particulars: age approximately fourteen months, Jewish, light brown hair, blue eyes; dressed in blue jersey, brown muffler, white bonnet, white socks, light blue shoes. The child was wrapped in a pink blanket." Then a request for information.

Particularly in January, such reports increased in number. Almost without exception the abandoned children had been well cared for; they were warmly dressed and left with toys or trinkets. Sometimes there was even a letter giving the child's first name, and adding "we have no alternative". And then, suddenly, the whole business ceased, no doubt as a result of the new German measure. Another explanation may have been that people who took in such children no longer reported them to the Germans. On May 5, 1942, Dr. Harster mentioned these children once more in a secret report. All of them would have to be taken to the German security police which would see to it that the "proper racial and biological investigations were carried out".

### THE EVACUATION OF APELDOORN

The events at Apeldoorn in January 1943 deserve special mention. Just outside this town lay a Jewish mental hospital, consisting of a large complex of pavilions and gardens set in lovely surroundings and enjoying an excellent reputation, even abroad. Since 1936 the hospital had been directed by Dr. Jacques Lobstein, who died in a Polish camp a few days after Germany surrendered. The inmates enjoyed a relatively quiet and peaceful existence and their peace increased even further when fewer and fewer visitors called as a result of the deportations. Here there was no curfew, here movement was fairly unrestricted, here there was what seemed perfect safety. The Germans were far away and rarely importuned the staff. There were lecture courses, all sorts of recreations; the patients were in relatively high spirits and indeed quite carefree. And so things continued until the Germans struck.

On December 31, 1942, the institute counted almost 1,100 male and female patients and this figure is unlikely to have changed radically before the catastrophe; the nursing, domestic and technical staff included some 400 to 500 persons—of those who did not go into hiding, only ten survived the war. The nearby Achisomog Training Institute housed seventy-four boys and twenty girls (another source gives a higher figure); we shall not dwell on the horrible fate of these educationally subnormal, invalid and mentally defective children.

We cannot tell whether Dr. Lobstein foresaw the disaster; in any case, like other Dutch Jews, he could not possibly have anticipated the full extent of the horror that lay in store for his charges. In retrospect, it seems difficult to understand why the Jewish leaders should have supposed that Apeldoorn would remain immune. After all, the Nazis had never hidden their intention of doing away with both Jews and mental defectives, and here they had the two together. The only astonishing thing is that they left Apeldoorn alone for as long as they did, especially as more than one German department had its eye on this comfortable lair so far from the exposed coast. Wielek[1] reports that when the chief of the German medical service visited Apeldoorn on November 6, 1942, he showed extremely keen interest in the equipment. Other Germans were much more interested in the buildings. An official of the Dutch Inspectorate of Mental Patients and Hospitals, though a member of the NSB, warned Dr. Lobstein, in the presence of Dr. Speijer, that the Germans were about to close the hospital; one month later he repeated this warning at grave personal risk. On both occasions Dr. Lobstein refused to take any counter-measures; he could not or simply would not believe that the Germans had any such plans, the more so as he had more than once been assured by the *Reichskommissar*'s office that he had nothing to worry about. Dr. Speijer, on the other hand, claims that he encouraged members of the staff, and those patients who were fit enough, to escape. On December 22, 1942, the German health chief, Dr. Conti, sent a telex report to Seyss-Inquart (with copies to Rauter, Wimmer and Harster): he had heard that Apeldoorn was to be cleared of Jews and made the urgent request that this institution be reserved for him.[2] On the same

[1] Wielek: *op. cit.*, p. 184.
[2] *Het proces Rauter* (The Rauter Trial) (The Hague, 1952), p. 440.

day, a meeting of the Secretaries-General mentioned the Jewish mental hospital at Apeldoorn as one of several places to which various government departments might be evacuated. One wonders if these gentlemen gave any thought to the fate of the poor inmates, let alone warned them.

The final order for the evacuation was passed on to Harster from Berlin (probably from Eichmann)[1] via Zöpf. It was then handed on to Aus der Fünten (Harster: "I thought that all these Jews would be put to work in Germany").

On January 11, 1943, Aus der Fünten, in civilian clothes, made a full inspection of the hospital and was given a comprehensive report of its various activities. A witness tells us that Dr. Lobstein believed Aus der Fünten had merely come "to find accommodation for Jews who had to be housed at all costs". Wielek reports that, on January 19, the local Police Superintendent let slip a hint to a group of people, including Dr. Lobstein, that the whole place would soon be cleared of Jews and mentioned what measures were being taken. By then it should have been obvious to anyone that the hospital, the nearby Achisomog Training Institute and, in fact, all Jews resident in Apeldoorn were in grave danger.

On Wednesday, January 20, a contingent of the Jewish Special Service Corps (OD) from Westerbork appeared at the hospital, followed soon afterwards by Gemmeker, the camp commandant, who ordered Dr. Lobstein to billet his men and expressed his astonishment that Aus der Fünten was not there to receive him. Gemmeker then assured Lobstein that his men would be leaving for Amsterdam the very next day. Though Lobstein himself seemed unperturbed, the rest of the staff and many of his patients drew the correct inference—with the help of the OD men (who were not under supervision), hundreds of them were able to escape just in the nick of time. A young member of the staff described it all in a letter to a friend in Amsterdam on January 20 to 21:

"This is probably the most agonizing night of my life. Here I am sitting on duty in the ward of a mental institution, doomed to be evacuated within twenty-four hours . . . Staff and patients alike are in a panic. Many have left their sick beds . . . We simply cannot cope with all the work . . . All the staff are busy packing suitcases

[1] B. A. Sijes: *Adolf Eichmann und die Deportation der in den Niederlanden wohnenden Juden* (Adolf Eichmann and the deportation of Jews domiciled in the Netherlands) (unpublished report), p. 34.

and so are many of the patients . . . Can you imagine the confusion? In a mental hospital of all places! A place full of helpless people, some—the psychopaths and schizophrenics—aware of what is happening but quite unable to do anything about it; others—the subnormal, imbeciles, idiots and demented, completely oblivious to the threat that is hanging over them. I am particularly afraid for D. (his fiancée, a nurse) who is taking it all very badly. Apart from that I am not too downcast."

Next night the Germans struck.

The Germans! After the war they were loud in their protestations that they had meant no harm to anyone, that they had merely acted on orders, and that even then they had tried to be as gentle as they could. The Jews had a different story to tell. But who can really say what happened on that January night in the dark corridors of a lunatic asylum? The raid was led by Aus der Fünten, that much he himself admitted, though he claimed that he acted on the orders of Harster or Zöpf. According to Jewish sources, Aus der Fünten behaved shamefully on that occasion; Wielek[1] called him a devil incarnate, who kept screaming curses in the infernal darkness, roared with laughter at the most harrowing episodes, shouted inhuman orders. Next day, he ransacked the whole place, an activity in which he was, no doubt, slightly hampered by the presence of Leo de Wolff, who was there on behalf of the Jewish Council. Aus der Fünten forced him to sign a slip of paper to the effect that the total sum confiscated at the hospital was 4,821 guilders and 18½ cents; of this amount, he transferred 4,610 guilders and 83 cents to Lippmann, Rosenthal & Co—the reader can decide what he did with the rest. According to Aus der Fünten himself, the difference was made up of postage stamps. In any case, he insisted that he had kept nothing at all for himself.

Did Aus der Fünten, in fact, curse, ill-treat people and steal that night? We cannot say. All we know is that someone did curse horribly, maltreat people abominably and plunder indiscriminately—and that someone certainly was not one of the unfortunate victims or nurses. The Germans did not stop at the hospital; they also attacked "normal" Jews in the town and children in the Achisomog Training Institute. Needless to say, they also set about the staff, the OD men from Westerbork, and a number of Jews who had taken refuge in the hospital in the mistaken belief that they would be safer there.

[1] Wielek: *op. cit.*, pp. 185–7.

The staff had spent the whole of the previous day baking the flour supplies into bread, boiling eggs, preparing food parcels, bundling up linen, etc.; the senior staff packed bottles of scopolamin and syringes for difficult patients. But most of these articles had to be left behind, as we know from a surviving doctor who was forced to accompany Aus der Fünten on a round after the raid was over.

"I am taking over the place myself," Aus der Fünten announced. He then had doctors and other senior staff locked up in a room away from their patients, who were given "further treatment" by the Germans.

The historian must leave the rest to the reader's imagination, and himself keep strictly to the known facts. But he cannot help repeating that the victims on this occasion were mental patients and that even normal people have been known to collapse under the strain of being dragged out in the middle of the night. First the poor victims were bundled into lorries and then into a train which stood ready for them in Apeldoorn.

They were escorted into the lorries with pushes and blows, men women and children, most of them inadequately clad for the cold winter night. As one eye-witness put it: "I saw them place a row of patients, many of them older women, on mattresses at the bottom of one lorry, and then load another load of human bodies on top of them. So crammed were these lorries that the Germans had a hard job to put up the tail-boards." Another eye-witness tells us that a German officer forbade one of the OD men to cover a very sick patient with a blanket. The same witness spoke of "horrible and bestial behaviour". Another OD man has stated that the lorries were so packed, that he had great difficulty not to trample on the face of a woman squashed between his feet. When one of the doctors spoke up for the children, and pointed out that they were not patients but backward pupils, Aus der Fünten is said to have replied: "No matter, they are all of them asocial elements." More than one document mentions pitiable screams. From the very start, the patients were thrown together indiscriminately, children with dangerous lunatics, imbeciles with those who were not fit to be moved.

The lorries hurtled to the station. The matter-of-fact, unadorned report of the station-master at Apeldoorn, who stood by the train throughout, gives us a few more particulars. At first everything went smoothly. The earliest arrivals, mainly young men, went quietly into the front freight wagons, forty in each. When the station-master opened the ventilators, the Germans quickly closed them again. At first, men and women were put into separate wagons, but later they were all mixed together. Although it was a very mild night, it was "not nearly mild enough for old people in night-dresses to travel in open lorries". As the night wore on, the more seriously ill were brought into the station. Some wore strait-jackets, "staggered into the carriages and then leant helplessly against the wall". The report goes on to say:

"Of course, a person in a strait-jacket cannot protect himself if he slips between the platform and the train. I remember the case of a girl of twenty to twenty-five, whose arms were pinioned in this way, but who was otherwise stark naked. When I remarked on this to the guards, they told me that this patient had refused to put on clothes, so what could they do but take her along as she was. Blinded by the light that was flashed in her face, the girl ran, fell on her face and could not, of course, use her arms to break the fall. She crashed down with a thud, but luckily escaped without serious injury. In no time she was up again and unconcernedly entered the wagon." "In general," the station-master went on, "the loading was done without *great* violence [his italics]. The ghastly thing was that when the wagons had to be closed, the patients refused to take their fingers away. They simply would not listen to us and in the end the Germans lost patience. The result was a brutal and inhuman spectacle." Did the Germans enjoy this scene? The station-master thought that the vast majority did not: "They showed no sympathy and did not seem to grasp that they were dealing with mental patients; they were rougher than the situation demanded, but I did not gain the impression that they enjoyed knocking these people about."

Early next morning Aus der Fünten called for volunteers among the nurses to accompany the train. Some twenty came forward; he himself chose a further thirty. The "volunteers" travelled in a separate wagon, at the back of the train. All were offered the choice of returning home immediately after the "trip", or else working in a really modern mental home. Not a single one survived.

Nor did any of the patients. According to the *Internal Information Bulletin*, they had all been taken to an "unknown" destination—did the editors really not know? A Dutch Jew who witnessed their arrival in Auschwitz has described it as follows: "I was on the station when the train arrived. It was one of the most horrible transports from Holland that I saw. Many of the patients tried to break through the barrier and were shot dead. The remainder were gassed immediately, but I remember that the doctors and nursing staff, who were in a separate wagon, were not taken to the gas-chambers but to the camp." According to another source, those nurses who refused to carry the corpses to the crematorium were sent straight to the gas-chambers as well; a third source reports that some of them were thrown into a pit, doused with petrol and burnt alive.

This is perhaps the place to remind the reader that Apeldoorn was not the only institution of its kind in the Netherlands. In the course of 1943 and 1944 most of the others were "evacuated" as well, and the patients sent to Auschwitz. So far as we know, not a single one of them has survived either.

## JANUARY–APRIL 1943

We must now go back to our main story, and look at the general course of events in February, March and April 1943. All the attacks on the Jews—from the house raids to the mass deportations "to Germany" during that period—were reflected in the *Internal Information Bulletin*, many of whose reports dealt with conditions in various Dutch localities with which the reader may be unfamiliar. What it all amounted to was that more and more of the Jews in the provinces were being driven into Amsterdam, or carried off to Vught Concentration Camp. In Amsterdam and other large cities, the Germans were meanwhile emptying Jewish old-age homes and hospitals. For those who were left, life went on—for some fearfully, for others with cherished illusions.

Here we shall merely try to present the reader with some typical glimpses:

In a telex message to Seyss-Inquart on February 1, Dr. Schroeder, the German Delegate in Amsterdam, reported a "reprisal measure" in Haarlem for the "political murder of a German soldier (suspected of being a Sicherheitsdienst informer) on January 30." Schroeder had ordered the "arrest of a hundred hostages, particularly from among Communist and Orange circles, together with three Jews". These last were the young Rabbi Frank and Messrs. Chapon and Drielsma, two prominent Haarlem citizens. Rabbi Frank was a regular participant in meetings of the Jewish Council, so that the report of his arrest caused consternation in Amsterdam, and the Presidents of the Jewish Council immediately contacted Lages. But "while we were still busy considering what further steps we could take, the meeting was interrupted by the arrival of one of our delegates from Haarlem, who pronounced the words 'Blessed art Thou, O Lord our God, King of the universe, the true Judge'—the blessing recited when someone has died. On hearing this terrible news we all bowed our heads in silence."[1]

All attempts to retrieve the bodies for Jewish funeral remained vain, the corpses had already been burnt. Instead, Lages promised to spare Mrs. Frank and her family—soon afterwards they were all carried off and not a single one survived. Several witnesses—including Germans—have testified to the noble bearing of Rabbi Frank. Thus Lages told Asscher that Frank had died "like a hero". More remarkably still, one Schröder, who was an intimate of Lages, reported that Lages came to him after the execution in a state of great shock. "I could see at once that, despite his usual military bearing, he was deeply shaken underneath. He obviously needed to unburden himself, and told me that he had had a long conversation with a rabbi that night, probably with one of the men who was shot. This man had behaved with outstanding courage and had told him (Lages) that he had forgiven him. After all, it was not Lages' fault; he was merely carrying out orders. Lages then said that he cursed the fate that had put him in this predicament . . ."

One of the non-Jewish hostages who was reprieved at the very last moment tells us that he roundly cursed the Germans in the presence of Rabbi Frank. "Mr. Frank, who must have known that his hours were numbered, then said to me quite calmly: 'My dear Mr. G——, they are little people, they cannot destroy our faith, they can only kill us. Judaism will still be there long after Fascism has gone, as we have seen so many times in our history. Spiritually we stand head and shoulders above them, and we must try to bear with them. I, as a rabbi, have only the one task of showing my people how to endure the ordeal that lies before them.' Then a high officer of the German Security Police, surrounded by his satellites, produced the death warrant from his formidable briefcase and read it out to the ten condemned men in German. We blenched, looked at one another bewildered and some of us began to weep, while others pleaded their innocence and begged mercy for the sake of their children. The German officer then ordered someone in civilian

[1] Cohen: *Herinneringen*, p. 100.

clothes to translate the warrant. The translator himself began to weep, strange though that may sound, and could not go on. All pleas by the condemned men were met with the reply: 'I know that you are innocent, but we have to make an example of someone . . .' This is the place to put on record the splendid bearing of Mr. Frank, who calmly brought out a sacred book and consoled his Jewish brothers . . . In the morning, at about 7 a.m., the ten condemned men were fetched from their cells and marched through the building, past the other hostages (who all stood to attention), with Frank making up the rear."

In the month of February 1943 attacks aimed particularly at the sick, the old and the orphaned continued unabated. On February 1, the *Internal Information Bulletin* told its readers that it was "pointless" to send reply-paid postcards to Theresienstadt; there were other postal instructions in the same vein. On February 2 the paper published an account of the work being done at the Jewish Business Training College, the scope of whose activities beggared imagination. A long report on February 5 gave some account of a very ambitious social course run, since February 1942, by Professor E. Kantorowicz; it was amazing what you could learn here, too. On February 8 a new venture by the Displaced Persons' Aid Bureau was publicized. It was now possible to make sure of a food parcel for oneself, one's family and friends in Westerbork, and readers were told just how many coupons were needed and all sorts of other details.

On February 12 followed another almost idyllic description of life in Vught Concentration Camp, together with a few less idyllic details, such as the total prohibition of correspondence "due to organizational difficulties". It seemed "most likely", however, that these difficulties would be removed "in the very near future". On the same date the *Jewish Weekly* gave detailed instructions of how to address letters to those serving in "German work-camps"; it was now the turn of those inmates whose surnames began with the letters D, I, J, U and V.

The issue of February 17, published a full report of the activities of the Youth Care Department which, the reader was told, would "continue to grow on its earlier foundations". The organizers were experiencing some difficulty in finding the right youth leaders since many of them were "no longer available". Luckily, "numerous leaders have remained at their post, even under the most trying circumstances". Singing and music were taught, there were holiday centres, physical training instruction, physical fitness tests and so on.

On February 18, the Medical Section published accounts of all sorts of work they were doing in recuperation centres for mental patients, the blind, etc. On February 19, came news from The Hague that 780 of these people in several institutions had been transferred to Westerbork; forty who were not fit to be moved were allowed to remain behind, but concentrated into two homes. The others had gone by passenger train, except for a few who had had to go in goods wagons. At a meeting of the Central Committee on the 19th, the chairman called this "a most disturbing report", one that might give rise to anxiety about the future of such institutions.

On February 19 came further reports about the impending evacuation of Jews to Amsterdam from Haarlem, Heemstede, Bloemendaal, Aerdenhout and Voorschoten, places in North and South Holland; some news of this had already been published on February 12, but there was now some modification in respect of mixed marriages.

This herding of the Jews into Amsterdam was, of course, an essential prelude to the mass deportations. As early as October 1, 1942, the Jewish Council had been told of Aus der Fünten's threat that "in the coming months" all except Amsterdam Jews would be evacuated to camps at Westerbork and Vught, "and if there was no room there, to Amsterdam"—the idea that there might be "no room" in these places may sound ironic today. We saw that, at the time, the Jewish Council had consoled itself with the fact that the people concerned were being sent to Dutch rather than German camps, and that "for the time being, a stop was being put to the deportations". That was October 1. The reader will remember that on October 2 the Germans rounded up thousands of Jews for just that purpose.

On November 23, 1942, Aus der Fünten repeated his threat to evacuate all provincial Jews; he reiterated it on December 10, 1942, and at an unspecified date before January 25. Then, on February 10, 1943, there appeared a decree ordering all Jews to Amsterdam, followed by Rauter's order of February 12. At first, both partners of mixed marriages were among those ordered to go to Amsterdam; later this was modified: the Aryan partner was allowed to stay behind, but the Jewish one and the children still had to go. A subsequent amendment allowed the children to stay as well. But amendments or not, it was a fantastic feat of the Jewish Council to house so many newcomers at such short notice.

On March 1, came the turn of the Jewish Invalid Hospital in Amsterdam. It has been said that the Germans had refrained from confiscating this building sooner, simply because the entrance was not imposing enough for them. Moreover, it was much too close to the Jewish quarter for comfort. We have a letter dated September 14, 1942, sent to the hospital board by the Presidents of the Jewish Council; the writers expressed their appreciation of the "titanic labours" of the whole staff, and assured the Board that they would be allowed to continue their work without interference. And indeed, the inviolability of this institution had become almost legendary among the Jews, so much so that many people offered their services as voluntary staff or even paid for the privilege of working there. Someone even called the place a human safe; at the end of February it held 416 patients, 197 full-time staff and 158 part-time staff.

On February 28 an operetta was due to be performed in the building, but one day earlier the Jewish Council had "leaked" the news that the place would have to be evacuated on March 1. On the 28th the rumour was confirmed, whereupon many officials made off; the rest got everything ready for the patients. The next morning, soon after 6 a.m. (when the curfew was lifted), another fifty of the staff left; the rest waited for the Germans, who were expected at 8.30 a.m. Instead there came a telephone call from Asscher who, with his usual optimism, let it be known that the whole thing had been a false alarm. A few minutes later the Germans arrived, almost as if to confound him. A. V. Hartogh, who was waiting in the porter's lodge with his wife, gave a prearranged sign and also dropped the telephone book on the buzzer to warn the Director, Dr. J. H. Buzaglo; the Hartoghs and two members of the staff then hid under the floor of the stage where they remained for forty-three hours before escaping through the back door. All the rest, including the Director and his wife and child, were arrested; the day's catch comprised a host of old, lame, sick, blind and otherwise incapacitated people—"there was no outcry from anyone; the SS did its ghastly work in terrifying and benumbing silence". Even so, they were disappointed to find that all but six members of the staff had got away. Perhaps it was to make up for this omission that they set to work plundering whatever they could, an operation that went on until 7 p.m. the next night, when they left the place in a shambles. According to one of their own number, they were looking chiefly for valuables, though they did not apparently mind laying their hands on anything they could get.

Next it was the turn of the Nederlands–Israelitisch Hospital (NIZ) which is said to have had 540 patients at the time. On Monday, March 1, 1943, the rumours of an impending German raid caused many of the patients to flee. Some 400 of them had to be helped away by family or friends using more or less improvised transport, including hand-carts, delivery bicycles, etc. Most of the staff fled as well, so that there was indescribable chaos.

On March 2 the Jewish Council let it be known that the Germans had given them assurances that nothing at all would happen to the hospital and that there was therefore no need for all this fuss. So it is hardly surprising that on March 3, at 9 a.m., the Germans drew up outside the hospital and the Old Age Home where they had a particularly good haul: 130 out of the 150 old people who had fled in the general panic on Monday night had returned after the assurance by the Jewish Council. In the hospital itself, the German doctor in charge of the raid asked that of the 120 patients present, fifty be picked out as fit for transport; when no more than twenty could be found, he made up the number "regardless of the patients' illness or condition".

On March 9 it appeared from the *I.I.* that postal contact with the *Ostland* (Riga, Minsk, etc.) could be resumed. On March 10 came the report that the remaining Jewish patients in the Hague Municipal Hospital and the Roman Catholic Hospital had been taken into custody on the night of March 5, "because a number of patients had left the hospital without permission"; the only ones to be spared for the time being were new-born children and patients suffering from infectious diseases. Not spared were the two remaining rest-homes in The Hague and the Jewish Orphanage there. In addition, the Germans carried off hospital patients from Leyden and Delft, and inmates of the Scheveningen prison—300 persons all told. Amsterdam also had raids round the clock that day. In the issues of March 9 and 11 the *Jewish Weekly* published a new order barring the Transvaal district (Amsterdam East) to Jews from outside the city; all those concerned were advised to consult the Jewish Council.

On March 12 the *Internal Information Bulletin* let it be known that on the morning of March 503 people—the sick and old and their families—had been sent from Groningen and Friesland to Westerbork. Twenty untransportable cases were left behind in Groningen, and a further five in Leeuwarden. Jewish partners of mixed marriages had been allowed to stay. The paper added that "apart from these two categories, the two provinces (Groningen and Friesland) are now practically cleared of Jews". We might add that this included most of the officials of the Jewish Council, which the Germans held had now become redundant. Professor Cohen nevertheless succeeded in getting a number of them transferred to Amsterdam (with their furniture), and in securing permission for a handful to stay where they were.

Perhaps this is the place to mention a few details about the deportations from Groningen. In an emergency hospital in that town—incredibly enough it had only one qualified nurse with several unqualified assistants—were a number of serious cases, so grave in fact that permission for them to remain in the hospital had been given by the notorious Jew-baiter Dr. L. M. ter Horst. But in the end, even these people—heart, kidney and bladder cases, paralytics and sclerotics—had to leave for Westerbork, as had a number of patients in private houses, among them a dying man.

The March 12 issue of the *I.I.* also contained the report that all Jews outside North Holland, South Holland and Utrecht provinces were about to be sent to Vught.

As usual, the Germans were not remiss in making their own contribution to the Jewish Festival of Purim (March 21). We are not so much thinking of the evacuation of the Central Israelitic Orphanage in Leyden, of the expulsion of all Jews from that city and of some sixty from Scheveningen, or the arrest of 700 Jews in Amsterdam from March 19 to 22, as of the address to which Rauter treated the Dutch SS on the day of the festival itself.[1] In it he reminded his audience that before the Germans had arrived, there were 140,000 "full Jews" in the Netherlands, including a number of foreigners whom "we could not touch for international reasons". However, "the whole of Jewry is due for expulsion to the East"; 55,000 had already been "shoved out" (Rauter asked his audience to keep this to themselves) and 12,000 were in camps, so that 67,000 of the 140,000 had been "purged from the life of the Dutch nation". But even that was not fast enough. From April there would be two trains a week, carrying a total of 12,000 Jews per month, with the result that in the foreseeable future no Jews would be "walking about

[1] *Het proces Rauter* (The Rauter Trial), pp. 41–3.

in Dutch streets". The only exceptions would be those married to non-Jews "to whom we shall have something to say later". Rauter added he would be "very glad indeed to see the end of the Jewish question", for the simple reason that—"as those of the security service will agree"—Jews invariably have a finger in all espionage and terrorist activities. "Until the Jews are gone we shall never get any peace." To get rid of them would not be a nice task, "it is dirty work". But this was not the time or place to show pity, for "behind us stand the Germanic peoples . . . who demand to be cleansed of this plague and to have the Jewish question solved once and for all". The Dutch police would willy-nilly have to go along, and the Dutch Churches would have to stop writing their pastoral letters. "Those who don't comply will get their knuckles rapped." He, Rauter, would take the entire responsibility: "I shall gladly answer with my soul for what crimes I have committed against the Jews." (Laughter)

In this Purim address, Rauter—as we saw—told his audience that he would have "something" to say about mixed marriages. On the orders of the *Reichskommissar*, all officials married to a Jew or Jewess had to be dismissed on April 1, 1943; this order did not apply to persons whose marriages were terminated before that date, through death, divorce or legal separation. The knowledgeable Dr. Calmeyer, to whom all difficult racial problems were referred, must have had his hands full . . .

The *Internal Information Bulletin* of March 24 reported that if anyone in Auschwitz should happen to die, the dependants could now apply for death certificates. "This may take several weeks but provides written proof to satisfy any authority." The fee and postage of 0·85 Marks had to be paid in advance by postal order—and this was thought to be big news as late as March 24, 1943! On March 26 the bulletin mentioned the arrival of fifteen postcards from Jawischowitz and one letter from Theresienstadt. The bulletin went on to discuss an earlier batch of letters and mentioned with satisfaction that even those undergoing punishment had been allowed to write. Unfortunately "all the letters come from men. There is no family contact." The reader will notice that there is no connection between the last two sentences, and wonder whether those for whom the bulletin was intended, namely the leaders of the Jewish Council, were really ignorant of what was going on, so ignorant, in fact, that they could continue co-operating in the transports.

On March 29 we find the usual reports of deportations from

Amsterdam ("labour service") and The Hague ("evacuation")—euphemism upon euphemism. The official Press of that day published Rauter's orders to clear eight provinces—all except Utrecht, North Holland and South Holland. On April 10 all Jews in these provinces were sent to Vught, together with their personal luggage and valuables. During his trial, Rauter[1] explained that he had been forced to take this measure because Jews from Amsterdam, "and particularly Jewish activists had gone to Groningen, Friesland and Drente, where they had caused 'extraordinary disturbances', acts of sabotage, shootings, etc.". As a result, he had had to send a whole regiment of police and had "endless trouble with this whole business". The only solution was the "dejudification" of the provinces as Zöpf so elegantly called this operation in a letter to Calmeyer. This beautiful word is also found in a confidential letter sent to Calmeyer on March 31 by the Central Population Office in The Hague. The same file also contains Calmeyer's list of provisional exemptions for provincial Jews: 174 names in all.

On March 31 the *Internal Information Bulletin* drew a full picture of Theresienstadt based on earlier letters. People there were said to have "a passable life" although "under very modest conditions". Everyone has his own bed, and "sometimes a family has its own room". "The post office in Theresienstadt is terribly overworked as parcels and letters pour in from everywhere." As for the old people, the bulletin explained that "as an example, we can only say (*sic!*—J.P.) that one man is continuing his scientific work and that another is having art discussions with like-minded friends . . . the many deaths mentioned in letters from Theresienstadt are readily explained by the large number of old people among the population there." This brings us to the end of March.

On Saturday, April 10, 1943, *Sturmscharführer* Fischer rang up H. Edersheim, the Jewish "spokesman" for South Holland, and asked him precisely how many Jews had been transferred to Vught from the proscribed provinces, and also for a "general survey and report on the attitude of Jews who have left the province".

Edersheim then rang up Professor Cohen, who could not answer the first question but added that many families who had been living in these provinces for generations felt terribly depressed about the evacuations; worse still, only a few provincial members of the Jewish Council had been permitted to continue their activities.

[1] *Het proces Rauter* (The Rauter Trial), p. 26.

On April 13 Rauter banished Jews from the three remaining provinces as from April 23; only Amsterdam was now open to Jews. On April 14 the two Presidents and Dr. Sluzker had an interview with Aus der Fünten, in which they told him that the small number of exemptions granted to members of the Jewish Council must be considered a "slight upon our work", and, indeed, made part of the work impossible. For instance, there would be no one left to care for the Jewish partners of mixed marriages. The answer was that "the Aryan partners of such marriages can, of course, travel to Amsterdam whenever it becomes necessary to obtain travel or removal permits". All other objections were overruled as well; only caretakers of cemeteries were allowed to stay behind. The Council then asked that those who had given good service to the Jewish Council should be sent to a separate camp. Impossible, said Aus der Fünten, though he was magnanimous enough to concede that such people "would be given important positions in the organization at Vught". "From this we gathered with gratification that we were to play some part in running that camp, a view which the Germans 'expressly endorsed'." (We are not told who was trying to deceive whom.) The Germans also promised to give "favourable consideration" to the suspension of raids during the first and last night of the Jewish Passover, indeed, they afterwards said that no such raids would occur throughout the whole of the Passover week, from April 19 to 26. Perhaps it would be of interest to quote some of the notices in the *Internal Information Bulletin* during the next few days. On April 14 the paper published the results of the hairdressers' examination held under the auspices of the Jewish Vocational Guidance Centre. Each of the five people who had passed, had given three haircuts and shaves, and received a diploma. At the same time, there was news of further round-ups, and so there was on the following day, when the *Bulletin* also let it be known that the various departments of the Jewish Council—with the exception of some emergency services—would not operate during the Passover. On April 16 came more reports of the usual raids, and the news that the youth services were holding an exhibition with the title: "What the Council Does for Jewish Children." "The exhibition was opened by the head of the Education Department, J. J. van der Velde, in the presence of many departmental directors. He expressed his great appreciation of the value and quality of the work done for the children by the youth services under the direction of S. Broekman. On a handsome stand, built by the staff, were arranged a number of models (fretwork, clay and cardboard, toys, etc.) made by the pupils. One special attraction was a loom constructed by the children to their own design, on which the girls had woven attractive materials. Excellent photographs and clear diagrams illustrated the whole range of activities. In particular, a graph showed that the number of participants in the month of March had gone up steeply. It is intended to display the exhibits in various large buildings of the Jewish Council."

The *Jewish Weekly* of April 16 advertised courses for young people aged fourteen to twenty years "for the furtherance of their general education and profitable use of their leisure time". It was also announced that it was now the turn of the K's and L's to send letters to "Germany". A second page included a high-toned article about "changes of occupation" which Jews were apparently making "with cool deliberation". A bachelor wished to meet other people.

The *Bulletin* of April 19 reported the usual transportations. That of April 22 mentioned the arrival of 2,040 letters from Vught, most of them written by women. Four Jewish markets and some dozen fishmongers would be distributing bloaters on behalf of the Jewish Council until April 28. On April 22 came the report that Jews from North and South Holland and Utrecht had been "evacuated" to Vught—in extra passenger trains provided "through the good offices of the representatives of the Jewish Council". On April 23 came the news that two Council representatives each had been given permission to remain in The Hague, Rotterdam and Utrecht. The *Jewish Weekly* of the same date published the "important" warning that kitbags and one blanket must be kept separate from the rest of the luggage, in case the latter was "delayed in transit". Elsewhere in the paper, and even in the religious article entitled "Reflection", there were unmistakable allusions to the desirability of "constant preparedness, readiness to move into a new environment". This piece of good advice also had its dangers, as we know from the case of a woman who was too ill to be moved when the escort came, but "was taken along all the same because her things were ready".

The number of advertisements in the *Jewish Weekly* constantly dwindled. The *Internal Information Bulletin*, too, became thinner and thinner; the issue of April 28 mentioned a few round-ups in Amsterdam and The Hague; it also published the news that, on April 22, an extra train with 500 passengers had left for Vught. In the *Jewish Weekly* on the same day, we read that the P's and W's could now write to "Germany". An unpaid advertisement called upon a Jewish reader to appear before the President of the District Court at The Hague, with a view to a reconciliation between him and his non-Jewish wife. The man was said to be of no fixed abode. There was also a marriage advertisement by a "Turkish subject" and one, moreover, of "good appearance". As if being Turkish and neutral was not a sufficient recommendation!

But April was not over yet. The Germans had still another anti-Jewish measure up their sleeves: the sterilization of Jewish partners of mixed marriages.

## STERILIZATION

Sterilization is perhaps the clearest illustration of how the Germans tormented the Jews before destroying them altogether, until their victims, ground down and crushed in mind and spirit, would bow to the inevitable. Once their morale was shattered, there would be little to impede their destruction. We do not say that the Germans clearly planned every move in this diabolical game; but the fact is that every one of their measures—psychological or economic—led remorselessly towards that end—whether they merely humiliated or actually plundered the Jews, they were steadily driving them towards the gas-chambers. Hence it is rather pointless to go at length into the German deliberations. Seyss-Inquart is said to have been in favour of the sterilization of all remaining Dutch Jews—it may well be so. Harster later claimed that the aim of the sterilization laws was merely to prevent the birth of children of "mixed descent", and he denied that the intention was to face Jewish partners of mixed marriages with the choice between deportation and sterilization. We may concede that this might have been the theory, but it certainly was not the practice. Sometimes it worked out that way, more often not, and when it did not the result was death. Whether Herzberg[1] was right in thinking that there were differences between Berlin and Rauter in this matter, or what precisely were the Nazi's pseudo-scientific theories about it, need not concern us. All that matters here is what actually happened with regard to the sterilization of Jews in Holland. On this subject we have a few, isolated documents. One dated March 20, 1943, suggests that the Germans

[1] Herzberg: *op. cit.*, p. 128.

had not yet quite made up their minds. On April 29 Rauter apparently discussed the matter with Zöpf, as part of his plan to rid Amsterdam of all Jews. The upshot was a letter sent by Harster on May 5 to various German departments offering the Jewish partner of mixed marriages with children a choice between voluntary sterilization and "forced sterilization in the camp at Vught".

On May 18 eight Germans, most of whom we have met before, assembled in conference at the offices of the *Zentralstelle*. There were two *Sturmbannführer* (Zöpf and Mayer), three *Haupsturmführer* (Aus der Fünten, Wörlein and Streich), one *Sturmscharführer* (Fischer) together with *Fräulein* Slottke (whom we shall be meeting again) and a *Fräulein* Winkelnkemper. The report of this meeting, as of all other official discussions of sterilization, was secret. It throws a great deal of light on what the Germans themselves felt on this delicate subject. There is no doubt at all that this particular meeting did wish to offer certain groups of Jews the alternative between sterilization and deportation. It is also interesting to see that other categories were not to be molested at all for the time being, among them Jews baptized into the Protestant faith, foreign Jews with double nationalities and "Portuguese" Jews. The meeting laid heavy emphasis on the fact that sterilization was, in any case, to be "voluntary". Another document of the same date dealt with the age of Jewish women: since some Jewish women were infertile though under the age of forty-five, and others above that age were still fertile, it would be best to submit all of them alike to medical examination. As for pregnant Jewesses, sterilization had best be deferred until after they had given birth.

On June 25, 1943, a different group of eight Germans met to discuss the same question. They were told that Rauter had stressed the voluntary nature of the measure, and also that it would be far better to have the work done by Jewish and Dutch rather than German doctors. "In that way, we shall cut the ground from under the feet of Church and hostile propaganda." However, "it is entirely up to the Jews to accept such medical intervention on the inducement that they might then be exempted from wearing their stars". The report does not tell us what was to happen to those Jews who refused to accept this most generous offer.

The whole sterilization operation has been described at length by Wielek who, *inter alia*, tells us that, at the Portuguese-Israelitic Hospital, the work was done by a doctor dismissed from Westerbork, "a palsied old wreck, physically and spiritually. He considered himself the saviour of mixed marriages in the Netherlands and in an address to the hospital staff compared himself to Judas Maccabeus."

A report dated July 7, 1943, gives some further details. It mentions a Medical Liaison Bureau (described as a department of the Jewish Council having special contact with the office of *SS-Sturmbannführer* Dr. E. W. P. Mayer, head of the medical branch of the German security service); this department of the Jewish Council had the task of dealing with applications by infertile people wishing to "enjoy all the advantages of sterilized people". There followed a host of unsavoury details which we will spare the reader.

Perhaps this is the place to mention the Jewish reaction to this new German outrage. We gather from a report of the meeting of the Jewish Council on May 20, 1943, that when the Presidents lodged a very strong protest against it, they were told by Aus der Fünten that the whole thing was purely voluntary and that anyone could choose between it and deportation to Poland. Aus der Fünten added that the whole matter was, in any case, not within the province of the Jewish Council. In his *Memoirs,*[1] Professor Cohen reports that many members of the Jewish Council objected to participation in an operation that "was in conflict with the spirit of Judaism and most certainly with Jewish Law". The strongest exception was taken by the orthodox wing which, nevertheless, continued to co-operate in what Professor Cohen so elegantly called the "administrative side", after assuring themselves that "no coercion was involved after all". Moreover, applications for sterilization did not pass through the hands of the Jewish Council, so that its members could argue that they had no real responsibility for what happened. "Yet I must admit that I was filled with utter revulsion, and that I only carried on because of what I felt was my duty towards those who came to us for advice."

It was probably due to this reluctant sense of duty that the "administrative department" concerned was kept as small as possible, and that it was "kept apart from the rest of the organization. I felt in this way I could overcome some of the objections that had been raised." The reader is best left to form his own conclusions about this matter, and also about such reports as the following:

"A meeting of the directors of the three Jewish hospitals was held in the council chamber of the Public Assistance Bureau to discuss

[1] Cohen: *Herinneringen*, p. 106.

the German order that their hospitals be made available for the sterilization of Jews, an operation that ran counter not only to all the principles of humanity and religion but also to the most basic medical tenets; some suggested wholesale resignations, but this was rejected on the reasonable grounds that the Germans would consider such resignations as sabotage and act accordingly. Moreover, the operation was voluntary and only to be performed on willing subjects, although, as the meeting recognized, 'voluntary' was not perhaps the right word when the alternative was deportation to a German concentration camp. The Jewish Council was asked to point out to the German authorities that the intended operation was godless and bestial."

Gertrud van Tijn[1] speaks with great respect of non-Jewish and Jewish doctors who refused to have anything to do with the new measure, the latter despite the impending threat of deportation.

We need not emphasize how much distress this new measure caused among every section of the Jewish population, schoolchildren not excepted. The word 'sterilization' became part of their ordinary talk, and what else could one expect when circulars were pushed through the door, stating in a matter-of-fact way where sterilization centres had been set up, where partners of mixed marriages could register for it, and the rider that if it appeared on investigation that the person concerned was sterile, the operation would obviously be omitted. The circular ended with the usual explanation that there was "no obligation to undergo this operation".

While it was true that the Jewish Council could keep aloof from this business to some extent, it was certainly more involved in it than Professor Cohen has suggested in his *Memoirs*. In particular, there was the question of who was going to pay for it all, especially when the "volunteers" were impecunious. One of the doctors performing the operation, a member of the Dutch Nazi Party, pleaded in mitigation after the war that his work had been paid for by the Jewish Council; the relevant court records throw a very harsh light on one of the saddest aspects of the Council's activities. We incidentally gain the impression that this Dutch doctor, whom the prosecution called "a vicious and blatant anti-Semite" was much worse than his German colleagues. He was even accused of having frustrated the attempts of some of his colleagues to sabotage the

[1] G. van Tijn-Cohn: *op. cit.*, p. 49.

measure. In sharp contrast to him, Dr. E. W. P. Mayer, the SS physician in charge of the whole operation, closed his eyes on "hundreds of occasions" when Jews turned up with doubtful sterility certificates signed by Dutch doctors; we have established that he and others like him helped as many as 2,400 Jews to the much-desired *red* 'J' on their identity cards. We know the names of many of the other doctors who did this, and Wielek reports that both Dr. Mayer and a Dutch doctor, whose name he gives, were suspected of "pro-Jewish sympathies" and that Mayer was even charged with this offence.

We must also give a few other examples of resistance to the measure, which were the more remarkable because they took place in Westerbork, where people were hovering on the brink of deportation. The sterilization question first cropped up in that camp at the end of May 1943, when Jewish partners of mixed marriages with children received an urgent summons to go to the assembly hall at 6.45 p.m. Of the 103 who came forward, the great majority thought that they were about to be released. Instead they were addressed by Aus der Fünten who offered them the alternative of sterilization or deportation. They had half an hour to make up their minds; those who left the hall were taken to have opted for deportation; discussion with a non-Jewish partner outside Westerbork was said to be completely superfluous. "Those in the hall, who had but half an hour to settle their fate, were stricken by panic as few human beings could have known it. Some collapsed on the floor, others had fits of hysteria."

The eye-witness to whom we owe this account managed somehow to contact his non-Jewish wife in The Hague, who was so incensed that she stormed to Zöpf's home. Luckily for all those concerned he did not know, or claimed he did not know, anything about Aus der Fünten's latest activities, and at the insistence of his visitor immediately revoked the ultimatum by telephone. As a result, those who had refused the operation escaped with a fright ("for the time being"). But the fifty or so who had offered themselves "voluntarily" for the operation were taken under heavy guard to Amsterdam where, according to one source, they were, and according to another source they were not, sterilized. Yet another source claims that by way of convincing the waverers at Westerbork, a number of people already sterilized were brought from Amsterdam as happy exhibits; they became known throughout the camp as mannikins.

The second Westerbork episode took place a year later, when Dr. Spanier, head of the medical service in the camp, sent for five of of the medical staff and told them—it was an order—that they had to sterilize all Jewish women married to non-Jews. Refusal was sabotage, and sabotage meant either deportation or death. One of the doctors—Rosalie Wijnberg—refused on principle and said that she was prepared to take the consequences. Another doctor said that for his family's sake he was reluctantly compelled to co-operate, but that in future he would look on himself as a criminal. A third said he would have to discuss the matter with his wife; the other two did not seem to mind so much and one of them simply wanted to know whether, after the German defeat, the women in question could claim compensation from him. This matter was referred to Professor Meijers, an eminent jurist then in Westerbork, who declared emphatically that, while he was not passing any judgment on the sterilization itself, no court would uphold such a claim since the doctors had been acting under duress.

Two days later, the commander of the camp himself resorted to veiled threats against Dr. Wijnberg and asked her colleagues to "make her see reason". We may take it that they complied, knowing as they did that the Germans punished even the least resistance with death. Still she remained adamant, and—instead of the expected sentence—received a message from the camp commandant a few days later, to the effect that The Hague felt sterilization ought not to be performed by order. The commandant added that he thought "he had expressed the general feeling of us all when he gave out that there was little enthusiasm for performing the voluntary operation in Westerbork, and that it would be best to choose a more suitable sterilization centre. And so an affair that had weighed heavily on our minds for five interminable days came to an unexpected end." As for her own action, Dr. Wijnberg simply said: "Had I acted differently I could not have gone on living with myself."[1]

As for the Churches' reaction, we know that though one parson asked the deacon's office for money to subsidize the sterilization of Jews (whom, admittedly, he was only trying to help), others—as Touw has pointed out—were thrown into camps for preaching against this "shameful measure". On May 19, 1943, representatives

[1] *Jaarboek Gemeentelijke Universiteit van Amsterdam, 1949–50* (Amsterdam University Yearbook) (Amsterdam, 1949), p. 57.

of the Dutch Reformed Church, the Roman Catholic Church, the New Reformed Church, the Christian Reformed Church, the Lutheran Evangelical Church, the Reformed Lutheran Evangelical Church, the Remonstrant Brotherhood, the Baptist Union and the Old Catholic Church lodged an official protest with Seyss-Inquart. The German text of this protest is quoted by both Touw and Delleman.[1] The former gives the names of the various signatories; the latter quotes the Dutch text as circulated to ministers by the New Reformed Church, with the addendum (by A. A. L. Rutgers, the president): "Though this address is not meant for publication or for reading from the pulpit, it is not confidential and, in my personal opinion, the congregation should be acquainted with its substance."

Touw calls this protest, drafted by Dr. Jan Koopmans, one of "the most moving documents in the struggle of the Church against godless National Socialism", and compared its tone to that of the noblest documents in the great days of the Church—of Guy de Bray and John Knox. We quote:

"Sterilization does violence to divine commandments and to human justice. It is the ultimate consequence of an anti-Christian and life-destroying racial doctrine, of overweening arrogance, of an outlook on life that is incompatible with true Christian and human existence . . . It is your Excellency's bounden duty to put a stop to this shameful practice . . ."

The reader must remember that this was written in the year 1943, at the risk of death. The Churches' attitude compared most favourably to that of the College of Secretaries-General. For when the non-Nazi members of that body met to discuss the question and were asked by the Secretary-General for Waterways, *mr.* Spitzen, to lodge a protest "on purely humanitarian grounds", they contended that such a protest would not help, and would only make matters worse. When Spitzen insisted, the meeting evinced "little enthusiasm for such a step" and felt that, in any case, Spitzen's letter would have to be "redrafted"—a favourite means of torpedoing inopportune suggestions.[2]

And what of those who submitted to sterilization? It would seem

[1] H. C. Touw: *Het verzet der Hervormde Kerk* (Resistance by the Reformed Church), pp. 150–151; T. Delleman: *Opdat wij niet vergeten* (Lest we forget), p. 615.

[2] Report by the Secretary of the College of Secretaries-General, p. 82.

that the Germans themselves had not yet quite decided what to do with them. Thus, according to a directive issued on August 28, 1943, they were allowed to use public transport, but not restaurant cars or wagon-lits; to be present at sports meetings, but not to participate in them; to order goods by telephone, but not to have telephones in their homes; to travel, but not to move house. Moreover, sterilized Jews were not allowed to have extra-marital sexual intercourse, to marry non-Jews, to employ "Aryan maids", to visit reference libraries as distinct from public libraries and museums . . . From a German document of June 15, 1944, we learn that of the total of 8,610 Jews married to non-Jews, 2,562 had already made use of the wonderful new opportunities—1,146 men, mainly after operative sterilization, and 1,416 women.

Did sterilization, in fact, confer permanent privileges on these people? The same German document contended that most of these Jews were shiftless, lived by the black market, fomented rumours, helped to hide undesirables, etc. The solution? To send them first to work on air-fields and similar projects, and later—to Westerbork. One advantage of sending them there was that the non-Jewish partners would be encouraged to seek divorces. But even before that happened, a number of sterilized Jews were seized and killed, possibly because they had broken some other regulation, possibly not.

### THE LAST RAIDS

By way of introduction to the subsequent events, we shall quote verbatim a report by the *Internal Information Bulletin* on May 28, 1943, of a message from the Presidents of the Jewish Council: "We have been told that this week's transports have been filled and that no further action is intended for the time being. The work of the Jewish Council will be carried on, although with a greatly reduced staff. How this can be done will be decided in consultation with the heads of the various Departments. We urge everyone to do his duty with devotion, so that the help which we must give to others is not relaxed or lessened for a single moment."

Clearly, something momentous had happened, though what precisely it was cannot be gleaned from the *Jewish Weekly* of the same day. That paper was much what it always had been, except that there were only half as many advertisements as usual.

But we know now that a week previously, at 10 a.m. on Friday,

May 21, to be precise, Aus der Fünten had suddenly informed Asscher, Cohen and Sluzker that 7,000 of the staff of the Jewish Council must go: the Council had twenty minutes to make up its mind. When the triumvirate protested, Aus der Fünten referred them to Lages who (in the presence of Aus der Fünten and Blumenthal) insisted that they must "carry out orders" or else face such measures as the Jews in the Netherlands had never even imagined. Further protests were waved aside and the Council was directed to pick the 7,000 itself.

At 2 p.m. on the same day the Jewish Council held an emergency meeting. After a report by the Presidents and a promise that they would try to carry out the orders "as considerately as possible", the members were given five minutes to collect their thoughts. Some held—but not for long—that Jewish honour demanded a blunt refusal; others agreed at once that these orders must be carried out for fear of worse. The Council concocted all sorts of "practical advice" which we spare the reader. In the end, it unanimously empowered the Presidents to select the 7,000.

Herzberg[1] reports that some members nevertheless refused to have anything to do with the new measure and threatened to resign. He even asserts that Asscher was one of them. But when Mrs. van Tijn actually submitted her resignation and the Council declined to accept it, she did not press the matter further. Many members told the Presidents that the orders were impossible, that the Council could not force any of the 7,000 to report to the Germans. There were particularly violent discussions in a number of offices. One departmental chief decided to draw lots. Here and there attempts were made at sabotage—some employees of the Jewish Council even cut a stencil countermanding a large number of call-ups.

To say that things did not go quite smoothly at the Jewish Council would be an understatement—there was once again utter chaos and panic. A commission was set up with the invidious task of sorting the staff into three categories: A. the absolutely indispensable; B. those doing important work; C. those who could be spared. The resulting demoralization must be left to the reader's imagination.

One eye-witness reports that on the evening of Saturday, May 22, the headquarters of the Jewish Council were "lit up from top to bottom as if it were a festival", while the commission deliberated within. "I still see them sitting there, with huge indexes before them,

[1] Herzberg: *op. cit.*, pp. 113–14.

as secretaries kept rushing in with new trays of cards and other members of the staff pleaded for those already doomed." A young man, who was part of a team carrying forms from one room to another, found his own among them. "He ran away in a panic, abandoning the Jewish Council to its own devices." The work continued throughout the night; the call-up papers—which the Council had solemnly vowed not to issue itself—were typed throughout the Sunday. On Monday many of the victims reported for transportation; others went into hiding, while others again had already been seized by the Germans—their call-up papers were returned on Monday night by an over-correct official, and a further dozen or so employees, including our eye-witness, had to be picked. Called in one by one before the Presidents, all but one of the new victims refused.

The full consignment of 7,000 had to be handed over to the Germans by the evening of May 25. The tension continued throughout the day—so much so that a detective was posted to chase people out of the passages with a revolver. Our eye-witness, who was watching all this with two colleagues, said: "We could think of nothing more heroic than to stand about defiantly in a remote corridor and blubber over the misery around us and our powerlessness to do anything about it." In the end he walked out, but the fear of missing something—"that's what it was, I don't want to embellish my motives"—drove him back again to the Nieuwe Keizersgracht in the afternoon. There he was set to work beside a German lawyer preparing new lists of Amsterdam Jews, some of whose names were unpronounceable to a German and ridiculous to a Dutchman. "Even while the building was resounding with the cries of distress, we, two fully grown men, were sitting together reading tongue-twisting names and having fits of laughter; I don't know why, but I shall never forget it."

To round off the story we must mention the arguments used by Professor Cohen and others to vindicate their behaviour.[1] There were several excuses, *inter alia*, the suggestion that the Germans would have deported thousands with or without the co-operation of the Council (in that case, the reader may well ask, why co-operate?), and that the call-up papers gave those who wanted to go into hiding ample warning and time to do so. The last argument does not

[1] Berkley: *op. cit.*, p. 85; Examination of Professor Cohen on April 10, 1947, November 24, 1947, November 26, 1947, and December 17, 1947.

sound very convincing, the more so as the call-up papers informed the conscripts that, if they failed to appear, others would have to go in their place. Professor Cohen himself afterwards conceded this point, so that his claim that, by co-operation with the Germans, 4,000 people were helped to go into hiding, is a hollow one. Professor Cohen's third argument was that, like the commander of a military operation who knows that he must sacrifice some of his soldiers, he tried to preserve an "élite" [his own word]. "I fully realized that this decision would be appreciated only by a few and that it was bound to cause resentment. A leader must not, however, allow himself to be deterred when he duly places the interests of the community above that of the individual."

Professor Cohen also contended that less than 7,000 were in fact called up, and that a very much smaller number still responded. This may well have been the position of May 25, 1943. But that evening the two Presidents were summoned before the "grim-faced" German leaders who told them that, as the numbers had fallen far short of their requirements, they had ordered a punitive raid for May 26.

As a result some 3,000 Jews were rounded up in Amsterdam, and it was remarkable how quietly they went. Most of them had clearly been expecting the raid and were fully packed and prepared. So were the Germans, who mounted special guards at the railway station. The people of Amsterdam, normally so "pro-Jewish", remained quite passive on this occasion. Otto Bene tells us that when it became known that two prominent Jews had managed to slip through the German net, many of the less fortunate ones became greatly incensed and demanded the immediate dissolution of the Jewish Council "which, under the cover of neighbourly love, is merely trying to save its own skin". Bene also declared that the Jewish Council looked upon the whole operation as a "Jewish Dunkirk". Another German made similar observations and also spoke of the "smooth" course of events; thus, a Jewish doctor who tried to swallow a dose of cyanide had the poison snatched from his mouth by a vigilant policeman. Unfortunately when the air-raid sirens sounded at 2 p.m. some Jews managed to escape across the roofs. We also know that Voûte, the Burgomaster of Amsterdam, was deeply offended that he, as the highest authority in the capital, had not been informed of the raid well in advance; as a result of the unexpected operation, a number of municipal services had been disrupted.

A Jewish view of the raid was given by Gertrud van Tijn[1] who lived right in the heart of the Jewish quarter. She tells us that from midnight, policemen and soldiers in SS uniform, armed to the teeth, poured in, as though into battle. The Great Synagogue was used as a registry; most of the people had to spend the rest of the night and part of the following day in the square outside. According to her, this "punitive raid" rid the Jewish quarter of most of its residents; after that it was as quiet as the grave.

On May 27 the two Presidents informed Lages, Aus der Fünten and Blumenthal that the raid had played havoc with their organization, and asked for the recall of a number of colleagues who, though absolutely indispensable, had been sent to Westerbork. Lages refused. When asked how he expected the Jewish Council to do its work with untrained personnel, he replied that Germany had the same problem in war-time. But there was the usual salve: the assurance that "the operation was over" and that "for the moment" there were no plans for any further action. "We were given permission to divulge this news."

This was precisely what the Presidents did at the meeting of the Jewish Council on June 2. Professor Cohen had already assured the Central Committee at its meeting on May 28 that "the German authorities attached great importance to the continued work of the Jewish Council".

On June 5, 1943, the Presidents met Lages again, and he repeated his assurances. "We told him that we were extremely grateful for this wonderful news and only regretted that he was unable to give any guarantees in the matter."

On June 18 the Central Committee expressed its great satisfaction that Lages' "reassuring declaration still held"—two days before the next raid.

This was the "big offensive" of June 20, which did so much to carry off the great bulk of the Jews living in East and South Amsterdam. In his report of June 25 Otto Bene boasted of the remarkable way in which the preparations for this raid were kept secret, with the result that the Jews were taken completely by surprise. The *Merkblatt für die Raumungskommandos* (Memo to Evacuation Commandos) ordered that all the victims were to be taken to specified assembly points. Only those whose identity cards bore numbers in the series 10,000, 30,000 and 100,000, or red 'J's' were to be spared.

[1] G. van Tijn-Cohn: *op. cit.*, pp. 59 ff.

White arm-bands issued by the Jewish Council did not themselves protect the wearers. All persons whose identity cards were not in order or who looked like Jews must be brought along as well, together with Jewish-owned bicycles, motor-cycles, radios and pets. Every place had to be searched, but closed shops must not be broken into unless there were special grounds for suspicion. "Every consideration must be shown to premises and barracks occupied by the *Wehrmacht*, the Security Police and other German departments." The reader may make of this what he will. Hospitals were to be left alone, but bed-ridden Jews elsewhere must be brought to the assembly points. "Aryans" had to be kept indoors throughout the operation.

We gain the impression that the Germans set to work with their usual thoroughness. Perhaps one incident deserves special mention: the fact that when Asscher cycled home, he was repeatedly stopped by the German police.[1] "Just before I came to Schubert Street, I began to get fed up with it all and told one of them that I had been showing my identity card so many times in a few hundred yards that I was sick and tired of it all. He then hit me on the nose and it began to bleed. I got hold of him by the throat, and punched him several times until he went down. A group of soldiers then placed me under arrest. What pleased me most about this whole episode was that a large number of people, watching from the windows in Rubens Street, shouted encouragement and asked me to come inside." When Asscher was brought before Aus der Fünten on Olympia Square, he was told "that they were not going to arrest me, but as I had once again proved a danger to the peace of Amsterdam, I must keep away from the vicinity that day". On arriving home, Asscher apparently found his house crowded with all sorts of people wanting his help. "To my sorrow I had to tell them that there was nothing I could do for anyone with these German barbarians."

From the assembly point, the Germans drove their victims to Muiderpoort Station; as at Apeldoorn, they used Jewish OD men as auxiliaries. According to several eye-witnesses, that evening was particularly harrowing. When Professor Cohen arrived at 6 p.m., a heavy rainstorm broke, forcing all those present to take shelter. "Our dear Lord apparently made no distinction between Aryans and Jews." He added:

"We were all sitting together on little chairs at tables. Opposite

[1] Examination of A. Asscher, November 8, 1947.

me sat someone I did not know. Whenever I went to a raid, I used to slip into my pocket a book called *Die Tröstung Israels* (The consolation of Israel), which contained the prophecies of Isaiah, in Hebrew on one side and in the Buber-Rosenzweig translation on the other. I now turned to it in the twilight, and the man opposite asked me what I was reading. When I told him, he began to intone '*Tröste, tröste, Jerusalem*' (Comfort ye, O comfort ye Jerusalem). Since he was obviously from the *Zentralstelle*, I was most astonished, and began talking to him about anti-Semitism, its hideous consequences and our sufferings. I afterwards understood that he was a former pastor, who had become the head of Calmeyer's department in the *Zentralstelle* (his name was Schellenberg)."[1]

Speaking of the chaos at the station, Professor Cohen said: "The ghastliness of the scenes enacted by these desperate people devoid of all hope was indescribable . . . Even on the platform I pleaded with Lages to exempt this one and that, but all in vain; I had to watch the last of these wretched men leave for their final destination with a few miserable bits and pieces."

To their penultimate destination rather, for they went first to Westerbork. Here, as Otto Bene reported, these ex-officials were greeted with "undisguised glee" by the earlier arrivals, many of whom expressed their regret "that the top brass and particularly Asscher and Cohen, had not been thrown in along with their minions".

Bene revelled in the fact that the latest "round-the-clock operation" had bagged a further 5,550 Jews, bringing the total up to 100,000. The only Jews not in custody now, were those married to non-Jews, foreigners, Jews whose pedigree was still being investigated and a small number with special stamps. This glowing picture was somewhat spoiled by the fact that some 20,000 had gone into hiding, but fortunately, according to Bene, the "number of anonymous informers has gone up".

The top brass, as we have said, remained in Amsterdam—but only for another three months, during which time they alternated between hope and despair, optimism and misgivings, rebelliousness and resignation. There were rumours that the war would be over within a week, that the Allied invasion was about to start, that the Germans would exempt the Jewish leaders once and for all—Aus der Fünten had said so, Lages had said so, Wörlein had said so,

[1] Cohen: *Herinneringen*, p. 104.

Blumenthal had said so. Immediately after the raid of June 20, the two Presidents resumed their daily routine, and above all, initiated a series of talks with Aus der Fünten, with a view to obtaining the release of as many officials as possible. Professor Cohen went to Westerbork, where he heard many complaints from former colleagues, all of them deeply distressed at the appalling conditions in this now overcrowded camp (a state of affairs that naturally "improved" as the camps were gradually cleared). Aus der Fünten conceded ten exemptions to be picked at the Jewish leaders' discretion. After long discussions, they finally agreed on the names. The lucky ones were released but picked up again soon afterwards. Not a single one of them has survived—just one more illustration of German magnanimity.

After the raid Aus der Fünten also expressed the view that the number of Jewish Council employees ought to be a fixed proportion of the total Jewish population. There had formerly been 140,000 Jews and 17,000 exemptions; now that only 14,000 Jews were left, no more than 1,700 people were needed to look after their interests. By "mistake", Aus der Fünten put that figure down as 170, and when this was pointed out to him he refused to correct the error. As a result, the Jewish Council found it exceedingly difficult to staff its several dozen offices and deal with all its manifold business. A document dating back to that period averred that, if only Aus der Fünten had come to see for himself, he would quickly have changed his mind. We rather doubt the truth of this assertion, the more so since, as Professor Cohen[1] himself has admitted, "all the essential work could be done with the smaller but excellent staff that remained to us". Not, we might add, without a host of recriminations, for we still have the official complaint of one department, to which seventeen employees had been allocated. This department had apparently "carried out its work unperturbed despite the nerve-racking times". And what was their reward? "We learned that a far larger number of staff had been assigned to departments, whose scheming members clearly preferred dissipating their energies on internal machinations to hard work on behalf of the community as a whole." After all sorts of petitions and threats, the Council appealed for a further thirty-five exemptions, listing them, not in alphabetical order, but "in order of importance". At the bottom of the list was the least important of all, an ordinary Jewish man (born on May 21, 1891);

[1] Cohen: *Herinneringen*, p. 107.

in the event, it would appear that he, too, was granted the necessary stamp, since, in the absence of Aus der Fünten, Wörlein was kind enough to increase the number of exemptions from 170 to a miraculous 2,800.

Alas, Aus der Fünten returned soon afterwards from Cologne, where—according to Professor Cohen—he had seen the destruction wrought by the Allies. It is said that in his rage at this and also at the "deceitful" behaviour of the Jews in his absence, he ordered the night raid on July 23, 1943, which was chiefly directed at the staff of the Jewish Council. Next morning began the usual bargaining—Aus der Fünten replying to even the best arguments with a shrug of his shoulders or with the remark that circumstances had changed. The train, scheduled to leave at 11 a.m., stood waiting in the station until 1.45 p.m., while a number of people from the Schouwburg were added to the passengers. Among them were several of the original 170.

"This blow completely destroyed the sense of security that had prevailed for the past fourteen days," said one of the leading officials of the Jewish Council on July 25. He added that if the Germans wished to restore confidence to any extent they would have to issue not just another stamp but one that could be "absolutely depended upon". The Council discussed this matter with Lages, Aus der Fünten and Blumenthal, who agreed to grant absolute immunity to a small number of officials, provided the Germans could have all the rest. "We asked to be allowed to make the choice ourselves, after consultation with the various departments. This was granted. We were then ordered to submit qualitative lists with the various groups in different colours." Things had come to a very pretty pass indeed.

The stamp "that could be absolutely depended upon" was apparently in the series 120,000. Since this was looked upon as the great panacea, we must give it a few words more.

The whole thing was a strange story and one, moreover, that cannot be fully reconstructed from the records. Herzberg[1] says it all began with a memorandum by Ribbentrop in February 1943, requesting that certain Jews should not be sent to the East but kept back for possible exchanges. A circular by Rademacher of February 20, 1943, specified the categories to be used for that purpose, namely Jews "having relatives, friends, political or commercial contacts with

[1] Herzberg: *op. cit.*, p. 125.

subjects of enemy states or with prominent contacts of Dutch or Belgian nationality in these states". Such Jews were naturally the *crème de la crème*, and it was with good reason that the victims believed that, since these people had been issued with stamps in the 120,000 series, everyone else with such stamps must be perfectly safe as well.

Though the whole thing was supposed to be on the top secret list, many Jewish officials came to know about it and tried to obtain the stamp by hook or by crook. Professor Cohen later declared that when the Germans freely offered the special stamp to himself and members of his family he saw no reason to refuse the offer; in fact, the records contain a letter which he wrote on July 6, 1943, requesting the special stamp for his future son-in-law, "as granted to my other son-in-law"; there is, moreover, a list dated February 22, 1943, with twenty-six members of his family—all duly issued with stamps in the 120,000-series. Professor Cohen afterwards explained that he had been ordered to submit this list. Asscher, too, was prompt to obey a similar order and to supply an ample list on March 1, 1943. Why were these two gentlemen so favoured? As Professor Cohen put it,[1] "simply to enable them to perform their important duties in the Jewish community without the threat to their own families constantly hanging over them". And what applied to them applied equally to the other high functionaries. Needless to say, less fortunate Jews took another view of the matter. By April 1943, altogether 300 of the special stamps had been issued. Thereafter the number increased rapidly. On June 11 Zöpf decided that Jews handing in diamonds should be promoted from 40,000 to the 120,000 category. There was a tremendous rush. Alas, these "economically important" Jews and others who brought similar offers were running after a mirage, for as Zöpf himself said during a discussion in June 1943, he never told the Jews precisely what protection the new stamp conferred; all he had done was to hint that those holding the stamp would not be sent for labour in the East. The stamps continued to be issued until September 27, 1943; two days later the 1,500 or so holders all disappeared to Westerbork.

But before then something else was to happen. On August 13 the Netherlands-Israelitic Hospital was evacuated; the Germans said it was because of a possible epidemic. A number of the staff managed to escape; 130 infectious cases and six nurses were allowed to transfer

[1] Examination on November 26, 1947.

to the Jewish Invalid Hospital (according to another source they numbered 153, of whom four died during the transfer); all the rest, staff and patients alike, were sent to Westerbork. The records contain a report about a woman who stayed stark naked in her bed all day pretending she was having a fit—"in the morning, the doctors had drawn blood from my arm and spattered it all over me". Also left behind were a baby in an incubator and a two-day-old in a crib. At an opportune moment, the blood-spattered woman rose from her bed with a scream, slipped past the astonished guards and dashed out of the hospital.

Control over the hospital and its equipment was given to the Director of the Jewish Invalid Hospital, which in its turn was emptied of most of its patients on September 17. Professor Cohen who was present at both incidents, calls the second by far the more horrible of the two, for here not even the most serious cases were spared. A top storey of the building was henceforth reserved for routine checks on Dutch prostitutes—working in the interests of the German soldiery; Jewish doctors, assisted by Jewish nurses, thus found temporary employment; on September 21 the Director was able to note the arrival of "our first popsy".

The general expulsion of the Jewish community followed on September 29, shortly before the Jewish New Year, and, according to Herzberg,[1] "undoubtedly chosen for that very reason". Did the Jews know what lay in store for them? Some afterwards said that they did, and quite a few in fact went into hiding. One witness has stated that the expulsion was "expected all over the country". Professor Cohen, however, contended that it was just another rumour. Professor Brahn, the head of the German Jewish *Beirat* (Advisory Council) was tipped off on September 28 by a German, who even offered him false papers in case he wanted to escape. This was one clear pointer and there were many others as well. Thus, Professor Cohen learned in the small hours of the morning that the Germans had alerted all "key-men"—members of the NSB collecting and holding the keys of evacuated Jewish houses. Perhaps the shrewd reader would also have realized that the Germans were up to no good from the mere fact that Aus der Fünten had expressly told one of his boon companions (whom he knew to have Jewish contacts) that nothing at all was planned for that day.

That night, the Germans dragged the most indispensable of all

[1] Herzberg: *op. cit.*, p. 117.

indispensables from their houses and took them to Amstel Station, where there was "indescribable pandemonium". Elsewhere too, the few remaining Jews were rounded up—the total liquidation of Dutch Jewry was about to be consummated. Professor Cohen, who went to the station of his own accord, was told by Aus der Fünten to wait in his home where a special car called for him a few hours later. Gertrud van Tijn[1] was also among those seized: "It was pitch dark when we left my home. I was carrying a very heavy rucksack and my escort took it from me without a word. Only when we came close to the lights of the station did he give it back to me. Neither he nor I said a single word about it." Within two hours, her friends found her home plundered of everything except the heavy furniture.

How many Jews were in fact rounded up that night? The estimates vary between 3,000 and 5,000. The only ones left behind were the "Portuguese Jews", the "Calmeyer Jews" (i.e. those whose descent was still being investigated), Jews married to non-Jews, and a few special cases. At the same time, some inmates of Westerbork were sent back to Amsterdam—"for the time being".

Professor Cohen[2] "was elated when at last he sat in the train for Westerbork. He had always felt awful at having to sit by while others were being carried off . . . He was glad also to be put into a large barracks. It was against his wishes that his friends later found him a better hut and then a little house to himself. He himself would much rather have remained in the large hut."

Cohen and Asscher had to act just once more as Presidents of the Jewish Council—when Aus der Fünten and the Camp Commandant told them that the Jewish Council was dissolved. This, according to Professor Cohen, was the end of Amsterdam, nay of Dutch, Jewry.

But in fact the end was not yet. There were still a few Dutch Jews left in the Netherlands and many more in camps elsewhere, and their long ordeal must still be chronicled.

[1] G. van Tijn-Cohn: *op. cit.*, p. 62.

[2] Statement to the Jewish Court of Honour, March 24, 1947.

CHAPTER FOUR

# THE STATE WITHIN A STATE

## FACTS AND FIGURES

WITH the last round-up—on September 29, 1943—and the subsequent dissolution of the Jewish Council—the Germans had put an end to their own creation: the Jewish enclave in the Netherlands. Even so, a few scattered Jews were left at large and these they plagued to their hearts' content with new measures, round-ups, releases, new round-ups and all sorts of humiliations. The only purpose, if any, of all this minor activity, was that those in charge could claim to be serving the *Führer* and the *Vaterland* at a safe distance from the front.

But first we must revert to the earlier history of the Jewish enclave, that state within a state. A German creation—the Jewish Council—had conjured into existence a network of special committees, whose members were sustained not only by a desire to serve the community but no doubt also by the belief that their work was so important that the Germans would be forced to spare them. In this way there arose a bureaucracy which, in its structure and activities, had something of the semblance of a government. Not, admittedly, a government of the kind that would have caused a Machiavelli or a Hobbes to put pen to paper, no *Leviathan* this, but yet a phenomenon interesting enough to deserve greater consideration than the brief summary we can give in such a work as ours.

It might seem that this summary should have been written in the factual and purely objective style of an encyclopaedic article. If we eschew this approach, it is not so much because the available data are too fragmentary as because the writer feels too close to the events to forget the human beings behind all the facts and figures—if one has been on board a sinking ship one cannot be content merely to count the drowned.

An encyclopaedic treatment of a state would normally begin with an account of its area—in our case an ever-decreasing one. At the beginning it covered practically the entire Netherlands, but in 1942 and 1943—as the Jews were herded into ever smaller confines —the territory kept shrinking until in the end it covered only Amsterdam, or rather, little more than three districts of that city. This was the last citadel but not the last act—this took place far from the soil of Holland, where the victims' ashes were blown across the wastes of conquered Poland.

It is in this framework that we must look at the German ghetto plans in general. They have been treated at some length by both Berkley and Herzberg. There is also a comparative study of Nazi-inspired ghettos throughout the world by P. Friedman[1] who shows, *inter alia*, that the Japanese, in response to a personal appeal by Hitler, set up a "special reserve" for stateless Jews in Shanghai in February 1942.

The word "reserve" is perhaps not quite appropriate when we consider that the Germans intended these places as mere preliminaries to "the final eradication of a plague". We cannot tell, of course, how far this was apparent to the lower ranks of the German hierarchy—in the Netherlands at least, they seem to have hesitated a great deal before liquidating the total Jewish population.

And yet ghettos had great advantages for the Germans, as we know from Herzberg's account of what went on in Poland, for instance. To begin with, it helped them to perscute, humiliate, blackmail and finally murder Jews in the most clandestine and unobtrusive way possible. In some countries the Germans may have abandoned all scruples from the outset, but not so in the Netherlands. A decree by Seyss-Inquart, a proclamation by Rauter, an order from Berlin, and Amsterdam too would have seen a Warsaw wall of the kind described by John Hersey, with the Jews inside and—who knows?—a Warsaw uprising at the end. Those wanting such a wall were *Generalkommissar* Schmidt and possibly Böhmcker as well. Those opposing it were Rauter and the *Wehrmacht*. Both Asscher[2] and Cohen[3] spoke after the war of the extraordinary efforts of Burgomaster Voûte in opposing the German plans. The Jewish Council itself drew up a lengthy report for the Germans, stressing the disadvantages that would accrue to the non-Jewish population from

[1] P. Friedman: "The Jewish Ghettos of the Nazi Era", *Jewish Social Studies*, part XVI, No. 1 (New York, 1954), pp. 61–88.

[2] Examination of A. Asscher on November 13, 1947.

[3] Cohen: *Herinneringen*, p. 20.

the establishment of a ghetto proper. This report was inordinately bulky, unusually well-documented and extraordinarily elaborate; three full folios were devoted to facts and figures showing what precise losses the town of Assen alone (31,000 inhabitants) would incur if the Jews of that town were sent to a ghetto in Amsterdam. The reader knows that the Jews were expelled from Assen despite these convincing figures, and we might add on the authority of Professor Cohen, that this excellent report and its remarkably clear tabulations simply helped the Germans in organizing the deportation with greater efficiency.

Herzberg[1] mentions that, as early as 1941, Böhmcker ordered a map of Amsterdam to be drawn with the Jewish quarters marked in red and all sorts of other useful details. Many similar maps were prepared in due course. On one, issued by the Amsterdam Municipal Bureau of Statistics in May 1941, the Jewish population of the various districts was given in blue figures, the non-Jewish in red; on another map prepared by the same Bureau in the same month, Jews were marked in red, non-Jews in blue. The second map also gave the percentage Jewish population in black figures, whereas the first map showed the Jewish population density by means of stipples. In September of that year the Public Works Department prepared yet another map, and so did the Germans. Herzberg saw a very close connection between the original ghetto plans and the creation of the Jewish Council—except that a Dutch ghetto never materialized.

In the preceding pages we have had many occasions to refer to what we have called the Germans' cat-and-mouse game. Here, if anywhere, we must mention a very minor aspect of this game, namely the eviction of Jews from various towns and provinces. We shall not go into the details, lest the reader lose himself in the indescribable confusion of regulations, revocations and amendments. Still, all these petty persecutions led remorselessly to one end: the concentration of Jews in three districts of Amsterdam, one in the Centre, one in the East and one in the South; in this connection there arose a whole new terminology, and a host of different German "removal orders".

Now in February 1943, there were "voluntary" and compulsory removal orders. What could the term "voluntary removal order" possibly mean? Well, if an Amsterdam Jew wished to move out of his home "for whatever reasons", he could apply to the Jewish

[1] Herzberg: *op. cit.*, pp. 80–1.

Council for a "voluntary order" to go to East Amsterdam; once applied for, this voluntary order became a compulsory one and, moreover, irrevocable. Compulsory removal orders, on the other hand, were supplied by the *Zentralstelle* quite unsolicited. In March it appeared that the whole matter needed further clarification. Nevertheless, the warning was reiterated that the regulations must be strictly observed and that it was best to consult the relevant departments of the Jewish Council "so as to avoid serious difficulties". Today, it is hardly possible to imagine what stampedes, what masses of paper, what anxieties, all this involved. Whole bundles of such compulsory orders have been preserved: forms printed in two languages and bearing the names of all those ordered out and of their families, together with the instruction to leave the present homes at short notice, to repair to a new address in East Amsterdam —clearly the cat had no wish to lose sight of its mice. There was hardly a single Jew who did not have friends, neighbours and relations spirited away in this fashion.

Outside Central, South and East Amsterdam there was yet another, miniature, Jewish quarter—Asterdorp, in the far north of the city. The place looked like an enormous bunker and had, in fact, been specially built in the twenties for the isolation and rehabilitation of asocial elements. It was easily surrounded and cut off. In the spring of 1942, and not without a great deal of chicanery, a number of non-Dutch Jews were taken there; they were later turned out to make room for their Dutch brothers. The whole thing was a kind of miniature Westerbork though, oddly enough, those "interned" there had quite tolerable living conditions and even a fairly full social life; the writer recalls visiting Asterdorp in May 1943 and being told that many of the "residents" would be quite content to stay there until the end of the war. The Germans, of course, had other plans, and from a document of June 3, 1943, it appears that, by then, a large number of the internees had gone into hiding: only 112 were left. All these were suddenly ordered to East Amsterdam whence, just as abruptly, they were moved on to Westerbork. The documents contain a number of references to one Marianne van Stedum; some speak of her as a saintly woman who, a former housemaid herself, well knew how to minister to the poor.[1] When she was sent to Westerbork, the Jewish Council declared her indispensable and

[1] G. van Tijn-Cohn: *op. cit.*, pp. 50–1; Letter by Professor Cohen to G. van Tijn-Cohn on September 14, 1943.

asked for her return, but the *Zentralstelle* apparently "forgot" to hand on the Council's request to the camp authorities. In any case, Marianne van Stedum was bundled onto the train "for Germany" and taken off again on two occasions; the third time she herself refused to leave the train because she had promised her dying mother that she would not desert her sister.

One last remark about the "removals". The Jews were being ordered into Amsterdam at a time when there was a general housing shortage, and when the German authorities were being pestered for houses by a host of non-Jews as well. Many of these applications and complaints have been preserved; in general they do not make edifying reading. "The Jew (so and so) still living at such and such an address is married to an Aryan woman with a small daughter"—so began one applicant, adding that this Jew had sold much of his furniture (which, of course, was forbidden) and that his house was almost empty. The writer concluded: "We have not been very successful in getting them out because the wife is not a Jewess. But ought not such people be treated as Jews?" The letter ended on the confident note: "In any case I hope that, whatever her position, you will be able to do something for us." Another applicant described himself as "an old pioneer of the purest National Socialism"—his application was endorsed by Wörlein himself.

From what we have said, the reader may have gathered that the tragedy of Dutch Jews was virtually confined to Amsterdam. We did, of course, mention The Hague, Rotterdam, Enschede, Utrecht and Haarlem, but only very occasionally. However, it should not be forgotten that Amsterdam was not the whole of Holland, and that outside the city there were many Jews whose fate must never be forgotten.

Jews and non-Jews alike who have spoken of these unhappy people, have done so with sadness and dismay, compassion and regret. They all draw much the same picture: ruin and desolation, Jewish homes occupied by strangers, sacred buildings used as stores, no gravestones later than 1943. The writer has walked through some of these provincial cemeteries in numb silence: where are the many dead, where is justice?

Roughly speaking, one-third of Dutch Jewry lived outside Amsterdam in 1940. Did the war, when it came, strike at them as it did at their brothers in the capital? Not at first, it would seem. They enjoyed more peace, felt less persecuted and far less anxious. Here

Dr Gerda Kautsky-Brunn. 8. Juli 1942
Amsterdam Z.
Corellistraat 18

**Persönlich**

45 811

An Herrn Dr Seyss-Inquart,
Reichskommissar für die
besetzten Niederländischen
Gebiete.

Gestatten Sie, dass ich mich in einer für mich lebenswichtigen Angelegenheit an Sie wende. Sie erinnern sich vielleicht noch meines Mannes, Dr Benedikt Kautsky, der nun das fünfte Jahr in Buchenwald interniert ist.
Ich wohne seit 1938 mit meiner Schwiegermutter und meinen beiden Töchtern in Holland. Seitdem wir unser Familienoberhaupt entbehren müssen, ist der Zusammenhalt von uns vier Menschen der einzige Inhalt unseres Lebens geworden.
Die Einstellung in den Arbeitsdienst bedroht unser Zusammenbleiben. Freunde aus Schweden haben uns schon öfter den Antrag gestellt, uns eine Einreise dahin zu ermöglichen.
Darf ich nun an Sie die ganz grosse Bitte stellen, uns die Ausreise von hier zu ermöglichen. Es handelt sich um meine 78 jährige Schwiegermutter, meiner 17 und 18 jährigen Töchter und um mich. Darf ich vielleicht noch dazu bemerken, dass mein Schwiegervater rein arischer Abstammung war, meine Schwiegermutter nie der jüdischen Glaubensgenossenschaft angehört hat, ebensowenig wie meine beiden Töchter, die christlich erzogen sind.
Sie würden durch Ihre gütige Hilfe den Fortbestand der Familie meines Mannes sichern und darum bitte ich sie von ganzem Herzen.

Ergebenst
G Kautsky-Brunn

An den
Befehlshaber der Sicherheitspolizei und des SD
Den Haag
zur weiteren Veranlassung. Der Herr Reichskommissar ist in der Angelegenheit nicht interessiert.

Den Haag, 11. Juli 1942.

[stamp:] BdS ... Den Haag ... Eing. 15 JULI 1942

IV B 4

55/42

Petition by Gerda Kautsky-Brunn, daughter-in-law of Karl Kautsky, the well-known Socialist theoretician, for an emigration permit. Neither her mother-in-law nor her two daughters have ever belonged to the Jewish community. Seyss-Inquart's comment: "Not interested".

and there, however, in their reminiscences we find echoes of a growing sense of insecurity and isolation. But let us turn to the tell-tale figures. There is, for instance, the *Statistical Record of Persons of Jewish Blood in the Netherlands* compiled in 1942 by the Central Population Office. It was based on returns under Decree No. 6 of 1941 of the *Reichskommissar* for the Occupied Netherlands. Pages 6 to 18 are devoted to Table 1, in which Dutch towns and villages are listed by size of population. The number of Dutch and foreign Jews in each is shown. There were altogether 566 places with "full-Jews, half-Jews and quarter-Jews". Right at the top came Amsterdam and at the very bottom Papekob, a parish of 425 souls including one Dutch half-Jew; immediately above that came Schelluinen, 474 souls, with one full-Jewess—neither Dutch nor German; and above that again Ruwiel (580 souls with one German full-Jewess). As we read these figures, can we still imagine the life of the real people they expressed: a quarter-Jewess in Heel and Panheel, one full-Jewess in Posterholt?

And yet, we need the figures to gain an overall picture. To complete it, the writer has largely drawn on the work of Dr. A. Vedder, Dr. F. Grewel and Dr. A. Pais; their conclusions, which are only provisional and uncertain in several respects, are based on the census of 1930, the last comprehensive survey of the Jewish population in the Netherlands before 1940. It would appear that, in 1930, the Netherlands had a Jewish population of 111,917, made up of 106,723 (95·4 per cent) "German" Jews (Ashkenazis) and 5,194 (4·6 per cent) "Portuguese" Jews (Sephardis). Of the grand total, 82 per cent lived in the six largest cities; our own calculations suggest that this percentage had dropped to 75 per cent by 1941. The proportion of Jews in the whole population dropped from 2·15 per cent in 1889 to 1·41 per cent in 1930, the reasons for which do not concern us here. However, there are good grounds for supposing that the real number of Jews was greater, indeed very much greater, than the figures suggest, for the census of 1930 was based on religious affiliation and many Jews had registered "none". It must also be noted that, after 1933, many Jewish refugees settled in the Netherlands, thus swelling the numbers.[1]

[1] Dr. A. Vedder: 'Demografie van de Joden in Nederland' in *Nieuw Israelitisch Weekblad*, October 5, 1956; Arie Pais: 'De Joden in Nederland' in *De Joodse Wachter*, January 25, 1952; Dr. F. Grewel: 'De Joden van Amsterdam' in *Mens en Maatschappij* vol. XXX (1950), pp. 338–50.

The Germans, on the other hand, were not so much concerned with religion as with "race". We have already had much to say of this, and, in particular, have mentioned some of the results of their enquiry on October 1, 1941. We shall not dwell upon the incompatibilities of the two investigations, but simply tabulate the main results of the second:

| | *Male Jews* | *Female Jews* |
|---|---|---|
| Dutch | 56,970 | 61,029 |
| German | 7,106 | 7,275 |
| Other Nationalities | 3,975 | 3,646 |
| | 68,051 | 71,950 |

If we sum it all up, we arrive at the following number of "full Jews" in the Netherlands on October 1, 1941:

| | |
|---|---|
| Dutch Jews: | 117,999 |
| German Jews: | 14,381 |
| Other nationalities | 7,621 |
| | 140,001 |

In what follows we shall use the round figure of 140,000. (This figure excludes the 7,510 male half-Jews, 7,385 female half-Jews, 2,985 male quarter-Jews, and 3,005 female quarter-Jews.)

## THE REFUGEES FROM GERMANY AND AUSTRIA

Our picture of the Jewish communities in the Netherlands would be incomplete without further reference to the many German refugees who entered Holland after 1933, some directly and others by more circuitous routes. "I am now rebuilding my life for the fourth time," said one of them who had reached Amsterdam by way of Vienna and Prague, and who was to end his life in Auschwitz after a brief stay in Westerbork. And one more fortunate, who was able to build up yet a fifth life, had this to say: "Where do I belong? I am a German. I am a Jew. I am an American. I am a writer. I am a professor. Where do I belong?"[1]

In his book, *Zwervend en dolend* (Rambling and Roving), Professor Cohen has dealt at length with the history of these wanderers prior

[1] Ludwig Marcuse: *Mein zwanzigstes Jahrhundert* (My twentieth century) (Munich, 1960), p. 368.

to 1940. The present author cannot continue their story in the same detail since, by the very nature of this work, he must confine himself to the general catastrophe of Dutch Jewry. Perhaps one day someone will give them the particular attention they deserve. But at least, what we can say of them here will be said in a spirit of deepest sympathy. It is not without compassion that this writer remembers the sad fate of so many of them, not without pity that he mourns the loss of such excellent men, not without gratitude that he remembers their kindness. This group, too, counted but few, very few, heroes or saints. It, too, included weak and faltering elements who, under the pressure of circumstances, gave in to all sorts of temptations. We wish to make no excuses for these. However, let us get back to the figures.

On October 1, 1941, some 14,500 people put themselves down as Jews of German nationality; 85 per cent of these had come to Holland after January 30, 1933, i.e. after the beginning of the Hitler régime. There were also Jews of many other nationalities and 7,000 stateless ones. Approximately 7,000 of all these immigrants lived in Amsterdam; a fairly large number of them were also found in Utrecht, Hilversum, The Hague, Arnhem and Enschede, but there were remarkably few in Rotterdam. After the invasion in May 1940, all these people were faced with a string of special regulations; one of these was the compulsory registration, on June 28, 1940, of all people who had entered Holland between January 1, 1933, and March 1, 1938. The Germans even considered sending all Jewish immigrants to Westerbork straight away, but had to drop the idea because of practical difficulties. On August 21, 1940, they asked for a list of all Jewish refugees who had become Dutch citizens by virtue of naturalization or marriage. On September 4 German and stateless Jews (with a number of other foreign groups) were ordered out of the coastal area, including The Hague. The raid of February 1941 helped to catch many German Jews; the June raid was chiefly directed at them. On December 5 came the order that all non-Dutch Jews had to report for "voluntary" emigration to the *Zentralstelle für jüdische Auswanderung* and that they must submit detailed lists of all their possessions. German Jews predominated among those called up for the first transports "to Germany" on July 15, 1942.

These are just a few facts out of many; the writer does not pretend to be able to draw a full picture of all the unspeakable suffering they entailed. It was not exactly a privilege to be a Dutch Jew in those days but it was still vastly better than being a German Jew, whom the Nazis considered natural guinea-pigs and whom they had already plagued in the Fatherland. Anxious for their families, often scattered over the face of the earth, subject to all sorts of humiliating regulations, hounded from pillar to post—one can only admire the way so many managed to carry on at all. To make matters worse, some—though by no means all—Dutch Jews kept their distance from them, much as the German Jews had formerly kept aloof from their Polish brethren. It is a sad fact, but one that is well documented, that many Dutch Jews mistrusted their German coreligionists and even hated them in a way that was almost anti-Semitic. We might add in parenthesis that Zionists had no such reservations.

What particularly annoyed so many Dutch Jews was the alleged ease with which German Jews insinuated themselves into key positions. They seemed to work much too assiduously for the invader and, in the circumstances, stood out like so many sore thumbs.

The leaders of the Jewish Council realized that something would have to be done to heal this rift, and even considered setting up a special commission to promote harmony. This was, no doubt, also the reason why a special *Beirat* (Advisory Council for non-Dutch Jews) was formed, with ten, and later twenty, non-Dutch Jews on its committee. The chairman was the eminent Professor M. Brahn, a man of nearly seventy, whom the writer remembers with very great respect. The first time Professor Brahn attended a meeting of the Jewish Council was on July 9, 1942, and here, too, he was held in high regard. He was arrested "by mistake" on December 24, 1943, sent to Theresienstadt and thence to a gas-chamber. Before then, and particularly from October 1942, Professor Brahn and his secretary, Dr. H. Eisner, were always available for consultation in two special rooms allocated to them by the Jewish Council. The committee also included the two German Zionist leaders, Dr. A. Klee and Dr. H. Goslar—Jews from Eastern Europe were represented by Dr. B. Mahler and Dr. J. Tauber. It is said that the *Beirat* often took strong exception to the policy of the Jewish Council and its administration. The writer still has a great feeling of warmth for one of its members, H. Bier, a former German civil servant from Cologne, who even in Westerbork continued to clutch his familiar briefcase. He died of blood-poisoning from the rusty wire while trying to pick a few flowers. Bier was the guiding spirit of a cultural centre in Amsterdam, an island of humanity in a sea of despair; it is almost incredible what was made possible there by his inspiring influence. That influence prevailed until July 1943, then the centre was closed by the Germans.

### OTHER GROUPS

When it came to the treatment of non-Dutch and non-German Jews in the Netherlands, we find that the German authorities at home and abroad, though often at loggerheads, were always agreed on one point: that their common enemy was the Jew, of whatever nationality he might be. If, nevertheless, they discriminated in favour of some categories, it was purely from fear of reprisals and for reasons of economic expediency. In any case, those German departments in the Netherlands expecially charged with the "solution" of the Jewish problem and the *Reichssicherheitshauptamt* (Reich Security Centre) had to keep in constant touch with the German Foreign Office, lest any offence be caused to foreign governments.

Who were these foreign Jews? There are no records from which we can cull a full answer. The nearest we can come to one is by consulting the *Statistical Record of Persons of Jewish Blood in the Netherlands* already mentioned. On p. 18 we find that on October 1, 1941, the Jewish population, excluding Dutch and German Jews, consisted of:

3,975 male and 3,646 female Jews
230 male and 207 female half-Jews
67 male and 58 female quarter-Jews

—making a total of 8,183. A small summary on pp. 38–9 gives us some idea of the varied composition of this Jewish group; there were eleven Argentinians and quite a few citizens of Paraguay and Honduras—whose number kept increasing during the war for reasons to be explained later. Several of the forty-five nationalities represented were numbered in ones and twos: there was one female Finn and one male Esthonian, eight Bulgarians, two Japanese, one Jew from New South Wales, two from Uruguay and one from Luxembourg.

Another table, compiled in 1942, shows that Amsterdam harboured Jews from such diverse places as Haiti, Honduras, Nicaragua, San Domingo, Guatemala and other exotic countries. Here, too, the list was topped by the Argentinians. On March 23, 1943, the Germans announced that "for obvious political reasons no disabilities whatsoever must be imposed" on this inviolable group. The announcement added that "as little publicity as possible must be given to this exemption, so as not to arouse claims from other neutrals . . . The temporary granting of immunity to Jews of Argentinian nationality is unavoidable, lest the Argentinian Government be given grounds for submitting to the importunities of our enemies and make common cause with them against Germany." In January 1944, Berlin ordered the arrest and transportation to Bergen-Belsen of all Argentinian Jews in France[1] (nineteen altogether); despite allegations to the contrary, it would appear that a similar order was not sent to The Hague, for from a memorandum by Otto Bene, dated July 20, 1944, we gather that the eleven Argentinian and several other foreign Jews were still "at large" in the Netherlands. The memorandum went on to say that "it would be a good thing if we could send them packing too, even though they are giving us no trouble and are behaving themselves". However, another report[2] states that nine Argentinian Jews from Westerbork were found in Belsen in 1944. We have not attempted to get to the bottom of this matter.

All these foreign Jews were, in any case, earmarked for the *Heimschaffungsaktion 1943* (Repatriation Plan 1943),[3] something of a misnomer, since what Eichmann really had in mind was to send them not home but to the gas-chamber. The only spoke in the wheel was, as we have said, the German Foreign Office, which constantly entreated the governments of Neutral and Allied States to recall their own Jews, lest they be treated like the rest.

In general, the Germans distinguished between three large groups of Jews: those from friendly states, those from neutral states and those from hostile states. In the course of 1943 it was decided to repatriate those in the first of these three categories. Swiss Jews were apparently treated with kid gloves until February 1, 1943, when the Germans proposed "in the interests of their own security", to apply the same regulations to them as to Dutch Jews; a later circular stipulated the conditions governing the transfer of Swiss-Jewish property from Holland, and a document of February 19, 1943, reported that on February 9, 11 and 13, sixteen Swiss Jews left for Basle via Heidelberg. Several Swiss Jews from Holland were, however, sent to Bergen-Belsen.[4] The repatriation of the Danes was scheduled for

[1] *Le Monde Juif* (Paris, June 1960), p. 48.
[2] E. Kolb: *Bergen-Belsen . . . 1943-45* (Hanover, 1962), p. 66.
[3] *Ibid*, pp. 22 ff.
[4] *Ibid.*, p. 24.

February 27; they comprised the households of two mixed marriages, making seven persons in all. Next came the turn of the Liberians, who must have caused the Germans quite a headache. They were first mentioned on August 10, 1942, when three Liberian men applied for permission to take their wives and (four) children to Switzerland. Their passports were "perfectly valid", as Bene discovered; nevertheless, Friedrich Knolle of the Security Service felt that there were "grave security reasons" against the transfer. The Hague then instructed Lages to leave them alone. That was probably the end of the matter for, on February 19, they were still "at large" in Amsterdam. On March 23, 1943, a letter from Berlin told Bene that Liberian Jews, of whom there were so few anyway, might be used for advantageous exchanges of prisoners.

Herzberg[1] has called the treatment of Russian Jews "almost droll". The Netherlands had never recognized the Soviet Union, so that those Jews who had settled in Holland before 1917 were still considered subjects of the Tsar and, under Tsarist law, they could never lose their Russian nationality. Things were further complicated by the fact that Germany, unlike Holland, did recognize the Soviet Union; as a result of this "conundrum in international law" (Herzberg), the Germans continued to leave these Jews unharmed "for quite a long time", although as Russians-cum-Jews they must have been doubly odious to them. It was not without irony that Bene[2] could write of these people that, whereas they had previously kept their Soviet citizenship secret, "now that Dutch Jews were being deported from Holland in large numbers, they could not protest it enough". Here and there Jewish women of Russian origin and married to Dutch Jews used this opportunity to pass their unions off as mixed marriages; the author can still remember how several of their offspring, unmistakably Jewish in appearance, were removed from the Jewish Lyceum, one in the middle of a lesson, after the headmaster had been given telephonic instructions to send them to a non-Jewish school.

Not all foreign Jews were equally fortunate. Worst off were citizens of countries allied to Germany, though the Germans did not treat even these alike. What with having to distinguish between Jews from allied, neutral and hostile states, the German Foreign

[1] Herzberg: *op. cit.*, p. 123.

[2] Letter to the Commander of the German Security Police on August 17, 1942.

Office got into endless difficulties. This is well illustrated by the cases of Turkish and Hungarian Jews. The former enjoyed special protection until January 1, 1943, when Berlin informed Ankara that all privileges would be withdrawn. Many of them who, by Turkish law, could lose their Turkish nationality after being abroad for five years, were in very great danger of deportation to the East. References to them occurred throughout 1943 and also during 1944. Thus a letter of March 16, 1944, mentioned the names of twenty-four Turkish Jews who had been sent to Westerbork and whose Turkish nationality the Germans refused to recognize. The letter was signed by Zöpf, who also contended that these Jews were nothing but stateless people and, as such, "ought to go East with the very next transport".

As for Hungarian Jews, their interests were "protected" by a "Hungarian representative" in Amsterdam (as he is called in one of the documents), who did his best to collaborate with the Germans. In a letter of July 3, 1942, Bene insisted that something would have to be done about the 193 people concerned—they must either be sent back to Hungary or treated as stateless persons. Bene returned to the subject the very next day, when Berlin told him confidentially that the Hungarian Government had let it be known that they did not care what became of these Jews. Needless to say, their possessions were confiscated there and then, and Bene informed the *Generalkommissar* for Finance and Economics accordingly. The precise fate of these unfortunate people is not clear, though we hear a good deal of them throughout 1943, for instance, the report on August 20 that some were on a transport to Budapest—probably on a round-about route to the gas-chamber.

Other Jews made more or less fictitious claims to Latin American citizenship. Thus in a letter dated July 3 Bene complained of the presence of one "highly undesirable and provocative Latin American Jew", whom he himself knew to have come from Düsseldorf. "We should be glad to get rid of him," the letter ended.

From the last sentence we may gather that the German authorities in Holland had been expressly told to keep their hands off Latin American Jews. No wonder, then, that so many Dutch and particularly stateless Jews gave out that they were of South American nationality, and that one cynic referred to Camp Westerbork as the capital of Honduras. One of the inmates was said to be in possession of seven passports, all issued by South American countries, whose capitals he kept mixing up. And so Jews tried desperately to become citizens of Bolivia, Paraguay and Haiti—though they could not always spell these names correctly. The passports were smuggled to them from abroad, or forged in Holland. Forgery had, in fact, become a large-scale industry, as we know, for instance, from Lidya Winkel: "Eduard Veterman, the author, was a specialist on Brazilian documents—though he had never been there; the sculptor Gerrit van der Veen was an expert on Paraguay, Poland and Czarist Russia. Frans Duwaer, the printer, gave them the authentic appearance of age."[1]

We get the impression,[2] that it was thanks to these forgeries that many Jews survived the holocaust; a study of this subject reports that 200 "Latin Americans" were released from Bergen-Belsen and sent to Philippeville, Algeria, via Switzerland, in exchange for German prisoners; other sources given further instances. Did these Jews really succeed in fooling Berlin? On November 11 the German Foreign Office informed Bene that the possession of a Paraguayan passport was no proof of Paraguayan citizenship, but that Jews with such passports must nevertheless be detained for possible exchanges against German citizens in Paraguay. If such exchanges could not be effected, there was time enough to treat them like ordinary Jews. On June 26, 1943, Eichmann wrote to Zöpf: "Though it is undesirable that Jews otherwise designated for deportation should acquire such nationalities by legitimate means, there is nothing we can do about it." At a later stage[3] the German Foreign Office intervened once more in the hope that the Latin American countries concerned might be persuaded to release German internees even against these pseudo-compatriots. In fact, many "citizens" of Honduras and Paraguay survived in Bergen-Belsen to the end; some were, in fact, released by way of exchange.

There were also a number of cases of double nationality; thus Wielek[4] reports that many women born in England, married to Dutchmen, and thus entitled to hold Dutch passports, yet retained British nationality. Moreover, the story went round[5] that in the

[1] Lidya Winkel: "Papieren vervalsen om te leven" (Forging papers for life) in *Den Vaderland getrouwe* (Amsterdam, 1962), p. 146.

[2] *Yad Washem Studies on the European catastrophe and resistance*, Part I (Jerusalem, 1957), pp. 151–2.

[3] E. Kolb: *Bergen-Belsen*, pp. 49–51.

[4] Wielek: *op. cit.*, pp. 266–9.

[5] J. T. Veldkamp: *Het Amsterdamse Bevokingsregister in Oorlogstijd* (The Dutch Population Record in War-time), p. 12; E. Kolb: *Bergen-Belsen*, p. 59.

1880s a Jewish police superintendent in Amsterdam had given Jewish criminals the tip to disappear to England; when there was no longer a danger of legal proceedings, these men had returned with their children who, though British by birth, had been issued with Dutch papers by the Public Records Office in Amsterdam. The Swiss Consul-General, who looked after the interests of American and British Jews, took many of these doubtful cases under his wing, and the Germans could do nothing about it, except have the Consul recalled for his "pro-Jewish bias".

Yet double nationality was not devoid of dangers, either. Thus during the winding up of Westerbork in 1942–3, the charm had worn off. Indeed, double nationality now became a handicap, inasmuch as those who insisted on it were simply packed off, regardless of the merits of their case. In general, the German authorities became highly sceptical of the authenticity of foreign passports held by Jews. A draft article of April 4, 1944, gave a list of such people, with the heading "Jews returning to their so-called 'homelands' ". In point of fact, the list was a very short one: 8 Danes, 1 Finn, 17 Italians, 10 Swedes, 18 Swiss, 1 Spaniard and 78 Hungarians.

Herzberg has asked whether the Allies could not have done more than merely shed tears for all these foreign Jews, not to mention the rest. The present writer can only echo that question.

## THE CAMPS AT ELLEKOM, AMERSFOORT, SCHOORL, OMMEN AND DOETINCHEM

We must now tell the reader something about a number of Dutch camps, of which we have so far said little or nothing, and which ranged from the relatively permissive (Doetinchem) to the strictly repressive (Ellekom).

"One hundred and seventy-five people have been sent for relief work to the camp at Ellekom, where an SS police school is quartered. No further details are known." Thus read the minutes of a meeting of the Central Committee of the Jewish Council on September 4, 1942, and this is the first mention we have of the camp. The last was found in the minutes of the same body and was dated November 27, 1942: "A number of utterly exhausted workers arrived (in Westerbork) from Ellekom."

This camp was officially known as *Palestine* and sometimes as *New Palestine*, which conjures up images of milk and honey. Unfortunately, Amsterdam was unable to verify this image, since the place was hermetically sealed off from the outside world in general and the Jewish Council in particular. Relatives were sent the usual postcard, of which Wielek[1] quotes a typical example: "I am very well indeed. We get lots to drink and eat, and it all tastes good."

But, as we have said, the place was, in fact, a training school for the Dutch SS, where professional torturers were given expert instruction, learning within a few months how to work over defenceless victims, how to drive them to the point of exhaustion, starve them, beat them with sticks and whips and prod them with bayonets. "Now and then a German boxer would appear, using human beings as punch-bags." Let us quote an eye-witnesses of the arrival of a batch of wretches in Westerbork:

"*November 21, 1942*. These people were hardly recognizable as human beings. They looked more like walking skeletons. Skin and bones. Utterly spent. So thin that they could hardly stand up. In the reception department, they were given helpings of porridge, and when they saw the food, they could hardly restrain themselves. They fell upon it like wild beasts." Another eye-witness mentioned a Dutch police constable by name and said that he "set about them with his truncheon". Yet another said: "Instead of leaving these famished men to their bit of porridge, they set about them with sticks, though the victims hardly seemed to notice it. 'At least, let us have our porridge first,' they cried. In the end the guards gave in, and left them to their bit of food. For many even this food was too much, and after a few painful gulps they brought it up again. Quite a number collapsed on the ground and had to be taken to hospital . . ."

Here they were given time to recover before they were packed off to the gas-chamber. On the initiative of Dr. Spanier, the head of the camp medical service, the Camp Commandant did, however, report the men's condition to his superiors; Professor Cohen claims that the Germans were "most indignant" at the excesses of the Dutch SS, and that they closed Ellekom as a result. Dr. Harster, with whom the writer discussed the whole episode in 1955, could not remember ever hearing about this camp. And none of the victims, it seems, lived to tell the tale.

Though the amateurish behaviour of the Dutch SS in Ellekom may have offended German sensibilities, the more professional persecution of the camp inmates at Amersfoort Concentration Camp

[1] Wielek: *op. cit.*, p. 88.

was no different in its effects, and has been described by some who were able to make the comparison as "worse than Poland". From the written reminiscences of many non-Jews we know that, in this camp, a truly incredible technique of humiliation and torture was used by guards, who had been imbued with the doctrine: "No softness to Jews."

"Eckhoff revelled in kicking his victims often—his eyes sparkling with pleasure and his peasant face flushed with lust—and viciously. The testicles of the victims were his favourite target . . . If an old Jew, bowed under the weight of a bucket of sand—Eckhoff had seen to it that it was more than he could carry—could not run with it 'at the double', Eckhoff would order him to put the bucket down and drag him into the bushes. But if the ensuing sexual assault was kept out of sight, it was not out of hearing; the old man's screams could be heard hundreds of yards away . . . and sometimes it was even done in full view."

This and many more stories like it are corroborated by a great many witnesses.[1] We also have the admission of Commandant Berg, who freely confessed that Jews had been ill-treated in his camp, but claimed that he himself had only taken part in it "when the prisoners disobeyed orders or shirked the work". However, it would appear that "shirking the work" was a euphemism for physically impossible tasks, since whenever a Jew with an inordinately heavy load of sand nevertheless succeeded in covering the required 250 feet, the Commandant would "add another few spadefuls of sand" while "spurring the Jews on to greater speed by beating them with a stick". "On several occasions" Jews had been forced to do physical jerks for hours on end "when the Jewish Sabbath was just beginning"; on those occasions, too, "I used my stick".

Moreover: "I admit that in 1942 I made the Jewish prisoners draw up in two lines some 250 feet apart, on opposite sides of the parade ground, and forced them to take turns in carrying me to and fro on their backs. The Jews had to do this on all fours while I spurred them on with my boots . . . I regarded this as punishment drill."

[1] H. L. Lieve and K. R. ter Steege: *Predikant achter prikkeldraad* (Parson behind barbed wire) (Nijkerk, undated); M. van Leeuwen: *Kamp Amersfoort* (Amsterdam, undated); J. F. Hunsche: *Polizeiliches Durchgangslager Amersfoort* (The police transit camp of Amersfoort) (undated); L. W. Schmidt: *Modern Bagno* (Rotterdam, 1947); *Onderdrukking en Verzet* (Oppression and Resistance), part I, pp. 642 ff.

What did the Jewish Council do about all this? On December 31, 1942, the Presidents discussed the ill-treatment of Jews in Amersfoort, first with Lages and later with Böhmcker; the Germans promised an investigation. The writer rather doubts that anything more was done in the matter.

Our first reference to the camp at Schoorl dates back to 1941, when the victims of the two raids in that year were locked up there for some time in the company of a number of Jewish Communists who, needless to say, had a particularly horrible time of it. For although Schoorl was more given to humiliation than to torture, the Communists were forced to do such jobs as "getting down on their hands and knees to clean a swastika on the ground with a toothbrush". Here, too, ill-treatment was not unusual and the inmates were often "drilled" to exhaustion. Nevertheless, the then Acting Secretary-General of Justice, *mr.* J. P. Hooykaas, who was not a Nazi, said of those taken to Schoorl in February 1941: "The boys were quite well off there."[1]

From Ommen, too—with its notorious camp called "Erica"—we have reports all too like those from Amersfoort:[2] "We were forced to witness the most horrible outrages against these people . . . The things that were done to them defy description and all their pleas for mercy were met with derision and curses. Everything had to be turned into a torment for them. Half naked, with swollen faces, they made a sorry sight. The main thing was not to kill them off too quickly, even though many begged for death on their bended knees." Another witness speaks of the "excesses of perverse bestiality".

Doetinchem, another camp, was said to be reserved for those Jews who, before 1940, had shown themselves sympathetic to the new Germany and had supported the call of the Dutch *Führer*, A. A. Mussert, for a New Europe under the leadership of Nazi Germany.

This is perhaps the place to say something more about these "Mussert Jews".[3] In the beginning, the NSB (*Nationaal-Socialistische*

[1] Enquiry Commission, part VIIc, p. 601.

[2] *Nederland gedenk* (Let Holland remember) (1946), p. 20; C. Uyttenboogaard: *In de Klauwen der SS* (In the claws of the SS), (Amsterdam, 1945), pp. 13–15; D. C. A. Bout: *In den strijd om ons volksbestaan* (In the struggle for national survival) (The Hague, 1947), pp. 18–20; *Je Maintiendrai*, January 31, 1943.

[3] *Het proces Mussert* (The Mussert Trial) (The Hague, 1948), p. 157; H. W. J. Sannes: *Onze Joden en Duitland's greep naar de wereldmacht* (Our Jews and Germany's bid for world domination) (Amsterdam, 1946), pp. 233 ff.

*Beweging in Nederland*) was not at all anti-Semitic. In fact, the movement expressly repudiated "false accusations" to this effect, adding that "every good Dutch Jew is welcome as a member". It is said that by 1935, 150 Jews had in fact joined the movement, particularly in Amsterdam. However, by then things had begun to change, and though Jews were still accepted as members they were no longer given any responsible positions. From the surviving correspondence it appears that Mussert had been unable to withstand the pressure from his own ranks and from Germany. After autumn, 1937, no more Jews applied for membership; on October 22, 1938, on the occasion of a provincial membership drive, Mussert closed the NSB to new Jewish recruits, even though on November 18 he still declared his abhorrence of the *Reichskristallnacht* (the German pogrom of November 9): "Vandalism and injustice are repugnant to our nature."

Under German pressure Jews were formally expelled from the NSB in October 1940, with the exception of those who had joined before May 1940. Mussert is said to have told his friend Woudenberg that the expulsion of so many "good and faithful Jewish comrades was the worst thing I have ever done".

It is clear that with every new anti-Semitic measure taken by the invader, these Jewish "comrades" and ex-comrades" found their loyalties more strained. However, some remained faithful to the NSB to the bitter end, and bitter indeed their end must have been.

Thus, a non-Jewish woman had this to say about her "full-Jewish" husband on August 25, 1942: "Putting aside all selfish considerations, he joins in the momentous events of the present with a devotion to the ideal of German victory that cannot be exceeded by even the most ardent Aryan. His fervour is expressed by his unshakeable faith in the magnanimity of the *Führer* . . ."

In May 1943 a lawyer from The Hague, and a member of the NSB Legal Front, appealed to Rauter on behalf of a number of Jewish families whose pro-German sympathies he described as unassailable. With boundless eloquence he asked that twenty such Jews be found a place at Doetinchem. On May 13 *Fräulein* Slottke noted in the margin of this letter that Rauter could not be bothered with it.

As for Doetinchem itself, all we can say is that, as the war went on, its numbers dwindled; so much so that, as one reliable document indicates, by March 15, 1943, there were only seven NSB Jews left—and they, too, were destined for Theresienstadt.

### THE CAMP AT BARNEVELD

The story of Barneveld is really the story of a privileged group of prominent Jews, whose special treatment made them the envy of some, and objects of hatred and envy to many more. In his apologia (*Op de bres*) K. J. Frederiks, the Secretary-General of the Department of the Interior, has told the first part of this story, which boiled down to the fact that he succeeded in protecting this group, thanks largely to tension between Rauter and Schmidt, who respectively opposed and supported him. This claim strikes us as implausible, because Schmidt was a notorious anti-Semite. Moreover, had Schmidt really opposed Rauter, the latter would most certainly have canvassed and obtained the support of Himmler. Finally, if there was tension between the German leaders, how would Frederiks have come to hear about it? On his own admission, all that Schmidt did for him in practice was to grant five exemptions, and it was only when Professor Van Dam, the Secretary-General for Education, Science and Culture, added his voice to Frederiks' that the number was increased, and that Seyss-Inquart gave the official promise that all these Jews might remain in the Netherlands.

Frederiks packed them all off to *De Schaffelaar*, a castle in Barneveld, and when that was full, housed the overflow in *De Biezen*, a large villa in nearby Ede. Barneveld had a "good" burgomaster, Ede a "bad" one; hence Frederiks changed the boundaries between the two boroughs in such a way that all "his" Jews came under the aegis of the "good" one. We still have the text of the letters Frederiks sent to his happy band; on December 11, 1942, he told them that Barneveld would be ready on December 16 to 26, and gave them detailed instructions as to their luggage. Those wishing to avail themselves of his good offices had to make up their minds by December 14, which gave them a whole weekend. There were many pros and cons, and though some of those concerned told the writer after the war that they knew what risks they were running, they all felt that going to Barneveld was safer than going into hiding. Quite a few, however, started to plan their escape on the very day of their arrival.

And so these Jews moved into the castle, some fully expecting to get a room with a bathroom attached. The children, above all, were full of the highest hopes, and quite unperturbed by the removal.

We have a great deal of information about the number and sort of people who lived in its ivory towers. One of the many surviving lists, that of August 2, 1943, gives 640 names. It is difficult to find a single formula to describe this group. Was it, in fact, a Jewish élite? The answers vary. Frederiks and Van Dam selected mainly people from their own social sphere, but there were others as well, including a number of men thought "indispensable" by the Jewish Council. Moreover, there was a special camp dentist, a camp shoemaker and representatives of a host of other trades and professions.

Life in this remote castle, cut off from the rest of the world, and with its strangely assorted community, must have been full of tensions. To begin with, there was friction between the residents in *De Schaffelaar* and those in *De Biezen.* The former was considered to be a socially superior and more elegant place, the latter the more sociable of the two; the former more stylish, the latter better organized—and so on. In particular, the Jews in *De Biezen* were less assimilated, and had no exaggerated opinion of their own importance. But possibly that was the very reason why there seemed to be what a visitor called "greater solidarity" and a more homely atmosphere at *De Biezen.* Some of the tension was merely the continuation of differences between Jews everywhere, but exacerbated by their close confinement. Thus some Jews wanted to celebrate Christmas soon after their arrival, while others were violently opposed to this idea. As a result of this and similar differences, there was a struggle between the "Assimilationists" and the "Pojos" ("Positive Jews"). There were various other factions as well: the old against the young, the rich against the intellectuals and so on. As one witness put it, the whole thing must have seemed to the outsider like a lunatic asylum, the more so as there was also a small clique of alcoholics. A whole world in miniature, we might say.

Everyone was full of praise for the cultural activities—there were concerts, lectures and various courses of instruction. It was at Barneveld that Dr. E. A. M. Speijer did the groundwork for his *Entomological Studies in Nazi Camps.* The children were taught by men of high standing, and all their examination results were accepted after the war. One of the teachers wrote: "Education is taken very seriously here . . . There are day-long debates on whether or not a given child should be upgraded, or whether another should be given a bad mark for German in his report."

Some of the school records have survived. They are almost touching in their ordinariness. Each pencil is accounted for. The children led normal school lives, except that freedom of movement constantly dwindled. "But still I was never conscious of being a prisoner," wrote a thirteen-year old girl. From Westerbork she later looked back nostalgically at Barneveld: "What could be worse for a child of that age than the complete loss of privacy?"

From its very beginning, Barneveld was a thorn in the Germans' flesh. As we have said, it is at best an open question whether Schmidt favoured the establishment of this camp; what is certain is that when he died, the other German leaders began to clamour for its closure. On April 29, 1943, even before Schmidt's death, Rauter asked Seyss-Inquart to send all the inmates to Theresienstadt. He repeated this request on May 5. Others, too, had a finger in this pie, including *Fräulein* Slottke, who, on the orders of Zöpf, accompanied Fischer to Barneveld on May 11 on a tour of inspection: she found 363 Jews (147 males, 216 females and 77 children under eighteen) in *De Schaffelaar* and 175 (74 males, 101 females and 36 children under eighteen) in *De Biezen*. All of them had apparently got there "without the requisite papers", so that there was good reason for the Security Police to "look into their antecedents". And as *Fräulein* Slottke, who had a good nose for these things, put it: "Few of the Jews resident in Barneveld will be able to stand up to such scrutiny."

It seems ironic that while these "chosen Jews" were sitting unsuspecting in their castle, surrounded by all their possessions, and counting on a very long stay, the *Fräulein* should already have been thinking how to dispose of their furniture.

Now that "Schmidt's happy family" was at the mercy of Rauter and the SS, the Dutch storm-troopers, too, felt free to cock a snook at them. Thus, on June 11, 1943, their weekly *Storm* came out with an article attacking Frederiks for having provided these "Jewish vermin" with a comfortable roof over their heads and with a pleasant park to walk in.

On September 10, 1943, the Jewish Council was told officially from The Hague that Barneveld would remain inviolate. This official promise was reiterated soon afterwards. Such promises should, by then, have convinced anyone that the end was at hand. Yet when it came, Barneveld was taken completely by surprise. On September 29 the very day the Jewish Council in Amsterdam was dissolved, the Germans arrived and gave the inmates thirty minutes to pack; an eye-witness reports that the German leader also gave the young people ample opportunity to escape—he left the fence unguarded. Not many made use of it, for according to a German list only twenty-five people were missing by the time the contingent arrived at Westerbork, and three of them had died at Barneveld. When some of the survivors were asked why they had not taken the chance to get away, quite a few replied that they were afraid of exposing the others to reprisals. One of them blamed it on the sense of false security that had built up in the place.

On October 30, 1943, Frederiks was attacked from another quarter. On that occasion the illegal *Het Parool* accused him of "naïvety, gullibility, vanity and spinelessness"; the Germans had "promised" him to keep the Barneveld Jews in Westerbork, and Frederiks had not only been ingenuous enough to believe them but had spread the news and even boasted that it was the result of his good offices. "Naturally the Germans left him out on a limb . . . A weak, misguided and unpatriotic figure. The sooner he ceases to meddle, the better . . ."

An eye-witness[1] has reported the arrival in Westerbork of these "last of the Mohicans", who were bundled into Hut 85, behind barbed wire and without any amenities—"a vile pig-sty, enough to make one vomit; in a trice, they had fallen from the relatively luxurious life at Barneveld to the degradation their fellow-Jews had suffered all along". Several sources agree that the Camp Commandant wanted to have them deported as soon as possible. He failed to get this done, but could his new charges really have doubted what lay in store for them? Frederiks had given them the most reassuring promises when they went to Barneveld, and he had done so in the name of Schmidt. But Schmidt was now dead. On October 25, 1943, Frederiks had again told one of them that none would be sent to work abroad. But were his promises now worth anything? Eichmann's department in Berlin kept a sharp eye on them; as early as October 21, 1943, Zöpf was informed that a special camp for prominent Jews had been established at Bergen-Belsen on Himmler's orders. This is where the Barneveld Jews must go; Zöpf would have to discuss this matter with Seyss-Inquart. Some of the men even volunteered for the new camp in January 1944 because, as they believed, they had every chance of being exchanged for German

[1] P. Mechanicus: *In depôt, dagboek uit Westerbork* (In depot, diary from Westerbork) (Amsterdam, 1964), p. 175.

prisoners of war and sent to Palestine. Meanwhile Rauter kept nagging Frederiks and Van Dam for the transfer of the remaining Jews; he had to have them all in Theresienstadt by June 1944 since, if the course of the war made it necessary to send them to Germany instead, he could not guarantee where precisely they would end up. On September 4, 1944, a train was accordingly made ready to carry this "privileged" group and others out of Holland; of the 654 original names on the passenger list, sixteen had been struck out.

A few of the rest managed to reach Switzerland in the spring of 1945, a few had died and the rest were liberated by the Russians. Why was this group so much more fortunate than most of their fellow-Jews? None of those we asked could give a satisfactory answer; in any case, the war ended just in time for them; another month and they might all have shared the common fate. According to Herzberg,[1] they all owed their lives to Frederiks and Professor Van Dam, and in January 1954 many of them, in fact, paid homage to the former at a private gathering in The Hague. Of the various reports published about this meeting, we should like to quote that which appeared in the Zionist paper, *De Joodse Wachter* (Jewish Watchman).[2] "We wish to state emphatically that we do not blame anyone who tried to save his own life in 1940–5. However, there were quite a few ways of doing so. The Barneveld group elected to do it under the aegis of an official who protected them for no better reason than that they were members of the middle-class intelligentsia. The class distinction this measure introduced belongs to the most horrible pages of the history of Dutch Jewry during the Occupation."

To this comment the writer has nothing to add.

### THE JEWISH COUNCIL

Having looked at the population of the Jewish "State within a State" in the Netherlands, it is time that we paid close attention to its government, if "government" is the right word for it.

The Jewish Council and its history have been mentioned frequently throughout these pages; in what follows, we shall be more concerned with its internal organization. We hope the reader will forgive us if, in so doing, we may have to cover some of the old ground. We have shown that the Jewish Council kept expanding throughout most of its existence and at the same time changing its

[1] Herzberg: *op. cit.*, pp. 132–3.
[2] February 19, 1954.

very nature. Perhaps nothing can give us a clearer impression of the proliferation of this organization than the *Handbook of the Jewish Council for Amsterdam*, which reflects the state of affairs on March 15, 1943. Even during the printing it was found necessary to add a host of addenda and amplifications—one surviving copy has such corrections marked on practically every page.

The *Jewish Weekly* of April 11, 1941, published the list of the Council members, twenty men, including the two Presidents. As time went on, some of the original members resigned (Messrs. Kan and Kisch, for reasons of principle). The Germans carried the rest off one by one; in 1943 three members had to drop out because it suddenly appeared that they were "not of the Jewish race". All in all, when the final liquidation came in September 1943, there was hardly anyone left besides the two Presidents.

The Jewish Council's activities are closely mirrored in reports in the *Jewish Weekly*. Thus the issue of June 27, 1941, published a small list of offices under the heading "addresses to be remembered". That list had grown quite a bit by November 7, 1941; on December 19, 1941, came the report that new offices had been opened in Nieuwe Keizersgracht; many of the older departments were retained as well. On April 10, 1942, in the first issue of its second year, the paper published yet a further list of offices; on September 25, 1942 (an issue we have picked at random), the list of offices fills a whole column; there were yet more on December 11, 1942.

The round-ups of 1943 took their toll. On April 1 some 8,000 staff were still listed for Amsterdam and some 560 for the rest of the Netherlands. After the great raids in May and June, the *Jewish Weekly* (July 23) mentioned a "reorganization", and published an "amended list of offices" which even then was larger than any published in 1942. On July 17, the list of higher officials in these offices included 1,091 names (409 salaried and 682 unsalaried), on August 1, the number was 1,013 (369: 644), on August 8, it had dwindled to 988 (369: 619). We also have an alphabetical list of all the leading officials—the Jewish nobility of that period. It was dated August 30 and gave the office telephone numbers of all but one of the ninety-two chiefs concerned. They did not have much time left: on September 24, 1943, the paper announced that all the offices would be closed for the Jewish New Year on September 30 and October 1, and they never opened again.

We have seen that the Council's work, originally confined to

Amsterdam, gradually spread over the whole country; the most interesting internal changes were those affecting the relations between the Presidents and the other members of the Council, on which subject Professor Cohen later made a deposition. With the exception of cases in which immediate decisions had to be taken, the Presidents invariably consulted all members, and "it never once happened that the members disagreed with the Presidents, at least on questions of principle". However, Professor Cohen had to agree that Messrs. Kan and Kisch had resigned on matters of principle, "although both continued to serve the Jewish community".

Possibly the best way of giving the reader some idea of the chaotic conditions prevailing in the Council offices is to take him step by step through the *Handbook*. The Internal Information Department (which published the *Bulletin* from which we have quoted at such length) had another great, awe-inspiring achievement to its credit, namely the publication of three types of registers, all arranged in alphabetical order and listing "staff as well as the names of departments in every building and the streets in which the various departments were located". The reader will appreciate that the compilers felt impelled to deviate from their alphabetic principle on the very first page, seeing that several offices so outdistanced all the others in composition and importance that they had to be given pride of place. These were the offices in 58 Nieuwe Keizersgracht, 50 Jan van Eyck Street, 366 Lijnbaansgracht and 74 Oude Schans. For the rest, it was an orderly procession from Afrikanerplein to Zwanenburgwal.

The list of names was headed by the two Presidents, the members of the Council, of the Secretariat and of the *Beirat*. The Presidents were installed in Room 101 in Nieuwe Keizersgracht. Asscher appears under only one other heading, but Cohen is listed as chairman of three special committees.

The list should by rights have continued with the name of one who was generally considered to have ranked in importance with the Presidents, but who does not figure in the *Handbook* of March 15, 1943, because he had been sent to a camp nearly six months earlier. This was M. H. Bolle, an Amsterdam accountant, who, on October 2, 1941, when the work of the Council was greatly expanded, was appointed joint Secretary with Dr. A van der Laan. His undoubted organizational genius quickly earned him a position of great power; this was recognized by many and feared by not a few. Particularly at the beginning of the mass deportations, an acknowledgment in his own hand that one was associated with the work of the Jewish Council, the so-called "Bolle-letter", was a valuable safe-conduct, though in the end it could not save even Bolle himself—the Germans carried him off on October 15, 1942, and all attempts by the Presidents to get him and his family back proved vain.

No doubt a brilliant organizer such as he must have made many enemies. How much this was due to his own personality is difficult to tell today. True, the Jewish Council machinery worked without a hitch under him, but those being packed off to Poland cannot really be blamed for having taken a somewhat less rosy view of his efficiency. Hatred of Bolle followed him even into the camps, where he is said to have been ostracized by many Jews. Some witnesses, however, say that his behaviour in Blechhammer, where he was a camp-prefect, was generally, if grudgingly, admired. Two witnesses tell us that, when he arrived in Allach-Dachau in March 1945, he gave a full explanation and vindication of his work in Amsterdam. He died of typhus in Feldafing (Germany) on about May 15, 1945—after the Liberation.

As we have said, his name did not appear in the *Handbook* for 1943; instead we find the name of another important figure, that of Meijer de Vries, a former high government official. The Jewish Council invited him to become "general adviser" in 1941, and delegated to him a great deal of responsibility, particularly in 1942 when so many Jews were sent to the labour camps. He had no official position in the Jewish Council, and was only paid his travelling expenses. His name nevertheless occurs on several pages of the *Handbook*; he was not only active but extremely versatile. Needless to say, as one of the top brass in the Nieuwe Keizersgracht he, too, was hated by many people who did not appreciate his unsuccessful attempts to delay their final departure. "Without him . . . the social work we were doing would have been impossible," Professor Cohen[1] later declared. In point of fact, the objects of his "social endeavours" proved so unappreciative of what he was doing for them that, on more than one occasion, the doors of the Council's offices had to be locked on them and the police called in. It would, however, be unfair to suggest that their wrath was directed at Meijer de Vries alone. J. Brandon, Bolle's successor, had much the same experience. We have already mentioned the other General Secretary, Dr. A. van der Laan who, as a former market superintendent, was given the

[1] Cohen: *Herinneringen*, p. 122.

task of provisioning Jews in the city; according to Professor Cohen, it was thanks to him and his staff that "no Jew went hungry in those days". We shall be returning to this point.

As we have said, the *Handbook* opened with the offices in the Nieuwe Keizersgracht, where all these great men sat in state. There followed a list of departments under Meijer de Vries, including Accountancy (which incidentally dealt with the issue of yellow stars), Central Buying and the Treasury. There was also a personnel office and one for staff social activities; after March 15, 1943, a cleaning and domestic help section was added as well. All departments had their own chiefs and often deputy chiefs, who were listed in the *Handbook*; here and there we also find the name of a secretary or clerk. Page 9 dealt with the Social Affairs Department, a branch of the Jewish Council concerned with the social life of Jews not only in Amsterdam but throughout the country. Its several subsections included one for employment, one for accommodation and one for special services, e.g. help in emergencies. In fact, everything was taken care of—except what finally happened to the Jews.

Dr. Van der Laan was in charge of only a few departments, together with a number of "external sections" (bread supplies, central kitchen, distribution of vegetables, meat supplies, supervision of ritual slaughter and fish supplies). Here, too, there were all sorts of subsidiary departments and chiefs.

Although it was not very spectacular, the work of all these bodies must have been considered very important by the Council. We lack the necessary data to determine whether Professor Cohen's praises were entirely justified; but it must probably be admitted—and that is admitting quite a lot—that the Jewish poor were, all things considered, not much worse off than their non-Jewish fellows. Scenes, as they were described from the Warsaw Ghetto, where children and adults were apparently left to perish in the streets, did not take place in the Netherlands. Even so, it remains an open question how much this was due to the efforts of the Jewish Council—we stated earlier that in the East, German anti-Semitism enjoyed far greater popular support than it did in the West. But when all is said and done, the Jewish Council did deserve some praise for its relief projects.

We could give the reader a fair idea of what precisely the Council did do by quoting from Berkley's short work,[1] and from some of the

[1] Berkley: *op. cit.*, pp. 38–40.

surviving minutes, letters and documents. But how can we give him even the most rudimentary idea of the grim reality, the petty persecutions and anxieties that could not be relieved by anyone? We have already given many instances of the Germans' repressive measures. Yet these can give only a pale image of the atmosphere in which the Jewish Council vainly attempted to soften blow after blow.

To take but one example: the reader will remember that Rauter's proclamation of September 15, 1941, barred public markets to Jewish traders, with the exception of a few greengrocers who were, however, forced to buy from NSB wholesalers; by the end of November 1941, the total number of such exemptions amounted to ten, seven of whom were in Amsterdam. The Jewish dealers were generally fobbed off with the poorest-quality goods; or else, when there was a glut on the market, they had to take far more than they required. All in all, Jewish shopkeepers became so impoverished that the Jewish Council had to give all of them financial assistance.

At the beginning of June 1942 a telephone call from Böhmcker's office told the Council that henceforth Jews would only be allowed to buy vegetables from Jewish greengrocers. This was confirmed during a telephone conversation a few days later and published in the *Jewish Weekly* on June 12. It was to take immediate effect. A circular on this subject gives us some idea of the great hardship involved. "Make the best of the new restrictions," it read (cold comfort this) and, as we know from a surviving draft, even this inspiring formula was only arrived at after many revisions. The task of the Jewish Council was not eased by the fact that Gombault (the German official in charge of the whole vegetable operation) kept on making further telephone calls; thus on June 15, he informed the Council that vegetables would be allocated first to the *Wehrmacht*, then to Aryans and finally to the Jews, who ought to get a fair share—if there was anything left for them at all.

As for the transport of vegetables, the only means available to the Jewish Council were motor vehicles. There were no horses and the few hand-carts were quite inadequate to this task. Imagine what happened when another German department, this time the one in charge of the Four Year Plan, ordered the confiscation of all these vehicles! The Council immediately sent letters of protest (on April 19 and 26), to which Gombault luckily replied on May 6 that he would "temporarily" exempt the vehicles in question. On May 5, the same official wrote an irate letter to the Jewish Council complaining about a Jewish greengrocer who had sent thirty boxes of rotten spinach to the municipal rubbish dump. The letter ended with a threat that supplies would henceforth be severely restricted. When the Jewish Council protested that the spinach was unfit for human consumption, the only result was that they were told to pay higher prices in future.

Jewish butchers did not have an easy time either; in 1941 there was talk of cutting down their supplies, but the Jewish Council itself had little to do with the distribution of meat until July 1943 when, as Berkley[1] tells us, it was ordered to take charge of this matter, as well. Here, too, the worst thing was not so much the new regulations as the chicanery that went with them.

Jewish poulterers had naturally been forbidden to continue the ritual slaughter of birds, but the leading one among them had apparently so impressed the Germans with the quality of his meat that he was unexpectedly ordered to carry on. Jews who refused to eat non-kosher meat could not even get fish as a substitute: for as Berkley[1] reports, Jews were not allowed to enter ordinary fishmongers' shops, and no special ones had been set aside for them. Be that as it may; on Sunday, May 31, 1942, some fifty WA-men still had occasion to chase Jewish buyers out of the fish-market for buying eel. Now though eel is not a kosher fish, Jewish traders had previously been allocated 3 per cent of the available eel supplies; clearly Mussert's henchmen thought even that was too much. The Jews were henceforth debarred from the fish-market, which meant no more fresh-water fish for them; salt-water fish, in so far as there were any supplies at all, remained "freely" available.

We have already mentioned that a Central Kitchen was opened by the Jewish Council on January 20, 1943. The records show that plans for this project had been made long before; thus, towards the end of 1941, there was a Central Kitchen Committee which apparently had its eye on the Jewish Invalid Hospital. When the kitchen was eventually opened in East Amsterdam, it had a chief, a deputy chief, an administrator, a chief cook and various other officials; there were three distribution centres with the appropriate cashiers and one inspector. There was also a number of nameless helpers, all with a stamp exempting them from transportation "until further notice".

[1] Berkley: *op. cit.*, p. 40.

This brings us to J. Brandon who, in addition to being General Secretary to the Jewish Council, served on heaven knows how many committees. The two copies of the *Handbook* consulted by us differ greatly in respect of the departments under him. We shall merely try to follow the main thread in the tangled web of his activities. He had a secretary, a consultant, an office manager and a deputy office manager. Much of his work was concerned with the German removal notices and with help to the many evicted families. When one reads a summary of his various departments and subsidiary departments, one wonders if even the most ingenious could have added to them. In addition, as General Secretary, he was, of course, in charge of all sorts of administrative departments: the messenger service, the postal dispatch department, the typists' pool, the personnel department, the canteen and so on. Just to round off his activities, we must mention that eight committees on which he served, were in regular session at headquarters. Does this exhaust the activities in Nieuwe Keizersgracht? Perhaps it does as far as the various officials are concerned, but then there were also the many people for whose sake all this impressive activity was supposed to go on, who kept milling in the corridors and on the stairs, who queued outside offices asking help for themselves, their families or friends, who sometimes broke down completely, or ran riot, for instance when an official in the umpteenth room was able to do as little for them as were the many officials they had seen before.

Their resentment must have been very much stronger still when it came to the offices at 15, 19 and 21 Jan van Eyck Street, which had no queues outside (it had been impressed on all Jews not to hang around), but instead provided its clientele with real consulting-rooms, private cubicles, and had a much more obvious hierarchical structure. This was the headquarters of the *Expositur*, which we have met on some occasions and which was perhaps the most formidable arm of the Jewish Council. Over it all reigned Dr. Sluzker, an Austrian advocate, to whose pleas the Germans listened with far greater attention than they did even to the two Presidents, and whose unobtrusive ways so often succeeded in wresting concessions from them —"until further notice".

Dr. Edwin Sluzker—or Edwin Israel Sluzker as the Germans liked to call him—entered the Netherlands in December 1938 as an illegal immigrant from Vienna, and was sent to a Dutch refugee camp. At the end of 1939 he joined the staff of the Jewish Refugee

Committee, on whose behalf he was able to arrange the emigration of small groups of Jews from Holland as late as 1940 and 1941, and even without their having to pay foreign currency into the German coffers. In the spring of 1941 the Germans opened their special *Zentralstelle für jüdische Auswanderung* (Central Office for Jewish Emigration), and ordered that Jewish officials must henceforth accompany and check the papers of all Jewish applicants. The Jewish community accordingly set up a special department, which was originally run by L. de Wolff, and soon afterwards by the much abler Dr. Sluzker. At first, the work was relatively unimportant and few would have predicted that it would one day be turned into the all-powerful *Expositur*. Similar organizations in Prague and Vienna were also dubbed *Expositur* by the Germans, a name, we might add, that hardly anyone associated with a body whose task it was to act as an intermediary between Jews who wanted to emigrate and the *Zentralstelle*. Who can say to what degree the unfamiliar cadences of this word made it sound the more ominous to the Jews. All they knew was that, somethow, at the "*Expo*" decisions were being made that meant life or death to them.

Yet it was soon enough to become part of their everyday vocabulary. At the beginning of 1942, when the evacuation of Jews from various parts of the Netherlands got into its stride, it was the *Expo* which succeeded in obtaining a number of exemptions; in many other respects, too, Sluzker was able to wrest concessions from Aus der Fünten when everyone else had failed. No wonder he got the reputation of being something of a miracle worker. He knew the right channels, understood the German orders and the terminology of their printed forms—of which latter the "emigrants" had to fill in thirty-two in all (even at a time when the chances of emigration were practically nil). Moreover, he could address the *Zentralstelle* in the homely Austrian dialect which so many of its officials spoke. He not only knew how to talk to Aus der Fünten, he knew when to listen. He was never pushing; despite his high position he lived very simply, kept in the background whenever possible and officially never did more than carry out the orders given to him by the Presidents of the Jewish Council. His tact was only equalled by his patience. According to Wielek,[1] "he would often hang about uncomplainingly in a corridor of the *Zentralstelle* while waiting for a suitable moment to buttonhole Aus der Fünten".

[1] Wielek: *op. cit.*, p. 256.

Not a few of his staff envied his position. The records contain a letter from which we gather that the Jews in The Hague would have liked to have an *Expositur* of their own: they felt no less threatened than their brethren in Amsterdam and hankered after the extra protection they thought such an organization would afford them. Unfortunately, the Germans would recognize no more than one *Expositur* in each country, and it was difficult enough to keep that one going. No wonder that a position in this organization, and the stamp that went with it, were prized beyond all possessions. *Expo* members were allowed to wear a special arm-band with which they could slip in and out everywhere—"until further notice".

The all-powerful signatures and initials of the upper echelon of this august body have been preserved for posterity in duplicate; each of the leaders had his own department, and one of them in particular, W. Süskind, whom we shall meet again, used his exalted position to save a very large number of Jews. Incidentally, members of the organization, particularly those who called at the *Zentralstelle*, were often able to gather useful information, for instance the names of people whom the Germans intended to arrest in the near future. A former pupil of the writer even had the delicate task of, now and then, "dropping" a 100-guilder note behind the typewriter of Aus der Fünten's secretary.

The work of the *Expositur* must not be disparaged. On occasion, particularly on critical days, the staff would have to remain at their posts for twenty-four hours at a stretch and even longer. The greatest strain fell on Sluzker who, moreover, had to adapt himself to Aus der Fünten's sudden changes of mood. What passed between them may be compared to a game of bluff for, if Sluzker hoped to obtain the release of twenty Jews he would ask for forty, and if Aus der Fünten needed eighty he would arrest 100 and "reluctantly" hand Sluzker back the balance. According to Professor Cohen, the *Expositur* was a necessary buffer between the Jews and the Germans and one the Council could not have done without.

Here and there we catch some glimpses of the atmosphere in which all this was taking place. Thus one eye-witness, who was present at the *Expositur* offices when a number of the staff returned from the *Zentralstelle*, where they had been typing out the particulars of those who were being deported that night by the Germans, had the following story to tell: "A strange spectacle unfolded before my eyes. A mirror was quickly unscrewed from the wall and put down on a table. Next, the carbon paper that had been used for typing out the lists was held in front of the mirror, and the reflection copied out at a furious pace. This was because the Germans issued no lists of those whom they deported, so that the mirror method was the only way of recording the names, birth-dates and last places of residence of the victims. The atmosphere in Jan van Eyck Street on such occasions was truly nerve-racking."

This almighty department of the Jewish Council was, of course, scrapped during the general close-down of September 29, 1943. Its members, too, were sent into exile from which many never returned; four or five were kept back by the Germans for the task of filing records at the *Zentralstelle*; they could easily have finished the work within a few weeks, but somehow managed to stretch it over eleven months. It is said that, in early September 1944, they succeeded in going underground and thus saving their own lives and those of their families. Dr. Sluzker survived the war. So much for the *Expositur*.

Our tour of the offices of the Jewish Council now takes us to 366 Lijnbaansgracht. The building itself has disappeared, but the writer can still remember the sinister industry of deportation that went on there. For while the *Expositur* could put up a minimum of resistance, occasionally obtaining the release of a few men, the Lijnbaangracht was dealing with *faits accomplis*, with people whose deportation "to Germany" or Westerbork could no longer be revoked. This was not the only activity, but as time went on it came to overshadow everything else. Here, too, there was a great gulf fixed between those who efficiently made the arrangements, and those who could only helplessly suffer the consequences. In March 1943 the writer himself called at these offices in the (foolish) hope of being able to save the life of his wife who had been sent to Westerbork. He was referred to one of the highest officials there, a widely respected man, who on that occasion was deeply engaged in conversation with a secretary. The conversation was not only animated but, judging by the laughter, amusing as well, and it went on and on. What could one do but wait, wait, wait—and finally cough politely and attempt a deferential interruption? But there was more laughter, and the conversation went on—in German. One tried to remember that the German Jews were Jews as well, if anything worse off and more persecuted than oneself, that nothing must be allowed to destroy Jewish solidarity, and so—patience, patience, patience. The telephone rang and there was more chit-chat, again in German, very amicable, apparently with a woman—was she perhaps his wife? And the woman the writer had come about was in Westerbork, in a punitive block; he knew that only a telegram from the Lijnbaansgracht could save her and that he must at all costs control his anger. Only that morning he had been told at the *Expositur* that if anyone could do something, it was this lot . . . this man, who was now chuckling over the telephone. It is only fair to add that, in the end, the man not only sent the indispensable telegram but took a real interest in the case, and proved most sympathetic. But in this case, as in so many others, all his efforts were in vain—my young wife was deported to Sobibor ex-extermination camp on March 23, 1943 . . .

At Lijnbaansgracht, the reader could have met a number of important figures in the Jewish Council hierarchy. Yet when the *Handbook* appeared, one of the most important of them, A. de Hoop, was no longer listed. The Germans had unexpectedly seized him in spring 1943, sent him to Westerbork and then deported him as a "special case", probably after a denunciation by a member of the Dutch Cinema Union of which he had been the Director. His place in the *Handbook* was now taken by E. Spier, whose task was described as: "Registration of the personal and financial particulars of all those called up for labour service, and processing the relevant data." The Lijnbaansgracht offices also housed the *Beirat* for non-Dutch Jews, which we have met before, and several other departments.

Then there was the Central Information Service. A surviving but undated memorandum stressed the essential, indeed the indispensable, character of this branch, which had to provide so much more than mere information, notably spiritual comfort. Its activities proliferated so widely that a host of subsidiary departments had to be opened; a document dated November 6, 1942, declared that it was impossible to give a comprehensive account of all the work in which the department was engaged. This is understandable when we consider that it had to publish innumerable rules and regulations, even unintentional breaches of which were punishable by death; when we think of all the matters, large and small, on which the Jews needed information; the many petty problems for which they needed assistance (for instance, writing official letters or filling in forms); the unavoidable translation of a host of documents and papers; the impossibility of finding one's way in a maze of offices with a constantly changing population; the problem of deciding what luggage, documents, etc., were needed for deportation; the disposal of the effects of those already deported and assistance to those left behind —if we think of this and all the many related activities, it becomes clear why this branch of the Jewish Council increased its original staff from just a few at the beginning (January 1, 1942) to almost 200. In November 1942, the Lijnbaansgracht offices as a whole housed 600 to 800 people; this number later increased to somewhere between 1,200 and 1,600.

Also at the Lijnbaansgracht were the Department of Emigration and the Displaced Persons' Aid Bureau, both under the same director. This is the only place in the *Handbook* where we find the name of Gertrud van Tijn-Cohn, and this despite her high rank and eminent role in the hierarchy of the Jewish Council. She was undoubtedly one of the most controversial figures we shall mention in these pages, and as such deserves a few words to herself. The writer must preface his account with the statement that, before he commenced this work, her name was entirely unknown to him. The earliest reference to her he could dig up was an article the *Jewish Weekly* published on the occasion of her fiftieth birthday (July 4, 1941); from it he learned that her whole life was devoted to Jewish social work and especially to the welfare of Jewish immigrants in Holland. The article also praised her work in connection with the Jewish labour camp at Wieringermeer, and spoke of her many journeys abroad. In fact, in as late as spring 1941, the Germans gave her permission to travel to Lisbon via Berlin in connection with emigration problems; inconceivable though it sounds today, prospects for emigation from Holland still looked very good at that time, and there was every hope that the so-called Domingo colonization plan (the offer by the Dominican Republic to take in 100,000 Jewish refugees) [1] would be fully implemented. What is remarkable is not only that the Germans allowed Gertrud van Tijn to travel to Lisbon during the war but also that they let her out from Bergen-Belsen in July 1944, i.e. at a time when Holland was still occupied. Soon afterwards she wrote a report for the Jewish Joint Distribution Committee, which she called "Contributions to the History of the Jews in the Netherlands from May 10, 1940, to June 1944". This report is a mine of general information, and also casts a great deal of light on the relations between this extraordinary woman and the other leaders of the Jewish Council, with whom she was often at

[1] J. Tenenbaum: *Race and Reich* (New York, 1956), p. 472.

loggerheads, and who were not slow to criticize her report—and her character and conduct.

As we have said, one of her jobs was to direct the Emigration Department which, according to the *Handbook*, had the task of "advising on the procedure for obtaining visas; investigating the validity and duration of existing visas; helping with the completion of emigration applications as required by the German authorities; advising and helping with applications for so-called 'exchanges and repatriation; and obtaining dollar-passages for those in possession of exit-permits".

The attentive reader will have noticed that many of these activities fell into the province of the *Expositur*. The resulting overlaps caused a great deal of friction between the two departments, particularly when, as the German threat grew, both had to fight for survival.

The promise of emigration was kept alive by the Germans throughout 1941. Things took a sharp turn for the worse on December 5, 1941, when the *Jewish Weekly* published an "important notice to Jews of non-Dutch nationality". It announced that all of them must forthwith apply to the *Zentralstelle* for "permission" to emigrate. This report caused panic among many foreign Jews and there were quite a few suicides among those who had an inkling that "emigration" was a euphemism for deportation.

Their suspicions were increasingly confirmed in the course of 1942, when the Germans came more and more into the open and began to send Jews in large numbers to their so-called "work-camps". Nevertheless, the Emigration Department continued its work, if on an ever-decreasing scale. Thus we know from a surviving document that, in April 1943, the department dealt with applications for emigration by twelve Dutch Jews and with the exchange of "one English lady". No one could say that it was being overworked.

Quite the contrary applied to Gertrud van Tijn's other department. On August 28, 1942, the *Jewish Weekly* let it be known that the Displaced Persons' Aid Bureau had begun its work of "rendering help and advice to all those going to Germany on labour service". Unfortunately, the bureau never gave the advice not to go at all—today we know what that cost those concerned. We cannot refrain from adding the bitter rider that by advising others to go, the staff of the bureau was able to stave off their own departure for a time.

But though its advice was questionable, the bureau certainly rendered help in many ways: by organizing domestic service, running errands, helping to pack and caring for the deportees' depenants. To that end, the city was divided into various districts with special branch offices. The department also had permission to collect clothes, etc., for distribution among Jews, and to provide food for those awaiting transport at the various assembly points. There was also a subsidiary section to deal with the business affairs of those who had "gone away".

A document dated November 11, 1942, tells us that of the 416 people working under Mrs. van Tijn, 396 were unpaid. We also have an instruction to the staff signed by Mrs. van Tijn herself: "The name 'Displaced Persons' Aid Bureau' speaks for itself, and we fully expect you to treat everyone seeking your help with goodwill and the greatest tact. Do not forget that most of those needing your help are in a state of great nervous agitation; be prepared, therefore, to *serve* selflessly and do not even take it amiss if those whom you serve forget to thank you . . ."

Another circular urged the whole Jewish community to give whatever they could spare—especially blankets, clothes, shoes, etc. The appeal ended with the words: "Do not send worthless cast-offs, but only what you yourself would use." No doubt the appeal was the more successful because many knew that it would soon be their turn to "go away".

Yet another circular gave "practical hints on what to take with you"; it left little to the imagination and ran to two closely typed foolscap pages. It even included such articles as "a favourite book", a modest writing-case, and postcards with international reply coupons. We should really have to quote the whole document to give the reader a proper idea of the insidious way in which the deportees were being persuaded that, though they were facing a hard future, they and their families would get by, provided only that they took the right equipment along with them. Nor is it easy to imagine today what fantastic organization was needed to provide all these people (and also those in Westerbork and Vught) with everyday necessities. This was largely made possible through the help of non-Jewish manufacturers and businessmen—and, mark you, at a time of unrivalled scarcity and restrictions, of control and treachery.

Here we must mention another leading department of the Jewish Council, namely the one in Oude Schans. Its main task was to look after the people in Westerbork, and this in the widest sense of the word (stores, workshops and clinics); the department employed a large number of buyers, ran a dry-cleaning and repair shop; made up camping equipment of all kinds and saw to its dispatch. (One non-Jewish merchant not only made no charge for the goods he supplied but also delivered them to the camp gratis.)

The leading figure in the Oude Schans was C. Blüth, a German Jew who had come to Holland in 1919 and became a naturalized Dutch citizen in 1935. He paid regular visits to Westerbork and later to Vught; *inter alia,* he would hold weekly consultations in the camps and try, with his staff of 300, to do everything in his power to ameliorate the conditions there. It is almost unbelievable how his department managed to conjure up all the supplies, and indeed how it contrived to get them delivered.

In the *Handbook* we find an impressive list of the various branch offices, depots and store-houses run by Blüth's department. We shall not here go into detail, but merely mention that one section alone looked after the medical care of the entire (non-hospitalized) Jewish population in the Netherlands. In addition, the department dealt with social work, maintained special nursing-homes, cared for the blind, ran a psychiatric consultation bureau, and looked after schoolchildren and infants.

The medical care section shared a building with the Postal and Sorting Department, which dealt with all correspondence to and from the camps. It was established when the first batch of letters arrived in Holland about a month after the departure of the first group of deportees, and had the additional task of giving the Jewish Council a general picture of conditions abroad, as described by the correspondents. It is impossible to assess the accuracy of these summaries, for we have only a few of the letters themselves, and we cannot tell how representative they are. Moreover, we know that since the majority of the deportees were murdered soon after their arrival, what few letters reached Holland were written only by a relatively small number of "privileged" prisoners. Nevertheless, we gain the impression that the gentlemen in the Postal Department were more zealous in hunting up encouraging details of camp life than in reporting the more sombre moments. When they did glance at the seamy side they were quick to add a few cheering details. Thus, references to "harsh conditions" were immediately "balanced" by the rider—"harsh but not unbearable—there is apparently no work on Sundays". One of the summaries contained the assurance that the incoming reports had been scrutinized with the greatest possible reserve—not, mark you, for possible embellishments (under German pressure) but in order to "offset unjustified complaints". In other words, the gentlemen at the Post Office were doing their best to reassure the next batch of deportees.

"The letters from Germany are not bad on the whole," we read in the minutes of a meeting of the Jewish Council on October 1, 1942. The only trouble was that there were so few of them. Luckily, by the end of November the flow increased again; there were ninety-three letters and letter-cards. Another document tells us that, shortly before, another forty-three had arrived with "crushing effects on the spirits of those left behind", though, as the Postal Department added, the writers had not so much complained of conditions in the camp as of being separated from their families. As for the ninety-three, their content was of "no great significance", notwithstanding the fact that (as the writer of this book discovered) one of them bore the word "Sof" (Hebrew = it's all up with us) beside the signature. On January 22, 1943, there were apparently 308 letters, once again with "quite favourable" news, although two of the senders had meanwhile "passed away". In all the letters from Monowitz the food was said to be "satisfactory", though one writer added the word *blanes* (boloney). People also remarked on the fact that no news whatsoever was received from children, women with children or old people.

We saw earlier that Jews in Holland were only allowed to address letters to selected alphabetical groups of deportees, and to these they wrote with "a gullibility and simple faith that now strike me as completely insane", as one survivor has put it. They continued for months on end to address the dead, the murdered, and they even had to write these letters in German, or to have them translated and censored! Who can say what happened to all these hundreds and thousands of letters? No doubt the Germans did not even bother to forward them to the camps.

And so the gentlemen in the Postal Department laboured on. The records still contain a report on March 26, 1943, of incoming mail from camps Jawischowitz, Monowitz, Birkenau and Theresienstadt, of which the first three were subsidiaries of Auschwitz. We do not know how many such letters there were, though, according to the Dutch Red Cross,[1] a last batch of letters was received in Holland

[1] Dutch Red Cross: *Auschwitz*, part III (The Hague, 1952), pp. 85–6. part IV (The Hague, 1953), p. 18.

on July 25, 1944. In any case, most of the writers were dead or dying by then.

Having discussed the activities in the four main buildings we must now turn to some of the subsidiary addresses in the *Handbook*. The first of these is 125–127 Tolstraat, the Jewish Care and Nursing Association, whose task it was to "look after minors, old people, invalids; to nurse the sick and to supervise all Jewish nursing institutions in the Netherlands". According to Berkley, this organization came into being when the Germans, having first disbanded and plundered a host of Jewish charitable institutions, discovered that they had caused so much dislocation as to jeopardize the continued functioning of the Jewish Council itself. They accordingly ordered the Council to merge all surviving charitable organizations into one body, the Jewish Welfare Association, and it was this body which later became the Jewish Care and Nursing Association. Herzberg does not say that the Association was founded on German orders, but A. van den Bergh, who was closely involved in all the negotiations as a member of the Dutch Israelitic Poor Relief Board, agrees with Berkley's version; another reliable source states that the Germans ordered Asscher to found the Association. We also have a copy of the constitution, in two languages and dated November 4, 1942, in which there is a clear reference to the orders of the Delegate of the *Reichskommissar* for the City of Amsterdam. Moreover, model statutes laid down by the German authorities were incorporated in this consitution; the German influence also makes itself felt in the stipulation (Article 5) that all the assets and liabilities of the various institutions incorporated into the new body were henceforth vested in it. A survey of November 27, 1942, shows us just how many such institutions were involved: 8 hospitals, 8 orphanages, 6 children's homes and 13 public old age homes. The *Jewish Weekly* of November 13, 1942, published a full report on the new body, together with a list of its chief officials (A. Asscher, President; Meijer De Vries, Membership Secretary), the address, consulting hours, sub-committees, etc.

For an institution such as the Dutch Israelitic Poor Relief Board in Amsterdam, which had a distinguished record of service over 120 years, the loss of identity came as a great shock, and there was talk of mass resignation—only a sense of responsibility to the old and sick prevented this in the end. Another factor which might have influenced the Board was the fact that all subsidiary bodies of the new organization were allowed to keep their own management committees, which, moreover, were all given the necessary exemptions from transportation "until further notice".

We also know something of the finances of the Jewish Care and Nursing Association in the middle of 1943, including estimates for the third quarter—by which time most of the subsidiary organizations had ceased to lead even a shadow existence. The latest estimates included an ominous new item: "Cost of operations in connection with sterilization". This was put at 12,000 guilders. A further 3,000 guilders was expected to be recovered from the patients. That is how far, in the summer of 1943, the concept of "care and nursing" had been stretched. The Association disappeared altogether in October of the same year.

The victim was down, but not yet completely out. A proclamation published in all newspapers on December 6, 1943, gave the *Reichskommissar* control of all remaining synagogues and their congregations, on the grounds that as "non-commercial organizations" they fell to him. Dr. Wimmer, as *Generalkommissar* for Administration and Justice, apparently took some exception, evidently fearing that the *Reichskommissar* would soon lay the same claim to Christian Churches and thus cause great unrest in the country. But whatever might be the implied threat to the Christians, the blow had already fallen on the Jews.

From the offices of the Jewish Care and Nursing Association in Tolstraat, we now go on to 17 Tulpstraat which housed the offices of what one might call the Jewish Ministry for Education, under I. van der Velde and J. J. van der Velde. We have voluminous records of its activities, from which we know, for instance, how many Jewish schools there were in the country at a given date, and how many teachers were employed; the records also include a map of Amsterdam (1 : 10,000) dated November 1941, on which all the Jewish schools are marked, and an alphabetical list of all teachers, indicating their places of work, probably dating from the spring of 1942. All this gives us the impression of a large and smooth-running organization which, though it had to work with unqualified teachers and was impeded at every turn by the Germans, nevertheless produced results bordering on the miraculous. At the time, those involved still felt confident enough to share the view of S. Broekman, the leader of the Youth Department, who declared in September

1942 that, if only the work were built on solid foundations, it would endure.

Solid foundations?

The writer remembers the first anniversary (July 1942) of the founding of the Jewish Lyceum, when the pupils were solemnly assembled in hall and the chief speaker, the invariably punctual Professor Cohen, was very late in arriving. At the end of his address, he turned to the writer and said: "This war grows worse with every hour it continues." At the time, he gave no explanation of a remark which, from a man usually so impassive, was highly charged with emotion. Only much later did the writer learn that Professor Cohen had just heard of the impending mass deportations. These were to involve first some of the students, then more and more, until finally even the teachers, who had supposed themselves relatively secure, disappeared never to be seen again.

We have spoken on several occasions of the Youth Care Department. A document of October 23, 1942, set out the advantages of this organization. They were so self-evident that we need not dwell on them here. In another surviving report the Department boasted of the fact that despite the few and generally inadequate meeting-places (bicycle-sheds, a tobacco warehouse, etc.) and very modest means, it had been able to create "a very nice atmosphere"—for instance, by means of murals, etc. It had even been able to establish a children's library. A document of January 11, 1943, refers to the difficulties in the organization's path. Chief among them was the fact that some of the handful of leaders had "ceased to be available" at short notice. The document added that it had been possible to rent a number of cart-sheds in East Amsterdam and that "everything necessary had been done to transform these decaying and neglected places into friendly halls". At that time there were six such halls, each with its own piano and most with a stage; there were also two peripatetic projectors and an epidiascope. Altogether 2,000 children were enrolled in the organization.

There was also the winter vacation school, where professors and artists held discussions and gave demonstrations and performances. Not the least valuable aspect of this work was that Jewish children, who were denied access to public playing-fields, were able to take part in gymnastics, boxing, table-tennis, volley-ball, basket-ball and other games. There were also medical fitness tests; on January 10, 1943, for instance, 360 children were examined and only thirty-one found to be unsound. Finally, the records also include a number of documents dealing with competitions and handicrafts for youth leaders, and we even have one of the diplomas that were given out —an accompanying letter explained that one of the signatories was "no longer available as a result of last week's events". (This was the great raid of May 26, which rendered not one but many hundreds "no longer available".)

Herzberg[1] has devoted many pages to the subject of Jewish schools, or rather, as he so precisely put it, to schools for Jewish children— to mark the fact that religious instruction was an optional subject in most of them. Moreover, until March 5, 1943, a number of half-Jewish children still attended these schools, and until March 1 there was even a half-Jewish teacher. A telephone call by the Germans quickly put a stop to this state of affairs.

A great many of the teachers in these schools were either unqualified or semi-qualified but, if the writer's own school was at all typical, this in no way diminished their devotion to their onerous task. The atmosphere in the staff-room was very much like that in any other staff-room, except for the ever-present threat from the outside. Thus the writer remembers that, on the morning after the introduction of the Jewish star, most of the staff were agreed on what the children should be told: though the star was intended to humiliate them, they must wear it as a badge of honour.

In many ways there was little to distinguish these schools from any others. There were the usual forms, 1A, 1B, etc., a headmaster, a senior master, a janitor, registers, impositions and absentees. Of course, the last were not quite the ordinary absentees, since for the usual reasons some were never seen again. Thus class 2B which, in the autumn of 1942, counted twenty-eight pupils, was reduced to four in May 1943. The writer will never forget the look on his pupils' faces when names were called from the register and there was once again no voice to answer.

Nor were the large gaps in the classroom the only differences between Jewish and normal schools. Thus the latter were closed not only on Sundays but also on Saturdays and Jewish holidays. Some children considered this a great boon; not so the fact that they had to travel to another part of the city for physical training, and to brave the ever more dangerous streets. In some cases, the distances were so large that, as Herzberg tells us, the Jewish Council had to

[1] Herzberg: *op. cit.*, pp. 184 ff.

supply a hand-cart for the transport of the heavy satchels. Perhaps it is also true to say that the relationship between teachers and pupils in the Jewish schools was somewhat unusual. Thus, at a time when it was difficult for Jews to buy fish, the writer was surreptitiously presented with neat little packets of skin and bones by anonymous donors who knew that he kept two cats. The writer also remembers that during one of his history lessons, a boy quietly put on a skull-cap and, on investigation, was found to be working at his Hebrew. Was he to punish the boy for being more in awe of the Almighty than of this teacher? A colleague reported a similar case of a boy who put on his skull-cap in class—but this time only in order to say a blessing over the sweets he was secretly eating. Here, the boy could be reprimanded, since the sweet was smaller than a pigeon's egg and therefore did not need a blessing said over it.

The education given to the pupils at the Jewish schools was in no way inferior to that enjoyed by other children of the same age, so much so that the Dutch Government subsequently recognized school-leaving certificates issued by, for instance, the author's own Jewish Lyceum. But if not inferior it was sometimes unorthodox, to say the least. Thus, at the Lyceum, eight Friday afternoons in the early part of 1943 were devoted to a series of lectures on the Romantic movement. This was a matter of some concern to an elderly mathematician, who was afraid that his pupils would have no time to prepare for their algebra examination in the summer. Still, he did not press his objection, no doubt realizing that most of his pupils would have "left" well before the examination.

This particular course of lectures was not without its dangers. Thus, a group of musicians, with the best Dutch Jewish violinist as their leader, treated the pupils to a Schumann quintet—and since Schumann was a good Aryan composer, the Jewish musicians were, of course, forbidden to play him. On another occasion, a group of pupils performed a play based on Nicolaas Beets's *Camera Obscura.* Would they have to wear stars on their nineteenth-century costumes? One of those taking part was Freddy S., the ablest pupil in Class 3A, whom the author remembers as a particularly bright boy. Shortly before the performance was due to begin, the headmaster entered the classroom and asked Freddy to go with him to his study, where the author joined them a few minutes later. There he found two strangers, one with a stony face, the other with an incredibly stupid expression, both in uniform. The first explained that Freddy's mother had been charged with a petty offence (buying eggs from a barrow, or something like that); Freddy's father, who was working at the Jewish Council, had been arrested immediately afterwards, and now Freddy had to come along because—and the writer remembers the precise words—"we like to keep families together'. Freddy was sent to fetch his coat, with the injunction that if he disappeared the headmaster would be taken away in his place. The poor boy was taken to the Schouwburg, where the writer and some pupils spotted him behind a window on the day that the performance took place. This was the sort of school-leaving that fell to the lot of many of the boys and girls. Little Carla G., one of the last children from the Lyceum to be seized, belonged to a small group who used to walk home with the writer every afternoon. One day, when the writer had to leave school earlier than usual, he noticed the squad-car outside her parents' house. He immediately turned back in the hope of saving the child, but in vain. She had already left school, and he never saw her again.

Another offshoot of the Jewish Council, the A. B. Davids School, where the boys were trained in metalwork, electrical engineering, automobile repairs, furniture-making, upholstery, woodwork, catering, tailoring, etc., was housed in 39 Valckenier Street. Many of the pupils owed their survival in the camps to the training they were given here. Thus, one of the author's colleagues in the Jewish Lyceum, an excellent historian, was trained as a baker, and as such worked, ate and survived in Bergen-Belsen.

From Valckenier Street we go to 10–11 Vening Meineszkade where there was found one of the mightiest—if so we may call it—organs of the Jewish Council: the finance department, or, as some wit called it, "the Jewish Treasury". It is interesting to make a comparison between the staff listed in the *Handbook* as at March 15, 1943, and that given in later editions. Thus, one of the leaders of the "Treasury" had meanwhile been "Aryanized", so that the Jewish Council lost the services of a man who was described as having a lucid mind, great critical acumen and expert knowledge. His right-hand man, the banker P. Hendrix, also "withdrew his services"—he and his entire family were murdered.

The "Treasury" had strange antecedents for which we must turn back to the beginning of the Occupation. At that time, the Committee for Jewish Refugees was caring for some 6,000 people, and with the outbreak of the war, they soon found themselves short of funds.

In early June 1940 the directors, led by Professor Cohen, had a discussion with Frederiks: the Dutch Government had voted 1,200,000 guilders for this work, and Frederiks had seen fit to cancel this arrangement—without any German pressure so far as we can tell. Instead, he advised that the Jews themselves should find the necessary money, the better to "conceal from the Germans the presence in this country of so many refugees" (Berkley). This was also more or less the view adopted at a subsequent meeting of the two main Jewish religious congregations; as Herzberg[1] put it, ". . . 6,000 needy God-fearing German Jews was the very last thing one wanted during the first months of the Occupation". The reader may well ask whether this was not perhaps the first step down the slippery slope. In any case, the result was the formation of the "Committee for Aid to Foreign Jews in the Netherlands", which continued as an independent body until the middle of March 1941, and whose main task was to raise and administer funds for and on behalf of the Jewish Refugee Committee. Their task should not be underestimated. There were needy refugees living at home, and needy refugees in Westerbork—the Jewish Community was compelled to pay for the building and upkeep of this camp, although it was not exclusively used for Jews. The Catholics and Protestants offered to pay for their own people, but only if they were removed to other places deemed more suitable. Since the Germans refused to do anything about the matter, the Jewish community had to stand good for the lot, or nearly so—what contributions various Christian bodies did make, says Berkley, were disproportionately small.

To raise all this money, a levy was imposed on the Jewish population as a whole, based on the 1939–40 tax assessment. The levy was 1 per cent for incomes up to 5,000 guilders; 1½ per cent for incomes from 5,001 to 10,000 guilders; 2 per cent for all higher incomes. In addition, there was a capital levy of 1 per cent for the first 30,000 guilders; 1½ per cent for the next 45,000 guilders, and 2 per cent on the rest. All those housing a refugee (or an evacuated person) were entitled to deduct 1 guilder per person per day.

It is clear that this kind of taxation was more easily put on paper than translated into practice. There were many defaulters, some on principle, some by evasion, and the newly established Jewish Council had to deal with them one by one and by personal visits. We have a copy of a letter which was sent to the more obdurate

[1] Herzberg: *op. cit.*, p. 187.

cases. These were told that they were "exposing the Jewish community in the Netherlands to serious dangers", that they "were deliberately placing themselves beyond the pale of the Jewish community, for which reasons the Jewish Council felt free to take whatever action against them was deemed necessary". Many readers will no doubt consider this tantamount to blackmail.

Were there any real sanctions behind the Council's threat? Well, yes, for those who paid up were issued with a "grey card", without which no one could make use of the services of the Jewish Council—and very soon it was a choice between seeking the Council's help, going into hiding or committing suicide. Those exempted from paying the levy, because they were too poor, also received grey cards, and, as Berkley reports, the Council would, in emergency cases, help even those without the card. Here, as so often, principle was in direct conflict with humanity. Be that all as it may, the Committee for Aid to Foreign Jews in the Netherlands, as an independent body and later as a department of the Jewish Council, did outstanding work until December 31, 1942, says Berkley, collecting, administering and distributing 6,000,000 guilders and thus bringing much needed relief.

In 1942 the situation deteriorated rapidly, as we can see from a statement issued by the Jewish Council's financial department for the months of May and June. At that time there was the first of many suggestions that a second levy would have to be raised. A special sub-committee was set up to study this question and its conclusions were, of course, greatly affected by the Decree of May 23, by which all Jews virtually lost control over their resources, having been forced to vest them in Lippmann, Rosenthal & Company. On September 18, 1942, the Central Bureau of the Committee for Financial Administration of the Jewish Council for Amsterdam (to give the reader its full title) sent a circular to all local departments, instructing them to increase the original levy by one-twelfth. All Jews accepting the new levy would have to send in Form A, together with their grey cards which would be returned immediately with a new stamp . . . Unstamped cards would lose their validity on November 1, 1942. The assessment would follow, on Form B. In addition to the circular, the Committee also issued a very clear set of rules and regulations. On October 22, came the news that new assessments were being prepared "at full speed"; on January 12, 1943, followed the announcement that the second assessment would not be levied after all. Hence we need not go into detailed financial calculations.

Something had clearly happened in the meantime.

On December 17 the Germans decreed that as from January 1 Lippmann, Rosenthal & Company would no longer be able to make direct payments to Jews, but that all such payments would have to pass through the Jewish Council. The Council would henceforth be entitled to draw on the Company each month for the amount of the levy and for its own expenses. This decision did not entirely come out of the blue; in a discussion of December 3, 1942, J. A. Rombach, the financial expert in Böhmcker's office, had instructed Professor Cohen to produce an estimate for the costs involved in acting as trustees for all Jewish property. This estimate the Jewish Council did, in fact, produce; they would require 945,000 guilders per month (for their own work). But it soon transpired that the Germans wanted the estimate to include private withdrawals from capital accounts. They conceded that this work would involve the Jewish Council in heavy additional responsibilities—"all Jews engaged on this task will be exempted from labour in Germany". Moreover, new employees recruited from outside Amsterdam would readily obtain removal permits. The conversation of Thursday, December 17 must have been cordial in the extreme, for the German Delegate "expressed his full confidence in the work of the Jewish Council", while Professor Cohen "declared his appreciation and said that we should try to prove worthy of the trust reposed in us." On December 19 Asscher and Cohen had another conversation with Rombach (who was later joined by Böhmcker); this time it was hard bargaining, with the Council asking for as much money as possible, and the Germans refusing on the grounds that "circumstances" and the "authorities" stood in the way.

Just before then—on December 18, 1942—the "Treasury" had published an announcement in the *Jewish Weekly* calling on all those making regular withdrawals from Lippmann, Rosenthal & Co. to make application for the January instalment directly to the Jewish Council. The Council received 3,750 such applications for a total of 589,000 guilders; in addition, there were countless requests for special payments, so much so that despite its best efforts the financial department could not satisfy everyone. From a surviving document we know that the Council established a brand-new inspectorate with 7 chief inspectors, 32 ordinary inspectors, 50 provincial inspectors and 5 district inspectors, who were given full instructions on two successive Sunday mornings and who were regularly supplied with special bulletins thereafter; it is a great pity that none of these documents has survived.

In order to form even a vague picture of what this work involved, the reader would have to feel some of the tensions and fears that prevailed at the time. Chaotic though the circumstances were, the Council was nevertheless able to pay out 90 per cent of the approved sums in January and even 100 per cent in February and March; all these payments had to be made in two instalments, for that is how the Council itself received the funds. During these three months the Council transferred a total of 1,428,000 guilders in 18,964 cheques.

It goes without saying that the Jewish Council had to finance the work of its own vast organization and, since the Germans had released no more than 800,000 guilders in January 1943, and the same amount in February, there was a serious deficit. Far from alleviating it, the Germans kept reducing the monthly payments, on the ground that so many Jews had "departed"—even so, the reduction was proportionately greater than that resulting from the number of deportations. In other words, everybody got less and less until finally, with the disappearance of the Jewish Council in autumn 1943, no one got anything at all.

Before we finally put down the *Handbook*, we must answer what is perhaps the most difficult question raised in this entire work: what judgment are we to pass on the work and continued existence of the Jewish Council?

"We believed that the Jewish Council let itself be used for the liquidation of Dutch Jewry. They collaborated with the Germans by compiling registers [of deportees] and in many other ways, all of which facilitated the final murder of the Jews. I was firmly convinced of this at the time and I still hold this opinion today."

This was not simply the view of an individual Jewish survivor, but the sworn declaration,[1] made a decade after the war, by Professor Gerbrandy, statesman, jurist, former Minister of Justice and a Prime Minister of the Netherlands. Others have accused the Jewish Council of being the Jewish arm of the German machine, of urging the victims on to destruction, of inspiring them with confidence in what had so clearly proved itself a diabolical tissue of lies, in tempt-

[1] Enquiry Commission, part VIIc, p. 783.

ing them to submit to a fate that they could have avoided at relatively small risk.

More than once the writer has wondered where precisely the line between the historian and the jurist must be drawn, but though this question has weighed heavily upon him throughout his labours, he was unable to find a satisfactory answer. In theory it is, of course, possible to draw such a line, though we might add that this task is much easier for the jurist who, no doubt, can dig up some precedent in law to decide, for instance, whether or not the very foundation and continuance of the Jewish Council constituted collaboration with the enemy, and whether the claim made by apologists for the Jewish Council, that if they had not carried out various German orders, those orders would have been still more ruthlessly imposed, can be accepted as a valid defence. But clear as the issue may be to the jurist, it is anything but clear to the historian.

To begin with, he cannot isolate the problem of the Jewish Council in the Netherlands from that of Jewish Councils in other occupied countries. There, too, an apparently innocuous beginning was everywhere followed by a steep decline into the abyss. Everywhere the same questions: could they have done otherwise? Should they have done otherwise? Would they have done otherwise? Where lay the boundary line between self-sacrifice and treachery, between help to one's fellows and help to the enemy? And everywhere the question of the moral responsibility of those who implemented the policies of that enemy, however reluctantly; everywhere the same tragi-comedy of a clique of jacks-in-office who had power over life and death, yet whose own skin was worth nothing as soon as they left their desks. The fact that this happened in Amsterdam later than in Berlin, Vienna and Prague, only makes it worse for a Dutch historian, who must surely feel that his own Jewish leaders should have learned from the terrible experiences of the rest—in so far, that is, as they knew about them, could know about them, or, indeed, wanted to know about them.

In the Netherlands these leaders were the Jewish Council, and particularly its two Presidents, Messrs. Asscher and Cohen, on whom lies the heaviest responsibility of all, for though it may have been more or less by chance that they were appointed in the first place, it was certainly no accident that they were allowed to remain at their posts. We hardly need the subsequent testimony of such German officials as Rauter, Lages and Aus der Fünten to realize that the two Presidents proved highly satisfactory to their masters—had they been otherwise, the Germans would have got rid of them quickly enough and replaced them with more "useful" men.

Abraham Asscher (September 19, 1880–May 2, 1950) was a prominent figure in his native Amsterdam before the war, playing a leading role in the diamond world, in public life and in the Jewish community. From 1917 onwards he was a member of the Provincial Council of North Holland; he was head of the Netherlands Israelitic Congregation and of the Council of the Netherlands Israelitic Chief Synagogue, presided over the Committee for Special Jewish Affairs, and was a member of many other important bodies.

"When the Jewish Council was founded, the [German] attitude to the Jews was by no means clearly hostile"—anyone who could make this claim in all seriousness and even put his name to it, as he did,[1] raises serious doubts as to his powers of insight—to put it mildly. "I had no afterthoughts about the foundation of the Jewish Council"—and this from a man who stood at the helm of the Jewish ship in a raging sea . . . When the writer questioned Lages on this point after the war, the latter replied with a quotation from *Julius Caesar* (Lages was always one for quotations): "Let me have men about me that are fat." And indeed Asscher was no Cassius. Moreover, even those who defend him in all other respects speak of his gullibility, impulsiveness, lack of discernment, his inability to keep a secret. In the course of this book the reader has met more than one instance of this impulsiveness and, we might say, naïvety; he has only to recall Asscher's physical attack on a German soldier. Clearly, such a man was quite unable to face the problems of his day in all their grim reality, let alone to solve them—though his courage was such that not even the Germans questioned it. Yet it seems impossible to doubt that they found him a suitable tool, so much so that they were prepared to tolerate his outbursts; "I fully believe that Lages was well disposed towards me. He once asked me if he made me sick and I said: 'Worse than sick.' He then told me that he thought this very frank." Or again: "One evening, when we had got to the end of our agenda, Lages asked me what I thought of the war. I said: 'If I told you what I really thought I would never get out of here alive—I am in the lion's den.' 'We have known each other for years now, Asscher,' he answered, 'you can speak to me as a friend and not as an SS officer.' Blumenthal, who was also present, said much

[1] Examination of Asscher on November 7, 1947.

the same thing. Lages then told me again to speak out freely, which I did: 'Germany is completely lost and will be smashed to smithereens—and all because you have put an arch-criminal like Hitler at the helm—Hitler and the rest of his gang, Goebbels, Streicher and Himmler. The only one who might still save Germany is Goering. Were he to sue our allies for peace terms, he might save something from the wreck.' That is what I truly believed at the time. And I added: 'Either string Hitler up or, if you haven't the will or nerve to do so, lock him up in a villa with 2,000 rooms for all I care.' The three of us then had the devil of a row but I was not arrested . . ."

To this strange and revealing self-portrait we might add that during the war, when Asscher received Goering in his Amsterdam factory, he would not let him sign the golden visitors' book: "That would have been too much, and so we quickly snatched the book away . . . We had a most pleasant chat with Goering."

A gullible man, an impulsive man, a courageous man. This is also evidenced by the fact that when his chance came to escape he let it go: he would rather put a bullet through his brain, he said, than leave his fellow-Jews in the lurch. Was he, then, an optimist? His reaction to the imposition of the yellow star on April 29, 1942, strongly suggests that he was, and there is also other evidence, some of it astounding. What the true explanation of this optimism was, the writer does not feel qualified to say, but Herzberg[1] has suggested that Asscher merely tried to reassure himself by reassuring the rest of the Jews. Undoubtedly, he told his co-religionists what they wanted to hear; people sought him out and clung to him—surely the great Asscher must know better than they themselves? Others reacted violently in the opposite direction. After one of his glib pronouncements, he was called an idiot by a leading Jew and promptly offered to knock the man down. Nor was that the only such offer he made, for he was invariably quick off the mark. According to Professor Cohen, he was merely trying to keep up his own courage. And yet there is no doubt that he raised the courage of many others as well; thus, when he died an obituary expressed the effusive thanks of "the many he saved during the war".

The writer must add that not all the survivors were quite so grateful, and who can speak for those who did not survive at all? Something of this must have percolated through to Asscher himself, and one must suppose that it deeply shocked and grieved him; how

[1] Herzberg: *op. cit.*, pp. 101 and 104.

else explain that a man who had been a religious Jew all his life—and an orthodox Jew at that—did not wish to be buried in a Jewish cemetery?

The other President, Professor David Cohen, was the more rational of the two; it was on him that Asscher depended for day-to-day guidance and also for the general plan of campaign. Moreover, Cohen was at his desk all day long, while Asscher never stayed for more than a few hours at a time, and was often absent at the most crucial moments. Cohen, who was born December 31, 1882, had taken part in Jewish life from his early youth. He moved to Amsterdam in 1926, where he pursued his profession as a classicist and occupied various positions in the Jewish community; after 1933, he was particularly active in refugee work.

"I have what a French philosopher once called *l'amitié sociale*. When communal interests are at stake, I completely forget myself, my position and my own interests." This is a telling revelation of his own character which Professor Cohen gave after the war.[1] But as he himself added: "These were characteristics highly disagreeable to their owner, bringing much trouble upon himself and his family." Moreover, "this irksome trait makes one lose a great deal of pleasure in life, and leads one to ask at the end of it what one has really lived for . . . The most annoying thing is that others ask the same question."

The reader will not miss a certain bitterness in this remark, a bitterness that need not surprise us, and which reflects some of the criticism that was made of Professor Cohen. It is difficult to distinguish, in the attacks on Asscher and Cohen, what is directed at them as Presidents of the Jewish Council and what is meant for their own persons; there is no doubt that Cohen's personality came under as much criticism as Asscher's, yet it would seem—although the evidence is inconclusive—that it was Cohen who on occasion earned more sympathy and certainly more respect. His qualities were recalled on the occasion of his leave-taking from Amsterdam University, when the Rector Magnificus, weighing his words, spoke of the affection felt for him by "very many" of his colleagues and of their "unshakeable faith in the rare qualities of his character . . . it is utterly inconceivable that he should have done anything dishonourable".

This statement evoked a number of adverse reactions. One man

[1] D. Cohen: *Curriculum vitae* (unpublished).

of rank in the community even said in private that Cohen's conduct during the war was, "to put it mildly, not free from guilt"; Cohen has also been reproached with "a childish love of power, an exaggerated opinion of his own work, and lack of character". This charge and others like it are to be found again and again in the records. Cohen (like Asscher) was blamed for breaking the February strike—as "the tool of the Germans"; for failing to realize even after the raid of June 1941, that the Jewish Council was merely being used by the invaders for the destruction of Dutch Jewry; that he held on to office even after the raid in the Eastern Provinces of September 1941; that he lent his name, in the columns of the *Jewish Weekly*, to the endorsement of infamous German orders and deceptions; that he encouraged Jews in 1942 to go to the Dutch work-camps, but saw to it that none of his own family or friends ever got there; that he started a "run on Vught" by singing its praises as a "better" camp; that he organized the distribution of yellow stars in what the Germans called a "splendid" way—and, moreover, in as many days as the Czechs took months over it, no in less . . .; that he was indefatigable in helping the Germans to organize deportations; that he collaborated in the system—rotten through and through—of exemptions, favouring his friends and relations; that in May 1943 he took upon himself the notorious choice of the 7,000, threatening all those who did not toe the line; and that making surrender after surrender he broke the last vestiges of Jewish pride and honour in the Netherlands. His subsequent conduct in Theresienstadt also aroused a storm of criticism. As to that, he himself afterwards confessed his "utter unsuitability" when it came to the leadership of the so-called Hamburg barracks in that camp. As for his work in the Netherlands, he admitted to failure only in respect of the final phase, when he was overwhelmed by the misery around him.

The reader will no doubt bear in mind that what criticisms were levelled at the two Presidents came from survivors—the views of the many tens of thousands who were murdered in the gas-chambers can only be imagined. Yet, surely, they would have added their voices to the clamour of the living: "You were the tools of our deadly enemies. You helped them to carry us off. You owe your own lives to this ignoble activity. You saved yourselves, your families, your friends and those of your own social class by sending us to our deaths. Your Council broke our resistance, deluded us with false hopes, misled, hurt, humiliated and on occasion even ill-treated us. You continued to serve the enemy even when he had plainly shown himself to be the butcher of our young people and the future butcher of us all. It was not we who appointed you as our leaders but the murderer—and yet you refused to lay down your office, indeed used it to deliver us to destruction, driving us with threats to the shambles. Perhaps we would have perished even without you, but can you truly say with the Bible that 'our hands have not shed this blood, neither have our eyes seen it'?"

But let us stop speculating, and turn once more to the living. In November 1947 the two Presidents were arrested on charges that constituted a comprehensive indictment of collaboration with the enemy, under fifteen headings. (The proceedings were subsequently dropped and the two Presidents never brought to trial.)

Some time previously the Jewish community had made its own investigation of the conduct of the two Presidents. A special commission of the Jewish Co-ordination Committee in the Netherlands appointed a Jewish Court of Honour, under the chairmanship of *mr.* M. Bosboom. Needless to say, this Court of Honour caused quite a stir in Jewish and other circles, not least because Asscher refused to recognize its competence. The findings were published on December 17, 1947, in a very lengthy document covering the historical facts, and presenting the case for and against the two Presidents. It did not omit to point out that the "Presidents of the Jewish Council were found wanting, but in a world that was itself gravely at fault". The Court concluded:

"That it was dishonourable to form an Amsterdam Jewish Council on German orders, and to have accepted the Presidency from the Germans (thus becoming answerable to them).

"That it was dishonourable to continue publishing the *Jewish Weekly* once it became clear that this publication could only serve German rather than Jewish interests.

"That it was dishonourable to lend support to anti-Jewish measures such as the issue of Jewish stars, and to the herding of people into Westerbork.

"That the Presidents acted dishonourably in the way in which they dealt with those who refused to pay the first levy.

"That they acted very dishonourably by co-operating in the selection of deportees, and particularly by their co-operation in May 1943."

The Court of Honour accordingly recommended the exclusion of both men from honorary and stipendary offices of all kinds in any Jewish organization or institution for the remainder of their lives.

Central to the whole problem, as we have said, was the question of collaboration. Here, too, the Presidents' (and the Jewish Council's) actions must be judged within the framework not only of the collaboration of Jewish Councils everywhere but also within the much vaster frame of collaboration as such, in its clearest, most undisguised and shameless form: that of the behaviour of willing tools in all Occupied countries, of Quislings, in short. Clearly, a distinction must be made between various groups of collaborators (among non-Jews we need only think of Mussert, Laval, Subhas Chandra Bose and, to some extent, of Franco). Similarly, among Jews, the spectrum of collaboration ranged from utterly corrupt elements, determined to save their own skins by deliberately and knowingly sacrificing their fellow-Jews, to those who, although collaborating, tried to save as many innocent people as possible.

No one has accused the two Presidents and the Jewish Council of being in the former range. They collaborated, and in so doing found themselves in a position where they could no longer choose between good and bad, but only between two evils. This is true even of Asscher, who to the end of his days apparently thought that he had, in fact, chosen the good; Cohen's possible human failings in Theresienstadt need not concern us here, for he was then no longer a President of the Jewish Council and we are here concerned only with his responsibility in that capacity.

As to that, we can do no better than quote the following dialogue with Lages:

"How was the Jewish Council used?"

"In every possible way."

"Did you find them easy to work with?"

"Very easy, indeed."

And Eichmann stated in Jerusalem that Jewish Councils everywhere helped to implement anti-Jewish measures, thus releasing German officials and policemen for other work.

The evidence was given after the war, when the Germans were intent on whitewashing themselves. But we also know what they said and did at the time. For instance, they felt no qualms in giving the Jewish Council a free hand in a number of ways—and quite especially in how it presented the German orders through the

*Jewish Weekly*. That this was collaboration, nobody can deny. They also appreciated the Council's work in registering Jews, in helping to concentrate them in Amsterdam, thus isolating them from the rest of the population before they could be sent, first to work-camps, and then "to Germany". Thousands of Jews were engaged in the work of a mighty machine and, even if we make allowance for the fact that much of their work was fictitious, they nevertheless made it possible for the Germans to deploy their resources elsewhere. Frequently, Asscher and Cohen urged their fellow Jews to obey the German regulations to the letter, an exhortation that was lent particular weight by their standing in the community.

Where did collaboration end and opposition begin? The Council continuously fluctuated between these two extremes. This was im-implicitly recognized by Professor Cohen, when he said that one could only go to the Germans when one had something to offer them. And what they had to offer was the services of the Jewish Council, an organization of extraordinary, one might almost say admirable, efficiency, and as such capable of throwing its great weight behind or against the Germans. We have examples of both actions. When it became clear that nothing would move the Germans, and that all further appeals would be in vain, the Council would work day and night both to implement the orders and to soften the blow. The unhappy victims who were snatched up with little more than what they had on, were richly supplied with goods, services and comforts. In addition, as Herzberg[1] has pointed out, the Council maintained "religious, social and philanthropic institutions, a Poor Board, orphanages, Old Age Homes, hospitals . . . schools, and a very important Youth Movement". Clearly, all this work could not have been done without a great organization and leadership. The alternative might have been the complete disorganization of Jewish communal life—and that was a risk no one was willing to take. Yet, once engaged on its task of alleviating the miseries of the moment, the Council all too readily forgot where all this was leading, and its own share of responsibility for the final outcome.

The Jewish Council played for time. Was that wrong? To answer that, we must once again try to imagine ourselves back in those days and, above all, remember that very few people thought that the war would last as long as it did. Even the most unselfish people would surely have hesitated to shelter and hide Jews if they had known that

[1] Herzberg: *op. cit.*, pp. 163–5.

their self-sacrifice would drag out over so many long years. And it has been said that had the war in fact ended in 1942 the Jewish community would have built a monument to Asscher and Cohen, as the brave and resourceful leaders by whose hands Dutch Jewry was saved.

On the other hand, it has been argued—after the war—that if the Jewish Council expected a speedy end to the war, it would have been politically expedient as well as morally imperative to refuse all collaboration. What could the Germans have done? Take ruthless measures? But in those days the Germans were still afraid of non-Jewish reactions. And in any case, the deportations would have been delayed, the feeling of solidarity between Jews and non-Jews would have been strengthened, and more Jews could have gone into hiding. As against that, it has been argued that the Jewish Council did, in fact, employ delaying tactics, and that, moreover, they had no idea what the Germans were doing to the deportees. Yet when all is said and done, Asscher and Cohen should have learnt the lesson of the treatment of the Jews in Germany in 1933. After all, they themselves had been responsible for bringing enough of them into Holland, and should therefore have been chary of sending a large volume of Jewish traffic in the opposite direction.

It has been said that they tried to soften the blow, that they tried to form a "wall" or a "barrier" between the Jews and the Germans. This barrier, Herzberg[1] has said was: "no thicker than the paper on which I am writing". And behind it, he went on to say, was not a garden "but a ghetto in the making". As for the claim that the Council saved Jews unpleasant contact with Germans, it must be remembered that this was hardly the case after the deportations. In any case, it also reduced contact between Jews and the rest of their fellow-Dutch citizens.

Now these, like the Jews, were oppressed by the enemy, and the Jews should have tried to make common cause with them. If we reproach the Jewish Council with not having seen to that, must we not reproach the Gentiles for their own lack of overtures in that direction? Did not Dutch municipal officers collaborate in the registration of Jews and in placing the letter 'J' on Jewish identity cards? Did not virtually all officials sign the "Aryan" declaration? Did not the Dutch authorities collaborate in the dismissal of Jewish civil servants? Did not the Dutch Bench implement many of the

[1] Herzberg: *op. cit.*, p. 169.

German decrees? Did not the Department of Social Affairs, the municipalities and the District Labour Offices allow themselves to be used to draft Jews to the work-camps? Did not the Amsterdam municipality play an important part in herding the Jews together? Did not the municipal transport system, the railways and the police, help in the deportations, and the gendarmerie in guarding Westerbork camp? Did the Dutch authorities refuse to collaborate in the confiscation of Jewish radios and bicycles, in depriving Jews of telephones? Did banks and clearing-houses refuse to hand over Jewish effects to Lippmann, Rosenthal & Company, or did the Stock Exchange refuse to transfer Jewish shares? Did the Government Textile Bureau refuse to cancel the permits of Jewish textile merchants? Did not the *Nederlandse Unie*, that organization of hundreds of thousands of loyal Dutchmen, try to co-operate with the Germans? What non-Jew had a clear conscience? And what Jew, for that matter? Did not the signatures of two Secretaries-General, proud of their anti-German attitude during the war, appear under a proclamation to the Dutch people, in which resistance-fighters, scores of whom were facing the death sentence in 1941, were described as "reckless and criminal elements"—and this at a time when Dutch Jews were already being exterminated as vermin in Mauthausen? Were there not traces elsewhere as well of the "unprincipled opportunism" with which the Jewish Council had been reproached?

Small wonder, then, that Asscher and Cohen felt completely alone. Sure enough, there was sympathy for the Jews, compassion, indignation and even some protest. But was there much more? Everyone else was protesting—and going along, all the same. And what of the Dutch Government in London? They, too, issued no clear directives to the Jewish leaders.

There are a number of other things that have a direct bearing on the attitude of the Presidents. As we have said, they assumed office in the certainty that they were the right men for the job. As far as Asscher, in particular, was concerned, he remained convinced of his suitability throughout his presidency. No doubt both men felt what Friedman has called a Messianic hope—the hope that they were the chosen instruments of their people's redemption—who can say? As for Cohen, he has compared himself to a leader who, in time of war, "must have the strength to sacrifice a hundred so as to save three thousand", to "the general who must sacrifice a company in order

After the great raid of May 26, 1943

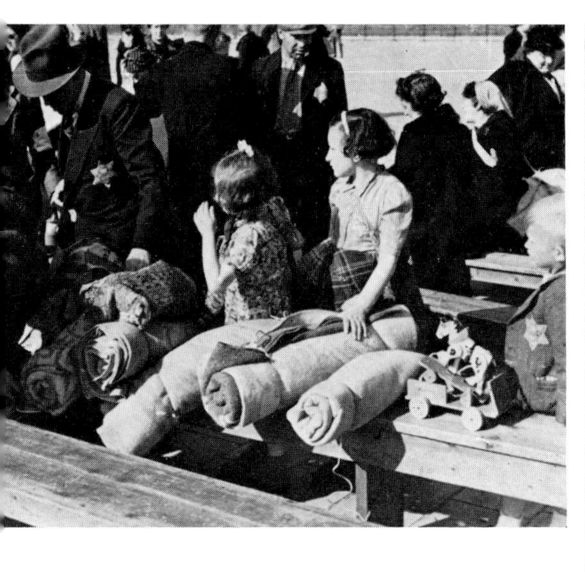

Lorries being boarded in East Amsterdam

De Schaffelaar Castle, Barneveld

The Jewish Council of Amsterdam.
A. Asscher and D. Cohen sitting at left of table

The Headquarters of the Jewish Council in Amsterdam

Displaced Persons' Aid Bureau

Class at lessons

to save a division". Again and again we find in Cohen's apologia the plea that if he had not been there, someone else (for instance, De Leon) would have done infinitely worse. This is a moot point. All we can say is that the Germans did not push De Leon to the fore, and that, had they been dissatisfied with Asscher and Cohen, they would have had no hesitation in dismissing and breaking them—much as they did Chief Rabbi Sarlouis. And it is just as well to emphasize once again that these two leaders were appointed not by the Jews themselves but by their enemies; when they took decisions on which the life and death of their fellow-Jews depended, they did so not by virtue of the powers vested in them by the community, but because they had been put there to do so by the Germans.

How little insight Asscher had into all this, is betrayed by the way he took as no more than his due the privileges conferred upon him: the continued use of his bicycle and telephone, permission to ride in motor-cars or trams ("front platform only"). He even asked Lages—(much to Cohen's dismay)—for permission to travel first-class on his visits to the camps—"I simply refused to travel in over-crowded, second-class compartments." (Cohen added: "I myself only used taxis and trams when it was absolutely essential for my work. When travelling by train, I generally did what everyone else had to do—I stood in the second-class compartments.") It is revealing to read how Asscher, wearing the yellow star, surrounded by Germans in uniform, was received in Vught, where so many fellow-Jews lived under such horrible circumstances: "There was a lot of bowing and scraping, everyone was terribly polite, and anti-Semitism was swept under the carpet for a few hours." "For the rest," Asscher said, "I had no single advantage and was treated as badly as all the other Jews." We must not, however, forget that both he and Cohen were allowed to put their families on the safety list, and that they were left in Amsterdam until the very end. In a German report of March 20, 1943, we can read that a number of Jews would not have to go to the East after all, but would be sent to Theresienstadt instead. The men in question all had a record of "distinguished service during the 'dejudification' of the Netherlands, and included the organizing staff at Westerbork and members of the Jewish Council."

"Distinguished service"—that is what the Germans themselves called it. After the war, Asscher said, not without some self-satisfaction, that when Jews were denied access to all but Jewish hairdressers, he had told Lages straight out that he would continue to visit his non-Jewish barber; if Lages did not like it he could always arrest him. We can imagine the Germans' reaction to this: why bother about this petty incident, when Asscher was proving so useful in far more important respects?

Just one further question: did the two Presidents never want to throw in the towel? As we saw, during the raids of June 1941, Asscher had the impulse to do it, but no more. By that time, many other leading Jews, including *mr.* L. E. Visser, had already sounded the alarm. From more than one side, people had begun to speak out against having anything to do with "the German butchers", as the illegal Press called the invader. In the spring of 1942 many more associates of the Jewish Council asked themselves whether it was right to continue the work, now that the so-called labour service was more and more appearing in its true light. When the same question was raised at a meeting of the Central Committee of the Jewish Council on September 18, 1942, after the round-ups had begun, Professor Cohen opined that it would be criminal to leave the community in the lurch at the hour of its greatest peril . . . "Moreover we must do our utmost to keep the most important people here as long as possible." (It is illuminating that there were two versions of these minutes, and that this passage occurs in the first, but not in the second.) Hardly a month later, the same Committee met to discuss the arrest of two outstanding leaders of the Jewish community, Chief Rabbi Sarlouis and Secretary Bolle. Was this not the time to resign? The answer was no—the rest would have to continue "in the interests of the community". It must have been at about this time that the writer first heard a joke that was then doing the rounds: Asscher and Cohen are the only Jews left, and the Germans demand the deportation of one of them. Says Cohen to Asscher: "It had better be you, Abraham—lest worse befall the rest of us."

Even in May 1943, when the Jewish Council was ordered to select 7,000 people for deportation, the cup was apparently not yet full, and the Council tried to "preserve a core". They apparently had no doubt who constituted it: the intelligentsia and the well-to-do of yore—it was to save this dwindling group, to which they themselves belonged, that an ever greater number of sacrifices were fed into the mouth of Moloch.

It has been said that most of the guilt should be squarely laid upon the Jewish community itself which, although it did not choose these men, accepted them as leaders, "idolized and indulged them", and indeed encouraged them in the feeling that they were "higher and better than the humble fruiterers whose interests they were supposed to serve". But if the Presidents liked to see themselves as captains of sinking ships, they should have remembered the captain of the *Titanic* who did not take to the boats—but perished in the waves. In May 1943 the Presidents of the Jewish Council agreed to supply the list the Germans had demanded of them—much against their own will and fully aware of the monstrous nature of their task. The writer must put on record that among the 7,000 names, two were conspicuous by their absence—those of Asscher and Cohen.

Let that fact speak for itself.

CHAPTER FIVE

# ASPECTS OF PERSECUTION

## JEWISH RESISTANCE

HOLLAND witnessed no ghetto uprising on the Warsaw pattern, no last-ditch stand by a group of desperate men, cut off from the rest of the population. In our country, Jewish resistance, by and large, was part and parcel of the common struggle against the enemy. The chief difference was that Jews ran additional risks; they were under far stricter surveillance, more conspicuous and, once caught, invariably done to death. However, as one non-Jewish author[1] has put it, "the greater danger did not in the least deter those who had dedicated themselves to this task". Understandably so. For while non-Jews could resist or submit, Jews could only choose between resistance and deportation. Hence it is not surprising to find that Jewish resistance had none of that playful nature typical of so much non-Jewish resistance work, particularly at the beginning. As early as February 1941, when Jews were first attacked by Dutch storm-troopers, they knew that they must fight for their existence, for their very lives. And how much more hopeless must the situation have appeared to them as the war dragged on! What comfort could they have taken from the victories at El Alamein and Stalingrad? They welcomed them, of course, but no doubt they must have had the nagging feeling that, for them at least, these victories came too late. And then Dutch Jews lacked a common rallying point. Many identified themselves fully with the general Dutch struggle, and derived great comfort from this act of national solidarity. Others, who incidentally proved no less valiant in the fight against the common foe, adopted quite a different attitude. What sustained their efforts? The Jewish community? No group could have been more heterogeneous—anthropologically, economically, socially, politic-

[1] A. de Froe: "De psychologie van de verzetsstrijder" (The psychology of the Resistance fighter) in *Onderdrukking en Verzet* (Oppression and Resistance), Part III, p. 499.

ally, culturally or in religious outlook. The Dutch synagogue, from which many Jews had, in any case, become estranged, had grown into a respectable, conservative institution in a respectable bourgeois country, and as such was utterly unfitted to any form of violent or revolutionary struggle. There was no single body to embrace Dutch Jewry as a whole, no body that could have supplied the leaders in this hour of need. Hence Jewish underground fighters, inasmuch as they did not merge into the Dutch Resistance Movement, were left more or less to their own devices.

How large a part did Jews play in the Resistance? There was no lack of testimony, during and after the war, that the Jewish contribution to the struggle was greatly exaggerated by the Germans, but seriously underrated by the Dutch. There can be no doubt that resistance by Jews was proportionately greater than that of other Dutchmen.[1]

The Germans, of course, smelt a Jew behind every hostile act. Thus Lages said after the war that "Jews lurked in all anti-German organizations; they worked deliberately and with personal animus".[2] Rauter likewise saw Jewish machinations behind dozens of acts of espionage and sabotage.[3] Other Germans claimed that the Jews were the saboteurs *par excellence*, the driving force behind the entire Dutch Resistance, and blamed them for every attack on pro-German Netherlanders.

After the war, the Jewish part in the Resistance was played down by many people both at home and abroad—the reader must decide for himself how much of this, too, was due to anti-Semitism. But even among those who cannot be suspected of this bias, many have deplored the fact that Jews apparently failed or feared to fight back. Still, these critics have had to concede that this impression is largely due to the refusal of many (though not all!) Resistance organizations to admit Jews who, as we have said, were under close and constant German surveillance, and thus a potential danger to their comrades. It has also been alleged that Jews went like lambs to the slaughter, with a meekness that must arouse astonishment and even indigna-

[1] J. Presser: "Het verzet van joden in Nederland 1940–1945" (Resistance by Jews in the Netherlands in 1940–1945) in *Schrijfsels en Schrifturen* (Essays) (Amsterdam, 1961), pp. 138, 146.

[2] W. Lages: *Gedanken und Aufmerkungen zur "Kroniek der Jodenvervolging* (Reflections and Notes on the "Chronicle of Jewish Persecution"), p. 52.

[3] *Het process Rauter* (The Rauter trial), p. 47.

tion; many no doubt find it more convenient to dwell on this than on the failure of their Gentile countrymen to make any strenuous attempt to save them. They also find it convenient to forget that a Jewish group was the first one to strike a blow at the Germans, and that, even before the war, Jews were in the forefront of the struggle against Hitler: many of them fought Fascism in the Spanish Civil War.

Before going into further details, we must mention the existence of a militant Jewish organization, the Society for the Defence of the Cultural and Social Rights of Jews (SRJ), which was founded in Amsterdam a year before the war. This society set out to teach Jewish youth—particularly young Jewish workers—how to defend themselves in the inevitable struggle against the Nazis. It strove to raise the morale of the Jewish population as a whole, and even tried, without success, to supply them with arms.

Until May 1940 it was still possible to discount the German threat; afterwards it could at most be played down. Every Jew then had to make up his mind precisely where he stood. The Jewish Council had its own answer, and, even with the best will in the world, no one can say that it set its heart on militant opposition. Yet there was no lack of Jews who did just that, chief among them L. E. Visser, the President of the Dutch Supreme Court.

His name has been often mentioned in these pages. Lodewijk Ernst Visser, born in Amersfoort in 1871, was the son of a merchant, alderman and deputy mayor. In 1894, after having studied in Utrecht and Paris, he earned his doctorate with a thesis on International Law. In March 1915, at the age of forty-three, he was made a member of the Netherlands High Court and on January 3, 1939, became its President. On Friday, May 10, 1940, Visser read a declaration from the Bench, in which he spoke openly of "murder" and "treacherous attacks". He was dismissed late in November 1940, after attempts to exempt him from the anti-Jewish legislation. Visser treated the failure of these endeavours as a high compliment, for he was well content to share the lot of the humblest of his people.

In the fourteen months of life that remained to him Visser resisted the Germans at every step; he became one of the contributors to the resistance paper, *Het Parool*, interceded with the Secretaries-General on behalf of the Mauthausen victims, and even tried to do so with Rauter, who refused to receive him. He then addressed a letter to that *Generalkommissar*, signing himself "President of the Supreme

Court of the Netherlands, retired". In December 1941 Visser protested against the illegality of instituting separate schools for Jews; he refused to accept his identity card on the ground that the letter 'J' made a false distinction between Dutch citizens, thus violating the Constitution. He had been a director of many Jewish organizations and Governor of the Board of Control of a Zionist body, the *Keren Hayesod*. Now, though by no means a religious man, he made a point of walking about The Hague on Saturdays "in Sabbath clothes, with a prayer book (which he could scarcely read) tucked under his arm—simply to defy the new Haman". There is small doubt that the Germans would have destroyed this courageous man, had death not claimed him first.

Visser was the leading spirit of the Co-ordination Committee, a body we have mentioned on several occasions. According to Herzberg,[1] it was set up by the two main Jewish religious communities on the initiative of the Dutch Zionist Federation. The Committee refused to deal in any way with the invader, unless directly forced to do so, in which case it would "decide beforehand precisely what line it was going to take". We saw that the Committee was afterwards dissolved, but even then it met in secret on a number of occasions—unknown to Cohen and Edersheim, two of its more "respectable" former members.

A few other highlights of the Jewish Resistance may be mentioned here. We have already spoken of the Koco affair. The Amsterdam *Schouwburg* and the crèche across the road from it also deserve attention. Both were under strict German supervision but . . . *quis custodiet custodes*? If the guards were not drunk already, the joint efforts of the Jewish conspirators inside and their non-Jewish helpers outside soon put that right. The result was that not a few incarcerated Jews were spirited away, together with all their records. A host of children likewise "disappeared" from the crèche—in crates and potato-sacks. It should be recorded that an SS man, one Zündler, was glad to assist the kidnappers. He was detected and died in a concentration camp. One witness says that more than a thousand children were saved in this way.

Inscribed in the Roll of Honour is the name of Walter Süskind, a thirty-nine-year-old former company director, who was the heart and soul of the whole kidnapping enterprise. He would first treat the German guards to drinks, and then take the suicidal risk of rifling

[1] Herzberg: *op. cit.*, p. 151.

the records behind their backs—he was not even on the staff of that department and, if caught, would have been shot out of hand. When he and his family were eventually removed from Theresienstadt, Professor Cohen begged Murmelstein, the Jewish "elder" in the camp, to intercede with Kommandant Rahm, who had known Süskind in Holland.[1] Murmelstein refused. Süskind and his family tried to hide in the camp, but were eventually discovered and sent to Auschwitz, where they died. "Very many owe their lives to him." In this book we are proud to proclaim Walter Süskind not only as a Jewish hero but also as the type of all that was best in the Dutch Resistance.

This may be the place to mention one of the most heart-warming episodes in our whole story, that of the so-called Palestine Pioneers and their many non-Jewish helpers. Not all the Pioneers were active in the Resistance; some even believed that all this suffering was God's will and must be endured. But that, of course, was a minority view.

Among the Palestine Pioneers one name stands out—that of Joachim ("Schu-Schu") Simon. Intelligent, knowledgeable and highly educated, this young man (who, incidentally, was plagued with asthma) proved a veritable dynamo. Not pausing even to eat or sleep, he would work ceaselessly for days on end, and cover long distances on foot[2] rather than draw on the group's dwindling fund. With a few non-Jewish friends, he devised a bold plan for shepherding forty-eight Pioneers from one of their training camps across the Belgian border. When the time came, he rallied their flagging spirits, met every emergency and spared no thought for his own safety. In January 1943, when he crossed the border for the third time, he fell into the hands of the enemy and, realizing that he knew too much and that the Germans had ways of making even the bravest talk, he took his own life in Breda prison.

With no less pride we pay homage to a non-Jewish hero—who continued Simon's work and also laid down his life—to Joop Westerweel, born on January 25, 1899. This Socialist teacher and conscientious objector first came across the Palestine Pioneers during the war. He was deeply impressed by their dedication and single-mindedness, and even thought of emigrating to Palestine himself. Meanwhile, he decided to help Simon's comrades across the border. On March 11, 1944, he was seized (he had been captured before but

[1] Cohen: *Herinneringen*, p. 63.
[2] M. Syrkin: *Blessed is the march* (New York, 1947), pp. 282–3.

had managed to escape), taken to Vught Concentration Camp, and subjected to horrible tortures which failed to break his spirit. In detention he wrote and recited poetry, played mental chess through the wall, and wrote many letters that were smuggled out of the camp. Unfortunately, the doctor who acted as his courier was caught by the Germans, who then set a spy in the organization. This man proposed an escape plan. At the appointed rendezvous, four Palestine Pioneers and two of their non-Jewish helpers fell into enemy hands. On August 11 Joop Westerweel himself was executed just outside the camp by a firing squad.

It is said that, during 1943 and 1944, the Pioneers succeeded in getting about 150 young people (including non-Jews) to France, where it was easier to survive. Quite a few joined the Resistance there, but eighty managed to reach Spain and seventy of these eventually got to Palestine.

Similar work was done at Westerbork, involving the forgery of papers, stamps, etc. One audacious Jew, pretending to be a messenger, went freely in and out of the camp to make the necessary arrangements; another, no less courageous, though barely twenty years of age, worked on the small railway serving the camp. He pretended to be simple, but all the while used his train to smuggle boys and girls past the guards. Other members of the group helped as well, and paid for it with their lives.

The reader may care to have a few figures. Out of a total of 821 Palestine Pioneers, 361—44 per cent—were saved. An even higher proportion was saved from Loosdrecht Camp—34 out of 48—i.e. 70 per cent. These proportions would have been even higher, but for the fact that some of those rescued were later recaptured. Else, the entire Loosdrecht group would have got away.

There was no branch of the Dutch Resistance in which Jewish men and women were not active. Jews were involved in, and died during, the February strike. Among the agents dropped into Holland by parachute, there was at least one Jew, and he took that risk three times. Jews guarded arms-stores and supplies of ration cards, and stole or forged baptismal registers and other documents. At least one Jew was involved in the raid on the Amsterdam Registry Office. Jews helped their co-religionists and others to escape into neutral countries. A Rotterdam Jew was the leader of a very active sabotage organization—the Dutch People's Militia—and committed suicide when he was caught. One of the writer's own pupils, Leo Frijda, who was involved in attacks on high NSB officials, lied while facing a firing-squad rather than betray his comrades—the German report was highly indignant about this—and a street in Amsterdam is now named after him.

A plaque in another street commemorates the name of Gerhard Badrian "a German Jew by birth, who was shot at this spot on Friday, June 30 1944, as a fighter for Dutch freedom".

Elsewhere, a resistance leader known as Jan de Geus was in fact a Jew, and Jews organized resistance groups across the border in Belgium—in the Walloon area as well as the Flemish. Jews wrote resistance poems, played an important part in the underground Press, and even published their own resistance paper, *Hashalsheleth* (The Chain). Had more Jews survived, a whole body of legends about the deeds of the Jewish Resistance would no doubt have grown up. Suffice it to say, that Jewish Resistance heroes were second to none in stature and in number.

## ESCAPE

"We got out in July 1942. We went via Brussels, where we stayed for fourteen days. Then we crossed the French border and the demarcation line. We spent some time in the camp at Château Neuf-les-Bains and worked in the area. When the Germans came, we crossed the Pyrenees, and were imprisoned at Pamplona. My husband was sent to Miranda camp; I myself remained in Pamplona and later went on to Madrid. About half a year later, my husband was released from Miranda. We were together for some time in Madrid, and then crossed into Portugal where we spent a few more weeks, until (in July 1943) we took a plane to England."

This odyssey by a Dutch Jewish doctor is no doubt typical of many experiences, most of which will never be known. Some refugees managed to reach Switzerland instead; many more were captured at some point on their journey. Treachery was everywhere, but there was also unselfish help, often at grave personal risk. Generally the refugees had to fend for themselves, to be heroes willy-nilly. They had to swim rivers, cross high mountains, bluff their way past guards, and go without sleep, food and other necessities. One false step and they ended up in the gas-chambers.

Theirs was a horrible story. But it must be told. It belongs to the history of Dutch Jewry, of the 140,000 men and women caught in a ghastly trap.

Many made use of an ancient remedy: they paid ransom, trying to buy safety for money. Some succeeded; Wielek puts their number at 200. Himmler discussed the matter with Hitler, as we know from a memorandum dated December 10, 1942: "I have asked the *Führer* about the release of Jews against foreign currency. He gave me powers to make what arrangements I saw fit, provided only that appreciable sums from abroad could be obtained in that way."

The release of two Jewish art-dealers from Dieren makes very strange reading. Goering had given them permission to leave for Switzerland, and when Rauter demurred, Goering telephoned to ask for an explanation in "a very irate tone". Rauter told him that, after consulting the representative of the German Foreign Office at The Hague, Bene, and the Security Police, he had decided to refer the whole matter back to Security Headquarters in Berlin. A few days later, Harster arrived with a favourable decision.

Not everyone was so lucky. A well-known banker's family, five in all, was able to offer a ransom of 100,000 Swedish crowns; this time Security Headquarters refused on the grounds that the ransom was 100,000 Swiss francs *per person* and, in any case, applied to old people only. And so the family was wiped out in the gas-chambers. Or take the case of an elderly violinist in Westerbork, whose poor family in Switzerland scraped together 10,000 francs for the German "winter relief", while a Swiss lady, who was the daughter of a Prussian major-general, vouched that the musician was a respectable woman, in no way concerned with politics. Another Swiss organization offered a further 10,000 francs; we do not know to what avail.

On November 24, 1942, London broadcast a talk on "Modern Racketeers": Dutch listeners were told that the Germans now demanded a ranson of 40,000 guilders per person. (We know now that this figure was an under-estimate.) There had also been an alternative proposal to release 500 Netherlanders *en bloc* against payment of 5,000,000 Swiss francs, to be underwritten by the Dutch Government. The broadcast went on to say that the Dutch Government had "regretfully decided that it could not be a party to these German practices"—they could not buy safety for a few with money that would only help the Germans to continue enslaving the many. Moreover, once their terms were accepted, the Germans, like all blackmailers, would merely be encouraged to raise their price. The Dutch Government went on to threaten action against anyone who participated in such exchange for profit. Even those who were willing to find ransom money from purely altruistic motives were warned that they would be breaking the law. There was an English language broadcast on the same day and to the same effect. Rightly or wrongly, this attitude of the Dutch Government was widely criticized after the war, *inter alia*, by the Parliamentary Enquiry Commission.

The fate of those ransomed falls outside the province of this book, though one episode deserves special mention: some Jews serving in the Dutch Legion that was being trained in Canada insisted that, for the duration of the war, members of their families in Holland be offered asylum to Canada. The Dutch Government expressed its willingness to pay for the maintenance of these families and to arrange for their repatriation after the war. However, the Dutch Minister in Ottawa reported to Minister Van Kleffens that Canada opposed the immigration of Jews and coloured people on principle. "The chief criterion for admission to Canada is race. The United States, where the criterion for entry is country of birth, has been swamped with Jews and other undesirable elements. It is a fact that Jews, having once obtained permission for their families to join them, if only temporarily, are exceedingly difficult to get rid of again."

This remarkable document was dispatched on May 26, 1943, the very day that Amsterdam witnessed its worst anti-Jewish raid, the day on which the invader had no difficulty in "getting rid of" thousands of such "undesirable elements". But when all is said and done, Canada was not a country for which the Dutch Government could be held responsible. What of the countries under its direct control? Let us hear what the Parliamentary Enquiry Commission had to say: "The Commission deeply regrets that the Governments of Surinam and Curacao—the first at the beginning, and the second throughout the war—opposed the admission of Dutch refugees, and that the Dutch Government, which must have realized the disastrous consequences of this policy, did not insist upon its reversal. It must, however, be admitted that Surinam—but not Curaçao—dropped its objections in 1942, and took immediate steps to admit a fairly large number of refugees."

But let us turn from these unwholesome political wrangles to the story of a few who managed to get away. Thus in her *Mijn Spaanse Grootmoeder* (My Spanish Grandmother) Suzanne van Thijn, who as early as May 22, 1940, left her studio and cycled into freedom "as fearful as a lonely child in the dark" but determined to succeed because she had "little to lose and everything to gain", tells us that what kept her going was the deep conviction that "as a Jew I was lost in any event, and so I would rather die fighting in England than quietly await the end where I was".

We also have the oral report of two brothers who crossed into Switzerland unaided. They first tried to make their get-away in December 1941, with very little money and without false papers. They reached the French border after a glorious hike through the Ardennes; in Namur, they even went to a dance and feasted on omelettes and wine. But near Givet things went wrong: the elder hid for hours under a railway truck while the younger was caught and cross-examined by a German officer. When he kept insisting that he was looking for work in France, the officer said: "There's something fishy about the whole thing; you are a Jew and much too young for such dangerous games. Go back to your mother—and God help you if I see you again." So three days later they were home again, but in March 1942 they made another attempt, and this time they were successful. The mother stayed behind until August 19, 1942, when she received a letter from Geneva, with the greeting: "Dearly beloved mother"—instead of the usual "Dear mother"—telling her that the letter was written in code. The message read:

"If you don't want to board with the Polaks or the Schlesingers (i.e. in Poland and Silesia—J.P.) try to get to Namur as quickly as possible. Madame Petit, who runs a photographer's shop at 18 Rue Cuvelier will give you, and you alone, full details of the route we took in December 1941. Go quickly and go alone. We know you can do it and we are waiting for you."

And she did it—a woman alone—or should we simply say a heroine? Let the sceptical read her report with care and accompany her in imagination through all her trials until finally she crossed the border: "There I spotted a tiny little man, almost a dwarf, with a broad, kindly face. He wore an apron and was picking large bunches of grapes which he put carefully into a basket. He gave me a friendly look and when I asked him '*Est-ce que je me trouve en France ou dans le canton de Genève?*' he answered '*Vous êtes sur terre libre, madame.*' And pointing to the fruit, he added, '*Servez-vous-en, madame.*' But before I tucked in I took his two hands in mine and kissed him on both cheeks."

Then there is the story of one of the writer's ex-pupils. This boy realized as early as 1934 that things looked black indeed, and in 1935 volunteered for service in the Officers' Training Corps. In the war he fought in the Dutch Army. After the capitulation, he considered —and rejected—all sorts of plans to escape by sea to England. Then, in July 1942, he escaped via Belgium into France with his wife. Despite many tight corners, their luck held until they reached Perpignan. Not far from the border a French gendarme stepped into the compartment to inspect their useless papers: "He looked at my wife's passport and at mine and returned them to us without further comment, but with a quizzical look. I had been asking myself what I should do with him if he asked us to come along. One thing was certain, I would not have gone quietly, particularly as we were in a separate compartment and there was no corridor."

Others, as we saw, tried to get away by paying ransom. This meant making cautious offers here and there, paving a very careful way to the *Zentralstelle*, and then for weeks, nay months, hovering between hope and despair. The *Zentralstelle* wanted to know every last detail—and one had so much to hide—and in any case their answer was generally the same. The writer has seen hundreds of packets of letters all stamped with the same "No"—a veritable cemetery of papers.

But the Germans were not the only ones who could be bribed. Strangers rang up and suggested the most wonderful plans—at the most fantastic prices. The writer himself got at least one such proposition a month before he went into hiding, and much the same happened to most of his friends. All this quite often went hand in hand with treachery—a pile of surviving documents bears witness to a miserable morass of blackmail and theft. A host of "travel bureaus" sprang up at the time—good, bad and indifferent, but all alike in being expensive. There was talk of messages over a secret cable link with England, which, of course, cost even more—and the Jews paid. There were Hebrew passwords, Slavic codes and what have you. One ex-pupil said: "They told us that crossing the border cost 20,000 guilders for the first person and 10,000 guilders for every additional one of us; later they added another thousand guilders per person. But Else, who led us across, was furious because K. (the intermediary) had only handed her 9,000 guilders per person . . . Jan, who had set up the whole organization, was even more furious —he had set the price at 5,000 guilders per person. In any case they smuggled us across as if we were so many sacks of tobacco. To get the money in the first place, we had had to sell diamonds and, needless to say, people made a good profit out of that as well."

But while this group did at least get across alive, many others were led straight into the arms of the Germans—on the platform at the border town of Maastricht, in a railway compartment, or at the foot of the Pyrenees. Some of the escape lines were known to the enemy, who could choose his own moment to strike. People crossed the Belgian border with or without a guide, often with no more than a rough sketch map and some sort of address to go to. The Roll of Honour bears the name of Benno Nijkerk, a thirty-seven-year-old merchant, who organized wholesale crossings into Belgium: the Germans put a price on his head and he was eventually caught in Paris and killed in Germany, after keeping his secrets under torture. In France there was Sally Noach, of whom hundreds speak with gratitude, and who, at great personal risk, managed to spirit untold prisoners (including many Dutch Jews) out of various Vichy prisons. Needless to say, things got much worse when the Germans occupied Vichy France in November 1942; approximately 1,000 Dutch refugees, most of them Jews, were now in the trap. Some escaped across the mountains, a few were left unmolested, some were deported—the latter without any protest by the Dutch authorities in France, whose lack of sympathy was extraordinary, to say the least.

One escape route from Occupied France led to Spain which, on principle, did not admit male refugees between the ages of eighteen and forty-one; everyone who entered that country illegally was arrested and interned for longer or shorter periods in Miranda del Ebro camp. All those released had a spell of forced residence in Madrid. There they had to remain until they obtained a Portuguese visa, and this was only issued when they already had an entry permit for another country. Some preferred not to wait and tried to cross into Portugal illegally—with or without success.

And once in Portugal? We have the evidence of a non-Jewish Dutchman, who tells us that the refugees kept besieging Consulate after Consulate in their anxiety to get away. Time and again they were asked—"Why don't you go back to the Netherlands", to which, on the advice of the Dutch Consul at Oporto, they answered, "For the same reasons that Her Majesty the Queen refuses to do so." This Consul's attitude was helpful, certainly more so than that of some men in the Dutch Foreign Service abroad who, to put it mildly, did little to alleviate the lot of their Jewish fellow-citizens.

Another goal for those who escaped was neutral Switzerland. We do not wish to discuss the attitude of the Swiss to Jewish refugees in general, but only to those from Holland. According to the Swiss author[1] of an important book on the subject, "there can be little doubt that a much less reserved policy towards the admission of refugees would have saved the lives of countless people". And as General Van Tricht, the Dutch Military Attaché in Berne, told the Enquiry Commission, the Swiss "tried to keep out all refugees in general, and Jews in particular". Ludwig,[2] while not attempting to estimate how many were turned back, contends that they must greatly have outnumbered those who, knowing the dangers, did not even make the attempt to escape to Switzerland, and of these there were many thousands.

The total number of Dutch refugees in Switzerland, including the 400 or so released early in 1945 from Theresienstadt, was approximately 2,500; if Ludwig was right, the number of Jews among them must have been less than half. The reader may care to know how these refugees were treated. Many were first put into prison, then into a reception camp, and finally, generally after a short time, into a hostel or work-camp. Not a few were given exemption for medical reasons or to pursue their studies. Some 250 were spirited out of Switzerland, thanks mainly to the good offices of General Van Tricht and such men as Dr. Visser 't Hooft, who were in touch with *Dutch-Paris*, an escape organization operating in France and led by the intrepid Jean Weidner. It is impossible to say how many of those rescued in this way were Jews.

Not all the Swiss work-camps treated their inmates equally well and while the living conditions in the hostels were good, the presence of such a heterogeneous mixture of people was bound to lead to a great deal of friction. One witness described it as follows: "The communal spirit is penny plain. Taken individually most people here are fairly decent. It is just that they have been completely thrown off their balance and placed into a completely new environment which obliges them to put on a show of toughness . . . Last week, one of them turned up with the latest slogan, saying that he was neither a Dutch Jew nor a Jewish Dutchman but 'an irreligious Dutchman of the Jewish faith, which he does not practise'."

[1] C. Ludwig: *Die Flüchtlingspolitik der Schweiz in den Jahren 1933 bis 1955* (The Swiss Refugee Policy in 1933–1955) (Berne, 1957), p. 372.

[2] *Op. cit.*, p. 319.

Needless to say, not all refugees in Switzerland were as flippant as that. We have only to remember how far most of them had come already, their racking anxiety for those left behind or in Poland, how they had to adapt themselves to a completely new life, and we cannot but feel deeply for them and admire all those who persisted in their attempts to join the Dutch Army in England, or devoted all their time and energy to helping their fellow-Jews.

This brings us to the work of the Jewish Co-ordinating Committee, or JCC, in Switzerland which deserves credit for what it tried to do, even though many of its efforts were thwarted—by circumstances, as well as by a combination of impotence, ignorance and ill-will. These are hard words, and the author realizes that once put down they will always be on record. But such is the evidence that he feels it to be his duty to pronounce them.

Our main source of information on the activities of the JCC is M. H. Gans who was working in Geneva at the time and who may be called the "conscience" behind the Committee.[1] "Without Shakespearian irony," he later wrote, "but in all seriousness, I must say that the scores of people everywhere who could have helped and shirked their duty, were, with the exception of a few criminals, 'honourable men, all honourable men' but men who failed to rise to the occasion. Considering what was at stake, failure here was inhuman, a crime for which they will have to answer to their own conscience . . . I am not being dramatic if, with my hand on my heart, I declare: *It was through their lack of responsibility that thousands of human lives were lost unnecessarily.*"

What was the JCC intended to do, and to what extent, if any, was it successful? It made available large funds for the maintenance of those who had gone into hiding in Holland; it persuaded South American States to claim as nationals many Dutch Jews; it sent food parcels to the deported. All this work was made possible through the generosity of Jews living in relative safety and aware that something terrible was happening to their brethren. But these were few and far between, and the rest, who did nothing, justified themselves by claiming that the others were merely being officious. What, they demanded, was the need for sending food parcels to Jews in Holland

[1] *Report of the Commission of Enquiry into the dispatch of parcels by the Red Cross and other organizations to Dutch political prisoners abroad during the time of the Occupation and also on the evacuation of Dutch prisoners shortly before the end of the War*, (The Hague, 1947), p. 108.

when there was already the American Joint Distribution Committee, the Jewish World Congress, the War Refugee Board, the *Hilfsverein für jüdische Auswanderung* and similar organizations—and when four Dutch Jews were working in the International Red Cross? And why in Heaven's name did Jews have to bother about getting South American passports and other papers? Had not a group from Bergen-Belsen been brought to safety without all that fuss in 1945 . . .?

"The Dutch Government proved lethargic, as well. But our desperate efforts to establish contacts wherever we could had one bright result. Despite the scowls of Dutch officials, we made free to sign declarations 'on behalf' of a favoured few, to the effect that they would not make use of their new nationalities after the war. Unfortunately, many of our (South American) allies, no doubt afraid of an invasion by a horde of new citizens after the war, were unwilling to take these declarations at their face value. This fatal news was communicated by the Spanish Ambassador in France, whereupon some 300 'South American' citizens were immediately deported from the French internment camp of Vittel. The Jewish World Congress informed me of this development the same night. There was great consternation. I tried to get in touch with Dr. I. Löwenstein (the Chief Rabbi of Zürich—J.P.) and Dr. Visser 't Hooft. A joint telegram was sent to the Queen, with the immediate result that Her Majesty's ambassador in Buenos Aires was ordered to intervene. The upshot was complete success soon afterwards. The only time that we appealed to the Queen was also the only time during the entire aid programme that the famous Dutch tradition, so admired by other countries, was publicly upheld."

This story involves a number of people who did not falter in the execution of their human and often official duties. Once again we must speak with the deepest respect of Dr. W. A. Visser 't Hooft, Secretary-General of the World Council of Churches in Geneva. It was very largely thanks to him that one of the leading chroniclers of this whole sad story was able to repudiate the jibe that anti-Semitic Poland did more for its Jews than pro-Semitic Holland. Luckily, he was not the only Dutchman of his kind to be found in Switzerland and elsewhere. But we must also pay tribute to the American Joint Distribution Committee, represented in Switzerland by Saly Mayer in St. Gallen. As we page through his letters, we find constant complaints about the "completely passive attitude" of the Dutch

Government in London—this "worries and concerns us a great deal". Elsewhere he wrote, "the Dutch Government does next to nothing for its Jews". This letter was addressed to Gans, who replied on July 31, 1944: "We are reluctantly forced to take full cognizance of your criticism." In another letter, dated November 16, 1944, Mayer wrote: "Do the Jews in Holland have to die just because their Government will do nothing for them?" This was a cry of despair to which Gans added in 1947, that it fell on deaf ears. "And time has only served to darken the picture."

Far more glorious was the fate of those Dutch Jews who, despite all obstacles, managed to reach the shores of Britain, where quite a few of them did outstanding work in the Army of Liberation.

There was also another small hole in the iron fence through which a few Jews managed to escape.[1] In the spring of 1943 we find several references to a request by the German Foreign Office to the Head of the Security Police "to refrain, for the time being, from deporting some 30,000 Jews of Dutch, Belgian, French, Norwegian and Soviet nationality". Not, mind you, because the Germans were suddenly overcome with remorse, but "to keep these persons available for possible exchanges". As we saw, this group was mainly to be drawn from Jews with relatives, friends and political or business contacts in Allied countries, and also from leading members of the Jewish Council.

This brings us to the so-called "Palestine-certificate" episode. In 1942 a number of "Palestinian" women were ear-marked by the Germans for exchange against Germans living in Palestine. A former Jewish banker, calling at the Swiss Consulate, spotted the passport of one of these women and seeing that, in fact, she was a stateless person, devised a plan that "at the time looked exceedingly far-fetched":[2] the Swiss consul was persuaded to transmit lists of eligible persons to both the British and German Governments, with the rider that a Palestine certificate had been applied for on all these people's behalf. When these lists seemed to "work" with the Germans, i.e. when it appeared that the bearers were left unmolested, it was decided to extend the scheme. After an initial misunderstanding, the authorities in Palestine realized what was happening and agreed to play ball. Two of the leading spirits in this whole affair were Gertrud van Tijn-Cohn and Helmuth Mainz, a German Jew.

[1] E. Kolb: *Bergen-Belsen*, pp. 204 ff.

[2] G. van Tijn-Cohn: *op. cit.*, p. 39: cf. Herzberg: *op. cit.*, p. 125.

A memorandum of June 21, 1943, mentions six categories eligible for such exchanges, including veterans (*Vatikim*) who had given distinguished service to the Zionist movement; it is said that the names of some 1,500 people were put forward. "But in July 1943, after a closer check in Westerbork, the Germans found that only 350 of these 1,500 were *bona fide* applicants; many of the others ended up in Auschwitz. Then, in the second half of 1943, new certificates became available, with the result that altogether 1,297 people were ear-marked for exchange and, from January 1944 onwards, were sent to Bergen-Belsen 'for that purpose'."

Let us quote S. de Wolff: "On May 21, 1943, a Red Cross telegram bearing the names of the first *Vatik* list, reached the Netherlands. It made an incredible impression. Everyone, even the most rabid anti-Zionists, felt that it marked an important point in the history of the Dutch Jewry. Palestine, the land of their forefathers, had opened its arms to the children of Israel, nor had they been forced into making the usual humiliating and false supplications. They were welcome simply for what they were. This was not a favour from a Frederiks or a Van Dam, men whose patriotism has been questioned; they did not have to sully the memory of their mothers or deny the faith for which their fathers had gone to the stake. This was 'Jewish' salvation, and the only one worthy of a Jew . . ."

This quotation reflects something of the emotional atmosphere prevailing at the time. De Wolff was, in fact, one of the few Jews lucky enough to reach Palestine. Many others holding Palestine certificates were less fortunate, though it is true to say that the majority were sent to Bergen-Belsen and not straight to the gas-chambers. The majority, but not all, and on one occasion when a transport from Westerbork was a few hundred men short, many of those whose Palestine certificates had not yet arrived were used to make up the numbers. Herzberg[1] places the chief blame on Britain; Gans does the same, but adds that in Switzerland, too, applications on which human lives depended would often be sent from office to office, or delayed "because of indifference on the part of the Red Cross and the Dutch Government in London".

There was also talk of exchanging children; this matter is referred to in various documents, but the figures differ. The Germans were in favour of the idea, for though "the brave and noble Arabs were being driven out from the native Palestine by the Jews", there was a good

[1] Herzberg: *op. cit.*, p. 126.

chance that most of these children would end up in England and not in Palestine, with the result that British anti-Semitism would be given a great boost. Moreover, Britain's very acceptance of the plan, if only in principle, was bound to incense the Arabs even further. Kolb reports a proposal in 1942 by the Dutch Association of Palestine Immigrants to send 1,000 (elsewhere we are told 500) Dutch children to Palestine;[1] the Dutch Government in London seemed prepared to bear all the costs and even to pay for the children's maintenance throughout the war. This time Berlin apparently decided against it. We need not therefore pursue the matter further, nor shall we go into the details of the abortive plan to exchange Germans interned in the Dutch West Indies against Jews in the Netherlands, except to mention G. A. Boon's evidence on this matter to the Enquiry Commission:[2] "It was proposed to exchange these people, in whom the Germans were not really interested, for Jews in the Netherlands. Several suggestions were put forward, but all of them were ignored. I can still remember a proposal by a Dutch Jew living in New York. He was told by the (Dutch) Government that Jews could not be treated differently from other Dutchmen who 'are in the same position'; in other words, the Government failed to realize, what should have been obvious to a child, that the Jews were in a far worse plight, though no one could have known just how bad it really was."

In conclusion, the reader will want to know how many Dutch Jews were, in fact, exchanged for Germans from Palestine and exactly how this was done. As we have said, all the people with Palestine certificates were sent first to Westerbork and then on to Bergen-Belsen. It was there that the penultimate scene of a drama that may be called the comedy of exchanges was played out. It is strange how the reports of eye-witnesses and others disagree about the facts and figures. But the following general impression emerges:

In the middle of April 1944, 1,100 inmates of Bergen-Belsen had papers entitling them to enter Palestine. On April 25 the names of some 275 candidates were made known to the Jewish camp population. These candidates were put into special quarters for a time and exempted from all heavy work; the camp officials treated them with improbable consideration. At the end of May they were told to make ready to leave on June 1, that is all except fifty, who had to go back

[1] Kolb: *Bergen-Belsen*, pp. 295–8.

[2] *Enquiry Commission*, Part IIc, p. 217.

to the general camp. Nothing at all happened on June 1, but ten days later the whole group was ordered back, with fresh instructions to keep their luggage ready for immediate departure. Three days later, they were sent back to heavy work; Herzberg[1] tells us that several of them died and that their identities were surreptitiously adopted by others. Then, on June 29, came the news of imminent departure; all the luggage was weighed in again and carefully examined. There was a medical examination as well; women and children at 3 p.m., men at about midnight. Finally, at 3 a.m., and to their utter astonishment, all of them were taken out of the camp. "We could not believe what we saw at Celle Station. A proper train with five wagon-lits, two buffet cars and first- and second-class compartments had been made ready. The SS and the railway guards were on their best behaviour. When the train started we all burst into the *Hatikwah* (the Zionist anthem). Then we stormed into the buffet cars . . ."

The train carried them via Fulda, Würzburg, Nuremberg, Passau and Linz to Vienna, where they arrived on the morning of Saturday, July 1, and were their contingent of 221 was joined by sixty-one people from Vittel (France). All of them stayed in a hostel until Sunday afternoon, and the leader of the whole group (Dr. I. Taubes), from whose reports we have freely quoted, was able through an intermediary to make contact with Dr. Loewenherz, the head of the Jewish congregation in Vienna, who was not, however, permitted to visit them. They were vaccinated once again and were then allowed to take off their yellow stars (according to another report they had to wear the stars until they crossed the Turkish border). On July 6 the train reached Istanbul, via Budapest, Belgrade and Sofia. A whole saga could be written about this journey, but the climax was, of course, the arrival in Haifa at 5 p.m. on July 10, 1944. There are lists, necessarily incomplete, of these fortunate few, and also of very small groups of others who reached Palestine before and after them. For the rest, we need only add that the Palestine stamp helped several Jews to survive the war in Bergen-Belsen. But they were few, and all too far between.

### CALMEYER

In the German trap there was yet another hole through which a handful of Jews managed to get away: since Jews were doomed, one

[1] Herzberg: *op. cit.*, p. 235.

could always try to pass oneself off as something else. It was sometimes said that the Jews suffered from not having an Eleventh Commandment: "Thou shalt convert thy grandfather and thy grandmother from Judaism." At any rate, this is what many Jews now did.

We had best begin our story with Decree No. 6 of January 1941, by which all those with at least "one Jewish grandparent by race" were required to register as Jews. The reader will also remember that a grandparent by race was anyone who at any time belonged to the Jewish religious community. For what follows, the third Article is the important one:

"(1) Whenever there is a doubt whether a person must be considered a full or a part Jew in accordance with Article 2, the matter must be referred for decision to the *Reichskommissar* for the Occupied Netherlands territory or to his nominee.

"(3) There is no provision for appeal against the decisions mentioned in (1)."

We have already said that only a few "full-Jews" failed to register as such. Had they but known at the time that by registering they were signing their own death-warrants, many would no doubt have preferred the risk of non-compliance. When the awful truth eventually dawned upon them, the Germans were showered with petitions from people who had suddenly discovered that they were not full-Jews after all. All these petitions were passed on to the *Generalkommissariat* for Administration and Justice, and in particular to the section headed by Dr. Stüler. So overwhelmed was the latter with paper work that he was forced to engage an assistant. This job was first held by one Kroll and later by Dr. Hans Calmeyer, a German lawyer, who will play the principal role in what follows.

Dr. Hans Georg Calmeyer was born in Osnabrück on June 23, 1903. He was never a member of the National Socialist Party, and indeed had a number of differences with the Nazis. It is said that they mistrusted him and constantly spied upon him, and we have ample evidence to show that they did just that. There is unanimous testimony that Calmeyer was highly intelligent, extremely conscientious and utterly incorruptible. It is also certain that, though he knew that many Jews were trying to pull the wool over his eyes, he nevertheless let all of them go unpunished. In addition he went to endless trouble to prove helpful to all petitioners. Thus on April 6,

1943, he put through a telephone call to the Mayor of Goldap in East Prussia to confirm that a certain man with a Jewish-sounding name had lived there between 1880 and 1885 and that he had in fact attended a Christian church. Most witnesses are also agreed that he served the Dutch cause in many other fields—for instance, he was able to reduce the number of provincial and municipal officials conscripted for "labour service". There is little doubt that hundreds of Jews owe their lives to him, that it would have been a disaster if his place had been filled by a good Party man, and that he ran untold personal risks.

In one report, he is quoted as describing himself as "a typical lawyer and therefore inclined to believe the opposite of what I am told". Still, in the *Reichskommissariat,* he was careful to keep his scepticism to himself, accepting on trust whatever could somehow be made to pass muster. Conversely, if an absolutely hopeless petition was presented to him, he would do his utmost to look for a possible loophole. It was in a lengthy addendum to the above-mentioned report, that Calmeyer tried to defend his actions during the Occupation. The crux of his plea was that he found himself in a hopeless position, comparable to that of a doctor "in a lonely post, cut off from the outside world, and left with a mere 50 phials of medicine for the treatment of 5,000 critical cases". There he was, a small "scientific assistant" swimming against the stream which, without noticeable protests by German scientists or jurists, was pouring out of Germany and threatening to engulf all of West European Jewry. The whole thing was much too big for him, and since he could not save all, he did what he could for the few. Jews claiming to be the illegitimate offspring of non-Jewish fathers had become so much the fashion that it proved quite impossible for him to accept all their claims—doing so would have undermined the work he was trying to do and would have placed even the few he tried to save in danger. From morning until night, his office was besieged by lawyers putting in special pleas for their clients and by people who came to plead their cause in person. Among the documents that have come down to us, one is the heart-rending appeal of a mother for her son ("an old, sick, nearly blind, poverty-stricken, lonely mother, for her completely innocent, deserving boy") who asked Calmeyer to "remember your own mother". Another petitioner used a different line of attack. He told Calmeyer in no uncertain terms what he thought of his "utterly indefensible decision"; we still have Calmeyer's reply

—it says much for him that he answered this insulting letter, and did not report its writer to the authorities.

People have argued for and against Calmeyer's conduct. The writer of this work, for one, has not the least doubt that Calmeyer was skating on exceedingly thin ice, that he was working under duress and that, had he gone any further than he did, he would, in fact, have jeopardized what little help he was able to give to the Jews.

It is quite clear, for instance, that particularly after the beginning of the deportations, Calmeyer was inundated with so many obviously bogus applications that there was little he could do about them. In any case, Seyss-Inquart had decided to set an early terminal date for these applications—December 1942. Those who were "in doubt" about their descent after that date were too late. Subsequent investigations could take place only on the initiative of German departments, or where "the public" (read, an informer) had lodged a complaint that someone had failed to register the full extent of his Jewish origin.

Another factor worked against Calmeyer. "Aryanized" Jews, i.e. Jews who turned out not to be Jewish after all, had the right to ask for the return of all their assets from Lippmann, Rosenthal & Company. Needless to say, the Germans were reluctant to allow this to happen, and spilled much ink on the subject. One of their memoranda, dated July 27, 1943, deals with the case of a prominent Jew, an ex-member of the Jewish Council and, moreover, married to a Jewish woman. It was indeed a "strange case": the man, now become an Aryan, asked for the return of his assets, including *objets d'art*, etc., while his wife demanded that her estate be transferred to their daughter—now a half-Jewess. Lippmann, though "naturally" convinced that the authorities had looked into the matter very carefully, could not help expressing his "utter astonishment" that this man "who until this day has played a leading role among local Jews and most probably belongs to the Jewish faith, should quite suddenly have discovered his Aryan origins". And Lippmann was right to be bewildered for, as he went on to point out, the man had at least one Jewish parent, was married to a Jewess and must in all conscience be regarded as a full-Jew. Imagine his dismay when he was told that the man's credentials were perfectly in order, down to a blood test carried out by Professor Weinert in Kiel. Another painful experience for Lippmann was the case of an Amsterdam medical specialist, married to a Jewess, who declared that not only had he an Aryan mother but also (and this had been a secret all along) an Aryan father, who had died in 1898. It was exclusively on the oath (Lippman underlined these words) of the mother that this man had been declared an Aryan, and this without even a blood test and despite the fact that the man made an "unequivocally Jewish impression".

Small wonder then that German doubts of Calmeyer's competence increased day by day. On May 27, 1943, they ordered a complete re-examination of the list of "Calmeyer Jews", many of whom had been found to be of "a pronounced Galician type". This was not as yet a direct attack on Calmeyer, but certainly served as a warning. A "highly confidential" document from the spring of 1944 was more directly critical of Calmeyer's work and ordered a full examination of his activities; unfortunately for the Germans, the destruction of the Central Population Registry by the Royal Air Force on April 11, 1944, made this extremely difficult. Another document, dated July 5, 1944, signed by Dr. K. G. E. Schöngarth, Commander of the Security Police, again referred to the necessity of "unmasking the many full-Jews who, by all sorts of manipulations, have succeeded in passing themselves off as Aryans or part-Aryans in the Netherlands", and of exposing the "extensive swindle" that enabled several thousand people to "run about in the Netherlands as unrecognized Jews". In a document of August 14, 1944, Zöpf, too, spoke of countless cases in which deception was suspected, and ordered the setting up of a committee of three. The reader will see later why nothing came of this.

Calmeyer was in charge of a whole department, which Herzberg had described with a measure of irony. Among his assistants were some who were rabid anti-Semites. However, there were also quite a few staunch anti-Nazis, chief among them Dr. G. Wander, who was later shot by his compatriots. Wander deserves special mention, if only because he ventured to warn many Jews whose applications had been refused to take to their heels, and because he helped the cause of the Netherlands in many other ways as well. According to Herzberg, there was also a secretary who helped Jews wherever she could, and others who rendered assistance when they were in the mood to do so.

In this connection we must mention the colourful figure of Professor E. H. Weinert from Kiel, an "anthropometrist" whose duty it was to evaluate racial reports and who also carried out tests of his own. Luckily, he was corrupt, and hence "approachable"; according to his colleague Professor A. De Froe, this "scientist" charged up to 10,000 guilders for a favourable opinion. Others claim that he did it for peanuts; Herzberg calls him a drug-addict who could never get enough morphine. It must not, however, be thought that Calmeyer was limited to this one "expert". A long list of men capable of giving reliable opinions on questions of racial descent was published in the *Allgemeines Sachblatt für Sippenforscher* (Journal for Research into Consanguinity), Vol. 6, No. 5, May 25, 1942. And Calmeyer had other helpers, too. There was, for instance, the Dutch Central Populations Registry, under the leadership of the indispensable J. L. Lentz, whom we have met before. This Office produced a "List of Family Names of Persons of Jewish Blood" dated March 1942, ranging from Aa to Zijttenfeld, and including some 11,000 to 12,000 entries; the Germans found this list so absorbing that Rauter alone ordered no less than twenty copies. The Office also issued a reserve list of names whose Jewishness was still being investigated.

This brings us to the actual figures. Of the many lists and interim reports compiled by the busy Registry, that dated March 20, 1943, strikes us as the most detailed, and we shall accordingly quote from it. At the time, 2,197 cases were being investigated. Of these 1,362 had been decided: 25 per cent had been declared full-Jews, 50 per cent half-Jews and 25 per cent quarter-Jews and Aryans. In other words, Calmeyer had rejected one in four of the applicants. Of the remaining 837, 196 were in Westerbork, 31 in Vught, 220 were at large in the Northern, Southern and Eastern Provinces, and 338 in Amsterdam and the Western Provinces. The report added that it would take many months to decide their cases. It came to the curious conclusion that it would be inadvisable to send these people to a "Jewish camp" because . . . if their applications were successful their possessions would have to be restored to them and this would cause great difficulty. In the circumstances, such persons had best be left where they were, or else ought to be concentrated into Amsterdam. There seems little doubt that Calmeyer was behind this advice, and that he intended to give those concerned every opportunity to go into hiding.

In Herzberg's book, the reader will find a concise summary of all the ruses and tricks used to get round the Nazi genealogical and "race-biological" experts. There arose a whole industry for forging papers, with photographs, medical declarations as to blood groups and so on. There was a rush to dig up old baptismal and marriage records, which is not surprising at a time when the right papers could mean the difference between life and death. The Amsterdam municipal archives remained open to Jews throughout, because the Chief Registrar "knew of no regulation which prevented Jews from exercising this ancient right". Burgomaster Voûte supported him in this stand, although "certain visitors" were heard to utter threats, and a police officer put in a "kindly warning". In the end, however, the pressure became too great and, in order "to prevent ugly scenes" the Registrar allocated a special room to Jews, which they were quick to name the "Star Chamber".

The Red Cross also helped Jews by giving them *carte blanche* when it came to claims involving alleged blood transfusions; if asked, the Red Cross would invariably declare that a transfusion had taken place and that the relevant card was kept in its archives. "Old love letters were forged on paper that was fifty to sixty years old and had been rummaged out from some merchant. Ink that looked in every way as though it were many years old was concocted. Ingenuity was boundless, particularly when it came to rubber stamps, for which it was said that all German officials had a weakness; letters from various Consulates bearing foreign postage stamps were collected by Resistance workers pretending to be Post Office employees and the postmarks altered" (Herzberg). One of De Froe's colleagues manufactured whole files of correspondence with German genealogists. False baptismal certificates were available and one could choose between fifteen Christian denominations; best of all was the so-called Synodal imprint which was a pure fiction and which, oddly enough, was the one that most impressed the Germans.

It is easy to smile at all this today, but less easy to recapture the atmosphere in which these things went on. Take, for instance, the predicament of an anthropologist, faced with an unmistakable Aryan who claimed that four equally unmistakably Jewish girls were his illegitimate daughters. Needless to say, men who were prepared to swear that they were the Aryan fathers of Jewish children were in great demand. "These men had to learn to play their parts to perfection; some sported photographs of their so-called sons and daughters and even managed to develop the appropriate feelings towards them. By all appearances, morals in even the highest Dutch circles must have been not unlike those prevailing in Sodom and

Gomorrah or in the late Roman Empire—there would have had to be adultery all round the clock. Even Professor De Froe began to imagine that these people looked more like their fictitious fathers than their real ones." "I could find a score of points in which the child differed from its legitimate father and another score in which it resembled the false one. I hardly had to lie at all." Moreover, as Professor De Froe told the Enquiry Commission: "There are always points of resemblance between people, some of them quite striking. I even began to convince myself."[1]

The records contain many reports of the courageous attitude of a number of lawyers; one finds nothing but praise for such men as Nijgh in The Hague and Kotting and Van Proosdij in Amsterdam. At the age of only twenty-one, the latter displayed a degree of reckless audacity that is well-nigh incredible. It was a very great privilege indeed to meet Van Proosdij after the war and to hear him discuss his anti-German activities. The Dutch Bench as a whole co-operated as well: "It admitted quite irrelevant evidence and declarations about adulterous relationships, when everyone—advocates, judges and clerks—knew that the whole thing was nothing but perjury."

By a fortunate chance, things became still more complicated, and hence more impenetrable. While Calmeyer was on holiday, Dr. Wander had to solve a particularly thorny problem. We saw that those grandparents were considered as full-Jews who had been members of a Jewish congregation. Was this a disputable or an indisputable legal fact? Dr. Wander decided that though it was the latter in Germany, it would have to be the former in the Netherlands. For instance, if it could be proved that one such grandparent, though a member of a Jewish congregation, was himself the child or grandchild of an Aryan, then he could not have been a full-Jew and his grandchild could no longer be said to have had four Jewish grandparents. "And Wander assumed that whoever had three Aryan great-grandparents and was thus three-sixteenths Aryan could not be regarded as a Jew. This decision meant salvation for quite a few families."

All sorts of other complications were discovered, for instance the relatively simple case of the "full-Aryan widow" who alleged that she had joined the Jewish congregation simply to get financial help for her son's studies. There was also the case of the man with two

[1] Enquiry Commission, Part VIIc, p. 343.

Aryan grandparents on the father's side who, in 1866, became converted to Judaism in order to be eligible for a bequest. Their son, although racially a "pure Aryan", remained a Jew by religion and married an Aryan Roman Catholic according to the Jewish rite. Their grandson, though a full-Aryan by race, was nevertheless circumcised. He cared nothing for his religion but had married a Jewess in Munich. He now wished to volunteer for the Hermann Goering "Ack-Ack Regiment", to which Calmeyer replied: "This accumulation of Jewish influences, although not of Jewish blood, is remarkable."

To give the reader some idea of the bizarre stories that got into the records we shall quote in full, although not, of course, with the actual names, a sworn declaration lodged with the Public Registrar in Amsterdam during the autumn of 1941:

"On . . . (date) Johanna Maria Nanninga, aged eighty years, the widow of Juda Polak, of . . . (address) made the following declaration in my presence:

"'You see, Juda Polak was really my second husband; he died last summer; he was a very good man and I was married to him for forty-three years. Muller, that's what I always called my first husband, was the real father of my children, though I was never married to him. He kept saying that he was older than me, but that was not true, he was about my own age; he came from out of town. I had four children by him, two sons and two daughters. All I know about him is that his name was Wilhelmus Adrianus Muller and that he was a Roman Catholic, just like me, although I never go to Church. He never spent a whole night with me, for he had to look after his old mother, who lived outside the city, I don't know where. After I had my fourth child he suddenly disappeared. Once someone brought me money from him but—as I heard from his friends—he died after an operation, for hernia, I think. I was letting rooms at the time. But I had nothing but trouble until I married Polak who was, you might say, a café companion of my first husband's, and I was only too happy that my children were getting a father, for he adopted them all and gave them his name.'

"To this solemn declaration the granddaughter of the applicant, Miss C. B. Polak, has herself added that, to the best of her knowledge, there are no circumstances, other than the aforementioned, suggesting that she is descended from one or more grandparents who can be deemed full-Jews by race, etc.; should she learn otherwise she would immediately report the matter to the Secretary-General of the Department for Internal Affairs."

The official who forwarded these declarations in triplicate added that "my personal impression was that the testimony was not implausible" and that "judging from the appearance of Miss Polak there can be no question of her Jewish descent".

This was the sort of thing Calmeyer had to deal with, and if he was not of the race of Solomon he certainly needed that king's proverbial wisdom. What, for instance, was he to make of the following expostulation by young Van Proosdij after the step-daughter of . . . had been refused "Aryanization" by Calmeyer. "This happened shortly before Christmas and so I exclaimed: 'You are not Herod!' A conversation followed, during which I laboured the Christmas message, until in the end I obtained the 'Aryanization'." On another occasion, Van Proosdij was dealing with "a man, a woman and two children, not a very prepossessing lot, but with all their papers in order. Calmeyer refused their application. I burst into tears and Calmeyer said to me: 'They must be friends of yours.' I replied: 'No, they are a rotten lot, but it's an outrage all the same.' Decision revoked, more people saved . . ."

Unfortunately Calmeyer was not the only one who made such decisions. At Westerbork, Van Proosdij tells us, Gemmeker (the Camp Commandant) himself used to screen the applicants for 'Aryanization'; his standards were highly personal, for when it came to women he went chiefly by the hips . . .

Another busy advocate, Dr. Benno Stokvis, had this to say: "I well remember a case in which Calmeyer—who was often unpredictable—hesitated for a long time. It was that of Ruth P., a sixteen-year-old girl. When for the umpteenth time I looked sadly through her papers I suddenly had an inspiration. Had not Ruth the Moabitess been adopted into Israel although a stranger? I had got it! The Jewish couple had chosen the name Ruth symbolically, to show that she was adopted and not Jewish by birth. Calmeyer was enthusiastic and immediately gave a favourable opinion." If only Calmeyer had always had the final word!

## THE PORTUGUESE JEWS

We now come to another painful episode in our story: the destruction of the Portuguese Jews, of those who joined in the hazardous business of claiming Aryan descent—and lost. They claimed—and according to Herzberg[1] tried vainly to prove—that they "had nothing to do with the Jewish race or with what went by that name, except for the trifling matter of sharing their religious faith". Herzberg speaks ironically of this whole matter, but adds that Jews from the Caucasus who lived in France and took much the same line, found their efforts crowned with success: "Not a hair on their heads was harmed. How hard it was to decide what or what not to do in this war!" True though this may be, there is little justification for the means used by some Portuguese Jews to placate their persecutors. They claimed that they had all along been sympathetic to the NSB or the New Germany and even appropriated Nazi terminology by referring to their co-religionists from Eastern Europe as "parasites", as people who had come to the Netherlands only for what they could get out of it.

According to the census figures, 4,303 people had registered as Portuguese Jews on October 1, 1941. We know that they were a very heterogeneous group—economically, culturally and even in matters of religion. In some places they had completely merged into the local population. In the nineteenth and twentieth centuries, assimilation had gone so far that only a very few Portuguese Jews of pure descent remained.

They presented Calmeyer with interesting puzzles. On one occasion, for instance, he was told that though "several grandparents of an applicant had been members of the Portuguese Israelitic Congregation, none of these grandparents had, in fact, been more than one-sixteenth a Jew by race". He was even told that it was reasonable to suppose that "the proportion of Jewish blood in Marranos living at the turn of the sixteenth century was no more than 1 in 32 . . . and that this proportion did not subsequently increase. Until 1750, mixed marriages between Marranos and, for instance, Jews from Eastern Europe could be counted on the fingers on one hand. Even Spinozza (*sic!*) was not a Jew by race, etc., etc." No wonder Calmeyer had his hands full.

In the autumn of 1941 *mr.* N. de Beneditty, a prominent Portuguese Jewish jurist, asked *mr.* Van Krimpen to interest himself in the matter. In the course of 1942, this work proceeded apace—most of the genealogical research was done by *mr.* Nijgh, the anthropological investigation by Dr. De Froe, the "legal" work by *mr.* Kotting and *mr.* Van Proosdij.

[1] Herzberg: *op. cit.*, p. 140.

Mr. L. E. Visser

Walter Süskind

Joop Westerweel

"Schuschu" Simon

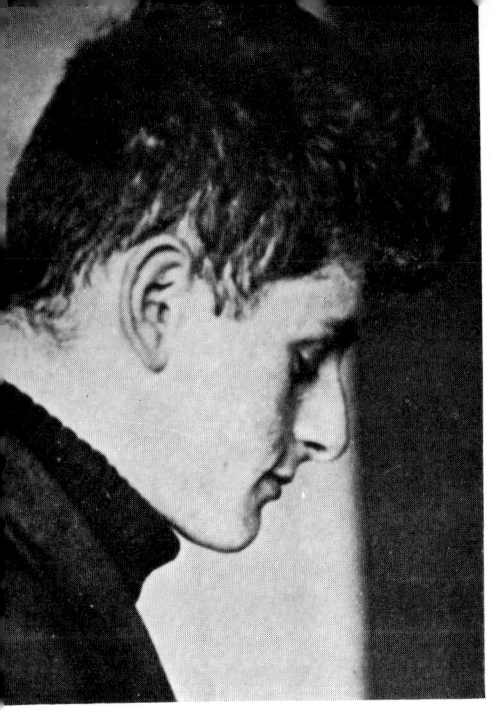

Hans Katan

Leo Frijda

Gerhard Badrian

Sally Noach

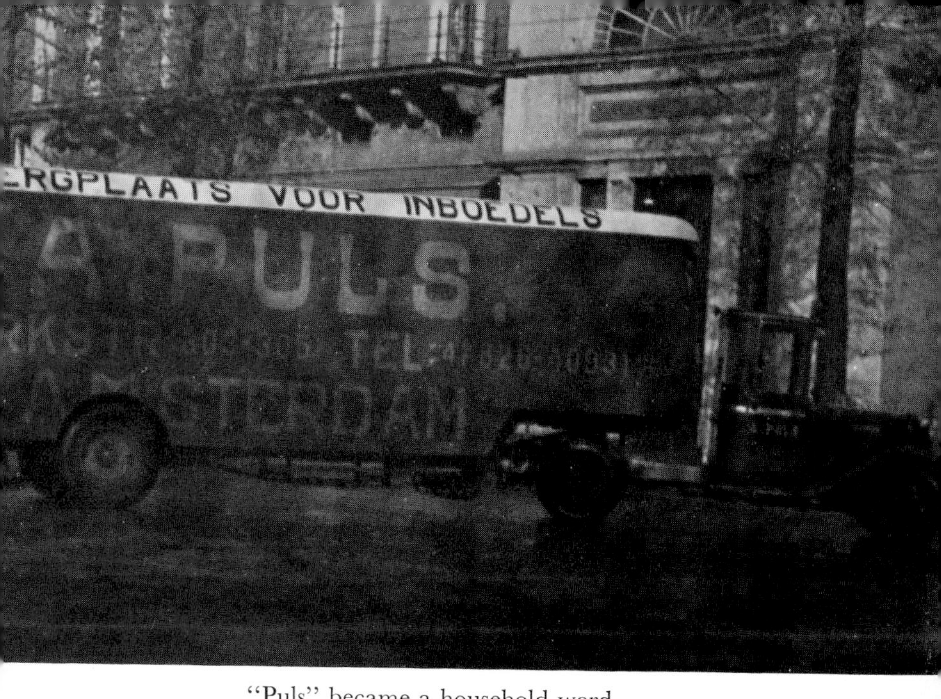


"Puls" became a household word

Jewish homes being emptied

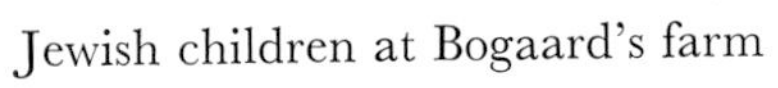

Jewish children at Bogaard's farm

Johannes Bogaard

An improvised hide-out

When Dr. De Froe, who was besieged by a host of Portuguese Jews with requests to establish their non-Jewish status, suggested that it would save a lot of time if the problem were considered in its entirety, Calmeyer insisted that each case must be treated on its own merits. As a result the Germans were swamped by a further flood of applications.

It is impossible to do more than sketch all this frantic activity. Suffice it to say, that the fate of most of the applicants was no less dreadful than that of their co-religionists. One of the efforts to come to their aid was the compilation of a report entitled *Die Herkunft der sogenannten portusiesischen Juden* (The Origins of the So-called Portuguese Jews), with appendices by Professor J. M. van Bemmelen and Professor C. U. Ariëns Kappers. It ran to 34 pages and 8 chapters and quoted such great "authorities" as Houston Stewart Chamberlain who on pp. 275–7 of his *Die Grundlagen des Neunzehnten Jahrhunderts* (1899; translated into English, 1910), spoke highly of the Portuguese Jews, while having nothing but scorn for their German co-religionists. Another document was addressed to Seyss-Inquart. In it there was reference to a strong mixture of West Gothic blood; it also listed a series of noble Iberian families (read Portuguese Jews), including knights, counts, dukes, barons, etc., who had settled in the Netherlands in the seventeenth century. Yet another document emphasized that Portuguese Jews had always been great patriots and had done yeoman service for the House of Orange (not perhaps the best recommendation during this War). Then there was a document giving irrefutable proof that the whole group was of non-Jewish origin. The Germans were supplied with a list of names borne by Portuguese Jews and still prevalent in Portugal. Someone else collected the names of Portuguese Jewish artists, compiled records of their work and so on.

Two further documents claim our very special attention. One was drawn up in July and August 1943 and came from the pen of Dr. A. de Froe (with the help of various experts). It was the imposing "Anthropological Investigation of the Composition of the So-called Portuguese Jews in the Netherlands", prepared at the Anatomical and Embryological Institute of the University of Amsterdam. It tried to answer the following questions:

(*a*) Must Portuguese Jews in the Netherlands be deemed Jews or as belonging to another race or mixture of races?

(*b*) If they are deemed Jews, must they be regarded as indistinguishable from other Jews or as a separate group?
(*c*) If they are not deemed Jews, what race or races do they belong to?
(*d*) In case of (*c*), do they form a separate group of a mixed race or are they an anthropological part thereof?
(*e*) Does the finding apply to all pure Portuguese Jews?
(*f*) Does it apply to those who are not pure Portuguese Jews and, if so, to what extent?

The authors based their answers on the investigation of 203 men and 172 women; ninety-two of them were photographed and all were examined for thirty-one special characteristics. The processing of the data formed a chapter in itself. Another was devoted to graphs. Skull measurements showed convincingly that these "so-called Portuguese Jews cannot by any stretch of the imagination be classified as Jews and that they show strong affinities with Western Mediterranean races".

Was all this entirely spurious science? The men responsible for this work were scholars of great renown; their research and conclusions could, on the whole, have passed muster, except for a few exaggerations here and there. They did not, incidentally, try, as so many have claimed, to prove that these Portuguese Jews were "Aryans"—that word does not occur in De Froe's work. Everything he put down was true as far as it went and was, in any case, difficult if not impossible to refute. The only question was whether the Germans would swallow it.

As to that, we have a letter from Calmeyer to *Generalkommissar* Schmidt dated August 6, 1942. All the arguments are discussed at length; while accepting most of the historical material adduced on behalf of the Portuguese Jews, Calmeyer challenged the conclusions. Thus he argued that these people had always followed the Jewish faith—and religion after all was an important criterion, since "what we call a Jew is really the product of a race mixture" (an odd thing to come from a German!). But he conceded that a number of these Portuguese might well have "less than 25 per cent Jewish blood"; this fairly small group ought to be set apart from the rest, and, being non-assimilable in Western Europe, be sent to the "Celto-Iberian area" for possible exchanges against Germans or Dutchmen.

From a document dated October 13, 1942, it would appear that

Calmeyer's department had "investigated" 1,015 of the 4,00
Portuguese Jews; only 400 of these could be considered eligi
a special stamp. "As for the rest of these so-called Portugues
they cannot be given permanent protection or exemption."
another document it appears that Calmeyer was merely handi
the views of Seyss-Inquart.) Elsewhere we learn that Rauter insisted on screening even the favoured 400.

In short, the future of even this small group was far from secure. Their Dutch advisers realized this full well and kept on begging them to go into hiding. The writer fails to understand why so many of them, who had the means to do so, failed to heed this good advice while there was still time. He remembers one professor, a respected man of exceptional intelligence who, in the staff-room of the Jewish Lyceum, declared emphatically that he for one would never be sent to a camp—the Germans themselves had given it to him in writing. Nor will the writer ever forget the looks that the rest of the staff exchanged. There was not a single one of us who could claim to be this man's intellectual equal, yet not one either who was simple enough to believe that German promises could be trusted.

The subsequent fate of the 400 can be followed in a number of documents. One of these is a list of exemptions dated March 1, 1943; on another the number of names was already down to 370—according to *Fräulein* Slottke, quite a few of these had by then been deported or sent to camps. By April 16, 1943, the number had shrunk to 300, and all these, it was rumoured, would be sent to the transit camp of Vught. Meanwhile Calmeyer was asked to prepare a memorandum for Himmler with whom the ultimate decision lay. Once in Vught, all Portuguese Jews would be inspected by Rauter, who desired "to form a racial impression about these Jews for himself". On May 5 came the news that they would be sent not to Vught but to Westerbork and that Rauter would examine them there. Then, in June, all of them were given a stamp in the 10,000-series. To get it, one needed at least seven "Portuguese" great-grandparents. A document from that time shows that Calmeyer's list at that stage consisted of only 201 persons; it also stipulated the precise methods that must be used by his assistants in dealing with these men. The document was quite unnecessarily elaborate and we can only suppose that Calmeyer was playing for time. Meanwhile, he was overwhelmed with so many new applications that he asked *mr.* Van Proosdij to revise the whole list. Van Proosdij found this a particularly unpalatable commission, but discovered a loophole: he asked the Jewish Council for a list of those already deported or dead and removed these from the list without further ado. Did Calmeyer realize what was happening? There seems little doubt that he did. In any case, he allowed all the names to remain. On September 20, 1943, came the news that all of them would be "inspected" in the very near future. According to Rauter, Himmler was still deciding their fate. On October 2 we hear again that Rauter was about to inspect all Portuguese Jews in Westerbork. On the 20th came the news that the inspection would be postponed until further notice, because of an outbreak of infantile paralysis in the camp.

Then in 1944 came the final catastrophe. On January 26 Zöpf instructed Aus der Fünten to include Portuguese Jews in the "deportation measures", and to send them to the Jewish camp at Westerbork. In this document, the words "immediately" and "urgently" were crossed out by Zöpf himself. Did this mean that Zöpf was still in two minds? From a telegram by Aus der Fünten we see that, at 11 p.m. on February 1, 1944, Portuguese Jews were rounded up "throughout Holland". A further telegram, of February 2, reported that of the 180 on the Amsterdam list, 108 had been seized, and that they had left Amsterdam "in the direction of Westerbork". In Rotterdam, too, Wölk reported a "lightning success". His telegram mentioned thirteen names and three children aged three and a half years, two years, and fourteen days respectively.

On February 20, 1944, the long-mooted inspection of Portuguese Jews finally took place—twenty-two families, 273 persons altogether—were paraded before *SS-Sturmbannführer* Zöpf, *SS-Sturmbannführer* Aust and *SS-Obersturmführer* Gemmeker. Aust summed up his overall impression in few words: "A sub-human race." As such, they must not be sent to Spain or Portugal, but treated like all other Jews. As for the arguments of the learned professors, these men were "apparently lacking in political understanding". Less laconic were the views of Zöpf, whom Herzberg[1] has called "a highly literate man". This erudite German contended that the Portuguese were Jews and had always been so, that the photographs purporting to show their non-Jewish characteristics were merely due to lighting effects, as anyone who saw the men in the flesh could easily tell. The pro-

[1] Herzberg: *op. cit.*, p. 141.

fessorial arguments were mere "Jewish evasions". Zöpf's final conclusion was that "since these people were quite unfit for work (as a result of inbreeding and soft living) they would have to be put on the train for Theresienstadt that very week". And so 308 Portuguese were deported on February 25, 1944. Their names alone survive. As for the people themselves, they were among the last to be gassed at Auschwitz.

## "THE BLUE KNIGHTS"

To Calmeyer belongs the honour of having introduced the "blue knights", i.e. that group of privileged Jews whose record cards at the *Zentralstelle* bore a blue device. They were exempted from wearing the yellow star and their identity papers were endorsed to that effect. The first man to be favoured in this way was a famous German-Jewish art historian; this probably suggested to Calmeyer the choice of a symbol used by Kandinsky and Franz Marc in 1912. It was said that Marc liked horses, Kandinsky liked knights and both loved blue. In any case, the story appealed to Calmeyer.

The first reference to this device is found in the records of March 30, 1942. The matter was apparently discussed with typical German thoroughness, but those concerned were far from unanimous on what precise privileges the blue knights should enjoy: whether they should be left in Holland, sent to a separate camp, to Theresienstadt, etc.; and a number of them did indeed survive the war.

As early as June 10, 1942, there appeared a list of twenty-seven Blue Knights, including two known Dutch Nazis, and a woman whose husband was serving with the SS at the front. In the spring of 1943 their number increased to forty-five. About twice that number was rejected. Three "blue knights" were allowed to emigrate (the well-known violinist Flesch, his wife, and an art-dealer). The records explain how the forty-five had been picked: thirteen were ex-members of the Dutch Nazi party, five were married to non-Jews and had boys at the front, three were art experts working for Goering; three were married members of the Conservatoire Orchestra; one was a German Olympic champion of 1896; one was the wife of a leading Dutch economist; one was the son-in-law of a former librarian of the Royal Library at The Hague, etc. From the documents we can reconstruct their fate until the end of 1943. As for Calmeyer, he stated after 1945 that while he could propose new "knights" and give advice on how to become one, the final decision was not in his hands.

### BAPTIZED JEWS

We said earlier, when speaking of the Portuguese Jews, that though they were sent to Theresienstadt as a privileged group, they nevertheless finished up in the gas-chambers of Auschwitz. The same fate also befell Jews baptized into the Catholic faith, who were seized on August 2, 1942. Protestant Jews, on the other hand, were allowed to escape the holocaust.

Herzberg[1] has stressed that the number of baptized Jews in Holland was very small indeed. Thus on October 1, 1941, 390 Jews of Dutch nationality and 300 foreign Jews had registered as Roman Catholics, a total of 690 persons; for the Dutch Reformed Church these figures were respectively 460, 131 and 591. In addition, there were a further 600 Jews baptized mostly into the Lutheran, New Reformed and Remonstrant Churches.

The fate of these people was the subject of many discussions, arguments and contradictory orders on the part of the invader; in any case, Jews once again went scurrying for the necessary certificates—true and forged. Many of the persons who helped them ended up in the concentration camp; others were given grey hairs by their would-be converts. "To give but one example," one of them explained. "I spoke to a Jew, a wealthy merchant and a great businessman. A gentleman through and through, but one who knew nothing of Jesus except that he had once listened to the St. Matthew Passion."[2] On August 22, 1942, came the report that the General Synod of the Dutch Reformed Church was compiling a list of Christian Jews who, by virtue of a German promise, were exempted from deportation; these were Jews:

1. Whose parents were Church members.
2. Who were being instructed for confirmation.
3. Regularly attending church services and with whom the Church Council was in spiritual contact.
4. Already baptized.
5. Who had made a confession of their Christian faith.

[1] Herzberg: *op. cit.*, p. 133.
[2] C. W. Koolsma: *Gekooide vogels* (Caged Birds) (The Hague, n.d.), pp. 168–74.

But all this applied only to those who had entered these categories before January 1, 1941, and even then the Germans kept trying to whittle down the lists.

When praising the Protestant Churches for their efforts on behalf of this group, we must remember that it formed only a very small part of the total Jewish community. And even in their case, can we truly say that they were saved by Church pressure? It was certainly no greater than that exerted by scholars and jurists on behalf of the Portuguese Jews, and yet all these efforts came to naught. On the other hand, the "Barnevelders" championed by Frederiks and Van Dam survived the war in Theresienstadt. Who can presume to allocate credit in such circumstances?

We know the number of exemptions (in the series 20,000 to 30,000) issued to Protestant Jews at various times; in 1942, it barely exceeded 1,000 (1,156 on December 2); the number rose to 1,575 on March 20, 1943. These figures do not help us very much, because numerous baptized Jews were exempted not by virtue of their religion but because they were married to Gentiles. In any case, a telegram from Berlin dated October 21, 1943, ordered all Protestant Jews (whom they put at 1,100) to Bergen-Belsen.

On September 4, 1944, some 500 of them left Westerbork for Theresienstadt in cattle-trucks. We have a list of all their names. In Westerbork they had been treated fairly well; there were three primary classes for the children, and one intermediate one. Divine service was held in a separate barrack, with the minister preaching from the top of a three-decker bunk, his lectern a cross-beam draped with a white sheet. The Dutch Bible Society which, until November 1942, issued Bibles and sections of it to Jews, ran into difficulties thereafter. We shall leave it at that. And of their stay in Theresienstadt, we shall say only that 150 of them were sent to Switzerland by way of exchanges in 1945.

## MIXED MARRIAGES

In more than one place we have mentioned mixed marriages, and described the fate of a group of Jews which more than any other must have been an abomination in the eyes of the German race fanatics. Their writings are full of expressions of disgust at those "bow-legged Jew boys", whose only ambition it apparently was to become united to the golden-haired Thusneldas of the higher Germanic race. Seen in that light, every Jew married to a Gentile was guilty of race-pollution, a crime for which Jews were normally punished with death. Strange, therefore, that no other group caused the Germans so much perplexity as this one. On June 15, 1943, Otto Bene recorded the following passage from a secret report by Harster to Seyss-Inquart: "Time and again we find that Jews in mixed marriages have no regular work and, particularly in the poorer town quarters, spend their time almost exclusively in black market activities."

Rauter, too, had very little doubt that the Jewish husbands of mixed marriages ought to disappear to Poland since, as he told Himmler on September 10, 1943, "we are bound to have endless trouble with these cases".

In view of all this, it seems almost miraculous that these people, of all, should have been saved; certainly, no one would have ventured to predict it at the time. There is every indication that they owed their survival to differences between the various departments of the Security Police in Berlin and The Hague; so confused were the Germans on this subject and also on the problem of half- and quarter-Jews, that even so shrewd a man as Calmeyer was utterly baffled. Not that those concerned were left in peace, far from it. They survived, but not without being hounded almost to death. More than once it appeared that their end had come. Not a few of them went into hiding. Did the powerful voice of the Protestant Churches[1] contribute to their survival? Once again the question is difficult to answer.

From a document signed by Calmeyer on November 27, 1942, we gather that on September 12, Jews married to Gentiles fell into two main groups:

A. Those with children, numbering 6,008 (the Dutch Census Office made it 6,038 on March 15, 1943).
B. Childless Jewish women married to non-Jewish husbands, numbering 928 (March 15, 1943: 1,024).

Calmeyer went on to give the number of childless mixed marriages where the husband was Jewish as approximately 10,000, and based his figures on a survey of August 1941. He fully realized the absurdity of this figure (it was, in fact, due to an arithmetical error) and eventually reduced it to 6,000, though someone added in ink that the real number must be "1,000 to 1,200 at the very most".

[1] T. Delleman: *Opdat wij niet vergeten* (Lest we forget), pp. 627–8, 637.

As we have said, the Germans were gravely troubled by the whole problem, so much so that the Jewish Council was forced to hand on most of the German orders in this field with a host of clarifications. The reader will also remember the repugnant way in which the Germans put an end to further mixed marriages in the spring of 1942, and their obnoxious proclamation on the subject in September of that year. We have also mentioned that in January 1943 the Netherlands Department of Justice sent registrars throughout the country directions to report to the Security Police all marriages in which one of the partners was a Jew—with certain exceptions. As Wielek has explained:[1] "G.I's (half-Jews) were allowed to marry Jews and would then be regarded as Jews themselves. Aryans were allowed to marry G.II's (quarter-Jews). Marriages between G.I's and G.II's required special permission, which was never granted, by the *Reichskommissar*'s Office. The same was true of marriages between G.I's and Aryans. Marriages between G.II's were forbidden. (Wielek forgot to add that marriages between G.I's were permitted.) And such things were happening in Anno Domini 1943, in the country of Erasmus and Spinoza . . ."

Wielek's book also gives us a glimpse of the general "line" (or, as he himself calls it, "the devious labyrinth") followed by the Germans. In brief, they never knew what they were doing, nor for that matter did the Jewish Council know when to expect permissions, revocations, exemptions or deportation orders.

A whole book could be written on the subject of quarter- and half-Jews—the *Führer* himself was keenly aware of the dangers of impure blood; in fact, so sensitive was he that, on July 1, 1942, upon meeting *Freiherr* von Liebig, a man of impeccable national sentiment, he suspected the presence of Jewish blood immediately. And the *Führer* must have been clairvoyant indeed, for soon afterwards it transpired that the noble Liebig race had been polluted by the intrusion of a Jewess in the seventeenth century—just another proof of what the *Führer* called Jewish infiltration. The reader may guess what happened to the *Freiherr*; much more interesting was the observation by Dr. Henry Picker, who kept a record of all important conversations in the *Führer*'s headquarters during 1941 and 1942: "During this animadversion, an orderly brought me a note by *Reichsleiter* Bormann. It read: 'Dr. Picker—Make a precise and full note of what the *Führer* has to say on the treatment and danger of

[1] Wielek: *op. cit.*, pp. 299–300.

our Jewish half-breeds, and in particular why they may not enter the *Wehrmacht* or be treated as equals.—B.' "

Clearly, even so rabid an anti-Semite as Bormann was at a complete loss when it came to the treatment of these unfortunate people, and had to hang upon the lips of the oracle, lest he make a false move.

### MUNITION JEWS

For thousands of Jews, there was yet another possibility of saving their skins; like the vanquished throughout history, they could offer their services to the conqueror. When the deportations began in the summer of 1942, many grasped at this straw. Few if any of them were not tormented by the invidiousness of their position, or failed to realize that they were working for an enemy who plotted the total destruction of their people. Nor were Jews the only ones faced with this dilemma.

In any case, in a discussion on September 2, 1942, Seyss-Inquart decreed that all skilled Jewish workers capable of doing useful service for the *Wehrmacht* or the German war effort must be spared, provided only that this did not interfere with the policy of concentrating all Jews in Amsterdam. The military authorities declared in the spring of 1943 that they failed to understand why "it was thought so urgent to remove Jews actively working for the German war effort, when so many useless Jews in the Netherlands, who did nothing for Germany, were exempted from deportation and kept in special camps, for instance in Barneveld". In Germany itself, the authorities added, Jews working for the war effort were always the last to be deported.

But there was another German way of looking at the matter. We might epitomize it in the words of Lessing's *Nathan the Wise*: "No matter, the Jew must to the stake." For fanatics like Rauter, who saw a Jew behind every broken cable and every displaced railway sleeper, there was only one solution. All Jews must be cleared out of the coastal region at the very least, and this applied *a fortiori* to Jewish workers. All of them were Communists, or at best fellow-travellers. No doubt Rauter had read a book by Hitler's friend Dietrich Eckart, entitled *Der Bolschewismus von Moses bis Lenin* (Bolshevism from Moses to Lenin), for only thus can we explain his great reluctance to spare 3,800 for the war effort at a time when so many other categories were still exempt from transportation. It was certainly not Rauter's fault that this figure went up to 6,420 on October 15 and 6,716 on November 3.

Then chance came to his aid. In the autumn of 1942, the Germans dissolved the so-called Dutch People's Militia, in which they discovered a number of Communist Jews (as well as other Jews and non-Jewish Communists). We know from a surviving document that on October 18 and 19, 1942, Rauter appealed to Himmler; the nature of his request may be gathered from Himmler's reaction. Through Rudolf Brandt, his secretary, he informed Rauter that Speer, the Minister of Armaments and Munitions, would be told that a host of Jews working for the armament industry were part of a sabotage organization; meanwhile Rauter was given orders to "investigate" all these Jews and to weed them out; Himmler wanted to know within fourteen days how many others were left.

Now, from various documents referring to the activities of Resistance members in the Hollandia Works in Amsterdam, we know that Rauter's complaint was not entirely without substance. For, as we said earlier, there was sabotage in that plant, and Jewish workers did their bit as well.

The bombshell burst on November 12 when Rauter, apparently in a great rage, told a number of officials of the Arms Inspectorate that their so-called munition factories were hotbeds of Jewish terrorism and sabotage. He demanded that as many as possible be released for transportation. On November 31, 1942, Rauter asked *Generalkommissar* Schmidt to transfer as many Aryans as possible into the clothing industry, "for else we shall never be able to get rid of the Jews there". On December 2 the Arms Inspectorate sent a list of Jews "released for immediate transportation". We give it below and leave the reader to judge the reaction of these unfortunate people who, in possession of the envied stamp in the 60,000 to 80,000 series, had thought themselves absolutely safe:

| | |
|---|---|
| 1. Army List: | 6 Jews |
| 2. Navy List: | 6 Jews |
| 3. Air Force List: | 3 Jews |
| 4. Administrative List: | 744 Jews |
| 5. Scrap-Metal List: | 34 Jews |
| 6. Metal List: | 21 Jews |
| 7. Leather List: | 15 Jews |
| 8. Rag Collection List: | 87 Jews |

| | |
|---|---|
| 9. Chemicals List: | 10 Jews |
| 10. Tobacco List: | 1 Jew |
| 11. Clothing Industry List: | 810 Jews |

The Inspectorate promised further lists on January 1, February 1 and March 1. At the same time, it was preparing lists of names of those whose services were to be retained. But on March 26, 1943, they were asked to refrain from doing so—since "all that interests me is the total number of male and female Jews working in various branches of the armaments industry".

On March 20, 1943, *Fräulein* Slottke noted that the "general elimination" (of Jews) was being hampered by the urgent need for their services; on that date there were still 1,842 "unrestricted" armament Jews, of whom 792 worked directly for the *Wehrmacht*; in addition, there were 600 in the clothing industry, and 574 in the diamond industry. On January 19, 1943, Seyss-Inquart held a meeting, during which it was decided that all Jews must be removed from army work by the end of May. The response of the Minister of Armaments and Munitions was to insist on retaining eighty of them.

On April 24 we hear that of the 5,475 Jews working for the *Wehrmacht* only eight months before, 4,082 had been placed "at the disposal" of the Security Police; the remaining 1,393 would be removed at the end of May, except for a few "very special cases". On April 27 Zöpf told Eichmann's department in Berlin that, families included, there were still some 5,500 "munition Jews"; these would be sent to Vught, where a special "armament industry" would be started. On May 5 Harster gave orders that all "munition Jews" without exception would have to be put to work in Vught or else be sent directly to Westerbork for subsequent deportation. On May 10 Zöpf contended that it was best to seize the lot, send them to Westerbork, and on to Poland before the month was out. He fully realized that this would come as a psychological shock to those who felt so safe in Vught, but Security Headquarters in Berlin were demanding 8,000 Jews in May, and however hard he tried (even by offering premiums for the capture of Jews), however he scraped and saved, he was still 200 short . . . On May 21 the Arms Inspectorate confirmed the revocation of all exemptions as on May 31, but haggled over two Jews, and these were, in fact, spared "until further notice". For one of the two, a new plea was entered on April 17, 1944, when he was given permission to stay on until July 1 . . .

Once again the writer must appeal to the reader to look beyond the cold facts and figures and to remember that behind them, behind all the permits and revocations, behind all the harassment, fears and tribulations, were men of flesh and blood, they, their wives and their children.

## OTHER EXEMPTIONS

What it was to have a stamp! What it was to be on the right list! Of these latter, one achieved particular fame—that bearing the signature of E. A. P. Puttkammer, an assistant manager of a large bank who, as early as 1941, had supported the application of several Jewish clients for emigration permits to the Foreign Currency Control Bureau. These were granted and, what is more, without foreign currency having to be paid in—something on which the Germans afterwards insisted. Now, while any such applications were being considered by the authorities, the applicants were safe from deportation. At a later stage, Puttkammer handled the delicate negotiations of buying exemptions against valuables. After the Liberation, when Puttkammer was arrested on complaints made against him, many written and verbal testimonials were given to the effect that he had at all times protected the interests of his clients and had actually helped them in various ways.

Then there was the so-called Bühler list, named after Dr. Albert Bühler, the German Delegate in the Netherlands Bank, and covering "Jews who played an important role in economic life and had considerable international contacts". There was also the Bondy list, so-called after a Viennese Jew who, with the help of a Security Police Chief in The Hague, was able to grant "immunity until further notice" against payment of 1,000 guilders. In addition, there was a Rietveld list, a Six list and a Weismann list, as to which last S. de Wolff has given us a number of unsavoury details. Just think what it must have been like to fall into the hands of a Weismann, a former bank-robber, a man who admitted that he had made so much money out of the Jews—125,000 guilders, he claimed—that he could keep a mistress in great luxury, a man who was a member of the NSDAP and had two sons—one by the name of Wodan—in the *Waffen SS*. Then again there was the "Indies Military List", a very brief one indeed, for which one had to register with J. Brandon, the Secretary of the Jewish Council. As to that list, it was officially stated that "no great expectations should be placed in it". That was on February 23, 1943; on March 8—less than two weeks later—came the news that the list as a whole had been rejected by the commander of the *Wehrmacht*. By a stroke of luck, a number of other lists have been preserved, the so-called Westerneng lists, with 26, 22, 47, 22 and 18 names repectively. Nearly everyone on it was issued with stamps in the 40,000 series and was thus "fairly safe"; even so, Westerneng wrote about a woman nearly in her nineties: "Not exempted. I personally would give a great deal if this lady could remain here . . ."

Did the Germans lend an ear to such requests? Sometimes they did, more often not. Very few of the people whose names appeared in any of these lists escaped deportation; at best, their departure was delayed for some time.

### THE UNPROTECTED

Repeatedly in this book we have spoken of the way in which the Germans played cat and mouse with their victims. They kept them in a constant state of doubt, under a tension that never relaxed. They created an atmosphere of depression, exerted pressure, drove the mouse farther and farther into the corner. No one could ever tell whether or not to believe a German promise, and even those that were kept were kept only as long as it suited them. Hence we can understand the exclamation of a German Jewess: "If only I could be sure that things would not go on getting worse . . ."

Here and there in the story we have referred to various psychological reactions on the part of the Jews. We must leave the last word on this subject to people more qualified to treat it in its entirety; suffice it to say that the reactions ranged through the entire scale of human emotion, from noble endurance, brave resistance to complete resignation, utter demoralization and disintegration. There are some documents that are almost unbearable to read, for instance, the one written by the Jewish woman whose twenty-year-old son had been carried off to Mauthausen and who herself was about to be deported: "I felt completely free from everyday cares; above me the sky and in my head nothing but my own thoughts; there was no longer anything to hold me back from the life of the spirit . . . All round me was the invisible world; I had deliberately and systematically brought myself to face death happily."

But she survived the war—must we say alas? "Had I been gassed I should have died at peace with God. Then I believed that the sacrifice made sense, surrendered my judgment to God, much as Abraham had done. Today I am far from that. Today death will find me unreconciled and embittered—my faith in Jewish destiny is no more."

We could tell many similar stories, and at least as many of people who accepted their fate far less stoically. This is reflected in quite a few of the jokes that were doing the rounds at the time. One of these had it that when the leaders of the Jewish Council were told by the Germans that all Amsterdam Jews would be gassed forthwith, they asked if they might put just one question: would the Jewish Council have to pay for the gas? The same grim brand of humour was prevalent in the Warsaw Ghetto.

There was towering optimism and abysmal pessimism. Remarkably enough, the former prevailed throughout the war. When we read in Churchill's war memoirs that, in December 1943, many experts believed in an imminent German collapse, then it is not surprising that so many Jews thought likewise. There must be few surviving Jews who cannot recall hearing utterances of this kind; the writer himself remembers that when, in December 1942, he met a well-known economist wreathed in smiles and asked him what he had to be happy about, the answer was: "I know for certain that the war will be over in four weeks." No wonder that the Jewish Council and the Co-ordination Committee felt it necessary to issue a special warning through the columns of the *Jewish Weekly* against passing on rumours that might arouse false hopes, or for that matter false despair.

As we have said, the victims' reactions ranged from deepest depression to highest hope, so much so that it would take a psychologist to give a complete analysis. All the historian can hope to do is to report the unembellished facts.

But at the time it was not so much a question of the facts themselves as rumours about facts, and no one could tell which was which. Thus Anne Frank had this to say on October 9, 1942, about the deportees: "We assume that most of them are murdered. The British radio speaks of their being gassed. Perhaps that is the quickest way to die. I felt terribly upset. I couldn't tear myself away while Miep told these dreadful stories; and she herself was equally wound up for that matter."

May we, then, take it that Anne Frank and Miep, the non-Jewish woman who looked after her, actually *knew* what was happening to the Jews? One man informs us that he was told about the gassings by a German. He handed the story on to his fellow-Jews—can we, then, say that he actually *knew* it, that they *knew* it? In the autumn of 1942 a Jewish advocate was told by a Gentile barber that he knew a German soldier "who got drunk every night to forget his part in gassing Jewish children in trains. He could not put it out of his mind and kept thinking of his own five children."

In Westerbork, similar stories were circulating among the Jewish leaders; and the illegal Press, too, published terrifying reports—in January 1943, about the gassings themselves, and in September about the actual methods used. One lady harbouring Jews on the run was told in the late autumn of 1943 that "the women were issued with a towel and a piece of soap and sent to the gas-chambers, believing that they were about to take a shower; that men too exhausted to continue doing heavy work were killed by a bullet in the neck, and that innocent children were thrown straight into the ovens".

The leaders of the Jewish Council were inundated with stories of this kind. Did they, could they, give credence to them?

The vast majority of deported Jews, it is probably true to say, had no inkling of the real horrors awaiting them in Poland. This is amply born out by the records. Philip Mechanicus was told by a blind man in Westerbork: "I cannot see, but I know that the sun, the moon and the stars shine in Poland, as well." There is also a good deal of evidence that, even while they saw the flames pouring forth from the chimneys, many did not know what was happening or simply refused to do so. One survivor wrote that even in Sobibor he had no idea that everyone was about to be murdered.

Some people affected a degree of realism and laughed at those who, on the way to Auschwitz, still hugged their musical scores; they knew that things were not going to be quite as good as all that, there would be terrible deprivations, but they felt that the young people at least would come through: "In the train, we felt that they would make short work of the old ones." And even that thought was not shared by all. For the fairly tolerable treatment of the older prisoners in Westerbork gave grounds for hoping that everyone might yet be spared.

What, then, of the pre-war reports about German concentration camps? What of the young men who had died at Mauthausen? There was an answer to that as well. All of them had been punished for crimes they, or their fellow-Jews, had committed. But if one was submissive, one was sure to survive.

And what of the reports, in 1941 and 1942, about the massacre of Polish Jews? What of Anthony Eden's declaration on December 18, 1942 (to which we shall return)? Some dismissed the whole thing as "propaganda". Others claimed that it was a purely Polish affair, which is not so surprising when we consider that much the same view prevailed in England, where Eden's speech was not only heard but could also be read and pondered at leisure. Had not Aus der Fünten told Professor Cohen that he was at liberty to inspect Auschwitz for himself? And in Westerbork they said: "We have cottoned on to the fact that the Germans always use the same train, and we have told some of the deportees to hide messages in pre-arranged places. They write that the journey itself is horrible, that there is a shortage of water and space. But they also tell us that they are travelling through beautiful country, and that Auschwitz, where they all get off, is a large industrial place, full of factory chimneys."

Did they really learn no more than that? A German *Brigadeführer* arrived in Westerbork from Poland with his two small children who told their Jewish gardener: "You'll be going away before Daddy comes, won't you? He can't stand the sight of Jews." And in the repair shop, where they used to play, the children said: "In Poland, things were quite different, there the Jews were driven into the marshes and as their bodies sank people kept shooting at their heads." (Gemmeker, the Camp Commandant, dismissed the whole thing as a horror story.)[1]

And as similar stories kept reaching the camp, most of the inmates simply refused to believe them. "Now (after the war) that reaction strikes me as quite inexplicable. Was it perhaps a defence mechanism?" The reader will recall that the Jews in the Warsaw Ghetto reacted in much the same way.

A prominent member of the Jewish Council claimed that all the fears were greatly exaggerated. Others contended that the Germans killed only Communists and *agents provocateurs*. Some said that it only happened here and there. And another leading Jew declared that he had enough trouble already without having to listen to such depressing stories. The reader will remember our lengthy discussion of the way in which the letters from Poland were dealt with. We can hardly believe today how people allowed themselves to be deceived

[1] Unpublished report by H. Ottenstein.

in this way. Let us again quote a few of the relevant minutes from the so-called Central Committee, which included many of the high command of the Jewish Council:

September 18, 1942: "The meeting received the first report of a death in *Auswitz* (*sic!*)."

October 30, 1942: "From time to time there are reports of deaths in Auschwitz."

February 19, 1943: "Several reports have been received from Silesia, not all of which are unsatisfactory."

April 13, 1943: (The meeting noted that "hardly" any letters were received from women and children.) "This matter will be discussed with the German authorities."

For those who wanted to believe at all costs, these letters were, in fact, the only straw at which to clutch. One letter from Poland weighed more than all the rumours about German horrors there. Moreover, all those who believed and spread "horror stories" were not only thought to be inordinately irresponsible but criminals guilty of undermining Jewish morale. Only fools paid heed to such people.

## JEWS AND GENTILES

The Germans in the Netherlands persecuted Dutch Jews. They also persecuted Dutch Gentiles. Did that fill the latter with a fellow-feeling for their Jewish compatriots, with the wish to come to their aid? We have already said a great deal on this subject, reporting both what was done—and what was not done—by various departments, churches, individuals and groups. What follows is merely a kind of summing up.

Ideally, of course, every Dutch Gentile ought to have sided with the Jews, not only to defy the common enemy but also as a witness to human decency in general. Ideally, every Dutchman ought to have been in the Resistance, the more so as, almost from the start of the Occupation, it became glaringly obvious that the persecution of some of his fellow-citizens was not just a minor feature, not something that could simply be ignored. But to realize that meant to take a stand. And to take a stand meant to take action, in this case, identification with the Jews.[1] How far did the reality fall short of the ideal?

[1] R. de Jong: "De voorwaarden voor een radicaal-pacifisme" (The prerequisites for radical pacifism) in *De Nieuwe Stem* (December 1958), pp. 692–3.

Even on superficial examination, we find that there was a host of contradictory attitudes and opinions. Undoubtedly, many Dutchmen showed the right attitude and acted accordingly, but there were also those who did not, and those whose right attitude did not express itself in action. In fact, there was every possible shade of behaviour.

What, after all, do we mean by the wrong attitude? Weakness? Thoughtlessness? Hostility? Cowardice? Perhaps the answer could not be the same for any two people. In the Netherlands, Jews and Gentiles had been living at peace for centuries; pogroms were completely unknown. True, here as elsewhere, anti-Semitism was not entirely absent, but there was so little open hostility in Holland that—as we saw—a number of Jews were even admitted into the Dutch Nazi party. There were some who held the Jews in high regard, others who distrusted them; by an unwritten code Jews were debarred from holding certain offices and joining certain institutions, but by and large discrimination in the Netherlands amounted to no more than a slight nuisance. No wonder, then, that so many Dutch Gentiles had openly denounced the persecution of Jews in Germany.

And now that the Germans were persecuting the Jews in Holland itself, quite a few Dutchmen failed to "notice" or, when they could no longer close their eyes, found all sorts of excuses for standing aloof. Some lulled their conscience by telling themselves that though the Jews were having a bad time, they were not actually dying. "When peace comes, things are bound to settle down again and, what is more, they will get full compensation."[1] Elsewhere we read: "One felt sorry for the Jews and congratulated oneself on not being one of them. People gradually got used to Jews having the worst of it."[2] And the underground paper *Het Parool* said on May 10, 1942: "Even now many of our people are undisturbed. They hear nothing, know nothing and would prefer to see nothing. They are blind to the criminal acts by which our Jewish compatriots are persecuted, by which a part of the Dutch population in our own, hitherto safe, country, is gradually being forced to live like hunted animals, without any protection from the law, fearing for their lives, without

[1] J. T. Veldkamp: *Het Amsterdamse Bevolkingsregister in Oorlogstijd* (The Amsterdam Registry Office in War-time) (Amsterdam, 1955), p. 9.

[2] R. Rijksen: *Criminaliteit en bezetting* (Criminality and the Occupation) (Assen, 1957), p. 22.

knowing what the morrow may hold for them and what new chicanery the satanic Hun will not think up."

They did not know, they did not want to know. And Hitler made it very easy for them—they did not have to know. Everything went so smoothly, so easily—most of the time. And people had their own problems, or so they told themselves. How often was the writer told after the war: Don't forget what *all of us* had to go through! He did not—and does not—need the reminder.

And then people could always use that alibi that the Dutch authorities had failed to give them any kind of a lead. When dealing with the Jewish Council, we cited a number of instances of Dutch officials actively assisting the Germans. This was not, of course, the general rule, but how useful it was for the Germans that Dutch officialdom had such a high regard for prudence! "A great deal of inner resistance had to be overcome. Officials had been trained to believe that records must be correct down to the last detail, that mistakes, however small, were quite inadmissible, and that they were personally responsible for the accuracy of their work . . . However, the desire to snatch fellow-citizens from the jaws of the enemy won out in the end . . ."[1]

Not in all of them, of course—we have only to leaf through the illegal Press to know that; thus on September 22, 1941, *Het Parool* pilloried Dutch officialdom as "this miserable spectacle of men huddled together on a sinking raft and clutching at each other's coat-tails, in a vain effort to keep up their flagging courage". "Had they but adopted a principled stand right from the start," *Trouw* wrote on June 23, 1943, "they would greatly have strengthened the morale of the Dutch people." And this they certainly failed to do. As early as the autumn of 1940, Pieter 't Hoen (F. J. Goedhart) attacked the civic leaders of Holland's great cities in these words: "The behaviour of many burgomasters is more than shameful—it is nothing short of scandalous. Each day anew they defer to the disgraceful demands of the Germans . . . and vie with each other in their eagerness to lick the invader's boots . . ." Yet was the average Dutchman set a more inspiring example by the Secretaries-General, now the highest authority in the state? Did they, at least, try to keep the Germans to the letter of the Occupation Statutes? Did they draw the line between legitimate and illegitimate collaboration? And when, after 1940, they were forced to serve two masters, did they not

[1] Veldkamp: *op. cit.*, p. 20.

fawn upon the new one? And what of the Churches? How circumspect were they not at first! How many of them submitted to the despicable demands of the Invader (often appealing to the Bible for justification)! How often did they not concentrate their efforts on saving the baptized Jews while leaving the rest to their fate! And what can we say of our police force, except that it gradually became a tool of foreign brigands?

The Germans hated the Jews and the Resistance hated the Germans. Hence, if logic were any guide to human conduct, there should have been a united front. And indeed it often was so, despite all the perils, and the story of this common struggle ought to be inscribed in golden letters in all Dutch history books. What then of Sartre's dictum that "all non-Jews are wholly culpable, indeed, criminal; the Jewish blood shed by the Nazis is upon all our heads"?

In fact, even where there was open opposition to the Germans, there was not always sympathy for the Jews—some Resistance fighters were, in fact, notorious Jew-haters. In Amersfoort and Ommen camps many of the non-Jewish prisoners scorned their Jewish comrades. Nor was anti-Semitism entirely unknown among those who escaped to join the Dutch forces in England. Quite a few Jews were betrayed to the Germans by underground workers. How murky the feelings were, may be gathered from such books as Anne de Vries's *Het opgejaagde volk* (The Hunted People), in which the writer confesses that "nearly all of us" hated the Jews, that "National Socialism successfully appealed to the evil within us, finding fertile soil for its anti-Semitic seeds . . . The prevalent attitude here (in Amsterdam) differed in no way from that in the rest of the country: none of us wanted to be bothered with the Jews."

Though this candid confession is greatly to Anne de Vries's credit, it is only fair to say that the author went too far in imputing the same ignoble motives to everyone else—we have only to remind the reader of the courageous stand made by Dutch workers on the occasion of the February strike.

Of course, there was the other side of the picture as well. We know of Dutchmen who denounced Jews to the Germans, openly or anonymously. Calmeyer kept a "personal" letter sent by one of these in 1941: "Nobody but you can rid our private and communal nursing homes of Jews and Jewesses. They are an offence to every civilized person and they make life galling for all of us." The letter was signed with an assumed name.

We know of a firm of forwarding agents in Hilversum who supplied the Germans with the names of Jews who were apparently trying to take some of their possessions to safety. A businessman (full name known) denounced a Jewish competitor for making insulting remarks about the Germans. A citizen of The Hague (full name known) protested on November 21, 1941, to the "honourable and learned *Herr* Doctor Seijs-(*sic!*)Inquart" against the appointment of a Jew ("a young man hostile to Germany and the Dutch Nazi party") to a government post; he further alleged that one of the departmental chiefs had more than once told the young man that he was on his side. The informant offered to give any further details that might be needed ("I am only sorry I cannot give them in German"). Meanwhile: "I do not wish my name to be disclosed."

A particularly sad chapter in the history of the Occupation was the work—or rather the inactivity—of an institution expressly founded for the alleviation of human suffering: the Dutch Red Cross. The records contain many complaints and accusations against that body, and even the most moderate were agreed on one thing: "Everyone in Theresienstadt received parcels, except the Dutch." And one witness, speaking of a post-war transit camp, had this to say: "The French Red Cross was there, of course, and so was the Belgian Red Cross, but the Dutch Red Cross was, as ever, conspicuous by its absence." Or take yet another complaint: "The Dutch Red Cross did not even have the excuse that it was impossible to make contact with Auschwitz. Why, then, did they never send any parcels there?" Even after the Liberation, the Red Cross could "still have done much good by dispatching adequate medical and food supplies . . . I feel sure that (had they done so) many a Netherlander who died after the Liberation would have survived." In these circumstances, what are we to think of the memorial tablet in Westerbork Town Hall, showing "an exhausted, prostrate Jew receiving a beaker from a female figure", flanked by the emblems of the Dutch Red Cross and those of Westerbork?

But let us revert to nobler figures. We have repeatedly spoken of protests, resistance and active support—over the dismissal of Jewish officials, the terror in the Amsterdam Jewish quarters, the introduction of the yellow star and the beginning of the deportations. Later we shall have occasion to speak of the many Dutchmen who gave asylum to Jews. On a few occasions, Dutchmen even snatched Jews out of jail. Here and there, people acted on their own initiative. Not all officials played safe; many of them—not least among the police—paid with their lives for the active help they rendered the persecuted. Many Dutchmen acted from the very highest of motives, and quite ordinary people rose to unprecedented heights of heroism.

Others had to keep their thoughts to themselves:

"This morning I met a former patient, a Jewish man of about seventy. He told me that his four children had been sent to Poland a few months ago and that he had heard nothing from them at all. When I shook his hand at the end of our conversation, a German NCO who was passing by yelled out: 'Dirty Jew-lover.' I did not answer and simply walked on. But that a Hun can talk like that in our country and we can do nothing about it . . ."[1]

He did not feel free to speak out, but what of those who were? What of the Netherlands Government in exile, or the many Dutchmen who had settled or had fled abroad? What did they say? What did they do?

## LONDON

The actions of the Dutch Government in London cannot be treated out of context. The Netherlands was one of several Allies, a somewhat weak member of an association led by the United States, Britain and the Soviet Union. The inactivity of these powerful countries was a cover for Dutch inactivity—though not entirely.

Millions of Jews were being murdered. The civilized world heard about it, and either disbelieved the news or stood aghast, 'stood' being the operative word. Not only God, it was said, helps those who help themselves, but man as well. And so the Jews were left to die in their millions, men, women and children.

Possibly the Allies could do little about it. But we are still entitled to ask why they failed to do even that little. Why did they not look upon the Jews as comrades-in-arms, why did they not make the Jewish cause their own? Why did every initiative founder in an ocean of political, economic and military excuses? Why was everything left undone, or done too late? "It is not that they do not care, it is just that they do not care enough," said a British Jew during the war.

There was no lack of explanations, certainly—arguments of military necessity, and so forth. And then, of course, there was

[1] H. Mees: *Mijn oorlogsdagboek* (My war diary), p. 335.

general incredulity; as Thomas Mann explained, all the incoming reports were simply dismissed as so many propaganda stories.[1] The truth was too horrible for most of them to face. Even Jews in Palestine could not, would not, believe it.

And what was the main issue for the Jews was for the Allies but one of many. Still, was that a legitimate excuse for stressing the "difficulties of disposing of any considerable number of Jews should they be rescued from occupied countries", as a British source put it? Were such sentiments merely the results of a deficient imagination or were they reflections of something much worse? Was the Jew so very far wrong who said in November 1943 that Hitler could have scored a magnificent propaganda victory had he offered all his Jews to the unwilling Allies? On May 12, 1943, S. M. Zygelboim, a leader of Polish Jewry, committed suicide in London as a protest against the inactivity of the democratic nations and governments in the face of the complete extermination of the Jewish citizens of Poland: "Perhaps my death will accomplish what my life could not: get something done."

In the course of 1942 the Nazi leaders, Hitler and Goebbels above all, left little doubt as to their plans for the Jews. On December 18, 1942, Eden made an historical declaration (simultaneously released in Washington and Moscow) to the House of Commons in which he proclaimed that the Allies had received numerous reports of Nazi atrocities against the Jews. Eden mentioned the wholesale deportations from all Occupied countries to Eastern Europe "in conditions of appalling horror and brutality". In Poland, "which has been made the principal Nazi slaughter-house, the ghettos established by the German invaders are being systematically emptied of all Jews except a few highly skilled workers required for war industries". The declaration spoke of many hundreds of thousands of victims. When Eden was done, the House of Commons stood in silence.

The British Government was immediately showered with petitions by Jews and non-Jews alike to open the doors of the Empire, and of Palestine in particular, to Jewish refugees. British newspapers published the most horrifying details, but were unwilling to make a sustained campaign on the grounds that the horror stories had lost their news value. Meanwhile the gassings continued.

From April 19 to 29, 1943, the whole problem was discussed at the

[1] Thomas Mann: *55 Radiosendungen nach Deutschland* (55 Broadcasts to Germany) (Stockholm, 1945), p. 48.

Bermuda Conference. It opened with a number of speeches. Referring to the deliberations, *The Observer* wrote in a leading article that what was so appalling about them was not only their utter lack of compassion but the humiliating protestations of the two greatest Powers on earth that they could do nothing to help.

It is impossible to read the records of this Conference (from which Jewish representatives were excluded!) without anguish and a feeling of shame, especially when we remember that all this speech-making went on at the very time that the Jews in the Warsaw Ghetto were nearing the end of their hopeless struggle. Not without reason did the *News Chronicle* of April 26, 1943, call its report on the Bermuda conference: "How not to hold a Conference on Refugees."

On January 22, 1944, President Roosevelt founded a War Refugee Board, with John Pehle as its Director. One is immediately struct by the fact that the word "Jew" does not even occur in the name of this Board. But then there had been a precedent. The St. James Conference on German War Crimes (January 1942) had refused to recognize crimes against Jews as being in a class by themselves. On March 30, 1944, Eden made another declaration to the House of Commons. At about the same time, the Russian *Politburo* explained the extermination of the Jews as a phase in the historical struggle between Fascism and Progress; in other words, Jews were not being massacred because they were Jews but simply as anti-Fascists. And while East and West were busy refining their interpretations, the Jews died.

What was the attitude of the Dutch Government in London during all this time, during the years when tens of thousands of Dutch Jews were being deported and done to death? At the Enquiry Commission, the former Minister of Internal Affairs, *mr.* J. A. W. Burger, tried to defend his colleagues with the following plea: "It would be quite wrong to assume that the Cabinet Council was not deeply concerned with the plight of the Jews; it was just that the majority of the members failed to appreciate how serious the situation really was."

*Mr.* B. Stokvis: "Would you say they lacked a sense of reality?"

Burger: "That is precisely what I felt at the time. It was not that they had no feelings for the Jews. In my opinion, they simply underestimated the seriousness of the situation."

Tens of thousands of Dutch Jews, men, women and children, were being dragged away in the most horrible circumstances; there were reliable reports that all of them were destined to die a horrible death in Poland. This was the "serious" situation which the Dutch Government "under-estimated"; and it is poor consolation indeed to hear that they bore the Jews no animosity. What precisely did they feel for them? Let us see what transpired at the Enquiry Commission:

The President: "Are you saying that though the authorities were worried about the fate of Dutch Jewry, they felt they could do nothing about it?"

Reply: "Indeed . . . no one could have hoped for a hundred per cent result in the circumstances . . ."

Stokvis: "But, in fact, the result was nought per cent."

Reply: "Yes."

And what of Prime Minister Gerbrandy himself, a man whose utter integrity and devotion no one has ever questioned? If others did nothing, surely he would? Before 1940 Gerbrandy had evinced deep respect for the Jewish people, for the People of the Book, and had even put on record his firm belief in the ultimate failure of the Nuremberg Laws, if only "because they run counter to the highest reality, the ultimate source of all justice".

Let us quote two excerpts from his evidence to the Enquiry Commission:

Professor Gerbrandy: "Let me say just this, Mr. President. I was visited by one of the champions of the Jewish cause who told me personally, in the presence of my Secretary-General, that no other Government took as keen an interest in the Jews as did the Dutch."

Stokvis: "Theirs was a purely Platonic interest, was it not, Mr. Gerbrandy?"

Gerbrandy: "No."

Stokvis: "Then might I ask you what was actually done about these sentiments?"

Gerbrandy: "As my visitor admitted, there was very little we could do. But then one should judge by the intentions rather than by the results."

Stokvis: "Indeed."

President: "Why could so little be done? Was it because of British pressure on you?"

Gerbrandy: "No, it was because action was physically impossible, Mr. President."

What did the President himself make of all this? "The strange thing is that when we asked Mr. Gerbrandy: 'Was this matter not preying on your mind all the time you were in London? Were you not constantly worried about the victims of the German terror, not only the Jews but all the others as well? Did you not keep asking yourself, what you could do about it?' He replied: 'Yes, naturally,' and enlarged upon this answer. He told us: 'It is all in the minutes of the Cabinet Council.' When we asked him to give us further details, he promised to look it up at home. Later we asked him if he had discovered anything and he told us: 'I could find nothing.'" No wonder the President ended: "This was something of an embarrassment to us."

A few documents from the autumn of 1943 help to throw further light on the actions of the Dutch Government. From a circular sent to all Dutch Ministers of October 6, 1943, we see that as early as February 1943, there were discussions about the possible exchange of Dutch Jews against interned Germans in Surinam. This plan was rejected by the Cabinet on the grounds that, although Jews were probably much worse off than the rest of the population, "it is questionable whether this entitles them to privileged treatment".

At a time when the Dutch Government knew full well that tens of thousands had been deported to Poland under appalling conditions, and when their fate hung in the balance all it could say was that they were "probably" worse off than the rest!

However, in a broadcast on October 21, 1943, Professor Gerbrandy proclaimed: "No matter what our nation as a whole has had, and may yet have, to suffer, the blows aimed at the Jews are not only more general but very much harder as well." He added: "Some day the Jewish section of our people will resume its rightful place among us, their heads bloody but unbowed. Alas, we cannot undo what has been done to them, but the Dutch people will surely bind up the wounds of the stricken Jews, even as they will relieve the sufferings of others."

The Director of the Netherlands State Institute for War Documentation, Dr. L. De Jong, who served in London during the war, remembers that in December 1943 he presented Professor Gerbrandy with strong documentary evidence that the Germans were systematically exterminating the Jews in Eastern Europe. Professor Gerbrandy was so overcome that he exclaimed: "Then that will be the end of the German people too." (Or words to that effect.)

Clearly until that moment, he had been unable to believe the awful truth. In 1954 Professor Gerbrandy said that he could still remember reading a convincing document (dated October 5, 1943) and finding himself, even at that late stage, utterly unable to believe in the mass extermination of West European Jewry.

What, then, *did* London know? The Polish authorities, for one, were fully informed on what was happening to their own Jews as early as the summer of 1942, but Zygelboim's suicide shows that they did little—if anything—about it. And the Dutch authorities? On July 29, 1942, Radio Orange proclaimed that "Jewish Poles" were being gassed by their thousands and warned that "our own Jewish citizens will fare no better". For the rest, as we saw, the Dutch Government, too, did very little.

What of the many Dutch Jews in London? This is what Meyer Sluyser, a leading witness to the Enquiry Commission, had to say on the subject: "In the middle of 1942, people in London *began* [my italics—J.P.] to realize how seriously Dutch Jewry was threatened." A number of people—Sluyser included—took "a very pessimistic view of the outcome right from the start". But it was "difficult to take in the thought that people were actually being carried off for gassing in Poland". One day Professor Gerbrandy said that an officer who had escaped from Poland had told him that Dutch Jews were being gassed in that country. "Do you think it can possibly be true?" Professor Gerbrandy asked Sluyser, who replied that he "could not believe even the Germans would stoop to such inhuman methods". In any case, Sluyser subsequently made contact with two Dutch Jews in London, J. L. Polak, a director of Unilever and S. van Zwanenberg, a Dutch industrialist. Their attempts to persuade the Dutch Government to create an Advisory Committee for Jewish Affairs fell on deaf ears at first, on the "completely *bona fide*" grounds that the Dutch Government refused to make distinctions between Dutchmen.

The writer knows that comparisons are odious, but cannot help remarking that a good doctor who does not distinguish between individual patients, nevertheless distinguishes between a cold and appendicitis. Perhaps this was also the view to which the Dutch Government eventually came round, for on February 22, 1943, the three men we have named were appointed to a special committee. At the Enquiry Commission, *mr.* Stokvis told one of the expert witnesses: "I never really understood what the Jewish

Advisory Committee was about." "Nor did I," came the reply, "but, then, there were many things I did not understand in London."

We fully endorse the verdict of an authority on the subject:[1] "Nowhere is it stated clearly and unequivocally what precisely the Dutch authorities did do." Nowhere, the writer would like to add, has there been an acceptable refutation of the verdict by the Relief Parcels Commission:

"That the Dutch Government in London shifted on to others the responsibility of caring for political prisoners and Jewish deportees, and that it failed to make certain that this work was properly carried out.

"That the Dutch Government and the London Committee were guilty of crass neglect because, until June 1944, they took no steps whatsoever, not even the registration of the names of known political prisoners and Jewish deportees, towards the organization of help to these prisoners, and at a time when other countries were doing just that.

"That in 1944 and 1945, the relief activities of most official Dutch agencies in London were so puny, and that even the promised financial help was paid so tardily, that every attempt to render aid was doomed from the start . . .

"That all the above shortcomings, great and small—most of them due to lack of initiative, courage and imagination and a surfeit of bureaucratic rigidity—led to the death of thousands of Dutchmen, people who, as far as it is humanly possible to tell, might have been saved had help reached them in time."

Herzberg[2] has called "characteristic" the reaction of the State Repatriation Commission to a request on March 8, 1945, that help be given to Jews in Bergen-Belsen. The Commission's spokesman replied that he would need time to consider "whether the matter was of sufficient urgency and importance".

What of those representing Dutch interests in Berlin—in this particular case, the Swedish Ambassador and a minor Dutch official who had stayed in Berlin when the rest of the Dutch Legation left in May 1940? From the hearings of the Enquiry Commission and from

[1] M. H. Gans: "Parlementaire Enquêtecommissie en hulpwerk aan Joden" (The Parliamentary Enquiry Commission and Aid to Jews) in *Nieuw Israelitisch Weekblad*, October 17, 1952.

[2] Herzberg: *op. cit.*, p. 237.

a number of post-war letters to Professor Cohen (which he has kindly made available to us) we get some idea of what these men tried to achieve, and to what extent they succeeded. On the whole, their intentions were good, although one leading official in the Swedish Embassy was said to be "no friend of the Jews" and "to cut a rather poor figure". On the occasion of the Mauthausen massacre in 1941, Professor Cohen appealed to A. J. T. van der Vlugt, the honorary Consul-General for Finland in the Netherlands, who had a permanent permit to travel to Berlin, and asked him to see the Swedish Ambassador there. But the Swedes had to proceed with caution for fear of jeopardizing the extremely delicate position of their own country, and after "the Germans had expressed their annoyance" at such intervention, the Swedish Embassy became extremely reluctant to intercede on behalf of Dutch Jews. No doubt the Germans were afraid that, once the Swedes became familiar with the real facts, the bubble of German "legality" would quickly have been burst.

## THE PERSECUTORS

No account of the life of the Jews during the Occupation would be complete without at least some reference to their enemies. Perhaps "enemy" is not the right word, because the Germans persecuted rather than fought the Jews, by means in which eventually the whole German nation was implicated, actively or passively. Much could be said of this, but the present work is devoted to events in the Netherlands themselves, and to these we must confine ourselves. The treatment of Dutch Jews may have differed in tempo from that meted out to their East European brethren, but the aim was everywhere the same: the "final solution" of the Jewish problem, the destruction of all "Jewish parasites".

In the Netherlands, the German apparatus for achieving this end worked chiefly on directives issued by the notorious Section IV B 4 of the Berlin State Security Headquarters; its leader, *SS-Obersturmbannführer* Adolf Eichmann, born March 19, 1906, SS No. 45326, was obsessed with the task of eradicating every Jew "without mercy and with cool deliberation". He initiated a Terror whose description would need the pen of a Malraux or a Sartre. "I shall leap laughing into my grave, for the thought that I have five million human lives on my conscience is to me a source of inordinate satisfaction"—it was the man who said this (and there is little doubt as to that) who gave the orders sealing the fate of Dutch Jewry; the guilt of his superiors, Heydrich, Himmler and finally Hitler, need not detain us here.

Nor need we give a full account of the workings of the German war machine as such. All that concerns us is that part of it which perpetrated one of Germany's foremost war aims, the annihilation of the Jews—in our particular case the annihilation of Jews living on Dutch territory.

As we pointed out earlier, the occupied Netherlands was put under the control of *Reichskommissar* Seyss-Inquart by Hitler's decree of May 18, 1940. Seyss-Inquart was assisted by Rauter who, on Himmler's suggestion, was given the job of *Generalkommissar* for Public Security; by Schmidt who, on the suggestions of Hess or Bormann, was appointed *Generalkommissar* with special responsibilities; and by Wimmer and Fischböck, two old colleagues of Seyss-Inquart's from Austria, who were given the jobs of *Generalkommissars* for Administration and Justice and for Finance and Economic Affairs respectively. Another German luminary was Otto Bene, the representative of the German Foreign Office, who was appointed at the special request of Ribbentrop. Then there were the territorial Delegates for the eleven provinces and for the two leading cities. It will be noticed that not one of these men was explicitly charged with the persecution of the Jews, but, then, they all had a hand in it.

"The worst regression of a civilized state to conditions of despotism . . . took the guise of zealous bureaucratism."[1] The extermination of the Jews was first and foremost an administrative feat—it was genocide by the civil service. We shall leave it to those more qualified than ourselves to decide why the process of destruction was not absolute; perhaps one of the reasons was what W. Hofer has called "the innate absurdity and pseudo-scientific and manipulative character of anti-Semitism"—perhaps there were other causes, as well. In Berlin alone there were four Chancelleries: a Reichs Chancellery, a Presidential Chancellery, a Party Chancellery and the *Führer*'s Chancellery; of these, the second and fourth had no direct dealings with the Netherlands. Here the German apparatus was at sixes and sevens as well or, as Harster called it, "a heap of odds and ends"; here the *Reichskommissariat* "was not a cohesive unit but a conglomerate of people posted to the Netherlands by various departments in Germany and hence, by and large, more concerned to carry out the intentions of their own chiefs than to work in the spirit

[1] W. Hofer: *Der Nationalsozialismus* (Frankfort, 1957), p. 271.

of the *Reichskommissar* himself". But while these Germans were at loggerheads, it is true to say that the extermination of the Jews was one subject on which all of them showed an unusual degree of harmony, and it was this factor which made the deportations such a successful operation. The instructions were often so wide that few knew how far their powers extended, and no one could have told you precisely what he was expected to do in particular situations. The only thing that apparently mattered was that whatever steps they did take were suffused with a "good" dose of anti-Semitism.

Were the Germans, in fact, the devils in human form they have been called during one of many trials? If this was true of anyone, it must certainly have applied to Rudolf Hoess, the Commandant of Auschwitz, this dutiful, subservient Prussian Philistine, this rubber stamp without a soul. Wielek[1] takes an equally poor view of the *Zentralstelle*: "All of them were more or less unbalanced. There was Aus der Fünten, a thorough-paced cynic; Wörlein and Stumm, two moronic dunderheads; Stübe, who later replaced Aus der Fünten, a brutish mercenary; together with such cretins as the obese, gasping Klausnitzer, and the dwarfish Irler, Aus der Fünten's head chauffeur, whose speciality was hitting and kicking tall and well-built Jews." All in all a thoroughly nasty gang of thugs.

Once again we must raise the question, how far knowledge about the final fate of the Jews was prevalent—this time among the Germans in Holland. Many people have endeavoured to provide an answer. There are so many degrees between full knowledge and complete ignorance—thus on April 21, 1943, when Ernst Jünger wrote about the gassings in his Paris diary, can we be certain that he *knew* that Jews (even French Jews) were dying in this way? It is, of course, more than unlikely that the upper echelons of Seyss-Inquart's entourage had heard nothing of what was going on in the East, that they had not seen photographs of camps or heard reports of mass executions. We have a declaration, made long after the war, by a German to the effect that the mass extermination of Jews in Poland was openly discussed in The Hague (he used the term "large-scale industry").

And this is what Eichmann's judges had to say: "By 1940, at the latest, it must have been clear to anyone not completely ingenuous that the Nazi system did not shrink from criminal acts. Those who participated in these cannot now claim that they did not act in full

[1] Wielek: *op. cit.*, pp. 329–30.

awareness of the facts." All they could do was repress that knowledge and shelter behind the veil of secrecy that surrounded the extermination of the Jews. Here in Holland, they could pretend that they were no more than forwarding agents, sending Jews from one address to another; what happened to the consignment at the end was none of their business. Moreover, it was better—and safer—not to ask any questions. As Herzberg has put it:[1] "The question is not so much what they knew about the actual fate of the Jews as whether they cared one scrap about what became of them. To that question we can only answer in the negative . . . That was their crime."

Let us once again heed the word of Eichmann's judges: "The legal responsibility of those who deliver the victim to his death is, in our eyes, no less than that of those who kill the victim; indeed, it may be greater still . . . The process of extermination was a single, all-embracing operation and cannot be divided into individual deeds or acts performed by individual persons at different times and in different places."

We know that everyone asked about his share in the extermination, has protested his ignorance or innocence, as, for instance, did Rauter in a conversation with the writer at Scheveningen prison. Speaking passionately, and more or less repeating what he had already said during his trial, Rauter denied that he had been a knowing accomplice; again and again he claimed that he would rather have torn his general's epaulettes from his shoulders than participate in mass murder—during the trial he had even asserted that anyone guilty of that heinous crime ought to be "burned alive at the stake". Alas, we also have access to the writings, letters and speeches of this man, and to many of the letters addressed to him, all dating from the time when he, his superiors and underlings, felt free to express themselves with impunity, when assurance of victory drowned all sense of responsibility or culpability—they tell an altogether different story. Here words fail, and there remains only the bowed head and silence.

And then it was all so neatly done. As we saw, there was no special Jewish Commissar, so that the whole operation was directed by the *Reichskommissar* in The Hague, about whom it now seems necessary to say a few words.

There is no doubt that Seyss-Inquart was a faithful servant of his master, carrying out Hitler's orders to the letter and omitting

[1] Herzberg: *op. cit.*, p. 104.

nothing. Whether or not he rejoiced in his heart as he went about this work we cannot tell; he simply did what he thought to be his duty—so well, in fact, that, in his last testament, Hitler appointed him Minister of Foreign Affairs. (For lack of a land in his gift this proved a hollow honour.) Seyss-Inquart was hanged at Nuremberg, and no real plea in mitigation could be found. He never achieved high rank in the Nazi Party itself, and depended entirely on the support of Hitler and those the *Führer* had appointed as his aides: Rauter and Schmidt—all three were received by the *Führer* on May 25, 1940. It should be remembered that as far as Seyss-Inquart was concerned, Holland was merely a stepping-stone to greater things—to fame in Berlin, and only by obeying the *Führer*'s every whim could he achieve them. In the event, obedience meant ruthless persecution of the Jews.

According to Rauter, Seyss-Inquart would hold a number of annual *Judenkonferenze*, during which he would discuss the latest anti-Jewish measures. Rauter would send full reports of the proceedings to Heinrich Himmler, his own chief, and Lages has given us some striking details about the atmosphere prevailing at these conferences. Seyss-Inquart, who was an Austrian, had brought a few henchmen from his own Fatherland, for instance, Fischböck and Wimmer, two old comrades from the *Anschluss* days; Rauter, too, was an Austrian—no wonder that their enthusiasm for the Austrian-born *Führer* was so great. The chats were cosy, there was high good humour, as so often happens when Austrians get together, although, according to Lages, Seyss-Inquart would soon bring them back to the stern realities of the Party line. The others, for their part, used the path of least resistance, would invariably "agree with alacrity and be all smiles", particularly on the Jewish question.

Let us look briefly at the other mighty men in the land, the four *Generalkommissars*. Among them Rauter has loomed large in these pages, not least because we know so much about him from his trial before Dutch judges. He was *Generalkommissar* for Security and Higher *SS*- and Police-Leader in the Netherlands, in which last capacity he was in charge of all German police units in this country. It is probably true to say that of all German high officials in Holland, he was the one the Jews most feared, and rightly so, for Rauter was one of the mainsprings of the whole machine, although even he is known to have had his moments of moderation and was, in any case, less directly involved in the deportation of the Jews than Dr. Wilhelm

Harster, of whom more below. Nevertheless, as Himmler's cat's-paw in the Netherlands and as representative of the SS, as a man who had served his apprenticeship in the dangerous jungle of Austrian politics, Rauter was in fact the persecutor *par excellence*, especially after the death of his great rival Schmidt (June 26, 1943), and the promotion of Heinrich Himmler to the post of Minister of the Interior (August 24, 1943). Seyss-Inquart is said to have called him "a great child, with all a child's cruelty"; needless to say, the Jews experienced more of his cruelty than of his childishness.

Fritz Schmidt was *Generalkommissar* "for special purposes". This former street-photographer had been given the task of representing the Nazi Party in the Netherlands, which, in fact, meant representing Martin Bormann. He was not an Austrian; was he therefore devoid of Austrian *bonhomie*? It has sometimes been said that "behind his desk" he was not the "bloodthirsty bully" he pretended to be when making public speeches. Be that as it may; we have sufficient evidence to show that he, too, was busily working away at anti-Jewish measures "behind his desk". Nor could it have been kindliness that prompted him to open Barneveld to the Jews—if indeed he was concerned in that. His motives must in any case remain a mystery since on June 26, 1943, he fell, jumped or was pushed out, of a train and lost his life.

The third *Generalkommissar* is another figure by now familiar to us: Friedrich Wimmer was a Doctor of Law, Doctor of Philosophy, a prehistorian, an archaeologist and a jurist, who had risen to the rank of *SS-Brigadeführer* in Austria and now, as *Generalkommissar* for Administration and Justice in the Netherlands, committed so many crimes against the Jews that it would take us much too far afield to list them in detail. As for Dr. Hans Fischböck, the *Generalkommissar* for Finance and Economic Affairs, holding the rank of *SS-Gruppenführer*, there is little doubt that he, too, was deep in the machinations surrounding the extermination of the Jews, the more so as he was a close intimate of Seyss-Inquart and had won his spurs in Austria long before the war.

Deeply implicated though all these martinets were in the destruction of Dutch Jewry, none was more closely involved than the man of whom Abraham Asscher declared after the Liberation that he had never even heard his name: Dr. Wilhelm Harster, *SS-Gruppenführer* and *General-Leutenant der Polizei* and, from July 15, 1940, to August 29, 1943, Chief Commander of the Security Police in the Netherlands. Nor was Asscher the only one; the average Jew, too, had reason to know—and to know only too well—what the names of Seyss-Inquart, Rauter, Lages and Aus der Fünten stood for, but they knew nothing about Harster, to whom Himmler and Heydrich had entrusted the organization of the German police forces in the Netherlands, this dutiful, precise and very intelligent policeman, this right-hand man of Rauter and Eichmann. There is no question that he was an interesting character, as the writer found during a conversation with him on September 6, 1955, in the Breda penitentiary.

What precisely was his job? In 1941 Harster was proposed for the post of *Kommissar für die Judenfrage*, but Seyss-Inquart refused to accept this appointment on the grounds that he did not wish to be excluded from the handling of the Jewish question; hence Harster was put in charge of "police measures against the Jews". Rauter, who greatly esteemed him, declared during his trial: "All Harster had to do was to organize the deportations." A 1944 report referred to him as the man who speeded up the "dejudification" of the Netherlands on Himmler's orders. And though "all" Harster had to do was to organize the deportations, we gather from his own evidence that he played a very central part in the extermination machine. Harster was sentenced to twelve years penal servitude, but did not serve the full term.

These six may be called the leading figures in the Jewish tragedy. Their underlings make up a large cast of extras. Must the writer deal with all of them? All he can hope to do here is to make a somewhat arbitrary choice, even an unfair one. He will only pass in brief review the fanatical Rodegro, a hateful and obnoxious man; Otto Bene, Ribbentrop's representative, whose reports to Berlin are by now sufficiently familiar to the reader; Naumann and Schöngarth, Harster's successors; Wölk, chief of the Rotterdam branch of the Security Police from October 1942 onwards, and praised by Naumann for the "necessary firmness" with which he did his duty; Otto Kempin, in charge of a group of Dutch police officials in Amsterdam and sentenced to ten years for his part in the persecution of the Jews (including the ill-treatment of Jewish prisoners); Willi Zöpf, an "expert" on the Jewish question, who worked under Harster and who, as *Sturmbannführer*, represented his chief at some ten conferences in Berlin during 1941–3. Zöpf's first task in Holland was to deal with the possible emigration of Jews. On January 1, 1942, he was appointed head of the new department IV B 4 in The Hague. By his side worked *Kriminalsekretär* Franz Fischer, director of the Department of General Affairs of IV B 4, and organizer of the deportation of some 13,000 Jews from The Hague, a *Hauptscharführer* who had so thick a dossier against him that a death sentence seemed inevitable, but who escaped it. Then there was Seyss-Inquart's delegate in Amsterdam, Dr. Böhmcker; much as Harster was the representative of the Heydrich group in Holland, so Böhmcker was the representative of the *Reichskommissar* on Jewish matters, a sort of co-ordinator for anti-Jewish measures, whom Rauter ironically called the "Jewish *Kommissar*".

Böhmcker had little to do with the actual deportations, but was involved in the ghetto plans, the herding of Jews into Amsterdam which made the deportation possible; moreover, he was present during many raids and also during the expulsion of Jews to Westerbork.

Next we come to *Fräulein* Slottke, the only representative of the "gentler sex" in this sinister catalogue. As a clerk employed by the police, she kept the ledger in which was recorded the number of deportations, and apparently also played an important part in some decisions. She would regularly appear in Westerbork, where an eyewitness has given the following description of her: "She was of small stature, a brunette, with a long pointed nose and many of the camp inmates thought she was a Jewess. She insisted on seeing everyone whose case she had to review; on the whole, she was to the point and friendly, although more often than not she would give a negative decision. Sometimes she could be brought round by pleading, but I do not think that she herself ever said anything that was true . . . While she pretended to be friendly, she was in fact an inhuman automaton, working from early morning to late at night." Herzberg[1] has called her "Our very own *Fräulein* Slottke . . . whom we shall always remember as a nightmare come to life . . . Probably embittered by loneliness she was an old parchment bag, the perfect hiding-place for the devil who possessed her. Over what was probably her breast she wore a crimson decoration, a carmine order, the emblem of her distinguished service during the dejudification of Europe . . . A witch who, unfeelingly, filed and sorted the 'material' and saw to it that the goods were dispatched on time to the East. Whenever she noticed the despair she caused to other women, torn

[1] Herzberg: *Amor Fati* (Amsterdam, 1946), p. 34.

away from their husbands, children and mothers, something like pious satisfaction would often play about her mouth. Children whom she hated, because she had none of her own, happiness which she destroyed because she herself was without it . . ."

She was an apparition, in drab clothes, a bat-like presence, her bag crammed with life-and-death decisions, who would flit in and out among the legion of the doomed, always affable and with a brisk efficiency, a ghastly figure stepped from the pages of Poe or Hoffmann.

Two other characters command our attention: Lages and Aus der Fünten. Willi Lages, a trained policeman, came to Amsterdam in February 1941, as Harster's personal representative in the city. His first task was to ferret out the instigators of the February strike, and this he did so well that Harster soon afterwards put him in charge of the *Zentralstelle für jüdische Auswanderung*. Here there was a certain division of labour between him and Aus der Fünten, who was more concerned with the day-to-day routine, or to be more precise "with certain administrative matters such as the proper registration of Jews, the implementation of such measures as the wearing of stars, the travel restrictions, the curfew and the expulsion of Jews from certain institutions."[1] After the war, Harster was loud in his praises of Lages, unlike the leaders of the Jewish Council and above all Professor Cohen, who took a very poor view of both his conduct and his character; someone even referred to him as an "intellectual criminal".

This could not be said of his deputy in the *Zentralstelle*, the Cologne merchant, or more probably small trader, Ferdinand Hugo aus der Fünten, who gave many signs of being a reluctant henchman but was at the same time a thorough-paced cynic. Thus he told an arrested Jew that "all roads lead *through* Westerbork", and he had many of these delightful jests. We have seen him in action on many occasions; to all intents and purposes, he and Lages *were* the *Zentralstelle*. Hence we shall say nothing about their underlings: Wörlein, Blumenthal and a host of lesser lights.

For the Jews, the *Zentralstelle* was charged with much the same indefinable aura as the *Expositur*. For them, the *Reichskommisariat* in The Hague hardly existed; the *Zentralstelle* was *the* enemy citadel within Amsterdam, the crater from which all evil poured forth over them. And rightly so. For, according to the Germans themselves, it

[1] Examination of W. Lages on May 9, 1949.

was here that the "essential part of the dejudification process took place". Here, Harster received his orders from Berlin via Zöpf, and saw that they were carried out. Here the persecutor was entrenched, here he did his ghastly work, here the plunderer, the thug and the murderer were at home. A witness at the Eichmann trial has described the Vienna *Zentralstelle*, the model on which the Dutch one, was later based, as "a conveyor belt . . . a Jew is fed in, with all he possesses, at one end, pushed through the entire building, from counter to counter, from office to office, and comes out at the other end deprived of all his rights, robbed of all his money, and bearing only a scrap of paper telling him to leave the country within fourteen days, lest he be sent to a concentration camp". In Amsterdam, it was all much the same, except that the victims were no longer given an alternative.

The Vienna *Zentralstelle* was formed in July 1938, a few months after the *Anschluss*. The next country to be graced with this splendid institution was Czechoslovakia: the Prague branch opened its doors on July 15, 1939, and had specific instructions to speed up the emigration of Jews from Bohemia and Moravia. However, by March 5, 1940, its original scope was vastly increased; this process gained further momentum under the impetus of the German *Zentralstelle*, which had been established on Goering's personal orders on January 24, 1939, and was led by Heydrich and Eichmann. The Prague *Zentralstelle* under *SS-Sturmbannführer* Hans Günther was soon afterwards attached to Department IV B 4 in Berlin, the headquarters of the extermination machine. In Prague the Jewish leaders with whom the *Zentralstelle* did most of its negotiations were Jacob Edelstein and Richard Friedmann, whom we might call the Cohen and Sluzker of Czechoslovakia.

As a result of the Germans' practice of sending an occasional "expert" from one country to the next, Edelstein and Friedmann arrived in Amsterdam on March 17, 1941, ostensibly to pave the way for Jewish emigration and to advise the Jewish leaders. Their's was a more or less secret mission, for although they saw many prominent Jews (they even joined some of them in celebrating the Passover), the first mention of their visit in the minutes of the Secretaries-General is dated May 12; moreover, the minutes show how little the College really knew about the emissaries' activities. The two men left again on May 17. From a surviving but undated document we know that Friedmann introduced Asscher and Cohen to a number of Germans, including the notorious Rahm; on that occasion *SS-Obersturmführer* Dr. Rajakowitsch informed the two Presidents of the Jewish Council that a department for the emigration of Dutch Jews had been established.

Our sources differ as to what precisely happened during the meetings between Edelstein and Friedmann and the leaders of Dutch Jewry. Thus, Asscher declared after the war that he simply had a number of chats with them but himself took no notice of their advice. Cohen complained that the men from Prague had failed to tell him anything about the gassings. However, there is reliable testimony that the two emissaries spoke out "in an exceptionally courageous and open way", sounding the alarm and "predicting in every detail what happened later".

A document dated April 18, 1941, throws light on the actual setting up of the Dutch *Zentralstelle*; it would appear that its emergence was the direct result of a request by Heydrich to Seyss-Inquart when the former paid a visit to The Hague in the spring of 1941. The Dutch *Zentralstelle* was to serve as a model for "the solution of the Jewish question" (though not yet the final solution) throughout Europe. It was given no less than three distinct tasks: to ferret out all Jews, to control all Jewish activities, and to supervise Jewish emigration. Part of this "supervision" was, of course, the "direction" of the so-called emigrants' property; this part of the work Heydrich entrusted to Zöpf. Zöpf was later joined by Dr. Rajakowitsch, who had gained experience in this field in Prague, and by Dr. Wohlthat, *Kommissar* of the Netherlands Bank, who, in a letter to Seyss-Inquart of February 21, 1941, suggested that all rich emigrants be compelled to take "a certain number of indigent Jews" with them. But on February 26, 1941, the Economic Control Bureau, a branch of the *Generalkommisariat* for Finance and Economics, informed Wohlthat and Fischböck that, in matters of emigration, security considerations far outweighed foreign-currency considerations. No wonder, then, that the Security Police gradually gained ascendancy over the Economic Control Bureau.

When it was first set up, the *Zentralstelle* was a very small affair—one, as we saw, that was exclusively concerned with Jewish emigration and related problems. Its subsequent change of role was intimately connected with Seyss-Inquart's refusal to endorse Harster's appointment as *Kommissar für die Judenfrage*. On May 19, 1941, this question was discussed at length in Seyss-Inquart's office, and it was then that Seyss-Inquart made it known that the *Zentralstelle* would be responsible not to the Security Police but to himself.

Oddly enough, the material contains a reference to a *Sonderreferat Juden* (Special Jewish Department), led by Dr. Rajakowitsch. We may take it that the founding of this department on September 15, 1941, was closely connected with Berlin's plans for a Final Solution, and that these plans called for a further tightening of the grip on the Jewish population. It is significant that, shortly before that date, Seyss-Inquart, Fischböck and Wimmer received a memorandum from Rauter in which the term "expatriation" appears for the first time. Many of the duties of the Special Jewish Department were in fact closely connected with this change of emphasis, particularly the genealogical investigations, the treatment of foreign Jews, and the deportation plans, which were then proceeding a pace. At the beginning of January, all these tasks were delegated to Harster by Department IV B 4, and Rajakowitsch was transferred to Department II B, which had nothing to do with the Jewish question.

In practice, as we saw, there was a division of labour between the Amsterdam Delegate and the *Zentralstelle*. While the former dealt more or less with administrative questions concerning Jews (provisions, finances, *Jewish Weekly*), the *Zentralstelle* occupied itself with the round-ups and deportations. The Delegate employed civil servants, the *Zentralstelle* policemen. As a result, the Presidents of the Jewish Council and members of the *Expositur* would often have to deal with two authorities at once.

The archives of the *Zentralstelle* have yielded a number of lists with the names and personal data of Jews in alphabetical order and by area of residence. Were these the lists the Germans used in rounding up their victims? The idea of compiling such lists seems to have occurred to them early in 1941—if not earlier—though a start was not made until October of that year, when the Presidents of the Jewish Council were given instructions by the Public Record Office to help the *Zentralstelle* compile a register of all Jews—apparently on the initiative of Aus der Fünten, who wanted his victims safely in his files by October 15. To that purpose, the Jewish Council was ordered to supply the *Zentralstelle* with all the necessary secretaries, typewriters, furniture and filing clerks. On October 16 the first three Jewish clerks reported for duty, and on October 20 the work began in earnest. On October 21 another German department put a spanner in the works: it objected to the use of Jewish secretaries on the grounds that they would certainly falsify the lists. But on October 23 it was agreed that the work could proceed, provided that a member of the *Zentralstelle* was constantly present. From a document dated January 1942, we may take it that the records were finished before that date. We cannot tell with certainty whether it was these lists that the Germans used as a basis for the deportations though, lacking the necessary staff for compiling another set of lists, it seems more than likely that they did use them.

It has often been asked, not without reproach to the Jewish leaders, why they never appealed for help to General Christiansen, the C.-in-C. of the *Wehrmacht* in the Netherlands. Though formally on an equal footing with Seyss-Inquart, he was in a much weaker position and it is, in any case, doubtful whether, even had he had the power to do so, he would have come to the aid of the Jews. All we do know is that one Jew who sent him a written appeal was snatched up by the police and deported to Poland. Possibly there were some exceptions to the rule[1] that "no distinction can be made between the National Socialist ideologists and Hitler's generals". But Christiansen certainly was not one of them.

### THE DUTCH AUTHORITIES AT HOME

We shall preface our discussion of the role played by the Dutch authorities in Holland during the war with two observations, one brief and the second somewhat longer. The first concerns the College of Secretaries-General upon which, in May 1940, was suddenly thrust the main responsibility for civil administration, or rather such part of it as the Germans conceded to them. It is no part of our task to judge how they acquitted themselves. Once real power had passed into the hands of the Occupier, all the College could hope to do was to restore and maintain public order within the framework of the existing civil laws, or rather within the part of the framework left intact by the Germans. Undoubtedly, what began as German discrimination and ended with deportation was a fundamental breach of the laws of the land, a breach that could not possibly be excused on the plea of needs must when the devil drives. Can it be said that the Secretaries-General, fully realizing the gravity of that breach, nevertheless continued in office in the honest conviction that they were serving their country and people as best they could, and that

[1] W. H. Nagel: "Twee Vragen" (Two Questions) in *Maatstaf* (December 1963), p. 575.

their actions did not conflict with what has been called their "primary duty"? This may well be true of the non-Nazis among them. To them, staying at the post was the lesser evil; the alternative was to let the *Reichskommissar* make good his threats and take charge himself. As a result, they became unwilling accomplices in the deportation of the Jews, and though they could not possibly have known at first what lay in store for the victims, the writer cannot help wondering whether even that knowledge would have caused them to choose the alternative.

The other observation concerns the Dutch police. It seems best to begin with the time when the persecution had become so intensified that the Jews were constantly brought face to face with policemen, and especially with those of them who had been specially trained for the task by the invader, men whom *Het Parool*[1] denounced as "bloodhounds", and who, according to Lages himself, bore themselves "exceptionally well".

The resistance of Dutch gendarmes in the Eastern Netherlands during the autumn of 1941 failed to dissuade the Germans from involving the Dutch police in their anti-Jewish measures. Thus, in early November 1941, Rauter asked the Secretary-General of Justice to pass on instructions to various Dutch police departments regarding their actions when called upon to search Jewish homes, and especially when confiscating cash and valuables. On November 25 the Amsterdam police was ordered to supply 100 men in plainclothes to supervise the closure of Jewish shops. In 1942 Dutch police officers were attached to the *Zentralstelle*; during that year, various circulars gave them all sorts of detailed orders and instructions; we need only remind the reader of the many police telegrams sent on the occasion of the great raid on October 2.

On May 15, 1941, the "Police Battalion Amsterdam" (PBA) was established on the orders of Major-General Schumann, Commander of the German *Ordnungspolizei* (Ordinary Police) in The Hague. Soon afterwards, in July 1941, a "Police Training Battalion" (POB) was established at Schalkhaar, near beventer, under German supervision. During the first two months, the PBA was rarely used to implement anti-Jewish measures, but in the spring of 1942, many of the old officers and men were replaced by National Socialists, with the result that the situation changed radically—from October 3, 1942, the PBA was used increasingly during the round-ups of

[1] September 25, 1943

Jews; it then came under the direct control of the German Security Police and seized Jews on German orders. For this purpose three-man patrols were set up, each of them led by a member of the PBA who was also a member of the SS or the NSB; the patrols had section-, company- and battalion-commanders. The men were given orders to bring in every Jew they discovered at a particular address and the officers would even make unscheduled raids—whether from excessive zeal or just for the fun of it we cannot tell.

Here it is only fair to remind the reader that most Dutch policemen found themselves in a grave dilemma; they had become the cat's-paws of the ruthless invader, who used them for his own purposes and threatened them with summary punishment for disobedience.

Let us look at the difficulties of an "ordinary" policeman tried after the war. It was against his will that his superiors transferred him to the Bureau of Jewish Affairs, and when he went for advice to various "good" men among his seniors, he was waved aside with "you'll manage somehow". He saw the trams carrying off Jews night after night, saw the trains bearing them away. Was he to go into hiding? Every policeman had a detailed identity record, and if discovered, would come before a German military court which might well condemn him to death on the pretext of illegal possession of arms. If, on the other hand, he simply refused to participate in the anti-Jewish measures, the Germans would employ someone else who would treat the Jews much worse. And then one could always console oneself that one was really working for the Bureau of Jewish Affairs and not for the Germans themselves . . .

On October 30, 1942, the German "plenipotentiary" for the reorganization of the Dutch police issued a set of directives regarding the "implementation of German orders for the arrest, transportation and detention of Jews, hostages and other persons". This purpose was to "leave no room for misapprehension"; henceforth, State as well as Municipal Police would have to carry out all these German orders to the letter. All previous regulations were superseded. On February 24, 1943, when six Roman Catholic policemen in Utrecht informed their Superintendent that, because of a pastoral letter read out from the pulpit on February 21, they would refuse to arrest Jews, the Superintendent threatened to dismiss them without pension or notice, adding that if anyone else intended to disobey orders, he would "be treated as a saboteur with all the grave consequences

VAN DER HAL,
Petrarcalaan 75
UTRECHT

-9 OKT. 1942

DER REICHSKOMMISSAR
Eingel.: -8 OKT. 1942 Beilg.: 2
Zahl:
Zuteil.:

Utrecht, 5 October '42

Unterzeichneter ist als holländischer jüdischer Infanterist bei den Gevechten (Mai 1940) am Grebbeberg derart verwundet worden, dasz er für Lebzeits schwer-Kriegsinvalide ist (Siehe beiliegende Atteste).

Unter den gegebenen Verhältnissen bitte ich Eure Excellenz ergebenst, wenn möglich, der „Zentralstelle für Jüdische Auswanderung" gefl. Weisung geben zu wollen, dasz mein Name (und von Frau und 1 Kind) bei dieser Instanz gestrichen wird und ich somit für Emigration nicht in frage komme.

Eurer Excellenz im Voraus verbindlichst dankend, zeichne ich,

8-6-43 8-11-43

Mit vorzüglicher Hochachtung,

J A v d Hal

-8. OKT. 1942

Seine Excellenz den Wehrmachtsbefehlhaber für die besetzten niederl. Gebiete,
den Herrn General der Flieger Christianssen,
's-Gravenhage

Appeal for exemption by J. A. van der Hal, who lost one of his legs in battle during the German invasion, May 1940. General Christiansen's comment: "A Jew is a Jew with or without legs".

that entailed". We might add that the Germans came for the six men soon afterwards and, when they could not find them, arrested their wives and children instead. It is estimated that 180 other policemen declared their solidarity with these men, but all of them were put under such strong pressure by the Germans that, in the end, only twenty-three remained steadfast. These went underground for the rest of the war. (The Superintendent himself, one Kerlen, was shot dead in the street a few weeks later.)

Or take the case of Major van der Hauw:[1] "In March 1943 I was serving with the gendarmerie near the village of Grootegast. My group included both rural constabulary and gendarmes. On March 12 we received a telephone call from the Security Police in Groningen, ordering us to arrest a Jewish family in the vicinity and to take them to Westerbork; all of us felt that it would be wrong to obey this order. In the afternoon we met for further discussion and decided to stick to our decision. But while we were still assembled, German and Dutch policemen came to arrest us and took us to Groningen, where we were told that our declaration was an act of insubordination, punishable by death. We refused to budge. Then we were told: 'You can have a night to think it over,' but next morning we all found the strength to go on, and we were sent to Vught concentration camp. There we had to share the ill-treatment and solitary confinement of so many of the other prisoners. My older colleagues were sent to German concentration camps, Constable Boonstra among them. I can still remember his getting into the car at Groningen and being counted by a German policeman, who said: 'All eleven present and correct.' Then Boonstra objected that there were, in fact, twelve of us: 'You have forgotten that God is with us.'"

The writer would like to pay his own tribute to this noble man, and to the many Dutch police officers who died rather than still the voice of their conscience. Others again committed small acts of sabotage whenever they could; they saw nothing, heard nothing, found nothing. They, too, took considerable risks. Quite often they were denounced by anonymous informers; the notorious Jew-baiter, Dahmen von Buchholz, boasted that on May 19, 1942, he had "shopped" two policemen for talking to a Jew in the street.

So dissatisfied were the Germans with the reaction of the Dutch police force that at the beginning of 1943, they transferred responsibility for the seizure of Jews to the Auxiliary Police, founded by

[1] *De Bezetting* (The Occupation), part III (Amsterdam, 1963), pp. 30–1.

[illegible] [illegible], den 17. März 1943.

Der niederländische Staatsangehörige [illegible]      3541

[illegible] übergibt am 17. März [illegible]

1. [illegible]

2. [illegible]

3. [illegible]

4. [illegible]

5. [illegible]

Für die Zentralstelle für jüdische Auswanderung Amsterdam richtig übernommen:

[illegible]

Wachhabender

[illegible]

1. Für die Richtigkeit der Übernahme:      ꟻ-Hauptsturmführer.

2. Verwaltung

zur Zahlung von –37.50 Gulden, in Worten [illegible]

[illegible] Gulden.

Amsterdam, den 17. März 1943.

Festgestellt

Polizeisekretär

Sachlich richtig

ꟻ-Sturmbannführer

B. d. S.
Zahlstelle-Aussenstelle
Amsterdam

Amsterdam, den 17. März 1943.

Empfangsbescheinigung:

Von der Zahlstelle des B. d. S. — Aussenstelle Amsterdam — habe ich 37.50 Gulden,

in Worten [illegible] Gulden erhalten.

Dieser Betrag ist vorschussweise aus Judenvermögen gezahlt worden.

[illegible]

(Unterschrift.)

[illegible]

K 372

"Receipt" for blood-money paid to members of the Keyer-Column. They received 7½ guilders per Jewish captive.

Decree No. 57 of May 21, 1942, and made up of volunteers who (by Article 2 of Section 1) had to be "supporters of the New Order in Europe and ready to defend it to the best of their ability"—in Amsterdam alone, 1,047 such volunteers offered their services.

This is perhaps the place to mention the special police, or should we say semi-police, detachments that went out of their way to hound the Jews. There was, for instance, the notorious Henneicke Column, which specialized in ferreting out Jews who had gone into hiding; we have a whole file of statements by some of the Column's members. We can also peruse their internal memoranda, for instance the one dated June 30, 1943: "You are urgently requested not to blot the register, not to scribble in it or in other ways unnecessarily to soil it." There is also mention of the money these men were paid for each Jew—or Jewish child—they handed over to the Germans: 7½ guilders.

We have already spoken of the "bloodhounds", the collaborators among the regular Dutch police. How far were they given a free hand? On one occasion, thirty policemen, including fifteen NSB members, were dismissed for misappropriating Jewish property—for usurping what was clearly their masters' prerogative. There is a copy of a survey compiled for Lages on March 3, 1943, by the Presidents of the Jewish Council, and listing several blatant cases of blackmail. At the time, anyone speaking German, not necessarily in uniform, had only to enter a Jewish house and utter veiled threats to get practically anything he asked for. The writer remembers how, on a Sunday evening in early March 1943, at about 9 p.m., two members of the Auxiliary Police, after a loud ring at the door, stamped into his room in big boots, and how terribly disappointed they were to find a few non-Jewish visitors there; the raiding party immediately changed their tack and, after some humming and hawing, insinuated that the writer and his wife were on a list of wanted persons, but that they could help us if it was made worth their while. All we could do was pretend that we had not the least idea what they were driving at and, in the end, they left with empty hands—no doubt to try their luck elsewhere. The writer has also been through the diary of an auxiliary policeman which, though much the worse for wear, gave a fair record of his day-to-day activities:

(Date) "Caught eight Jews tonight. Later, with G. and De V., caught a further twenty-four Jews in Weesper Street."

(Date) "Jew-hunt tonight; a very successful evening. Must have bagged several hundreds of them during the past few weeks. Got home at 3.30 a.m."

(Date) "Caught a few men plundering Jewish houses."

(Date) "Jew-hunting again tonight. B. came along and had a full bag."

(Date) ". . . on Jew work. Rotten, squally night. Sergeant J. R. was A.1. A particularly good catch."

(Date) "Jew-work in the North this evening. A huge crowd of children followed us. Set out in the company of V. V. Sergeant W. shot three Jews."

This man obviously warmed to his work, and it must have been one like him who was present at a house not far from the writer's own when, late one evening, the police came to fetch a ninety-three-year-old Jew "for labour service in Germany". A non-Jewish lady who intervened earned herself a few slaps in the face, accompanied by a stream of abuse. (One of these men gave his occupation on a tax form as "Jew-catcher".) Many of their excesses were mentioned in the "personal and strictly confidential" report by the two Presidents of the Jewish Council to Lages, and the records are full of their harrowing deeds. Thus when a non-Jewish woman pleaded with three of them for the life of a fourteen-year-old girl, she was told: "No, we're getting rid of all this rubbish." (The witness added: "The same scoundrel who spoke these words is now free to walk about as though nothing had happened.")

What of the German police, of the notorious *Grüne Polizei* (Green Police)? It has been said that some of them were revolted by this type of work, and three are on record as having protested to their superiors. We also have the evidence of Henrietta von Schirach, the wife of Baldur von Schirach, leader of the Hitler Youth who, during a stay in Amsterdam in the spring of 1943, was awakened by the screams and moans of Jewish women. She took the first opportunity to complain to Hitler, whose only answer was: "Mere sentimentality! Humanitarian nonsense!"

While a few Germans behaved most creditably, this is not, alas, true of a number of Jews. Sad to relate, members of the OD, the Jewish Special Service Corps, quite often assisted the "Jew-catchers" in their dirty work. Dispatched by the Jewish authorities to lighten the load of the sick and old during round-ups, some of these young men misbehaved so disgracefully that their conduct drew protests even from non-Jews: "They would hang about on street corners exchanging pleasantries with the Green Police, offering them cigarettes and, in short, being as thick as thieves with them."

Perhaps this is the place to say a few words more about the Dutch Nazi party or NSB. Before 1940, responsible people thought that, even in case of an invasion, it would be unnecessary to arrest Mussert, their leader—he was thought to be "far too insignificant". That judgment hardly needed revising after the war, except that the Judge-Advocate-General accused Mussert of "boundless arrogance" and of being morally obtuse. This is mildness itself compared with the German opinion of him. Otto Bene was just about prepared to put up with this "little man without drive", but Himmler thought him "on about the same mental level as his lowliest follower" and made fun of his "stupid Dutch notions". The Germans particularly blamed him for his failure to deal with the Jewish problem; some even called him a Jewish lackey.

We might also say a few words about the Dutch Goebbels, Max Blokzijl, one of Mussert's close associates, and a great champion of pan-Germanism and of Aryan purity. Imagine his embarrassment when the fanatical Ten Cate, a leading expert on family trees, ferreted out the information that one of Blokzijl's grandmothers had borne the ominous name of Hanna Heimans, and that the good Max was himself a quarter-Jew! Nor was he the only NSB man who stood on shifting sands: the leader of the NSB Education Department was found not only to have a Jewish grandmother, but a Negro great-grandmother to boot!

And then there were the Jewish traitors, those unspeakable men and women who worked hand in glove with the German butchers. A few of them were brought to justice after the war and one of them, a woman who had betrayed scores of people, was sentenced to death. The excuse of these persons was always the same: they were threatened with deportation, they acted under duress. In one particular case, the judge contended that the traitor's being a Jew made his crime doubly heinous—as to that, the reader will have his own views. It is shocking to read the names, pseudonyms, addresses and birth-dates of these Jews in the German records, sometimes with the information that they were double agents in a sabotage group; on one of them, in particular, the Germans built high hopes, not least because his wife worked for the Jewish Council. Another Jewish collaborator was so dangerous that the underground had to do away with him. We have the diary of a man who, while hiding in Amsterdam, kept in constant touch with this traitor, whom he considered a devoted friend and to whom he divulged all sorts of confidential information. The man had not seen his wife and child for ages and was overjoyed when his "friend" arranged a family reunion. Alas, the expression of his joy in the diary was cut off in mid-sentence—the Germans appeared on the scene to take all three of them away. The traitor is said to have betrayed his own family as well . . . for money.

## ROBBERY

One aspect of the Germans' activity which has been mentioned in passing now claims our closer attention: the seizure of Jewish property.[1]

As is well known, the Nazis had every intention of saving mankind from the Jews, but not, mark you, without first claiming material benefits from this outstanding piece of philanthropy. Years before Hitler's accession to power, they had threatened their enemies with the "Night of the Long Knives". When that night eventually descended on the Jews, they had also to contend with the Night of the Light Fingers. They were robbed of everything they possessed, but not, of course, without due formality. The Germans were loud in their protestations that they did not so much exterminate the Jews as find a final solution to the Jewish problem; similarly, they did not rob the Jews but merely "transferred" their property or held it in trust. Everything was written down and carefully credited in the appropriate books. Scores of special offices were set aside for this work, and it is not surprising that some of the labourers in this vineyard were not beyond collecting a few windfalls. But only some; most of them did their work meticulously and honestly, with devotion and with that satisfaction that comes of a task well done. It must not be forgotten that particularly in the case of these "accountants", an unblemished character was an "absolute necessity" to the Germans. They had to observe the proper decorum in what they wore and in how their hair was cut. Here in the Netherlands they formed the vanguard of an army that in Poland brought up the rear—"conscientious officials who pulled the gold

[1] We are glad to acknowledge our indebtedness to A. J. van der Leeuw, of the Netherlands State Institute of War Documentation for the invaluable help he gave in the preparation of this section and the following one (*Jews in the Diamond Trade*).

teeth from the victim's mouth and made a careful inventory of all the toys they took away from the doomed Jewish children, gentlemen who saw to it that not a single silk blouse was lost, no corset, no truss, no scarf".[1]

All this demanded a vast organization, a host of clerks and a mountain of paper; this was the triumph of forms in triplicate, quadruplicate, sesquiplicate, and copies in even greater quantity. Nor was a single organization enough. As so often in the Third Reich, there was a host of separate departments, dependent or independent of one another, co-operating or in rivalry, but in any case all dedicated to plundering the Jew, from the greatest industrialist down to the poorest widow and orphan. Wherever the smallest item of Jewish property was found, it had to be seized "quickly and resourcefully"—those were the actual words.

The whole thing was not only legitimate, it was also justified. Legitimate inasmuch as the Jews were the enemies of Germany, and justified inasmuch as they had not earned their possessions by honest work but as mere parasites, and used them to the ruin of unsuspecting Aryans. Moreover, all Jews were capitalists and Communists at one and the same time, and had to be rendered harmless. Was not this a noble task for all Germans, and an unselfish one at that? This, in any event, is what the Germans gave out, and we may take it that quite a few who lent their services to the work of what the Nazis so elegantly called their policy of "relentless redeployment", actually believed it.

Did the Jews in the Netherlands have much for the Germans to take? A 1940 report based on a 1930 census suggests that they did not. The Germans themselves must have noticed this soon after their arrival. Jews played a fairly insignificant part in the economic life of the Netherlands. Thus they accounted for only 0·1 per cent of those engaged in agriculture and fishery; in the shipping industry there was not a single Jewish employer and Jewish workers amounted to less than 0·5 per cent of the labour force. Of the 14,159 employers in the inland waters traffic, only two were Jews, and of the 29,069 employees seventeen were Jews. What of banking and insurance? Here there were only 236 Jews among the total of 3,426 employers. In trade, there were 12,088 Jews among a total of 170,572 businessmen —less than 7 per cent. Moreover, a large proportion of these were

[1] Marnix Gijsen: *Lucinda en de lotuseter* (Lucinda and the lotus-eater) (The Hague, 1961), p. 32.

street-vendors and traders whose incomes were considerably less than that of the average worker. The only spheres in which Jews were more prominent were: the diamond, clothing, dry-cleaning and food industries. But even there Jewish employers accounted for only 2,539 out of a total of 69,552 (3·6 per cent), and Jewish workers for only 11,572 out of a total of 291,358 (3·9 per cent).

All in all, it is true to say that by far the great majority of Dutch Jews belonged to the proletariat and few of them had anything that it was worth the Germans' while to take away. They, however, were not the people to despise the widow's mite and seized even that with alacrity.

This last fact is so eloquent that the writer must interrupt his chronological account to dwell upon it at some length. History has known greater depredations and far greater robbers. Thus, some historians have admired the taste shown by Napoleon in making off with the Horses of San Marco and the Chariot from the top of the Brandenburg Gate. What was so original in the behaviour of the German predators was that they used an almost scientific method for milking millions of physically and economically defenceless people as a stepping-stone towards their extermination. They were so brazen about it, that of all their actions this was the one that attracted most notice and the one they could least disguise. Everyone in the vicinity, even those who had not seen the victims dragged away under cover of darkness, could not but observe the furniture vans being loaded up in broad daylight.

Here, too, every observer could not help being struck by the bureaucratic earnestness and devotion with which the invader did his job, chiefly under the aegis of the *Einsatzstab Reichsleiter Rosenberg* (National Leader Rosenberg's Action Group). This title was significant. The bands of murderers whose liaison with the Army was tenuous and who, in Poland and Russia, were butchering defenceless Jews by the thousand, conferred upon themselves the proud name of Action Groups. Was not "readiness for action" . . . "the loftiest of the virtues, comprising courage, determination, self-denial and, above all, high earnestness—male, mature and deadly earnest"?

Courage, determination, self-denial, seriousness. What of these do we find in the thieves, great and small, who had the safe job of plunder far behind the battle-front? Courage? Determination? Self-denial? Perhaps none of them, but they certainly set to work in deadly earnest. After all, they were an Action Group, and did not a list of Jewish rare booksellers singled out for plunder bear the heading: "Action stations of the Netherlands Working Detachment of the *Einsatzstab Reichsleiter Rosenberg*"?

As we have said, they worked with earnest devotion. As early as September 18, 1940, Rosenberg sent a letter to the National Treasurer of the NSDAP, Franz Xavier Schwarz, in Munich, with the following triumphant message: "You will see that we are very busily at work, and that we are making hay while the sun shines, knowing that we may never get another chance like this." The only cloud on this bright horizon was that so many other departments were also trying to "act" in a field where so much could be gained at so little personal risk.

During the first two months, the great work was largely confined to libraries and similar institutions—not the kind of combat the "Action Groups" really relished; their greatest campaigns were fought in the living-rooms of Jewish houses. It was a little difficult to see oneself as a hero when all that was involved was the dull business of collecting and cataloguing old books and pictures. But when it came to seizing furniture and dragging away the owners for dispatch to the gas-chambers, men came truly into their own. Then "Strength Through Joy" was verily joined to "Joy Through Work".

Of the many competitors in this field, one deserves special mention: the *Hausraterfassung* (Department for the Appropriation of Household Effects) which, according to a statement by Lages, was founded in the course of 1941 for the specific purpose of registering ownerless Jewish possessions. This august body was soon afterwards affiliated to the *Zentralstelle* and placed under the personal control of Wörlein, a German, and P. Docter, a Dutchman. It was their job not only to register goods but also confiscate them on behalf of the *Einsatzstab Rosenberg*. When the deportations were nearing their end, some of the staff were assigned to other duties, for instance, the ferreting out of concealed Jewish valuables. At the height of the deportations, the Household Effects Branch was so overwhelmed with work that it was forced to create a special "key department", whose task it was to guard the keys of unoccupied Jewish houses. All these keys were subsequently handed over to the *Einsatzstab Rosenberg*. No doubt, the men did not always find it easy to sort out the large bunches of keys, many of them unlabelled. There were eighteen Jewish helpers in this work; on June 6, 1944, they and their families were sent to Westerbork (forty persons in all) with the prospect of being transferred to the preferential camp of Theresienstadt. The *Hausraterfassung* also employed a team of loyal Dutch officials, who sabotaged the work wherever they could and opposed the Germans in every possible way. For the rest, there was a great deal of confusion and . . . corruption.

As we page through the voluminous dossiers we get the impression that the *Einsatzstab Rosenberg* was very hard at work in our country, and that many of its members did a great deal of overtime in the service of the Fatherland. From the many returns that have survived we have singled out one list; that of houses cleared of furniture during the period March 26, 1942 to May 31, 1943. There were 17,235 of them (9,891 in Amsterdam alone), with a total capacity of 479,726 cubic metres; the contents were loaded on 449 barges (438,095 cubic metres) and 136 goods-wagons (6,423 cubic metres) and sent to Germany; the estimated value was 4,854,944.87 guilders. A later return shows us that by the end of June 1944, 29,000 dwellings in all had been cleared. As we page through the various lists of "appropriated" goods we are struck with some of the items. Whoever would have thought that there were so many tea-strainers?

Were *all* the confiscated goods sent to Germany? Most of them undoubtedly were; "Jewish movables" left the country by all sorts of routes, sometimes treated with touching care, sometimes not. One example of the care was the construction of special crates, for instance of No. 51, designed to hold the kitchen furniture of a "larger family", or of No. 101, made for the contents of a kitchen–dining-room for four persons (including linen, cutlery, crockery, etc.)

According to Lages, these goods were often "placed at the disposal" of the various German services in the Netherlands, of people who needed them to make themselves comfortable in this foreign land. He himself "had made use" of such goods, including gardening tools.

However, not only Germans benefited from the "wonderful opportunity". We have a number of documents dealing with *SS-Standartenführer* Feldmeijer, a Dutchman, who was the head of the Germanic SS in the Netherlands and who, on May 26, 1943, let it be known that he was looking for an apartment with a reception-room, a drawing-room and a bedroom and that, since he had to entertain prominent guests, the place would have to be "something fairly decent". He needed other things as well—on loan, naturally. The inventory has survived and was far from Spartan in its simplicity.

All in all, this "head man" made himself as comfortable as he could and, what is more, with Rauter's entire approval. We also have the customary form of receipt, which began with: "The following articles have been removed from the residence of the Jew . . . . . . ." There followed a long list of the most common household effects, from which those not applicable were to be deleted. But, as we have seen, the lion's share went to the Party leaders in Germany itself; when Bunjes, a high official in the *Einsatzstab*, mentioned the possible legal difficulties that might arise from the export of works of art, Goering told him: "My dear Bunjes, let that be my worry; after all, I am the highest legal authority in the State." This was a characteristic saying by one who, in the last phases of the war, was so much more concerned with saving his art collection than with saving the German Reich.

The saying may have been characteristic, but it was not entirely correct. For there was an even higher authority in the land. It is almost touching to see how many beautiful "presents" were showered on the *Führer* himself; on April 16, 1943, for instance, Rosenberg sent him a portfolio of photographs showing what magnificent works of art had been "saved" from the Jews—this was for "you, my *Führer*, in the hope that it may give you pleasure on the occasion of your birthday". There were also the six night shirts which Rosenberg himself obtained from the Netherlands and which, he was able to tell himself, were not necessarily from a Jewish home, nor, it may be, were the thousand tulip bulbs for his garden, for which "several couriers" were needed. Undoubtedly of Jewish origin, however, were the six pianos which Dr. Schroeder, the new Delegate for Amsterdam, placed at the disposal of *Gauleiter* Hildebrandt in Schwerin on January 14, 1943; he even offered to fill the truck with "other Jewish furniture". By comparison with this, we can feel something like sympathy for Dutch SS corporal W. H., who —back on leave from the front and finding that his wife had run off to Germany after selling all their furniture—discovered that his home was not fit for a hero to live in. "I then thought of getting some Jewish furniture but was told that everything had to go to the Reich . . . This is how it should be, of course, but I have heard that some things have also been given to Dutchmen and why not to me?" He wrote all this to Mussert, begging his pardon, "but what can you do if you don't even have a chair to sit on . . .?" And anyway, the neighbours were busy helping themselves to Jewish possessions.

This was only one of the reasons why the Germans did not manage to lay their greedy hands on everything. Many Jews must have had the same experience as the writer of this book. Before he went underground, several of his friends and acquaintances rescued whatever they could. This sort of assistance was not unknown to the Germans, and the records are full of their complaints in this matter. They deplored this even more than the fact that so many Dutchmen were thieving goods from empty Jewish houses—between the round-up of the Jews and the official collection of their furniture. Unfortunately, the distinction between the two groups was not absolute. Though most of the former returned the property immediately after the war, quite a few did not. Thus, one survivor complained bitterly that his family had lost more to the Dutch than to the Germans. Another was told on his return from Auschwitz: "What a pity you are back." There were few Jews who could not tell you stories of this kind—and worse ones, as well. Let us quote some actual cases.

A housewife, aged fifty-one, wrote in her diary on July 3, 1943: "I and Truus went over some Jewish homes, but there was little to get—all the essentials had gone, including underclothes and linen. The next-door neighbours had got there first; all I could find was a few trifles and Truus got a pedal-car and some other toys. But the whole business is highly dangerous, for if they catch you they send you straight to Vught concentration camp."

A typist, aged twenty-eight, wrote on June 27, 1943: "There are many Jews, of course, who give all their things away to Christians—neighbours, acquaintances and friends. But there are many who don't. I can understand why. For if you watch these compassionate and neighbourly Christians swooping down like vultures and seizing everything they can get their hooks on, it makes your heart sick. All they can think of is what they can grab. No one spares a thought for the poor Jews. Is it any wonder, then, that the Jews prefer to leave their things in the hands of the known enemy rather than to their so-called friends? At times like these you discover what human nature is really like. And the worst thing is that you learn things about yourself. For even while you are judging the others, you discover that in many ways you are no better yourself. In fact you are just like them, you, too, put aside all scruples when it serves your turn. There are only too few who are steadfast and who stick to their principles, come what may. And I'm certain that I'm not one of them, much as I would like to be. And that is the worst of it all, to know that you are no better than those you so readily condemn."

Imagine a street scene, full of furniture vans, with men running to and fro, lugging Jewish goods and chattels for all they are worth. The reader may not be familiar with the verb "to puls", coined during the war in honour of Abraham Puls, one of the biggest removal men in Amsterdam. (His vans bore the simple legend A. Puls, lest that "Abraham" caused anyone to mistake this pure Aryan for a Jew.) But few of the Jews who lost everything will have forgotten what "pulsing" was all about, how their precious, or at least, dear, possessions were manhandled or left standing about in the rain. Nor was the writer's own experience uncommon. Soon after an elderly aunt had committed suicide he was inundated with forms, and visited by two Dutch gentlemen, closely followed by Puls's pantechnicon. The men told him to make sure he kept his fingers off these Jewish goods, which were now the *Führer*'s property. They made it sound as though it always had been. Next came Puls's own men, one of whom whispered encouragement—he would make sure that, come what may, "they" would not get hold of the magnificent Persian rug, the aunt's greatest treasure. He would personally see to that. And, in fact, he placed the carpet in a corner where it remained after all the rest had been taken downstairs. "There you are, sir, that's one thing the Boche isn't getting"—thus spoke the good patriot, as he finally absconded with the extremely valuable item. The writer himself also managed to cheat the *Führer* out of something—his aunt's Bible which still stands in his room, a silent witness to the indelible Commandment, "Thou shalt not steal."

So far we have spoken of the possessions of Jewish house-holders, but there were other Jewish assets, too, that awaited the invader's attention. For instance, there were the horses, the cars and carriages, which had all been registered at the *Zentralstelle* in accordance with Decree 58/42—and whose total value cannot now be estimated. Then there were the farms belonging to Jews, which were registered with the Land Registry in accordance with Decree 102/41. All these were now offered for sale to the tenants or to Dutch farmers approved by the Land Registry, the whole operation supervised by the German Department of Food and Agriculture. Estates remaining unsold were, by Decree 92/43, transferred to the *Niederländische Grundstücksverwaltung* (Department for the Control of Dutch Estates) for liquidation under Decree 154/41 (August 11, 1941). The total area of these lands came to 46,550 acres and was valued at 17,000,000 guilders. The *Niederländische Grundstücksverwaltung* was, by the same Decree, also designated as the place where all other real estate and mortgages had to be registered; by Decree 37/43 of April 19, 1943, all such mortgages had to be paid up within three months. Altogether some 20,000 properties and 5,600 mortgages were involved. The combined value can only be guessed at; the unmortgaged immovable property alone was estimated to be of the order of 150,000,000 guilders, and the mortgages must have come to at least another 22,000,000 guilders. And remember, these figures were not the real value, for most of the property was knocked down at greatly deflated prices.

Little purpose would be served in giving a detailed account of the endless chicanery and misery that these measures brought in their wake. We get some idea of it from a memorandum compiled by the Legal Committee of the Jewish Council in the spring of 1942, after they had vainly tried to discuss some of the problems with the *Niederländische Grundstücksverwaltung*. The burden of the Jewish complaint to the Germans was that the new regulations were tantamount to . . . "partial expropriation", which, "surely was not the intention of the German authorities".

What of Jewish art collections and other valuables? By Decree 58/42 all of them had to be deposited with Lippmann, Rosenthal & Co., and in nearly 13,000 cases this was, in fact, done, either by the owners themselves or else by the "Department for the Appropriation of Household Effects" which obtained these articles via Puls, or finally through the "Foreign Currency Department". Here, too, the total value cannot be reckoned—the realized figure of 6,000,000 guilders was much too low, not least because all the silver articles were sold by the kilogramme and at the price of unworked silver.

Decree 54 of June 11, 1943, laid down what was to be done with all life insurance policies deposited with Lippmann, Rosenthal & Co. in accordance with Decree 58/42. Most of the registered policies (22,368) were "bought up". The total yield was approximately 25,000,000 guilders.

What about debts to Jews? All of them had been blocked by Decree 58/42, and by Decree 89 of September 25, 1943, had to be paid to Lippmann Rosenthal & Co., within three months. Altogether some 8,500 such debts and claims were registered with a value of some 38,000,000 guilders, of which Lippmann, Rosenthal & Co. collected some 6,200 (value approximately 90,000,000 guilders), while 8,000,000 guilders had to be written off as bad debts.

The reader will appreciate that the above process of milking the Jews, though it brought the Germans a great deal of money, was only a fairly minor part of the whole operation; far more important was the collection of Jewish cash assets, bank accounts and shares, all of which had to be deposited with Lippmann, Rosenthal & Co. under Decree 148 of August 8, 1941. No one can say precisely how much money was involved. But we know that by February 7, 1942, the latest figures in our possession, the Germans had netted well over 26,000,000 guilders in cash alone. As for the 500,000 shares handed in to Lippmann, Rosenthal & Co., they were estimated by them at 300,000,000 guilders, but by that time (May 1944) a large part of them had already been "sold" to various German departments.

The money held by Lippmann, Rosenthal & Co. was not only used to pay the considerable costs of the German Appropriation machinery but also to maintain the Jewish Council and allied institutions. Thus some 26,000,000 guilders were made available for the construction of the camps at Vught and Westerbork. In addition, Jewish money was used to "advance" funds to the notorious Henneicke Column, i.e. to pay for the capture of Jews at so much per head.

One day someone should write a monograph on that den of thieves, the offices of Lippmann, Rosenthal & Co. in Amsterdam. No doubt he will wish to refer to one of the directors, whose income of 100,000 guilders a year shows how much credence must be given to attacks on Jewish materialism by the Nazis. Nor did the other directors fare much worse; all those who had any dealings with them could have told you that much of the flow of Jewish money passed their way—no doubt by legitimate channels. Nazis or otherwise, all of them played an essential part in the merciless machine of plunder. Every book-keeping entry, every message, every note, every letter they wrote, advanced this process one step further, until the victims, stripped of everything, were packed off to the gas-chambers.

There was yet another field in which Nordic heroes could show their mettle: the expropriation of Jewish businesses. Unfortunately, the Germans were often too late in this field, and we hear many complaints that the wily Jews had been able to transfer their businesses to Christian front-men, just in the nick of time. By Decree 198 of October 22, 1940, every business had to be registered with the *Wirtschaftsprüfstelle* (Economic Control Bureau). The relevant form deserves to be preserved as a remarkable piece of literature in its own right. It is about as clear as mud. But then it was only a beginning, and was followed on March 12, 1941, by a new Decree (48/41), governing the control of businesses subject to registration.

The most important stipulation (Section 7) was that the *Reichskommissar* could appoint a Trustee who would take over all the functions of the proprietor or manager. The implementation of the Decree was put into the hands of the Economic Control Bureau, and it was thus that the active "Aryanization" of Dutch business life may be said to have begun.

The Trustee was a mighty man. He could, for instance, enter a rare book shop, built up with loving care and great expertise over many years, and simply put the owner into the street. He could then sell all the books at bargain prices to "Aryan" book-lovers. What a feast for true German lovers of culture! Some of these Trustees were conscientious, others were common thieves. But no matter which they were, the result was much the same.

A few months before the appearance of Decree 48/41 the German Chamber of Commerce and Industry supplied German enterprises with forms by which they could make application to "merge their capital" with enterprises in Belgium and Holland. These forms were subsequently scrutinized by the Chamber itself and also by the Territorial Economic Adviser of the NSDAP and forwarded to the *Reichskommissariat* in the Netherlands. At the same time, there were animated discussions between the Economic and Technical groups of the German Organization for Trade and Industry (*Organisation der gewerblichen Wirtschaft*) and the *Reichskommissariat* on the allocation of the most important available concerns. The Aryanization Department of the Nazi Party Chancellery also busied itself with this problem, and issued directives to the District Economic Advisers as to the selection of Party comrades for the running of Jewish enterprises in the Netherlands. Finally, there were the many German and later Dutch applicants who applied directly to the *Reichskommissariat* for a share of the booty; many of their letters have been preserved to us.

There was, for instance, a man from Berlin-Steglitz, who was prepared to try his hand at anything. He would have preferred a tobacconist's, but was prepared to make do with a perfumery or even a drapers. Alas, all three applications were refused, but he was promised that attempts would be made to find him a restaurant. The owner of a "National Socialist model enterprise" in Halle desired to "merge his capital" with a very large multiple store, but sad to say, there was no Jewish one to be found. Hence he had to make do with a wholesale food business. These men would make any sacrifice for Germany—until it came to getting something for themselves. The records contain complaints by District Economic Advisers who for "some completely inexplicable reasons" got no prizes in the lucky dip. On that score, the *Gauleiter* of Thuringia felt impelled to write: "It strikes me as incredible that the wishes of the Party are slighted in this way." He accordingly asked the Party Chancellery in Munich to instruct the Economic Control Bureau in The Hague "with all emphasis" to ensure that "my people's applications are satisfied without delay". Needless to say, Munich forwarded this complaint, with warnings against incurring their own displeasure, to The Hague. The answer was that The Hague was doing everything in its power, and that one of the Thuringian Party comrades had already been put down for a factory. The Party's wishes would be respected "in every way", but their implementation must be left to the discretion of those in The Hague, who were dealing with each industry in turn.

The applications by German front-line soldiers should have a chapter to themselves. We may take it that no stone was left unturned to satisfy them, and, in fact, the surviving documents show that The Hague expended a great deal of ingenuity in working out a special *Frontkämpferunterbringungsverordnung* (Front-line Soldiers' Redeployment Decree). This was apparently in hand even before Hitler attacked Russia, which greatly complicated matters, seeing that the number of front-line soldiers was greatly increased overnight.

In July 1942 it was said that twelve "front-line soldiers" had already been "redeployed". Another 178 had businesses reserved for them, and forty-three places were held open for potential management personnel or "partners". The twelve lucky ones were inducted by the Party before the Russian campaign began; after that, places were "reserved" until after the war. The odd thing is that the number of such reservations was reduced on September 28, 1942, but increased in October and again in December, when there was a total of 392 "openings". This is little enough when we consider that there were millions of front-line soldiers. One veteran could not be found a place—and this was said to be an unkind thing to do to a man who had set his heart on a factory in Tilburg; in the end, however, he was offered a partnership in the factory, which had fallen to a more fortunate Party comrade. Unfortunately, that offer had to be withdrawn again when it was discovered that he had been a front-line soldier in the First World War and not in the Second. In the end, The Hague "fobbed him off" with a large laundry in Amsterdam. The veteran declared himself satisfied with this, but then there were a number of "formal" complaints, so that he was thwarted again. In the last letter by this poor man—there is a whole file full of them—he seems quite dispirited: first no Jewish factory, and now no Jewish laundry. We can only hope that ultimately he did find some Jewish corner-shop or fish-barrow in appreciation of his services and sacrifices for the Fatherland.

What of the Dutch claimants for prizes in this keen competition? After all, many of the NSB, too, had made sacrifices in the fight for the new Germanic order, and here was the Germans' chance to show their appreciation. Let us see how they rose to the occasion.

On October 22, 1941, Rost van Tonningen, the financial expert of the Dutch Nazi movement, complained to Mussert that too many Aryanized enterprises were falling into the hands of Germans: "I find myself in the extremely embarrassing position of being overwhelmed with letters from comrades, all of whom hoped they would be considered for businesses as they became available." In April 1942 another Dutch Nazi, H. C. van Maasdijk, wrote an article for *De Nederlandsche Volkshuishouding, Tijdschrift voor het Economisch Front* (The Dutch Journal of the Economic Front) from which Herzberg has quoted at length. In it the writer expressed his disquiet at the possibility that "very important Dutch fortunes and industries, with a great potential . . . seemed to be falling *exclusively* into German hands". One of the reasons was that "Dutch financial institutions had held back from such transactions on principle" but, as this great patriot warned his readers in italics: "It is in the Dutch interest to arrive as speedily as possible at a generally positive viewpoint with respect to the process of Aryanization in our country." As Herzberg[1] commented: "It is written, 'Thou shalt not steal' but where is it written 'Thou shalt not receive'? And receiving is in any case so much better." And it should not be forgotten that among those who

[1] Herzberg: *Kroniek* . . ., pp. 72–3.

queued up to be receivers there were many who were not beyond stripping even the victims of the gas-chambers.

We may take it that the Dutch Nazis never ceased their efforts to claim their place in this unsavoury queue. Even towards the end of 1944, a Party comrade from Drente was still pressing his claim for a hotel or a cinema, and one from The Hague was no less loud in his demands for an accountant's office. At that time, when things looked far from rosy for the Germanic cause, this persistence could only have been a sign of "unshakeable faith in German victory" and of "love for the *Führer*"; the man who wanted the cinema was particularly admirable, since he pressed his claim long after the Economic Control Bureau had let it be known that there was little prospect of an audience boom.

From all this, the reader will have gathered that the Economic Control Bureau was never idle, indeed, that the staff laboured hard in the sweat of their face. The surviving documents leave us in no doubt that these gentlemen knew perfectly well what they were about, and that they were bent on the total spoliation of the Jews—the man chiefly responsible for this work, *Generalkommissar* Fischböck, was able to elude justice after the war by going into hiding.

The records include a detailed plan of campaign dated December 22, 1941. It laid down that all recommendations for business transfers had to be submitted to the Planning Committee of the Economic Control Bureau, which would draw up special lists for the disposal of the various commercial categories. All decisions were made at a special planning session at which various departments of the *Reichskommissariat*, the NSDAP and German experts on whichever trade was under discussion, were represented.

The general view was that small Jewish businesses had to be liquidated at all costs; businesses with a minor Jewish share in the management were generally allowed to carry out their own "Aryanization"; large and economically important businesses were reserved for German applicants, while medium-sized enterprises were open to Germans as well as to deserving Dutchmen.

Altogether some 22,000 enterprises were involved. Of these, about 2,000 were left to "Aryanize" themselves; another 2,000 were forcibly "Aryanized", i.e. sold to German (75 per cent) or Dutch (25 per cent) interests. The rest was liquidated. While it is difficult to estimate the total value of all these enterprises, we know that the 2,000 or so forcibly "Aryanized" businesses brought in some

75,000,000 guilders, and that the liquidation of the 13,000 smaller businesses brought in a further 6,500,000 guilders.

Do these figures really tell us everything? Since we must assume that most of them were sold at ridiculously low prices, the answer is largely in the negative. For one thing, no allowance was ever made for the goodwill, which must have come to several hundred million guilders. In any case, there were few left to feel the effects of this robbery, for most of the Jewish shopkeepers, merchants and manufacturers concerned had been destroyed—liquidated like vermin.

## JEWS IN THE DIAMOND TRADE

We come now to a subject we have mentioned several times in passing but which, as the greatest prize in the German liquidation, deserves special mention: the diamond industry. Here, if anywhere, we have an example of how the demoniacal fanaticism with which the Germans persecuted the Jews invariably triumphed over all rational considerations. For had they heeded reason alone, they must have appreciated that the retention of a small number of Jewish diamond experts and diamond workers was in the best interests of the German war machine. And, in fact, many Germans did appreciate this and tried their utmost to keep these Jews where they were. But all they achieved was to postpone their demise.

Before the Second World War the diamond trade could, by and large, be divided into three major branches: diamond mining in South Africa, the sale of rough diamonds in London, and diamond cutting and trading in Amsterdam and Antwerp. In Amsterdam, 80 per cent of the employers, and 2,100 out of the 3,400 registered workers were Jews; of these latter, less than 1,000 were actually employed in the trade in 1940, and of this number a full 60 per cent were Jews. All these men were very highly skilled and could certainly not be replaced at short notice. Now, since Germany was desperately short of diamonds—both of cut stones that could earn foreign currency and also of industrial diamonds for machine-tools, etc.—it is not surprising that some German authorities did their utmost to protect what they called the "diamond Jews".

When the *Reichskommissariat* was formed in 1940 it co-opted a number of diamond experts, and also appointed a number of external consultants, including Councillor Lemberg of the War Administration Department in Antwerp and, after 1941, Arthur Bozenhardt, a diamond merchant from Hamburg. In general, the

*Reichskommissariat* would refer questions involving the diamond industry to the *Hauptabteilung Gewerbliche Wirtschaft im Generalkommissariat für Finanz und Wirtschaft* (Industrial Division in the General Commissariat for Finance and Economy) and soon afterwards to the Department for Special Industries, under Assessor Carl Hanemann. There is no point in giving the names of all the other officials, the more so as it was not only the Economic Control Bureau which had a finger in this pie but also the Security Police and especially their important Department IV B 4 in Berlin, the power-house of the whole machine for the destruction of the Jews.

The first attempt to protect Jews in the diamond industry was made by Councillor Lemberg of Antwerp, who apparently tried to set up a "united defence front" of diamond workers and diamond experts with the aim of frustrating the plans of the politicians, for instance, the application of Decrees 189 of October 22, 1940, and 48, March 12, 1941, two "Aryanization" measures that we have discussed at some length. And, indeed, on the advice of Bozenhardt, the *Reichskommissar* decided not to apply these measures to the diamond trade, with the result that most of the Jewish experts (though not the workers) were saved until 1944.

The real tug-or-war between the various German interests began at the start of the deportations in July 1942. Originally, the Germans agreed to exempt all those who were actually working on diamonds and, in fact, 500 workers and 300 employers, together with their families, were granted a temporary respite and, in the autumn of 1942, they were issued with a special stamp. Even when the "munitions-Jews" were "weeded out" after the Hollandia Works incident, the "diamond-Jews" remained untouched and this happy state of affairs continued until the middle of January 1943, when the Germans insisted that the list of exemptions be halved. When the State Diamond Bureau and its industrial advisers refused to co-operate, the German officials in the Bureau did the work themselves. Those removed from the list were arrested on February 12, 1943. (The records also contain Seyss-Inquart's order of October 16, 1942, to have all essential "diamond-Jews" herded into a ghetto in Amsterdam; we need say no more about it because it came to nothing.)

What does deserve mention is the fact that, during 1943, Bozenhardt Bros. contrived to buy up all available diamond supplies, by what were ostensibly quite normal trading operations. This they did on the orders, and on behalf of, the Berlin Directorate of the German

Four-Year Plan. The details of this exceedingly complicated affair cannot be discussed here; suffice it to say that it was thanks to this operation that part of the diamond industry and, what is far more important, the lives of those employed in it, survived for another year.

We must now say a few words about what the Jews called the "Hanemann gift". During the great raids in May and June 1943, quite a few "diamond-Jews" were carried off to Westerbork or even deported; those needed for the Bozenhardt operation were allowed to return in July and August at the insistence of *Assessor* Carl Hanemann. He gave them to understand that out of gratitude they ought to offer up a present to the German Reich. No doubt he hoped thereby to raise his own standing in Berlin. Naturally the Jews felt little enthusiasm for this piece of blackmail, but there was nothing for it but to comply. Some twenty firms put their heads together, and produced a "present" of precious stones worth 600,000 guilders. Hanemann promised to use his good offices on behalf of the donors and on about September 23 left for Berlin. Five days later the co-operative twenty were all seized in Amsterdam and sent to Westerbork. In all fairness we must add that this had nothing to do with Hanemann, who did, in fact, try his utmost to get them released. Some forty "diamond-Jews" remained in Amsterdam until May 1944, first working in a factory set up in the Jewish Invalid Hospital and later in Asscher's diamond works. Those packed off to Westerbork—213 including dependants—did not remain there indefinitely, they were "transferred" to Bergen-Belsen on May 19, 1944.

This is perhaps the place to say a few words about the German plan to set up a diamond industry in Vught and in Bergen-Belsen. This plan was probably concocted by Heinrich Himmler himself, who was, at any rate, responsible for the order of December 3, 1942, to set up such an industry in Vught. His ultimate aim was to train disabled SS men as diamond cutters. The wheels and other machinery arrived in June 1943 from disused factories in Amsterdam. In February 1944 Himmler made a tour of inspection. In March, when the invasion seemed imminent, he gave orders to have all Jews removed from the Netherlands; he intended to continue the work in Bergen-Belsen. This scheme was discussed by the Dutch Diamond Bureau and non-Jewish diamond manufacturers with *Obersturmführer* Meyer of the Chief Economic Directorate of the SS

(WVHA)—the organization responsible for running the Concentration Camps. In a last attempt to do something for those now in Bergen-Belsen, the Dutch representatives declared themselves ready to supply the necessary machinery, and to let the camp inmates polish stone for various Amsterdam merchants. Two-thirds of a parcel of rough diamonds, received in Amsterdam in August 1944, was reserved for Bergen-Belsen; here several departments had been set up, supervised by a well-known diamond expert, and all under the control of a Jewish merchant by the name of Henri Soep. On September 13, 1944, a further team of diamond workers arrived from Westerbork; they, too, were left idle and were therefore in peril of their lives, the more so as the war was drawing to its close and the Germans had other things than diamonds to worry about. After enjoying special privileges for many months (they were housed in a separate barracks and exempted from hard labour) the "diamond-Jews", too, had to pack their bags. On December 4, 1944, the men were sent to Sachsenhausen. Next day the women and children were ordered to Beendorf, but when they had already left the camp, instructions came that the children must be sent back. As one witness put it: "This parting was the most dreadful thing of all. I shall never forget it." Even so, the entire group was given a further lease of life —because of the men's special qualifications they were sent not to the gas-chambers but to factories needing precision workers. Two families were left behind in Bergen-Belsen: the Asschers, probably in recognition of Abraham Asscher's services as a President of the Jewish Council, and the Soeps, probably because they were of Paraguayan nationality. For the rest, most of the men died, while quite a few of the women survived—we had better not enquire how. It should also be mentioned that some time in 1943 or 1944, diamond workers in Vught were "accidentally" sent for extermination to Auschwitz instead of Bergen-Belsen; we have been unable to fathom precisely why.

## THE LEGAL REMNANT

On October 5, 1943, less than a week after the deportation of the leaders of the Jewish Council with all their families, friends and relations, and thus of the last large group of Jews remaining legally in the Netherlands—that is not counting those detained in Westerbork—Seyss-Inquart informed his chief henchmen that the solution of the Jewish problem had reached a position that might be called "stable". Before that happy state arrived it was, however, necessary to compile a list of all the remaining full-Jews, for instance those exempt from wearing stars, those baptized into the Reformed faith and those in Barneveld. It appeared that he was prepared to leave the first group alone and send the second and third to Westerbork. The letter had a singular ending: since he, Seyss-Inquart, had given a clear promise to keep all these people in the Netherlands, their deportation would undermine his authority as *Reichskommissar*. So remain they must at all costs.

Alas, it must be said that, by and large, the *Reichskommissar* did not have his way. The two Jewish groups in Westerbork—those from Barneveld and the baptized Protestants—were deported all the same, with no apparent loss of authority on his part. In short, the desired stabilization did not materialize; it was a goal that was always approached and never quite reached. The causes of this failure are partly outside the scope of this book—they were to be sought in Berlin, where, despite desperate tinkering with the problem, no satisfactory answer was found to the question of what to do with even German half- and quarter-Jews or, for that matter, with Jews married to Gentiles. In the Netherlands there was another factor militating against the complete liquidation of the Jews: the longer some vestiges of the Jewish population remained behind, the longer those busy with its persecution were kept out of the front lines. And out of the front lines they wanted to remain. No doubt this was one of the reasons why there was such a flurry of regulations and counter-regulations, all for the benefit of the few remaining Jews, and why this whole process rose to a crescendo as the war neared its end. In this process we saw that group after group disappeared until only those of "mixed blood" were left. Luckily for the invader, there was still quite a lot of loot to mop up.

As early as March 1942 the Germans put forward a scheme to rebuild every synagogue that lent itself for other uses, and to demolish the rest. This seemed to have the full agreement of Dr. Schröder, the German Delegate in Amsterdam, who suggested that the work should be tackled in the spring of 1943, when the deportation of Dutch Jewry had got well under way. The same idea was also put forward in October 1943, with the rider that, once all synagogues had been demolished, there would be no offensive reminder of the existence of the Jews. Surviving documents suggest that the Dutch Nazi party went out of their way to save the historic Portuguese synagogue in Amsterdam. Synagogues and Jewish cemeteries still figured largely in many of the German records during 1944.

As to the cemeteries, many were desecrated and laid waste; here and there someone (the burgomaster?) made a little money on the side by selling tombstones to masons who erased the wording and resold them. The Germans did their bit of vandalism as well. Thus, on the day after Christmas 1944, a number of high German officers in the village of Aalten near the German border, under their leader von Hütz "drove in procession to the Jewish cemetery. There they vented their rage on the building and reduced it to ruins."[1] This, no doubt, was their way of celebrating Christmas. Oddly enough, the custodians of a number of Jewish cemeteries were allowed, under an order made in 1943 (probably in April) to remain at their posts, where one of them even continued until the very end of the war.

They must probably be counted among the handful of Jews to be left in office after the liquidation of the Jewish Council, ostensibly for the benefit of their remaining brethren. Wielek, who has called these officials "a miniature Jewish Council", has also given us details of their weird activities.[2] There was, for instance, a Jewish Hostel next door to the *Expositur* and reserved for some of this strange assortment. It is almost beyond the wit of man to imagine what scenes were played out there during this final phase of the war. The inmates must have been completely taken aback when, with the approach of the German defeat, their oppressors suddenly became positively affable, and when some of them began to break their own laws and did them little favours. It finally came to the point where Germans would ask Jews to recommend a suitable hiding-place. Wielek reports that Henneicke, that Jew-hunter extraordinary, hastened to tell a group of Jews that he had torn up a list of 190 men whose hiding-places he had recently discovered. We know, too, that this Saul turned Paul a little too late for his own salvation: the Resistance finished him off late in 1944.

We do not wish to deprive the reader of the end of "the miniature Jewish Council": "Its final dissolution took place on September 19, 1944, and the end was greatly reminiscent of the grand finale of a Punch and Judy show. Two Jewish bicycle-makers, working for the Security Police and who had survived everything, suddenly went

[1] Be de Joode: *Aalten in bezettingstijd* (Aalten during the Occupation) (Aalten, 1946), p. 77.

[2] Wielek: *op. cit.*, pp. 256 ff.

into hiding, and, what is more, had the impertinence to abscond with the keys of the shed where the great Lages kept his bicycle. Lages was livid and promised to shoot them on sight. He would, in fact, put the 'whole Jewish Council' against the wall, and so forth. When those still working for the *Expositur* heard of this, they, too, thought it was high time to go into hiding."

We may laugh about this episode, but we must remember that the two practical jokers knew that they might drown even while in sight of dry land. Nor must it be forgotten that they, like most of the survivors, realized that, after all that had happened, the Germans could not afford to let them tell their terrible tale. To make things worse, all sorts of rumours and threats were spread about. Thus Wielek[1] tells us that Aus der Fünten let it be known "in strict confidence" that if any of those married to Gentiles stepped out of line, the whole group would be dealt with—thus deliberately increasing panic among Jews. Perhaps this was his motive, who knows? In any case, it is impossible to recapture the atmosphere of uncertainty, pressure and fear that prevailed at the time. Each day seemed like a year, and still the war went on—the winter of hunger came and after it the spring. And only then, at long last—Liberation.

## MIXED MARRIAGES

Though Jews married to Gentiles were kept in Dutch camps throughout the war, they, too, had their share of suffering and constant fear. On the credit side, we must add that Dutch officials went out of their way to frustrate the German plans regarding these people. The reader might remark that when they were finally packed off to the camps the war was entering its final phase, so that what help was rendered was rendered at small personal risk. But he should remember that while he knows this to have been so, no one could have counted on it at the time.

Here, too, we must largely rely on the evidence of Wielek, though there is much other testimony as well. But despite the wealth of material, it is impossible to give a full and coherent account of what mental anguish these people suffered, as the Germans kept on issuing orders and counter-orders in chaotic profusion. Nor is it even possible to establish some sort of chronological order. At one point they would order hundreds to do one thing, only to tell tens to do something quite different; each group was divided and subdivided

[1] Wielek: *op. cit.*, p. 304.

*ad nauseam*; some people were called up for labour service and then sent back home again; some were sent to camps; others again were not called up at all but simply seized, and even some of these were sent back. Men would be selected for one camp and sent to another, sometimes with pay and sometimes without; men would be ordered to report for immediate deportation, sometimes with travelling permits and sometimes at their own risk, and so on. All we ask of the reader is to believe that all this madness is but a pale reflection of what really went on.

Let us take but a few cases. On December 16, 1943, some 2,500 Amsterdam Jews married to Gentiles were ordered to report for selection in the Atlanta Buildings, the headquarters of the Labour Service; people between forty-five and sixty-five were told to work on the "Forestry Project" near Amsterdam, those below forty-five were allocated to "various camps in the Netherlands". However, anyone able to prove that he was doing useful work in Amsterdam was exempted. On January 5, 1944, some 250 people over forty-five were actually drafted to the Forestry Project; 210 turned up, the rest applied for exemption or pleaded sickness. Wielek reports that the selection took fifty seconds per person; but even those few seconds were wasted, since a German Jewish girl who was active in the Resistance carried a tray of index cards out of the building ("I pretended that I was going about my business, and nobody asked any questions") and threw it into a canal. (The writer happens to know about this because the girl's father was a close friend of his.) On January 18, there was another selection in the Atlanta Building. This time, Jews were to be chosen for work at Schiphol airport. Some 900 were selected (those exempted from wearing the star were turned away, and so were all those doing useful work elsewhere). A telephone call to Burgomaster Voûte and the Director of the Tramways Department, and they all had permission to use trams for travelling to and from work. Absentees were arrested by the German police and so were a number of those who had been expressly exempted. Of the 120 so caught, the Germans sent thirty to Weteringschans Prison and thence to Havelte Camp.

Havelte is a name that appears repeatedly in the records during this last phase of the war. The first reference to it occurs in a document of February 29, 1944, emanating from the *Hauptabteilung Soziale Verwaltung* (Head Office for Social Administration) in Amsterdam. This body claimed that, since Jewish men married to

Gentiles had now been put to work in the three leading cities, the time had clearly come to extend the practice to provincial Jews between the ages of eighteen and sixty. These should be sent to Havelte airfield and work under the direction of the German expert in the Meppel Labour Office nearby.

A German document of April 19 tells us something about the set-up. The men were put to work in gangs of sixteen, from 8 a.m. to 6 p.m., with a 1½-hour lunch break, during which they could buy a mug of soup for 5½ cents. The Germans admitted that "the soup is said to be very bad". The wages were 47 cents per hour and the work was carrying sand. The promised holidays were never granted, but the men were given three days special leave for the Passover.

Next came the instruction that those who had been rejected in Amsterdam and the Hague would have to report for reselection in Meppel; of the 101 who did so, eighty-eight were sent to Havelte. At the beginning of July came orders for a number of "non-star wearers" to report to the Selection Board. When they turned up, they were told that the whole thing had been a mistake. In the autumn of 1944 many "workers" from various places were sent home, but 200 were transferred to Havelte. Our last report about that place comes from Wielek,[1] according to whom those vacating the camp now had to walk on foot—no more trains were running. "On the way, many of them were picked up by the Security Police and sent to prison."

Now back to Amsterdam. In the spring of 1944 a few Jews were working at nearby Schiphol, others were engaged in the Forestry Project; all used to be taken to and from their work, and their "temporary" wages were 5 guilders per day. Selection was by an officially appointed doctor; all certificates by unofficial Dutch and even German doctors were ignored on principle. At the beginning of April 1944 eighty-five of those working in the Forestry Project were temporarily transferred to the harbour to unload potatoes. At the end of April one group was transferred from Schiphol to Het Zandt near Den Helder in North Holland; then, at the beginning of May, some fifty men from the Forestry Project and the harbour were transferred to De Kooy, also near Den Helder.

As to life in Het Zandt, Wielek[2] gives us a number of interesting details. The guards were Georgians, pressed into service by the

[1] Wielek: *op. cit.*, p. 306.
[2] Wielek: *op. cit.*, pp. 355 ff.

Germans and, though somewhat rough, very friendly gaolers on the whole. More than once they let it be known that they had remained Communists at heart. One of them, however, turned out to be a fanatical Nazi and a traitor. While wages and food were far below the average, the inmates were allowed to receive parcels and to buy provisions from the farmers in the neighbourhood, at fair prices. They had Sundays off and frequently received visits from their wives and children—though not for long. Meanwhile the threat of deportation hung constantly over their heads—on one occasion they were even ordered to pack their bags. In September 1944 the Germans began to wind up this camp—and also the Forestry Project; hardly any work at all was done in either during the winter, though a handful of Jews are reported to have continued preparing the fields until February 10, 1945. On January 1 Lippmann, Rosenthal & Co. stopped paying the small allowances granted to non-star-wearing Jews; luckily for this group the Amsterdam Municipality decided to make up the loss only five days later—clandestinely, of course. This is but one of many examples of Dutch assistance, and we gladly pay tribute to it here.

CHAPTER SIX

# INTO HIDING

WE return now to September 29, 1943, the date on which the last group of "privileged" Jews was sent from Amsterdam to Westerbork. In the preceding pages we have dealt with those married to non-Jews, those exempted from wearing the yellow star and other categories of Jews allowed to reside "legally" in the Netherlands (outside Westerbork). In what follows, we shall be discussing the fate of those who did not bother to seek German permits or favours, and went into hiding instead.

The writer is tempted to point out that in so doing they were not departing from Jewish tradition: we have only to look at *2 Samuel* 17:17. Or we may think of Josephus, the Jewish historian who, in the company of forty prominent Jews, hid away in a pit. (Here, too, there was a traitor, and a Jewish traitor at that.) Indeed, we do not have to go back so far in time for our precedent: from 1933 onward, when the Dutch authorities went in search of illegal German immigrants—Jews among them—many of the refugees found shelter in the houses of Dutch sympathizers—"protective custody", as they called it.

Let us say a few words about our sources. We have been able to consult a host of books on the subject, some of which make fascinating and absorbing reading, together with diaries, reports and, last but not least, the memory of many survivors.

But though our sources are abundant, it is impossible to tell whether they are representative, the more so as most of those who were caught did not live to tell their tale. What, for instance, do we know about the bodies of Jews found floating in the water? Were they thrown in—alive or dead—or did they jump in of their own accord and if so, why?

Again, while we know that most Dutch Jews went to ground in Holland, it is extremely difficult to determine precisely where. All sorts of rumours were rife on this subject. A report to London suggested that the fugitives kept to the countryside rather than to the towns, where it was more difficult to get food. In the country, however, there was a different danger: here, local Dutch Nazis, with intimate knowledge of local conditions, would organize "hunts" and hand hosts and fugitives alike over to the Germans. Scores of good men fell victim to these traitors, whose deeds constitute one of the darkest chapters in the history of the Occupation. Luckily, their crimes were more than offset by the actions of Dutch patriots, many of whom were able to persuade their district to absorb more than the "normal" quota of Jews.

We have used the word "normal", but it is of course, impossible to determine norms in situations that are essentially abnormal. Still, many people seem to think that much more could have been done at the time. Thus Dr. Drees[1] felt that, in this respect, the Dutch people as a whole were found wanting; Touw[2] has deplored the "most shameful fact that Christians should have stood by while more than 100,000 Jews were being deported"; H. M. van Randwijk[3] has spoken of the "historical failure of the Dutch people to render to Dutch Jews that help which, as Netherlanders, as human beings, as compatriots and neighbours, they had the right to expect." And this is what J. Meulenbelt[4] had to say: "While Jews, more than anyone else, needed the help of the illegal organizations and the hospitality of Dutch families, one is forced to conclude that, by and large, they received far less help than the rest. Thus the facts published in *Onderdrukking en Verzet* (Oppression and Resistance) show that an "Aryan" had five and a half times as great a chance of finding shelter, while non-Jewish captives ran only one-sixteenth of the risk of being sentenced to death. This gives a ratio of 1 : 88. Lack of insight, human shortcomings—all added up to a pitiful lack of assistance. Those small groups, mainly run by artists and students, who ever since the summer of 1942, tried to hide as many Jews as possible in the Netherlands, and hence at least keep them alive, were for ever short of reliable helpers and of places where the fugitives, great and small, could be brought to safety . . . The whole thing was unspeakably squalid and sad."

[1] W. Drees: *Van mei to mei* (From May to May) (Assen, 1948), p. 132.

[2] H. C. Touw: *Het verzet der Hervormde Kerk*, pp. 433–43.

[3] H. M. van Randwijk: "Het Grote Gebod" (The Great Commandment) in *Vrij Nederland*, November 10, 1951.

[4] In: *Voormalig Verzet Nederland*, March 26, 1955.

Similar criticisms have come from the Jews themselves. There was, for instance, the Jewish university lecturer, a man who took enormous risks and who explained that many Jews could not or would not go into hiding, simply because "Dutch people were neither able nor willing—I am not allotting blame—to harbour them. With the notable exception of that relatively small proportion of them who, from the very beginning, sacrificed money, goods, and even their freedom and their lives, in the cause of justice, the Dutch looked on while the *Netherlands police* herded Jews through side-streets . . . For many, the whole thing became a familiar spectacle, on which they turned their backs."

A doctor from Arnhem, the only one of his family to return from Auschwitz, had this to say: "I had to struggle very hard to get over the dislike I felt towards my fellow-citizens. This aversion to non-Jews, making every allowance for the good people among them, persisted for a long while—to my mind, my non-Jewish neighbours all bore a measure of blame for the great massacre we had suffered. Sometimes I still feel bitter as, on my rounds in the country, I see a house that, in my opinion, would never have been searched. Perhaps I am quite wrong, this might have been the very first place in which they looked; I really do not know, and yet I ask myself: 'How many Jews could not have been hidden there . . .?' "

The actual number of those who went into hiding is problematical, too. There is no lack of estimates: a Jewish source put the figure at from 25,000 to 30,000 in June 1943; Berkley[1] also speaks of 25,000, of whom 10,000 were subsequently caught; according to Herzberg, however, no more than 8,000 escaped. In short, there is no agreement, and all we can say is that thousands went into hiding, thousands were caught and thousands were saved. The writer himself gets the very tentative impression that 10,000 at most survived in this way and that an equal number was caught—though the latter figure is particularly speculative.

How did people set about finding a hiding-place? Perhaps many fared like the writer, whose own decision to go into hiding was the combined result of his determination to keep out of the enemy's hands and of his having definite offers of help—in the course of 1942 he received at least half a dozen of these, some of them fantastic enough to have sprung from the pen of Baroness Orczy. (He remembers with grief one of his pupils who played the Scarlet Pimpernel

[1] Berkley: *op. cit.*, p. 94.

with the Germans and paid for it with his life—as did many of those he so nobly tried to rescue.) In the autumn of 1942 the writer accepted one of the more feasible offers, and, during the Christmas vacation, he and his wife spent a few days with his future host; now, even after so many years have past, he still cannot understand how he had the audacity to venture there without his star and with false identity papers.

False identity papers! The writer had seven of these altogether, each more implausible than the last. One of the earlier ones still bore the photograph of another man, and would not have deceived anyone who could use his eyes, unless he chose to turn a blind one. His various names were Cornelis Klaassen, Jacob Hans Willem Klasen or Johannes Claessen. The writer cannot remember how much he had to pay for all these papers, but he does recall that the first lot cost him 350 guilders and that the man who had "lost" it (people were always "losing" identity cards at that time) got cold feet, asked for it back, and kept the money—no doubt by way of compensation for the anxiety he had suffered. On the other hand, some of the false papers were given to him for nothing. Nor was money generally the greatest difficulty; much worse was the scrupulosity of Dutch bureaucrats whose records were kept so meticulously as at any moment to expose the fraud.

And so one passed as Cornelis Klaassen or as Benjamin Jacobus Johannes Piekar.[1] And then one had to assume a more or less plausible occupation. The writer certainly could not have acquitted himself with credit in several of the trades he was supposed to practise. A few of his Klaassens were clerks, others were teachers of the Christian religion; the last two were vocational guidance officers. The teachers and the vocational guidance workers carried documents, letters and other papers to "prove" that they were what they seemed to be—all of them bore the requisite stamps and were written on official letter-heads. In retrospect, it is obvious that the sense of security all these false identities provided was almost entirely illusory. A little efficiency in examining the documents, and the fraud would easily have been exposed.

To make things worse, one had to remember one's fictitious birthdays and birth-places—among his own, the writer remembers a town of which he had never even heard. One acquired a large new

[1] J. Hemelfijk: *Zeven maanden concentratiecamp* (Seven months in a Concentration Camp) part I (Alkmaar, 1953), p. 12.

family and, on changing one's first name, which poor Piekar had to do a few times, there was always a new lot of birthdays and relatives to remember. Sometimes one was married, sometimes a bachelor. All this had not only to be memorized but also to be recited convincingly under a quick fire of questions. Thus, though the wife of one of the Piekars had deserted her "husband", he still had to support her and, needless to say, to know all about her. Friends, too, had to know who precisely one was at a given moment, and it sometimes happened to this "Piekar" that he was addressed by his last name but two. In a way, the whole thing was a game, but the stakes were life and death, as the "Piekar" who wrote *Seven Months in a Concentration Camp* found out to his cost.

Thus Jews walked about with false identity cards, false names, false relations, false friends and false occupations; sometimes they even had a false face. In a Rotterdam beauty parlour, for instance, people had their noses, lips and other features changed, and their hair dyed—usually blonde.

Plastic surgery was a great help in what was perhaps the riskiest part of the whole business: moving from one part of the country to another. This particular manoeuvre faced the Jews and their helpers with almost insuperable difficulties, and the literature is full of them. To begin with, the fugitive had to reconcile himself to the fact that when he shut the door of the home he knew so well, all he left behind was forfeit. His wife would never again see their bits and pieces, their linen, their kitchen utensils; there were so many objects one would miss, old photographs, old souvenirs, the precious little things that go to make up a life. We know of many Jews who could not bring themselves to take this irrevocable step, to tear off their stars, to walk up the dangerous street or enter the still more dangerous railway station. It was often as much as their non-Jewish helpers could do to drag them reluctantly away; on one occasion, a man known to the writer used the expedient of "arresting" his charge: he turned up wearing a white band with a red swastika and escorted the Jew to the train. Not everyone could have recourse to plastic surgery; some tried to change their fatal physiognomy with strips of plaster or a bandage. The best thing, naturally, was to travel after dark. "Jews were conveyed in crates, cases and baker's carts. Some were removed in ordinary cars, handcuffed and driven by a chauffeur in SS uniform. On one occasion such a car was stopped by a German patrol. 'Jewish dirt for Westerbork, on their way to Heaven,' said the chauffeur and the Germans waved them on with a knowing grin."[1] One Jewess was solemnly driven to her destination in a mourner's carriage. "We had a good laugh about it afterwards. But it is easy to laugh when the danger is past."[2]

Quite often, too, Jews would have to change one hiding-place for another. The writer can remember the strain of a journey from Ede to Wageningen; he and his host were on bicycles and for a large part of the way they were followed by a young man. When they went fast he went fast, when they slowed down he did so too. Upon reaching Wageningen they dared not make straight for the new address and kept circling round the streets until they were certain they had lost their pursuer. On another occasion, the writer had to go from Lunteren to Ede and had the uncanny experience of suddenly coming face to face with a Jewish acquaintance, another person on the run who, in accordance with our code, gave as little sign of recognizing me as I did of recognizing her. The writer also had the strange experience of cycling through Northern Holland in the vague hope of finding a new hide-out. He had this sort of experience only once, but his parents-in-law, who were no longer young, had twenty-six different addresses after September 1942—if the word "address" can be used for some of them. Like Ahasuerus, Dutch Jews wandered from place to place and, what is more, in constant fear of betrayal.

An "address"! There was magic in the word for people whose very lives depended on their finding one. In theory, any Dutch house might become such a haven, but in practice, "addresses" were very few and far between. Moreover, your new host might turn out to be good, bad or indifferent, and you could never tell in advance.

Let us look first of all at the good ones. The records are full of the noble deeds of men of high integrity and warm humanity, and their actions are among the brightest rays of light in that dark period. Those they helped and sheltered remember above all the small but so infinitely welcome kindnesses, the tact, the sympathy, the understanding. Often such hosts were so concerned with the fate of their protégés that it was they who had to be comforted. There was the hostess who gave her Jewish lodger, lonely and separated from his family, a little cat to care for. There was the couple who greeted the

[1] *The Great Commandment*, Part II, p. 8.

[2] J. A. Slempkes: *Rozendaals rampentijd* (The trials of Rozendaal) (Velp, 1946), p. 28.

newcomer—the writer of this book—with a home-made cake and who, when asked if it was someone's birthday, replied that it was to celebrate his arrival. There was the hostess who, though having her hands full with her own family, knitted her lodger everything he needed to keep him warm, at a time when wool was almost unobtainable. There was the hostess who discovered that her Jewish lodger liked to have soup on a Friday night, and gave up her own meat coupons to provide it for him. A fitting tribute to such hosts was paid by Anne Frank: "Whenever Mr. Kleiman comes in, it is like the sun breaking through the clouds"—words that her father quoted at Kleiman's funeral in 1959. Indeed, for the lonely Jewish exile and fugitive, the host or hostess were, like the sun, the only source of human warmth and comfort.

Many were the stories of complete selflessness. There were the hosts who would take little or nothing for board and lodging, with "We'll talk about that when the war is over." Even working-class families with little enough to live on themselves would not take a penny. What need to mention more cases; it is enough that there was such a spirit abroad. Yet we must single out one host who, for two long years, harboured a whole group of Jews in his farm. In March 1944 seventeen German police raided the place and when, after five hours searching, they found nothing at all, threatened that unless the Jews they knew were hiding there were handed over by next day, they would raze every building to the ground. When the Jews decided to leave that very night, their host refused to let them go, saying: "God is with us today and he will not desert us tomorrow." And indeed, every one of these Jews survived the war.

Were such people the exception or the rule? It is a well-known fact that only late in the day did people begin to help Jews on any considerable scale, and even then only after much soul-searching. We need merely quote from the very moving post-war letter by a Dutch host to his Jewish protégé, in which he admits that at first he had shrunk from the idea of harbouring any Jews in his house. But: ". . . the subject kept cropping up . . . I consulted my wife and we again decided against it; some time later I spoke to my wife about it once more and told her: 'Think how we would feel if it was us . . .' I decided to visit you (the prospective lodgers), but though I observed you carefully I could not make up my mind. I went home and said to Anna: 'It seems incredible to me that such people should want to pig it with an ordinary working-class family.' " Still, offer them his home he did, and when they came, the host confessed that he and his wife kept asking themselves: "How on earth will they manage? All this sudden change, the separation from their children, driven from hearth and home, hunted like wild beasts, and now huddled in a humble room and at the mercy of an ordinary worker and his wife . . ." Then he recalls his embarrassment, for instance when food was getting short, how they tried to hide this from the lodgers, and what a strain it was for his wife to have strangers living always in the house; nevertheless, on Saturdays she would often hand over the cakes she had made because it was their Sabbath. And that was only one of the many things she did for them. "But," he went on to say, "in all the twenty months you were with us, you behaved with the utmost tact; neither Anna nor I have a word to say against you—there was never a complaint, but always gratitude and the wish to make things as easy for us as possible . . ."

Or take the case of the local official who hesitated about offering hospitality to a Jewish couple and their dog, and who decided to sleep on it. Before retiring, he and his wife asked God for guidance: "Neither of us slept very well that night, but when the morning came we awoke with our minds made up. We knew that we simply had to help these people, and that the Lord would watch over us all. Of that neither of us had the slightest doubt."

Others saw it somewhat differently. Thus, an artist, asked to take in a Jewish child, commented: "They're a lousy lot, but of course we must help them." Then there was the grave burgher who said: "Of course, you can't let them be burned in concentration camps, but I don't much like them, that's a fact." From there it was but a short step to a blank refusal to help. A minister of the church even declared that he would rather be locked up with ten English pilots in one hut, than with one Jew in ten houses. Then there were the perennial excuses. Of course one wanted to help, but it would make the house too noisy, the neighbours were untrustworthy, the servant wouldn't hold her tongue, the postman was inquisitive or the husband irritable. On July 14, 1942, in a blazing article, the underground paper *Het Parool* declared that it was most often the people in the poorest homes who threw them open to the hunted, while those "with plenty of money in their purses, their cellars crammed with hoarded food" and living in comfortable country villas would not even have Jews in their outhouses. The writer remembers only too well a saying of the times: "The poor offer you shelter, the rich someone else's address." Or as one witness put it to the Enquiry Commission:[1] "It was very hazardous to harbour Jews; hardly anyone took them in."

Now, it must be admitted that the risks were far from negligible and that the Germans left no one in any doubt about that—there were warning notices everywhere, the price they put on Jewish heads was always going up, they not only threatened punishment but meted it out and, applying their peculiar ethical standards, came down far harder on those who helped from conviction than on those who did it for money. In all fairness, therefore, it must be said that some of the excuses we have mentioned were all too well grounded. In fact, no hiding-place was altogether safe: even if they were not positively hostile, the neighbours *might* talk, the maid or a workman *might* try to blackmail the host, the postman *might* get suspicious. There is, in fact, not a single Jewish survivor who went into hiding and did not have a narrow escape; the writer, who incidentally thinks himself among the lucky ones, remembers at least four, and in each case his hosts were also in danger.

Moreover, all the hosts had relatives—parents who paid a call and had to be kept in ignorance. And then there were the children: "For eighteen months we never left our room; we hardly ever came downstairs, for the two oldest boys, aged six and eight, must not and did not know anything about our existence. For children are bound to talk."

Indeed they are. Thus some village children were overheard to say: "We've got two Jews at home." "That's nothing, we've got three, real dirty ones." Children could be a trial for the fugitives, and they could be a solace, as well. There is the story of the utterly lonely Jewish mother who, upon hearing her host's children noisily greeting their parents and romping about with them, burst loudly into tears. There was the Jewess who lived in the house of a widower and was only too glad to have his children to look after. The widower himself knew neither that she was Jewish nor that she was married. He could not understand why she refused all his advances; it was only after the Liberation that she felt free to tell him.

It is perhaps worth reiterating that, almost without exception, the hosts did not bargain for having their guests stay as long as they did. Weeks turned into months, months into years. All sorts of

[1] Enquiry Commission, part VIIc, p. 262.

things they wanted to do had to be abandoned because of the constant presence of strangers, and all sorts of things they did not want happened all the time. They could never let themselves go completely. If the guest ate with them, they never had their family to themselves at meals; if he did not, there was all the trouble of taking meals to him. They could never rely on their guest's coupons coming in time, and in any case, the food situation was always getting worse. One did not dare to take a holiday, it was hardly even possible to leave the house. Worse still, host and guest were thrust into each other's company day in and day out, whether they wanted it or not. And everyone has some idiosyncracies.

Most hosts had no idea what would be demanded of them, and nor had their guests. The best sort of relationship, and the writer was fortunate enough to have such, was one in which people felt completely free with one another, free if necessary to tell a few home truths. Often, however, the relationship was far from easy; neither party could find out exactly what was expected of them. Where was the host to draw the line between concern and meddling? "I could never understand why some things were right and others were not, but the people with whom I lodged said to me: 'You can leave all the thinking to us.' And of course I had to, for they were running all the risks."

In fact it was a good thing, in the circumstances, to be overcautious, although this sometimes developed into quite a little comedy. For instance, there was the case of a woman whose daughter came home every weekend but was never told there was a Jewess in the house. Yet the daughter, for her part, was sheltering Jews, and was afraid to tell her mother.

From meddling it was but a small step to importuning. An eighteen-year-old girl was so pestered not only by her host but also by his son that she had to keep her door locked all the time. One hostess who, incidentally, showed exemplary self-sacrifice in sheltering a whole group of Jews, saw fit to mete out punishment for even the smallest peccadillo—on one occasion, all these grown-up people, including a seventy-two-year-old woman, were sent to bed immediately after supper; when the old lady's daughter stayed behind to protest, she was given a severe dressing-down.

Visitors and correspondence were problems that were settled in a great number of different ways. The writer remembers two hosts, one of whom had no objection to visitors (within certain limits) but drew the line at sending and receiving letters—not surprisingly, since he thought it safer to post the letters from another village and had to take them there himself on his bicycle. The other host had no objections to correspondence, but reduced the number of visitors to the absolute minimum. Both undoubtedly acted from the very best of motives, in the interests of all concerned. Some insisted on reading all the incoming and outgoing mail.

But perhaps the hardest hosts to bear were those whose ideas of hygiene were, to put it mildly, rudimentary: "They used the milk-pan as a chamber-pot. I had to empty it in the morning before putting the milk in. We had a special bottle in which to put all the fleas we caught. [This was in a lower middle-class home in Amsterdam East.] Their two little boys were not yet potty-trained. In the morning their rubber pants were hung up to dry over the saucepans on the cooker. Whenever I took them off and hung them beside the cooker they were put back in the same place within a few minutes." Then there was the woman who pricked the potatoes with a dirty hairpin, or the one who did not wash at all, but whose bed a Jewish girl had to share: "You can't say I'm dirty—I change my clothes every week!"

Sometimes the hosts would exploit their helpless wards. Some charged 200 guilders a week per person for board and lodging; one Jewish lady, who could not go on affording it after a year, was thrown out and ended up in Auschwitz; after the Liberation, some Jews were still paying off arrears. One man charged his guests 65 guilders for coupons that he himself bought for 5 guilders. Group J of the National Aid Fund, which subsidized the maintenance of fugitives, had on record cases of Jews asked to pay 500 and even 1,000 guilders a month for board and lodging.

We have spoken of the hosts; what of the other helpers? There were the many who brought the two parties together, transported the fugitives and kept them in touch with the outside world. The dangers these people ran were enormous; their work took them from town to town, past countless patrols, each one of whom might discover that the helper was bearing coupons, identity cards, letters, illegal newspapers or, worse still, accompanying Jews. We do not know how many of these brave men lost their lives in that way.

We have previously mentioned the inner resistance that Jews had to overcome before they went into hiding. They lacked energy, contacts, money, played down the dangers of deportation and exaggerated those of going underground; they were frightened, terribly frightened; they were unsure of their own strength, they wanted to remain with their families, they did not want to depend on others or endanger them. Probably there were many other considerations as well—at this distance we cannot say. In any case, those who were not content to take a purely passive attitude had sooner or later to make a decision, for themselves and for their families. They had to make up their minds to ignore the many whispers: "Poland is not so bad." "The war will soon be over." "If they catch you, you will be sent to Westerbork." "Informers are lurking at every street corner." Worse still, the Jewish Council was opposed to people going underground and had ordered its staff to remain at their posts. They contended that going into hiding was "impracticable for very many on financial grounds and quite impossible for the vast majority". And if everybody could not go into hiding, nobody must—that is precisely what the Jewish Council told all those who sought its advice.

Herzberg[1] claims that the relative success of the rescue operation exceeded the expectations of 1942 and 1943. This seems indisputable, but we must repeat that even when they were hidden from sight, the fugitives remained in constant danger of discovery. It is certain that thousands of Jews lost their lives as a result of denunciation, anonymous or otherwise, sometimes even by their hosts; not seldom the supposed sanctuary was a trap set up by the landlords (Jewish traitors among them) working hand in glove with the Dutch and German police—the reward was shared out among them. The *Algemeen Politieblad* (Police Gazette) kept publishing lists of missing Jews sent in by various burgomasters (some of whom must have been as keen as mustard) and calling for their capture. On one occasion, the Germans published an appeal to Jews in hiding: those who gave themselves up would be pardoned. We do not know how many were foolish enough to believe this promise, but all who did come forward were deported. We have spoken of the Henneicke Column on more than one occasion. Its activities brought about the deaths of hundreds of Jews. The men were paid piece-rates and their blood-money was, in time, raised from 7½ guilders to 37½ guilders per Jewish head. While a few Jews were rescued from their clutches by the Resistance, most of their victims were deported or butchered on the spot; in Zwolle, a few fugitives, together with other Jews, were shot

[1] Herzberg: *op. cit.*, p. 245.

down after being forced to dig their own graves. We also know of a few cases of killing for plunder, sometimes with the host as an accomplice. When caught, did these criminals go unpunished? Of course not. They were infringing a German monopoly, and the Germans could not allow them to get away with it.

In view of all the hazards, it is surprising that so many did in fact survive. One had only to put a finger wrong to lose one's life, and yet there were places where the "whole neighbourhood" knew about the presence of fugitives among them; one such place, a centre of underground activities, ran a noisy cabaret which was, in fact, a centre for the distribution of illegal newspapers and unauthorized supplies of food. In Hoorn, "Auntie Dieuw", the tenant of a house used by the German Town Commander, kept eight Jews hidden there for a long time, before sending them on to a safer place.

What the Netherlands lacked was a heavily wooded countryside where one could go to ground. And where Nature refused to provide hiding-places, man had to make his own. During the war, this sort of thing became legendary, and in fact some people were extraordinarily resourceful. The writer, to give one small example, has lived in a loft measuring no more than 13 feet by 5 feet, in which four men, with all their belongings (including a radio) spent seven long months; they could hardly stand up in it and, during warm weather, hardly breathe—the only ventilation was provided by a loose piece of glass.

In a house in Amsterdam South, the fugitives decided to extend their hiding-place, ". . . so that we could get some physical exercise . . . This place was right under the roof-tiles and was obstructed by a heavy cross-beam. The roof is still on, though one day we sawed through that beam and pushed it out of the way." In a house in Leyden a cupboard was ingeniously fitted out to accommodate two persons, but when the number of fugitives increased, the loft above it, too, had to be put to use. A ladder could be drawn up and a trap-door closed. "In the loft there was a radio and other illegal articles, such as identity cards, coupons and even a pistol. The cupboard seemed safer than the loft; when danger threatened, the most Jewish-looking of us had first claim to it."

In retrospect the expression "when danger threatened" must raise a wry smile. Many hide-outs could not have escaped detection in any thorough search, and while there are stories of fugitives who did, in fact, elude their pursuers, it remains an open question whether the searchers really wanted to find them—whenever they were in earnest they usually succeeded. In a place near Amsterdam, for instance, numerous fugitives were discovered in their man-made shelter, because they had left a piece of string hanging out of a trap-door. Then there is the story of the German policeman who danced and jumped up and down on the floorboards of a corridor until he located a Jew hidden underneath: "Come on out of that, you so-and-so! You can't be all that comfortable," said the man, in tones of mock consideration and with a twisted grin on his face. "Slowly Max rose out of the ground—with the fear of death on his face . . . My heart stood still . . ." Then "Max" was horribly maltreated, while his landlady, to whom we owe the story, was taken away.

A memorial tablet in Santpoort Provincial Hospital tells us that 200 refugees were hidden there until the autumn of 1944. Then the Germans found out, and some 150 lost their lives.

We have said that the Netherlands lacked a heavily wooded countryside; yet it did have some scrubland. There some fifteen Palestine Pioneers lived in a hide-out 65 feet long, 5 feet wide and 3 feet high. The place was very well fitted up, and after six months was even wired for electricity. "One day, one of the 'troglodytes' came to visit me . . . I was astonished and glad to see how well my friend looked, and how full of bounce he was. He had come to buy a few books and then hastened back."

In Soeren (Northern Veluwe) where a large number of fugitives were encamped and had to forage as far afield as 10 kilometres for food, it took the Dutch SS one and a half years of persistent effort to find them. Eight of the eighty captives were forced to dig their own graves. And just outside Winterswijk, a number of Jews succeeded in building a few wooden shacks in the thick scrub, almost under the noses of a group of keen Dutch Nazis. On November 28, 1942, the whole place was surrounded, and only six of the twenty-three fugitives could make their escape—three of them survived the war. An ex-pupil of the author's and her little brother took shelter in the house of what turned out to be a kleptomaniac and psycho-path and decided to look for more "pleasant" surroundings. From August 1943 to December 1944 they and their parents hid in a hut on the borders of Friesland and Drente; this hut was some 16 feet by 5 feet, and one could stand upright only in the middle of it. The first few weeks they slept on straw which, for safety reasons, could not be replaced since any trace of it might have given away their presence. Soon afterwards, they added a few more huts, and though the nervous tension and boredom proved almost unbearable, the thought that "anything was better than Poland" helped them to endure it. The clergyman who called on them from time to time "came from a strict Calvinist family, in which he had always been taught that the Jew was a usurer and one condemned to suffer for the Crucifixion. But when, during the war, he met his first Jew, he realized that he had all along been holding to a false doctrine".

Many reports give us some idea of the atmosphere and attitude of the fugitives, though we shall never, of course, know the whole story. The reader must remember that all these people had, until 1940, been part of a normal community, in a country where life, on the whole, was peaceful and civilized. And then quite suddenly they were hounded out of their homes, away from their familiar surroundings into a completely new and alien environment, where they went in constant fear of their lives and where other attitudes, norms, customs and values prevailed. Dangers lurked everywhere; they were separated from their loved ones and now lived in enforced idleness, in tiny hovels unfit for human habitation; they were utterly dependent upon others and constantly forced to face up to their hosts' whims and their own shortcomings.

Day after day dragged out its miserable length. One woman made a little cross on the wall for every one of them; on October 17, 1942, she wrote in her diary: "It has been thirty-eight days; pray God it won't be that much again." In the end it was not seventy-six, but 933 interminable days in the same small unheated cubicle, facing the cold east wind, often not daring to move because there were visitors downstairs. Or what of the woman who, with her husband, lay hidden in a tiny corner beneath the roof: "The skylight was so small that your head would blot out all the light . . .; whenever it admitted a thin ray of sunshine I quickly moved my chair and lifted my face up towards it." A simple Jewish girl made this entry in her diary: "This spring, a flycatcher built its nest on the terrace. The female laid her eggs beside the flower-pots. When Mrs. —— [the owner] discovered it, she warned us not to keep peering at the nest and not to move about too noisily lest we disturb the birds. Unfortunately, Bert knocked against the nest with his broom and out tumbled four or five small pale green eggs: so easily are lives broken even before they begin! The desolate parent birds kept flying from the nest to a nearby tree and back again, seeking hour after hour for what they had lost. But for them there was hope, they still had each other. How different it was for the many hundreds of Jewish parents torn apart and robbed of their children—irrevocably. Suddenly I was struck by the enormity of all their suffering. I sobbed uncontrollably and my tears were their tears too."

Day after day . . . and ever on the watch. This writer—and he was one of the lucky ones—had to keep away from the window for months, curtained though it was; at all times, he had to keep his voice down and steal about in slippers. And if chance visitors arrived —luckily this did not happen very often—he had to watch his every word, and moreover, try to talk in the local accent. Not far from the place where the writer was hiding was a married couple who were only allowed to visit their little boy at Christmas, disguised as Santa Claus and his attendant: "My husband could at least take him on his lap, but I could not, desperately though I longed to do so." Some diaries betray the pressure of sexual tensions. One fugitive, formerly a very busy general practitioner and now forced into complete idleness, was overcome by a feeling of drowsiness throughout the day. His fatigue apparently gave him a respite from his constant "preoccupation with negative emotions". According to him,[1] this was "a very general phenomenon".

The sudden change of environment was particularly hard on religious Jews. For many, their new life was the first direct experience of Christian mercy, compassion and love. Delleman (quoted by C. B. Bavinck) has stressed that even the "very slightest acquaintance with the Gospels, handed to them as they set out on their journey, the sincerity and compassion shown them in the hour of their deepest need—all that made a deep and lasting impression on them". To which Bavinck himself added: "Difficult though it was to understand how the Lord could allow so much evil and injustice, we felt that it was all part of His plan, and that comforted us in those dark days."

Luckily, there were many, very many, reports in a less sombre tone. Take, for instance, the recorded impressions of a seventy-year-old Friesian woman, who did not worry in the least about walking about without an identity card: if stopped, she would just pretend to be stupid and what could they do to her then? Two young girls who hid together told the writer: "We gradually acquired a voca-

[1] H. Musaph: *Doodsdrift, castratie-complexen en depressie* (Death-wish, castration-complexes and depression), 1948.

bulary that we would not have been allowed to use in our homes. Here we would make free with 'God', 'In God's name', 'Gosh' 'By Gosh', 'In Heaven's name', 'Honest to God', 'Lord in Heaven' and—probably worst of all—with 'Christ Almighty' . . . Lottie always claimed that living on the run was something that you could not learn, and I would say grandly that we drew on forces of which we had not been aware until then." And while telling this story to the writer, this girl—the same one who had wept over the bird's nest—was laughing merrily.

But inevitably unpleasant feelings predominated and, needless to say, the hosts, too, came in for their share of misery, not only from the Germans but also from their "guests". The writer remembers the case of one of his non-Jewish friends whose lodger ate him out of house and home and, what is more, at fantastic speed, and who got a good telling off every time he brought the wrong kind of grapes—after all, wasn't he being paid for them? Another non-Jewish friend took in an old Jewish lady who had to have the last word in everything, never let anyone speak and drove the family to desperation. Many of the fugitives would stand on the dignity of their former social position; one of them was highly incensed because the farmer who was sheltering him presumed to address him by his first name—he, whose father had been a general! What annoyed the hosts even more was the recklessness with which some of their lodgers not only ran unnecessary risks themselves but imperilled their benefactors too. At one address some twenty Jews would congregate almost every evening, and it was only by a miracle that they were not discovered at once. "One evening, Mr. —— even gave a film show, and the neighbours objected because the noise could be heard halfway up the street." Needless to say, the miracle did not last.

One woman's family was asked to take in just one more Jew, "for only a few days". "Once more we agreed, but imagine our surprise when, next day, he appeared with a removal van from Rotterdam. We were all completely flabbergasted Out of the van came a large number of cases and a piano. Our Ikey, that's what we called him, stood on the steps and gave instructions. One of the removal men asked me if I knew what I was doing. 'That Jew is as bold as brass,' he said, and when I protested he merely shrugged his shoulders. I knew the neighbours were bound to ask us what we wanted with yet another piano, and that I would just have to lie my head off . . .

Ikey was a real horror. He kept going out with my son's identity card and when we pleaded with him not to do it, he just laughed at us and said he was born under a lucky star. And right opposite us lived a German woman, and we didn't know if we could trust her. One day she asked us how long we intended keeping the Jew with us. He was always taking unnecessary chances, and the last straw was when he informed us that he was a musical genius. I myself never got farther with my music than *Grossmütterchen*, and here we were harbouring a great virtuoso! The neighbours were bound to notice the difference. In the evening, when we used to look at snapshots, he kept wriggling closer to me and wouldn't be put off."

It was one thing for a Jew to be a nuisance, quite another for him to be a traitor. Two such men among a group of forty fugitives were found to be corresponding with the Germans. "After long deliberations it was decided to do away with them. The executions were carried out by Resistance fighters from outside. The baron (on whose grounds the group was living and for whom this was, no doubt, an unprecedented experience) later asked the Resistance men if he owed them anything for their work." There were also quite a few cases of Jews threatening their hosts with: "If I go, you go with me."

The guests were of all sorts. They might be amusing, boring or overbearing—the reader can easily imagine what varieties of behaviour might be expected from people locked up for months on end together. No wonder that sometimes they felt they had to give vent to their pent-up emotions. In a provincial town where five Jewish girls were hiding, the "great event was the arrival of Kees H. (a well-known psychiatrist) who took all our hearts by storm. He could not venture into the streets in daylight and so he came to us in the evening. Whenever he was expected, we would prepare the daintiest morsels we could manage and shower all sorts of other attentions on him. He took it all as no more than his due. There was always something we had to say to him in private, and though he would often spend the whole night with us in conversation, ours was not the only house he visited. Perhaps that had something to do with his decision to become a sexologist".

Women guests indeed often posed quite special problems. "I did not know what to do," said one Jewish lady after the war. "I went from one place to another, but who will take in a pregnant woman? Even a clergyman, to whom I had a letter of recommendation, was unable to help. I knelt down at his feet, clutched his knees and sobbed." A few weeks later her child was born—clandestinely in a hospital. And to the writer's questioning look, she said: "I know what you mean, but we were only in our early twenties. My husband and I thought about it a great deal and we did so want a child."

We have already mentioned the special difficulties of orthodox Jews, the problems of keeping the dietary laws. Not every host found an easy answer to this and similar questions, as witness the case of the devoted helper who went cycling round with all sorts of baggage, including a set of prayer-straps, tied to the back of his bicycle. Perhaps this is the place to mention the opening of a clandestine synagogue in a room in Amsterdam during the darkest year of the Occupation, a few small Scrolls of the Law, prayer-shawls and other ritual articles were "borrowed" from the Portuguese Synagogue. Many Jews still at liberty would join with some of those living on the run to celebrate the High Festivals. A non-Jewish fellow-conspirator would make sure that the "muted sound of the *shofar* being blown on the Day of Atonement could not be heard from outside" (1944). There was no rabbi. One week they would follow the Ashkenazi and the other the Sephardic rites, and "for the Feast of Tabernacles we had a palm branch and myrtle, and we stole a few willow leaves from the park". The last Sabbath service was held on May 5, 1945.

The non-Jewish conspirator we have just mentioned had yet another task: he would, with others, help to convey dead fugitives to the Jewish Cemetery; the official papers were easily obtained from the Dutch authorities who never made any difficulties. There were wooden boards instead of the usual grave-stones, and even these were difficult enough to obtain. Dead fugitives posed other problems, too, and few people knew how to solve them. According to one professor at the Medical Faculty in Amsterdam, the anatomy theatre often served as a mortuary.

One girl, a courier for the Resistance, found a dead woman in a house sheltering four other refugees. "I realized that they expected me to do something about it. I loaded the old woman in a hand-cart 'borrowed' from the neighbours and tipped her into a canal. I was then eighteen. In peace-time, I should probably have been amusing myself in a sports club or gone walking in a lane with a friend. Yet here I was, watching through a mist of tears, as a little old Jewish woman disappeared into the dark waters of the canal." In a small village in the east of the country a dead fugitive had to be conveyed to the cemetery on the front of a bicycle. "It was a macabre journey . . . then the remains were quietly interred."

We have already spoken of the financial arrangements between host and guest. To take but one case: "Not long after the Liberation a non-Jewish friend asked me how we managed for so many years without any income at all. My answer was, we lived on manna. Like so many others I had realized that it was important to get hold of a few jewels and similar articles before I left. The incredible prices which many were prepared to pay for these trinkets later, now provided us with manna and so rid us of at least our monetary worries."

The reader will appreciate that this sort of manna was not available to everyone—far from it. The majority were helped by the NSF (National Aid Fund) or rather by Group J of this resistance organization which, for security reasons, worked almost independently of the mother organization, and incidentally did a great deal more for its "clients"—it coped with births and deaths and would also act as peace-maker between hosts and guests in case of need. The funds distributed by this Group ultimately reached 400,000 guilders per month; the maximum allowance per person per month was at first 75 and later 100 guilders, but in many cases much less. According to Professor Sanders, who wrote a history of the NSF, the great majority of fugitive Jews benefited from this aid. This is true, provided there were only some 9,000 Jewish fugitives in the country as a whole but not if, as seems probable, the number was very much larger than that. In any case, we must give unstinted praise to this noble and dangerous work, particularly during the "hunger winter" of 1944–5.

What was done for the children deserves a few paragraphs to itself.

Not seldom, children would bear their life on the run with a resilience that makes us marvel even now. There was the story of the seventeen-year-old girl sheltering with her parents and little brother in a tiny hide-out in a copse. Luckily she was not entirely cut off from the company of young men: "And so I had a most enjoyable time, romantic strolls in the moonlight, walks farther afield and endless discussions on all sorts of subjects . . . during these talks my father saw his authority slipping a little, for he discovered that I could think for myself." Though the nervous tension and boredom were often unbearable, she could take comfort in the fact that her parents' happy marriage stood the test of all trials. "I never had any problems; nor did I ever ask myself if something 'special' was happening in the corner of the hut." During the Liberation a number of parachutists arrived with two German prisoners of war: "They threw dice to decide who should have the job of killing the Germans. One of the prisoners was ordered to take off his leather jacket. I realized at once that the man to whom the lot had fallen did not want a hole through the coat. We watched impassively while the two Germans disappeared up a path into the woods; then we calmly ate the hard-boiled eggs from the German's mess-can, while waiting for the two shots which we knew had to come. We had been present at too many raids to get excited over the death of two Germans."

We could tell many stories of the self-denial and devotion with which so many people cared for Jewish children. For to look after a Jewish child in those difficult circumstances did indeed make great demands. As one host, who one night deposited two Jewish boys with a woman who related the story, said to her: "I simply can't put up with these two ruffians any longer; this afternoon, they used my shot-gun to fire at birds sitting on the wires, just as a trainload of Germans was passing. And this evening, two sinister characters have been prowling up and down the street outside. I simply daren't have my house become a centre of attention. The boys don't understand what risks they are running, but I have a wife and two children". And no one else would have these boys either. In the end the elder said: "All right, then. We're going to turn ourselves over to the German police and you'll have to face the consequences."

But it was not always the children who were at fault. An eight-year-old boy who went into hiding in September 1942 was passed from hand to hand and lodged with eighteen different hosts in barely two years before he was finally caught in November 1944; from prison he was sent on to Westerbork where he was found alive at the Liberation. His parents had been killed in Rotterdam. Twice he was taken in by strict Protestants and twice by equally strict Catholics; one Catholic couple did their utmost to convert him—he had to tell his beads, learn the history of the martyrs and, apart from that, was taught little else than cleaning shoes, peeling potatoes and lighting stoves; the fourteen-year-old daughter of the house took all his sweet coupons. The mother of another boy told the writer after the Liberation how her little son was taken to safety in Oosterbeek by a fourteen-year-old girl. "Just as they got there, the battle of Arnhem began. They were right in the midst of it. They must have been through absolute hell. The house where they were hiding was razed to the ground. The British threw them into holes to save them. They were out in the open for ten days, trying to get away. All that time, the girl took care of him. The British and Germans both gave them chocolate." Then the child found some new foster-parents: "They were very good to him, but he was not allowed to cry. They lived in a very small house and were afraid someone would hear him. And, of course, one knows how they felt. But then, how could the child not cry? After all he had been through . . ."

A little girl was taken to the provinces by one of her teachers. Her grandmother had this to say: "The foster-father later told me that when she first came there she was like a shy bird. She was only nine years old, and hardly opened her mouth. At night, when she lay in bed, he would sit beside her and try to gain her confidence. In the end, he and his wife were successful. We owe these wonderful people an unspeakable debt." When the foster-parents were denounced to the Germans, they managed to take the child to safety just in time; their house, which had been a centre of illegal activities, was burnt down.

The grandmother also told us: "My grandson, who was only eight years old, had to hide in eleven different houses, and in every case got away just in the nick of time. A ten-year-old boy, locked up by himself in a little room, had quite forgotten how to talk after six months—all he could do was to babble incomprehensibly."

The mother of the boy who was caught in the battle of Arnhem also told the writer: "As for myself, I had to make do somehow, but it was extremely difficult to come to terms with it all. I helped with the cooking and ran errands. On a few occasions I found myself standing deep in thought in front of the house where we had lived before the war; it was just near by. I lived in the past, but did not talk about it. My thoughts were so often with my husband and my child. I was no longer young when I married and the child was like a gift from Heaven. He looked so frail when he was born, I hardly dared to touch him. We had an anxious time trying to keep him alive. But then he began to thrive. I was a nervous mother, but all the same I did not stop him from cycling, swimming or skating. At school he was one of the best pupils, good in every subject. And how he loved his books! Why did they have to take my child from me? Why? I know that there are many who could ask the same question. When I was in Westerbork I once went into a hut with forty children. They used to call it the orphanage. Many of these children were less than six years old. All of them had gone into hiding and had been caught. They had committed the same crime as my son—they had Jewish parents and four Jewish grandparents. And that was a capital offence. In the terrible night of February 6, 1944, the hut was cleared and all the children were deported. That's what they told me."

And so we could go on. But perhaps we may spare the reader more of these harrowing details and pass at once to the Liberation and the survivors' return to a Netherlands that would never be the same for them again. Everywhere the Jews came out of their corners. Were they happy? Were they elated?

In the writer's experience this was not the mood of most survivors: "Germany has surrendered. Our country has been liberated. I felt very old, happy and sad at one and the same time, sad because, whatever happens, the Jews have lost the war. My first reaction was to burst into tears. I thought of the thousands and tens of thousands who had been carried off and did not live to see this great, unforgettable moment. But gradually I was drawn into the boundless joy all around me. It was as if I had been given a holiday and the feeling stayed with me for several weeks."

The woman who said this worked on a farm, and shortly before the Liberation she decided to reveal that she was a Jewess: "I did not have the faintest idea how they felt about Jews, and for all I knew they might have been rabid anti-Semites. I did not even admit to myself how frightened I was of their reaction, or their possible change in attitude. One evening, when I was in the farm-house, I gathered up all my courage. My heart was in my throat. My hands were clammy and the tension was so great that, when finally it all came out, the farmer's wife had to get me a glass of water to keep me from fainting. I told them that I was Jewish, that I did not know what their attitude to Jews was and that they might now be sorry for having helped me. But all my hostess said to me was: 'I am sorry, but only because, had I known, I should have tried to help you even more.' The farmer himself said he was happy that he, too, had been able to do something for the Jews, albeit unwittingly. They realized that I had kept silent in everyone's best interest."

And so the Jews returned.

"During the triumphal entry of the Princess Irene Brigade into The Hague, a Jewish girl just out of hiding and still wearing her yellow star, presented the victors with a garland of flowers. The Burgomaster tore off the star with his own hands amid the loud jubilation of the crowd." In some places, the fugitives were given a hero's reception. They entered in decorated coaches and were greeted with flowers and warm addresses of welcome. Elsewhere the reception was less than cordial: "At the first house I visited, they wept with happiness to see me. Others, who had been looking after some of my things, were rather taken aback. 'What, you're still alive?' they said in great consternation. Even some of my own family were not pleased to see me, they had some of my things, too."

Another homecomer said: "Outside, I could see a few motor-cars with people who had been brought back from Theresienstadt. A whole crowd of non-Jews—I deliberately do not call them Christians—had stopped to look. I expected them to feel sorry for what these poor people had been through. Instead, I heard someone say. 'You can see they're still scared stiff.' Another remarked: 'They've got nothing now—but mark my words, it won't be long before they're rolling in it again.' And then someone said something about Jewish cowardice during the Occupation."

Or take this account: "On Sunday, May 6, 1945, we went into town (Amsterdam), but it was so full of strange faces that we hardly recognized it. Soon afterwards the Canadians arrived. The day before I had got back my camera from a friend. I had some film for it, and now I wanted to take pictures of the Canadians. But it was all spoilt for me when I heard a voice in the crowd say: 'There they are again. You can see who's got the best cameras.' Yet my camera was really quite an ordinary one."

Perhaps this simple remark is a fitting ending for this chapter. Or perhaps we should rather give the last word to a Jewish historian who, speaking of survivors throughout Europe, asked whether people who had to spend twenty to thirty months in cellars, without light or air, living on the crumbs that fell from the tables of poor farmers, and always in fear of their lives, could retain their physical and spiritual health; whether people who had to fly from village to village and faced death every time they met a stranger, could ever again lead completely normal lives; whether the Viennese girl, hidden for four years by a sexton—during Gestapo raids she often had to lie among the corpses—could ever banish her deadly fear from her scarred and tortured soul.[1]

This girl may well stand as a figure of the European Jew during the war. It may be that Dutch Jews were a little more fortunate than some of the rest, but who will presume to grade the degrees of human misery and suffering?

[1] Jacob Lestschinsky: *Crisis, catastrophe and survival* (New York, 1948), p. 56.

CHAPTER SEVEN

# THE TRANSIT CAMPS

## WESTERBORK

THOSE Dutch Jews who lived on the run, and of whom we have just written, were so many individual cells of defiance. If they were a small group, was not the Dutch Resistance itself a minority? Many of these fugitives were captured by the Germans and sent to Westerbork to join the vast majority of Dutch Jews who had been rounded up in the "ordinary" way. Westerbork, indeed, was soon dubbed the "Jerusalem" of the Netherlands. All told, it "accommodated" 100,000 Jews, some for a few days, some for months and a very few for years. "All roads lead through Westerbork." That, the reader may recall, was how Aus der Fünten put it during a raid. And "through" was the operative word—most Jews went on to the gas-chambers.

"Westerbork was another word for purgatory. There was nothing to sustain one, materially or spiritually. Each was thrown on his own resources, utterly alone. Desperation, total and absolute, seized everyone. People sought help but seldom found it and, if they did, knew that it could not possibly prevail. Deportation to Poland might at best be postponed—for a week, perhaps, or for a few weeks at most. Husbands were powerless to protect their wives, parents had to watch helplessly while their children were torn away from them for ever. The sick, the blind, the halt, the mentally disturbed, pregnant women, the dying, orphans, new-born babies—none was spared on the Tuesdays when the cattle-trucks were being loaded with human freight for Poland. Tuesdays, week in, week out, for two interminable years."[1]

Judgment Day, the *dies irae*, the day no historian will ever be able to describe. Here we can only endeavour to give the reader a few facts and figures, a mere glimpse into the depths of this vale of tears. The rest he must try to picture for himself.

[1] A. Herzberg: Introduction to *De nacht der Girondijnen* (Amsterdam, 1957), p. viii.

We shall proceed in much the same way as we have done in following the general fate of Dutch Jews under the Occupation. First we shall make a brief survey of the history of the camp and then attempt to describe its "geography" or rather, "sociography".

Westerbork was, in fact, not a German but a Dutch innovation, and was originally intended for Jewish refugees from Germany. It was planned some time before the outbreak of war and officially approved in 1939. In the minutes of the meeting of the Netherlands Council of Ministers on February 13 of that year we read: "On the proposal of the Minister for the Interior it was decided to establish a camp for German refugees in this country." 1,250,000 guilders was voted for buildings and general equipment, the cost to be repaid by the Relief Committee for Jewish Refugees in annual instalments of 200,000 guilders. Many Jews argued at the time that this money would be better spent on settling the refugees abroad, though the sum involved would barely have sufficed.

On October 9, 1939, the first twenty-two German refugees arrived; by May 1940 their number had increased to about 750—their subsequent evacuation from the camp has been mentioned in Chapter One. Most of these evacuees were afterwards returned to Westerbork, except for sixty illegal Jewish immigrants who were discovered in the Hook of Holland in May 1940, and forcibly returned to Germany along with a number of German deserters who had been captured in the same area. But after passing through a series of German prisons, these refugees, too, landed up in Westerbork. Few of them understood how fortunate they were. Their turn had not come—not yet, that is.

The original Westerbork "Central Camp for Refugees" was under the control of the Ministry of the Interior. The land on which it stood had been made available by the Department of Economic Affairs. The total area measured some 250 acres, of which the actual camp itself occupied about 60 acres. A Dutch Member of Parliament called the place "a bare, desolate expanse, probably one of the most depressing stretches to be found anywhere in our country". It was a wind-swept plain, little better than a peat-bog. Moreover, it was completely isolated, one of the very few places in the Netherlands before the war where you could feel truly "God-forsaken". No wonder that Professor Cohen,[1] President of the pre-war Refugee Committee, felt obliged to point out to the Minister for

[1] D. Cohen: *Zwervend en dolend* (Haarlem, 1955), p. 139.

the interior that "this was no place to send old people and children". (His protest was ignored.) Dr. Ottenstein had this to say of Westerbork: "It was stormy all the year round. The wind smothered the camp with sand and dirt, which turned everything grey or black and got in everywhere. As soon as it started to rain, the paths became like swamps. Eye infections were common; many people wore goggles. In summer there was a plague of flies, which especially bothered the helpless babies . . . The camp at Westerbork was cheerless in every imaginable way."

Professor Cohen[1] states elsewhere that Westerbork was a model camp "until the Germans got hold of it". It seems unlikely that even its first occupants would have agreed with him. We have already spoken of insects—in the summer of 1943 every inmate had to hand in fifty flies per day. But the accumulated dirt could not be got rid of, and so the flies and other vermin kept breeding apace.

On July 16, 1940, the camp came under the jurisdiction of the Department of Justice, only to fall into the Germans' hands on July 1, 1942. From a Central Camp for Refugees it was suddenly turned into a *Polizeiliches Durchgangslager* (Police Transit Camp), an ominous designation that took some time to filter through to Westerbork itself. The true character of the new régime was recognized in Amsterdam as soon as it became known that the Germans had put barbed wire round the camp. At that time, ironically enough, most of the people inside would have been only too glad to stay there. Ottenstein tells us that the official description of the camp was changed to "work-camp" in March 1944, but, for all that, a transit camp it certainly remained.

A few incidents may be selected from the monotonous history of Westerbork to illustrate how tension continuously waxed and waned. In this, of course, Westerbork was a true reflection of what went on in the Netherlands at large.

We have mentioned that the Germans declared Westerbork a transit camp on July 1, 1942. Many things had previously suggested that something was in the air, and had increased the mood of panic inside. Within a fortnight, the inmates knew that their fears were only too well founded: the time of the deportations had come. For more than two years the transports to Poland determined the whole character of Westerbork as a vast clearing house.

When the first trains had left, those left behind walked about in

[1] D. Cohen: *Zwervend en dolend* (Haarlem, 1955), p. 137.

a daze. And how could it have been otherwise? Most of them had been there for nearly two years. If they were far from happy (what Jew in the Netherlands could be happy under the Germans?) they were at least relatively unmolested. Suddenly, the now familiar ground began to move under their feet, and they found themselves sliding to—God knows where. True, the Jewish Council had given assurances that the bulk of them would remain where they were, but quite a few of the inmates must have come to realize by then how little reliance could be placed in their leaders' glib assurances. On July 13 almost everyone who was not a "full" Jew was turned out of the camp. On July 14 all those born between 1902 and 1925 were declared eligible for "labour service". As Deppner, the German commandant, put it: "Your labour, too, is needed for our victory." There now began the sort of spectacle that would be repeated hundreds of times with ever-increasing horror: "One of those selected was a young man, who was to be separated from his aged father. The old man, a Polish Jew with a long beard, came to plead with them. We did not know, then, what sadists the Germans really were. 'So you want to stay with your son? All right then, you can go along with him tomorrow.' That was all he got out of them."

The reader knows that the Germans meant to use Westerbork as a reservoir on which they could draw whenever there was a shortage of "volunteers" from Amsterdam. In addition, they used it as a kind of sluice. Early on the morning of July 15, for instance, some 800 Jews reached the camp from Hooghalen, mostly on foot, to be "sifted" through within an hour. This pitiable procession—men, women and children—was then quickly packed off to Hooghalen again, where they were herded into cattle-trucks like so many animals. Next day a number of Jews from Amersfoort camp arrived in Westerbork, dirty and hungry, with no luggage, and were quickly dealt with in the same way. The whole camp was aghast. But so little did most of the inmates realize what lay in store for these people that they went to great trouble to buy from a bank in Assen what little German currency they could get. This they handed to the "labour contingents", together with such clothes and food as they could spare. Perhaps it was this very group of deportees whose extermination Himmler himself witnessed during his summer tour: "After the inspection in Birkenau, he supervised the extermination of a whole transport that had just arrived . . . He watched it all without a word."[1] When he sat down at table soon afterwards with his own entourage and the camp leaders, "he led the conversation in the jolliest of moods and was extremely affable . . . He held forth on all sorts of themes . . . child education and new housing, art and literature."

In the first week of October many thousands more, snatched up during Rauter's great raid, arrived in Westerbork for "processing", before being packed off to Poland.

We know quite a lot about this transport, since hardly anyone who witnessed it and survived to tell the tale has failed to do so. Most of the accounts agree down to the last detail. It seems almost unbelievable that the men who perpetrated all these unspeakable horrors belonged to the same species as their hapless victims.

One of the Jews who was forced to help the Germans in this ghastly work has left an extremely valuable legacy, in the form of his diary. He was an FK[2] man in Westerbork, one of those whose task it was to deal with the victims' luggage. His account covers that whole week of October 1–7, 1942.

"Two and a half months of deportation have completely altered us. When the first batches arrived, we could hardly bear to look at them, so deeply did their misery move us. And now? Now we just say, as a matter of course: '300 from Amsterdam today, 200 from Utrecht.' Not only those of us who have witnessed the whole thing from the start talk that way. One night in August, a batch came in from Amsterdam, in pyjamas or underwear, without shoes, and the old without dentures. Most were shipped off again next morning. We immedately whipped round the camp for clothes and managed to collect quite a lot . . . Yet the few Amsterdammers left in the camp rejoice whenever it is the turn of the provincials to go and they themselves are spared a little longer."

On October 1, our FK man felt terribly worried. Another 1,000 were due to leave next day, and there was great fear that many of the old inmates would have to make up the number. At 3 p.m. he heard the "good news" (*sic!*) that another batch was coming from Amsterdam—he and his comrades could "breathe again". "Nobody gave one thought to all the horrors awaiting the poor deportees next morning."

On October 2 there are no entries. On the 3rd we read: "I shall

[1] R. Hoess: *Kommandant in Auschwitz* (Stuttgart, 1958), pp. 176–8.

[2] *Fliegende Kolonne* (Flying Column).

always remember this day. It has been quite indescribable." (He was referring to his desperate attempts to sort out the luggage of all the people from the labour camps.) "As women and children were crammed into the barracks, all hell broke loose. No one could find anything or anybody; men, women, children and rucksacks were all one inextricable confusion . . .

"None of them had had anything to eat. People stood about outside and asked: 'Has my husband got here yet?' 'Where are the women from Amsterdam?' Or in voices charged with bitter hatred they told us all the wonderful things the Jewish Council had promised them about this camp. These people detest us, they think it is our fault they have no food or washing facilities, no bed or even a share of one. But what can we do? What can we possibly say to these wretches, who have every reason to be angry? Some of us began to shout at them, and that was unforgivable. There were scuffles outside the huts. The whole situation was quite hopeless. No one could be found. Absolutely hopeless. We went on with the farce of sorting out the baggage, but, in fact, anyone could just pick up anything he fancied; there were not nearly enough of us to keep an eye on the things."

Somehow these extra thousands were crammed into the barracks; two people to a single bed, no chairs, and even such tables as there were had to be used as beds. Many barracks had no electric lights, in others the lights were out of order. October nights were cold on this bleak moor. In every hut hundreds of people had to find their way in the pitch dark, "or grope about by the sad glimmer of a carbide lamp . . . No wonder everyone is so terribly depressed."

Then on October 4: "Today it was even worse than last night. Or did it only seem so . . .? The rush, which continued throughout the day, is over now. Altogether some 13,000 new arrivals, on top of the 2,000 already in the camp. Lorries and trains poured in from all directions and spat out their human cargoes—what the SS would call a splendid operation. Yet for us it was nothing but confusion . . . The people felt completely helpless and deserted . . . And here we were, trying to do our best for them. You might just as well try to bale out the ocean with a soap-dish."

And there they were—husbands and wives looking desperately for one another, everyone searching for his chattels . . . Most of their things were still stacked in Hooghalen and even farther afield. The road from Hooghalen to Westerbork was crowded with cars and carts taking luggage to the camp or so at least it was said. But . . . "today is Sunday, few cars and farm-carts are abroad, and tomorrow many deportees—we do not know precisely how many, but I think at least half—will have to leave without their luggage. Not only men and women, remember, but babies in need of clean nappies. I wonder if the farmers thought of that when they refused to drive on a Sunday?"

"October 5: A day of real horror. I can't imagine a worse one." Some 1,700 people were driven to the train by the gendarmes; they all went along "mechanically, as though in a dream". And when they got to the train, it turned out that the transport was incomplete. "It so happened that this very morning, some 200 to 300 women had come with their children to join their husbands. Their luggage had been left in Hooghalen and was expected later. The women were waiting in a side-lane near the camp entrance, guarded by gendarmes. When Dischner, the German Camp Commandant, heard that the trains were not full—that is, the standing room was not crammed to capacity—he gave orders for all the women to be registered and then hustled off to the station. The unsuspecting victims, waiting anxiously to be reunited with their husbands, gladly gave their names. But when, instead of being let into the camp, they were shepherded to the station, the awful truth began to dawn upon them. They all began to scream and some offered resistance. Dischner hurried to the scene and made liberal use of his riding whip." (According to some reporters, this man, a brute at all times, was also drunk on that occasion.) "Some of the gendarmes, too, kicked and pushed the women. A few succeeded in escaping into the camp; the others, particularly those with children, were shoved remorselessly into the train. The whole thing was horrible enough to behold, but worse still were the frightened screams of the bruised women and children, whose only wish was to catch just one more glimpse of the husbands and fathers from whom they had been separated for so many months. There were women from every rank of society and of all ages, though most were working-class wives between twenty and forty. Some were warmly dressed for the journey, others, who had clearly not been given enough time by the police, were in the flimsiest of dresses and slippers . . .

"Their screams attracted a gang of men, who were busy road-building near by, and some of whom suddenly recognized their wives. They raced to the spot, broke through the police cordon and, unable to bring their wives back to the camp, tried to board the train themselves. To make room for them some of the luggage had to be thrown out. When the train left, the whole platform was strewn with suitcases, rucksacks, perambulators and other articles. We rejoiced—it is an awful thing to admit, but I intend to tell the whole truth—once the train was finally out of sight. The whole thing had been too much for even our hardened nerves. The routine deportations left us almost unmoved, but this one was something infinitely worse.

"In the afternoon, I had to sort out the women's luggage, with the aid of a list. Men, anxious to discover whether their wives were among the deportees, crowded round me. Some gave horrible groans when they saw their wives' and childrens' rucksacks in the heap, and thus realized that their families were on the way to Poland; some appeared calm. But all alike clenched their fists in impotent rage. Some decided to volunteer for the next transport; others begged me at least to send the luggage on the next train . . ."

Our FK man next saw to the luggage strewn about the station: "I stood there in the darkness and rain, guarding their pitiful belongings, forlorn on an empty platform. If they could only speak, what tales of woe would these bags not have to tell? Here is the suitcase that I handed to an old woman only yesterday—and when I gave it to her she tried to kiss me. Now it is lying about and she is gone for ever . . ."

On October 6 he was too busy to make any entries, but on Wednesday, October 7, he had a breathing space. What had he been doing for the past twenty-four hours?—opening countless rain-soaked parcels in an effort to save what food in them had not been spoilt: food that had been lovingly packed and still bore such messages as: "To Father, with love" or "*Bon appetit*, my darling". There were moving letters, too (he had to read them to find out whom the parcels were for, since the outer labels had been soaked and were illegible). Often the contents had been saved up for years against just such an emergency, scraped together with great difficulty by some woman who wanted to help her husband. "We unpacked it all and sorted out the contents as though they were ordinary boxes in a grocer's shop . . ." Our FK man made a few further entries, and mentions another transport that was to take place on the 9th. The rest is silence. Of course, the deportations went on.

We must describe one other incident, if only because it touches new depths of infamy. It occurred on February 8, 1944. Four days earlier, Camp Commandant Gemmeker had sent a Telex message to *SS-Sturmbannführer* Zöpf, telling him that though Westerbork's population had been reduced to some 6,500 Jews, the hospital "still" contained some 900 of them. So, of course, it was "urgently necessary" to "organize the deportation of these Jews". He added that the presence of so many patients called for an unnecessarily large staff "which could have an inhibiting effect on the flow of deportees to Auschwitz". "I have the impression that, once the more radical deportation of sick people is ordered, all these Jews will suddenly regain their health and no longer seek refuge in the hospital." Gemmeker accordingly recommended that 400 to 500 patients be sent to Auschwitz, including cases of scarlet fever, diphtheria, jaundice and tuberculosis. The only ones who might remain were those of whom one could say "with certainty" that they would die within the first few hours of the journey. Even Gemmeker could hardly suppose that these were merely shamming sickness.

The transport of February 8, 1944, was made up of 1,015 persons. It included "no more" than 268 sick people; clearly Gemmeker did not reach his target of 400 to 500. When asked about it after the war, he protested that the initiative had come, not from him but from The Hague. He could not quite recall why he had failed to make this clear in his Telex message. He did, however, concede that the message was strangely worded, though the passage about those who would die within a few hours was obviously a typing error. What he had really meant was three to eight *days*. He would never have dreamt of sending people who were seriously ill on a long journey. The writer, a layman in medical matters, leaves it to those better qualified to judge whether or not a person whose death is expected within three to eight days must be regarded as seriously ill. And the scarlet fever and diphtheria cases? Here, too, Gemmeker had a ready explanation: such cases were "as a rule quite well in body during the second phase of their illness". Moreover, their removal helped to reduce the danger of infection in the camp. True, the patients travelled "in cattle-trucks, like every other transport", but were there not separate wagons for different kinds of infectious cases? Moreover, the sick could actually lie down. And so the apologia went on . . .

Eye-witnesses tell quite another story. Dr. Spanier, the head of the camp's medical department, may be right when he claims that no one in the trucks was actually dying. But many were so far gone that they hardly knew what was happening to them. According to P. Mechanicus: "Men of the Special Service, driving open, horse-drawn carts, loaded the stretcher cases as though they were so many coffins. All the while, wet snow was falling out of a dark sky, covering everything in white slush . . . A bleak winter morning . . . Children with scarlet fever and diphtheria . . . sick children from the orphanage . . . Of all these diabolical transports, perhaps this was the most fiendish . . ."

## ORGANIZATION

We turn now to daily life inside the camp. It is necessary to insist upon the obvious: a camp, however good, is a place of forced confinement; few if any of the inmates would have gone there from choice. In Westerbork, moreover, the barrack atmosphere was, as we saw, made still more cheerless by the bleak surroundings. According to Herzberg:[1] "The wash-houses were dingy, the barracks lugubrious and overcrowded, the sleeping accommodation unsalubrious and rudimentary; the lavatories and latrines were disgusting, the overcrowding unbearable . . . and the camp as a whole was hideous, hideous beyond description, just like every camp run by the Germans . . ."

Wieleck's more detailed account[2] confirms this impression. Westerbork was a filthy, ugly place. The only remark the writer feels disposed to add is that Auschwitz and Birkenau were still dirtier, more hideous, stony and hard. Westerbork, at least, was built of wood.

Everyone at Westerbork was struck by the fact that the place was so highly organized. "Organization" immediately makes one think of Germans, who seem to have a peculiar genius for that sort of thing. But if the organization of Westerbork was a German achievement, it is only fair to add that it was built upon foundations laid by German Jews.

Kurt Schlesinger, who must be considered one of the prime movers in this first community, wrote after the war that the inmates themselves decided to organize the camp under a Jewish leader, for fear of having a worse one inflicted on them. When the Germans took over, the organization was left practically intact; it was even thought

[1] Herzberg: *Kronick* . . ., p. 200.
[2] Wielek: *op. cit.*, p. 195.

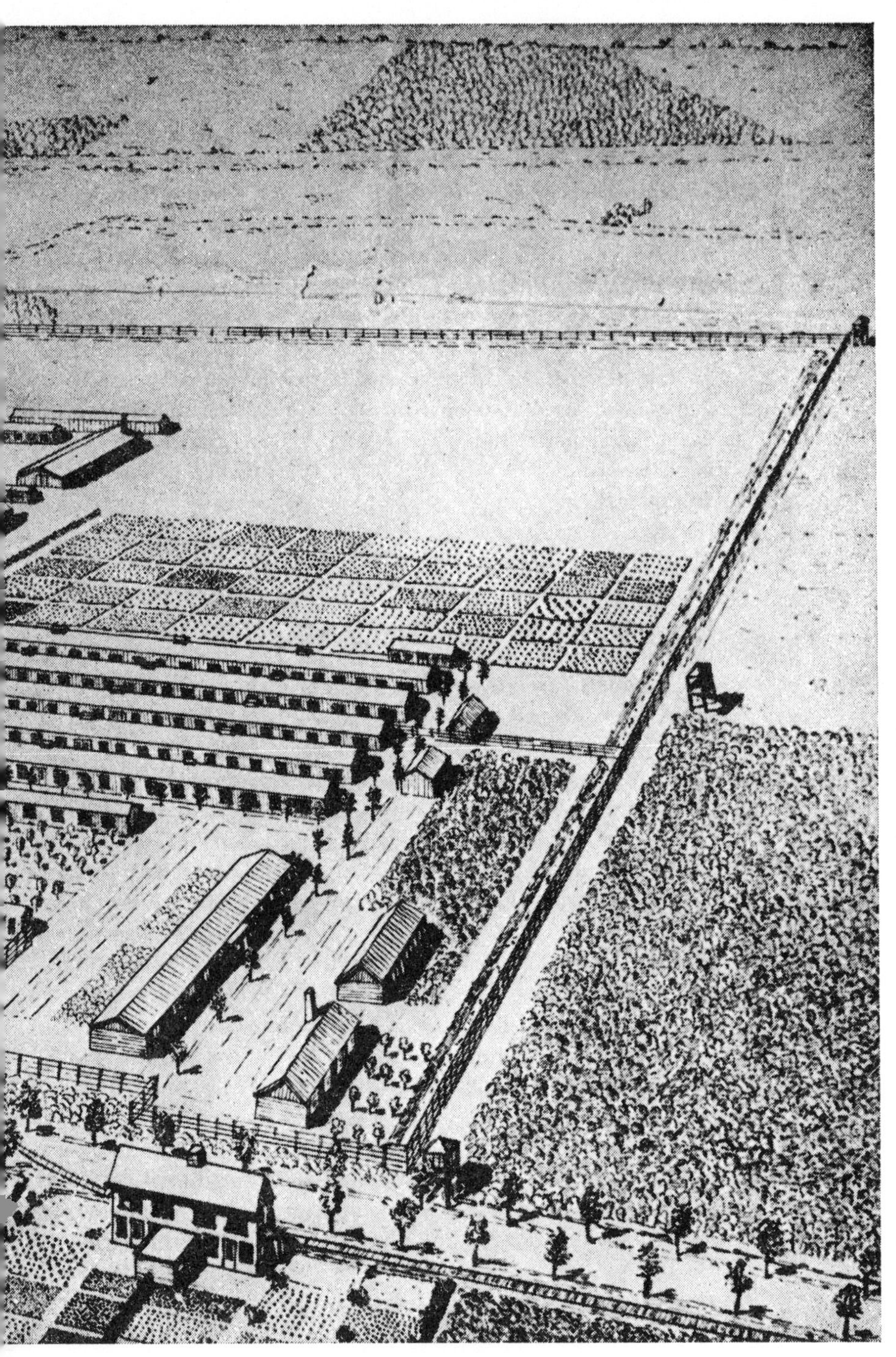

Plan of Westerbork camp.

unnecessary to bring the dreaded SS in to run the camp. According to Ottenstein, this self-reliance proved "successful to the very end", though the reader will be able to form his own opinion as to that. One point, however, is indisputable: this pre-German organization worked with maximum efficiency throughout—we have only to think how many hundreds of German personnel would have been needed to remove 100,000 Jews so smoothly and, so to say, silently, from the country.

Let us, then, look more closely at this organization, particularly at its hierarchy. The camp boasted a number of administrative sections (*Dienstbereiche*), each with its own leader and deputy; in addition, there were a number of *Dienstleiter zur besonderen Verwendung* (Section Leaders for Special Purposes), not attached to any particular section.

All these camp leaders would regularly foregather, exchange opinions, discuss internal matters and receive official notices and orders from their German masters. "In this circle, there was a great deal of manoeuvring for position and very many differences of opinion and attitude," says Ottenstein, of whose reports we have also made liberal use in what now follows.

Before examining the activities of some of these sections, we must note that when Gemmeker became the Camp Commandant, he did introduce a few slight administrative changes. His Camp Order No. 3 of January 25, 1943, gives us a clear picture of the prevailing conditions and a glimpse of the moving spirits among the Jews in the camp. We quote only from the last paragraph of this Order: "Section Leaders are personally responsible for seeing that everyone under them works to his full capacity, and will take all appropriate steps to that end." The reader need not be told what happened to those who disobeyed.

Nor will he be greatly surprised by the parallel between the behaviour of the Jewish camp leadership in Westerbork and the Jewish Council in Amsterdam. In both cases there was a semblance of autonomy—just as much as it suited the invader to permit. In both cases there was a proliferation of tasks, affording a maximum number of staff a measure of temporary immunity. But, if anything, the Westerbork leadership was even less effective than its counterparts in Amsterdam in opposing the German demands. They tried, of course, but here, at this last Dutch halt on the journey to destruction, the pressure was much greater. Here, the awful truth about collaboration—an ever-decreasing number of Jews helping to deport an ever-decreasing number of their fellows—stood out still more starkly, not least because at Westerbork this task was carried out with such exemplary efficiency.

Our brief review of the several administrative sections will do scant justice to the swarms of men in departments and sub-departments that merged imperceptibly into one another.

First of all, there was Section I, the Camp *Kommandantur*, with a welter of subsidiary divisions, including a Building Bureau, a Purchasing Section, a Messenger Service and an Outside Labour Office (we are picking at random from Ottenstein's catalogue). The Outside Labour Office was in charge of the various teams put to work beyond the camp but not released from it; usually the families had to be left as hostages. Here, too, there were all sorts of groups and sub-groups with special leaders and deputy leaders.

The second main arm of the organization was the actual Administration (Section II), whose tasks included the registration of newcomers and the compilation of sundry lists. "Probably the most important subdivision of the administrative section was the Central Registry. It kept cards giving full particulars of every inmate: his personal data, his camp history, including complaints, exemptions, hospitalization, barrack number, etc. The Central Registry also had to compile lists of deportees, based on German directives. In another index the cards of all deported, dismissed, escaped or deceased inmates were preserved." These indexes and files provide the historian and statistician with invaluable material.

We cannot here consider every other subsection of the Administration, and shall again pick only a few at random. Singularly enough, Westerbork had a Housing Bureau, though such "housing" as it allocated was generally a dirty barrack with two, or more usually three-decker bunks. But then there were also a few small houses allotted to highly privileged people and affording the only privacy that was obtainable in Westerbork. "There were incessant quarrels about the work of this Bureau," says Ottenstein. It is hardly surprising.

Some sections—for instance, the Central Food Distribution Bureau, the Central Registry, etc.—were under non-Jewish direction.

Two peculiar features of the camp were the *Lawa* and the *Larka*—short for *Lagerwarenhaus* and *Lagerkantine* (Camp Warehouse and

Camp Canteen). In the warehouse, camp inmates could make many purchases, including "household articles", toilet requisites, toys and even flowers. In the canteen, they could buy food that was not normally available—fish, cucumbers, pudding mixes, lemonade powder and so on. This was all the more strange because many of these articles had long since disappeared from the rest of the Netherlands. The privileged few who went home on leave could present their astonished families with what had come to be regarded as unheard-of luxuries. Bunches of flowers and little plants in pots were just the thing for birthday presents—particularly to one's section leader. One witness says that the amount of money spent in the canteen was quite astonishing, the more so as the inmates were not supposed to have any. The explanation may be that the Germans found it convenient to turn a blind eye in this respect—all that mattered to them was that the Jews should *leave* without any money. They even tolerated the existence of a so-called Exchange Bureau. Perhaps stranger still was the existence of a camp café with a string band and two crooners from Amsterdam, known as "Johnny and Jones".

The camp Post Office was another very busy section. We have said that some luxury goods could be taken out of the camp. Far more important were the incoming parcels; psychologically—each parcel was a sign that one was still remembered—and physically—the contents provided a change from the monotonous camp menu.

The Westerbork division of the Jewish Council deserves special consideration. For long it was led by Dr. S. A. J. Wachtel, a man of universally acknowledged probity, who had formerly been the Westerbork representative on the Jewish Refugee Committee; for reasons that are not entirely clear, this fatherly figure was replaced in 1943 and sent on to Theresienstadt in 1944.

In July 1942, that is to say when the deportations began, the Jewish Council opened a special department to deal with the financial affairs of the inmates. For a while the officials in this department enjoyed a certain measure of liberty; they were paid a salary and could spend their leave in Amsterdam. Ottenstein observes that this alone was enough to anger their less fortunate brethren, who too readily forgot that these men formed a vital link with the outside world—often illegal, but no less indispensable, for instance, when essential documents had to be fetched from Amsterdam and The Hague. When the Jewish Council itself was dissolved, its Westerbork division also disappeared. Vestiges survived in the form of the so-called Contact Commission, whose tasks, though ill-defined, were closely related to the work of the *Antragstelle*, of which we shall have more to say.

The records are loud with complaints against the Contact Commission. Its four leaders were said to live like princes, to stuff themselves with good food, to shower expensive presents on their families and friends, to be utterly corrupt. In short, the "Cognac Commission" provided living proof of how camp existence might pervert otherwise good men. Ottenstein, more circumspect about it, merely says: "Now, as then, there are many people who have hardly a good word to say about the work of the Contact Commission." On November 22, 1945, an official investigation reported that the accusations of bribery and peculation "certainly could not be substantiated", and characterized as merely "tactless" the style of living enjoyed by these officials in the camp. More than this, the four men concerned, who spent the spring of 1945 in Amsterdam in the hope of being exchanged for German prisoners abroad, made a secret deposition with a local notary, in which they gave a very detailed account of their own activities in the camp. They claimed that, at imminent peril to themselves, they had made frequent attempts to sabotage German transports and to hinder the enemy in other ways. To do so, they had had no choice but to use means that were bound to discredit them in the eyes of their fellows. They could not, for instance, make the German camp officials merry without dining and wining themselves—the end justified the means. The official investigation explicitly says that the Contact Commission "risked their own lives by the illegal methods they employed to help others".

We have already acknowledged out indebtedness to Dr. Ottenstein. This is perhaps the place to give the reader some idea of his character and stature.

"With great humanity, integrity, unselfishness and frankness, Dr. H. Ottenstein was a fine example of what a man should be . . . All his actions bespoke a noble, lofty and magnanimous soul. All too often he was powerless to help those who came to him in their hour of need, yet no one ever doubted that the will to help was there . . . Everyone felt this man's greatness of heart . . ."

To the writer who has had to delve into so much inhuman cruelty this rare spirit must, as Shakespeare said, "like a star in the darkest night, stick fiery off indeed", and there can be few who would not echo the sentiment.

In January 1942, during one of the "evacuations" of Hilversum Jews to Westerbork, this German-Jewish immigrant, then in his forties, arrived at the camp, together with his family. His academic eminence was rewarded with an office job—he was made responsible for registering the steady flow of new arrivals from the West. No effort to be of service to them was too humble or too great for Dr. Ottenstein. His efforts were directly responsible for the emergence of the *Antragstelle*, already mentioned, which was to become one of the most important departments in Westerbork. For it was the *Antragstelle* that applied for exemptions on behalf of many Jews doomed to deportation. In other words, the *Antragstelle* was a sort of Westerbork *Expositur*, the last straw at which one could clutch.

Ottenstein's staff would ask everyone coming into the camp: "Are you married to a Gentile? Have you any children? Are you a half-Jew or a quarter-Jew? Are you a Portuguese Jew? Are you baptized?—if so, when? Are you of foreign nationality—and can you prove it? Do you have a South American passport? Or a double nationality? Do you have close relatives abroad? An immigration stamp? Special qualifications? Have you done active military service? Are you eligible to go to Theresienstadt? Is your name on the Barneveld list? On the Palestine list? On any list that might help you? Are you in poor health? Is your wife pregnant?" And so on and so on.

Even those who had to say no to all these questions, and these were legion, must not give up hope. If they could only find a new pretext, however flimsy, they could, by all means, come back to the *Antragstelle*. Those who did so were immediately taken to the *Antrags-Vorbereitung* (Document Preparation Section), which helped them to get the necessary papers as quickly as possible. From the data thus obtained, another department would draft the petition and the whole process often went on deep into the night, up to the very moment of departure. Not a few were, indeed, snatched off the trains, just before the whistle blew.

The scene at Westerbork was sombre in the extreme, but nowhere more so than in *Dienststelle 3*, the Special Service Corps. This Corps was formed in March 1942, even before the Germans took over, under the Dutch Commandant Schol. It used to parade regularly for inspections by high dignitaries from The Hague; in between these great occasions it acted as a sort of camp police. Camp Order No. 27 of April 23, 1943, specified a new uniform for this Corps, known as the OD (*Ordedienst*, Special Service), and also for the FK, the *Fliegende Kolonne* (Flying Column). Henceforth, the OD would wear green overalls and the FK would wear brown ones. All other camp inmates who had so far worn those colours must now change to blue. OD men had until then been issued with red arm-bands. Now they were given special OD signs to place on the left breast. FK men might retain their yellow arm-bands, but must "keep them clean and firmly in place".

The OD, mostly Jewish ex-soldiers or young men, were drilled on military lines. An important part of their duty was to guard the punishment block. A great many of those who came into the camp were found guilty of some real or imaginary transgression; if so, they were sent to a special barracks, closely guarded and completely isolated from the rest of the camp. They were subjected to all manner of humiliating treatment—the men had their heads shaved, the women's hair was cropped, they all had to wear special clothes and so on. There is some evidence to suggest that approximately 10 per cent of all new arrivals in Westerbork were punitive cases—nearly 10,000 of them. Three out of four of these incorrigibles were deported. 1,750 were "rehabilitated" in the camp, and only 350 were dismissed from the camp or freed after the Liberation. Apart from the punitive barracks there was also a prison, a small stone building with detention cells, the notorious Barrack No. 51. To it were sent those guilty of the most heinous of crimes—such as trying, or even being suspected of trying, to escape. No one could help them, not even the *Antragstelle*; the prisoners saw no one except the SS and rumour had it that they were abominably maltreated.

Then there was the so-called Punishment Squad, which had to do hard labour outside the camp and then come back to punitive drill inside. In charge of this work, the Germans placed a special commandant, whom even gentle Ottenstein refers to as a "vile creature". According to Wielek,[1] he used to beat his prisoners and inform on them to Gemmeker. One report about the camp says that: "This man, a former German officer who had acquired Dutch citizenship, never tired of shouting and tormenting. He took great pleasure in inventing the most sadistic punishments and revelled in reporting people to the German commandant or to the gendarmes . . . whose

[1] Wielek: *op. cit.*, p. 235.

creature he was." In another document, the Jewish chief of the OD fares no better; he is called "probably the most hated person in the camp, one who took an absurd pride in his uniform and in his repulsive barrack-room manners and tone, a tone that even the Germans did not find it necessary to adopt".

According to Ottenstein, the OD consisted of 20 men in July 1942 (2 Netherlanders, 18 Germans); of 60 men in October of the same year (42 Netherlanders, 18 others); of 182 men (106 Netherlanders, 76 others) at its peak in April 1943; and of 67 men (32 Netherlanders, 35 others) in February 1944.

This was the "Jewish SS" as Mechanicus has called them. "The whole camp hated them like the plague." The FK was little better; though mainly concerned with the baggage, they were only too often assigned the sort of jobs which allowed them to lord it over their fellows. This corps, too, was small and remained so: in 1942–3 it counted eighty to 120 men; after September 1943, it dwindled to sixty and later to twenty-five. In September 1944 it disappeared altogether. The FK man already quoted had this to say:

"Many envy us. But the price we have to pay is high. We must stand idly by while our friends, acquaintances, comrades and families disappear into the trains . . . One day it will be our turn, and then there will be nobody to console us with the kind of fairy-tales we have been telling the others . . ." And: "How long can things go on like this? Some day the war will be over. Where shall we be then—if there at all? Can we ever again become like other people, after all we have been through? They say you can't afford to worry too much if you want to live, but we have seen far too much to remain calm. We can only wait and see."

A plea of mitigation for the OD has been entered by Ottenstein who points out that they were held personally responsible for any escapers, and also got the most obnoxious tasks—we need only to remind the reader of the rape of the Apeldoorn Mental Hospital. The OD boasted bullies, cowards and lickspittles, but not a few of them tried secretly to help their fellow-inmates, whatever the risks.

Strange though this may seem, Westerbork also ran to a large hospital, with 1,725 beds, 120 physicians and a general staff of over 1,000. There were isolation units, a mental ward, a first-class dispensary (liberally stocked by the Dutch authorities), a kitchen for special diets, stores, a special section for making anatomical diagrams, an orthopaedic clinic, hairdressers, photographers, laboratories, a welfare department, a chaplain's room, first-aid posts, a department of hygiene, dental clinics, messengers, porters, a postal service, magnificent operating theatres, and almost everything else that can be imagined. There was an out-patients clinic, open from 7.30 a.m. to noon and from 2.30 to 5.30 p.m., with special sessions for workers from 6.30 in the morning and from 7 to 8 in the evening. A patient might choose whichever doctor he preferred. Pediatricians were in attendance from 2 to 4 p.m., Sundays included. Visiting hours were from 7 to 7.50 p.m. daily. All inmates were X-rayed, as a precaution against tuberculosis, and immunized against typhoid and para-typhoid fever; their blood groups were recorded. The doctors would confer together every week and these consultations were conducted at the highest scientific and clinical level.

Most sources mention the Head of the Medical Service, the German-Jewish Dr. F. M. Spanier, who had a strange influence over the Camp Commandant. (The camp knew that the two men were both citizens of Düsseldorf and believed that this must have something to do with it.) Whenever the commandant entered the doctor's room, the latter did not even stand up—something that no one else would have got away with. Indeed, Spanier was sometimes said to be all-powerful, or, as one of his colleagues put it, to wield the powers of life and death. Some said that he did so in an arbitrary, not to say sinister, fashion. Were not trained nurses deported and their places filled with unqualified people who had "the right connections"? Yet the very same source concedes that "in this hospital one could meet doctors and nurses who, disregarding their own needs and anxieties, worked day and night with the utmost devotion, to do whatever they could for their fellow-men".

Do what they might, there was one thing that neither they nor their all-powerful chief could achieve—save the patients from deportation. So, when all is said and done, they were merely keeping people alive for the gas-chambers. At the time, of course, none of them knew it. The very presence in the camp of so splendid—and that is surely the word for it—a medical service seemed to give the lie to all the pessimists. Surely the Germans would not go to these lengths if the ominous rumours about Poland were true? But we know now that there was method in the Germans' madness.

In Ottenstein's survey, the next point of interest is the "Internal Service" with its barrack-leaders, kitchen workers, cleaning service and food distribution staff. "An important duty of all these camp officials was to settle the many quarrels, which arose from the lack of cooking facilities. There were also numerous disputes over accommodation. Thus, the so-called Old Age Home was much sought after—it was furnished with two-decker, not three-decker, bunks and even with tables—real luxury that. Some barracks were more "fashionable" than others. These were not for every Tom, Dick and Harry, though the Angel of Death was, alas, a frequent visitor there too. Ottenstein has given us a very detailed description of the barracks themselves—wooden huts, measuring some 275 feet by 33 feet and 16 feet to 20 feet high—and also of the little houses we mentioned earlier. The great attraction of the latter was, as we saw, their privacy. Less fortunate couples, too, were able to snatch an hour together there. The not so small token of their thanks, at one time took the shape of a pot of jam, and "pot of jam" acquired a certain overtone in the camp, something about which Dr. Ottenstein is discreetly silent.

We turn next to the "External Service" with its Agricultural Section and various Gardening Sections. For some time it also included the Flying Column, various excavation groups and others which had to maintain the railway line between Hooghalen and the camp.

Then there was the Latrine Column—made up of five people, according to a report of December 20, 1943. The External Service also had the services of four bricklayers, a number of carpenters and cleaners, a special old people's section employed on shelling peas and beans, and, last but not least, a veterinary surgeon. He was in charge of all the animals inside the camp and was kept busy all day. The private gardens of the camp staff, on the other hand, required nothing less than teams of three men and four women.

The Agricultural Section tended the farmland outside the camp and fed the horses and cattle on it. To give just a few figures, on December 20, 1943, the livestock of the camp comprised 10 horses, 7 cows, 6 calves, 10 sheep and 98 pigs; in addition, 51 head of cattle were being reared for slaughter. The crops consisted of potatoes (35½ acres), rye (22¼ acres), oats (15 acres) wheat (2½ acres), mangold (3 acres).

The Internal and External Services both had a share in running the workshops. Section VII was responsible for the so-called building department (with a special drawing-office), the electro-technical division, the garage and boiler room, the bath-house, telephone exchange and sewage works. In this Section worked furniture-makers, blacksmiths, locksmiths, watchmakers, opticians, book-binders, black-out experts and decorators. They were often used by the Germans for work outside the camp as well.

Section VIII was in charge of mending (clothes and shoes). This Section boasted a tailoring department, a dress-making shop, etc., and took outside commissions for stuffed toys and uniforms. "Thanks to the special buyers, there was always a good supply of leather for our soles." This section also helped to get up the costumes for the camp cabaret. Towards the end of 1943 the clothing department alone employed a thousand people; a special dress-maker and knitter worked continuously for Frau E. H. Hassel, the commandant's mistress.

We must on no account fail to mention the small stocking-repair shop, with special machines for mending ladders; thanks to this service, women from the camp could arrive in Auschwitz with glamorous stockings. A less romantic workshop manufactured makeshift windows—bits of glass cut into small discs and fitted into cardboard.

Section IX looked after the kitchens: here the servers from all the barracks would arrive with their little trolleys, load all the food into large mess-tins, and afterwards bring them back empty. The kitchen itself was excellent—modern, large and bright. The food it produced was, by contrast, monotonous in the extreme. Here, someone has annotated Ottenstein's report with the pertinent question: "What about the section leaders?" We can only say that some of them frequently dined on fare that would have flattered the most delicate palate.

Sections X and XI (Provision and Woman's Section) will be discussed in another context.

Section XII, the Industrial Department, was for long the largest in the camp. However useful this may incidentally have been to the inmates themselves, one thing is certain, it was even more useful to the Germans. The writer does not for one moment suggest that the Jews in Westerbork could hope to escape from a problem that faced every Dutchman in those years. Suffice it to say that the camp leadership was well aware of the implications. We might add that according to a 1945 report the German war potential was not very greatly strengthened by this work. In any case, the Jews in Westerbork were certainly entitled to do everything in their power to keep as many people as possible in the camp, even if it meant work of this sort. That they succeeded in this to some extent, we gather, for instance, from a letter written by Fiebig, the German Delegate for Non-Ferrous Metals, on February 29, 1944. It was essential, he insisted, that a number of Jews should remain in Westerbork, otherwise the salvaging of scrap metal would suffer.

This scrap metal included debris from aeroplanes that had been shot down. To break it up called for an army of workers—and exemptions. The labourers even made up songs about it. As one of them has put it: "We smashed the metal to a rousing chorus." Older people helped to remove aluminium foil from its backing and earned their exemption in that way. Men on punishment were given the dirty job of dismantling old batteries and extracting manganese. Others, again, busied themselves with sorting all sorts of refuse. Many pieces of furniture from Jewish houses in Assen and near by were sent to the camp for repair. All the wireless sets the Germans confiscated in the province of Drente ended up in Westerbork. According to Ottenstein, this must have been how news from the outside world circulated so freely, despite all prohibitons and threats of dire punishment. One inmate had a set hidden under the floor of his work-place and wired to the electric stove. "He listened by means of half a head-phone which would quickly disappear up his sleeve on a piece of elastic if anyone came in."

It is now high time to say something about non-Jewish officials in the camp, the Dutch and German overseers and gaolers. The fact that their number was so small need not, as we saw, be put down entirely to the German genius for organization, though far be it from us to belittle the ability of the Camp Commandant, Gemmeker. It was his aim to turn Westerbork into a model camp and he largely succeeded in doing so. And did he not also succeed in sending tens of thousands of Jews to their deaths with the minimum of resistance and unseemly disturbance?

We need say little about the Dutch leadership of Westerbork since, as we saw it was replaced by the Germans in July 1942. Captain Schol, the Dutch commandant, was generally regarded as politically reliable, anti-Nazi and anti-German, but even he was not always equal to the onerous task of leading a camp of this sort. His helpfulness, though occasionally marred by lack of self-control (Ottenstein says that he sometimes had bouts of tropical fever) was generally appreciated, but alas, he was not there for very long.

We must also mention the gendarmerie and other officials on guard duty outside the barbed-wire fence. From such data as we have, it would seem that many of them had no great relish for their work. But there were some consolations, food, for instance. Judging from their bills of fare, we may safely say that they went short of very little, even in the hunger-winter of 1944. Westerbork was also a convenient rest centre for a number of German officers, particularly when reverses at the front increased their mobility to other parts. The troops of uniformed security men even brought along its own *Brigadeführer*. It was this man's child who said to a Jewish gardener: "You'll be going away before Daddy comes, won't you? He can't stand the sight of Jews" (see p. 323).

As for Gemmeker, the Camp Commandant, he was executive, legislature and judiciary all in one. He had three predecessors: *SS-Sturmbahnführer* Dr. Deppner, "a typical SS leader, cold-blooded and remorseless, a murderer masquerading as an officer", *SS-Obersturmführer* Dischner, "the usual brutal type of SS man, no brains and usually drunk", and Inspector Bohrmann, "a nonentity". Oddly enough, Gemmeker prowled about the camp for quite a few days before revealing that he was the new Commandant, no less. We had better take a closer look now at this latter-day Haroun Al Raschid.

## GEMMEKER

Albert Konrad Gemmeker was born on September 27, 1907, and trained for an administrative career in the police. He joined the German Nazi Party on May 1, 1937, and the SS on November 1, 1940. On August 25, 1940, he came to The Hague as Personnel Officer to the Commander of the Security Police. Some time in 1942 or 1943 he was made an *Obersturmführer*. When asked for his opinion of the Jews after the Liberation, he brought out the stock Nazi propaganda: the Jews were parasites, wanted to rule the world, were unfair competitors, were responsible for Germany's defeat in the First World War, were corrupt, grasping, etc. No, he never met any before he took command at Westerbork and yes, once there he had to revise his opinions about the "Jewish menace". Then why the deportations? A necessity of war. "Naturally," he had not the faintest idea what became of them when they got to Poland.

We learn more of Gemmeker from the reports of camp inmates who knew him at close quarters for several years. Once more our chief authority is Ottenstein who, as leader of the *Antragstelle*, saw more of him than any other Jew. He thinks that Westerbork might have done worse: Gemmeker had no patience with brutality, was approachable and, above all, incorruptible. Compared to other camps, where torture was a daily pastime, Westerbork was positively "civilized". However, Ottenstein adds, Gemmeker was devoid of natural feeling, capricious, and, in short, incalculable. He also remarks on Gemmeker's memory: if anyone was ever brought to his notice, it was a case of once seen, never forgotten. Like most of his counterparts elsewhere, this petty princeling lived like a grand pasha. He had a large house—outside the camp of course—with any number of camp inmates at his beck and call: "tailors and shoemakers, a goldsmith, a cabinet maker, architects, draughtsmen, gardeners, chauffeurs and domestic staff—all kinds of first-class craftsmen worked for him and his friends. He was treated by Jewish doctors and dentists, and even had a Jewish hairdresser—privileges he did not permit to any of his SS subordinates, for a while, anyway. He had his own chicken farm and also flowers from greenhouses specially built for him."

An incalculable creature, we have said, and the more feared in that, exemptions apart, he could, says Harster, please himself as to whom he deported, so long as he filled the quota, that is. An Amsterdam jurist who saw a good deal of him at Westerbork alludes to Gemmeker's "highly personal" standards for deciding who was Jewish. Where women were concerned, he would always tell by the hips. The secret of this form of divination remains hidden from the present writer. Members of the Contact Commission, who for some time had to see him almost every day, found Gemmeker a strange enigma, outwardly very correct and indeed more like an English sportsman than a hulking Hun—"very polite, very dangerous". He never screamed at anyone. In his own admirable words, Gemmeker gave the Jews "the best treatment that was permissible under National Socialism". After his impeccable conduct in discussions with them, Mechanicus tells us members of the Contact Commission would often have to remind themselves that this man was, in fact, their mortal enemy—"lest they succumb to his singular charm". Mechanicus also says that, after the war, there were many who wanted to hang Gemmeker—with a velvet cord. A doctor has said that this was "no ordinary criminal but a gentleman crook". Thus when a group of gypsies was brought into the camp, Gemmeker said to him: "Ah, doctor, how different these people are from you and me." And would he have the goodness to disinfect the twenty-seven violins these people had now been relieved of? (The gypsies themselves, after much infamous ill-treatment, were packed off to Auschwitz.) According to Herzberg,[1] Gemmeker was not always so soft-spoken. He ranted and raged, punished, tormented and even shot people. This is fully borne out by the records. "And yet, when those arriving in Westerbork asked: 'What sort of man is Gemmeker?' they were often told: 'At least he has been decently brought up . . .' Quite often, he would speak to Jews on equal terms, particularly to the Palestine Pioneers, for whom he felt some respect . . . Occasionally, he even gave the impression that he no more hated Jews than a butcher hates cows."

Indeed, this man sometimes looked on the Jews with a positively amiable eye, and never more so than on the day of their departure to the East. They were not unappreciative. As one said when boarding the train: "Once I had a Camp Commandant who used to kick people off to Poland. This one sees them off with a smile." And yet he was considered to be fair and ready to act on all legitimate complaints. Moreover, as one Jewish lady has stated, he would never speak of anyone as "a Jew" but referred to them simply—even to his superiors and colleagues—as "camp inmates".

Not, as we said, that he was always quite so amiable. Thus once, when a six-year-old child, with a serious ear infection and a temperature of 104, was due to board the train, he was asked if this was not a suitable case for exemption: "No, the child will die anyway." Another witness spoke of him as a killer in kid gloves. A woman tells that when her daughter, watching a transport of children, said: "And this is what they call civilization," Gemmeker ordered her to get into the train there and then, although she was not due for deportation at the time. "I have only one wish left," the mother said, "and that is to see Gemmeker swing."

But did he swing? On April 11, 1945, when the Canadians were approaching, he left the camp for Amsterdam, where for a time he continued as an administrative officer. In May 1945 he was arrested. There were a few major charges and several minor ones. He got off with ten years in prison, for had he not always treated the Jews at Westerbork with some degree of propriety?

That, at least, is more than can be said for his "assistant" Frau Elisabeth Helena Hassel, if most witnesses are to be believed. She,

[1] Herzberg: *Kronick* . . ., pp. 203–4.

too, came from Düsseldorf, where she was born in 1905, and, like Gemmeker, arrived at Westerbork in October 1942. She became his secretary and, except for an interval of about one year (August 1943 to July 1944), remained so to the end. They conceded that they had been lovers, a fact that was in any case notorious throughout the camp. Frau Hassel's fatal influence on Gemmeker's decisions probably sprang from violent jealousy—woe to the Jewish woman to whom Gemmeker paid the least attention. At the cabaret performances above all, she would anxiously follow the course of Gemmeker's roving eye. Though she was not his official deputy, he nevertheless entrusted her with certain responsibilities. When he was absent, she would simply take over, to the great dread of the inmates, who knew that this rabid Nazi would show even less mercy, and grant even fewer exemptions. After the Liberation, she protested that she had felt strong compassion for Dutch Jews throughout the war and had gone out of her way to help them whenever possible. If so, no one can say that Frau Elisabeth Helena Hassel wore her heart on her sleeve. But let us return from this precious pair to the Jews, whose very lives depended, for two and a half interminable years, on their every whim.

## THE CAMP INMATES

Before we discuss the daily life of the Jewish population of Westerbork, we must remind the reader that, from about the middle of 1942 to the end of 1944 (when the mass deportations stopped), 100,000 people passed through the camp. They arrived, they stayed a while, they went. All who came, however heartbroken to be there at all, had one desperate desire: to stay on. For beyond Westerbork lay the unknown, "the undiscovered country from whose bourn no traveller returns". Only with that terrible prospect always before him can the reader have even the least notion of what Westerbork meant to its pitiable inmates.

We know how it all began. After weeks and months of mounting tension, the future inmates surrendered to the authorities or were dragged out of their houses. They were packed into trains for Northern Holland, where they found themselves in a world unlike anything they had ever known. They had heard about the camp, of course. Some had said it was like a prison. Others had called it a zoo. The threat of Mauthausen lay heavy on them all. And now they were actually there—at Westerbork.

Every new arrival in the camp was registered by a special Reception Department (*Transportaufnahme*) and at a special reception desk (*Aufnahmetisch*) where a number of forms and cards lay waiting for him. The Central Distribution Bureau would then take charge of the inmate's ration cards. After these formalities, the arrival would be passed on to a classification desk (*Listentisch*), where more details had to be given. Next he had to go to the accommodation bureau, not a mere desk this time but a separate office, where yet more forms had to be completed. Next came the *Antragstelle*, which we have mentioned before. This was the procedure devised by Section II, but, though elaborate, this was by no means the end in the inquisition.

Section II "showered kindness" on the newcomers. These words of Ottenstein's are not inappropriate because many, if not all the officials treated the arrivals to coffee and encouraging advice. They had been dumped in the camp, over-tired, deeply unhappy, dirty, hungry, thirsty, and there were many sick or old people and little children among them. As to these last, one eye-witness says: "For days, these poor mites had been kept in prisons or in the *Schouwburg*, amidst dirt and lice, until finally they were squashed into the train as cargo for Westerbork . . . Children without parents! Babies in cribs, their napkins unchanged, hungry, thirsty and screaming. Many of them were already ill. Then there were older children, large and small, some fearful and shy, others almost stupefied with exhaustion."

We have said that the Accommodation Bureau was not the end of the reception line. Next, the new arrival was ushered into the Quarantine Barracks, where he had to stand in line: "The whole thing took hours, more long hours of waiting before one was shown to one's place and could drop exhausted on to a bed." One of the worst features of this tortuous ordeal was the interview with the "Westerbork branch" of Lippmann Rosenthal & Company—the firm that practised robbery under the guise of banking. No one had a good word to say for its staff. Ottenstein, who first called their conduct sickening, later amended this to "outrageous". The Jewish Council in Amsterdam had no illusions about what this Company was doing in the camp. A document of November 16, 1942, gave a list of everything these "bankers" required their "clients" to deposit with them. In brief, it was whatever had even the slightest value. "A jar of butter per person," Amsterdam warned, "is more than will be admitted into the camp." Shoes, fountain-pens, watches ("if of good make"), dainties, none of these were safe. And the whole operation was accompanied by ranting, raving, kicks and every kind of humiliation: the victims were ordered to strip and to kneel down while their bodies were searched. And this to people who were already so tired that they could hardly keep their eyes open. "With their top boots, smart attire, well-groomed heads, manicured nails and reeking perfume" these "officers" would pounce upon their helpless prey. And not only the "officers". The team also included a female who was responsible for searching the women. Our sources agree that she was if possible worse than the men.

The leader of these bandits was brought to justice after the war. Had he manhandled anybody? Perish the thought! Well, he might have given someone a little push, no more. Had he stolen? Certainly not, though he might perhaps have accidentally acquired a fountain-pen. Had he slapped anybody? Yes, but only to "make some hulking young fellow carry an old lady's luggage". The colleagues who gave evidence at his trial admitted that he had occasionally been "harsh" and "overbearing", but hastened to add that he was not really a bad fellow. Of course, they had never seen him raise his hand in anger. What with so much money and so many trinkets being sent to Amsterdam from the camp, was it surprising that a few paltry articles or banknotes had been mislaid? The accused himself added that he had only accepted this work under protest. Once engaged in it, he had tried to do his duty to the best of his ability, so that "my work will stand the most critical examination". Obviously a dedicated man, this.

We have had several occasions to speak of the OD, Westerbork's Special Service Corps. It was men of this group who received the newcomers, accompanied them from department to department, willing to help, perhaps, but harassed by their leaders (who, in turn, were bullied by the Germans). They were touchy, peremptory. The fact that they, too, were wearing the star did not prevent them from swearing at other Jews. Take this description of incoming transports: ". . . The whole thing was sheer farce. They would usually arrive from Amsterdam at 2 p.m. At 1.30 the whistle would blow to summon all concerned to the Registration Hall. Before that we would all slick ourselves up for the occasion. I shaved, put on my best suit, a clean shirt and white coat, gave my shoes an extra rub and then went off to join my other friends on registration duty. The women went to

Westerbork

Children outside their school barracks

LEFT: Gemmeker (left) and Aus der Fünten

BELOW: Gemmeker, companion and dog

The *Boulevard des Misères*

Lippmann Rosenthal squad at cards after a successful day's plunder

The camp orchestra

Jewish youth in Westerbork

some trouble, too—rouged cheeks, painted lips, a spot of nail varnish. We would all have a quick drink together before we started, and over a cigarette—of the kind that had long since vanished from the shops—work out what we would do afterwards. Occasionally we would seek out someone with a relative in the kitchen, whom we would invite to join us, so that we could share a modest crust together. At half past one we would all saunter over to the Registration Hall. Some people would be there already. There was no strong drink, sad to say, but you could buy lemonade and there were cigarettes under the counter (at 20 guilders a packet). We flirted, made dates, swapped the latest news. We all had the right stamps, so what could happen to us? True, we were Jews, too, but somehow we felt more like super-Jews. If we ran short of news we fell back on scandal. When Schlesinger (the head of the Jewish camp administration) came in, we would all bow and give him the full German treatment, all heel-clicking and flattery. We did it as a mere stratagem, and believe me you needed a great deal of that if you wanted to go on living . . ."

Yes, it was all very sociable. You could smoke, the women could make up . . . And then the thousands of the plundered came into the camp, filthy, exhausted, only to find this waiting for them. It is hardly surprising that few of them were favourably impressed; their dislike of the OD would have turned into undisguised hatred had they but known that members of the same efficient team would one day put them on the train for Poland.

Ottenstein's vivid account of the devastating effect of the weekly deportations is only one of many. They invariably took place on Tuesdays, caused desperation, panic and then hopeless apathy, followed by sudden relief. The very people who had been showering all sorts of gifts on the deportees would begin to squabble violently over their remaining possessions. By Tuesday evening everything was smoothed over; sociability and peace reigned once more. Wednesday and Thursday were days of calm optimism and euphoria. On Friday, fears again began to stir: was the exemption really safe, was the "list" on which one figured about to be scrapped? On Saturday everyone was edgy. On Sunday they were agitated. On Monday the panic spread and everyone would run around in circles, looking up relatives, trying to get information, keeping an ear to the ground. And on Tuesday—the next transport. And then a new round—but let Mechanicus paint the picture for us:

"Friday, July 30, 1943. Last night I took my first evening stroll through the camp after dark. The *Boulevard des Misères* (the main street of the camp) looked like a Promenade: tittering girls, arm in arm, mingled with more sedate pedestrians, others lounged about at street corners. In the centre of the camp, a mighty chimney stretched up into the lilac sky. On one side, groups of people romping, on the other, pairs of lovers disappearing into the shadows, stealthy as cats. In one little street, the cabaret orchestra could be heard playing *Bei mir bist du schön*, a popular hit proscribed in Germany because of its Jewish origins. The whole scene was like a primitive shanty-town, set right in the middle of the prairie, and making its first contact with 'civilization'."

All the same, the camp inmates were anything but a homogeneous group. They differed socially, culturally, denominationally and nationally and, what is more, in the degree of "protection" they enjoyed. Most of them as we have pointed out, did not "go" to Westerbork but were "taken" there, after having been forced, step by step, to abandon the life they knew, often losing their self-confidence, self-respect and self-discipline in the process. If we want to form a complete picture of the mood and rhythm of life in the camp we must remember that, unlike life outside, it did not begin with birth and end with death, but with forced removal. This subject is dealt with at some length in Adler's important reflections on Theresienstadt.[1] The writer must leave it to the psychologists to judge how far Westerbork was the beginning of the process of demoralization or depersonalization so characteristic of the Polish terror camps. One thing, however, is certain beyond all doubt: erosion of personality threatened—and often consumed—the inmates, with a resulting decrease of energy, initiative and mental power, and a gradual decline of vitality into mere vegetation. This may not have gone nearly as far as it did in Bergen-Belsen, but it is nevertheless something that must be taken into account—notwithstanding the strange fact that trains leaving Westerbork would sometimes be filled with singing people. Anything, absolutely anything, could happen at Westerbork . . .

Let us turn next to the positive side. A doctor once assured the writer that he had the time of his life in this and other camps. There were no decisions to be made, one just existed. Of course, there was the chance that one might die—but that was always a chance any-

[1] H. G. Adler: *Theresienstadt 1941–1945* (Tübingen, 1960).

way. This stoic view may not strike the reader as a very positive philosophy, and he may well find more inspiration in the attitude of Rabbi Levisson, nicknamed "Rabbi Simchah"—the man of joy, who found so much solace in his faith. The Palestine Pioneers, as we said, bore themselves proudly. (Gemmeker simply could not understand it, he had never met such characters in *Der Stürmer*.) There were great friendships, deep affections: "One's friends were the only redeeming feature in a concentration camp," said a deported woman. "No effort was too great for them in one's hour of need." Another woman had this to say of her arrival in Westerbork: "I was overjoyed to find that I was with Jews again, among my own. In the room [where she had been hidden for two years] Jewish friends were only memories. How one had longed for them! And now here they were, a community, people who shared one's suffering, who could tell you what had happened to your other friends. After the registration we were taken to the Punishment Block, given a bed and told what work we would have to do next day. And already, friends at large in the camp knew about our arrival and sent or brought us some of the things we most needed. They knew they might be punished for it, but they did it just the same. They even wrote little notes to give us courage. I shall never forget the bread that arrived unexpectedly from a friend. Others sent pyjamas and tooth-brush, even an aspirin tablet. Someone sent a chemise—all these precious gifts made us feel wanted again, part of a community."

Still, one had to perform prodigies of adaptation. "One could even cultivate the feeling that this was a summer holiday, spent under somewhat difficult circumstances. It was all a question of imagination." That, at least, was the view of Mechanicus. And a doctor took a similar view: "Life in the camp was sometimes positively enjoyable. We had a cabaret and, for a time—for instance, round about Christmas 1942, when no transports went out—the place was like a holiday camp. Here there was no need to be afraid of raids, of entering the wrong shop, or of breaking the curfew. On New Year's Eve we were allowed out until 1 a.m., while the people in the rest of the Netherlands had to be in by 10 p.m." After which we are not surprised to find references, at least in the earlier camp proclamations, to small front gardens outside the barracks, in which a variety of flowers were grown. Flower-gardens in Westerbork. What an idyll!

One factor above all kept up the camp spirit, namely the rumours spread by the JPA, the "Jewish Press Agency", as people liked to call the camp grape-vine. At the end of November 1942 it was whispered that the deportations would stop in mid-December. In August 1943 came a report of Hitler's resignation and of his replacement by a triumvirate. The whole camp was agog. And so the rumours went on, month after month, and even the most intelligent people—in Westerbork and outside—would credit them. They believed because they wanted to believe, because the alternative was too horrible, because in any case the war must end some time . . .

Perhaps this is the place to say something about camp humour, often harsh, cynical, and appealing simultaneously to the sense of the ridiculous and the pathetic. The names chosen for the main street of the camp were *Boulevard des Misères*, *Rachmones* Street or *Tsores* Avenue (Hebrew for pity and misery). The camp itself was often called Westerbork-*les-Bains*. What is "a privileged position"? ran one conundrum. Answer: "A front seat in a cattle-truck for Poland."

Ottenstein even mentions a special camp language, consisting chiefly of Hebrew or Yiddish words "mixed with terms taken from Nazi jargon and with private allusions". An MSW man was somebody who blew his own trumpet ("*Macht sich Wichtig*"); the barracks of the baptized Jews were called *Schmaddenau* (*schmadden* = to become converted); the NB (Emergency Squad), became known as the *Nebbich* Brigade (the Sorry Squad); the leader of Section I was known as "Leather-Arse" (he wore leather trousers; no reflection on Elijah); a cabaret revue had the title *Dogs are Lucky* (the implication being that men were not). It has often been remarked that this type of "gallows humour" was more than mere fun. By "restoring the link with the past it did something to alleviate the unbearable present". It "helped one to rise above one's situation and thus became a bulwark against despair". It was no less essential than food and a bed, and like these two it bore the unmistakable stamp of its environment.

Humour could tide one over all sorts of crises, but in the long run, of course, it could not prevail against the flood of misery all around, against the wretched life everyone had to lead, against dirt, noise, back-breaking slave-labour, lack of privacy and, above all, the ever-present threat of deportation. Someone has compared it all to Job sitting among the ashes, but Job, however sorely afflicted, did not have to squat in the midst of a swarm of screaming, quarrelling people. Job was in no danger of deportation. And last but not least, Job could argue back.

Of course some people were less able than others to endure camp life. One eye-witness had this to say: "Some lived like pigs. I saw one pick up a cat and throw it into a pot of soup. That shows you what depths of degradation we had sunk to." Camp life broke or twisted people's spirits, undermined all norms; it made one prickly, unmanageable, difficult and disagreeable. Some of the quarrels were all too well grounded, as Mechanicus has clearly shown. According to Ottenstein, however, many of the inmates refused to feel guilty, arguing that the enemy, not they themselves, were responsible for the condition to which they had been reduced. That was one way of looking at it. Mechanicus describes a scene in Barrack 85, which housed the privileged men from Barneveld. One day, a camp guard came in and ordered a grey-haired gentleman to doff his cap to him. "Do you realize that I was a general in the Dutch Army?" asked the old man. "General, my foot. As far as I'm concerned you're just a bloody Jew." And the guard, a former meat-porter at the municipal abattoirs, sent the old man's hat flying. "Damn you," muttered the General through clenched teeth. "I'll teach you to swear at me," yelled the porter, and the old man got three weeks in Barrack 67, where he did slave-labour under the supervision of the OD. Of course, he knew he had done nothing to feel ashamed of but, as Ottenstein himself had to admit, ". . . this sort of knowledge did not avail anyone against feelings of dejection, hatred, anxiety and misery, longings and hunger". And there were many, indeed, who suffered hunger and who were tormented with longing.

Westerbork was not a healthy place—least so for morals. Men and women were thrust indiscriminately into each other's company, with the threat of deportation constantly hanging over their heads. "Utterly dissolute," one reporter has called them, adding that "there were few marriages in which both partners did not commit adultery. This was the inevitable result of the lust-laden atmosphere gripping the camp." Perhaps Herzberg was nearer the truth when he said : "People used to couple with sensuous, mindless abandon."

Westerbork was unhealthy in other respects, too. Many people have complained about "the complete loss of respect for other people's property". Yet what could you hope from men who had been stripped of most of their possessions before ever they came near the camp? How could one ask anyone to respect other people's belongings in a world where nobody owned anything at all? Taking other people's things, "organizing" them as it was called, was held to show a sturdy self-reliance. Food, especially, was pilfered on a grand scale. Not only in Westerbork, of course, but in Westerbork it was all so simple—here, the only place where people could hide things was under the bed.

Two more reports are of special interest. One was written by Mechanicus on August 5, 1943, and appears in his published diary.[1] It is the story of a day no different, in most ways, from any other. A day in Westerbork, beginning with weariness after a restless night (fleas and other insects saw to that). At 6 a.m. 300 men started to shuffle to the wash-house and the three WCs: "There was no room to put down one's things or to hang up clothes or towels. The floor was filthy, slushy and full of puddles. People began to squabble." That was how the sordid routine always began. "At 8 a.m. someone screamed the order 'Everybody out. Get the place cleaned up.' Then came a few hours of aimless lounging about outside, with a lot of boring small-talk, all of it repeated *ad nauseam*. At 10 a.m. the barrack was clean, or at least swept, but still as grubby as the inside of a tram, the floor oozing with mud. Everything one touched was dirty and dank. Groups of people with nothing to do would sit around, gossiping, flirting, writing. But the clack got on one's nerves. It was impossible to write. If only one could shut oneself up, find a bit of privacy." As for walking about: "One soon gets to know everybody. At about ten o'clock, you pass a few friends: 'Any news? How long do you think the war will last?' One of them says it will be over tomorrow, another that it will go on for at least ten years. You would like to say, 'Go and drown yourself,' but you have to keep a civil tongue in your head, otherwise you get a bad name." Back in the hut they quarrel about whose turn it is to use the stove, about opening or closing a window, about the laundry, about God knows what besides. Then it is time to fetch the food. Afterwards you wash up in cold water and everything is still greasy. A nap? "Chatter to the right and to the left—a woman, reliving one of yesterday's squabbles or starting a new one—two malingerers lying in bed and shouting across to one another—a young man and his fiancée, who have climbed into the upper bunk, giggling together—a group of men wrangling about politics or playing cards and conducting the usual post mortems. Someone else is busy knocking in

[1] Mechanicus: *op. cit.*, pp. 330–2.

nails. Or there is some other sort of infernal row going on . . . And all the time the din keeps getting worse, worse, worse . . . it is nearly midnight before everyone has quietened down."

Mechanicus was a trained journalist who knew his job. Let us now quote from the private letter written by an ordinary young man whom his friends had accused of making cynical and sarcastic remarks in his previous correspondence. He does not deny it, but goes on to ask: "How else can you defend yourself against all the misery, dehumanization, egoism, degeneracy, in short against this breeding-ground of human vice? Would you feel any different if you saw people robbing one another, saving their own skins by making others miserable, swindling and cheating one another, and, if, to top it all, you yourself were nearly round the bend with worry—would you feel any different if you saw hundreds of people herded into wooden barracks, sleeping on iron bedsteads without proper mattresses, often without even a decent blanket? Would you feel any different if you saw crowds constantly streaming into the camp, old people, blind people, invalids, robbed of everything, exhausted, all too often kicked and beaten, and torn away from everyone they love? Would you feel any different if you saw "our good old gendarmerie" hounding the self-same people into trains, towards a future that is no future at all but certain death? Would you feel any different if you saw young people being packed off to work as slaves for the enemy far from their homeland? Would you feel any different if you saw people having sex in front of all and sundry, utterly without shame, without the least pretence of reticence? Would you feel any different if *your* life were governed by three things only: fear, despair and never-ending misery?"

The young man went on to say that his cynicism was merely a protective shell, a means of self-defence. Nor was he entirely free of Jewish self-hatred. His mother was in the sick-bay, where she had to do her morning ablutions in a pan. "By some peculiar irony of fate, the kitchen had been declared kosher and these damned Jews were so steeped in their antiquated ways that, of course, they would not hear of anyone washing there. What, in a religious kitchen! How do you like that?—It's enough to make the angels weep blood. I have sworn two things. If I should somehow live through this rotten war I won't see or speak to a Jew for at least a month. And I will never, never, eat stew again. And that's about all you do get here . . ." He, too, admits to stealing—cigarettes: "I'd break open drawers to get them." He goes on to list a whole catalogue of miseries . . . "Once again I've started an uproar. They got going on one of their interminable prayers again when I wasn't expecting it. When that happens, you always have to cover your head and stop writing. Well, you know me. Right now, they are all sitting or rather sprawling on their beds, chanting and mumbling away, and here am I, with my under-pants over my head but writing furtively all the same—what you might call a sensible compromise."

The young man has much more to say, but it does not make very pleasant reading. He, too, disappeared in the gas-chambers.

It is against this sort of background that we must judge the desperate attempts of many inmates to keep up their flagging spirits. The marvel is that any of them succeeded. Learned men somehow found the heart to give lectures on all sorts of subjects. Section X, the welfare department, managed to lay on religious services, no easy matter, since there was compulsory work even on religious festivals. Ottenstein actually speaks of a "very active religious life in Westerbork". Even in the death-camps in Poland, the Jews would often have to make music, so it is not surprising that Westerbork could manage a full-scale concert now and then. We still have some of the programmes, on which, of course, Mendelssohn and Saint-Saëns loom large. Mechanicus reports that at first the orchestra was also allowed to play "Aryan music". That was soon put a stop to.There was light music, too, of course, and last but not least, the cabaret.

This cabaret was a singular feature of life in Westerbork. It is no exaggeration to claim that for costumes, sophistication and performance, it was then the best entertainment of its kind anywhere in Holland. Most of the artists had come to Westerbork towards the end of 1942 or early in 1943. They quickly formed themselves into a company which put on variety shows, chiefly but not only for the camp inmates. Their much-coveted reward was temporary respite from deportation. The Camp Commandant was appreciative of their efforts, afforded them all kinds of facilities and appointed himself script-censor. In fact, Gemmeker was so keen that it proved possible to form a choir and a ballet troupe. Moreover, when the artists were finally deported, they were lucky enough to find themselves at Theresienstadt and not in one of the Polish death camps. Admittedly, Gemmeker's patronage was something of a mixed blessing. Not content with vetting the scripts, this accomplished ringmaster would often "drop in" during rehearsals and give everyone the benefit of his advice. We have said already that the wardrobe was dazzling. We might add that, according to one witness, 25,000 guilders went on dressing the first production alone. Another witness had this to say: "In the fourth year of the war, when everything was in short supply and millions of people had to walk about in rags, at a time when the inhabitants of many German cities had lost their all, when millions of people were suffering and dying in Polish and other concentration camps, Westerbork could put on a show whose decor would not have disgraced a world capital. Special buyers were allowed to scour the country for precious dress materials and returned with rolls of velvet for the curtains. The stage was enlarged, the most modern lighting equipment brought in . . ."

"First nights" were great events at Westerbork. The whole company was on its toes, the dancers cavorted to the latest jazz hits —on a stage knocked up with timber taken from the synagogue at Assen. Glittering dresses, fantastic wigs, elaborate scenery, all added glamour to the occasion. One such scintillating first night took place after a day that had seen another deportation. An altogether splendid affair it was, too, and there was a scramble for tickets. Another time, Gemmeker had the entire hall redecorated—to celebrate the deportation of the 40,000th Jew. For this festive occasion, he invited forty high officials from The Hague. Forty Jewish girls must wait on them. The girls chosen were the least Jewish-looking and were told to take off their stars. In the rows immediately behind the guests of honour sat the Jews—many of whom had, only a few hours before, been nearly out of their minds with grief for their loved ones.

Gemmeker was a regular patron at his favourite entertainment. He would often command special performances, at which the section leaders and their ladies, dressed to kill, had to put in an appearance: *Le roi s'amuse*. Even a court fool was not lacking, for one of the artists was dressed up as a jester. Some of his gags have come down to us. One evening, when Gemmeker and his crew were occupying the front rows as usual, he piped up: "Gentlemen, we are all descended from Abraham—I am *so* sorry, this only goes for that lot at the back." Such a crack would go round the whole camp next day. The hit tunes, too, were on everybody's lips. Like the great Maecenas that he was, Gemmeker would sometimes treat his artists to cognac and cigars after a performance and chat with them until the small hours. We still have a few of the old programmes and, poor-quality lettering and bad printing apart, no one would connect them with life in a prison camp. A possible exception is the programme of the *Grotesque Revue*, given in June 1944 and appropriately sub-titled "Quite Round the Bend". The star turn, after the interval, was a "real" opera, "Ludmilla, or Corpses on the Conveyor Belt", which naturally had a happy ending. Not so Max Ehrlich and Willy Rosen, who starred in this show and were mainly responsible for it. A few months later they were transferred from Theresienstadt to Auschwitz, where they were gassed on arrival. To the Nazi conveyor belt there was no happy ending.

Etty Hillesum tells us what happened during one deportation: "Men of the Flying Column, in brown overalls, were bringing up the luggage in wheel-barrows. Among them I discovered two of the Commandant's court entertainers—a clown and a song-writer. Here they were, having landed the safe job of transport duty. Only a few evenings previously the song-writer's fate still hung in the balance as he burst his lungs to please an appreciative audience, including the Commandant and his retinue. He had sung: '*Ich kann est nicht verstehen dass die Rosen blühen*' (I Do Not Know Why the Roses are Blooming) and other topical ditties. The Commandant, a great connoisseur of music, almost had to wipe away a tear. (One eyewitness spoke of the tormented look on the performer's face. As someone else said, that night he had indeed to sing as though his very life depended on it—J.P.) He got his exemption. He even got a little house, where he now lives behind red check curtains, with his peroxide-blonde wife. She sweats out her days behind the wringer in a steamy wash-house. He himself walks about in khaki overalls trundling a wheel-barrow piled high with the baggage of his fellow-Jews. He looks like a walking corpse. And over there is another court entertainer, the Commandant's favourite pianist. Legend has it that he is so brilliant that he can play Beethoven's Ninth Symphony as a jazz number and that certainly is saying something . . ."

And so people flocked to the revues. In Theresienstadt they even held a masked ball on the eve of a transport. Shades of Edgar Allen Poe! In Westerbork they did not go to quite such lengths, but here too the scene was sufficiently macabre. Too much so for some people. Others could only absent themselves from felicity awhile. Sooner or later they were drawn there by the all-too-human craving for sociability and the wish to lose themselves for an hour or two. After all, what else was there to do? Some of the luckier ones, particularly the young, could engage in outdoor sports. A programme from

August 1943 includes gymnastics, sprinting, high-jumping, long-distance running, putting the weight, tug-of-war and various competitive games between the different Sections. On September 25, 1943, there was a boxing tournament, with proper referees, seconds and doctors in attendance. The heaviest contestant weighed 11 stone 9 lb. and the lightest, 5 stone 13 lb. One can only hope that the losers were not sent straight off to the gas-chambers, much as short work used to be made of gladiators who bit the dust in the arena.

By Camp Order No. 86 of August 3, 1944, the orchestra was disbanded and the cabaret closed. Some time earlier, on June 20, 1943, a Sunday, Mechanicus had observed a more grisly show: "A macabre procession of crippled, blind and arthritic men and women hobbled into the camp, supported by members of the Reception Service. The whole thing was a heart-breaking sight." This Breughelesque scene, a parade of the sick and dying, was a fitting reminder to one and all that the Germans spared no one from labour service—not even the halt, the lame and the blind. A woman aged 102 was, according to one report, at first allowed to stay in Amsterdam, but . . . "if we we left her alone, she might last to 110," joked the German officer in command of the detachment that took her to Westerbork, much to the amusement of his subordinates.

This is a fitting introduction to Section XI, the so-called Women's Section. Lest this name conjures up any romantic visions, we must say at once that these women's chief tasks were peeling potatoes and doing similar chores from morn to night. All the same, they would often sing at their work and, as Ottenstein tells us, "quite a few camp choruses were first heard in the potato kitchen". Some of the women also worked as domestics in the houses of the SS.

And their children?

"For our children—poor mites—the train departures were the events of the week; every Tuesday, my little boy would badger me: 'Mummy—please!—*can't* we go on the train?' And when it was grandmama's turn, he jumped for joy on his bunk: 'My grandma's going on the train, but your's isn't!' " So wrote a mother who, with her son, was fortunate enough to escape the longed-for joy-ride.

Another mother was heard to say to her little daughter, who made a face at the pudding: "Just you mind—if you don't eat your pudding you'll have to go off on the train without me." (This fine example of Westerbork education is quoted by Mechanicus.)

Luckily this was not all the children learned at Westerbork. There was, in fact, regular schooling and a child welfare service and, if we read Camp Order No. 40 of July 14, 1943, we might well ask ourselves if children under fourteen lacked for anything at all. The Child Care Department looked after those between one and six throughout the day; all children from six to fourteen attended classes and there were even special inspectors whose task it was to apprehend truant pupils. Occasionally, however, there would be no school, for instance when the hut was wanted for other purposes, or, more often, when there was a lack of teachers. That tended to happen on Wednesday mornings, the day after a transport, before there was time to "recruit" new instructors. Ottenstein tells us that there were three schools, one founded before 1942. For the benefit of the earliest arrivals, German was the language of instruction here, but "all" languages—except Dutch—were taught. There was also an elementary school and a Church school for baptized Jews.

We have just spoken of old people, women and children, but these were by no means the only special groups in the camp. To a large extent, indeed, inter-group tension was characteristic of life in Westerbork. This is hardly surprising when we consider the motley composition of the camp. There were veterans and new arrivals, religious Jews and non-believers (both of various shades), the baptized of various denominations, Zionists and anti-Zionists. Dutch Jews and foreigners. There were even some Nazi sympathizers. We have a dossier on a half-Jew threatened with deportation, formerly married to a Jewess, but divorced too late to lose his perilous status as a full-Jew. But was not his father a rabid NSB man, whose five other children were "dedicated pioneers of National Socialism"? As such, they "held several offices and were unswervingly loyal to the ideal of pan-Germanism". The father moved heaven and earth to get his "Jewish" son out of Westerbork, appealing to Seyss-Inquart and bringing pressure to bear on Fischböck and Rost van Tonningen —in Westerbork the absurd was positively commonplace . . . And what could you expect in a camp where there were good and bad, men of character and scoundrels, rich and poor, celebrities and humble workers, assimilationists and traditionalists, Catholics, Protestants, Liberals, Socialists and Communists? There were rifts, and rifts within rifts, fierce resentment of the others merely because they happened to be different.

Even before Dutch Jews, with whom this work is primarily concerned, were shunted off to Westerbork, there was serious tension between the German-Jewish inmates and the Dutch-Jewish leaders, whom they distrusted. The evidence goes to show that this tension often amounted to open hatred. The chief target was Professor Cohen, then one of the leading members of the Committee for Jewish Refugees, but he was by no means the only one on the black list. Anyone who has read Cohen's *Zwervend en Dolend*, in which he describes his work at the time, will understand the feelings of the German Jews but will certainly not share them. Let us simply say that people did things and adopted attitudes that must have been intolerable to the German refugees and the assurance by *Mevrouw* Colijn that she and her husband, Dr. H. Colijn, a former Prime Minister, felt great compassion for them, was small consolation for the general failure to take action on their behalf on the usual plea of political expediency. And how utterly inhuman, to their ears, must have sounded the words of C. M. J. F. Goseling, a minister in the pre-war Dutch Government—who was later to die in a concentration camp himself—that "a concentration camp is not a death sentence"! That was his excuse for refusing to allow more of them to enter Holland. How craven must have seemed to them the attitude of those, ostensibly concerned with their welfare, who yet would not stand up for even the most elementary human decencies! Truly, the early arrivals at Westerbork would have needed saintly dispositions if they were expected to maintain a tolerant objectivity and abstain altogether from that natural anger which their would-be benefactors were quick to interpret as base ingratitude. However, these benefactors were all too soon to have a taste of Westerbork themselves. When that happened, it was small wonder that the early arrivals did not welcome the newcomers with open arms.

As we have said, similar differences made themselves felt even outside the camp. But in a camp where the various groups were thrown inextricably together, friction was, of course, far worse. Various witnesses even speak of unbounded hatred. When the first Dutch contingents arrived, the men already in the camp felt that their hard-won privileges were being threatened and reacted accordingly. The Dutch Jews, in their turn, resented being thrust into a camp full of German-speaking people. The first camp order, passed in 1943, made German the compulsory language for all documents, forms, stamps and signs. Camp instructions and orders would sometimes be issued in both languages, but never in Dutch only. The new arrivals soon found themselves at the receiving end of the "big stick" wielded by all sorts of officials, wearing the yellow star like themselves, but barking orders at them in German. German Jews were people with quite a different cast of mind and far too often showed a "German" predilection for bossing people about, dressing them down, and other parade ground manners. The two factions were at daggers drawn, despite attempts by more sensible people to establish a united front against the common enemy. These attempts were doomed to failure for a variety of reasons (which we shall discuss), but mainly because power was so unequally divided between them. To take just one instance: the deportation of Han Hollander, the best-known radio sports-commentator who held a privileged position in the camp, was clearly a direct result of these tensions. According to Mechanicus, his downfall came when his wife, after a quarrel with a German Jewess, shouted: "It won't always be like this, you know. One day we'll get even with the whole damn lot of you." The Camp Commandant who must have heard about it, quickly wrote *finis* to what Mechanicus describes as "until then the biggest success story in the camp". "That is how women bring misfortunes upon their husbands' heads," is his moral, though at that time he could not have know the full horror of what lay in store for Hollander. When this and many similar stories were told round the camp, with additional comments best left to imagination, they only helped to make bad feelings worse. We may take it that more than one Dutchman in Westerbork had visions of what someone had called "a Jewish Day of Reckoning".

The early arrivals were German, and as though that were not enough they had to behave like a caste, an oligarchy, or in Herzberg's felicitous phrase, "a nobility"[1]—knights, barons, margraves, earls, a major-domo even—all that was lacking was the *roi fainéant* and, alas, a Charles Martel. But there were scores of slaves and serfs, *taillables et corvéables à merci*, men without rights, without help and without protection. The oligarchy provided the enemy with a convenient and efficient apparatus whose willing service was to be had in return for the much sought-after respite from deportation. In this way there arose that subtle system which turned some of the slaves themselves into slave-drivers—in the eyes of the former, no better than mere collaborators. More than that, these men even

[1] Herzberg: *op. cit.*, pp. 198 f.

aped their German masters, behaving as though they themselves were pashas.

Members of the oligarchy were all in possession of the coveted red stamp, so naturally their children would often decline to play with others whose parents had not attained to this honourable degree. The oligarchs also had better houses and other privileges, which, small though they were, made all the difference under camp conditions. Being charged with the maintenance of internal order, the camp leaders would always choose the best men for the best jobs—themselves, naturally; they set the tone, ruled with a rod of iron over a staff of officials and helpers (often referred to as the middle class) and, *a fortiori*, over what we might call the camp proletariat, the vast majority who had no privileges at all. Herzberg has given us a clear picture of this sinister set-up. He tells us that the oligarchy as a whole, and particularly Kurt Schlesinger, the head man, "had the power to influence the choice of deportees". Only an influence, mark you, but that was quite enough to give them the whip hand. For, while Gemmeker himself would make it known how many Jews would have to go and when, the selection of individuals was left almost entirely to his Jewish paladins. This privilege they defended tooth and nail against all comers.

Such was the "nobility". Almost everybody else was a pariah, an outcast of absolutely no account. One of them a Jewish woman, puts it in a nutshell: "Because we enjoyed no protection, owned no diamonds, lacked the right stamps, or the right contacts among the Germans, we were only in the camp four days before we were put on the train."

All sorts of witnesses have condemned the activities of the men who thus lorded it over this little bit of Dutch soil hedged in by barbed wire. Were they really as bad as these reports make out? They were no doubt subject to many and varied temptations. It is easy to say that they should never have yielded to them—to bribes of money, goods, diamonds and last, but not least, feminine favours —that they should constantly have borne in mind that, in the last analysis, their powers derived from a source that was inexpressibly evil, that they should never have had a single thought for themselves. How few of us could do this in any circumstances, let alone over a long period and under the conditions prevailing in such a camp? Even the barrack-porter was above the barrack-dweller, for he could stay on a while longer. It is easy to say that those in power, however little of it they really enjoyed, should not have abused their position, that they should not have lost their tempers when others infringed the orders they were responsible for maintaining. How quickly, then, would they have been left to take the rap! The camp inmates may not have seen it that way but we, looking back at the events from a safe distance, can speak of the Jewish camp leadership with a measure of compassion, for we know that even the most arrogant of them was a mere pawn in the hands of those who wielded the real power in the camp, that the word of even the great Schlesinger, uncrowned king of the camp, weighed nothing against that of the lowliest SS men.

It has been said that Westerbork was a moral morass or even worse. No one can tell to what extent this is true, for when all is said and done, the vast majority of all those who tried, by whatever means, to remain in Westerbork, were sent to their deaths, and those who were able to save themselves by devious means are unlikely to be communicative. To escape from deportation, people would do anything, sacrifice their last hoarded halfpenny, their jewels, their clothes, their food, or in the case of young girls, their bodies.[1] "The most abominable wrongs were inflicted," declares another source, "for instance, all the parents of those on a deportation list would suddenly be ordered to go with their children. Not one might remain behind and yet, somehow, when the train left, the parents of X and Y (two of the Jewish élite—J.P.) were not on board . . . No one can blame a son for saving his family, but what of all the other parents? Is it right that some should be spared and others not?" How we all sympathize with Etty Hillesum's anger at the officious way in which several of the "oligarchs" flaunted themselves beside the train crowded with deportees: "No doubt the outside world thinks of us as a grey, uniform, suffering mass of Jews, and knows nothing of the gulfs that yawn between us. How could they even begin to understand?" Mechanicus, too, has much to say about the conduct of these Jewish princelings. Thus on July 9, 1943, he wrote in his diary: "One Jew went to A., a man who has a pull, and begged to be kept out of the next transport. A. looked him up and down and said (in German): 'Why shouldn't you go? You're just the sort of stuff they want.' " Mechanicus also tells us that, when one man, who had a serious stomach complaint, appealed to B., another "oligarch" to get his name taken off the list of deportees, B. told him: "The

[1] S. van den Bergh: *Deportaties* (Deportations), p. 13.

trip is just what you need. It'll help to put you out of your misery."

On Sunday, September 12, 1943, Mechanicus made the following entry: "Yesterday we celebrated a friend's fortieth birthday, a woman journalist who lives (or rather sleeps) in the women's section of my barracks, but looks after the one-room house of a camp veteran, where she usually takes her meals. In that house, six people, like the jolly shipmates they are, were gathered round a festive table—here, in this camp sunk under its weight of human misery! The menu: *hors d'œuvres* consisting of egg with salmon, followed by Frankfurters and peas with vanilla pudding for dessert. The Frankfurters were a gift from the gods: the tin merely read 'green peas', but when we opened it we found six Frankfurters inside. The guests nearly went crazy over the sausages and almost swallowed them whole. At the end of the meal (as though by design, but in fact it was purely chance) a wheel-barrow with six parcels from Amsterdam arrived from the post office, a veritable cornucopia of bread, cheese, butter, jam, truffles, writing paper and what have you. Everybody was so happy for the lucky recipient, though not a little envious. Then came coffee—real coffee from one of those providential parcels. It was sipped slowly and given the highest praise. Real coffee was practically unknown in Westerbork. While we were still at it, one of the guests, another camp veteran, rose and said: 'Fellow-guests, what would you say to a bottle of apricot brandy?' To which the host replied, without batting an eyelid: 'Yes, excellent idea.' I was completely dumbfounded. Five minutes later it appeared, a gigantic bottle, its golden fluid gleaming in the lamp-light. Soon it was sparkling in crystal liqueur glasses. We tippled and smoked. An excellent bouquet!—a glass disappears at a gulp, as though there was plenty more where that came from. Yarns were swapped about drunken fights in the camp. The woman whose birthday it was told me later: 'The bottles were brought in by the official camp buyers.' "

As the reader will readily suppose, the story of this little get-together spread quickly round the camp, and grew as it went until rumour turned it into an orgy that would not have disgraced Heliogabalus himself. So that is how they amuse themselves, these people who send others to Poland and speak German just like the enemy . . .!

We have deliberately named no names, but for the inescapable one of Kurt Schlesinger. This German-Jewish refugee was officially admitted to the Netherlands in 1939, when he was in his early forties. In February 1940 he was sent to Westerbork, where for a time he did "ordinary" work. He was then taken into the office of Dr. S. A. J. Wachtel, the head of the Administration Department, where he played an important role in the organization of the camp and, in February 1942, was appointed "Camp Elder" under the then Dutch Commandant. The Germans simply took him over, along with the rest of the existing organization. When this was reshuffled, on January 25, 1943, Schlesinger became the leader of the powerful Section II, the Administration. By a special camp decree of August 12, 1943, Gemmeker put him in charge of all the other Section Leaders. In that exalted position he remained to the end.

The records are full of bitter accusations against him. Every conceivable charge is laid at his door, above all that he was inordinately servile to the Commandant while being utterly ruthless to his subordinates and to the so-called "transportation material". Much vaguer and less provable was the charge that he was open to corruption. As to the criticism voiced by one eye-witness, that he professed himself helpless when asked to intercede on behalf of one of the worst transports, we can only say that he was probably speaking the truth. He was powerful and quite powerless at one and the same time. Thus, Mechanicus tells us that on one occasion this mighty Camp Leader was publicly dressed down by an ordinary gendarme who "revelled in his ability to make the boss of all this rabble look small".

Well, Schlesinger was small: "He stood there stuttering and stammering, while the gendarme gloated over his confusion." And this was the mighty man of whom the camp jested: "Have you heard the latest? Gemmeker is being sent to Poland. Let's hope Schlesinger can save him."

But if he could be made to look puny, Schlesinger knew how to act big at other times. This small-time German manufacturer had put on a giant's robe. We may tell the story in the words of Mechanicus, as reported by Herzberg:[1]

"One fine day, Schlesinger broke his leg. For the whole camp it was like the Queen's birthday. People would have put out flags if only they could. 'Schlesinger has broken his leg.' He had been cycling through the camp with the Commandant and they had both fallen off. Some, though highly delighted, were not completely satisfied;

[1] Herzberg: *op. cit.*, p. 207.

they complained: 'It happened to the wrong one.' Others said: 'No, it should have happened to both of them.' But the most popular comment was: 'Why not both legs, or, better still, his ruddy neck?' " (This dislike of Schlesinger notwithstanding, his bedside table was covered with fruit and delicacies from everyone who wanted to keep in his good books.) Herzberg goes on to quote Mechanicus's report of his visit to the sick-bed on October 13, 1943 (actually October 14): "Saw Schlesinger in hospital. Last night, half past eight. Room full of people. Schlesinger in a night-shirt. When he noticed me, he made a sweeping gesture, like a dictator bestowing largesse, followed by a hearty handshake, and a theatrical: 'Ah, my dear friend!' Then, throwing off the blankets with a dramatic gesture, he proudly exhibited his plastered hip, showing me with great pride that the plaster has been covered from top to bottom with pencilled scribblings, all going different ways: dedications, poems, autographs of friends and admirers. And his expression asked: 'There, what do you think of *that*? Isn't it marvellous?' I gave him a fatherly look. Every fresh visitor had to marvel anew at the plaster, as though it encased an Egyptian king, some priceless historical treasure."

We have mentioned the fact, and will have occasion to mention it again, that Westerbork received very little help from the outside. What help there was had to be clandestine and consequently few records of it have survived. Moreover, some of the helpers did not act from purely altruistic motives. There was, for instance, the case, in the summer of 1943, of a gendarme who hid a Jewess underneath the seat of an incoming train, with the idea of taking her back to Amsterdam. His ruse was discovered by another gendarme and so came to nothing; in any case, the first officer had been bribed by the woman and his actions cannot therefore be considered "illegal help to Jews" in the proper sense of the words. Nor for that matter can the behaviour of the three police officers who let two Jewesses off a train in Houghhalen, in return for their favours. Moreover, when it came to Westerbork, the illegal organizations that were so active elsewhere seem to have been strangely unenterprising. And what of our Allies? On May 30, 1944, Westerbork underwent an air attack; two people were killed and a few wounded in the Barneveld barracks and there was some damage to property. This was the only air attack on the camp and probably unintentional at that. In any case, the Jews did not think that salvation was at hand, or that the world had suddenly begun to care for them. For them Westerbork remained completely cut off from the outside world. That was probably one reason why there were so few escapes—some fantastic claims to the contrary notwithstanding. Ottenstein does not put the number of escapes higher than 210 out of a total of 106,000 inmates, i.e. at 0·2 per cent. When group after group of Jews who had gone into hiding was captured and brought into the camp, the feeling of hopelessness increased even further: what was the use of escaping when you were sure to be picked up again? And then there would be punishments and who knows what reprisals against others as well.

There was, for instance, Camp Order No. 5 of February 11, 1943, decreeing that if anyone escaped, everyone sharing his barracks would be deported, and "special measures" would be taken against the barrack leader. (According to Gemmeker, this order had to be enforced on only one occasion.)

We have said that the German system in Westerbork worked much as it did outside: Jews were made to regiment other Jews—"in their own interest". On August 23, 1944, there came a sweeping new regulation. All those leaving the camp on official business (including labour projects) would have to name five sureties, beginning with their nearest relatives. Bachelors would not, in general, be given permission to leave the camp at all. A Protestant could only stand surety for other Protestants. There were special provisions for school outings and similar excursions, and many more details to the same effect.

One Camp Order (No. 52 of October 13, 1943) announced that H. v. d. G. having escaped while working outside the camp, his mother and sister would be deported. (Needless to say, Gemmeker's defence after the war was that he had acted on orders from The Hague.) Mechanicus mentions a few other cases and adds: "On the orders of an OD man, one Jew, who was found behind Barrack 73 near the barbed wire (which was forbidden, although this was not generally known), was sent to prison and deported." Comment would be superfluous. There is also the strange case of the Jew who dodged the transport by hiding in the camp with the aid of a barrack leader. He was caught during a roll-call and deported, but survived the war.

One escape story makes us wonder why everybody did not try it, it sounds so simple. You just made a few arrangements, crawled under the barbed wire in the dark, shortly before evening roll-call, crept into a ditch, were taken by a helper to the house of a farmer who had been paid to help. What if the farmer had chance visitors? So what, you just hid in the barn. You burnt your camp papers and stars, and fixed up with false papers, you went from A to B and B to C, and so on until you finally got to your hide-out. It was almost child's play, at least as the story was told to us. Nor was our narrator in the least disturbed by the appearance of a special "Wanted" notice in the *Police Gazette*.

By way of contrast, we may quote the horrible case of four Jews who were caught while trying to escape from Westerbork on the night of September 7, 1944. Numerous eye-witnesses tell us what happened. Gemmeker ordered all four to be shot out of hand (no doubt out of pure obedience to The Hague). One, not fatally wounded, shammed dead and later made his way to the camp hospital, where Jewish doctors bandaged him up. Then they dutifully reported the case to Gemmeker, who ordered them to finish the man off with an injection. When they refused he recalled the firing squad, whereupon the doctors gave the hunted man something to make him unconscious. He was then laid out with the corpses of his three comrades and burnt together with them—unconscious but still alive. In his file, we read that he was shot "while trying to escape".

That was in September 1944, when the camp had entered its final phase, and the Germans were still clinging to the fiction that the *Führer* was hovering on the brink of victory. Meanwhile, Gemmeker continued to probe various "exchange possibilities" and to promulgate a few new decrees—a mere half dozen between August 10, 1944, and March 30, 1945. By that time it was obvious that the days of Westerbork were numbered: the store was closed down, the camp currency was scrapped, and many of those married to non-Jews were even sent back to Amsterdam. We have a number of lists giving the camp population in this final period (and shortly thereafter). On January 1, 1945, there were 670 Jews; on February 7, 742 and on March 1, 848 (clear proof that people were being sent to the camp right up to the last moment, most of them no doubt, dragged out of hiding). On April 12, 1945, there were 918 camp inmates, 909 Jews and 9 "Aryans"—this was the official number liberated from the camp, but we cannot say with certainty how many had refused to wait for the count, had refused to remain among the tragic remnant of the 100,000 who had passed through Westerbork in their time.

### DEPARTURE

"Each week the cry went up: 'This is a terrible transport.' All transports are terrible." So says Mechanicus, and so indeed they all were. Every week the train came. Without fail. Clearly the deportation of Jews had priority over victory at the front—thousands of wagon-loads of Jews were shunted off, while the fighting forces went short of supplies. W. F. Hermans[1] quotes a German as saying: "The greatest blow the Jews dealt Germany was to fill so many of our goods-wagons and cattle-trucks."

The train. Every Monday, one of the Section Leaders had to ring railway enquiries at Groningen, to find out precisely when it was due. "This man," one informant tells us, "would sit for hours at the telephone—often right through the night—until he could proudly report to the Commandant that the train was on its way."

The train. What sort of human being was it that drove the engine? Since the Dutch railway authorities did everything they knew to keep control of the system, naturally they had to play ball with the Germans, but only—they insisted—as long as the German demands did not conflict with "our most cherished principles". The trade unions stretched their principles as well, the more so since, as a resistance fighter, J. H. Scheps, unkindly put it, they knew on which side their bread was buttered. But he could not help wondering just what they felt when they heard the moaning of their passengers: "Don't you understand what they're doing to these helpless Jews? Don't you know how they torture our Jewish comrades? Have you bread-and-butter patriots never heard the voice of Rachel, she who mourns and will not be comforted for her children—the children you help to carry to their death?"

It was a waste of breath—"hardly any resistance was offered to this damnable traffic in human lives".[2] The trains went on running on time. And what, the reader may well ask, did the Enquiry Commission have to say about all this?[3] It expressed its regret at the "laconic manner in which the Railway Board and the representatives of the staff organizations reacted to the deportation of workers

[1] W. F. Hermans: *De donkere kamer van Damocles* (Damocles' dark room) (Amsterdam, 1958), p. 238 f.

[2] A. J. C. Rüter: *Rijden en staken* (The story of the Dutch Railways during the War) (The Hague, 1960), pp. 94 f., 117.

[3] *Enquiry Commission*, part VIIv, pp. 684, 694 and 748.

and Jews". The Board was all injured innocence. The question of "Jewish deportations" had been raised with them, they admitted to the Commission, but they were quite unable to recall that anyone had ever urged them to refuse co-operation. Other evidence, not surprisingly, suggests that their memory was playing them tricks. However, the Enquiry Commission did not confront the Board with anything so disagreeable as a conflict of testimony. No less an authority than Adolf Eichmann told his judges in Jerusalem that at first the trains "ran like a dream". Later there were difficulties. He did not go into details, but certainly said nothing to cast doubt on the reliability of the Dutch railway authorities. However reluctant they may have been to follow the German line, they apparently saw no sense in going clean off the rails. And so the trains ran on "like a dream".

What of the Resistance fighters? There has been vague talk of sabotage from that quarter, but we have been unable to verify it. All we do know is that the Germans saw fit to set a special guard on the railways. In Belgium that did not stop the Resistance movement ambushing a train and rescuing the Jewish deportees. Then why not in Holland, too? Was it because the Resistance knew that no matter how many engines they derailed, the Germans were so dead set on the deportations that they would have found others? Was it because the Allies failed to bomb a single one of these transports, when systematic bombardment would no doubt have made many railwaymen remember their cherished principles? "That would have made them feel something—those men who with monotonous regularity manned the engines dragging thousands of Jews with them," one fugitive wrote in his diary in October 1943. But no—not so much as "a single pint of petrol, one oil-can, or one bullet was spent on behalf of these 120,000 Jews".

One of the then Railway Regulations has been preserved to us; it was published in 1942 and laid down the schedule for trains leaving the Netherlands via Nieuweschans. At first, all the deportees left from Hooghalen, but from November 2, 1942, onwards, they could embark from Westerbork itself, whence a line had been built to Hooghalen, by Jewish labour, needless to say. Ottenstein reports that the early transports were made up of old cattle-trucks; afterwards, for a time, dilapidated carriages were used. On March 10, 1943, the cattle-trucks came back (some call them goods trains), but even then the privileged few, those destined for Bergen-Belsen or

Theresienstadt, continued to travel in carriages. The Jewish leaders in Westerbork, realizing the cruel hardship of long journeys in the trucks, made plans early in 1943 to fit them out with benches. Unfortunately, the benches were not sent back from Poland and so the travellers had somehow to make do with straw. When even that returned stinking, filthy and unusable, the only "amenities" provided were a vat of drinking water and a lavatory bucket, and just occasionally a bit of straw or thin paper mattresses for the gravely ill.

A few holes in the roofs of the trucks were the only ventilation, and the "passengers" had to squat on their suitcases and lean against the wall. In June 1943 the transports were so arranged that, according to a message reaching Amsterdam,[1] "there was room for 3·6 Jews per square metre". What the Jewish Council thought about it all we do not know, except that they decided to supply everyone leaving for Westerbork with as much baggage as possible—even if the deportees could not take it to Poland, someone in Westerbork might benefit by it and there would soon be no one left in Amsterdam, anyway. Every trainload was given a marshal and a special doctor and there was a group leader in each truck. No doubt these arrangements helped to lull the worst suspicions of those being taken to their deaths . . .

Before we trace the course of one such journey, we must first look more closely at what happened before the actual departure. The preliminaries were brief. Gemmeker would summon a few of the most prominent inmates, Section Leaders and such like, and order them to make up a transport consisting of so many people within two days. Ottenstein, as leader of the *Antragstelle*, was invariably present. There they would sit, he tells us, at a round table—the *SS-Obersturmführer* and a few Jews wearing the yellow star upon their breasts. Officially the talks were secret, but there was no one in the entire camp who did not know all about them. Gemmeker had to be given the latest totals on all the lists, and whenever there were more people eligible for deportation than Gemmeker needed (correction—than The Hague needed, of course) the meeting would decide who was to be spared this time. We do not have to say again who was likely to be lucky, even though the general directives kept on changing. Sometimes pregnant women and the bedridden were exempted as a matter of course, sometimes they were the very ones

[1] Minutes of meeting of Jewish Council, June 4, 1943.

who had to go. Etty Hillesum reports that a simple woman from Rotterdam, spared two months earlier on the grounds that her time was near, was ordered out in the ninth month of pregnancy because someone else had failed to report. This woman, too, went in the cattle-truck, lying on the floor.

The situation was "much worse" still when Gemmeker's needs exceeded the "available" number. Then exemptions were worth nothing. The quota had to be filled, and devil take the hindmost. For that reason—mark it well—the Jewish élite would give Gemmeker a list that had a surplus of names on it, thus making doubly sure that they and their friends were in no danger of having to make up the balance. This margin was also a safeguard against unexpected exemptions put forward by, for instance, The Hague, Amsterdam, Gemmeker himself or the Medical Service, who would add or subtract names up to the very last moment. It quite often happened that more people left with a given transport than the Germans decreed; the opposite occurred rarely, if ever. The notorious Fischer, from The Hague, was heard to roar at a Subsection Leader that if the list was even one man short he and his family would do to make it up. Small wonder that it was a case of every man for himself.

At the "Round Table Conference" all sorts of technical details were discussed as well; the "allocation to trucks, the equipment to be carried, the precise time at which the trains had to be boarded or loaded (this delicate distinction will not be lost upon the reader—J.P.), the provisioning, the permissible luggage, etc.". The Registration Department would once more issue cards, so that all who left the camp had to go through the whole registration rigmarole again. No doubt everything went like clockwork—the clockwork of an infernal machine.

It is impossible to depict the scene on the night before a transport, and, remember, there were scores of these. Etty Hillesum has tried to do it, so has Mechanicus, but the whole thing defies description. Neither the feelings of the oligarchs nor those of the people they had helped to consign to their deaths can ever be fully fathomed. The former, driven by the primitive craving for self-preservation, were putty in the hands of the enemy. No doubt some of them tried to alleviate some of the worst suffering. But even the *Antragstelle*, which was working flat out to save anyone they could, must always have been haunted by the thought that every one held back from the train (and perhaps only for a week) meant another doomed in his stead. Impotence to do any real good coupled to a very real feeling of guilt and complicity oppressed even those who were not concerned only to save their own skins. Perhaps the staff of the *Antragstelle* might have tried to console themselves with the fact that they were at least trying to do something. But what of the others? Mechanicus made the following entry on August 31, 1943: "Every transport was a loathsome spectacle, not least because of what was going on around. This time, while the train was being made ready and, indeed, even as it started to pull out, some people in the camp were dancing. Imagine it—actually dancing! A new revue was in rehearsal. That was just what we all needed! The *Obersturmführer* had seen to it that 2,000 guilders from the camp funds were spent on the costumes. The wardrobe women had been kept at it all through the night before the transport. The dancers themselves had started their ballet rehearsal first thing in the morning. It would never to do flop on opening night."

So much for those who had a stay of execution. What of those who had to leave? All through Monday, rumours would snowball, fear would give way to panic. Once more we must insist—the scene is indescribable. Then came evening and the long vigil of waiting in torment. At last, the die was cast. They knew it, yet some continued to hope against hope. A mortal fear settled on the victims. Last desperate efforts were made to escape the net, by any means—money, diamonds, relatives, anything. Some tried to deceive themselves with the argument that they had been called up so many times before, only to be sent back, so why not this time? Large numbers had so often been kept in reserve on the stage of the Assembly Hall (soon to be loud again with song and dance), wondering as the long hours dragged by—are we going, are we not? The record was held by a young girl, listed sixteen times, only to be recalled. In the end, she was placed on a special list and allowed to stay. We can guess at what cost . . .

The things that could happen! A friend of the writer, a highly gifted man in a "safe" job, was suddenly ordered to join a transport, despite all his chief's efforts to save him. Why? Simply because the head of another department, who had lost one of his own staff, felt that a *quid pro quo* was called for and did not hesitate to tell the Germans so.

One youth, who thought himself safe and then found that he was listed for deportation, went nearly out of his mind, ran away and hid. According to Etty Hillesum, his fellow-Jews were ordered to ferret him out. Find him they had better, otherwise scores of them would have to take his place. The boy was discovered in a tent and dragged out. Fifty extra people had to go with him all the same, on the orders of "our Commandant, of whom it is often remarked that he is a real gent". "But what," the same writer added, "will that poor boy feel when he begins to realize what he has started? And how will the other Jews on board the train treat him? One thing is certain, he won't have an easy time of it."

Heart-rending, too, was the way in which some people paced about in anguish while others sat motionless, all hope abandoned. The climax came when at last the Barrack Leader read out the final list. "The scenes that followed defy imagination. The piercing shriek of a mother almost demented with panic, the sobbing of children, the stricken looks of the men, the anguished cries of those whose dear ones were to be torn from them—all this sends a shudder through one's very bones," wrote one eye-witness. "Those who had to leave," wrote another, "set about packing or dressing their children, while those who had been allowed to stay, often wept with relief or capered about in ecstasies of joy." A third witness wrote: "It was always the same. While some threw fits or burst into loud tears, others would pack their bags and quietly obey the orders. Others again would make a last despairing effort to get exemption. But not seldom one was struck by the proud bearing of people whose fortitude put to shame the abject creatures of the Nazis . . ." *Requiescant.*

Once more our thoughts turn to the children. We think not so much of the four-year-old who, as we said, pestered his mother every Tuesday to let him go on the train (but who had the sense all the same to add: "Once I'm inside with the door shut I'll yell out, 'You rotten old Commandant,' at the top of my voice."). Rather, we have in mind the Children's Department at Westerbork which, from the time of the very first transport, was inextricably caught up in the catastrophe. One night Deppner, the then Camp Commandant, suddenly declared that all but six of the camp's orphans were liable for deportation. Indescribable panic broke out (Westerbork was not yet inured to such horrors). When *Mevrouw* Schol, wife of the former Dutch Commandant, begged Deppner to spare these poor children, his only answer was: "They will be better taken care of in the orphanage at Auschwitz." The most poignant moment came when Salo Carlebach, a young teacher, who had somehow managed to gain the children's confidence, offered in vain to waive his own exemption to go with them.

Indeed, children's transports invariably left without an adult in charge, since the Germans knew only too well that a grown-up might stop at nothing to protect the lives of his wards. Left to themselves, however, the children might just fall asleep and cause no trouble during the journey, which, after all, was the main thing. Preparations usually began at 5 a.m.—the older children would write a few letters, leave messages about what should be done with their few things, and pack. "Some boys and girls stood in a corner deep in prayer, drawn-faced but not weeping." To the very last moment, our eye-witness kept on trying to hide a four-year-old boy, but an OD man raised the alarm and the would-be rescuer himself was nearly seized by the SS. He escaped, but as he puts it: "The pitiful cry of the child, 'Mr. Birnbaum, don't let them take me!' still rings in my ears and always will." As though that were not enough, the Jewish camp leadership gave Birnbaum a sharp reprimand. When the train finally pulled out, the adults and remaining children stood by, helplessly struggling with their own anger, misery and despair: "Almost unconsciously, somebody began to chant a prayer and, hardly knowing what we were doing, we all joined in. From the train we could hear the children, singing away happily . . ."

Only a very few of these orphans survived: "It was a glorious moment when, arriving in Amsterdam by lorry, I was recognized by one of them. He was walking with his mother in the street and, when he saw me, he sprang forward and embraced me with real affection. But then other mothers came up to me: 'Why isn't my child here too?' I shall feel for every one of them to the end of my days."

There were other eye-witnesses, too. One of them recalls: "The train was standing there. A long chain of trucks had rolled in during the night, right into the middle of the camp. Now it was waiting, motionless, like a masked executioner concealing his bared axe. Men, women and children, with their bags and baggage, were herded in. Good weather or bad, at 7 a.m. they were driven out of their barracks, their names were called out, their camp papers collected . . . They were all lined up; a deadly hush fell on the camp. The utter calm with which these people faced their dark future could not but evoke everyone's heartfelt admiration . . . Parents seemed to have no thought but for their children and the older children thought only of their parents."

Another eye-witness had this to say: "Once again a silent procession moved towards the train. Every time this happened we thought 'things can't get any worse', but somehow they always did. Here stood a mother with a new-born babe. There, a few old women wearing slippers and groaning under the weight of their few bits and pieces. I cannot say which was the more harrowing: a woman in her seventh month of pregnancy going proudly to the train, telling us with a defiant smile: 'We'll be all right'; the men and women who sang 'Holland for ever' as they stepped into the trucks for Poland; or the poor girl with deformed hands . . . But if I gave you a hundred more such instances, you could never understand what it was like—for you, no transport to No Man's Land ever stood waiting. A film of the infernal regions could have no apter setting."

According to yet another witness, the victims all felt like animals about to enter the slaughter-house, except that in a slaughter-house there is usually someone to see to it that the killing is humane . . .

Mechanicus tells us that the exiles were marched three abreast to the train, to that "long, cruel crocodile of dilapidated, grimy wagons that cut the camp in two". The *Boulevard des Misères* was cordoned off by OD men, "to keep back the crush". And then the victims: ". . . Lugging a haversack (suspended from the shoulder by a strap and rubbing against the hip), a rolled-up blanket (tied to the other shoulder with a string) flapping against the back, shabby emigrants, owning nothing but what they stood up in and what hung about them. The men silent, with set faces, the women often quietly sobbing, the old faltering and stumbling over puddles on the uneven ground, stretcher-cases helped on their way by OD men." On the platform, almighty Gemmeker himself, generally with his dog, German police and a number of camp dignitaries, including the ubiquitous Schlesinger "in riding-breeches and top-boots, his straw-coloured hair crowned with a flat cap". Ottenstein would be there too: "I am not ashamed to say that when the first transports left I wept bitterly. But you can get used to most things. I noticed later on that, after having worked through another of these interminable nights, after all the commotions and seeing so much misery, you found that you had quite an appetite."

But to return to Mechanicus's account: "Men and women, old and young, whole and sick, children, babies and all were bundled into the same truck. Healthy men and women between old people who could not look after themselves, next to people who had lost control of their bodily functions; between the halt, the deaf, the blind, and the insane. All huddled together on the floor, between and on top of the luggage, helplessly entangled. One small bucket in the corner of the truck where they all had to relieve themselves in front of everyone else, just one little bucket for all those people. Next to it stood a sack of sand, from which everyone could scoop up a handful to cover the excrement. In the other corner stood a vat of water with a tap to it, from which you could quench your thirst. The agents of Lippmann, Rosenthal & Company would follow the exiles hotfoot into the train and wring from them their last remaining treasures—small banknotes, fountain-pens, watches—with threats and even blows . . ."

Then, an interminable pause. At last it was eleven o'clock, the whistle blew and the tension was broken. More than one eye-witness has told us that the "passengers" burst into song. *Morituri te salutant.* The sliding doors were shut; only a faint ray of light could penetrate into the truck crowded with some sixty people, all crouched with their luggage against the walls. Our faithful chronicler sat next to a family of four. "Where are we going, mummy?" asked the oldest child, aged four. The mother gazed blankly before her and said gently: "You'll see, dear, just try to get some sleep." *Requiescant.*

The final word may be given to Herzberg:[1] "Tuesday passes and everyone has a lump in his throat. Then comes Wednesday—and with it fresh squabbles, new hopes, political discussions, a cabaret, all the ups and down of the daily round, the jostling about the stove for a place to heat one's pan or to get a mug of soup—the never-ending intrigues . . .

"That was what happened after every week's transport—and there were ninety-three of them, all told."

## VUGHT

During the Occupation, Holland had yet another camp for Jews, with a character and history of its own, although it, too, served the one main purpose: to act as a waiting-room for the Polish gas-chambers.

Unlike Westerbork, Vught was a German creation, it was from the outset a Nazi concentration camp. Its official title was *Konzentrationslager Herzogenbusch* and it was intended to be a complement to the Police Transit Camp at Amersfoort and likewise of Wester-

[1] Herzberg: *op. cit.*, p. 212.

bork. To its very end (September 1944) it was controlled by the *SS-Wirtschaftsverwaltungs-Hauptamt* or WVHA (Headquarters of the Economic Administration) in Berlin and not, like Amersfoort and Westerbork, by the Security Police—which, of course, did not mean that the latter took no interest in it. This further complication does not make the historian's task any easier, nor does the fact that "Vught"—as we shall continue to call it in accordance with war-time usage—comprised a number of sections for quite distinct categories of prisoners, only one of which was exclusively Jewish. This is the part of "Vught" on which we shall concentrate—the rest, the so-called *Schutzhaftlager* (Protective Custody Camp) was largely made up of non-Jews of all sorts of nationalities, but included a few Jews whom the Germans had accused of various crimes, or what they considered as such. These notorious wrongdoers were subsequently kept in a separate barracks, Block 15, though, for the rest, their treatment differed little from that meted out to the "ordinary" Jews in the camp.

Who precisely were these "ordinary" Jews? They fell into two distinct groups: the first was chiefly made up of those who had previously enjoyed exemption by virtue of their work (e.g. in the diamond or textile industry); the second mainly of those who in April and May 1943, were cleared out of the "dejudified provinces". All of these now ended up in what was originally called the Jewish Reception Camp, but which only too soon became a Jewish Transit Camp, a name first used on February 26, 1943, although the prisoners themselves only learnt about it later. And then, as the diarist David Koker put it: "We were given all sorts of explanations, which would have been very reassuring—had we believed them; but of course we did not."

We have definite evidence that Rauter[1] for one, and Security Headquarters in Berlin, had every intention of sending these Jews, too, to Poland from the start. In particular, Rauter's letters of September 10 and 24, 1942, leave little doubt about his designs, and what few reports there are of discussions on this topic in The Hague tend to the same conclusion. For example, in a document of April 29, 1943, Rauter revealed his plan to concentrate all remaining Dutch Jews in Vught; the place held altogether 18,000 people, so that various batches would have to be cleared out from time to time. At Vught the families would be split up. Those deemed unfit for

[1] *Het proces Rauter* (The Rauter trial), pp. 27 ff., 139 ff.

productive labour would be deported first; the others would follow in due course. As for the industries established in Vught, the Germans never intended these to be permanent, although that, of course, was not quite what they told the Jews.

This brings us to what we might call the "illusion of Vught", the threefold misconception held by many Jewish inmates during 1943: that Vught was "permanent", that it was an indispensable "industrial centre", and that conditions there were "better" than elsewhere. In the autumn of 1942, when it became known in Amsterdam that the camp was about to be set up, the Jewish Council did its utmost to get to the bottom of the whole business. De Winter, their representative in 's Hertogenbosch (who later rendered invaluable service to the Jewish inmates) reported that, judging from a great deal of reliable information, "and from the impressive extent of the sanitary preparations, it looks as if the Germans are setting up a model camp on the most modern lines". Quite a few drew the conclusion that the camp was intended for the SS, rather than for Jews and other prisoners, so much so that Vught ceased to be a subject of general discussion (or rumour) among Jews for quite some time.

It was soon to make up for this lack of general interest, for in no time at all the Jewish Council had its hands full with plans for industrial training and other work in this new (and "permanent") camp. After the war, Professor Cohen insisted that he never had reason to doubt that Vught was anything but an industrial centre, a conviction that was only strengthened by his visits to the camp. He claimed that many of his colleagues thought the same, but we know that there were, in fact, other opinions even then. Thus, whenever C. Blüth, whom we shall meet again, was asked whether he preferred Vught to Westerbork, his invariable answer was that he himself would choose Amsterdam—in other words, he would rather take his chance and go into hiding than risk being sent to either of these places. Another illusion seriously entertained was that Vught was meant to house the old, the sick and the incapacitated. No doubt this is just one more example of how little most people could, or would, allow themselves to believe in the barbarous plans of the enemy.

Let us now look at the events in chronological order. It all began on January 13, 1943, when the first prisoners arrived, the advance guard, as it were: some 250 men, a motley throng from Amersfoort

OVE: The OD in action

RIGHT: The train in Westerbork

Departure from Westerbork

Selection on the platform at Auschwitz-Birkenau

Selection on the platform at Auschwitz-Birkenau

Auschwitz

Bergen-Belsen

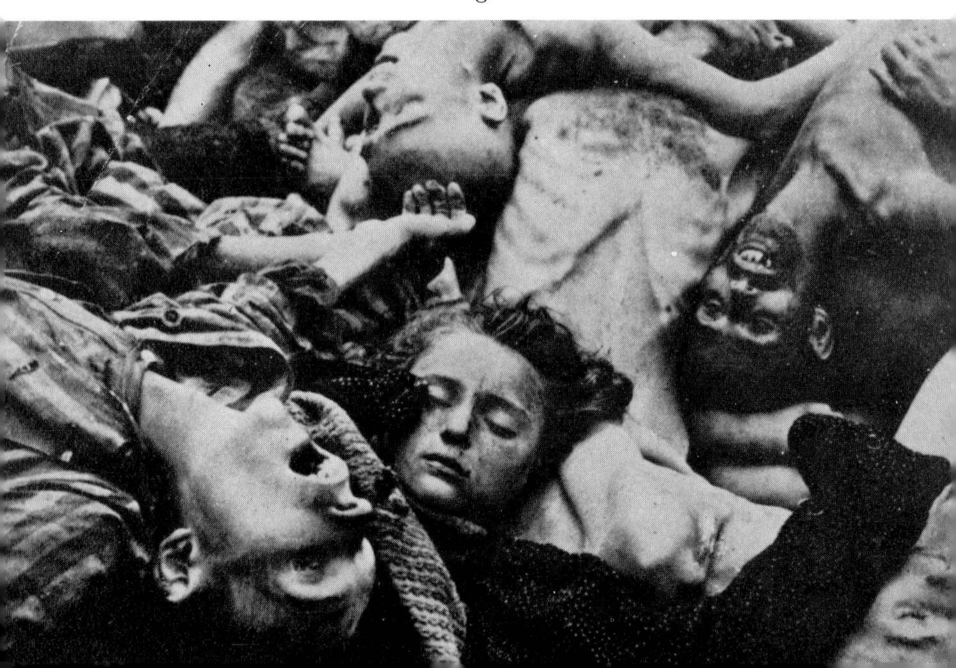

Camp, most of them non-Jews. Of the Jews among them, one eye-witness has said: "Compared to the way they were treated here, they would have been far better off in Birkenau." We shall have more to say about that.

On Friday, January 15—once again a Sabbath eve—the Germans herded a few hundred Amsterdam Jews into the *Hollandse Schouwburg*. That very night, 453 of them were taken by tram to the Central Station, and put on a train for Vught, where they arrived on the Saturday morning. Their advent was completely unexpected, and the camp was quite unprepared for their reception. We leave it to the reader's imagination to picture how they fared, bereft as they were of all essentials, and in mid-winter at that. (Since most of these men had been "exempted" because of the "indispensable" work they were doing, they had thought it superfluous to take any luggage to the Schouwburg.)

This first batch was followed by very many more, with greater or lesser degrees of hardship, depending on the humour of their escorts—many of the Dutch SS saw fit to use their rifle butts on these helpless people and then threatened to shoot them if they did not get up instantly. For weeks on end, Jews would stream into Vught, mainly from the provinces, and their number included a great many elderly (some more than ninety years old), lame and infirm; the whole thing, declared one witness, was heart-rending, and we may well believe it.

From the very start, the Jewish Council in Amsterdam tried to help (this body must be distinguished from the 's Hertogenbosch Jewish Council, with which it shared only its name). The Council in Amsterdam employed its whole machinery to render aid on a large scale and, with the assistance of non-Jewish businessmen, managed to supply the inmates with nearly everything they needed; much of the credit must go to C. Blüth, who knew how to deal with the easily corruptible SS.

Like Westerbork, Vught soon established its own organization; here, too, with the aim of keeping the enemy at bay. Various sections quickly sprang up, though on a much smaller scale than in Westerbork.

It is with some diffidence that we raise the delicate question of the Jewish "élite" in Vught. There was no camp without them, and we have seen how important a part they played at Westerbork; in Vught they were fewer in number and not nearly so important. To avoid any misunderstanding, we would emphasize that, besides a few less attractive types, there were many who stood up boldly for the rights of others, and who—particularly in the beginning, when so much had to be done—jumped to it, created order, lent help and alleviated suffering. Let us here mention two of them, by way of example.

Dr. A. Lehmann, a Jewish lawyer from Germany and a member of the Jewish *Beirat*, has been praised by one and all for his deep humanity, great sympathy, sense of reality and contempt for cheap and dangerous illusions. Until March 20, 1944, this "Professor" (his nickname) remained *Leiter der Inneren Verwaltung und Lagerschreiber I des JDL* (Chief of the Internal Administration and Chief Camp Clerk). Koker[1] tells a typical story about him. When the whole camp was ordered to kneel as a punishment, Lehmann . . . "quickly made for the office and sat down ostentatiously with his hands in the air. This, and his questioning look, made many people laugh. But he succeeded in his purpose of persuading the other clerks to join him."

Far less flattering stories are told about Richard Süsskind, the Camp Elder, who was in daily consultation with the German camp officials; in the beginning, he did a great deal of good work, particularly in organizing the OD, but he was criticized for his oafish manners and his craven efforts to curry favour with the Germans, if need be at the expense of his comrades. He was a young, Herculean figure, one who revelled in his physical fitness and in his position. The harder was his fall: he was deposed in October 1943, and deported to Auschwitz on November 15.

The leader of the Vught Labour Battalion was Map Rosenberg, a Dutch Jew whom Dr. Lehmann has called a "very capable and brave man". His job was to find men for the so-called commandos, whose main work, as distinct from the ordinary camp industries, was heavy labour outside (clearing rubble, building, etc.), generally under German supervision. Even worse, according to Dr. Lehmann, was the lot of the special commandos, who worked exclusively on military projects (tank-traps, air-strips) and were generally not only less well fed than those in the camp but also had to live away from their families and friends.

We shall refrain from giving a detailed account of the industries set up in the camp. The most important "branches" were the

[1] D. Koker: Diary (unpublished MS.), pp. 49 f.

Philips (electrical), Escotex (clothing and fur), Menist (rag-sorting) workshops and, later, a special shop for salvaging aeroplane parts.

A rough calculation shows that on about March 1, 1943, that is within the first six weeks, more than 4,100 people arrived in the camp, while some 800 were "discharged"; according to Lehmann,[1] the camp reached its peak figure on May 8, with some 10,400 people, including 1,876 children under thirteen. Lehmann also estimates that a total of 12,000 people passed through Vught. From the many surviving counts, we can follow the fluctuations in number over a long period. We shall be returning to the subject.

In Vught, as in Westerbork, the impending deportations overshadowed everything else. They did not take place with the same mechanical regularity, but were probably not the less feared on that account. "Probably" we say, because the train from Vught left for Westerbork instead of Poland, and there was always the hope that one might be allowed to remain there. We know today that this was an idle hope—indeed, people would often pass straight through Westerbork on their journey to the East.

Before we come to the deportations themselves, we must make just a few comments about conditions in Vught. Here, the guards, both male and female, played a far greater part than they did at Westerbork. Because Vught was part of the WVHA, SS men were assigned to it as guards from the beginning of 1943, and were drawn from such camps as Mauthausen and Sachsenhausen. We know quite a bit about these men, who figure in many reports as corrupt, brutal, primitive, violent and depraved. The camp commandants were on a par with them; two men, Chmielewski and Grünewald, inaugurated a veritable reign of terror. Reports of ill-treatment come from all quarters; here we need mention only two cases. The first is told by a survivor, whose testimony is corroborated by a great many other witnesses:

"Whenever I wasn't working at Menist, I had to join the outside commando, which involved, among other things, the sweeping of the camp square and street with pine branches. For this task they would usually pick 200 Jews from the 'protective custody' camp and twenty of us. On one occasion my pine branch broke and I was too afraid to ask for another. However, an SS guard spotted me, let fly a stream of abuse and set his dog on me. I fell on top of the dog, and next I had to do punishment drill. Then he asked me if I was

[1] Unpublished MS., p. 20.

hungry and I said no but it did not help, I had to close my eyes, open my mouth and was ordered to swallow a live frog. When I refused, I was beaten mercilessly and had to be helped back to the camp by two men. At noon, I was just about able to stand up again, and was ordered to pick up bits of paper with a nailed stick. That day, two Jews from the outside commando were shot dead, one of them sixty-five-year-old Mr. Israel from The Hague. They said he had stopped outside the boundary, but that was not how it happened, for I was standing right next to him. It was the SS themselves who led him there. They put three bullets in him, and he died on the spot. The other victim was working within ten yards of the wire, which was forbidden. He was shot without any warning."

The second case has been reported by Lehmann: "Benni Brill, the Dutch boxing champion, and a Block Leader in the camp, was the only man I saw, or even heard of, during two and a half years of concentration-camp life, who dared to disobey a formal SS order, indeed who flatly refused, and what is more, in the presence of the entire high command and all the prisoners on parade. This was the order to pick up a bull's pizzle and to flog another prisoner with it."

The female camp guards really merit a chapter to themselves. Some said they looked like seedy charwomen. Others complained of brutal ill-treatment at their hands, and of base behaviour, calling them furies, hyenas, shrews, viragoes and she-devils.

Our picture of life in Vught is naturally based on personal testimony, of which we have already given a few examples. Dr. Lehmann has called it a compound of "pressing anxieties, profound sorrows and not seldom just a little cheerfulness". He recalls that camp life, by its very nature, kept every inmate in a state of continuous tension and that, depending upon each man's nature and disposition, he might find life there merely hard, just bearable or quite intolerable. "However, outsiders will never be able to grasp the full extent of the misery, for which the feeling of humiliation, of being an outcast, of having lost one's freedom of movement and sense of security would have been quite sufficient causes. But on top of all that came concern, indeed fear, for the fate of one's family in other camps."

One might call "normal" many of the tensions that, in Vught as elsewhere, expressed themselves in all sorts of ways. We shall not go into details, though it is pleasant to record that the strife between German and Dutch Jews, which was so marked in Westerbork, was far less in evidence in Vught—and this despite the fact that here, too, a number of German Jews were conspicuous in the camp hierarchy. It would, however, be untrue to claim that there was no such tension at all, and Dr. Lehmann, who did his best to reduce it, admits that the matter caused him some anxiety.

From a number of accounts we gain the impression that the daily round in the camp was unbearably monotonous, with small breaks, sometimes for the better, more often for the worse. People got over it, lived on, sought solace, fell into despair and, in one solitary instance, tried to escape . . . but one cannot exhaust all the variety of human nature in a brief summary.

Diversions? Yes, even in Vught. Some came from the outside world, but there were others, inside the camp, as at Westerbork. The most important outside diversions were, of course, the little signs of sympathy that friends were able to send. And when, in mid-February 1943, the Germans prohibited normal correspondence, people did their best to maintain some contact by means of the German stock letters still permitted to them—with greater or lesser success. On one occasion, the "*Oberhauptscharführer*" tore up an entire batch of outgoing letters:[1] "We had apparently made too many requests for food parcels, thus reflecting upon the catering in our fine hotel. As if anyone needed telling!" Did many food parcels reach the camp? At Christmas 1943, Jews in Vught actually received gifts from the Dutch Red Cross. It was the only time they ever did so, because on all other occasions the German commandant had another use for such windfalls. As for parcels from relatives, friends and acquaintances, which were allowed in, the reader does not need to be told what they meant in spiritual and material solace.

Another, less pleasant, form of diversion was the visit of high German dignitaries. Lehmann[2] has reminded us that Vught was singularly honoured in this way, if only because it was a labour camp and as such had to be constantly inspected and controlled. For the inmates this was just another chore: whenever a VIP was coming, the whole place had to be spotless. On one occasion, when Himmler was expected with a large staff, every available carpenter was set to work on countless frames for the portrait of this great leader. Lehmann associated this visit with an anecdote involving a Jewish woman and Rauter:

[1] David Koker: *Diary*, p. 44.
[2] MS., p. 20.

". . . One fine day, Rauter arrived, suddenly there he was, right next to me. No doubt he picked on me because I am a blonde.

" 'How long have you been working here?'

"Under German discipline, I was not allowed to look up, so that he failed to spot my star.

" 'Seven months.'

" 'You must be here for helping a Jew,' he said almost kindly.

" 'No, you see, I'm a Jewess myself!'

"Rauter could not get away fast enough; he had clearly made a fool of himself . . ."

So much for the "external diversion". What of the internal ones? Lehmann has spoken of the "happy days" in Vught. What were they? Well, for a while—a little while—the Sundays, on which the men were allowed to visit their families in the other blocks, to sit with them at tables brightened up with mats and flowers, and share coffee and cake (God knows where all this came from). When the signal came to leave, many of them pretended to be deaf and the OD had endless trouble getting them back into their own blocks. "But the SS knew only too well how much these visits meant to us; they used them as a form of blackmail and threatened to punish even the smallest transgression by banning the next visit."[1] This happened more and more often, until in the end all Sunday visiting was stopped.

In Vught, too, attempts were made to organize religious services. On the eve of the Passover, Naomi Kohn conducted the Seder meal for 700 women: "The Jewish Council had provided a packet of matzos. There was a wonderful atmosphere in the barracks. The whole thing was fantastic. We had arranged two tables, and the women sat round it on the 3-tier bunks. It was all very impressive. Later I heard that my father did the same thing in the men's camp." Elsewhere[2] we read that a *Scharführer* was present throughout the service, a cigarette dangling from his mouth, while each part of the service was explained to him: "He even accepted a piece of matzo from us and later nibbled it with apparent relish, although the matzo was terribly stale."

We have just mentioned a German observer: on other occasions there were whole rows of them. Vught, too, had an orchestra, the

[1] Lehmann: MS., p. 14.

[2] *Vught, Poort van de Hel!* (Vught, the Gateway to Hell) (Hilversum, 1945), pp. 49 f. (anonymous).

Jewish Council supplying all the missing instruments, including a grand piano. One authority has praised the orchestra as being much better than the one at Westerbork; oddly enough, they were not allowed to play any Jewish music at all. Lehmann deplored the fact that Vught, too, had a cabaret. To the end, the SS made available a whole barracks, and had it tastefully done up by Jewish decorators. Each evening there would be some 300 in the audience, including, as we have said, many of the guards; it was a night out for everyone.

We could give many more details of this and other camp diversions, but must return instead to what was the most grim reality: the remorseless, unceasing flow of deportations, unceasing, that is, until the last Jew had gone.

Vught was—or was said to be—a labour camp. That faced the German guards with the thorny question of what to do with the sick, the aged and the children. They had a ready answer—deportation. As early as January 28, 1943, the first batch of 436 was packed off to Westerbork and thence almost immediately on to Poland. A further 179 people left on February 20; both batches included eighty-year-old men and women. On May 8 there followed another contingent of old people and families with more than four children. Quite often, the deportees would leave under the most pitiful circumstances, waiting for hours in all weathers only to be driven on with blows. The contingent of May 8 had the aim of thinning out the swollen camp population; as a result, the population of the Jewish Transit Camp was reduced from 8,684 to 7,874.

Let us look at some later figures. On June 4 there was a total of 7,088 inmates, made up of 2,451 men, 3,181 women and 1,456 children under sixteen; on June 11 there were 4,158 inmates, made up of 2,075 men (376 less), 1,893 women (1,288 less) and 190 children (1,266 less). We need not dilate upon the tragedy revealed by these figures—the massacre of the children of Vught.

The massacre of the children. It had begun months before, but the June transports were the climax of the whole operation. Immediately after the opening of the camp, the Jewish Council had asked the German authorities whether children sent to Vught would be allowed to stay there. They were given positive assurances . . .

Surviving reports and other data tell us much about the educational work organized by the Jewish Council in Vught and about the care of youth in general. One such report states that open-air exercise was essential to health and made all sorts of suggestions on how to organize it. Koker[1] tells the following poignant story: "Something terrible happened today, something that depressed me very much. The men were ordered to take down the barbed-wire fence. I did not want to take part and went across to the children. They were having a matinée. The whole place was beautifully arranged. Built up like an amphitheatre. A touching sight. The children with their hands in their laps. Their gaze fixed in rapt attention. There was a compère and a puppet show. A girl with a little grey cap came on. And went off again. Then the roll-call. All children out. Five in a row. Such tiny rows. And so they stood for nearly two hours, as they always had to. Drilling children like soldiers is even worse than beating them. This afternoon, when I watched the children stand outside for so long, so very long, the matinée that had given them so much pleasure utterly spoilt, I realized *for the first time* what other people had been saying for so long, to what depths we had sunk . . ."

Koker must also have seen what was obvious to all at Vught: the plight of the sick children. We know much about this subject from Professor Dr. S. van Creveld, who heard in April 1943 that scores of children were dying in the camp. When he tried, with the help of Blüth, to get permission to see for himself, the German camp doctor, Mayer, merely replied: "A Jew and a Dutchman to boot—it's out of the question." But Creveld persisted, and through the Jewish Council managed to persuade Camp Commandant Chmielewski to allow him to make ten visits between May 4 and June 10. The conditions he found were indescribable—food, care, hygiene, the state of the children in general and of the youngest in particular, everything was appalling. The utter indifference of the German staff caused more havoc than their pilfering (they would "confiscate" all the food and medicaments sent in from Amsterdam). Infants often had to go without milk altogether or were given sour milk, the drinking water, which the camp leadership considered excellent, was found to be polluted. Toddlers with every imaginable infection were thrown together; only scarlet fever cases were "isolated" by a dirty curtain. There were no washing facilities whatsoever. "Two miserable shacks contained a number of small lavatory bowls; it was here that the cooking was done, unwashed nappies were dried and the corpses of small children laid out for burial." And in a post-war lecture, Professor van Creveld had this to say: "Can you imagine dying,

[1] Diary, p. 70.

emaciated babies or older children, all being dumped together on a mattress without sheets, without napkins, almost without any other clothing, plagued by hundreds of flies which settled on the stinking secretions from the children's noses and ears and on their excrement? And from there they would go on to the milk if there was any—and to other food, thus closing the vicious circle."

We shall spare the reader further details, say nothing of the children's last death pangs. We shall merely add that, even though the brave intervention of Professor van Creveld produced a great improvement in the conditions, the benefits were short-lived—soon afterwards all the children, sick and healthy alike, were packed off to Sobibor and exterminated.

Many desperate attempts were made to save these children from the grave. Early in 1943 came the order that all children then in Vught must be sent to "special children's camps in Holland" where the mothers could come "to satisfy themselves that the children were well looked after". The Jewish camp leadership, who were not taken in for a moment, made the counter-proposal that a special camp for children be set up just outside the main one. Camp Commandant Chmielewski seemed sympathetic, and Professor van Creveld was even asked to draw up plans for their accommodation (which have been preserved to us). On June 5 he had a discussion with Hulshof, the Amsterdam city architect, about converting barracks into a hospital; contacts were even made with a firm in Amersfoort which promised speedy construction. On June 6, however, Professor van Creveld was informed by the Presidents of the Jewish Council that all children under sixteen had been ordered out of Vught. This was to happen on Sunday and Monday, June 6 and 7, once again a Jewish holiday (Creveld had been preparing presents for the occasion).

This order was communicated to the inmates by the Jewish camp leaders on June 5. Children under three could be accompanied by their mothers, those from four to sixteen by either parent, except in cases where one of the parents was working in one of the camp industries; if both were so employed, they might choose which one should go. There was a small number of exemptions (particularly for people whose Jewish descent was under investigation). According to the Jewish camp leaders, there was still "good reason to hope that the children would remain in this country", but they nevertheless called for eight days camp mourning. Dr. Lehmann made vain efforts to get all the fathers working in outside commandos recalled to Vught. These men had, of course, heard rumours about the impending deportations, but when they were assured that it was a false alarm, "they were so overjoyed that they staged a celebration". Soon afterwards they received the shattering news that their worst fears had been only too true. One eye-witness tells us that as the children left, the SS men either beat them or stood about laughing; some were taking films or snapshots, while their dogs sat obediently at their heels. And what a picture it was: a five-day-old baby, for instance, who weighed under 3 lb. at birth, thrown in with children suffering from pneumonia.

This is what a non-Jewish eye-witness, who watched it all from the punitive block, had to say: "My impression was—and still is—that this was one of the rare occasions when the whole camp was united and when the latent anti-Semitism of so many turned into human compassion and a touching desire to help. Even such doubtful characters as A, the block elder, had apparently climbed through the wire to hand out pieces of cake. Everyone gave bread, butter, chocolate and whatever they could spare; at the back of one of the huts a full-scale distribution centre had been set up. No one knew precisely what was in store for these poor mites, but there was a general feeling of warmth for them and revulsion for their tormentors . . . The indescribable barbarism of the Germans was revealed in all its naked horror when you looked at your own baby or any little child and realized that such lovable little creatures were being gassed like vermin."

According to Dr. Lehmann, it was to be a long time before laughter was heard again in Vught. However, in the minutes of the meeting of the Jewish Council in Vught on June 21 we can read that the nightly cabaret performances "are loudly applauded and are also approved by the Camp Commandant". But perhaps we had best let the statistics speak for themselves once again. On June 25 the Jewish Transit Camp numbered 4,276 "ordinary" inmates and 95 prisoners (the last figure rose to 153 on July 2); on July 9 the figures were 2,778 and 115 respectively; the last figure rose to 262 on September 10 and to 292 on September 17, but between these two dates, the number of people in the Transit Camp itself dropped from 2,707 to 2,084 and to 1,724 a week later. On October 15 the figures were 1,717 and 366; on October 22, 1,496 and 360; on November 12, 1,492 and 391; on November 19, 677 and 39—a drop of 1,667.

This large drop was caused by the deportations of November 15. Thanks to the attentions of Grünewald, Chmielewski's successor, that particular transport was even more repulsive than its predecessors. To begin with, the unfortunate victims were stripped of everything; the women were made to undress completely by the worst of their guards who, after the degrading search, ordered them outside, so that they had to put on their thin clothes in the pouring rain (in the middle of November). Wearing only dresses and clogs, without underwear, they were herded into the cattle-trucks, strewn with scraps of dirty straw. One of the witnesses who stayed behind wrote that even the women's brassières were stolen. He sent the whole story to the illegal *Het Parool*,[1] adding his repugnance that Dutch railway staff should have lent themselves to such an outrage. According to a telegram received in Vught on November 18, the transport, consisting mainly of Escotex workers, arrived in Auschwitz at 1 p.m.; two men had escaped on the way. Of the rest, only one in twenty saw Holland again.

There were then some 700 people left in Vught, including seventeen children. Practically the whole camp organization had collapsed; there was a host of new restrictions, but for the time being Dr. Lehmann was allowed to remain the nominal Camp Leader. On January 16, 1944, the first anniversary of Vught, he summoned all the men to his hut; of those who had come to the camp when he did, only fourteen remained. He delivered a brief address, in which he described the events of the last twelve months. Soon afterwards it was his turn—Lehmann was deported on March 20, 1944. He was one of the few in this transport whose family was still there to wave him goodbye. "I never saw my wife and children again."

On March 24, 1944, 387 persons (10 men, 360 women, 17 children) were left in the transit camp, and 22 in the prisoners' block. Some who had been deported were subsequently sent back to work for Philips, and there were other comings and goings. But the day arrived when even this small remnant had to go, and when the Jewish Transit Camp was closed for good. Of the last transport, Professor Cleveringa, who was locked up in the camp at the time, wrote: "The Jews were driven like beasts, and had to stand for hours in the scantiest of clothes. Many of them were sick and infirm. I saw that some of them were pulling up tufts of grass, only to have them snatched out of their hands. They were treated like dirt."

[1] *Het Parool*, January 10, 1944.

The transport leaving Vught on June 2 consisted of 90 men, 389 women and 17 children. Their subsequent history is known: because of their technical skill, they were kept out of the gas-chambers. As for the rest, the many, many thousands who passed through Vught to Poland, we can only say that, with few exceptions, they, like the majority of Dutch Jews, were murdered in cold blood and with malice aforethought.

CHAPTER EIGHT

# MURDER

## THE JOURNEY

We have quoted Herzberg's account of the departure from Westerbork, to which he added: "What happened in the trucks themselves, we cannot tell." Even at the time, however, many camp inmates had at least an inkling of the truth. Admittedly, they had no personal testimony, but there was quite a bit of other evidence. Thus, a medical orderly in the camp noticed that, during the first half year of the deportations, the same train was always used. He accordingly fitted up a little hiding-place in which messages could be sent home. He dutifully passed all these messages on to the addresses, but not before he had made copies and smuggled them out of the camp. It is thanks to his resourcefulness that we know of the contents of several letters written in December 1942. Another camp inmate told his brother, who was deported on April 6, 1943, to hide a report beneath the truck. This message, too, has come down to us.

The first batch of letters gave a clear account of the journey across Germany; at that stage, carriages were still being used and the travellers could see out. One report began: "The first day of the journey was terrible; the carriages were crammed full, and whenever we wanted to go to the lavatory we had to climb over all the others. For the bedridden the whole thing was a nightmare; they had to be helped in and out all the time. When the door was shut, the smell was unbearable and the air oppressive; when the door was left open there was a horrible draught. At night the carriage was pitch dark and the cold was quite unbearable . . . Next morning, the German police came to ask if a few more Jews had 'kicked the bucket', and in fact two had died of cold and misery. They were taken to the luggage section."

This journey lasted three days and two nights, and the destination, as we know only too well, was death.

But what do we know of what went on in the minds of the victims during that terrible journey? The number of testimonies is pitifully small. Quite clearly, many must have felt like the Jewish woman who, on crossing the border, exlaimed: "Now we've left Dutch soil, it's all over with us." Another wrote: "At first, a plucky Amsterdammer kept up our spirits with a few jests, but as we came nearer to the border, one by one we fell silent." A doctor: "I had a terribly sad journey and the fact that my wife's parents were with me only made it worse. The whole thing was pathetic. I did not mind nearly

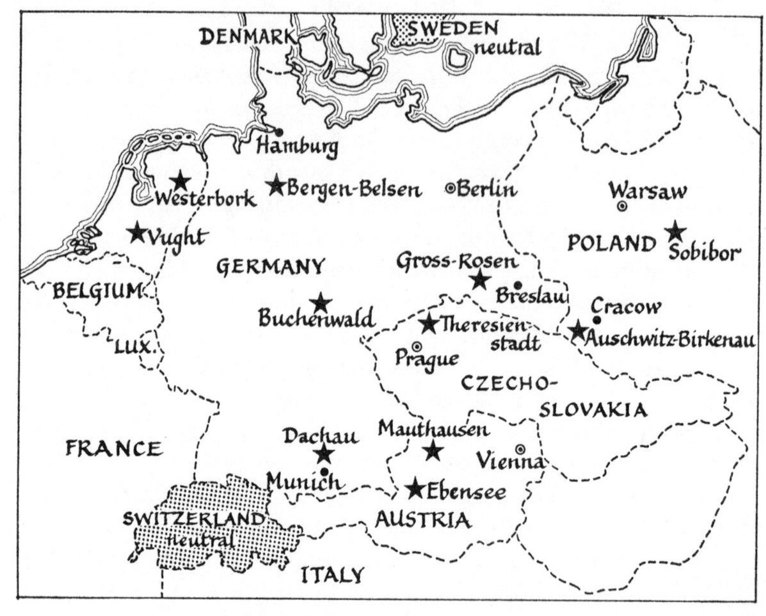


Map of Concentration Camps

so much about my wife herself as about these two old people. And what was true of them was true of ten thousand others as well. All these people, who had worked so hard throughout their lives, who had been such solid citizens, were now being carted like cattle into a dark future." Or: "Many people found it agonizing that they had to perform their bodily functions in front of others, and were desperately ashamed. But later no one seemed to care about that. Everyone was afraid, and moreover afraid to say so." And yet: "I was completely taken aback by the optimism of the people all round me; the more difficult the situation the more cheerful they became. Everyone was convinced that things would not go on like that for very much longer."

That was in September 1943.

Another witness reports that people were in such "wonderful spirits" that a "cabaret" was organized in their truck during the first night out . . . "I shall always remember a girl of sixteen, singing *Nederland* in the flickering light of a makeshift candle."

During one journey, a barber shaved all the men, not without protest on his part for, as he pointed out, it was his early closing day; a teacher gave "an inspiring lecture on Zionism, which took everyone's mind off the journey. Afterwards, we all tried to get some sleep, and some of us actually snatched a few winks standing up."

Only a few people managed to escape, possibly because the Germans let it be known that they would hold the truck-leaders responsible for the safe delivery of all their charges. "The whole thing was sheer farce, however, for on arrival in the East, the doors of the trucks were thrown open, and, not stopping to count, the Germans let everyone out, indeed drove them out; they could not clear the trucks fast enough. To them Jews were less than cattle, for cattle are worth something and must be counted . . ."

How were the travellers treated during the journey? What few data we have conflict; there were surprisingly few complaints, but there were, of course, some: "The worst thing was that (in our truck) there was not a drop of water. Let me give just one example. At one station, the father of twins aged six and a half months asked one of the guards for permission to fill a feeding-bottle. The guard said he would do it for him. He took the bottle, but instead of filling it with water, smashed it against the wall of the truck. Throughout the journey not one of us saw a single drop of water."

And the German people? Let us hear what Jacob Lestschinsky[1] had to say on this subject: "Hundreds of trains, consisting of thousands of cars, jammed with Jews from Western Europe, being taken to the extermination centres in the East, passed through Germany. These trains would stop at German railroad stations for days and sometimes for weeks. Many Jews were suffocated in these trains or died of hunger. Yet not a single instance of assistance to these unfortunates on the part of the Germans is known."

This is how a nurse ended her letter: "We're there! Just past Auschwitz . . . In the distance we can see a building all lit up . . ."

[1] Lestschinsky: *Crisis, Catastrophe and Survival* (New York, 1948), p. 40.

Was it perhaps the flames rising from the chimney of the crematorium? We shall never know. She barely had time to hide her letter; one or two hours later she was no more, she and all those with her.

### SOME FIGURES

All in all, ninety-eight transports left the Netherlands, including ninety-three from Westerbork alone. Twenty-six of these transports had no survivors at all; from many others, only a single person returned. It is difficult to give precise figures, because so many trains were split up on the way; all we know is that of the 60,000 persons sent to one camp (Auschwitz) in sixty-seven trains, only 500 returned. These figures are not precise, we said, but in all conscience they are enough.

Between June 1947 and March 1952, the Dutch Red Cross published the results of an investigation into the fate of deported Jews. Here, too, the data were not complete, but the following picture emerges clearly enough.

From July 15 to August 24, 1942, thirteen transports left Westerbork with some 11,000 Jews (approximately 6,200 men and 4,800 women)—an average of two trains a week. In these early transports, the age group sixteen to thirty-two was predominant, since, as we have said, the Germans pretended that the deportees were needed for labour service. Next came the Cosel-period (August 28 to December 12, 1942), so called because a number of trains, including some from Belgium and France, stopped at Cosel, 80 kilometres west of Auschwitz. Here the Germans disembarked the "labourers" and allocated them to various camps in the neighbourhood. During this period a total of twenty-nine transports left Holland, at a rate of two per week. Of these, eighteen were split up in Cosel; the other eleven went straight through to Auschwitz. The first eighteen trains carried some 16,000 deportees, of whom some 3,500 (men between the ages of fifteen and fifty) were taken off at Cosel. Of these, there are 181 known survivors, including 126 from Blechhammer camp, which was taken over by the SS on April 1, 1942. It would appear that every single one of the women and children from these twenty-nine transports was exterminated. There were no survivors at all from five of the eleven trains that went straight through to Auschwitz, and only twenty-six men from the six others.

After the deportations of December 12, 1942, there was a Christmas break, no doubt to enable the murderers and their henchmen to celebrate the birth of the Prince of Peace in the bosoms of their families. On January 11 they returned to the strict line of duty, giants refreshed, as we shall see.

In 1943 one can distinguish three periods, of which we shall treat the middle one, the so-called Sobibor period, in another section. The first period, from January 11 to February 23, witnessed nine transports, eight from Westerbork and one from Apeldoorn. There was no longer any attempt to pretend that these were labour contingents. Security Headquarters in Berlin had issued secret orders for the deportation from the Netherlands of 3,000 Jews between January 11 and 31, but so efficient were the German authorities in Holland, that they succeeded in producing an extra 600 (five transports carrying 3,600 persons). The next four transports accelerated the rate even further and produced a crop of 4,300. The transports of the first period included many unfit for work, 3,400 people over the age of fifty, 800 children under sixteen and some mental patients from Apeldoorn. From these nine transports there were thirty-three survivors: twenty-six men and seven women. The sole survivor of the train that left on January 23, to take but one example, owed his good fortune to the fact that he was selected to play in the Auschwitz orchestra. The eight autumn transports, from August 24 to November 16 (seven from Westerbork, one from Vught) carried a total of 8,127 persons, including 897 children under fifteen, 2,624 men from sixteen to fifty, 2,829 women from fifteen to sixty, and 1,777 people over fifty. In the case of these transports, the female survivors (121) outnumbered the male. The reason was that three of these transports (August 24, September 14, September 21) supplied the Germans with women for their notorious "medical" experiments. In three of the other five transports, no woman survived.

In 1944 eight transports from Westerbork and Vught went straight through to Auschwitz, carrying 5,500 persons—approximately 600 children, 1,650 men and 1,150 women aged fifteen to fifty years, and some 2,100 persons over fifty. Of this contingent, a total of 234 men and 315 women have survived (the transports included quite a few people married to non-Jews and half-Jews). The survivors of one transport (June 3, 1944) even included five children —three boys of about ten and two girls of about thirteen. The last transport from the Netherlands to Auschwitz left on September 3,

1944; it carried over a thousand people, of whom 127 have survived.

### AUSCHWITZ-BIRKENAU

The great majority of the Jews deported from Holland finished up in Auschwitz—"the end of the line".[1] What awaited them there was beyond anything that even the gloomiest among them could have imagined. When the train arrived (generally at night), the human cargo would either be unloaded at once or kept waiting till daybreak. Then the horrors began. One of the early transports was greeted by bully-boys armed with clubs, the so-called "reception committee"; on the arrival of another transport, a blind man aged seventy-eight, who failed to understand the orders screamed at him, was clubbed to death before the rest. But even the Germans had their milder moods and one mother recalls: "When we arrived in Auschwitz, they told me to pick up my child and carry it to the car, but one of them said that the cars were reserved for old people and children, and so I had to hand the child over to my mother. As I did so, I said to my husband: 'Do take care of his bottle.'"

And a man testifies: "We were lined up, and not far from us I could see a tall structure spewing out bright flames . . . This, I thought, was one of the strangest German symbols I had ever seen. None of us had any inkling of the awful truth . . ."

Generally a "first selection" would be held soon after the arrival, whereupon most women and all the children were sent straight to the gas-chambers. Naturally, the victims themselves were not told; indeed, they felt grateful for being taken to the "showers" in a car . . . Unforgettable are the many portraits of the German camp doctor, who, like a dancing-master rehearsing his troupe, gracefully directed people to the left or the right, to life or death. Husbands and wives waved to each other, "See you tomorrow," little knowing that this was the final parting of the ways, and that there would be no tomorrow for at least one of them. The favoured left-hand file had to strip naked in a quarantine hut, had their clothes confiscated, their forearms tattooed, and were then put through the mangle of the camp's registration system, which booked even their gold teeth. In the wash-house, the so-called Sauna, all body-hair was removed and some sort of bath followed. Next came the issue of "new" clothing, mostly torn and dirty rags. With minor

[1] Greet van Amstel: *Den vaderland getrouwe*, p. 160.

variations, that was the routine. Occasionally, the men would learn, even before they had gone any farther, that their wives and children were dead: "I don't know how I lived through the moment, half an hour after our arrival, when X (a Jewish name) joined our group and said: 'You don't know how lucky you are.' And when we asked him why, he told us: 'All the rest have gone up the chimney.' I was completely stunned by the news." Others did not hear until much later.

"(On arrival) I took my children by the hand and ran forward, to get them and my wife a place in the car. And they were among the first to get a seat. The children waved to me and were obviously looking forward to their ride. I myself was one of 259 who were told off to walk to the camp. I was marching on one side of the column and asked an SS man about my wife and children. He told me that I would be allowed to see them on Sunday."

In any case, the truth soon became obvious to all; they were no more than cyphers, torn from their country and people, robbed of their families and of everything but their wretched lives. The past had been wiped out for them; they had nothing, absolutely nothing, not even a photograph of their loved ones; and they themselves were no longer names, just numbers, doomed to slave-labour under the most pitiless conditions. This was to be their lot to the end of their days and these were few.

And if one did chance to survive, could one ever forget that first night in Auschwitz? There were the visions of the children's faces, those children whose ashes were blowing in the wind. "I shall remember to my dying day those flames, the flames in which my own faith perished for ever. I shall never forget the deathly hush of the night in which my will to live was extinguished, the moment that murdered my God and my soul, and turned my visions to dust. I shall remember, even were I condemned to live as long as God Himself."

Many times the stories of the gassings have been told. In all the extermination camps the process was roughly the same, and we need do no more than report what the Germans themselves considered the ideal method: simple, tidy, quick and effective (the shooting of prisoners, lined up on the edge of a flaming pit was another good method, but gassing was deemed to be more "elegant" —as someone put it during the Eichmann trial). This aesthetic solution the Germans had already perfected when dealing with mental patients at home. We know fairly well how it worked, not only from the reports of the survivors but also from the German sources which, in their prosaic officialese, kept congratulating themselves upon their efficiency.

The normal gas-chamber looked like—and was arranged as—a shower-room. First, everyone had to undress in an ante-chamber—grandparents, parents, children, all of them together in full view, embarrassed, astonished or perhaps unseeing. The clothes had to be folded neatly and the shoes tied together, for there must be no muddle. All sorts of other regulations completed the illusion; a piece of soap and the promise of a cup of coffee after the bath. And then into the shower-room itself they went, whole families together, as many as could be crammed in. The iron door was slammed shut and the gas turned on. This was the "Special Treatment". Fifteen minutes—by the clock—and it was all over. The corpses were thrown into the oven, but not before their gold teeth had been salvaged, wedding-rings pulled from dead fingers, the women's hair cut off. The clothes were sent as home comforts to members of the Master Race in the Fatherland. In Birkenau, there would be 10,000 to 12,000 gassings a day, though if need be the number could be stepped up. If need be—and there was such a rush of customers. Later the SS were told to go easy on the gas, and so had the inconvenience of having to wait a few minutes more until the last victim was dead. Perhaps this is the place to remind the reader that, according to the memoirs of Camp Commandant Rudolf Höss, the gas had a somewhat "calming" effect.[1]

The writer has been to Auschwitz to inspect this *Musterlager*, this model for all the others. He stood on the vast square of Auschwitz-Birkenau, that place of the dead without a single grave. The writer, we have said. Can one write, about this? It is not possible. If proof of that were necessary, the Eichmann Trial provided it. There was no lack of witnesses. They told all the facts, or tried to do so. But they, too, failed to find words for the hell they had gone through, for the hell they were now asked to relive. They could not. All one can say is that the freezing wastes of the Arctic cannot be more desolate than this square in Birkenau where men and women stared into the empty eyes of death, death in a shape of unimaginable horror.

Behind the barbed wire, once crackling with electricity, many of

[1] R. Höss: *Kommandant in Auschwitz* (Stuttgart, 1958), p. 122.

the Auschwitz barracks still stand. It is a museum now, piled high with articles that once belonged to living people. In one section are thousands of crutches, corsets, artificial arms and legs; another holds thousands of shoes, ballet slippers, babies' bootees; a third consists exclusively of prayer shawls, prayer straps, scrolls of the Law and prayer-books. Be silent awhile among these ghostly relics. Then go on to yet another section, stacked with pile upon pile upon pile of human hair, discoloured, greyed, lack-lustre.

We would not presume to add to this pyramid of horrors, except to give heed to the voice of one who came back: "On those last days in Auschwitz, I was put to work on the hair. It lay packed in several hundred bales and they had to be shifted. There were waves in the tresses and the pins and combs had not been removed." And among that lot was the hair of the woman he had married but a little while before.

Another show-case: tens of thousands of pairs of spectacles. Yet another: empty suitcases. Nico Rost[1] tells us that while he was reading the names of their owners—Budapest, Lyons, Ollmütz (Olomouc), Kaschau (Kosice), Erfurt and Pez (Pécs)—he suddenly came across the name and address of a Jew from Groningen: "May I be forgiven, but the name of one person you have known personally touches you, if not more deeply at least more directly than that of the many thousands whom you mourn but have never met."

Need one say more about Auschwitz-Birkenau? Perhaps just tell exactly where it lies: 50° 3′ 30″ N., 19° 13′ 30″ E., 50 kilometres due west of Cracow on the Vistula. It was the largest of all the camps, this combination of Auschwitz and Birkenau (3 kilometres away), the most notorious of them all, and the acme of everything the Nazis had attempted in thousands of smaller camps: death in an instant, death by inches, inhuman slave-labour, bestial punishments. The inhospitable climate suited the place: burning hot summers, drenching, freezing winters. The stable-like barracks in which the prisoners eked out their lives were quite uninhabitable, what with pools on the ground and sodden bunks: "We even envied the SS men's dogs, who were kept in dry, clean kennels." But worse, if anything, than the rain was the sun, which in the short Auschwitz summer parched the air over the plain. "Our skin, grown so thin and vulnerable, could not endure the blazing heat. During the end-

[1] Nico Rost: *Veranderend Klimaat in Polen* (Changed Climate in Poland) (Assen, 1957), p. 66.

less waiting on the parade ground, the merciless sun would burn holes in our skin, causing unbearable pain. Each step kicked up great clowds of dust. Tongue and mouth were dried up, and we all craved for water that was nowhere to be had."

The ground lay low, was marshy and the air was foetid—the whole region was notoriously unhealthy. A scientific report called the drinking-water there "so unfit for human consumption that it cannot even be used to rinse the mouth".

Above the gate, it was still possible in 1960 to read the slogan *Arbeit macht frei*—"Work sets you free". Was this sheer cynicism? Indeed not, for the Camp Commandant, the notorious Rudolf Höss, actually believed it. On his visit to the camp, the writer was shown the frame of the gallows on which they hanged this fanatical and diligent man—his master's devoted, most devoted, servant.

It was in this camp also that tens of thousands of Dutch Jews lost their lives, most of them, as we said, on arrival. But others lingered on for a while and some even survived the holocaust. We might add that not all of them stayed in Auschwitz itself, or in nearby Birkenau; Auschwitz had thirty-nine subsidiary camps in Silesia and beyond, and some prisoners were even transferred to camps outside this network. As early as January 1943, the Jewish Council knew about the existence of Birkenau, Monowitz, Buna and Jawischowitz; other names, too, became known but some of the worst remained secret until the end.

### OTHER CAMPS

The Germans had built up an enormous industry, with vast marshalling yards, a perfect technique and a standardized killing machine. It is in the interstices of this vast framework that we must now locate the Dutch Jews and try to speak with a little human feeling of their brief ordeal. We look at the map, at hundreds of names, most of them lacking any geographical importance. What can these hundreds of places, scattered in remote areas, have to do with one another? Or what are we to make of the sinister new descriptions that abound in the official documents: *Konzentrationslager* (Concentration Camp), *Arbeitslager* (Labour Camp), *Arbeitserziehungslager* (Labour Education Camp), *Judenlager* (Jewish Camp), *Judenarbeitslager* (Jewish Labour Camp), *Gemeinschaftslager* (Community Camp), *Sonderlager* (Special Camp), *Polizeigefangenenlager* (Police Prison Camp), *Familienlager* (Family Camp), *Schutzlager* (Protective Camp),

*Zivillager* (Civilian Camp), *Durchgangslager* (Transit Camp), *Judenumsiedlungslager* (Jewish Resettlement Camp), *Gefangenenlager* (Prison Camp), *Kriegsgefangenenlager* (War Prisoners' Camp), *Zwangsarbeitslager* (Forced Labour Camp), *Judenzwangsarbeitslager* (Jewish Forced Labour Camp), *Aussiedlungslager* (Evacuation Camp), *Internierungslager* (Internment Camp), *Zivilinternierungslager* (Civilian Internment Camp), *Anhaltelager* (Holding Camp) and *Sammellager* (Assembly Camp)? There seems to be a name for everything here and, to make things worse, the appellations kept on changing, more particularly in the worst camps, no doubt the better to disguise their real purpose. And that purpose never changed—the killers went on killing in all of them, in some places with gas, in others with slower means. The various designations might suggest that there were at least degrees of horror, but what differences there were were insignificant against the dark purpose that governed them all. Every Jew in every one of these camps had to die, and would indubitably have died had the war lasted just a little longer. As it was, the machine ground to a halt when it had swallowed 6,000,000, and the fact that a few thousand were liberated was not due to the internal collapse of the system but to its overthrow from without.

As we have said, among all these millions it is only the Dutch Jews who concern us here. We have sampled the official decisions, we have looked into the evidence of survivors, we have sifted, checked, compared and investigated. Of hundreds of camps, it can be said with certainty or near-certainty that no Dutch Jew was ever in them: about others we do not know enough to say this, but wherever there were Dutch Jews they suffered indescribably; the lot of most of them was humiliation, torture, starvation and every kind of ill-treatment at the hands of men who set about their task with cold deliberation.

We have spoken of Mauthausen. After loud protests in the Netherlands itself, the Germans promised in 1942 that no one else would be sent there. It did not take them very long to break the promise, for in that self-same years they sent some 400 to 500 prisoners to Mauthausen, mainly from Amersfoort camp. Again, during the evacuation of various Polish camps in 1944–5, numerous Dutch Jews were among those who landed up in Mauthausen, and only a few of them survived to tell the tale.

We shall have little to say about some of the most notorious camps, simply because they held few Dutch Jews or held them only for a very short while. This excuses us from giving a detailed account of, for instance, Buchenwald or Sachsenhausen, which last also bore the slogan *Arbeit macht frei* and which was plastered with the message: "*Es gibt einem Weg zur Freiheit; seine Meilensteine heissen: Fleiss, Sauberkeit, Ehrlichkeit Wahrhaftigkeit, Nüchternheit, Gehorsamkeit und Liebe zum Vaterlande* ("There is but one way to freedom and its milestones are: Diligence, Cleanliness, Honesty, Truthfulness, Sobriety, Obedience and Love of the Fatherland").

One milestone was omitted from this list: the crematorium.

In Monowitz, which we have mentioned previously, thousands of Jews were put to hard labour, ground down, beaten, tortured and finished off. All this in the service of the highly respectable IG-Farben Industrie, among the largest of the German corporations, and incidentally the supplier of Cyclon B, a gas used to kill millions. From time to time the directors of this splendid concern would visit the camp, to check on the production and to see that there were no complaints. The staple diet was Buna soup, so called after the Buna Works; it was a watery gruel made with potatoes and scraps. W. Dürrfeld, a director of the company, sampled it: "He praised the soup, but mentioned that it was capable of improvement." Another director told *Obersturmführer* Schwarz that the working hours could safely be increased from 10 to 12 hours, and that work need only cease when the temperature had reached 27° F below freezing point; he added that the prisoners' output left much to be desired, and that appropriate measures would have to be taken. Needless to say, these measures at once reduced the labour force.

Of the many other "death factories", we know only one—Sobibor—of which it can be said with certainty that many thousands of Dutch Jews perished there. As for the others, the records are inconclusive. This is true, for instance, of Belzec, of whose 600,000 inmates only a few here survived—the maximum output was 15,000 corpses per day. In this factory, on the Lublin–Lemberg road, Diesel engines would pour exhaust gases into the chambers. An eyewitness, Kurt Gerstein, has reported that on one occasion the motor would not start, and the victims—700 to 800 squashed into four chambers measuring altogether 270 square feet—were kept waiting for 2 hours 49 minutes precisely. At last the motor responded and, after a further 32 minutes, the watcher at the spy-hole could report that everyone inside was dead! Then the door were opened: "The dead stood like statues, pressed tight against each other. They could neither fall nor bend down. Even in death, one could still recognize the families, for in their agony they had clasped one another's hands so tightly that it was difficult to tear them apart and to clear the chamber for the next batch. The corpses, soaked with sweat and urine, covered with excrement, menstrual blood dripping down the legs, were flung outside. Two dozen people were busy with hooks, forcing open clenched jaws in a search for gold. If they found any, the corpse was thrown to the left, if not to the right; others set to work with hammer and tongs breaking the gold teeth and crowns from the jaws . . . Others again checked the female genitals for hidden gold, diamonds or jewels." Over the camp hung a sickly sweet smell, mixed with fumes. Belzec.

Next day our eye-witness went to Treblinka, 120 kilometres north-north-east of Warsaw, a "factory" that produced 25,000 corpses per day—a real bone-crushing mill this. And Treblinka, of all places, was dressed up as a Rest Centre, indeed as a Sanatorium. There was a proper "railway station" with signs reading "Restaurant", "Waiting Room", "Ticket Office", etc.—all of them bogus, for Treblinka was the terminus for Jews from the Warsaw Ghetto. As a Chamber of Horrors it was said even to surpass Belzec; Höss has described the place as only a true connoisseur could do. Here, too, motor exhaust fumes were used, a method that, apparently was not nearly as "good" as Höss's own Cyclon B: "In Auschwitz, I never saw or heard of a single person being alive half an hour after the gas had been turned on." The uprising in Treblinka of August 2, 1943, is justly famous—a glorious feat of heroism which, alas, failed to turn the tide.

In one breath with Treblinka we must mention the name of Majdanek, 5 kilometres from the centre of Lublin. This camp was solemnly inaugurated by the gassing of 8,000 Jews in the presence of prominent guests, soldiers and civilians, who declared themselves "highly satisfied with the results. The special spy-hole fixed to the door was in constant use. The visitors were unstinting in their praise for this new installation." No doubt they, too, were connoisseurs.

Belzec, Treblinka, Majdanek. We are unable to dwell upon them any longer, and indeed we must not do so. The number of Dutch Jews murdered there may not have been large, though we can never be sure. But there is one slaughter-house with which Dutch Jews were far more familiar.

The name of Sobibor first crops up in Dutch records on March 26,

1943—in the minutes of a meeting of the Central Committee of the Jewish Council: "Reports from Germany are not unfavourable. A few of the last transports seem to have gone to Sobibor and not to Auschwitz."

Sobibor was some 80 kilometres east of Lublin and the journey there took a little longer than the trip to Auschwitz. This camp, too, was honoured with Himmler's visit: to celebrate the auspicious occasion a number of Jewish girls were gassed, a process which this august visitor and his entourage observed through the spy-hole; Himmler also presided over the disposal of the corpses. Perhaps this was the occasion on which the notorious jubilee was celebrated: the gassing of the millionth Jew in March 1943 (one source makes it only the 500,000th). Sobibor differed from Auschwitz in that there was practically no "selection" at all; true, even here, a handful of people was picked for camp duties, but for the rest Sobibor was an extermination camp pure and simple. Between March 2 and July 20, 1943, nineteen trains from the Netherlands brought in some 34,000 persons. The trainloads varied between 964 and 3,017—the latter was the so-called children's transport from Vught (June 1943). Of all the Jews sent to Sobibor from the Netherlands, we know of less than twenty survivors; most of these spent only a few hours in the camp before being sent on somewhere else. Two women succeeded in escaping during the uprising of October 14, 1943, which was sparked off by the rumour that all camp inmates were about to be shot.

In Sobibor, too, there was an elaborate system of camouflage.[1] The whole place looked like a holiday resort, with canteens, parks and rose-gardens. The Commandant's villa was called *Gottes Heimat* (God's Home). Other villas bore the names *Schwalbennest* (Swallows Nest) and *Zum lustigen Floh* (The Lusty Flea). Above the door of the gas-chamber, was a plate reading *Seuchen-Bekämpfungsstelle* (Department for Combating Epidemic Diseases). The reception was cordial in the extreme; the guards would take the children on their laps and give them goodies; they were most helpful with the baggage, which they promised to put in store and for which they would issue an official receipt. On the square stood a table with pens and ink for the writing of letters. Incoming Jews were enjoined to look after their possessions, and quite a few called at the Registration

[1] Eva Lichtman: *Het dodenkamp Sobibor* (The death camp of Sobibor) (Polish publication).

Office to make sure that everything had been properly recorded. Occasionally, however, the Germans would drop the play-acting even at this early stage; it is said that those arriving from Westerbork on March 10, 1943, were "horribly ill-treated on the way to the gas-chambers; many were beaten to death or shot out of hand".[1] For the rest, the last act of the tragedy was much the same as elsewhere, except that here no doors had to be opened afterwards: the floor itself moved to tip the corpses out; just one more example of the resourcefulness of Germany's technologists and scientists.

In this utterly inhuman and obscene system of death there was an incongruous and temporary centre of peace, an improbable island in a raging sea. This was Blechhammer Camp, a subsidiary of Auschwitz. Its inmates included a great many Dutch Jews who worked there in the ersatz petrol factory and who, for a time at least, were fairly well treated. Moreover, through civilian workers, they could keep up contact with the Netherlands and even receive parcels and letters from home.

In this camp, practically everything was obtainable: chocolate, cocoa, fruit, white bread and rolls, English cigarettes, condensed milk, sardines and genuine vodka. There were even a few "camp capitalists" who had a Christmas goose on their table—a Christmas goose on a table, in a concentration camp, mark you! Two Dutch Jews served as undertakers and wore black gloves, for people went on dying, with or without German assistance. There were splendid meals; on one occasion, a visiting SS man was heard to mumble: "Well, well, you have it good, don't you?" Variety shows broke the monotony of camp life, and had Blechhammer not been evacuated quite suddenly, many more would have survived. Quite possibly, too, they would have returned financially better off, for Blechhammer boasted a full-scale bourse, where you could exchange practically anything—one Czech Jew imported watches, others dealt in diamonds and in provisions. All this was facilitated by the thoroughgoing corruption of the camp guards, some of whom even drew a regular salary from the Jewish prisoners. Occasionally, such arrangements would be discovered and the prisoners hanged. This happened, for instance, to someone who was found repairing his shoes with a bit of discarded leather, and also to the *Kapo* (Trusty) who tried to smooth the whole thing over. What with the gallows, therefore, Blechhammer too was no paradise, and in the end, when Blech-

[1] *Sobibor* (The Hague, 1946), p. 12.

hammer was evacuated upon the approach of the Russians, its inmates ended up in one of the beastliest of all camps (Gross-Rosen), after a long march in icy cold weather during which great numbers of them perished.

### LIFE ON THE BRINK OF DEATH

Let us now look at the few who were allowed to linger on for a while. Those murdered on arrival are counted by the hundred thousand; those put to work by the ten thousand; those who returned by the hundred; and those who came forward to tell their tale in tens. It is on their scant evidence that the historian must largely base his account, fully aware that this testimony, and all the other available data, can never reconstruct the whole terrible picture. All he can hope to do is to preserve for posterity a few characteristic glimpses of a tragedy that, as we said, defies description, of a horror that was more gruesome even than Kafka's *The Penal Colony*, with its machine for cutting the victims' sentence into their very flesh. But let a surviving woman speak for herself:[1]

"Every night, the past takes possession of me. I am helplessly delivered over to an irresistible force, and carried back to a place I would give anything to banish from my memory. Down to the least detail, I keep reliving a life that had really ceased to be any kind of life at all. Often it is as if I were moving through a painting by Hieronymus Bosch, a canvas peopled with fearsome monsters. I behold men and women caught in the jaws of winged horrors. The horizon is invariably hidden behind a red veil of smoke and flame. On other nights, the past rises up before my closed eyes, with all the sharpness of a film sequence. Picture follows upon picture, with a hideous clarity concealing nothing. I know not if I am awake or dreaming. Was it only yesterday, or so many years back? Time is dissolved, but on my skin there once more burns the weal of the whip . . . But then I often feel that I am neither asleep nor awake. In this half world, memories and dreams merge to engender a feeling of unbearable oppression. I am pursued by visions of impenetrable clouds of smoke, which press in upon me until I cannot breathe. And then I become part and parcel of them. With all my powers, I endeavour to resist the fatal embrace, but try as I will I cannot free myself. And then, when I finally do manage to open my eyes, I can still see the dark grey wisps of smoke creeping along the

[1] Greet van Amstel: *op. cit.*, p. 160.

walls, just as they used to rise up day and night from the chimneys, our only way out of the camp. The petty gods, who had been set over us as guards, had left us no illusions about that. Whenever, on the way to work, we would pass the crematorium, they would make us stop, and, pointing to the smoke, they would say: 'I don't know why we have to waste our time on you. Any day now, you'll be up the chimney with the rest.' And the burning of the corpses never ceased, night or day. Always the sky was fouled by an oily cloud that filled the whole horizon, covering the sorrow-stricken barracks that were our whole world. This smoke cast a pall over everything we did, until the world we had left seemed infinitely remote and unattainable."

The question has been asked whether Dutch Jews of whom this woman was one, fared differently from other Jewish deportees. One answer was: "The Dutch suffered more than all the rest. They thought too much of their wives and children, and that was the reason why they perished." This, as we said, was one answer. But was it really *the* answer? Another explanation was that the Dutch lacked "the animal cunning, the stubborn urge to survive at any price, if necessary at the expense of others". A doctor found the answer in the sudden change of diet—from the fatty meals of former days to the almost total lack of fat in the camp food. It was said that Poles and Russians, coming as they did from countries with a harsh climate and a lower standard of living, were better able to endure hardships, more capable of taking care of themselves, of escaping notice and of fending for themselves. Not much less adaptable were the Greeks, followed by the Slovaks, the Germans, the Czechs—in that order—with the Dutch at the very bottom of the list.

According to Dr. E. A. Cohen there were relatively few suicides in the camps, but at least some of them were Dutch: among a railway gang that had to toil twelve hours a day on a food ration of half a pound of bread a day and half a litre of rape-seed soup, with the worst thugs as overseers, two men, one aged 45, the other 23, had had enough after five weeks, and threw themselves in front of a passing train. "We were ordered to carry the remains of these men into the camp and to lay them out on the parade ground. During the roll-call, the *Lagerführer* warned us not to cause more accidents of the kind that happened today. We just stood there, saying nothing . . ." These were clear cases of suicide, but what of those who, worn out by the constant struggle, lost heart and spirit and abandoned themselves to a more gradual death?

In fact, what do we really know of the emotions of these doomed legions? "I must emphasize," a doctor had written, "that we were not unhappy in the camp all the time, that we were not always asking ourselves 'When in God's name will it all end?' . . . I myself have known times when I felt completely carefree." We have met something like this in the preceding pages. But there were also those who never stopped pining for the material and spiritual consolations of former days. "Blessed are the moments when you can forget where you are," wrote a young woman, "and dream of the past as you flop down on your bunk: of a beefsteak and green peas, of warm sand running through your fingers on the beach, of putting on a new silk blouse, of enjoying a good book—*Nacht ist wie ein stilles Meer*—of listening to the Jupiter Symphony, of shopping in Amsterdam . . . but here you are so desperately alone and left to your fate."

Of many, very many, if not of all, we must suppose that at times they lived a mere shadow existence, drained of all those violent emotions that people so often attribute to them. Again, to what extent were these people subject to depersonalization and disorientation? This subject, too, is treated at length in Dr. E. A. Cohen's study of concentration camp life.[1] In another report he emphasizes the great importance of camp friendships, of comradeship: "You prized above all the presence in a camp of a few people on whom you could rely absolutely and who relied on you in turn, people to whom you could open your heart and not be afraid that they would organize (= steal) your things, people who shared what little they had with you, who would protect you and help you whenever they could, and quite unselfishly at that. Because there were no women, friendships in the camp were of a purity such as I never expect to meet again."

We, who complain of the least draught, or of an open train window, cannot even begin to understand how a single one of the prisoners survived the Polish winters, undernourished, half naked and badly shod as all of them were. But some not only did so but escaped without so much as a cold in the head. On the other hand, the number of those who succumbed to disease was legion.[2] On average, 30 per cent of the camp population was in need of medical

[1] E. A. Cohen: *Het Duitse concentratiecamp* (The German concentration camp) (Amsterdam, 1952).

[2] J. Sehn: *Konzentrationslager Oswiecim-Brzezinka* (Auschwitz-Birkenau) (Warsaw, 1957), pp. 66 ff.

attention. Up to 80 per cent suffered from dysentery. There were repulsive infections, including scabies and the like. And then there were the lice. "I must say, this was something quite terrible. We could just about get through the day, but at night things became unbearable; we itched so much that we never got a wink of sleep. To make things worse, our feet were always cold and wet. We were always hungry, and the lice were just about the last straw. I myself was suffering from tuberculosis, though I didn't know it at the time," wrote one survivor. Typhoid epidemics were unavoidable, and so were malaria, skin infections and other things too many to mention.

Still, there were hospitals in the camps, even in Auschwitz. Originally, these were mere collection centres for corpses and the dying. In 1942, however, the Jewish camp doctor made his appearance, an innovation that saved the lives of many patients and of quite a few doctors, too. A Dutch-Jewish physician had given us a description of the block in which he worked for ten months:

"Every time one went in through the door that would not shut and in which most of the glass was broken, the first thing one saw was a line of jerry-built, two-tiered wooden bunks against the walls, in which the patients were 'bedded down'. In one bunk, 2 feet wide, you might find two—or in emergencies even three—cases. The bedding itself was a badly stuffed and generally torn sack of straw, placed on a few planks that were often broken up for spills or, when there was no coal, for fuel. A small corner had been partitioned off to make a lavatory. Not that it was a WC. Two zinc buckets were placed in a wooden box, and the floor was covered with calcium chloride; the contents were emptied several times a day into a cess-pool on the square. Even that was a luxury, for, at first, few blocks could boast anything like it; in most of them, patients would have to go outside, even in mid-winter, often running a high fever, badly clad in a thin shirt and torn, thin jacket, and relieve themselves in a latrine on the square. Not a single block had bed-pans or bottles. Whenever a patient was too sick to get up and messed his bed, he was sent to the *Scheissereiblock*, the Shit Block as the Germans so elegantly referred to Block 12. Transfer there was tantamount to a death sentence. Here you were given no care whatsoever, and your food was generally 'organized' away by the staff, under your very eyes . . ."

What about drugs? Incredibly enough, for a little while there was a small supply of "pain-tablets", which served for headaches, pleurisy, arthritis, rheumatism, stomach complaints, and what have you. Bandages? Perhaps we had better just leave it with the query. Someone from another camp (a makeshift male nurse) wrote: "We had no proper drugs at all, and so we had to prescribe permanganate for dysentery, for throat infections and for everything else as well. When first I saw some of the worse cases, I was sick myself, but later one learnt to control oneself and to do one's bit. We had no instruments either, and the whole place was one foul mess. I often witnessed frost-bitten limbs being amputated without anaesthetics and with a pair of rubber-cutters."

If one fears to be ill even in one's own home, how much more so in a camp, where the sick were generally cured in the gas-chamber! People even ran this risk if they so much as looked poorly or were not fit for work. And fear of such a fate was itself a potent cause of breakdown. The only defence against it was a sort of Oriental fatalism; people simply ceased to care. As one survivor put it: "I often came across men who really did not seem to be suffering from anything but who, at a given moment, stopped washing altogether, shambled instead of walking, until they finally would not so much as move a foot. They just went out like a light."

Those were the lucky ones. Most of these fatalists, or "Muslims" as they were called, had a rude awakening, when they were suddenly seized and flung into the gas-chambers. No wonder then, that so many did their utmost to avoid being mistaken for Muslims; they would stuff their clothes with old newspapers, and hide the pallor of their cheeks with anything they could lay their hands on. "In this camp you could see people in the throes of starvation oedema, of dysentery and tuberculosis, still desperately tottering round, in a frantic attempt to pass as fit. They all went in deadly fear of being 'selected'."

Selection—from many a camp memoir, we can see how highly charged with horror this word was, in Auschwitz and elsewhere. The reader will remember that a "first selection" was held immediately upon the arrival of a new batch of deportees, when those who had to die at once were separated from the rest. These powers of life and death were usually exercised by a doctor or some other camp dignitary. Everyone would have to strip and stand to attention and those not altogether fit were condemned to death there and then. Quite often, however, perfectly healthy men would be "selected" as well, particularly when a fixed death quota had been set beforehand. This is how one Dutch doctor has described it all: "Sometimes the naked people were squashed into a small lorry, fifty at a time. If they showed any signs of hanging back, the SS would start to belabour them . . . When the lorry started, the victims would often intone the *Hatikvah* (the Zionist anthem), or if they were Dutch, the *Wilhelmus* (their national anthem). The distance to the crematoria was a few hundred yards and within the half-hour we saw the smoke and flames from the burning corpses rise up from the chimneys." The victims did not, however, invariably end up in the gas-chambers; quite a few were shot in the neck or, if that happened to be more convenient, thrown alive into the fire. According to one eye-witness, the smell was comparable to a chicken being singed. "People got used to everything, but not to the selections," said a doctor. Another witness wrote: "Often, a selection would be made on the spur of the moment, when people least suspected it. One day ten of us were running behind the dung-cart. Right in front of me was a lecturer from Amsterdam. He was unshaven and looked old and tired. Quite suddenly I saw the crook of a walking-stick slide round his neck and he was yanked away from the cart. I think he had been selected."

A woman: "I was present at various selections. On one occasion, a girl (name given) entered the quarantine block and asked: 'Does anybody want to buy my pullover for a piece of bread? I am due for gassing tomorrow and I'd like to have some food inside me before I go.' And indeed she was thin enough to be mistaken for a skeleton."

A doctor: "I saw boys of fifteen and sixteen, condemned to the gas-chamber, prostrate themselves before an SS man and plead for their lives, promising to work even harder in future. One of them said: 'I am still so young.' "

Another doctor: "At the selection, the dreaded Hauschild (a notorious 'selector') asked a boy who had been standing in the cold for over an hour: 'What are you shivering for? Are you cold? Don't worry. We'll soon warm you up a bit—in the oven."

Doctors were invariably passed over during selections, though there was an occasion when one, whose block medico had forgotten to claim him as a colleague, was condemned in this way. There were many other "clerical errors" as well. Thus, "in September to October 1944—(name given) was selected for gassing. This was a very tragic case, for the whole thing was a mistake. The wrong number had been called out."

Let us quote just one more selection scene. Its chief character was Professor A., a highly respected teacher from Amsterdam. He was taken to the camp hospital where "he was far too modest to demand anything for himself". Only when he felt his time was up, did he ask the doctors (to one of whom we owe the story) for drugs so that he would not be fully conscious when he was taken to the gas-chamber. "This was too risky for me. If Professor A. had been found dead or unconscious in his bed, they might well have started an investigation, and then God knows what would have happened. In any case, I would not do it . . . This just shows how the first thought of everyone in those camps was to save his own skin . . . And we clung to the flimsy excuse—perhaps they won't take him after all . . . So Professor A. went to the gas-chamber in full consciousness."

Then came the day, the incredible day, the day of the last selection. The horror that seemed as though it would never end was almost over. By orders from Berlin all gassings had to stop from November 2, 1944—some even claim that they ceased before that date. For the Portuguese Jews, sent from Amsterdam to Theresienstadt and thence to Auschwitz, the order came just too late: for a few Dutch Jews it came just in the nick of time. One Jewish woman from Amsterdam tells us that when the order was received she was already in the "Sauna", going over her life for what she thought was the last time. Another Jewess from Amsterdam, due for the gas-chamber, had this to say: "First they locked me up in a special hut for two or three days, and then they took me to a place with a mass of horribly maimed and emaciated women on the floor . . . A few days later, we had to line up five abreast and march to the gas-chamber. In utter despair I found the strength to break away, and hurled myself into one of the deep pits with which the camp abounded. I lay there until dark, and then went to the nearest barrack, where they accepted me without a word. In this way I escaped the last gassing in Birkenau."

Dutch sources throw much light on the general attitude of the German officers and their henchmen. Clearly, we cannot treat this problem fully; those who want a more comprehensive account are referred to the autobiography of Rudolf Höss, the commandant of Auschwitz, or, for that matter, to H. G. Adler's account of the doings of the Master Race in Theresienstadt. Höss's name looms large in many of the records. One Thilo even calls him "a first-class paterfamilias", one who never raised his hand in anger. "Everyone spoke well of him"; he was "a worthy man, not at all a bully, a devil or a sadist". "He would get up and go to work, just like thousands and millions of others. He did his work well and thoroughly. That this work involved the extermination and selection of prisoners made no difference at all. He had his duty to do and he carried it out."

A worthy man indeed, of the same ilk as that other paterfamilias,[1] who carved the words "Genuine Jewish Bone" on the handle of his pocket-knife, as the one who would proudly take his wife and children for a "happy little Sunday morning stroll" round one of the most horrible hunger-camps, or as the one who, in a similar camp, looked on while the Jews started fighting over a few rotten turnips, slapped his thigh and exclaimed, with a jovial chuckle: "I've never seen anything to touch that!" Clearly a man with a sense of humour.

Not that good humour always prevailed. Take the evidence of an Amsterdam Jewess: "I had on me a little photo of my parents, the size of a penny, which I had managed to keep through everything. When the *Feldführer* saw that I was holding something in my hand and asked me what it was, I showed it to him, and asked him to let me keep it as a memento. But he simply tore it up, saying that this was no place for snapshots—he did not even carry a picture of his own family. He must have seen the hatred in my eyes, for he gave me a few hard kicks on the body."

A "trifling incident" one might say. But there were others. The same witness tells us of a youth who was caught singing a popular French song: "Lou was ordered to go the latrine, where he was plastered all over with excrement, and made to go on singing all the time it was being done. Then he was beaten. His lungs were so badly bruised that he died a week later." More than one camp inmate became familiar with the "twenty-five on the backside", which generally reduced the buttocks to a "raw beefsteak". There were also quite a few cases of people being forced to ill-treat one another. On one occasion, a father and son were accused of pilfering bread. "Each blamed the other. They were ordered to beat each other up. And this had to go on until the son killed the father." "As a punishment, specially for Netherlanders, they used to order the 'cold spray' in which a hose was directed at the heart." No one needs to be told what was the result, or how long the agony was drawn out.

[1] N. Blumenthal: On the Nazi vocabulary in *Yad Washem studies on the European Jewish catastrophe and resistance*, Part I (Jerusalem, 1957), p. 56.

One of the tribulations of the Jewish women resulted from their being guarded by men. The Germans did what they could to "protect" the latter against race pollution, as the writer saw for himself when inspecting the all-Aryan camp brothels in Auschwitz. But accidents will happen. "I remember," one Jewish woman told the writer, "Nelly waking me at about 2 a.m. and telling me of the terrible thing that had just happened to her. She had gone to the latrine and was suddenly attacked by an SS man who soon overcame her struggles. She was almost out of her mind with terror, and I can still see the red marks where he had dug his nails into her neck, and the bruises all over her legs and arms . . . I don't know how the story leaked out, but in any case the SS got to know about it and Nelly ended up in the gas-chamber."

Were female guards any less vicious? All the records show that the answer was no. The woman we have just quoted has described the arrival of a new female commandant, with a staff of SS girls: "She was a terrible creature and I shall never understand how a young woman could be so evil."

Comments about the complete unpredictability of the camp personnel, high and low, are legion. Take, for instance, the story of twenty-five-year-old *Untersturmführer* Bergmeier, a kind man by nature, who would go round the barracks at night to see if there were any complaints, and who even allowed one to answer freely. Yet . . . when in charge of a punishment squad he behaved like a wild beast and permitted the most indescribable atrocities; whenever his henchmen did not strike hard enough, he would himself pick up the rubber truncheon and, foaming at the mouth, would wildly belabour the victim's head, back and buttocks. Another high official, a "bull-necked major with a shaven head", suddenly, and for no apparent reason, gave orders that fifteen women were to be hanged. He picked his victims at random, whereupon the others fell on their knees before him and pleaded with him to show mercy: "What finally persuaded him to change his mind I do not know. In any case, the fifteen girls remained alive. The odd thing about this man was that he worshipped his horse and would not harm a hair on its head; his riding-whip was entirely reserved for us."

We come now to one section of the camp staff with whom many Dutch Jews and Jewesses had particularly bitter experiences. These were the camp doctors, and one must clearly distinguish between the Nazis among them, who generally helped to do away with their patients, the anti-Nazis of various shades, and the Jewish doctors, most of whom cared for their patients as for comrades in misfortune. No one can say enough in their praise. Here we shall only pay tribute to those of them who never flinched from their duty, and note with regret the failure of those who faltered, however much we understand the reasons why. The best among them steadfastly upheld the noble principles of their profession—just as consistently as the Nazi doctors betrayed them. As for the latter, their deeds are made even more unpalatable by the fact that many of their most repulsive human experiments were carried out as part of a profitable contract with various German enterprises. This is generally known, and the fact is sufficiently documented. But even these doctors were not all of a kind. Many were extremely amicable, helpful and careful as they carried out their orders with the utmost professional skill. Others, and their helpers, were, to put it mildly, less dexterous. Take, for instance, the case of a female block in Auschwitz, where one of Dr. Clauberg's assistants, an *SS-Obersturmführer* and a chemical expert on lemonades and toothpaste, invented some twenty different sterilizing fluids. These were injected into live subjects by his collaborator, an SS barber, who, completely ignorant of medicine, had to take short daily lessons in gynaecology from one of the physicians. Alas, he did not learn very much, for "he succeeded in giving most of the women extremely painful and long-lasting infections of the ovary". The chemist, evidently determined on a proper scientific verification of his results, later called for 100 men to cohabit with the women. To that end, he also wanted some of the buildings redesigned, but it appears that Berlin rejected the plan at the very last moment. One of his colleagues, working with X-rays, often so damaged the intestines of his women "patients" that most of them died in agony. The few who survived disappeared in the gas-chambers as so many laboratory waste-products.

No book on the destruction of Dutch Jewry can fail to mention Johann Paul Kremer, Doctor of Medicine and Philosophy, *SS-Obersturmführer* and Assistant Professor of Anatomy in the University of Münster, if only because his diary contains several references to deportees from Holland. On September 2, 1942, he was present at a "special action" and observed that, compared with what he saw there, Dante's hell was a paradise. On September 5 he witnessed two more "special actions", one of them involving Dutch Jews. He agreed with a colleague who called Auschwitz the *anus mundi*. On

September 6 there was an excellent luncheon: tomato soup, half a chicken, potatoes and red cabbage (20 grammes of fat), pastries and simply delicious vanilla ice; at 8 p.m. there followed another "special action". On September 9 he was doctor in attendance at a flogging of eight prisoners and at a firing squad for one ("with small arms"); in the evening there was another "special action" and again on the following morning. On September 20, from 3 to 6 p.m., the prisoners' band—eighty strong—gave a concert in glorious sunshine; at lunch there were chops, and in the evening baked tench; on September 23, two "special actions", followed by "a feast" of baked pike "as much as you could eat", with real coffee, excellent beer and sandwiches. On September 27 a social evening, with an address by the Commandant (Höss), followed by a floor show, music and all sorts of refreshments. On September 30 another "special action"; on October 3 work on "fresh human livers, spleens, and pancreas". And so the diary goes on, but we need select only a few further entries. On October 12 there was a "special action" involving 1,600 Dutch Jews, with a "gruesome scene" at the last bunker. When Johann Paul Kremer uses the word "gruesome", it must indeed have been a "special action"—possibly the victims realized what was being done to them and panicked, or perhaps the mothers and fathers refused to give up their children. Dr. Johann Paul Kremer, physician and Professor of Anatomy preserves a discreet silence. He continued with his experiments and his attendance at executions—in a medical capacity. On October 18, on a cold, wet day, came another "special action" against Dutch Jews: this time he is a little more communicative. "Ghastly scenes with three women, pleading for dear life." On November 8 his fourteenth "special action" (he kept count) followed by a "cosy get-together" over Bulgarian wine and Croatian schnapps. A physician. A philosopher. A cultured man, who could quote the poets and was passionately fond of music. And a man of initiative: whenever he needed material for his biopsies, he would not wait for one of the countless "Muslims" to die but would dispatch a suitable subject with an injection. Science must be served.

We have just spoken of some of the experiments. The writer knows only too well that human guinea-pigs are not a modern innovation, that even the Ancients used them. But there is good reason to suppose that never before were human experiments performed on such a scale and with such refinements of inhumanity as in Auschwitz, and certainly not with so much conviviality—experiments followed by get-togethers, good dinners and an abundance of wine. If we insist on this point, it is because so many of the guinea-pigs were Dutch Jewish women. Some of them survived, some have written reports, and yet others felt it their duty to speak freely of their experiences to the writer, to lay aside their feminine modesty so that the world might know the truth. Theirs is the story of Block 10, a cheerless, cold and musty stone building inside the lethal barbed wire of Auschwitz; it was here that "prisoners for experimental purposes" were kept, a hundred at a time, over a long period. Many believed that the women who went there were the lucky ones, for here the "only" thing that apparently threatened them was the deadly boredom of endless waiting in complete idleness, with nothing else to think about but the fear that they might end up in the gas-chamber after all.

Great experts have written at length of the painful and humiliating experiments themselves, most of them involving the sterilization of women. (Men, too, were sterilized in Auschwitz, but we know of no single case in which a Netherlander was the victim.) This "negative demography" (the inimitable German euphemism) was carried out with exemplary enthusiasm, though not always with complete success—many of the women died before the results of the operation could be ascertained; others writhed in agony and were in any case quite unfit for the sexual intercourse which would alone provide the requisite scientific corroboration.

The name of Dr. Carl Clauberg, SS Brigade-General and one of the leading surgeons in Block 10 has become universally notorious, and not least so in the Netherlands. We know a great deal about his "scientific work"; ten years after the collapse of Germany, he was returned with a batch of other prisoners from the Soviet Union. He was arrested in November 1955 and released, but such was the pressure of public opinion, that he had to be put on trial. When the indictment was being drawn up, much consternation was caused by the discovery that, legally speaking, he had been guilty of not more than maltreatment (maximum penalty three years imprisonment) and that "no more" than four fatalities (maximum penalty fifteen years hard labour) could be brought home to him. Luckily, the German people were spared the embarrassment of a trial, as Clausberg died before the hearing. Let us merely add that many of his colleagues, guilty of similar crimes, got away with short sentences or none at all, and that quite a few of them are again practising their honourable profession. Among them is the man who first devised the idea of breaking gold teeth out of the victims' jaws—he is now a respected dental surgeon in Berlin. Another medical luminary back in practice is the professor who supervised the refrigeration experiments in Dachau. Nor are they the only ones.

So much for the doctors. What of the patients who survived the treatment in Block 10? Medical reports, dated 1959, lie before the writer. They make sorrowful reading. Symptoms of all kinds speak of permanent physical and mental damage, to say nothing of the ruined lives themselves: depression caused by infertility, chronic stomach pains, nervous tensions, permanent confinement to bed, partial or complete incapacity.

Let us say a few words more about the general camp staff. Here, as elsewhere, the Germans applied their proven tactics and made Jews torment their fellows. This brings us to the *Kapos*, a general camp phenomenon and, in the case of the Dutch deportees, the successors of what we have called the Westerbork oligarchy. As in Westerbork, many of these men had good qualities, but others identified themselves with the enemy in return for certain privileges. The rewards of Judas, the victims called these advantages. The *Kapos* themselves felt entitled to some recompense for the risk they ran in providing a buffer between the victims and their persecutors, and it must be conceded that many of them did afford some protection, and sometimes more than that. The Dutch records mention one *Kapo* who, though he punished and kept strict order, did so to maintain morale—which was the only thing that kept his men alive. One witness has testified: "X (a Dutch Jew—J.P.) was a *Kapo* but a damned good fellow all the same; he often had to deal out a few cuffs, but none of us held it against him. While he was at it, the victim would yell blue murder, as he was told to do, though X barely touched him." The same witness was far less flattering about two other Dutch *Kapos*, one of whom has also been severely criticized by other witnesses, and praised by one for his "unforgettable services to the camp . . . He always worked for the safety of his men, forced them to keep clean, protected them against disease, sustained them physically and mentally. Those who could not understand what he was doing, merely thought of him as one who came into the barracks, slapping people, or turning up on the parade ground to take names . . . Naturally, he would often have to appear brutal, but if you only knew how many people died of typhoid and how many did not wash themselves, you would understand."

Alas, here as in Westerbork, the other type predominated. The Dutch records abound with examples of abuse of power, of domineering, of downright wickedness. Even Steinmetz, who claimed that human immorality was simpler to understand than morality, would have been hard put to it to decide what was moral and what was immoral in this half-world of damnation, where you had to be a demon to survive at all.

"The first impression that I gained (of Birkenau) will remain with me for the rest of my days," wrote a young Jewish woman, who was taken there from Block 10. "So much melancholy and desolation. Just imagine, long rows of desolate stables, and round them, half-dressed or undressed women—if women they could still be called—sitting in the mud. Farther away, women breaking stones, digging and carrying away corpses. The whole scene was unspeakably sombre and grey. Beyond them, the smoke of the crematoria cast its shadow over the whole of Birkenau."

This, as we have said, was the setting of Birkenau. By now, the reader will have some inkling of what happened there. But it can be no more than an impression. Nor shall we even try to tell the whole story, but must content ourselves with a few glimpses here and there, based exclusively on Dutch accounts. Thus we shall pass in silence over some reported instances of cannibalism, or rather of necrophagy, and merely mention that many Dutch men and women were given a temporary stay of execution while engaged in the removal of corpses—sometimes one at a time and sometimes by the cart-load. We know of one *Oberscharführer* who forced a young Jewish woman to dispose of a freshly killed Jewish family: "For this purpose, he took me to a foul barn, where I had to witness a horrible spectacle. Four people, a man, a woman and two children, bullet-riddled and fearfully mutilated . . . It was a gruesome task, loading these corpses on a cart. The *Oberscharführer* stood nonchalantly by, smoking a cigarette."

During a mass clearance of corpses: "Watched twenty Ukrainians remove the gold teeth from the corpses' mouths (with pincers). Then we had to place the bodies on a plank or ladder and take them to the pyres. The Ukrainians put all the gold into their own pockets, and whenever they felt we were not putting our backs into the work, would set about us with clubs and boots. It took us fourteen days to dispose of the bodies of 18,000 Jews, and Ruth went out of her mind. I think it was on the third day that I myself became so revolted by the work that I simply could not go on. I was just busy with the corpse of a fifty-year old woman, who looked so much like my own mother. One of the Ukrainians who saw me standing there, my face contorted with grief, came up to me, screamed something I could not understand, and then pulled out a knife and slashed at my face. I quickly backed away and when I bent down again to continue the work, Ruth was lying in a heap on the ground. Try as I might to raise her, I could not . . . All she did was mutter the words: frightened—knife—Miriam. I called the other girls and quickly returned to the gruesome work, but by then it was too late, for blows had begun to rain down on Ruth."

We might also mention that the "corpse squads" would often have to sing, or work to the strains of the camp orchestra. "Murder with music" is perhaps a fitting description of this twentieth-century *danse macabre*—whenever people were marched to the gas-chambers, or about to be hanged, the band would strike up.

A Dutch physician has described the orchestra: "The flautist was a Greek gynaecologist who, on one occasion, was still playing while his own daughter rode past in a lorry, on her way to the gas-chamber."

This orchestra also included a number of Dutch Jews and so did many other camp bands. In Monowitz there were as many as eleven Dutch players, all of them wearing white suits with red pipings and red caps. A young girl tells us how a Belgian Jew, who had been caught while trying to escape, was done to death to the strains of music; in another camp, the orchestra was ordered to play the "Death Tango" during all executions (we have a photograph of them doing so). In Blechhammer Camp, three Jews were hanged for a minor misdemeanour: "We all had to witness it . . . Later in the evening, we all had to go to a concert, and while Harry Pos was singing, you could see the corpses dangling outside." A Dutch musician was conductor of the Auschwitz orchestra for some time, and that is no doubt why he survived.

The vast majority of those deported to Poland was, as we saw, exterminated immediately upon arrival or soon afterwards; the rest lingered on, some only for a short while, some for longer, under what were generally inhuman conditions. Sometimes there were the most incongruous paradoxes: the occasional, very occasional, Christmas goose and even the odd helping of whipped cream. And then again the grey monotony, with people clinging desperately to life, trying to adapt themselves to impossible conditions, nurturing illusions, and some even reaching a degree of inner detachment, of mental equilibrium and spiritual peace. Strange though it sounds, even our sparse records bear witness to lofty experiences, for instance the emergence of a tender human love relationship which it would be a profanation to document, something that calls rather for the pen of Dante—a spark of calm radiance in a human hell. Even in these depths we meet man, our fellow-man, frail but invincible, full of noble aspirations in conditions that apparently left room for little more than self-abandonment to humiliation, cowardice and squalor.

We have just spoken of the enforced musical accompaniment. But the prisoners would also burst spontaneously into song. There was much singing in the camps, and in Poland there is now a whole heritage of camp songs. But not only the Poles, the Dutch too, had their prisoners' chorus. They intoned the *Wilhelmus* and other patriotic songs; they sang the *Hatikvah.* "They would make up songs about the soup, half of them now unintelligible to us, or about the cooks, who made the soup with mud from their boots (whether that was true or not, worse things certainly did happen to the food)." A German camp inmate (in Brande) was greatly put out when the Dutch guests he had invited for a social evening finished up with the *Wilhelmus*—German Jews were not allowed to sing their own national anthem; their doing so would, of course, have been "an insult to the German people".

One more report, again without commentary: "The Germans had a great predilection for holding their selections during Jewish festivals. Thus they held a great selection two days before the Day of Atonement in 1944, so that many of those who attended the special service knew they had only one more day to live. It was a most moving experience to be present at this service, held as it was by people in rags, but whose faith in God remained utterly unshaken under all the unspeakable horrors to which they had been subjected."

The material contains a few instances of what was, short of open rebellion, the supreme act of resistance—escape. Of unsuccessful attempts there were many, but few actually got away. If we consider all the precautions taken at Auschwitz, it is almost inconceivable that anyone at all should have escaped through the many cordons, the barriers, the electrified barbed wire and so on, the more so as all the prisoners were in camp uniform, with shaven heads and tattooed arms. When captured, they would be cruelly punished. Let us quote one example: "He was caught and sentenced to be hanged. The scaffolding of the kitchen bell was used as a gallows. We were surrounded by the SS and forced to watch the execution—our first hanging. Afterwards —— (a Dutch Jew—J.P.) had to cut him down."

On more than one occasion, Höss, commandant of Auschwitz, would lock up ten prisoners and starve them to death, as a reprisal for the escape of one of their hut-mates.

A special chapter should be devoted to the lives of Dutch women who were not selected as experimental animals. Their hair shorn off, frequently clothed in rags and tatters, tattooed, ill-treated, the small surviving remnant of women deported from Holland eked out their lives in miserable barracks, exposed to constant humiliation, beatings, rape, hunger, sickness and filth; they were set to do inhuman labour or left to rot in idleness.

For various activities connected with the gassings at Birkenau, the Nazis would specially select young women and girls. They were given better clothing and a little more food, and were housed in a hut to which no one else was admitted. They had to help the unsuspecting victims undress and put their minds at ease by asking innocent questions about age and occupation. Then they would hand them a small piece of soap, so as to make the victims think they were about to take a bath. Children would be given toys. Thus reassured, most of them would willingly enter the gas-chamber, where sprinklers in the ceiling completed the illusion. After the gassings, the bits of soap and toys had to be collected up from between the corpses—they were needed for the next batch which was already waiting in front of the building.

"One morning we stood shivering on the parade ground. A bitter wind, blowing from the Carpathians across the Auschwitz plain, froze in our places. We stood there waiting for the roll-call, with our heads huddled into our shoulders. It was a defensive attitude against the cold that had become second nature to us. When the SS finally appeared, we stretched our limbs again. This morning they were selecting young women for service in a gas-chamber commando. Compared with the unbearably hard labour on the land, in rain and snow, many considered this type of work almost a God-send, while the promise of more food overcame all possible scruples. A special order that members of these commandos were all to be gassed after they had served a few weeks was known only to the camp leaders.

"When a few women had been selected, the SS man stopped in front of me, and told someone at the back that she had been picked, as well. Then something quite extraordinary happened. This woman stepped forward and said emphatically: 'I cannot do it.' My blood chilled in my veins, for it was the voice of my own daughter. Utterly taken aback, the SS man asked her why. 'Because I refuse to gas my own parents. And even if they are not my parents, they are someone else's. I cannot do it.' Then the patience of this exemplar of the Master Race was exhausted. He rained blows on her face and had her number taken, for gassing before the day was out.

"All of us were utterly dismayed. And there was nothing we could do. Many of us were weeping.

"Before they took my daughter away I was able to say a few words to her. Overcome with despair I was craven enough to beg her to change her mind. 'Your refusal won't save a single life.' She looked at me with wide eyes and very softly asked me: 'Mummy, would you do it?' Then I had to admit that I would not. 'In that case, it's all right, mummy,' she whispered, as they took her away.

"From that moment, the smoke became an obsession with me. For weeks, on end, I dared not look up at the chimney. But at night, in the bunk, or by day, when I was working, that chimney belching smoke was always before my eyes."[1]

Another team of young women was put to work on the dentures of people who had been gassed. "They had been disinfected with hot steam, and we had to clear them of wax by boiling them in a small saucepan filled with hydrogen peroxide . . ." For this work, the women asked to be issued with white coats like some of the others: "Down and out though we were, we thought we should at least stick out for that. Other girls 'organized' bed sheets for me, and Beppie and I sat deep into the night making white coats out of them. Very nice they were, too, with neat pleats and high collars—we looked extremely *chic*." In the women's block, some people would even play hop-scotch. One of the participants was a fifty-year-old grandmother who took as much pleasure in the game as her grandchildren would have done. And while they were playing these and similar games,

[1] Greet van Amstel: *op. cit.*, pp. 166 f.

death was all the while waiting for them outside. One reporter has marvelled that these women should have had the strength to carry on at all, let alone amuse themselves with games.

All these camp reminiscences show clearly how large a part chance, mere luck, played here, where the dividing line between life and death was so very thin. Noble figures appear in these camp reports, figures that evoke the name of Florence Nightingale or the deeds of the great saints: "Take, for instance, *Mevrouw* Branco, a Dutch pharmacist; as fine a woman as you would expect to meet anywhere. Someone really out of this world. The things she managed to do behind the scenes were quite incredible . . . Nothing was too much trouble for her and, unlike the rest, she would never take even a slice of bread or a helping of sandwich spread for her trouble." And, the witness adds, *Mevrouw* Branco never tired of treating the most horrible illnesses and revolting sores.

Another witness had this to say: "Branco was an incredible tower of strength, and one of those rare beings ready to sacrifice everything for another; she was a real jewel. And what was more she knew her job, unlike all the others. For so many merely pretended to be nurses to save their own skins . . . She was sweetness personified, but (or perhaps for that very reason) could not 'organize' a thing for herself."

The reports are full of other heroines, to whom the writer would like to pay his humble tribute: brave Miriam, brave Ann, brave Greta, brave Hilda, brave . . . there were more of them than we can count. All these noble Jewish women have their names enshrined in records that few people seek out and that may soon be forgotten altogether. Let us here set down for all to see our thanks, our deepest gratitude, our warm affection, nay, our love, for those who were great sisters indeed.

### BERGEN-BELSEN

Our tale of horror is not yet at an end, for no book on the fate of Dutch Jewry would be complete without an account of two more camps. What little space we can devote to them, bears no relationship to the suffering they enclosed.

One of these was Bergen-Belsen.

"I do not know if any hand can ever describe the misery of the 4,000 Jews that lay dying in Bergen-Belsen on Christmas Day 1944. But if such a hand there were, there is surely no eye that could bear, no heart that could endure, no mind that has the strength to read it. The cold was unbearable. Before Christmas a few faggots were doled out among the barracks. The women huddled round the stoves for comfort, to warm up a mug of porridge or water. The children were running about with numb hands and feet, crying with the cold, only to be scolded by their nervous parents. Christmas 1944. Today, the second day of Christmas, ten of us died. Yesterday there were seven dead. The day before that there were three. And many more will die before the week is out."

It is only fit and proper that we should have begun this account with an excerpt from the writings of our chief witness, Abel J. Herzberg. We have taken it from his camp diary, published in 1950 under the title of *Tweestroomenland* (Land of Two Streams): "Two streams ran through this camp, and not through this camp alone; National Socialism and Judaism . . . Two irreconcilable principles here met in invisible combat, though the fatal consequences of that combat were all too apparent."

We know enough about Bergen-Belsen to give a fairly extensive description of it, though once again no one can ever hope to tell the whole truth . . . It should, moreover, be remembered that Bergen-Belsen has become a sort of symbol—the British troops who unsuspectingly stumbled upon it, received a shock that they could not forget all their lives. "Belsen" became an English synonym for "horror", and even the discovery of worse camps did not change that. People knew, of course, about Auschwitz, but it was Bergen-Belsen that hardened their hearts, that spurred them to strike the final blow against the crumbling German Reich.

We have mentioned that the Germans held out the hope that inmates of Belsen might be exchanged for German prisoners, and in fact, quite a few left the camp in that way.

A German document of August 31, 1943, signed by Kaltenbrunner, contains a number of directives for the running of the "Residential Camp of Bergen-Belsen near Celle (Hanover)". Why Residential Camp and not Internment Camp, as the camps for "exchange Jews" at Vittel (France) and at Tittmoning, Laufen, Liebenau and Biberach (Germany) were called? Quite simply, because under the Geneva Convention all Internment Camps were liable to inspection by the International Red Cross, and this Reich Security Headquarters did not desire for "tactical reasons". The German document also lists the groups of Jews who would be allowed to go to Bergen-Belsen as a kind of privilege; one of these consisted of "top Jewish functionaries". Their deportation would take place under the same conditions as ordinary "evacuations to the East", except that members of this group would enjoy certain concessions: "We are prepared to be generous regarding personal effects and particularly clothing, linen, provisions, etc." In Bergen-Belsen the Jews were treated not as prisoners but as camp-inmates. They were allowed to wear their own clothes—with a star. Moreover: "Work will be allocated in the normal way" (what "normal" meant in this context remains inexplicit). A certain amount of correspondence was allowed. "The dietary standards will correspond to those laid down for concentration camps."

A document of September 21, 1943, issued in The Hague, summarized these directives and also set out in detail precisely which groups were eligible to go to Bergen-Belsen. Among them were those with Palestine stamps, those with a double nationality, Jews who had bought (*sic!*) South American passports, etc. Some groups, though mentioned in this document, were nevertheless sent elsewhere, for instance, "Jews of so-called Portuguese descent" and the "Barneveld Jews". A week earlier, on September 14, 1943, a number (305) of Jews had already been taken to Bergen-Belsen in seven coaches, and the report of their journey ends with the words: "The camp itself cannot be compared with Theresienstadt"—a sentence in which the ambiguity is more apparent than real. ("There are no sanitary arrangements.") According to one source, these 305, detached from a train bound for Auschwitz, nevertheless ended up in the Auschwitz gas-chamber, after a brief stay in Bergen-Belsen; according to another source, some of them were sent on to Theresienstadt. The regular transports did not arrive until 1944, the delay being due to the quarantine in Westerbork.

Altogether eight batches left Holland for Bergen-Belsen: 1,037 persons on January 11; 935 on February 1; 773 on February 15; 210 on March 15; 101 on April 5; 238 on May 19; 178 on July 31; and 279 on September 13, making a total of 3,751 men, women and children.

A German source gives the figure of 908 for the transport of February 1; the difference is probably due to the fact that the train included twenty-seven Hungarians. Reliable sources tell us that of all those deported to Bergen-Belsen (including non-Dutch Jews and making a total of more than 4,000) 30 per cent were saved, so that

Herzberg was quite entitled to ask: "Was this a privileged camp or was it not?" The answer is that it was indeed—the Germans even referred to it as a recuperation centre. True, the only recuperation was working oneself to exhaustion and being left to die, but when all is said and done, 30 per cent of the inmates did survive, and compared with the other camps, that was a high proportion indeed.

During the war Bergen-Belsen was regarded by many as a veritable Mecca. Jews doomed for deportation to Auschwitz offered thousands to go there instead. All those picked for Bergen-Belsen were showered with congratulations by their less happy comrades in Westerbork. With good reason, as we know today, for in Auschwitz most of them would have died almost at once. And then they travelled in proper carriages, could keep their clothes, their luggage—and their head of hair. Families were kept together. Things were much better than in Birkenau, Sobibor, Majdenek, Treblinka and Belzec. Much, much better. But bad enough in all conscience. And as time went on things went from bad to worse,[1] until here, too, they became altogether unbearable. One did not die at once. Two out of every three, took a long time over their dying—after a process of slow decay, starvation, beating, torture, sickness and, all too often, of demoralization. And it was hardly dying, just a slow fading away. Very slowly, for this was a privileged camp.

The Westerbork illusions, Herzberg tells us, were dispelled even in the train, where the SS pilfered as brutally and with as much impunity as ever they did on the train to Auschwitz, and if there still were any illusions after that, these disappeared altogether on arrival at what turned out to be an "ordinary" concentration camp: "The dismal atmosphere that hung about the place, even when nothing happened, certainly cannot be understood by those who have never been there themselves, nor, in truth, can it really be comprehended by those who were there." And, we might add, what is left of the place today resembles the nightmare atmosphere we might expect to find a few years after a disaster has destroyed all life on earth: chill, decay, emptiness and death.

Though the authorities in Bergen-Belsen eschewed extermination as such, conditions were harsh in the extreme. The work commandos were set to the hardest of labour, sometimes for nineteen hours at a stretch, guarded by merciless SS men, who set their dogs on them,[2]

[1] Herzberg: *op. cit.*, p. 223.
[2] Wielek: *op. cit.*, p. 407.

and followed this up with blows. Old people, too, had to share in the work and one of them was a man of eighty-six. The Jewish *Kapos* in this camp were particularly brutal, so much so that the Germans felt free to delegate many of their tasks to them. Blind people would be driven to "work", and so were people running temperatures of 104°. Nor were beatings the only punishment—one might be ordered to stand for hours against the barbed wire, go without food, be locked in the bunker or be sent to an extermination camp. As Josef Kramer, the new Camp Commandant, a fiend known as the "Beast of Bergen-Belsen", told one of his henchmen: "The more dead Jews you bring me, the better I like it." Another favoured means of persecution was to order sudden changes of quarters; the whole thing had to be done at the double, and was speeded on with kicks. What with the continuous stream of newcomers, one always ended up with worse accommodation; the shock often proved fatal, not to mention the loss of provisions, clothes, etc. For old people, particularly, all such removals were tantamount to pogroms; they could do nothing for themselves and simply "flopped down in the dirt amid the chaos of their few belongings and died". And: "In a veritable wilderness of excrement, lice, rags and broken glass, old women lay swearing at one another." More than one report speaks of the murderous roll-calls, which even the oldest camp inmates had to attend—people had to stand from 6 a.m. in the morning, poorly clad, in streaming rain, in snow, in mud, sometimes for eight, nine or even twelve hours at a stretch—dreading all the time that they were about to be picked for an extermination camp. After all, one was in the hands of brutes who, from time to time, would send, nay kick, whole groups to their deaths. Why these and not others? When will it be our turn? When will they let the dogs loose on use? These were so dangerous that the SS trainers had to wear thick arm-guards and constantly went about with dog-whips and pistols. And this despite the fact that the dogs were specially trained to attack none but people out of uniform. (When Berlin wanted photographs of the dogs, the photographer had to put on an SS tunic.)

A monotonous litany, all this. But the historian has no choice, he must let his sources tell their tale. And of the merciless hunger during the last months in the camp they speak with one voice. Those who were fortunate enough to work in the kitchen could still just about fend for themselves and their own, but the majority, the overwhelming majority, wasted away and succumbed to one of the many diseases that ravaged the place. The filth was indescribable; towards the end, there was hardly anyone without lice; everywhere people were crawling with them, even to the eyebrows and lashes, and to plague these unfortunates even further, the Germans would often amuse themselves by cutting off the water supply. "The accumulation of faeces," wrote a medical expert, "in some of the wash-houses was so indescribable that people shunned them altogether; almost everyone suffered from dysentery, until all the barracks were oozing with it."

As early as July 1944 Loden Vogel noted in his diary:[1] "The man below me has a gangrenous leg, which smells like the cheese we were given yesterday. The whole thing is horrible, for the flies settle on it, and to make things worse he had dysentery again." And this, mark you, was in July 1944, almost a year before the end of the war. And the winter was much worse. In his account J. Weiss mentions fourteen (reported) cases of cannibalism; a doctor who protested to the Germans that the only way to eradicate cannibalism in the camp was to give the inmates more food, died within a week. The "cannibals" themselves were apparently hanged. A Dutch Jew speaks of flesh, brought in by the Section Leader—a chunk wrapped in paper drenched with blood; he was also shown corpses with their ears cut off or without their sexual organs. Other horrors abounded as well. This is what a young woman in Bergen-Belsen had to say:

"My diary stopped at Christmas 1944. I was too sick to continue, was running a high temperature, was racked by a bad cough and dysentery. People said it was camp fever. My temperature went up and down. Occasionally I would get up; sometimes to fetch water, when there was no one to bring me a bucket, or to be present at roll-calls, which even the sick had to attend. The roll-calls were often much longer than it took to count the people there. Sometimes the Germans would keep us for hours in the icy cold, by way of punishment they claimed. Such punishment often went hand in hand with the withholding of our rations. The new camp elder had been given orders by the SS to make sure this "star camp" was not turned into a pig-sty. And so he doled out punishments for dirt in the barracks, dirt in the street, dirt in the wash-house. But what can you do when you are squashed together, two to the bed, and both of you have dysentery? What can you do when you have to go to the lavatory,

[1] Loden Vogel: *Dagboek uit een Kamp* (Camp Diary), p. 27.

some 400 yards outside the barracks, when your body, shaken with cold and fever, is suddenly seized by cramps? What if you can't stop yourself? The lavatories in the wash-house (two!) were invariably blocked up, so that the whole place resembled a cess-pool . . . Early in the morning the camp would look like a living dung-heap. And still the camp elder doled out punishment. He kept us standing during roll-call and deprived us of food. His remedy against diarrhoea: 'If you don't eat, you can't shit either!' "

And the same witness also tells us of a death, a very ordinary death:

"The woman in the bunk below died after hours of bitter torment. I knew her when she was still beautiful and healthy. An elegant, vital sort of woman she was. And here she was all alone in a camp: her husband in France, or probably in England by now, her daughter on the run in Holland.

"She had wasted away until she was no more than a sallow skeleton. Her eyes were sunk into her oedema-swollen cheeks, she was in terrible pain. It was said that hers was no 'ordinary oedema' but a cerebral one. She would suddenly burst into screams, ranting and sobbing like a small child. At night, I could not get to sleep, in the day I could think of nothing else. She died after a ghastly night, and they fetched her away. When they turned her mattress over for the next claimant, a spotless crêpe handkerchief bearing her monogram dropped out of the filthy bed."

And what of those who survived in this hell? The same witness mentions cases of incredible selfishness and ruthlessness, and ends: "I knew all these people, I witnessed the worst demoralization, the desecration of corpses, prostitution, egoism and every sort of wrongdoing." But, she adds: "I am not putting this down on paper because I think that I myself was any better, it was simply that I didn't get the chance to do likewise . . ."

And this is what Herzberg had to say:[1]

"Time and again we were taken aback by the spiritual and moral decline, indeed ruin, all round us. Everyone stole, not only those from the poorer classes but leading businessmen as well. The deputy manager of one of the biggest Dutch banks was once caught cutting slices from a fellow-prisoner's loaf of bread. A cultured and charming lady was not above getting up in the night and stealing butter. Another, whose husband had been the director of an im-

[1] Herzberg: *Tweestroomenland*, p. 41.

portant concern, filched jam from a baby's crib. A third, from a highly respected circle, would rummage through the beds, which she could easily do as she was a nurse, pilfering sugar from hidden bags and tins. The chief buyer of a firm with a world reputation stole three bread-rations from one of his acquaintances; the son of a well-known figure from Amsterdam filched a case full of provisions and cigarettes from his best friend . . ."

That was in August 1944, and there were still eight months to go before the war was over!

Loden Vogel wrote on January 5, 1945: "After the war, I would like to live in a simple home for old age pensioners, and eat fancy cakes with my tea every day. I am old before my time."

On February 15 he added: "I am dead tired, hungry and at the end of my tether—but somewhere, a part of myself, the most important part, remains untouched, at peace . . . *Something in us remains forever immutable*."

For even in this inferno, where it seemed impossible that anyone could preserve his integrity, his honesty, his decency, his ideals and kindliness, somehow there were those who managed to do so. The Germans tried to turn all their victims into beasts, but try as they might, some, perhaps even many, remained profoundly human. Let the sources speak once more:

"About a hundred of us were working in a hut full of old shoes, and between all the dust and dirt we would sit together at the table and hold serious debates. Among us was a German professor, a sociologist, the Chief Rabbi of Salonika, a high German civil servant and a doctor. And while we were sorting the shoes, or at least pretending to do so, we would all listen to introductory lectures on sociology, under the suspicious eyes of the German guards, or hold debates on justice, religion and history, animatedly philosophizing about God and the world. Each afternoon a few children aged from fifteen to sixteen would come along to be taught history, biology and even the first steps in Latin. It all had to be done in whispers, but both teachers and pupils showed great enthusiasm."

The material abounds with examples of human solidarity, of kindliness, sympathy and compassion—"the flowers on this dung-heap" someone has called them. Here, too, there were the incorruptible; here, too, there were many kingly spirits. The whole thing seemed—we cannot stress it enough—quite impossible, and yet it happened. Let the reader attend with reverence to what Herzberg wrote on September 23, 1944:

"It is awful here. Any German camp for Jews is awful, awful in every way, inside and out. And yet . . . And yet . . . even here there is sometimes to be seen a noble profile proudly proclaiming that all the suffering in the world need not necessarily blight the human soul, but may raise to sublime heights what lies hidden even in the murkiest depths of human experience. Even here, you are sometimes greeted by radiant eyes, in which the miracle of love shines forth undimmed. Or by a face so fresh, so glad, so young, so full of faith and hope, that it seems illuminated with the dew of eternal happiness. Or again you may hear a word spoken, a word the tone of which resonantly proclaims the brotherhood of all men. You may see a man rendering help to his fellow, a doctor applying a bandage, a woman cooking for a suffering comrade, another quietly slipping off her own warm coat and putting it over a sick one, a mother taking orphans under her wing and caring for them with all the sublime self-sacrifice of the maternal impulse."

And in an earlier passage: "We salute you, little grandmother; you have not changed, you with your kind old face, your fine grey curls, your smiling mouth, you who give help wherever it is needed, who care for the sick, console the dying, strengthen the weak, giving a clean sheet here, a potato there, tucking in at night, bringing them hot water, giving them a tit-bit and never losing faith in them. We salute you, little boy, caring for your lonely baby sister, combing her hair every morning, sharing with her the few good things that come your way. We salute you, mothers, who—come what may—yet find the heart to keep your children clean and healthy. We salute you, all who have remained steadfast, who refuse to give in or to surrender, who have held high your heads in this unspeakable vale of tears."

In this passage Herzberg has referred to the children—in Bergen-Belsen too the Germans in their wisdom, saw fit to "keep families together", and, miraculously enough, some of these children emerged undamaged from this pit of hell. Undamaged in body that is, but what of their minds?

"The bed inspection was the worst of our terrors: who would be the next victim? This fear we could not help communicating to our children; for years to come, my little daughter—who was two and a half years old when we were liberated—kept playing at bed-inspection and, whenever I entered her bedroom, would cry out in a panic: 'Bed inspection, bed inspection,' as she tried, with frantic gestures, to straighten out a bedspread on the floor."

According to Vogel: "The children were hopelessly out of hand. Their education was a concoction of sloth, incompetence, bigotry and ill-digested Zionism. M. (who is now a school-teacher) tells me that the children would rattle off a Hebrew song, of which they did not understand a single word, whenever they were bored by a lesson."

And a doctor found that "the behaviour of a number of children very quickly became psychopathological . . . Within a few months, quite a few of them, from model families, began to act like the most neglected waifs and strays." Rowdiness, ganging up ("with elected chiefs"), and refusal to listen to anyone were the order of the day. Not surprisingly, when the youngsters were the constant witnesses of their parents' and teachers' humiliation at the hands of the Germans. Why should they respect people who could be treated like that? Moreover, the adults were irritable, hungry, sick, feeble and impatient. How, then, could their children remain cheerful, gay or obedient? "Bed-wetting was a veritable plague in the thickly crowded barracks." People did what they could to prevent it, often with some success. They also tried to teach and guide the children, more often than not without success. The incredible thing is that they ever succeeded at all.

In the spring of 1945 Josef Weiss presided over the Passover service in the children's home. Typhus, hunger and filth reigned supreme, yet his voice was steady as he read from *The Haggadah*: "Let all who come, eat at our table" and from every adult within earshot came the answering "Amen". Thirty children, all in their "best" camp clothes, sat round the table. The ritual questions were all put and answered. There were even the traditional dishes, almost entirely made out of swedes, but "beautifully prepared" by a devoted woman, and tricked out with all sorts of extras. And so at the nadir of their suffering, shortly before the evacuation of Bergen-Belsen, the Jewish spirit touched its zenith with this celebration, this time-honoured observance, this feast of freedom, this token of inviolable faith.

Shortly before the evacuation, we said, for Bergen-Belsen was evacuated like so many other camps, cleared of its prisoners by the Germans, even while the liberators were approaching. The basic pattern was the same in all the camps: the Germans drove all their flies to the centre of the shrinking web. No one must be allowed to get away. It was a constant trek from the periphery, sometimes in trains but mainly on foot. Let the reader imagine those first months of 1945, those last months of the war, when Jewish survivors (of the non-Jewish ones this book does not speak) were streaming through a country on which bombs were raining from all sides, and which was fast crumbling, struggling along in misery, cold, filth and disease. Their SS escorts had by no means lost heart—stragglers were shot down and the rest were kept together for delivery to camps which, in turn, would be evacuated soon afterwards. In that very spring, many who had somehow managed to keep alive until then, perished of hunger, sickness or just bloody murder. And their persecutors, though now fighting with their backs to the wall, yet would not spare men and materials from this satanic purpose, butchering tens of thousands, indeed hundreds of thousands of victims in a final orgy of senseless destruction.

The train from Bergen-Belsen is clearly visible in this cloud of darkness, because what happened on it is unusually well documented. The testimonies do not agree in every detail but the main points are clear.

In the spring of 1945 a *Hauptsturmführer* arrived from Berlin with instructions that some 7,000 people must be transferred to Theresienstadt. The Jewish camp leaders pointed out that, since 85 per cent of the prisoners were seriously ill, this was out of the question. But by early April the Allies were so close at hand that the Germans overruled all protests. We know of at least two trains carrying Dutch Jews out of the camp—the first left on Sunday, April 8 (according to Kolb, the author of an excellent monograph on Bergen-Belsen, on April 6), the second at midnight on Tuesday, April 10; only the worst cases and the dying were left behind. By that time, the camp was already full of the corpses of people brought to Bergen-Belsen from other camps: "They lay stacked up everywhere, like so many loaves of bread, only here a layer of heads was piled upon a layer of feet, and so on . . . Over the camp hung a miasma of stinking swedes, filth and decay, mingled with the all-pervading smoke from the crematorium."

On the first train, carrying altogether 2,400 persons, 179 were Dutch; this train was intercepted in Magdeburg by British (according to Kolb, by American) troops. "They came just in the nick of time. The train was due to be driven into the Elbe with every soul on board." We know much more about the second train. We shall spare the reader the ghastly story of how these terribly emaciated and sick people were herded to the train; we need only mention that the station itself was some five miles from the camp. The train had just carried a load of typhus cases and had been neither cleaned nor disinfected. One witness tells us that her own truck was full of "people with typhus, pleurisy, suppurating wounds, tuberculosis, all of them virtually dying of oedema and all covered with lice". For thirteen days, thirteen long days, they "travelled" through Germany, passing Berlin on the way. From time to time, the train would stop and those who could still stand would try to beg food or drink in villages or isolated farms for their families and themselves. They ate whatever they could lay their hands on; according to Herzberg, many lived on potato peel. "Worse even than the lack of food was the fact that they found it impossible to get any sleep for two long weeks. Practically everyone had dysentery, so that the train was an open sewer." Many, very many, died; they were buried by the wayside—"and those who had to do it demanded extra rations for their labours".

And even here, even under these conditions, even in this hell, there were those who did not falter. Stories of self-sacrifice and compassion abound. The adults looked after the children, the healthy (and who among them was that?) cared for the sick; people came to the aid of the old, friends helped friends. And all this when it was well-nigh impossible to fend for oneself.

This is how one young woman put it: "I have already said that it was quite a feat even to wash yourself in the morning. There was hardly room to remove a garment . . . Most of us thought nothing of stripping in the presence of all the men. It simply had to be done, we had no choice. But we could hardly believe our good fortune, when the train stopped and we came upon a little stream in a wood or meadow. Then my first thought was never 'how do I fill my tins?' but 'how quickly can I get myself clean?' It was early April and still rather cold for a bathe, and certainly for someone who had not been free from disease for months on end. I stood in the dark, cold water, beneath willows stirring in the spring wind. It was a glorious feeling. Everyone who was at all fit, got right in, and a few mothers set to washing nappies. Quite suddenly, all the misery, filth, oppression, hunger, deprivation and fears for the one who was fast fading away (her husband—J.P.) dissolved. Even the forebodings about our destination left me, as I stood in the water, scooping it up with my hands and pouring it over my shivering body. Bergen-Belsen was no more. There was no hunger, no corpses, no more suffering. I was alone. It was spring. And though I was exhausted, I felt the surge of life and was glad."

The endless, interminable journey came to an end on April 23 in Tröbitz, a village some 35 miles from Leipzig, where the victims were freed by the Russians. This memorable moment has been described by more than one witness. Free! Those who could went out to forage and took shelter in the village. The witnesses are all agreed about the helpfulness of the Russians, but even they could not liberate anyone from typhus. And typhus had so many in its grip! Most of the doctors and all the former hospital staff were down with it and, according to Weiss, had the Russians not helped, every one of them would have died. He estimates the number of dead between April 10 and the departure from Tröbitz to the Netherlands at about 600 (out of a total of 2,500).

And Herzberg[1] says: "For two months they remained at Tröbitz, in this warm spring, this blossom-time made melancholy by suffering. People crept about, shaken by fever, sickness, misery and longing, hobbled through the few streets of this lonely village. Would there never be an end to all this dying? With the help of the Russians, hospitals were set up and two large Jewish cemeteries laid out. The mood was sombre. Then slowly, slowly, the disease receded and finally disappeared. After two months, the repatriation of the handful of survivors to various parts of Europe began."

Two Jewish cemeteries. Let us end our report on Bergen-Belsen with a few details from a document that lies open before us. Many a Dutch and German Jew buried at Tröbitz is described as a citizen of Ecuador, Paraguay, Peru, San Salvador or Honduras. Here too were many stateless Jews, people whose first name could not be given, and some whose grave bore only a number. Let us look at their ages—there was a woman of seventy-six, a boy of eight months. There were names of people the writer knew. May they rest in peace. The train that carried all of them did not end up beneath the waters of the Elbe—that was meant to be its fate, as well; still death came to claim many of its passengers—in a little German village in high spring. *Requiescant.*

[1] Herzberg: *Tweestroomland*, p. 285.

## EVACUATION

It is hardly necessary to repeat that the evacuation of Bergen-Belsen was only one of many. Moreover, it was possibly, or even probably, one that took place under the least unfavourable conditions: The prisoners at least had a little breathing space, could fend for themselves on the way, were not too harassed by the guards and, when all is said and done—most of them survived. The "normal" evacuation by train or on foot was much worse. Many of those who went by train died of hunger, cold and suffocation; those who went on foot were exposed for months to the rigours of a cold winter. It has been possible to reconstruct the route of several of these death-marches; we know on which days the miserable processions straggled through what villages: hundreds of thousands being hounded through them under strict guard, as though they were so many dangerous criminals. One of the survivors has tried to give us some idea of the mentality of these guards, who were apparently pulled several different ways by their own interests: if they did away with all the prisoners, they themselves would be sent to the front and that was unthinkable; on the other hand, to get rid of the majority would make their task easier; if they succeeded in reaching a camp with however few, then they themselves would not have to go foot-slogging any farther and could still evade the perils of the front line. There were very many other considerations as well. No one will ever be able to reconstruct the full horror of this tragedy; official documents are few and far between and are, in any case, based on mere glimpses of the whole long ordeal.

Some records describe the prelude to the evacuation of Auschwitz. According to one witness, he and his circle of friends even contrived a few celebrations, with a full-scale New Year's Eve dinner ("consisting of mashed potatoes, baked liver sausage, and methylated spirits filtered through charcoal . . . I could not bring myself to drink very much of this stuff, for fear that I might go blind"). At 4 a.m. a few prisoners in Block 28 "made such a din that you didn't know if you were coming or going". A drunken SS leader delivered a speech in which he made free with the word "comrades", a term that had a strange ring in the ears of the prisoners. When they looked askance at him, he went on to say: "Of course we are comrades. It makes no difference now whether you are behind barbed wire or outside; we are all in the same boat."

The group to which this eye-witness belonged left Auschwitz about the middle of January, many of them behaving as though they were going on a holiday: "Though the snow lay heavy on the ground, we all burst into song." Many, who were too weak to move, had to be left behind, and others elected to stay. The Russians were said to be close by (some said they were only some 10 miles away). Remaining in the camp meant running the risk of being shot by the retreating guards, but that struck many as the lesser evil. Some contrived to hide themselves and spent a few agonizing days between the departure of the last German and the arrival of the first Russian. Agonizing, because the Germans could and often did come back, with dire consequences. No doubt, the choice between staying and going was but rarely taken on logical grounds. One stayed, one went, one did not know why.

Many, but by no means all, of our sources speak of a second dilemma: should one try to escape *en route* or go on with the rest. People were trudging through the land in long columns, crossing it in trains, often passing through wooded regions where a single bold leap might land one in freedom. Quite a few, indeed, leapt and survived. But the risks were enormous. The guards fired mercilessly at every fugitive, and even if one escaped them, there were always the dogs. And if one got clear of the dogs—one still had to go in search of food and shelter, and was thrown on the mercy of the local population. Though quite a few of these proved sympathetic, most were completely indifferent or actively hostile. Needless to say, the more hostile they were the more abjectly and loudly they professed their innocence when the tide finally turned against them.

". . . I think it had become a question of principle with me. Until then, I had lived in the camps as a Jew, and now I was determined to continue as a Jew and, if need be, to die as one. This was a deliberate decision and I never felt a need—though I did consider the possibility—to change my mind."

That was the response of one man.

What of the rest? Can we really hope to describe their death-march, their slow and painful procession through war-torn Germany?

"This death-march was one long horror. Just like the months that followed, during which one was deprived of even the last vestige of human feeling, felt struck to the very soul with insults and humiliation and was treated as though one were the dregs of the gutter. To survive at all, you had to stoop so low, that sometimes you prayed for death to come and release you."

Many knew almost from the start that it would be like this: "At first we tried to keep count of the corpses, but soon their number grew out of all reckoning . . . Women got mixed up with our group, old ones and young ones, walking in slippers or barefoot. You would try to help them along for 2, 3 or 4 kilometres, but in the end you just had to abandon them." And what happened then? "The callous indifference with which the SS would ask a woman, 'Can't you go any farther?' had to be seen to be believed. The victim would say nothing, and simply bend her head for the *coup de grâce* . . . And when (as we passed through Upper Silesia) the local people came out, bringing us hot tea, the SS tipped it away before our very eyes." Our witness went on to say: "The transports left behind them a ghastly trail of prisoners with smashed or bullet-ridden skulls and with faces beaten into a pulp."

This was the fate of those who went on foot. Were those who went by rail much better off? Let us listen to a thirty-four-year-old woman: "For three days and three nights, we had to march, in the freezing cold, without food or drink. Anyone who faltered was shot out of hand. Next we spent five indescribable days and nights in an open coal-truck, which finally delivered us to Ravensbrück."

Or take this report by a man: "Suddenly there was a shot. We peered over the top. A prisoner was lying with his face on the ground. Dead. We all thought, 'Well, his sufferings are over.' People said, 'They'll do that to all of us.' Then a madness seemed to seize them. Another man jumped off the truck. A shot. There he lay. 'They didn't get him,' someone exclaimed, 'he's just shamming. As soon as they're gone, he'll get up and run for it.' 'No, he won't—by then he'll be frozen stiff.' A guard approached. Picked up the struggling man, and then shot him several times in the face. It wasn't a face after that. A few more people leapt from the trucks. All the guards were standing on that side. The men ran, in a sort of jog trot. With wooden clogs. On the slippery ground. The guards fired. They aimed mainly at the legs. And the abdomen. Leaving their victims writhing on the ground and screaming in agony until they froze to death. Again, people jumped off the truck. Now they begged the guards to shoot them. One who had fallen on his knees some ten yards away screamed: 'Please, oh please, good sergeant, good people, won't you please shoot me? Do me that mercy!' There he knelt begging and pleading, for ten long minutes. The guards were tickled pink. They told him to sing for it. And then he began: 'Shema Israel, Adonai Elohenu, Adonai ehod,' and the whole truck joined in. All of us reciting the prayer of the dying. 'Put a bit of life into it,' called the guard. 'And you, up there, keep your bloody traps shut'. And on he sang: 'Adonai duhenu, our only God . . .' A shot. The prayer stopped. All was still."

The same witness tells us that of this column totalling some 13,000 prisoners, 6,000 died during the eight days' train journey.

What precisely happened when the evacuees reached the camps, we do not fully know. Sometimes they would be allowed to stay, but more often than not they would be shunted out again after a few days or even a few hours. Here, too, the dogs did their duty: "At one time, there were two young boys with us, with their father. One day, when we were passing through a village, the father said he would push the children into the first house with an open door. No sooner said than done. We hadn't gone much farther, when a local lad, who had seen it all from a window, told the SS. The scene that followed was blood-curdling: the SS set their eighteen dogs on the children. We had to stand by and watch. The children's shrieks pierced our ears. There was blood all over the road. The screams went on. Then a few pistol shots."

And those who somehow survived it all, and arrived at the very last stop? "We suffered hunger as never before. I supplemented my 'diet' with grass, young fir branches, charcoal and lumps of ordinary coal."

Here, too, there were reports of cannibalism, but these we shall not pursue. No less horrible is the story of a train that arrived in Buchenwald with the remnant of a group of 4,000 prisoners from Poland. Of the 4,000 who had begun the journey in open coal-trucks many weeks before, only 300 had survived. "Many arrived with frozen arms and legs, that simply snapped off as the trains were unloaded. The transport arrived on Friday at noon. It left again next morning."[1] The unloading of the corpses by the prisoners "proved a difficult task, since the bodies were frozen together". The reader may take it that these are not the only macabre details we could give. We have deliberately said no more than is absolutely necessary to intimate a reality that cannot possibly be described.

[1] Hemelrijk: *Zeven maanden concentratiekamp*, Part III, p. 28.

THERESIENSTADT

Nor do we mean to tell the full story of Theresienstadt, which was unique in that such large numbers survived their stay.

Let us at once begin with a few remarks about our sources. Of Theresienstadt we actually have a large quantity of illustrative material. This includes the famous children's drawings exhibited in many countries, and also drawings and paintings by adult prisoners. Their work speaks to us with the brush of a Callot or Goya, depicting the horrors of war, the ghoulish atmosphere in which a teeming mass of victims lived under the constant threat of hunger, degradation and cruel death. Bedrich Fritta and Karl Fleischman were only two among many such painters. During a visit to Prague, in 1958, the writer was able to see an exhibition of Theresienstadt drawings; a wall reserved for the work of the Dutch painter Jo Spier gives one the impression that the whole place was an idyll. This holiday camp atmosphere was precisely what the Germans were trying to pass off on the world, and particularly on the Danish Red Cross. They even took a film, for which purpose Theresienstadt was, for several weeks (from August 16, to September 11, 1944) turned into "the Hollywood of concentration camps". With a cynicism that beggars description the Germans forced the Jews to play out a charade. Here, all at once, was a happy little community, well-fed, sociable, carefree, well-dressed and spotlessly housed; here the butcher of Theresienstadt, Rahm, who was afterwards hanged, patted little boys on the head, and led them by the hand like a fond father. The title of the film was: *Hitler schenkt den Juden eine Stadt* (Hitler's gift of a town for the Jews). A town apparently rolling in money (worthless "ghetto crowns"), where there was nothing you could not buy, where Hoffmann's tales had come true, where people recuperated on deck-chairs in the sun, where children not only had a play-centre, romping merrily on rocking-horses and see-saws, but also a special pavilion made of wood and glass (materials that were difficult to obtain in war-torn Germany), with beautiful drawings of animals, with a fine kitchen, showers, day-beds and other brand-new apparatus. We could go on and on, but will merely add that the very manner in which the ground floors of the houses, into which outside visitors were only allowed to peep, were modernized and stocked with quality furniture and *objets d'art*, with flowers in large vases, etc., the way in which Jews were suddenly allowed, nay forced, to go in for gymnastics and all sorts of healthy outdoor sport, sufficed to show the lengths to which the system was prepared to go. And, of course, there was method in their madness. The film was, after all, intended to refute what Hitler chose to call the "atrocity stories". What better proof of the Führer's paternal care than this happy settlement? *Hitler schenkt den Juden eine Stadt.*

And barely had the film been made, when rumours about an impending deportation swept through the camp, and there was prepared "one of the ghastliest tragedies".[1] It is not the Theresienstadt of this catastrophe that Jo Spier has bequeathed to us. What he drew was a false façade and not the chambers of horrors lurking behind it. What he showed was only what the Germans wanted to be shown.

According to Leo Baeck, three things were typical of Theresienstadt. The first was that it deliberately created conditions under which life could not flourish: "Living space was replaced by dying space." Secondly, it brought out all the worst in people, as more and more of them were squashed together in less and less space. And thirdly, by indiscriminately herding together disparate groups from every part of Europe, it accentuated the tension even further. Theresienstadt was a ghetto, but it was more than that. It was one of the portals to Auschwitz, one of the sluices on the way to the gas-chamber. And in this sluice many, very many, Jews were caught. Theresienstadt, no less than Bergen-Belsen, was a station on the road to death. However, while this war ended too late for the millions in other camps, it ended just in the nick of time for many in Theresienstadt. Among them were a few Dutch groups, which is why Theresienstadt is included in this book.

One witness has praised Theresienstadt as being "incredibly beautiful in the spring, with all the trees and parks in full blossom". Another has spoken of the "picturesque little town" with "decorative walls". Theresienstadt was, in fact, a small garrison town with seven parallel streets crossed by five others, covering an area of some 700 yards by 500 yards. It contained a large number of barracks, imposing and built according to plans by Italian architects; particularly in spring, people said, one could imagine oneself in a North Italian village. In the centre, was a large square, set out with trees. In normal times, the town held 7,000 people, which was about the limit of its capacity. Yet during the war, this "Jewish settlement" held not 7,000 but 60,000 people at a time.

[1] H. G. Adler: *Theresienstadt 1941–1945*.

When the writer looked the place over in 1958, on a still September evening, after travelling some 40 miles from Prague, his main impression was one of a ghost town—where once so many thousands had been crammed together, hardly a soul was now to be seen. There was no sound at all, not even on the large central square. The writer went to the barracks, the crematorium, the fort, taking everything in, and listening to his two guides, who had been there as children.

One of them told how he was allowed to help clear the "mausoleum", the cellar where the ashes of the dead were stored. These ashes were due to be thrown into the river Eger, and for this work volunteers were given a tin of sardines apiece. "We had a rare old time and on top of it—sardines . . . The ashes were kept in three types of boxes, all with a label bearing the name, birth-date and date of death; prominent camp inmates had iron boxes, the less distinguished had wooden boxes, and the rest cardboard ones. The mausoleum was cleared a hundred boxes at a time. We would toss them to one another and, in the case of iron, yell out: 'Look out, here comes another celebrity.' Quite often a tooth or something would fall out, which we would throw into another box. The best fun of all was mixing together the big shots and the lesser lights."

He added that his sister, who was eight years old at the time, burst into tears when her mother would not let her join in. Our young guide, who claimed that some 30,000 boxes were flung into the Eger, further explained that the whole episode "made no impression on me at all". Probably because his mind was filled with another horror: he had witnessed a German being shot at close range. "The bullet entered his eye and it was a ghastly sight. Even though he was only a German, still it was terrible to watch his whole head split open." A number of adults were present at the Eger as well: one eyewitness says that, between them, they disposed, not of 30,000 but of 40,000 boxes: "The whole thing was like a ball game, with the boxes being tossed from hand to hand." One of the witnesses, however, felt that she simply could not continue, not even for the extra sardines. When she complained, the Germans allowed her to stop; an old lady was let off as well, but a third woman, who complained of a weak heart, was refused: "If I let you off, everyone's going to have heart trouble." Perhaps we might add that when Kaltenbrunner demanded the removal from Theresienstadt of 5,000 Jews over the age of sixty, he was told in Himmler's name: "The *Reichs-*

*führer* cannot countenance the deportation of Jews from Theresienstadt, since this might dispel the illusion that Jews can live and die in peace in this old-age ghetto."

Live and die in peace. It was easy enough to die there, very, very, easy, and one could even live in Theresienstadt. But in peace? Practically all the documents are full of the terrible overcrowding in this nightmare town, of conditions "worthy of the pencil of a Brueghel or the pen of a Kafka", what with its swarm of human flotsam, tortured by fears and hounded by merciless and demented tyrants. And in all this squalid tumult, in this vast crowd, you could be lonely as nowhere else, but never, never, alone. The work was filthy, long and soul-destroying, and there was the ever-present threat of deportation: "That fear followed us into all our dreams, and plagued us every day, from hour to hour." The mere rumour of an impending transport was enough to cause widespread panic. Let the reader recall that more than sixty transports, with almost 100,000 persons, were sent from Theresienstadt to Auschwitz. Under such circumstances, how could anyone fail to walk in constant terror? How could anyone retain his mental balance? Just listen to Utitz,[1] who tells us that the mental home—Theresienstadt had even that—held a patient suffering from delusions of grandeur: he imagined that he was a member of a Council of Elders, and as such he demanded unconditional obedience, behaved like a prince, or rather as he thought a prince would behave. A member of the Council of Elders, mark you, that completely powerless body, a convocation of shadows, founded on German orders and just as readily dissolved . . .

And then, just as in Westerbork, just as in Bergen-Belsen, and just as in all other camps, there were the various diversions, physical and otherwise—sports, games, concerts, cabarets, theatre, lectures. In almost every branch of art and science, Theresienstadt could boast first-class representatives, not a few Dutchmen among them. Lederer[2] claims, that on the cultural plane, Theresienstadt was the freest place in all Europe: he put this down to the German policy of keeping up appearances. According to him, all this "culture" served chiefly to lull the inmates into a false sense of security, acted as a soporific—here, too, people left for the extermination camps to

[1] E. Utitz: *Psychologie des Lebens im Konzentrationslager Theresienstadt* (Psychology of life in Theresienstadt Concentration Camp) (Vienna, 1948), pp. 5–6, 66–69.

[2] Z. Lederer: *Ghetto Theresienstadt* (London, 1953), pp. 4–5.

the strains of *The Bartered Bride.* (One of the lyrics asked: "Why shouldn't we be happy?")

We have said that some of the artists came from the Netherlands. This brings us to the Dutch inmates in the camp. Since their fate was not so very different from that of the others, we shall here concentrate on only a few facts and figures.

Once again, there is disagreement on some points and almost complete unanimity on others. For instance, Herzberg's total figure of deportees arriving at Theresienstadt exceeds the number actually registered there by seventy-two. A special difficulty is the fact that in some transports the Dutch were not clearly distinguished from others, and that in one instance their journey did not begin in the Netherlands.

A document signed by Aus der Fünten gives precise details about the first transport of April 21, 1943, by which 295 Jews left Amsterdam at 1.42 p.m.; the greater part—101 men, 79 women and 15 children—had arrived in the capital from Westerbork on the previous day; to them was added a number of people from the *Schouwburg*. They all travelled in seven third- and two second-class carriages (one of them meant for war invalids). We know a great deal about the composition of this privileged group; we have practically all their names and know that most of them, almost without exception, were German Jews. Fifty-three are said to have survived the war. The material also contains vague references to a train leaving Westerbork on September 14, 1943, and there are lists of names of those who were supposed to travel on it. This train deposited the 305 passengers destined for Theresienstadt at Bergen-Belsen, whence 281 of them are said to have gone on to Theresienstadt on January 25, 1944. It is also said that seventy-one of them survived, but the facts are far from certain. Later, on November 17, 1944, forty-eight Dutch children from the orphanage, with three people in charge, left Bergen-Belsen for Theresienstadt; we are told that all fifty-one of them survived, but this is too good to be true. We know much more about the transport of January 18, 1944; it left Westerbork at 10.42 a.m., and carried 870 Jews. We know their names—many of them Dutch—that 387 of them had been specially picked for their services "in the building up and running of Westerbork", and that a further 141 were parents of people who had made themselves useful in "the dejudification of the Netherlands and in Camp Westerbork". Of these 870, 132 are said to have survived the war. We have equally full information about the transport of 811 Jews (761 normal, 50 infirm) on February 25, 1944, also from Westerbork; it included much the same categories, but also carried 308 Portuguese Jews. All the names are known, and ninety-four are said to have survived. On April 5, 1944, another transport left Westerbork with 289 people of eight different categories. Of these, sixteen were infirm and twenty-six are said to have survived. On July 31, 1944, there followed 213 Jews on five lists, including 146 who had helped in "dejudification". There were forty-eight (?) survivors. We have previously mentioned the "great" transport of 2,087 deportees of September 4, which included baptized Jews and the Barneveld group; they travelled in goods-trucks with a few holes for ventilation and a few buckets as the only toilet facilities. "Oddly enough, in quite a few of these trucks, people were in high spirits. A number of them played cards on an improvised table, cracked jokes and sang songs."

This was the last transport to depart from Westerbork for Theresienstadt. Altogether, 4,897 (according to Herzberg, 4,969) people left the Netherlands for that destination, of whom 1,273 are said to have survived; a report of June 7, 1945, speaks of 1,400 Jews from the Netherlands in the camp at that date, but by then some of the old people had left and others had come in.

As we have said, the life of Dutch Jews in Theresienstadt differed little from that of the rest. They were put into the so-called Hamburg barrack, and settled down there as best they could. Adler speaks, on more than one occasion, of the tensions among the Westerbork group in Theresienstadt, tensions that were said to be due to the special character of this (the most disparate) group of all; here too, Dutch and German Jews were at loggerheads. Then again, many must have been sorely disappointed at what they found on arrival. Aus der Fünten had apparently promised them wonderful conditions (complete freedom, SS rations, cinemas), and even advised the women to take shoes that would stand up to country walks. But of this we cannot be sure.

One thing we are sure of is that, at the Liberation, some 75 per cent of those who had originally come to Theresienstadt from the Netherlands were no longer there. They had died or they had been evacuated—to the gas-chamber. In the autumn of 1944, when most of the inmates thought that transports out of the camp had finally ceased (there had been none for several months), thousands, including many of the healthiest, were packed off to Auschwitz. The Dutch among this group included many members of the Jewish Council hierarchy and other communal leaders. Two Dutch sections in particular were spared: the Barnevelders and those baptized into the Protestant faith. These latter numbered 433 (or 436); some 150 of them left for Switzerland in February 1945 by way of exchanges; the rest were liberated in May and gradually repatriated.

We have a number of news-bulletins in Dutch and German: the first is dated May 13, 1945, and contains a promise by the Dutch Government in exile: "We shall do everything in our power to help you." A Committee, under the leadership of Professor Meijers, tried to make contact with camp inmates, to collect names, etc.; on May 18 Professor Meijers addressed Dutchmen at home over Radio Prague. A letter sent by him to the Government in London gives some impression of conditions on May 30, with the reassuring report that "the Dutch among them are still free of lice, and without lice there is no danger of contagion"; no more than a handful of Dutch doctors and nurses had contracted typhus and only one woman had died. A report by Professor Cohen gave high praise to Russian efforts "if not to wipe out at least to control the scourge".

All who tried to approach the Dutch Government on behalf of these victims found that their appeals went unheeded, and if the French and Americans had not taken pity on the victims, they would have gone on languishing. This did not surprise the camp inmates. It was all of a piece with the conduct of the Dutch Red Cross during the war. An unbiased, non-Dutch observer has expressed the view that when it came to receiving parcels in Theresienstadt, the Dutch either got nothing or least of all. Perhaps we might plead, as an extenuating circumstance for the Dutch Government at least, that in May 1945 the Netherlands itself (or at least the big cities) was faced with complete chaos, and that the authorities had their hands full with other problems. Extenuating circumstances perhaps, but not a vindication.

# EPILOGUE

THE historian is fortunate indeed in that his task does not extend beyond the end of the war, beyond May 5, 1945. For the sufferings of Dutch Jewry continued long after that date, and it would be a painful task indeed to chronicle them. We would have to tell of a long, slow, painful convalescence, of laborious attempts to rebuild shattered lives. Tens of thousands had died, and the thousands who survived bore upon them the indelible mark of their terrible ordeal. That is soon said, but shall we ever understand its full meaning? Perhaps we glimpse it in the following testimony: "Simply to live, every single survivor had been forced to betray someone, to leave another to his fate, sometimes deliberately and sometimes willy-nilly. Each one of the survivors was, at a given moment, torn away from his helpless father or brother, from his wife or child. No wonder, they all felt guilty, no wonder so many committed suicide, or had the gnawing feeling that there was no justice in their own survival. Everyone who was spared by what must have seemed a succession of miracles knew that, to the end of his days, his every step would be dogged by a bitter 'Why?' . . ."

But as we have said, this is a story that we do not have to tell in full. Yet few people would deny that a book about the destruction of Dutch Jewry must contain at least some reference, however slight, to the aftermath of the war, to what has been called "the post-war Jewish attitude to life". The odd thing is that many Jews reflected and talked about this subject, even during the war, wondering whether, after the experiences they had already had or that were still in store for them, they would ever again be capable of behaving like normal human beings—a question that many of them answered in the negative. After all the fears, all the threats, all the shocks, the panic, the losses—home, family and even name—how could they hope to find their way back to everyday life, without mental anguish, suspicion, nameless terrors and nightmares? How could the Jewish woman who had seen her own daughter enter the gas-chamber, ever again face life with her head held high? How could the Jew, robbed of all his children and grandchildren, ever again feel himself an ordinary man among other men?

It has been said that, after 1945, every Jew stood alone, bereaved of his parents, children, family, friends, acquaintances, and deprived of everything that once made up his life.

It has also been said that every Jew who had been to a camp would always carry the memory in his very vitals. There were many cases of people who had somehow managed to keep up their spirits in the camps themselves, only to break down utterly after the Liberation, often because of unbearable loneliness and a terrible fear of strangers. Each of them was forced to build up his entire life anew, in an environment that all too often refused to receive him, in which he felt unwelcome, which took it amiss when he asserted his claims to former possessions, indeed which simply resented his very existence, and often treated him with suspicion, dislike and scorn. We must leave it to experts to discuss the psycho-somatic repercussions of the war upon those who were herded into the camps, those who went into hiding and those who took the risk of masquerading under false identities. Suffice it to say that all who returned from the camps had experienced unspeakable things, unbearable hunger, unbearable humiliation, unbearable ill-treatment, unbearable work, unbearable quarters, unbearable sights, unbearable mental tensions, had had to live utterly unnatural lives, endure never-ending days of cold, inactivity, tedium, dejection and above all, continuous fear, dread, humiliation, grief for their families and anxiety about their children. Mental disturbances? Physical disorders of every kind? It would have been astonishing indeed had they not shown themselves everywhere.

A Dutch doctor[1] had this to say—in 1964: "Possibly there is someone in your vicinity who has been to a concentration camp or who was locked up in a little attic for years. Perhaps he is difficult and a little strange in his manner, has a number of symptoms characteristic of the concentration-camp syndrome: he flares up, he becomes melancholic and cannot carry on a normal conversation without suddenly losing the thread, he likes to be alone at one moment and at others cannot bear to be left. Confining spaces, for instance telephone booths, oppress and frighten him; he may even refuse to enter a cinema. One drink, if only a glass of beer, and he is tipsy. Perhaps he cannot stand coffee; that, too, is not uncommon.

[1] Dr. J. Kater in *Algemeen Handelsblad*, May 30, 1964.

He is always tired and will sometimes burst into tears for no reason at all; he may start sweating, without any physical exertion. And this list is far from complete."

Are there, then, no positive, encouraging signs at all? Perhaps there are just a few. For instance, the emergence of a new Jewish community in the Netherlands. "Not what it used to be, less colourful perhaps, though hardly less many-sided; people once again perform their religious duties, celebrate the Jewish festivals, meet one another in favourite cafés and restaurants, at gala evenings and social gatherings. Girls once more dream of love; boys dream of girls and plan careers. People work in the traditional occupations, but also in jobs that are closed to Jews elsewhere." That, at least, is how it looks from the outside.

May we also class as positive those expressions of a deepened understanding, of a more profound appreciation of what life has to offer, of an increased awareness of what is good and beautiful in human nature and in the world? Or of the new turning towards Israel and Zion by some, and fresh attempts at identification with the Netherlands by others? Or the various combinations of these two? May we consider the many who, once again, lead "normal" lives, as completely cured of the wounds of war? To this last question, as we have seen, medical science is unable to answer in the affirmative.

We have spoken of a new Jewish community. Can we really call it that? The writer himself prefers to speak of a group. A group pieced together after the Liberation, from a host of fragments; a few thousand men and women married to Gentiles and spared for that reason, a few thousand who emerged from hiding, the survivors of Westerbork, the very small number who returned from Theresienstadt and the other camps. Among them is to be found every conceivable kind of misfortune: parents without children, children without parents, a preponderance of old people, a preponderance of women, and all too many who are left with no one in the world. In any case, the social and economic composition of Dutch Jewry has utterly changed; the working class, so strong before 1940, has been almost completely exterminated. A large number of family names has completely disappeared; the Jewish communities in the provincial towns have been broken up; only a handful of Jews have returned to retail trading; many artists and intellectuals have been massacred. In very many places the synagogues have been desecrated and only a single grave-stone or inscription stands as a reminder of the past; Jewish cemeteries everywhere lie completely abandoned. The spiritual life of very many has drawn away from the synagogue; the Portuguese-Jewish community, in particular, is sadly diminished. And that is not all.

During the Eichmann trial it was said that when other peoples counted their war losses, the Jews counted their survivors. Not that the Jews have forgotten their dead, but the task of counting them all can never be completed. It would take a whole treatise to show why that is so. All we can try to do here is to convey a vague idea of the enormity that struck down Dutch Jewry.

By October 1, 1941, 140,000 people had registered as "full-Jews" in accordance with the German race criterion. This figure also included a considerable number of non-Dutch Jews registered in Holland, but excluded Dutch Jews in colonies and other places abroad, particularly in England.

Even without the war, the Jewish population would not have remained static. But with the advent of the Germans there was a steep rise in the death-rate. To begin with there were several hundred suicides, followed by hundreds of deaths inside the Dutch camps, hundreds of deaths during attempts to resist, and then, of course, thousands of deaths at the hand of butchers in camps outside Holland. Altogether, some 110,000 people were deported from the Netherlands; of these, a total of 5,450 people (2,361 men and 3,089 women) returned (counting the 918 still present in Westerbork at the Liberation).

Even these figures are only approximate, and this for a number of reasons. Thus we do not know if all those who returned from the camps, or for that matter all those who emerged from hiding, registered their names as Jewish survivors. Who can tell how many emigrated immediately after the Liberation, or how many of those who escaped during the war (2,000?) returned to the Netherlands? Most estimates of the number of Jews from the Netherlands who perished under the Nazis range round the figure of 106,000, but this figure also includes persons of non-Dutch nationality. There are grounds for supposing that the German Jews among them fared slightly better than their Dutch brethren and, after taking this into consideration, the total of Dutch-Jewish victims may be put at about 90,000.

H. Wielek has rightly called his book *The War That Hitler Won.*

The almost total destruction of people over fifty and under sixteen is an indubitable fact. Many Jewish women had no alternative but to marry non-Jews after the war, not only because so many Jews had been butchered but also because quite a few of those who had survived preferred to emigrate. Who can say whether the ordinary mortality rate, mixed marriages, assimilation and emigration to Israel and elsewhere will not in fact finish the process that Hitler so cruelly began? Only the future can tell.

The writer does not find it easy to turn at once from human tragedy to the loss of mere possessions. For when all is said and done, things, unlike people, are replaceable. We have already spoken at length of the wholesale plunder carried out by the Germans, and once again count ourselves fortunate in not having to pursue the story into the post-war period. But there are just a few remarks we cannot help making.

To begin with, a comparison between Jewish wealth in 1940 and, for instance, in 1965, is inadmissible, if only because so many family fortunes disappeared altogether—there were no survivors to lay claim to them. Moreover, any such comparison would have to take into account the Dutch economic condition as a whole, and this too has changed radically since 1940.

For many Jews, and especially for the well-to-do among them, it was a strange experience to re-enter society without even the bare necessities, with not much more than the clothes—and what clothes! —in which they stood up. And it was precisely these "bare necessities" that they had failed to save: their tooth-brushes, raincoats, cups and saucers—but the list may be left to the reader. Many were forced to re-equip themselves with furniture and other goods from Germans and political criminals—for years to come, such terms as "Berlin bedsteads" and "Dutch Nazi chairs" were part of the everyday vocabulary. But this was by no means the worst—far from it.

For most Jews the immediate post-war period was one in which they tried to win back their rights and obtain some measure of restitution. In the former they were more successful than in the latter: clearly it was much easier for a civil servant to regain his post than for a businessman to build up his ruined firm from scratch, or for a professional man to rebuild his old practice. Particularly during the early years, the struggle was hard indeed. It should also be remembered that the enemy had driven a steam-roller over everybody's rights of ownership. Jewish shares had changed hands several times, mortgages had been redeemed, life insurance policies concelled, houses and effects sold, whole fortunes dissipated. Only too often, the claimants had to engage in costly lawsuits. A particular complication was the fact that, in the case of most deportees, there was no way of proving death; it was only by the law of June 2, 1949, that certain categories of missing persons could be deemed dead. This in turn raised many legal problems about next-of-kin. The Dutch Government kept strictly to the rule that no distinction must be made between Jews and any other Dutchmen which, in practice, amounted to an act of discrimination, since Jews had lost so much more than others.

Let us quote two sentences from a letter sent to us by a Jewish correspondent in 1951. After recalling the horrors of the war, he went on to say: "The years after 1945 really finished me. Everything seemed to conspire against the recovery of my spiritual and material self-respect. Above all, there was the trouble with the authorities. Where I would have expected sympathy, I met the curt, non-committal, forbidding amorphous mass that goes by the name of officialdom. I can only say that these years were a real nightmare . . ."

Once again in these pages, the writer must turn to the Jewish child, the child who came back to the world of 1945. From the extermination camps proper, scarcely a single one returned, but there were a few from Bergen-Belsen, from Theresienstadt—and from the free world. We have no figures, but there can only have been a few, very few. What the camp children must have suffered in physical and psychological damage may have varied from case to case; one thing is certain, not a single one came back unharmed. Most of those who survived into 1945 were, in any case, children who had gone into hiding, if that word can be used for the many who lived in a degree, and some in a very large degree, of freedom. Frequently they were tended with extraordinary kindness, with a selflessness and devotion that are among the most cherished memories of those dark days. Tended in the first place by their foster-parents, but also by the many underground helpers who ran the enormous risk of taking them to safety.

Taking children to safety during the war was an operation shrouded in secrecy and confusion. Quite often it called for the eradication of every possible link with the past, so that many important lines of communication were severed. Many were the parents who had not the least idea during the war where their children were. They simply did not know, and quite often the child owed its survival to this very fact. People just had to hope and trust, and all too often their trust was shamefully betrayed.

We shall say little more on this subject, but merely ask the reader to imagine himself in the place of those parents who, having gone underground themselves, suddenly heard that their child, deemed safe, had fallen to the Germans, parents who would for years be plagued by the terrible question—was it really our child, our son, our daughter? Or in the place of the children who emerged from their holes at the end of the war, only to find that they had no parents and no home to go to.

There is little doubt but that most of these parents would have wished their children to grow up as Jews after the war, as members of some sort of Jewish community—unless, of course, special circumstances arose that demanded a different solution. Even completely unorthodox parents would surely not have liked to see their children brought up as Christians—they had entrusted them to Christians but not for conversion to Christianity. Both Dutch law and the Jewish tradition supported this view; any infringement of this right was generally considered an infringement of the rights of the individual. Quite naturally, people understood that for safety's sake the children might have to go to church or even be baptized, that close bonds would grow up between the child and its foster-parents, bonds that would prove extremely painful to sever. Still, the Jewish leaders were firm in the view that this was a price that must be paid, if the child were not to grow up into a world in which it might come to feel a stranger.

Immediately after the cease-fire on May 14, 1945, the *Oorlogspleegkinderenbureau*, or OPK (Office for Wartime Foster-Children) set to work; it was dissolved by the law of August 12, 1949, which decreed that all its wards would come under the aegis of the Minors' Protection Boards. Let us give just a few figures. In the spring of 1947 it appeared that of the 3,481 OPK children, 1,540 were reunited with their parents. In the case of another 508 children, the committee proposed to the court that 421 be given to Jewish guardians; in eighty-seven cases, the court had already allocated the children to fifty-one Jewish and thirty-six non-Jewish guardians. Of the rest, approximately one-third grew up in Christian homes. The further history of the OPK falls outside the province of this book, but we might add that there were quite a few cases in which judges saw fit to set aside the natural right of parents, as though their suffering during the war had not been more than most people could bear. No doubt these incidents persuaded many of the younger generation to turn their backs on the Netherlands and to settle in Israel instead. Neither possessions nor a sense of solidarity, nor the tradition of Dutch Jewry itself, were there to restrain them, and the post-war atmosphere was not such as to encourage them to remain in Europe.

This brings us to a particularly difficult problem, which, painful though it may be, cannot be omitted here: the attitude of most Dutchmen to their Jewish fellow-citizens after the war. Clearly it is impossible to deal with this matter precisely, but there is small doubt that—after the Liberation—there was, to say the least of it, a certain hostility, so much so that in the summer of 1945 a number of people called for a special study group to assess the prevalence of anti-Semitism in the Netherlands. The original intention was to spend several weeks on this enquiry but, for whatever reason, the group disbanded before it could publish its results. Possibly many of its members were busy with other tasks, possibly they reached the conclusion that this question was best left alone.

"All the good Jews are dead. It is the bad ones who have come back." This is what one of the writer's friends, a teacher, was told after his return from exile and great personal suffering, by his headmistress, a "generally respected" lady of high academic standing. "There really are still too many Jews in the Netherlands." "There ought to be a fixed quota for Jews." "Jews should always remember how thankful they need to be—they could very soon exhaust our sympathy." "Jews ought not to be in such a hurry (to claim their possessions back)." "What happened during the Occupation was repugnant, but all the same we're better off without them." "Now that the enemy is gone, we still have the Jewish enemy within." And so we might go on; suffice it to say that these Dutch expressions of anti-Semitism did not go unnoticed abroad.[1]

The strange thing is that such sentiments were heard even during the war, when one might have expected all Dutch citizens to stand shoulder to shoulder. Herzberg,[2] who quotes a number of examples,

[1] H. W. J. Sannes: *Onze Joden en Duitsland's greep naar de wereldmacht* (Our Jews and Germany's reach for world domination) (Amsterdam, 1946), pp. 6–7.

[2] Herzberg: *Kroniek der Jodenvervolging*, p. 249.

rightly says: "One has only to read the illegal Press, to appreciate how far this went." How often was it not given out that a Jew had betrayed a non-Jew to the Germans? And can anyone honestly claim that there were no illegal organizations who refused to help Jews "on principle", or resistance groups who would not have a Jew as a member? What did "Jan Jansen", an honest official, write in his diary on March 15, 1943? When formulating his personal plans for the years after the war he said: "We must restrict the influence of Dutch Jews, so that they do not have too big a say in politics and in the social and economic field (*a bit tricky, this*)."

Naturally, Jews realized that they would be returning to a changed Netherlands, but they could not foresee how very different it would be. If they expected the world in general to show sorrow for the millions of innocent victims, to open its arms to the few Jewish survivors, they were soon to be cruelly disappointed. As if Auschwitz and Treblinka had never even existed, many Gentiles went back to their everyday tasks indifferent to, indeed impatient with, those who had come back, leaving the Jews to their solitude, their misery and the fear that it might all happen again. This feeling would always remain with them, not least when they saw how quickly their neighbours set about the task of renewing relations with the very nation that had perpetrated all those unspeakable horrors. And how could anyone forget that, even after the Liberation, Jews were still being murdered in Poland, where a daylight pogrom was organized, not by professional criminals, but by young mothers, by students of Polish literature, by devout Catholics who prayed to God before the massacre? And not only did they murder the Jews but they also indulged in an orgy of torture, in a veritable witches' sabbath—in July 1946, barely a year after the end of the war.

This was Poland, but the picture was not very much more encouraging in post-war Germany. Denazification was, to put it mildly, incomplete, and was soon followed by what has been called renazification; there was a prevalent wish to reject, or an inability to accept, the historical fact that millions of Jews had been murdered, and a suspicious readiness to reprieve a host of cold-blooded murderers ("so that they may spend Christmas in the bosom of their families"). That and the public recrudescence of "neo-anti-Semitism", the sweeping of the war crimes under the carpet—who can blame Dutch Jews if, despite sincere efforts by the West German Government to make financial restitution to them, they remained ultra-sensitive to the less salubrious manifestations, particularly since, as we have said, they found echoes of them even in their own country?

Many people have contended that the Dutch nation was contaminated by contact with the Nazis during the war, but a careful examination has shown that matters are far more complicated than that, and that there is still a great deal of truth in the old saying *proprium ingenii humani est odisse quem laeseris*—it is in the human spirit to hate whom it has wronged. No doubt, at the root of it all is a feeling of guilt, to which so many non-Jews have confessed. It has often been said that every Dutchman worth his salt ought to have been in the Resistance. Is it any wonder, then, that so many who were not, now vented their feelings on those whose very presence was a constant reminder of their shortcomings? "Generalizing vilification was the bad side of the medal which on the other side showed the gold of true compassion. Vilification and compassion were complementary. Both resulted from the same situation and ... both were to be found in the same human heart shortly after the occupation."[1]

And so we could go on. But we have said enough. Like history, life continues, "*but sometimes there must be one who remembers*".

The one who has here remembered has striven to be faithful.

*Requiescant.*

[1] L. de Jong: "Jews and Non-Jews in Nazi-occupied Holland" in *On the track of tyranny* (London, 1962), p. 154.

# INDEX

# INDEX